P9-ASI-548

CRITICAL COMPANION TO

# Tennessee Williams

CRITICAL COMPANION TO

# Tennessee Williams

GRETA HEINTZELMAN

ALYCIA SMITH-HOWARD

Facts On File, Inc.

**Critical Companion to Tennessee Williams**



Facts On File, Inc.
132 West 31st Street
New York NY 10001

**Library of Congress Cataloging-in-Publication Data**
Heintzelman, Greta.
Critical companion to Tennessee Williams : the essential reference to his life and work / Greta Heintzelman, Alycia Smith-Howard.
p. cm.
Includes bibliographical references and index.
ISBN 0-8160-4888-6 (hardcover : alk. paper)
American—20th century—Biography—Encyclopedias. I. Smith-Howard, Alycia. II. Title.

PS3545.15365Z459 2004b
812′.54—dc22 2004007362

Facts On File books are available at special discounts when purchased in bulk quantities for businesses, associations, institutions, or sales promotions. Please call our Special Sales Department in New York at (212) 967-8800 or (800) 322-8755.

You can find Facts On File on the World Wide Web at http://www.factsonfile.com

Text design by Joan M. Toro
Adapted by Erika K. Arroyo
Cover design by Cathy Rincon

Printed in the United States of America

VB Hermitage 10 9 8 7 6 5 4 3 2 1

This book is printed on acid-free paper.

*For our mothers*
*and in memory of Jennifer*

# Contents

# ACKNOWLEDGMENTS

Special thanks are due first and foremost to our two contributing researchers/writers, Sabine C. Bauer and Sarah E. Cook, for their tireless efforts and ceaseless enthusiasm; Jeff Soloway, our editor, and Danielle Bonnici, his assistant, at Facts On File, for their patience and sharp eyes; and our ever-supportive literary agent, Elizabeth Frost-Knappman (New England Publishing Associates).

Our thanks are also due to the librarians and reference staff of the Billy Rose Theatre Collection, New York Public Library; Bobst Library, New York University; University of Memphis Library; Mount Holyoke College Library; Sophia Smith Rare Book Library, Smith College; Cornell University Library; Rare Book and Manuscript Library at Butler Library, Columbia University; Harry Ransom Center, University of Texas at Austin; Monroe County Public Library, Key West, Florida; and the Key West Art and Historical Society.

We are indebted to the following individuals without whose support this work would not have been possible: Lois Brown, Dorothy H. Schnare, Jeanine M. Akers, Tom Lisanti, Helen M. Whall, Asalé Angel-Ajani, David Schuller, Sean Scheller, Carol and Marilyn Huffman, Vivian S. Howard, Clydia Warrix Heintzelman, Claudia L. Pennington, Steve Pratt, Laurie Callahan, E. Frances White, Ali Mirsepassi, Sheila Thimba, Laurin Raiken, Michael Dinwiddie, Nick Lycos, Kathe Ann Joseph, Sally Suttherland, Donal O'Shea, David Wolkowsky, Dann Dulin, Nydia Ferguson, Beth Weinert, Genevieve Davila, Jean Disrud, Candace Whitaker, Don Booth, and David Felstein.

# INTRODUCTION

Twenty years after his death, Tennessee Williams was heralded in *USA Today* as "the hottest playwright in America" (October 22, 2003). Elyssa Gardner's commentary in this publication revealed popular culture's recognition of the critical reassessment of Williams that has been percolating within the theater and the academy for many years. Williams is finally being acknowledged as America's greatest and most prolific playwright. Although his works are, and have always been, an integral part of the American literary, theatrical, and popular landscape, we are now witnessing a resurgence in the visibility and appreciation of his literary achievement.

Williams's literary career spanned a period of more than 40 years, and the sheer magnitude and volume of his artistic ambition make his work an inexhaustible study. Despite numerous critical and commercial failures in the latter part of his life, Williams never suppressed his drive to write and create. From childhood to the day he died, Williams wrote. He penned some 45 full-length plays and 60 shorter dramas, as well as screenplays, short stories, letters, essays, and volumes of poetry. Previously unpublished materials held in special collections and archives across the United States are being regularly uncovered, produced, and published by eager literary scholars and theatrical producers. Williams's creative genius continues to thrive, long after his death.

Noted for his poetic lyricism and often brutal frankness, Williams is celebrated as a "poet of the human heart" and as the "Laureate of the Outcast." Loneliness, social isolation, and the conflict between repression and release are primary themes in Williams's works, which are also characterized by eloquent dialogue and richly complex characters. Each of Williams's works challenges readers' perceptions of style, structure, society, and the meaning of literature, drama, theater, humanity, and, ultimately, life itself. The range of his dramatic and literary style is incomparable. Williams consistently tested the limits of realistic writing and theatrical production. His first major success, *The Glass Menagerie,* ushered in a new age of American drama and theater. Throughout his life, he continued to experiment with new forms and innovative techniques of expressionism to create a suitably vibrant world for his volatile characters.

His heroes, heroines, and antiheroes, such as Blanche DuBois, Maggie the Cat, Big Daddy, Amanda and Tom Wingfield, Stanley Kowalski, and Baby Doll, have become mythic figures in the American collective and cultural psyche. Beyond these well-known figures, the Williams canon is an unparalleled universe of intrinsically human characters: brave and battered, flawed and fallible, yet ever hopeful. From the vindictive landladies of such works as *Angel in the Alcove* and *Vieux Carré,* the crippled child of *The Chronicle of a Demise,* and the tormented artists of *At Liberty, Orpheus Descending, In the Bar of a Tokyo Hotel,* and *The Notebook of Trigorin* to the feuding brothers of *Kingdom of Earth* and the quarreling friends of *And Tell Sad Stories of the Death of Queens, Something Cloudy, Something Clear,* and *Clothes for a Summer Hotel,* Williams chronicles humanity in all its diverse and often painful complexity.

The American South, particularly the landscape of rural Mississippi, is featured prominently as a setting and background throughout the Williams canon. The Southern landscapes that appear in his works are invested with his deep-set affection and disdain for the region. In his works this part of the world is simultaneously revered and reviled as "the beauty spot of creation," and as a "dragon country, the country of pain . . . an uninhabitable country which is inhabited." But although he was Southern in his upbringing and outlook, Williams's voice and vision exposed deferred American myths and dreams beyond his regional locale.

As Lyle Leverich notes in his exceptional biography *Tom: The Unknown Tennessee Williams,* although Williams was so distinctly American in his art, "no other American dramatist is more universally recognized, admired or produced." In Russia, Williams is the second most often produced playwright after Anton Chekhov. Williams's major plays (*The Glass Menagerie, A Streetcar Named Desire, Cat on a Hot Tin Roof,* and *The Night of the Iguana*) are in continual revival across the United States and abroad, on Broadway, in the West End of London, and in countless regional theaters (not to mention college, university, and community theaters). Several theater companies across the United States have recently dedicated themselves to producing the Williams dramatic canon in its entirety over the next 10 years (Hartford Stage Company in Hartford, Connecticut; the Guthrie Theater in Minneapolis, Minnesota; and the Shakespeare Theatre in Washington, D.C.), and no fewer than three major Broadway revivals of Williams's plays have been scheduled through the year 2010.

The revival of interest in Williams can be credited to a shift in critical, social, and cultural attitudes. It is evident that throughout his career, Williams was a theatrical maverick, a poetic revolutionary who was clearly ahead of his time. There is now a greater appreciation for artistic experimentation and innovation. This new generation of Tennessee Williams admirers are a testament to his acceptance as a far more accomplished and pivotal writer than previous generations may have appreciated.

Although there are a variety of works dedicated to the life and works of Tennessee Williams, little has been written about Williams's literary output in its entirety. Much has been produced about particular works, pivotal productions, films, and so forth, but there has long been a need for a book that covers Williams's life, characters, and works comprehensively and cohesively. This book fulfills that need as an all-encompassing guide to Williams's body of work. In many cases this volume contains the only significant critical commentary available on numerous lesser-known Williams works, particularly his fiction.

The primary goal of this volume is to assist readers and students of Williams in their quest to understand, enjoy, and situate the works and life of this great American writer. It is also intended to provide scholars and those already familiar with Williams's oeuvre a convenient one-volume reference source. We are both literary scholars and active theater professionals. This experience gives us a unique perspective on dramatic literature and the nondramatic writings of a dramatist. Our sense of theory is tempered by our knowledge of practice and what Charles Marowitz calls "playable values."

Arranged alphabetically, the entries in this guide provide critical information on a wide range of topics directly related to the study of Williams's life and works: publication and production histories, characters, places, family, friends, artistic colleagues, themes, ideas, influences, and more. In addition, this reference guide also couples extensive plot synopses with engaging and accessible critical commentary. *Critical Companion to Tennessee Williams* is meant to serve as a research companion to enrich the reader's experience, and of course it is no substitute for the enjoyment of the dynamic works of America's greatest dramatist themselves.

## How to Use This Book

Part I consists of a brief biography of Williams. Part II contains entries on Williams's works, both major and minor, in alphabetical order. The characters in each work are listed as subentries within each work entry. Part III is made up of related entries on places, themes, topics, and people, including actors, friends, relatives, literary influences, and more. Part IV contains appendices, including a chronology, a list of resources important to the study of Williams's life and works, a bibliography of Williams's works, and a bibliography of secondary sources. Cross-references appear in SMALL CAPITALS.

# PART I

# *Biography*

# *Williams, Tennessee (Thomas Lanier)*

(1911–1983)

A gifted and prolific writer, Williams produced a creative output that encompassed plays, novels, poetry, short stories, screenplays, and essays. Noted for his poetic lyricism and vivid frankness, he was celebrated as a "poet of the human heart" and the "Laureate of the Outcast" (Leverich, 5). Loneliness, social isolation, and the conflict between repression and release are primary themes in Williams's works—which are also characterized by eloquent dialogue and incisive analyses of richly complex characters. The American South, particularly the landscape or rural Mississippi, is featured prominently as a setting and background throughout his work. His major dramatic works include *THE GLASS MENAGERIE* (1945), *A STREETCAR NAMED DESIRE* (1947), *SUMMER AND SMOKE* (1948), *THE ROSE TATTOO* (1948), *CAT ON A HOT TIN ROOF* (1955), *SWEET BIRD OF YOUTH* (1959), and *THE NIGHT OF THE IGUANA* (1961).

Born Thomas Lanier Williams III, in Columbus, Mississippi, on March 26, 1911, he was the second child of EDWINA ESTELLE DAKIN WILLIAMS and CORNELIUS COFFIN WILLIAMS, and the first grandson of ROSINA OTTE DAKIN and the REVEREND WALTER EDWIN DAKIN. His paternal ancestors included several distinguished leaders of the state of Tennessee, such as General John "Nolichucky Jack" Sevier (1745–1815), the state's first governor, and John Williams (1778–1827), the state's first senator. Williams's paternal grandfather, Thomas Lanier Williams II (1849–1908), was the Tennessee commissioner of railroads and at one time made an unsuccessful run to be governor of the state. His paternal grandmother, Isabel Coffin (1853–84), traced her Sevier family lineage to the French Huguenot descendants of Saint Francis Xavier. Williams was proud of his ancestry, which he classified as "a little Welsh wilderness, a lot of Puritan English and a big chunk of German sentiment." His artistic sensibilities were also present in such notable ancestors as the poets Tristam Coffin and SIDNEY LANIER (1842–81), known as "America's Sweet Singer of Songs."

Williams's father was a traveling representative for the Cumberland Telephone Company when he met Edwina Dakin. The rugged and blustering traveling salesman wooed the small-town belle, and after an 18-month courtship they were married at Saint Paul's Church on June 3, 1907. The bride's father officiated at the service. The couple spent their honeymoon in Gulfport, Mississippi, where they remained for 18 months. This was the happiest time of their life together. Their idyllic existence ended with the news of Edwina's first pregnancy and Cornelius's change in employment. Tired of being tied to a desk in Gulfport, Cornelius left Cumberland Telephone and accepted a traveling sales position selling men's apparel for Tate & Cowan. His return to the road gave him the freedom he craved but left Edwina lonely and alone. She returned to the refuge of her parents' home in Columbus in 1909. She, and later her children, would remain there for nearly a

Portrait of Tennessee Williams *(Friedman-Abeles)*

decade, with her husband visiting the family sporadically on weekends.

On November 19, 1909, Edwina gave birth to the Williamses' first child, ROSE ISABEL WILLIAMS. Their second child, Tom, followed on March 26, 1911. Rose and Tom's grandfather, Walter Dakin, more than adequately filled the void that resulted from Cornelius's significant absences. The Reverend Dakin was a powerful contrast to the children's father—he was a kindly, gentle, affectionate book lover who became the most important male figure in their life. Rose and Tom flourished in the loving parochial environmental of their grandfather's rectory. In addition to their doting grandfather, grandmother, and mother, Rose and Tom benefited from the care of a beautiful African-American nurse named Ozzie, who enchanted the children with tales of magic and folklore.

In 1913, the family moved to Nashville, Tennessee, where the Reverend Dakin had accepted a ministerial position at the Church of the Advent. The family returned to Mississippi two years later, in 1915, when the Reverend Dakin accepted a post at Saint George's Church, in Clarksdale. The Dakins would remain in Clarksdale, Mississippi, until the Reverend Dakin's retirement in 1931. A far cry from the excitement of Nashville, the rural town of Clarksdale, Mississippi, with its cotton gins, silver maples, and water oaks, would leave an indelible impression on the young Tom Williams. This locale would continually resurface in his writing throughout his life.

In the summer of 1916, at the age of five, Tom was stricken with diphtheria and nearly died. The episode damaged his eyesight and left him paralyzed for more than a year. This time of confinement significantly altered Tom: He changed from a rambunctious, bustling little boy to a more solitary, introverted child. He amused himself with imaginative and literary pursuits. He regained full use of his legs in 1918, just as he, his mother, and his sister were set to join his father in SAINT LOUIS, MISSOURI.

Since 1916, Cornelius Williams had been employed by the INTERNATIONAL SHOE COMPANY and was based in Saint Louis. In 1918, he was offered a managerial promotion within the firm at its Saint Louis headquarters. He sent for Edwina to join him and to assist in finding a permanent family residence. Because of Tom's recent and severe illness, Edwina would not leave Mississippi without him. She and Tom made the journey to establish themselves in Saint Louis, initially leaving Rose behind with her grandparents. This episode was traumatic for the family, and Tom endured the painful experience of "being separated for the first time from those he loved best in the world" (Leverich, 45). Edwina shared her son's anxieties. Not only had she left the comfortable pastoral setting of her parents' home for one of the largest, most industrialized U.S. cities, but she was faced with the challenge of living with Cornelius. Although she and Cornelius had been married for quite some time, they had essentially created separate lives that only collided intermittently. They had only lived alone together for 18 months. Edwina's fears were substantiated: From the start of their new life in Saint Louis, she and Cornelius were "bitterly at odds and equally miserable" (ibid. 47).

The family first moved temporarily to a boardinghouse on Lindell Street, then settled in an apartment at 4633 Westminster Place. Williams recalled this location as a "perpetually dim little apartment in a wilderness of identical brick and concrete structures with no grass and no trees" (Cuoco, 195–96). It was a far cry from his childhood in rural Mississippi. In this new locale Tom also became aware of the fact that there were "two kinds of people, the rich and the poor, and that we belonged more to the latter" (ibid. 196). This building has since been renamed the Glass Menagerie Apartments in Williams's honor. The family moved twice more, ending finally in a cramped apartment at 6254 Enright Avenue. This tenement building is in fact the model for the Wingfield home in *The Glass Menagerie.*

The Williams home life was strained by their frequent relocations. This challenging scenario was augmented by Cornelius's bombastic demeanor. He did not adjust well to the settled and responsible lifestyle of a company middle manager. He yearned for the freedom of travel and the open road. He compensated by indulging in heavy drinking and weekend-long poker parties with his friends. His drinking and gambling were an affront to Edwina's

Southern sensibilities and were the source of frequent arguments between them. The atmosphere was volatile and frightening to Rose and Tom, who also suffered from their father's temperament. Cornelius regarded Tom as a "sissy," and he taunted him by calling him, "Miss Nancy." All of this took its toll on Edwina physically. During this time she suffered a miscarriage, Spanish influenza, and a difficult pregnancy with the Williamses' third child, WALTER DAKIN WILLIAMS, who was born in 1919.

At age nine, the young Tom had still not adjusted to his new life in Saint Louis, he was not doing very well in school, and his home life was dismal. It was decided that time with his grandparents might help. In 1920, he gleefully returned to Clarksdale, Mississippi. Here Tom explored his former home from a new perspective. He was able to discern that the South had a way of life that he would always remember, as he would later recall, "a culture that had grace, elegance . . . an inbred culture . . . not a society based on money, as in the North" (Leverich, 54). As did his fellow Mississippian writer William Faulkner, who immortalized the territory around Sardis and Oxford, Mississippi, in his fiction as "Yoknapatawpha County," Williams depicted Clarksdale and its environs in his literary canon, often referring to the area as "Blue Mountain, Mississippi," "Glorious Hill, Mississippi," or "Two Rivers County."

It was during this time that Williams encountered many of the people, places, names, and events that he would feature later in his dramas and fictions. One such figure was Mrs. Maggie Wingfield, a matron who owned several boardinghouses and a noted collection of glass ornaments and figurines, which she kept displayed in her front window; another was an elderly woman in Columbus, Mississippi, who was said to have in her possession a letter written by Lord Byron. This was a magical place and time for young Tom, a time he never forgot. The year spent in Clarksdale captured his imagination and sparked his creativity. This was his spiritual home, as he explained, "home being where you hang your childhood . . . and Mississippi to me the beauty spot of creation, a dark, wide, spacious land that you can breathe in" (Kozlenko, 174).

After his glorious yearlong hiatus in Mississippi, Tom returned to his dreaded home in Saint Louis. On Tom's return, his sister, Rose, was offered a similar respite and was sent to spend a year with her Dakin grandparents. Alone and dejected, Tom found refuge and escape in reading and writing. His mother bought him a secondhand typewriter, and he began to compose poems and short stories. He submitted poems to the Ben Blewett Junior High School newspaper in 1925. However, his literary career officially began at age 16 with the publication of his essay "Can a Wife Be a Good Sport?" which appeared in *Smart Set* magazine in May 1927, followed by the publication of his short story "THE VENGEANCE OF NITOCRIS," which was printed in *Weird Tales* magazine in August 1928.

The year 1928 also marked another pivotal occurrence in Tom's life. During this year, he joined his grandfather on his parish's tour of Europe. Not only was this another opportunity to escape the environs of Saint Louis and spend time with his beloved grandfather, it was his first important experience of world travel. As an added bonus, before the tour group embarked from New York, Williams was treated to his first Broadway performance. His first glimpse of the "Great White Way" was a production of *Showboat.*

In 1929, he graduated from Saint Louis's University City High School and enrolled at the UNIVERSITY OF MISSOURI at Columbia with the intention of studying journalism. He was supported financially by his grandmother, from her earnings as a private music teacher. He wrote his first play, a one-act entitled *BEAUTY IS THE WORD,* and submitted it to the University Dramatic Arts Club's annual play competition. His play received an honorable mention, and he was the first freshman to receive such a distinction. Inspired by the response to his first dramatic work, Williams focused completely on his writing, to the detriment of his overall academic standing. Within three years at the university he had received four Fs. The last one was in the Reserve Officers Training Corps (ROTC). His father was outraged. Cornelius promptly pulled Tom out of the university, financed a short typing course for him, and obtained a position for him as a clerk/typist at the warehouse of Continental Shoe Makers, a branch of the International Shoe Company, located at 15th and Delmar Streets in Saint Louis.

Portrait of Tennessee Williams *(Photograph courtesy of the Billy Rose Theatre Collection, New York Public Library)*

Williams worked there from 1931 to 1934 and earned $65 per month. He detested the position and referred to it as his "season in hell." The work was monotonous and tiring: dusting hundreds of pairs of shoes each morning, carrying heavy cases of them across town in the afternoon, and typing endless lists of figures. What he did enjoy about the position was the camaraderie with his coworkers, the daily exchange of talk about movies, stage shows, and radio programs. He structured his time so that whenever he was not at work, he wrote consistently. He often worked through the night to complete his self-imposed quota of one short story a week. Occasionally, he would write poetry on the lid of shoe boxes during the day at work. His time at the shoe warehouse was invaluable to him as a writer. He learned firsthand about the life of the white-collar worker trapped in a hopelessly routine job. The experience endowed him with a compassion for the working class. Williams would eventually deduct the three years he spent at the International Shoe Company from his actual age, as he felt he did not truly live during those years.

His sister Rose's life was becoming increasingly difficult at this time. By 1926, Rose had continually suffered from psychosomatic gastric trouble. Their mother, Edwina, sought to remedy Rose's ailments through a regular combination of church visits, social outings, and gentleman callers. Frustrated and mortified by Rose's increasing hysteria, expressed in either outbursts or extreme withdrawal, her parents placed her in a private sanatorium in 1929. During the early 1930s her mental state declined consistently, and the psychological counseling and therapy she received in 1936 seemed to do little to halt the process. The situation reached a breaking point in the late 1930s, when she accused her father of being sexually abusive. The Williamses admitted their daughter to a state asylum in Farmington, where she was diagnosed with schizophrenia.

Tom escaped the trauma of his home life and the tedium of his job at International Shoe Company by making frequent visits to the theater and cinema. The principal legitimate theatre in Saint Louis at this time was THE AMERICAN. The American featured touring productions from Broadway and provided local audiences with an opportunity to see prominent actors, such as TALLULAH BANKHEAD and LAURETTE TAYLOR, perform in exceptional productions. Williams regularly attended performances at the American during this period, and his most profound experience there was seeing Alla Nazimova playing Mrs. Alving in HENRIK IBSEN's *Ghosts* in 1934. Attending this production was a pivotal moment in Tom's life. He was completely enraptured by Ibsen's play and Nazimova's performance. Williams would later recall that this was the defining moment when he knew that he must write for the stage. (In a remarkable coincidence, EUGENE O'NEILL had a similar experience in his youth. In the spring of 1907, O'Neill saw and was struck by his first production of an Ibsen play. The production was *Hedda Gabler,* featuring Alla Nazimova in the title role.)

The monotony of Tom's day-to-day existence and lack of sleep from staying up to write all night finally took their toll in March 1935. He collapsed of exhaustion and was sent to recuperate with his grandparents. In the interim, the Dakins had relocated to Memphis, Tennessee. Tom stayed there with his grandparents for several months, long enough to recover his strength, discover the works of ANTON CHEKHOV, and coauthor a one-act play, *CAIRO! SHANGHAI! BOMBAY!*, with Dorothy Bernice Shapiro, the daughter of his grandparents' neighbor. This light comedy was produced by the Garden Players at Mrs. Roseboro's Rose Arbor Theater, in Memphis, Tennessee, on July 12, 1935. The play and the production were modestly successful. More importantly, however, through this experience Williams became instantly enamored of the laughter and applause he could evoke in an audience.

He returned to Saint Louis during this same year and won first prize in the Saint Louis Writers Guild contest for his short story "Stella for Star." In the fall of 1935 he enrolled in WASHINGTON UNIVERSITY in Saint Louis. There he became acquainted with another young poet, CLARK MILLS MCBURNEY. McBurney, who would later publish under the name Clark Mills, shared Williams's passion and ambition for writing. The two converted a section of Mills's basement apartment in Saint Louis into a writing studio, which they called the "literary factory." Williams was quite productive in his writing at this time and was creating a career as a local dramatist.

Two of his short plays, *THE MAGIC TOWER* and *Headlines,* were produced in Saint Louis by local amateur theater groups in 1936. *The Magic Tower* won first place in a contest sponsored by the Webster Groves Theatre Guild, and *Headlines* was produced by THE MUMMERS, a local amateur dramatics society directed by Williard Holland. Williams recalled the Mummers as being a dynamic, if disorderly, theater group who guided his "professional youth" (Cuoco, 199). Encouraged by his work with the Mummers, Williams left Washington University to study playwriting with Professor EDWARD CHARLES MABIE at the UNIVERSITY OF IOWA. Williams remained in contact with the Mummers, who produced his first full-length plays, *CANDLES TO THE SUN* and *THE FUGITIVE KIND,* in Saint Louis in 1937.

When Williams returned to Saint Louis from Iowa City in 1937 to attend the Mummers' production of *The Fugitive Kind,* he discovered that his sister's condition had reached a devastating conclusion. Diagnosed with schizophrenia and institutionalized at a state asylum in Farmington, Missouri, Rose had been subjected to electric shock therapy and other treatments since the summer of 1937. Doctors suggested a radical treatment to end Rose's trauma, and in November 1937, with her parents' consent, she had a prefrontal lobotomy. This invasive surgery left her practically autistic and in need of permanent institutionalization. The controversial procedure was performed without Tom's knowledge. He was only made aware of it when he returned home for the Mummers' production and the Christmas holidays. He found his beloved sister permanently changed, resigned to a life that proved to be little more than a "living death" (Londre, 7) as the surgery had left her bereft of her personality and sense of identity. Tom would never forgive his mother for giving her consent for the operation and would blame himself, for just as long, for not being home to prevent it. The entire family was completely altered by this episode. As Donald Spoto notes, "Little of Thomas Lanier Williams's life after 1937 is comprehensible without appreciating the awfulness of [this] . . . irreversible tragedy" (Spoto 67, 68). Throughout his life and career, Tom would pay tribute to his dearly loved sister and retell her story.

Tom returned to the University of Iowa, where he continued his studies in playwriting under Professor Mabie. Their relationship was rocky, as Mabie had taken a dislike to Williams and frequently teased and humiliated him. As had Tom's father, Mabie often referred to him as a "sissy." Williams completed two plays under Mabie's tutelage, *SPRING STORM* and *NOT ABOUT NIGHTINGALES.* Mabie gave Williams harsh criticism for both works. Despite Mabie's ill treatment of Williams and his distaste for the young dramatist's early dramaturgy, Williams respected Mabie. He admired his intellect as well as his contributions to the Federal Theatre Project (Mabie was the regional director as well as a founding designer of the Works Progress Administration program). Tom completed his B.A. and graduated from the University of Iowa in 1938. As had his mentor, Tom sought a place on the Works Progress Administration (WPA) Writers Project, first in Chicago, Illinois, and then in NEW ORLEANS,

LOUISIANA. He was not offered a position with the WPA in either city; however, pursuit of a position with the WPA had taken Williams to his most pivotal artistic home.

Williams moved to a boardinghouse owned by Mrs. Louise Wire on 722 Toulouse Street, New Orleans, in 1938. There the vibrant environment of the French Quarter became a major influence in his personal and artistic development. This bohemian locale provided a community of fellow artisans and liberated Williams socially, artistically, and sexually. He would later describe New Orleans as "the paradise of his youth" (Holditch, 194). Far from the puritanical environment of his Saint Louis home, Williams was free to explore his craft and his sexuality within the confines of the French Quarter. Williams would later chronicle his experiences as a young artist living in the French Quarter in such works as "THE ANGEL IN THE ALCOVE," *THE LADY OF LARKSPUR LOTION,* and *VIEUX CARRÉ.* New Orleans would also serve as the setting for numerous works, such as *AUTO-DA-FÉ* and *A Streetcar Named Desire.*

During this time Williams successfully launched his dramatic career by submitting a collection of three one-act plays (*MOONY'S KID DON'T CRY, THE DARK ROOM,* and *THE CASE OF THE CRUSHED PETUNIAS*) under the title *AMERICAN BLUES* to a new play contest sponsored by THE GROUP THEATRE in New York City. Williams won a $100 prize for his collection and drew the attention of the talent representative AUDREY WOOD, who became his agent. By the time the prize was awarded in 1939, Tom had left New Orleans, was traveling extensively, and was writing under his new pen name, "Tennessee." During this year he published his first work, under his nom de plume, the short story "THE FIELD OF BLUE CHILDREN." The same year "The Field of Blue Children" was published in *Story* magazine, *Not About Nightingales* was produced in Saint Louis and Williams was awarded a $1,000 grant from the Rockefeller Foundation. This was also the year that Williams made his first professional visit to New York City. While there he saw a Broadway production of LILLIAN HELLMAN's *The Little Foxes.* The production featured Tallulah Bankhead in a play centered on a traditional Southern family at odds with modern changes of the "New South."

His New York adventures and newly acquired funds sparked a desire to travel extensively. His travels took him across the United States to California, where he spent time working on a poultry farm, and to Taos, New Mexico, where he visited Frieda Lawrence, widow of the English novelist D. H. Lawrence, one of Williams's literary icons. Williams returned to New York in 1940. In February of that year, his one-act play *THE LONG GOODBYE* was produced at the New School for Social Research. This was the first New York production of one of his works, and it sparked the Theatre Guild's interest in his new full-length play *BATTLE OF ANGELS.* Williams spent the summer of 1940 revising the play in Provincetown, Massachusetts. There he met a young Canadian dancer named Kip Kiernan, who became his lover. He would later dramatize the events of this summer in the late play *SOMETHING CLOUDY, SOMETHING CLEAR.*

Williams's blissful summer was followed by a winter of discomfiture. *Battle of Angels* premiered at the Wilbur Theatre in Boston, Massachusetts, on December 30, 1940, under the direction of MARGARET WEBSTER, starring Miriam Hopkins and Wesley Addy. The opening night performance was a complete disaster. More troubling than the critical reaction to the play was the moral outrage that quickly followed. The Boston City Council denounced the play and called its presentation in the city of Boston a criminal act. Webster and her producers persuaded Williams to make changes to the script. After his changes the production was allowed to continue, but it closed only 17 days after its opening. After the disastrous Boston "tryout," the Theatre Guild decided not to risk a run of the show in New York. At the tender age of 24, the young playwright's career had been launched with a highly explosive start. Williams was shocked by the public's response to the play and devastated that his career had taken such a blow. To compound his angst during this time, Williams also had to have the first of several eye surgeries for cataracts in his left eye. Williams recuperated and recovered from his first professional failure in KEY WEST, FLORIDA.

He returned to New York in 1941; at that time *Moony's Kid Don't Cry* was selected for publication in *The Best One-Act Plays of 1940.* In 1942, the New School of Social Research offered him his second New York production, this time of the one-act play *THIS PROPERTY IS CONDEMNED.*

As do many young artists when just starting out, Williams struggled to make ends meet. He drifted where he could find work—work that would allow him the freedom to write evenings and weekends—in such locales as New York; New Orleans; Macon, Georgia; and Jacksonville, Florida. He sustained himself for a few years working at odd jobs while trying to secure a place for himself as a writer. During this time he waited tables and worked as an elevator operator, movie usher, and briefly as a message decoder for the U.S. Department of Engineers. His luck began to change in 1943, when Audrey Wood secured a contract for him as a scriptwriter in Hollywood, California, for METRO-GOLDWYN-MAYER (MGM). The young Williams felt like a king earning a princely wage of $250 a week as a full-time working writer.

Williams and his canine companions at his home in Key West, Florida *(Don Pinder)*

Williams's six-month contract with MGM was simultaneously a dream come true and a nightmare. He was frustrated by studio politics—MGM solidly rejected a screenplay he had worked on painstakingly and to which he was desperately committed. The screenplay, *The Gentleman Caller,* was largely autobiographical and was the basis for *The Glass Menagerie.* Williams was also demoralized by what he saw as the inane projects he was forced to develop, such as a vehicle for the irritable child star Margaret O'Brien, whom Williams found to be a rather loathsome version of Shirley Temple, and lightweight fare for the glamorous Lana Turner. Williams described the Turner project as fashioning a "celluloid brassiere" for a "grammar school drop out." Williams's attitude toward his work put him in hot water. He was removed from the film, suspended, and then fired. Fortunately, his name was gaining currency in the theater. In October 1943, his collaboration with DONALD WINDHAM, on a full-length play inspired by the D. H. Lawrence short story "You Touched Me," had been successfully produced by the Cleveland Playhouse by MARGO JONES and then revived at the Pasadena Playbox, in Pasadena, California. Notification that he had also received a $1,000 award from the National Academy of Arts and Letters was further indication that his star was on the rise. Williams used the prize money to revise his screenplay, *The Gentleman Caller,* for the stage.

The year 1944 was a major turning point for Williams. He completed the revisions of *The Gentleman Caller,* now renamed *The Glass Menagerie,* during the summer of 1944. His agent, Audrey Wood, loved the work and submitted it to the actor-producer EDDIE DOWLING, who decided to codirect the play with Margo Jones. JO MIELZINER was the production designer, and PAUL BOWLES composed the incidental music. Dowling secured the role of Williams's self-portrait, the young artist-narrator Tom Wingfield, for himself. Julie Haydon was cast as Laura Wingfield, the delicate portrait of Williams's sister Rose. The part of Amanda Wingfield, the dramatization of Williams's mother, Edwina, went to the veteran theater star Laurette

Taylor. The 60-year-old Taylor, who had recently retired from the stage since the death of her husband, was considered a risky choice by many. However, after a rehearsal period dogged by problems, not the least of which was Taylor's bouts with alcohol, *The Glass Menagerie* opened for a trial run at the Civic Theatre in Chicago, Illinois, on December 26, 1944. Neither the date (the day after Christmas) nor the raging blizzard that hit Chicago that night was conducive to attracting audiences. By the afternoon of December 27, the box office had taken in only $400, and the producers had begun to prepare a closing notice. CLAUDIA CASSIDY, the drama and music critic of the *Chicago Tribune* and one of the most influential critical voices outside New York, rescued *The Glass Menagerie.* Cassidy actively promoted the work, characterizing it as "a dream in the dusk and a tough little play [that] reaches out tentacles, first tentative, then gripping, and you are caught in its spell" (Cassidy, 1944). Because of her enthusiasm, by mid-January 1945 *The Glass Menagerie* was playing to sold-out houses.

On March 31, 1945, *The Glass Menagerie* opened at the Playhouse Theatre in New York City. The production concluded to an extraordinary 25 curtain calls and shouts for the author to appear on-stage. By the following Monday theatergoers lined the streets to purchase tickets. New York reviewers were slightly more restrained than those in Chicago, but they were unanimous in praising Laurette Taylor's performance and the overall impact of the play. Less than two weeks after opening on Broadway, *The Glass Menagerie* garnered the New York Drama Critics Circle Award and was voted the Best Play of 1945. Williams also won the Sidney Howard Memorial Prize for the play. With this award-winning play Williams had created a new aesthetic for American theater, which he called PLASTIC THEATRE, a highly expressionist stage language and style that would replace the standard conventions of realism.

*The Glass Menagerie*—which ran for a record 561 performances in New York—transformed the landscape of U.S. theater and Williams's life. The play gave him the critical respect, popular acclaim, and financial success that he had long sought. On March 2, 1945, Williams wrote to inform his mother that he was receiving $1,000 a week in income from the play. He also informed her that his good fortune was also hers: Williams had assigned half of the royalties from *The Glass Menagerie* to her. The play that she had inspired sustained her for the rest of her life and enabled her to realize her dream: independence from her husband, Cornelius.

After the spring of his first great success in New York, Williams retreated to Mexico for the summer. He spent his days at the Lake Chapala resort writing poetry and working on a new play, another treatment of a Southern heroine suffering from the loss of and nostalgia for the Old South. Before settling on the title *A Streetcar Named Desire* for his new work, Williams had considered other options, such as "Blanche's Chair in the Moon," "The Moth," "The Primary Colors," and "The Poker Night." He returned to New York in September 1945 for the Broadway premiere of *YOU TOUCHED ME!* Since the success of *The Glass Menagerie,* expectation was high for Williams's new play, a farcical comedy about sexual liberation featuring the handsome rising actor Montgomery Clift. *You Touched Me!* was immediately and unfavorably compared to *Menagerie,* which was also still playing on Broadway, about three blocks away. Williams responded to the lukewarm reviews by traveling and throwing himself into a new writing project, another treatment of sexual repression and liberation, tentatively titled "Chart of Anatomy," which was later revised as *Summer and Smoke.*

The new year, 1946, found Williams living in New Orleans once again. There he celebrated the publication of his one-act play *27 WAGONS FULL OF COTTON.* This period in New Orleans was highly productive, and Williams completed the short play *TEN BLOCKS ON THE CAMINO REAL,* and the short story "DESIRE AND THE BLACK MASSEUR" at this time. By summer, he was on Nantucket, sharing a cottage with CARSON MCCULLERS. Williams became enamored of this fellow Southerner's writing after reading her novel *The Member of the Wedding.* The two spent the summer of 1946 writing together, each at an end of a long dining table. McCullers worked on an adaptation of her novel for the stage, while Williams revised *Summer and Smoke.* In the fall of that year, Williams returned to New Orleans, where he was joined by his 90-year-old grandfather, the Reverend Dakin. The elderly Dakin had lost his wife (in 1944) and by now much of his eyesight. His grandson was happy to provide him with a refuge away from the bitter Williams household, where the Reverend Dakin had been living since 1941.

The Reverend Dakin was accepting of his grandson's sexual orientation and immensely proud of his success. During the year the Reverend Dakin spent living with his grandson, Williams shared such exotic locales as Key West, Florida, with his grandfather. As his grandfather had taken him on his first trip to Europe in 1938, Williams treated his grandfather royally during his stay with him. The Reverend Dakin thoroughly enjoyed the rich, elite artistic world they inhabited in New Orleans and elsewhere. For Williams, having his beloved grandfather by his side was a source of "spiritual solace" (Spoto, 143). The year 1947 was also emotionally fulfilling for Williams for another reason: It was during the summer of this year that Williams met FRANK MERLO, a handsome New Jersey–born navy veteran of Sicilian descent. He was to become the single most important love of his life. Williams and Merlo remained committed life partners until Frank's death in 1963.

This year also saw the premiere of *Summer and Smoke,* in Dallas, Texas, and of *A Streetcar Named Desire,* on Broadway. *A Streetcar Named Desire* was another major success for Williams. The production, directed by ELIA KAZAN and featuring JESSICA TANDY and MARLON BRANDO, ran for a record 855 performances in New York (294 more than *Menagerie*) and yielded a second New York Drama Critics Award and his first Pulitzer Prize. Williams again celebrated his success by traveling extensively. On this tour of Europe, Williams was accompanied by Frank Merlo. Experiencing Italy in the company of an Italian was a remarkable adventure for Williams, one for which he was forever grateful. Frank enabled him to appreciate Italian culture intimately, and this opportunity had a profound impact on Williams's writing. The experience spawned his Italian-centered works, such as *THE ROMAN SPRING OF MRS. STONE.* (1950) and *The Rose Tattoo* (1951). On returning to the United States, Williams and Merlo settled in Key West. The Reverend Dakin joined the couple at their new home there at 1431 Duncan Street.

In 1950, Williams's estranged father, Cornelius, resurfaced in his life. In February of that year, *Flair* magazine published one of Williams's most autobiographical short stories, "THE RESEMBLANCE BETWEEN A VIOLIN AND A COFFIN." Cornelius had apparently come across the story and was so outraged by its contents that he wrote to his son's agent, Audrey Wood, and threatened legal action. In the letter he accused his older son of being "a liar and an ingrate" (Spoto, 180). Cornelius ordered Wood to warn Tom that if he ever made reference to him again in any of his writing, his father would "make him regret it as long as he lives" (ibid.). Williams was bemused by what appeared to be his father's somewhat delayed reaction to his son's dramatization of the Williams home life. It seemed ironic to Williams that this short story—in which his father is mildly chastised as a "devilish" man who was hard to live with—had sparked his father's unmitigated rage. Cornelius had been completely indifferent to *The Glass Menagerie,* which was clearly and openly autobiographical, with its cavalier and notoriously absent father figure. Neither Williams nor Audrey Wood responded to Cornelius's letter.

*The Rose Tattoo* opened on Broadway in 1951 and won the Antoinette Perry (Tony) Award for Best Play. This same year a film version of *A Streetcar Named Desire,* starring VIVIEN LEIGH, was released. This landmark film won the New York Film Critics Circle Award and numerous Academy Awards in 1952. Williams was also awarded a lifetime membership in the National Institute of Arts and Letters. *Summer and Smoke* was also successfully revived in New York at this time. Jose Quintero directed the benchmark production of the play at the Circle in the Square Theatre. The production featured the then-unknown GERALDINE PAGE as Alma Winemiller.

The success of *Summer and Smoke* ensured a stable financial future for Williams's sister, Rose. Williams arranged for half of the royalties for *Summer and Smoke* to be assigned to her. Tom was delighted finally to be in a position to care of his beloved sister. He was now able to take a more authoritative role in the decision making surrounding her and her care.

Williams was unhappy with reports that he received that Rose was still being subjected to insulin and electroshock therapy at Farmington. He ordered that she be released from Farmington and placed her in a private and more expensive sanatorium, first one in Connecticut, finally in Ossining, New York.

The next year, 1953, saw the publication of Williams's first volume of poetry, *IN THE WINTER OF CITIES,* and the premiere of *Camino Real.* This experimental and largely expressionistic (see EXPRESSIONISM) play was a striking contrast to Williams's previous works and major successes. As such, it was not well received by the press or the public. However, many of Williams's fellow artists, such as Edith Sitwell, appreciated and admired his poetic risk taking. Williams regained his critical momentum with the release of the film of *The Rose Tattoo*—which featured the incomparable Italian screen diva ANNA MAGNANI and Burt Lancaster—and the Broadway premiere at *Cat on a Hot Tin Roof* in 1955. *Cat on a Hot Tin Roof* reaped for Williams his third New York Drama Critics Circle Award and his second Pulitzer Prize.

Williams's immense public favor was challenged with the release of the film *BABY DOLL* in 1956.

Portrait of Williams *(Friedman-Abeles)*

*Baby Doll* was a cinematic composition of two one-act plays, *27 Wagons Full of Cotton* and *THE LONG STAY CUT SHORT, OR THE UNSATISFACTORY SUPPER.* The film, directed by Elia Kazan, was dubbed "the dirtiest American-made motion picture that has ever been legally exhibited" (Sova, 28) and officially denounced by the Roman Catholic Church. Francis Cardinal Spellman, then archbishop of the archdiocese of New York, and the Catholic Legion of Decency (LOD) attacked the film relentlessly. Cardinal Spellman—who had in fact not actually seem the film himself—warned Catholics not to view the film on pain of sin and admonished that the film was a potential threat to their very salvation. The clamor of controversy and censorship only served to promote interest in the film and increase box office revenues.

Controversy and conflict were also prominent thematic features at the heart of many of the works Williams produced at this time. The three principal works of this period, *ORPHEUS DESCENDING* (1957), *SUDDENLY LAST SUMMER* (1957), and *Sweet Bird of Youth* (1959), mirror Williams's own conflict with the critical and moral establishment. Each of these works is centered on a rebellious outcast artist in conflict with, and often at the mercy of, a ruthless, overbearing, and oppressive society. Ultimately, all three artisans suffer violently at the hands of their censors. Professional strife and public humiliation are also at the center of *Night of the Iguana* (1961), Williams's last major Broadway success. *Night of the Iguana* earned Williams his fourth New York Drama Critics Circle Award and prompted a *Time* magazine cover story (March 9, 1962) heralding Williams as "the world's greatest living playwright." *Iguana* also won the London Critics Award for Best Foreign Play in 1965.

Despite the success of *Iguana,* the late 1950s and 1960s were overall a time of crisis, affliction, and change for Williams. The death of his beloved grandfather in 1957 marked the start of a lengthy period of depression, grief, and loss in Williams's life. The Reverend Dakin's death was soon followed by that of Frank Merlo in 1963. For Williams the loss of these two most pivotal people in his life was cataclysmic, and the depth of his grief was immeasurable. He turned to drugs and alcohol for solace and consolation. In the hands of a thoroughly irresponsible physician, Williams become addicted to a variety of prescription medications. Despite this personal and physical turmoil, Williams continued to write daily. However, the lackluster reception of such works as *THE MILK TRAIN DOESN'T STOP HERE ANYMORE* (1963), *THE MUTILATED* (1966), *THE KINGDOM OF EARTH, OR THE SEVEN DESCENTS OF MYRTLE* (1968), and *IN THE BAR OF A TOKYO HOTEL* (1969) compounded Williams's sense of despondency and isolation. Richard Gilman skewered Williams in *Commonweal* (February 8, 1963) by declaring, "Mistuh Williams, He Dead" after the debut of *The Milk Train Doesn't Stop Here Anymore* in 1963. To combat his depression and chemical dependencies, Williams turned first to psychoanalysis and then to religion.

In 1969, he was baptized into the Roman Catholic Church. His brother, Dakin, who had converted to Catholicism during his tenure in the navy, encouraged Williams's conversion and served as his witness at his confirmation service. Williams chose Francis Xavier, a saintly ancestor, as his patron. In addition to this spiritual intervention, Dakin took drastic measures to save his brother's life. When Dakin pleaded with his brother to seek proper medical attention in Saint Louis, Williams initially agreed and then changed his mind once back in Saint Louis. His brother took charge and forced him to go to Barnes Hospital. Because of the severity of his chemical dependencies, Williams was placed in the Renard Psychiatric Division. The physicians at Barnes Hospital sought aggressively to combat Williams's addictions. Their method of total and immediate withdrawal had an adverse and violent effect on Williams. In the course of his first few days at Barnes he suffered three grand mal seizures and two heart attacks. That Williams survived and made a complete recovery was remarkable. Dakin had saved his life; Williams, however, viewed the situation differently. During his three months at Barnes, Williams had been forced to live his worst nightmare, that of being confined and hospitalized. His greatest fear was madness, his sister's fate. As far as he was concerned his brother had forged fear into reality. For this, he resented and never forgave Dakin. Williams went so far as to excise his brother from his will.

This new lease on life prompted a period of incredible creativity for Williams. His confidence was bolstered by the award of an honorary doctor of humanities degree by the University of Missouri and a Gold Medal for Drama by the American Academy of Arts and Letters. Williams galvanized his creative energies and expressed the trauma of the past decade in the writing and rewriting of *THE TWO CHARACTER PLAY* and *OUT CRY*. For roughly four years (between 1971 and 1975) Williams dedicated himself to this tale of a brother and sister trapped in a virtual wasteland. The work was not widely produced, nor very well received. Only now is it, as are many of Williams's later works, being critically reassessed and appreciated.

Williams's critical reputation continued to wane significantly in the 1970s. Critics were brutal and responded savagely to his efforts during this period. The critical rejection took a heavy toll. Ironically, the works of this period are some of Williams's boldest and most extraordinary dramatic renderings, which are now being appreciated for their vision and innovation. Works such as *THE GNÄDIGES FRÄULEIN* (1966), *I CAN'T IMAGINE TOMORROW* (1966), *Out Cry* (1973). *THE RED DEVIL BATTERY SIGN* (1975), *TIGER TAIL* (1978), *STEPS MUST BE GENTLE* (1980), *CLOTHES FOR A SUMMER HOTEL* (1980), *Something Cloudy, Something Clear* (1980), *NOW THE CATS WITH THE JEWELLED CLAWS* (1981), and *THE REMARKABLE ROOMING-HOUSE OF MME. LE MONDE* (1984) were drafted in an entirely different vein from Williams's earlier dramas and illustrate his evolution and maturity as an artist. Critics who expected, and wanted, Williams's "voice" to remain constant, reproducing his previous successes *The Glass Menagerie, Cat on a Hot Tin Roof,* or *A Streetcar Named Desire,* were sorely disappointed and expressed their disapproval vehemently and consistently.

Undaunted by critical opinion, Williams kept writing and even expanded his literary repertoire. He published a collection of short stories, *EIGHT MORTAL LADIES POSSESSED* (1974); a novel, *MOISE AND THE WORLD OF REASON* (1975); an autobiography, *MEMOIRS* (1975); a collection of poetry, *ANDROGYNE, MON AMOUR* (1977); and a collection of essays, *WHERE I LIVE* (1978). He was also encouraged by his continued popularity with audiences and the academic establishment, which manifested in the National Theatre Conference Award (1972), an honorary doctor of humanities degree conferred by the University of Hartford (1972), the Entertainment Hall of Fame Award (1974), the National Arts Club Medal of Honor for Literature (1974), and his selection as president of the Jury for the Cannes Film Festival (1976). In 1977, the Florida Keys Community College in Key West, Florida, dedicated the Tennessee Williams Fine Arts Center. The center opened with the premiere production of *WILL MR. MERRIWEATHER RETURN TO MEMPHIS?* (1980).

On February 25, 1983, Williams was found dead in his suite at the Hotel Elysée in New York City. He had choked to death, on a plastic medicine cap. Drama surrounded in him death as it had in life. Williams had stated repeatedly, and even in writing, that he wished to be buried at sea, off the coast of Florida, that his bones might rest in the deep, alongside those of his favorite poet, Hart Crane. His brother, Dakin, again intervened and ordered that his brother be buried in the family plot in Saint Louis. Williams's friends and admirers found Dakin's decision cruel and callous. Not only were Williams's final wishes being ignored, but he would also be placed at final rest in the city he loathed more than any other. Although Dakin respected his brother's wishes to be buried at sea, he adamantly believed that because of his brother's great literary status his remains should be in an accessible place. On March 5, 1983, Williams was buried beside his mother, Edwina Dakin Williams, at Calvary Cemetery, in Saint Louis, Missouri.

Williams's great legacy is that his art has stood the test of time. As Lyle Leverich noted, although Williams was so distinctly American in his art, no other American playwright has been more universally recognized, admired, or produced. The early 21st century has witnessed a renewed interest in Williams and his literary canon. Theater companies throughout the United States and abroad turn to Tennessee Williams for dramatic works that exude rich, seductive, and poetic language and possess remarkably human and complex characters. Some 20 years after his death, Williams had garnered the coveted position as "the hottest playwright in America" (Gardner, *USA Today*). On Broadway and in regional theaters across the country (not to mention community college and university theaters), there has been a continual stream of revivals of his most well-known works. *Cat on a Hot Tin Roof* was most recently produced on Broadway in 2003, featuring Ashley Judd as "Maggie the Cat." Productions of *A Streetcar Named Desire* and *The Glass Menagerie* were slated for Broadway in 2004 and 2005, respectively.

In addition to productions of the great Williams classics, there is significant interest in his lesser-known dramatic works and a drive to unearth these works for the stage. In 2003, Michael Kahn successfully premiered *AND TELL SAD STORIES OF THE DEATH OF QUEENS* at the Shakespeare Theatre in Washington, D.C. Some theater companies, such as the Hartford Stage Company (Hartford, Connecticut) and the John F. Kennedy Center for the Performing Arts (Washington, D.C.), have made a long-term commitment to produce Williams regularly and—in the case of Hartford Stage—ultimately to present his dramatic works in their entirety.

The scholarly community's commitment to the preservation of Williams's legacy is evident in the creation of two annual festivals honoring the playwright: the Tennessee Williams Literary Festival in New Orleans (established in 1986) and the "Tennessee in Key West Festival" (established in 2004). In addition, two academic journals are dedicated to the continued critical evaluation of Williams's works: the *Tennessee Williams Newsletter* and the *Tennessee Williams Annual Review*.

The revival of interest in Williams can be credited to a shift in critical, social, and cultural attitudes. It is evident that throughout his career Williams was a theatrical maverick, a poetic revolutionary who was clearly ahead of his time. There is now a greater appreciation for artistic experimentation and innovation. The overwhelming statement from this new generation of admirers is that Tennessee Williams was a far more accomplished and much more pivotal writer than previous generations appreciated. Contemporary artists, scholars, and audiences continue to affirm his status as America's greatest dramatist.

## FURTHER READING

Cuoco, Lorin, and William Gass, eds. "Tennessee Williams," in *Literary St. Louis: A Guide*. St. Louis: Missouri Historical Society Press, 2000, pp. 194–202.

Gardner, Elysa. "Tennessee Williams Is Hotter Than Ever," *USA Today*, October 21, 2003, p. A1.

Holditch, W. Kenneth. "Tennessee Williams in New Orleans," in *Magical Muse: Millennial Essays on Tennessee Williams*, edited by Ralph Voss. Tuscaloosa: University of Alabama Press, 2002, pp. 193–206.

Leverich, Lyle. *Tom: The Unknown Tennessee Williams*. New York: W. W. Norton, 1995.

Londré, Felicia. *Tennessee Williams*. Fredericton, Canada: York Press, 1989.

Sova, Dawn B. *Forbidden Films: Censorship Histories of 125 Motion Pictures*. New York: Facts On File, 2001.

Spoto, Donald. *The Kindness of Strangers: The Life of Tennessee Williams*. New York: Ballantine Books, 1985.

Williams, Tennessee. "Landscape with Figures: Two Mississippi Plays," in *American Scenes*, edited by William Kozlenko. New York: John Day, 1941.

# PART II

# *Works* A–Z

# "Accent of a Coming Foot"

Short story written in 1935.

## SYNOPSIS

Catharine, a young career woman, returns to her hometown after moving to the city. She visits her old acquaintances, the Hamiltons. It was planned that Bud Hamilton would meet Catharine at the train station; however, he has fallen behind schedule because, as the mother and sister presume, he now spends too much time alone writing. The Hamiltons are unhappy about Bud's preoccupation with his writing. A strange tension arises in Catharine as she anticipates meeting Bud again. Her relationship with him is unexplained, but sexual imagery is synonymous with memories of Bud. When Bud finally *does* arrive, she sees his shadow through the window and "she felt herself impaled like a butterfly upon the semi-darkness of the staircase." When he enters the house, Catharine freezes and stares down at him. He sees her, retraces his steps back out of the house, and closes the door behind him. Catharine begins to cry.

## COMMENTARY

This short story's appeal resides in its subtleties. It is written in a similar fashion to a scene that might appear in an Alfred Hitchcock film. The shadows on the wall when Bud arrives have a menacing and panicking effect on Catharine. Their history is quite vague, and before Bud arrives, it seems clear that she is in love with him. She reminisces about their college days and nervously adjusts her appearance. While Catharine anticipates Bud's arrival, she is overcome with emotion and left speechless, unable to confront or greet him. Bud exits her life once again, and Catharine is fraught with sadness and anxiety. Williams leaves their relationship unexplained.

In many ways this work resembles and foreshadows "THE IMPORTANT THING," another tale of strained romantic tension between a budding writer and an ambitious yet sensitive female counterpart.

## PUBLICATION HISTORY

"The Accent of a Coming Foot" was published in *Collected Stories* (New York: New Directions, 1985).

## CHARACTERS

**Catharine** A young career woman who visits her friends in the country. Catharine is disappointed when Bud Hamilton does not collect her at the bus station. When she does make her way to the Hamiltons', she learns that Bud locks himself away and writes. She nervously awaits his arrival and reminisces about their intimate moments of the past. When Bud finally appears, he causes Catharine to collapse and cry.

**Hamilton, Bud** Bud is an intensely dedicated young writer who, as was Williams, was criticized for spending all of his youth alone and writing. When Bud does not collect his friend, Catharine, as he had promised, his family becomes irate and embarrassed by his lack of concern for their guest. Bud arrives at his home long after Catharine has found her way there. He opens the door and sees her at the top of the stairwell. When he makes eye contact with her, he quickly departs.

# *All Gaul Is Divided*

Screenplay/teleplay written around 1950.

## SYNOPSIS

In Saint Louis, Missouri, in the late 1920s, the predominant action of the play takes place at Blewett High School and in the shabby apartment of Jenny Starling and Beulah Bodenhafer.

Jenny Starling is teaching her class to conjugate the Latin word for "love." The sound of a marching band that is practicing can be heard. The music upsets Jenny, as it reminds her of the man teaching the band, Harry Steed. One of her students, Eddie Peacock, taunts Jenny by mimicking her high-pitched voice. Jenny becomes irate, bursts into tears, and orders Eddie out of the classroom. Eddie confides in Mr. Paige, the school superintendent, that Jenny is "on another rampage" and that every time she hears Harry Steed's Victrola she "goes to pieces."

After class, Jenny calls her housemate Beulah at her job at the Universal Shoe Company. Beulah urges Jenny to stay at school and to visit the school nurse. Beulah calls Mr. Paige and warns him that Harry Steed is upsetting Jenny. Jenny encounters Harry in the school cafeteria. Harry sits next to Jenny and asks her, "How many parts is Gaul divided into?" Jenny nervously responds, "Three parts." Lucinda Keener joins Harry and Jenny at their table. Lucinda invites Harry to a bridge party on Saturday night. Harry responds that he has invited Jenny to see *Blossom Time* at the Municipal Opera. Jenny happily accepts his invitation. Lucinda openly criticizes Jenny's "little girl curls" and suggests she have her hair bobbed. Harry states that Jenny "looks like an angel with curls." Jenny, torn between embarrassment and euphoria, leaves the table to call Beulah.

Lucinda chastises Harry in Jenny's absence. When Jenny returns, Lucinda leaves to have a cigarette. Noticing Jenny and Harry alone, a group of female students whisper and giggle. Jenny overreacts and ferociously chastises the girls. Mr. Paige confronts Harry and suggests that he dress more appropriately before entering the cafeteria, instead of making a "public display" of his physique following his gym class. Harry challenges Mr. Paige's comments and threatens to quit. Mr. Paige urges him to be careful in his dealings with Jenny Starling.

Lucinda discovers Jenny crying at the chalkboard in her classroom. Jenny asks Lucinda to walk her home. Once outside, the two women discuss Harry Steed. Lucinda tells Jenny sordid details of Harry's previous romantic liaisons. Jenny naively disregards Lucinda's warnings. Lucinda changes the subject and pressures Jenny to leave her "fat, middle-aged typist" housemate and join her in a luxury apartment in an exclusive area of Saint Louis.

Jenny shares with Beulah the details of her lunchtime encounter with Harry Steed. Beulah tries to turn the conversation to her brother Buddy. Jenny confesses that she is not interested in Beulah's widowed brother or his daughter, Little Pretty.

Jenny prepares for her date with Harry. She waits for him wearing a snowy white taffeta ball gown. A rainstorm begins as Harry arrives. Jenny leaves with Harry, and Beulah phones Buddy.

Jenny and Harry are driving in his car, a "blood red" Bear Cat. They stop on Art Hill, and Harry asks Jenny for a kiss and she eagerly accepts. Jenny suggests they forgo the opera altogether and stay parked on Art Hill. Jenny sings a song from the opera for Harry. Harry decides they should go to the performance.

Harry and Jenny attend the outdoor performance and are caught in a violent rainstorm. Jenny is crushed as everyone runs for shelter. Harry carries Jenny home and delivers her to Beulah. Beulah ushers Jenny into her room. Harry sneaks out of the apartment while Beulah goes to answer the telephone. Jenny becomes hysterical when she realizes Harry has left without a word.

Buddy pays a visit to the apartment, where he crudely proposes to Jenny by suggesting that she's "not getting any younger." He tries to kiss Jenny, who becomes hysterical and leaves the room. Beulah chastises Buddy for "moving too fast." Buddy admits that he thinks Jenny is just a "prissy coldheart schoolteacher." Beulah tries to arrange a romantic picnic for the three of them the following Sunday at Creve Coeur. Buddy concedes and agrees to pursue Jenny.

Lucinda corners Jenny about her date with Harry and implies that Harry has been making fun of her behind her back. Lucinda once again pressures Jenny to move in with her at Westmoreland Place. She uses Harry as a reason for Jenny to move to Westmoreland Place—it will be a more fashionable place to entertain him.

The following Saturday, Lucinda visits Jenny to collect her deposit for the new apartment. Jenny and Beulah's living conditions mortify Lucinda. During her visit she is rude to Beulah and hounds Jenny for the apartment deposit and taxi fare. Beulah criticizes Lucinda and informs Jenny that she has arranged a picnic at Creve Coeur the next day for Jenny, Buddy, and her. Jenny attacks Beulah for matchmaking and accuses her of "not have a life of [her] own." Beulah apologizes and reminds Jenny how they met. (Jenny was a patient in the same sanitarium as Buddy and Beulah's mother.) Jenny takes a wastepaper basket and collects all of Beulah's tacky treasures and throws them away.

The next day, as Beulah prepares for the picnic, her upstairs neighbor quickly descends the fire escape to give her the society page from the Sunday newspaper. She shows Beulah a photograph of Harry Steed and his fiancée and their engagement announcement. The Upstairs Neighbor warns Beulah that the other teachers will be calling soon to tell Jenny. Beulah decides to disconnect the telephone and to hide the newspaper. Lucinda arrives to see Jenny. Beulah serves her coffee while she waits for Jenny. (Jenny is performing calisthenics in her bedroom.) Beulah makes a frantic call to Buddy, demanding that he join them for the picnic at Creve Coeur. Beulah urges him not to bring along his daughter, Little Pretty, as the little girl "makes Jenny nervous."

Lucinda asks Beulah about Jenny's mental health: whether she had previously had a nervous breakdown or something "mental." Beulah dodges the question and explains that Jenny is simply a person who "can't cope" with life. Beulah tells Lucinda about her plan to encourage Buddy and Jenny to marry. Lucinda asks for details about Buddy and ridicules the fact that he works at the Budweiser brewery. Lucinda slips into Jenny's bedroom, while Beulah takes her bulldog, Rosie, outside. Just as Lucinda starts to tell Jenny of Harry's engagement, Beulah rushes in, turns up the radio, and whisks Lucinda out of Jenny's room. She threatens Lucinda with a cactus plant, and Lucinda storms out of the apartment.

Jenny leaves her room and informs Beulah that she will not be attending the picnic at Creve Coeur and that she is moving in with Lucinda. Jenny explains that she will need a more refined place in which to entertain Harry Steed. Beulah counters by pleading with Jenny to give Buddy a chance. She informs Jenny that Buddy is "ready and willing" to accept her "on faith." Jenny becomes outraged by the implications of Buddy's acceptance of her "on faith." Beulah tries to explain delicately that this is in reference to Jenny's previous nervous breakdown. Jenny launches an attack on what she calls Beulah's "tyranny of kindness," which has robbed her of her independence.

Jenny goes through the Sunday paper and questions Beulah about the society section. Beulah confesses that she has wrapped the deviled eggs in that page. Jenny orders her to unwrap them and give her the page. Beulah leaves Jenny with the newspaper and goes to meet Buddy at Creve Coeur streetcar station. Jenny is dumbfounded and sits in silence for a few moments. She then places a call to Creve Coeur streetcar station. She asks the station manager to relay a message to Beulah Bodenhafer, whom he will recognize by her hat (a straw hat with silk roses) and the large poppy she wears over one ear to conceal her hearing aid. The Station Manager is advised to tell Beulah that Jenny is on her way to join the Bodenhafers at Creve Coeur station.

## COMMENTARY

*All Gaul Is Divided* is the foundation text for the play *A LOVELY SUNDAY FOR CREVE COEUR.* Williams penned *All Gaul Is Divided* during the 1950s, mislaid it, and subsequently recovered it in a file of old manuscripts in New Orleans around 1976. Williams believed the screenplay to be the superior text of the two because in the screenplay he "rectifies the major defect dilemma of the recent play: the giving away of the 'plot' in the first scene . . . the denouement is saved till the last few minutes of the final scene" (Williams, "Author's Note," 3). Although *All Gaul* may be structurally superior to *Creve Coeur,* the latter is a much more satisfying work in terms of form, content, and depth of characterization. In *Creve Coeur* Williams is also more concise with the material and employs farcical humor to drive the plot and relieve dramatic tension.

## PRODUCTION HISTORY

*All Gaul Is Divided* has not been filmed or produced professionally.

## PUBLICATION HISTORY

*All Gaul Is Divided* was first published in *Stopped Rocking and Other Screenplays* (1984).

## CHARACTERS

**Bodenhafer, Beulah** Beulah is a middle-aged German woman who works at the Universal Shoe Company in Saint Louis. She shares an apartment with a young schoolteacher, Jenny Starling. Beulah met Jenny while visiting her mother in a mental institution. Jenny had suffered a nervous breakdown. Beulah pitied her and took her in upon her release. Although Jenny is infatuated with Harry Steed, Beulah strives to convince Jenny to marry her brother, Buddy Bodenhafer.

**Bodenhafer, Buddy** He is the large beer-drinking brother of Beulah Bodenhafer. Buddy works at the Budweiser brewery in Saint Louis and is a single father. At his sister's insistence he is pursuing a relationship with Jenny Starling, an emotionally unstable schoolteacher. Although Jenny is attractive, Buddy often finds her to be snobbish and "prissy." Jenny becomes interested in Buddy only when Harry Steed becomes engaged to someone else. She decides that Buddy, and his nerve-wracking daughter, Little Pretty, are better than no family at all.

**Keener, Lucinda** Lucinda is a sophisticated art teacher at Blewett High School in Saint Louis. She pretends to befriend Jenny Starling, a fellow teacher at the school. Jenny is insecure, mentally unstable, and easily manipulated by Lucinda and others. Lucinda swindles Jenny and procures money from her for the down payment on a luxury apartment in a posh section of the city.

**Paige, Mr.** Mr. Paige is the principal of Blewett High School. He is concerned for the well-being of Jenny Starling, a mentally unstable woman who teaches Latin at the high school. Jenny has frequent outbursts in her classes; the source of her distraction is the attractive gym teacher Harry Steed. Mr. Paige confronts Harry about his behavior and his somewhat revealing attire.

**Peacock, Eddie** He is one of the students in Jenny Starling's Latin class. Eddie mocks Jenny by imitating her voice during class recitation. Jenny loses her temper, bursts into tears, and orders Eddie to leave the classroom. Eddie reports the incident to the school principal, Mr. Paige.

**Starling, Jenny** Jenny is a mentally unstable Latin teacher at a Saint Louis high school. She is older than age 30 and shares a tasteless apartment with Beulah Bodenhafer, a middle-aged office worker. Jenny dresses herself "like a grown woman playing a little girl" and is infatuated with the local playboy and high school gym teacher Harry Steed. She is easily toyed with by Harry, manipulated for her money by Lucinda Keener, and coaxed into a relationship with Beulah's beer-swilling brother Buddy.

**Steed, Harry** Harry is a handsome, well-built gym teacher at Blewett High School. He is a local playboy in the Saint Louis country club scene. He dallies with the affections of Jenny Starling, a mentally unstable Latin teacher.

**Upstairs Neighbor** She is a stout matron who lives in the apartment above Beulah Bodenhafer and Jenny Starling. The Upstairs Neighbor rushes down the fire escape to show Beulah the society page in the Sunday paper, which contains a photograph of Harry Steed and his fiancée.

## FURTHER READING

Williams, Tennessee. "Author's Note," in *Stopped Rocking and Other Screenplays*. New York: New Directions, 1984, p. 3.

# *American Blues*

A collection of six of Williams's one-acts plays published by Dramatists Plays Service in 1948. The plays included in this volume are *Moony's Kid Don't Cry*, *The Dark Room*, *The Case of the Crushed Petunias*, *The Unsatisfactory Supper*, and *Ten Blocks on the Camino Real*. These plays individually and collectively illustrate the plight of the American working class and their quest for freedom and a better way of life.

## Androgyne, Mon Amour

Poetry collection published in 1977. Profoundly personal, Williams's poetry is the truest reflection of the dramatist's psychological and emotional self. Although it is often thought that Williams candidly revealed his private life in his autobiography, *Memoirs* (1975), that work in no way corresponds with his conflicted views regarding his sexuality, which are fundamental aspects of this collection of poems. Just as he notoriously wrote his own life and experiences into his plays and fiction, he did so in his poetry. Moreover, the poems of *Androgyne, Mon Amour* are a testament to Williams's worries and fears as well as his inner visions of life and aging. As does the work of modernist poet Frank O'Hara (1926–66), Williams's poetry takes many midthought tangents, and he loosely interjects images, which often yield the most poignant moments of truth.

Much to his chagrin, Williams was never fully recognized as a poet (because he had already been defined as a playwright to the public). He wrote poetry his entire life, and he was often praised early in his career for incorporating a poetic aesthetic into his plays (such as THE GLASS MENAGERIE, A STREETCAR NAMED DESIRE, and CAT ON A HOT TIN ROOF). He would also be criticized and defamed for this convention in the 1960s and 1970s (in such works as CAMINO REAL, TWO CHARACTER PLAY, and STEPS MUST BE GENTLE). Williams defended his artistic innovations by proclaiming, "I am a poet. And then I put poetry in the drama. I put it in the short stories, and I put it in the plays. Poetry's poetry. It doesn't have to be called a poem, you know" (Radar, 98).

Williams constantly pushed the boundaries between the genres of playwriting and poetry, and like "a box of questions shaken up and scattered on the floor," *Androgyne, Mon Amour* invites the reader to investigate the personal lamentation of a disdained poet.

See also IN THE WINTER OF CITIES.

### FURTHER READING

Radar, Dotson. "Interview with Tennessee Williams," in *Playwrights at Work: The Paris Review Interviews*, edited by John Lahr. New York: Modern Library, 2000.

Roessel, David, and Nicholas Moschovakis, eds. *The Collected Poems of Tennessee Williams*. New York: New Directions, 2002.

Taylor, William E. "Tennessee Williams: The Playwright as Poet," in *Tennessee Williams: A Tribute*, edited by Jac Tharpe. Jackson: University Press of Mississippi, 1977, pp. 609–629.

## And Tell Sad Stories of the Death of Queens

A one-act play published in 2002. The date of composition is uncertain.

### SYNOPSIS

The play is set in the French Quarter of New Orleans, Louisiana. It is the weekend before Mardi Gras. The period is "possibly between 1939–41 or alternatively 1945–47." The action of the play takes place in the interior of a beautifully decorated apartment owned by Candy Delaney, a male transvestite. Candy's apartment is decorated in a Japanese style with bamboo furniture, grass mats, and delicate blue and white porcelain bowls. The adjacent patio garden is also fitted with a Japanese motif: a fish pool, weeping willows, and an arched bridge with paper lanterns.

#### *Scene 1*

Candy escorts Karl, a large merchant seaman, into her apartment. She insists that Karl have a look at the Japanese garden. Karl is unimpressed by its Oriental finery. Candy shares details about the rental property she owns in and around the Quarter and about her 17-year relationship, which has just ended. She tells Karl about her upstairs tenants, "a pair of sweet boys from Alabama." Karl confronts Candy about her sexuality. Candy reminds Karl that they met in a gay bar. Karl asks for a drink and warns Candy that he is not physically attracted to her. Candy clarifies that she would be happy just to have a "true friendship" with Karl. Candy goes into the bedroom to change "clothes and sex." Candy returns to the living room in drag. Karl is astonished by Candy's beauty. Candy recites a poem written for her by one of her upstairs tenants.

Karl becomes agitated and inquires whether Candy knows any "real" women; he adamantly denies any interest in Candy. Candy suggests they dance. Karl refuses, insisting that he cannot allow himself to forget that Candy is not actually female. They dance, and Karl tries to leave. Candy makes him an offer: In exchange for his companionship she will provide him with a place to stay in New Orleans, "unlimited credit at every bar in the Quarter," money, and freedom to come and go as he pleases.

Karl insists that he wants a woman. Candy includes that in her bargain. She informs Karl that all she wants is to lie next to him and "blissfully fall asleep with [his] hand in [hers]." Karl is willing to give Candy what she wants for $20. She places $50 in his wallet and calls her friend Helene, a stripper at a local club. Candy makes arrangements for Helene to stop by for Karl. Karl reminds Candy that she is not getting anything out of this deal. She explains that "getting nothing" is something she is used to.

Karl goes out to the garden, while Candy mixes him another drink. One of the upstairs tenants, a young drag queen in her 20s, Alvin Krenning, arrives at Candy's door. Alvin has arrived to warn Candy about her new acquaintance: Karl has a reputation for being "dirt" and for physically abusing queens in the Quarter. Candy dismisses the warning and throws Alvin out of the apartment.

### *Scene 2*

The location is the same; the time is a half hour later. Candy and Karl are outside in the garden. Karl slips into the fish pool as he tries to recross the Japanese bridge. Karl enters the apartment wet and cursing. Candy follows him back into the apartment, while trying to silence her giggling upstairs tenants. Candy offers Karl a Chinese robe to change into. Karl disrobes and threatens Candy with physical harm if she approaches him. Candy ignores his threats, calling him a "roughtalking two hundred pounds of lonely, lost little boy." Karl places a call and leaves a message for Alice "Blue" Jackson, a loose woman he met earlier. Candy implies that she knows Alice. Karl warns Candy not to malign Alice and again threatens to harm her. Candy reiterates that Karl will eventually grow fond of her. Karl goes into the bedroom to get some sleep before Helene, the stripper, arrives.

### *Scene 3*

The location is the same; the time is an early Sunday morning, one week later. Candy, dressed in drag, sits at the breakfast table having coffee. Karl is sleeping and snoring in the adjacent bedroom. The other upstairs tenant, a drag queen, Jerry Johnson, enters the apartment without knocking. Jerry wishes Candy a happy birthday and goes to the bedroom to take a peek at Karl. Jerry and Candy argue over Candy's state of affairs. Candy explains that she is striving for a life of "dignity" and permanence. Jerry leaves and slams the door. Karl rises and enters the kitchen looking for a drink. Candy tries to coax him not to drink.

Alvin stands in the doorway and overhears their argument. Karl confesses that he only returned to Candy because he is out of money. Alvin informs Candy that she has hurt Jerry's feelings. While Karl is in the bathroom, Alvin explains to Candy that Karl has been "shacked up" with Alice Jackson and has only returned to Candy because Alice threw him out. Candy is outraged and evicts Alvin and Jerry from their apartment.

Candy questions Karl about Alice and his recent whereabouts. She tells Karl about her plans for their future together. Karl demands money from Candy, and when she refuses, he attacks her. Frightened and stunned by Karl's violent outburst, Candy tells him her money is hidden in a silver teapot. Karl takes all of Candy's money from the teapot and leaves. Candy becomes hysterical, screams, and passes out. Alvin and Jerry rush in to rescue Candy. Finding her unconscious, they fear she is dead. Together they lift her from the floor and carry her to the bed. When she regains consciousness they offer her a glass of brandy. Jerry and Alvin sit beside Candy and try to comfort her, as rainfall can be heard in the distance.

## COMMENTARY

*And Tell Sad Stories of the Death of Queens*, as do many of Williams's New Orleans–based dramas (such as AUTO-DA-FÉ, A STREETCAR NAMED DESIRE, and VIEUX CARRÉ), depicts the broken but colorful lives on the fringes of society. The play's title is a reference to William Shakespeare's delicate and vulnerable outcast king, Richard II ("Pray, let us sit upon the ground and tell sad stories of the death of kings." [*Richard II* 3.2]). *Sad Stories* is, however, a significant and unique drama within the canon and a profound departure from Williams's other dramatic works.

*Sad Stories* features Williams's most overt depiction of gay characters and his most dynamic treatment of homosexuality. In sharp contrast to much of contemporary criticism, which has blasted Williams for what has often been seen as his "coded" or "closeted" treatment of homosexuality, *Sad Stories* is not a "sentimental apology" (Kahn, 392) but rather a gritty, realistic tale of a vulnerable drag queen who opens her heart and her home to a ruthless drifter.

The three gay characters—Candy, Jerry, and Alvin—form a close-knit community, a "sisterhood" that revolves around Candy's enchanted Japanese garden. This tranquil, delicate, and pastel Eden is a place of beauty and grace, where the monogamous Candy has mourned the loss of her long-term lover after a 17-year "marriage." Karl, an emissary from the outside world, a coldhearted sailor, slithers into Candy's world and throws all into disarray. Williams presents the three transvestites in such a frank, vulnerable, and endearing manner that the predictability of the plot can be overlooked for the sheer value of the tale. This remarkable and radically contemporary work confirms Williams's position as a visionary and political writer who was profoundly ahead of his time.

## PRODUCTION HISTORY

*And Tell Sad Stories of the Death of Queens* was first produced at the John F. Kennedy Center for the Performing Arts in Washington, D.C., in April 2004. Michael Kahn directed the premiere production.

## PUBLICATION HISTORY

*And Tell Sad Stories of the Death of Queens* was first published in 2002, along with NOT ABOUT NIGHTINGALES in *Political Stages: Plays That Shaped a Century*.

## CHARACTERS

**Delany, Candy** She is an elegant New Orleans "queen." Heartbroken and forlorn after ending a 17-year relationship with an Atlanta businessman, Candy pursues a relationship with Karl, a young merchant seaman. Candy dreams of love, security, and a prosperous and happy future with Karl. Karl, who is utterly homophobic, preys upon Candy's vulnerability, tenderness, and loving nature. He beats Candy and takes her money. In the end, she is left to grieve with the support of her closest friends, her fellow queens Alvin Krenning and Jerry Johnson.

**Johnson, Jerry** Jerry is a young drag queen from Alabama living in New Orleans. She shares an apartment in the French Quarter with Alvin Krenning, another young drag queen from Alabama. Their friend and fellow queen Candy Delaney is also their landlady. Alvin and Jerry try to prevent Candy from pursuing a relationship with Karl, an opportunistic and homophobic drifter.

**Karl** He is a young opportunist merchant seaman who drifts into New Orleans looking for someone to support him. He finds Candy Delaney, an elegant drag queen, in a gay bar and accompanies her to her apartment. Karl is cruel and homophobic. He bullies Candy, beats her, and takes her money. As does his fellow Merchant Seaman in SOMETHING CLOUDY, SOMETHING CLEAR, Karl has an unromantic view of love and intimate relationships. For them sex is merely a commodity to be bought, sold, and traded.

**Krenning, Alvin** Alvin is a young drag queen from Alabama. She shares an apartment with Jerry Johnson, another young drag queen from Alabama. Their friend and fellow queen, Candy Delaney, is their landlady. Jerry and Alvin try to prevent Candy from pursuing a relationship with Karl, an opportunistic and homophobic drifter. Alvin warns Candy that

Karl has a reputation for mistreating and physically abusing queens.

## FURTHER READING

Kahn, Michael. "Introduction," in *Political Stages: Plays That Shaped a Century,* edited by Emily Mann and David Roessel. New York: Applause Books, 2002.

# "The Angel in the Alcove"

A short story written in 1943.

## SYNOPSIS

The Narrator, a young writer who lives in the French Quarter of New Orleans. He rents an attic room in a boardinghouse owned by a ruthless and bitter old woman. The Narrator despises his shabby living conditions. There is an alcove in his room with a bench seat. The moonlight floods his room every night, and he is thankful for its beauty. Every evening as he is nearing sleep, an apparition, a Madonna figure, appears on the bench. The figure reminds him of his grandmother and he is comforted by her presence. One evening, the Narrator receives a visitor: a fellow tenant, a Young Artist who is dying of tuberculosis. The two young men have a romantic encounter under the gaze of the apparition sitting in the alcove. The young writer is surprised that she does not have a look of disapproval on her face, and she remains his guardian after this incident.

The Young Artist has an argument with the Landlady, who coldly reminds him he is dying and evicts him from her boardinghouse. The young man runs out of the building, hysterically yelling and coughing in the streets. The Narrator watches the painter from his alcove window. The Landlady's maid salvages the painter's belongings and places them under a tree near the house. Eventually the painter returns to collect his things. The Narrator once again watches him from his alcove window. For several nights after this explosive episode, the apparition does not reappear in the alcove of the Narrator's room. The Narrator decides this is a sign that he should leave the boardinghouse; he sneaks out and never returns.

## COMMENTARY

Largely autobiographical, "The Angel in the Alcove" is reminiscent of Williams's experience as a young artist living in the French Quarter of NEW ORLEANS, LOUISIANA, during the late 1930s. Williams moved to New Orleans in 1938, and the vibrant environment of the French Quarter became a major influence in his development as a writer. This bohemian locale introduced him to a community of fellow artisans and liberated Williams socially, artistically, and sexually. He would later describe New Orleans as "the paradise of his youth" (Holditch, 194). It was a paradise presided over by suspicious, unstable, and often violent landladies. One such landlady, Mrs. Louise Wire, who owned and ran the boardinghouse Williams lived in at 722 Toulouse Street, became the inspiration for the landlady character in "The Angel in the Alcove," *THE LADY OF LARKSPUR LOTION*, and *VIEUX CARRÉ*.

"The Angel in the Alcove" chronicles Williams's experience as a boardinghouse tenant coming to terms with his sexuality within the confines of the French Quarter. Far from the puritanical environment of his SAINT LOUIS, MISSOURI, home, Williams was free to explore his sexuality. Although he had left his prudish mother behind, Williams (and the Narrator of the story) found an equally domineering surrogate in the "paranoidal[ly] suspicious" (Leverich, 428) landlady, who made him feel guilty without cause. This tyrannical figure, simultaneously a stand-in for his mother and a personification of his own deep-set feelings of guilt and internalized homophobia, is juxtaposed with the compassionate and affirming apparition, the spirit of his grandmother.

In the story, the young writer is surprised that the Angel does not react negatively to his intimacy with another man. He is bewildered that she returns and remains his guardian. The Angel offers the young man acceptance, which comforts and relieves him. Williams received this same unconditional love and devotion from his maternal grandmother, ROSINA OTTE DAKIN. She was a source of beauty and light in his life, just as the Angel and her moonlight made the filthy surroundings of the Narrator's squalid room glow an iridescent blue.

Williams's grandmother is memorialized in this and numerous other works, such as *GRAND.* Her tragic death from lung cancer is also recalled in this short story and in other works such as "ORIFLAMME" and *KINGDOM OF EARTH.*

"The Angel in the Alcove," and its collection of colorful artists and sadistic landlady, served as the basis for two later works: the one-act play *The Lady of Larkspur Lotion* and the full-length play *Vieux Carré.* However, within the impoverished, lonely environment of this story, Williams creates a world that possesses instances of immense beauty quite unlike its successors.

## PUBLICATION HISTORY

"The Angel in the Alcove" was first published in the short story collection *One Arm* in 1948. It was subsequently published in the short story collections *Three Players of a Summer Game* (1960), *Collected Stories* (1985), and *The Night of the Iguana and Other Stories* (1995).

## CHARACTERS

**Landlady** The landlady is a miserable woman who owns a boardinghouse in New Orleans. She enjoys bullying her tenants and maintains a very strict curfew. The landlady is suspicious and accusatory, believing that many of the low-life characters who live in her house are committing the crimes that happen in New Orleans. The landlady especially enjoys accusing the Narrator of crimes she has read about in the newspaper. She evicts a young artist from her home because he has tuberculosis.

**Narrator** The Narrator is a young writer who lives in a New Orleans boardinghouse run by a tyrannical Landlady. He receives nightly visits from the apparition of his deceased grandmother, who comforts him. The Narrator has a secret rendezvous with a Young Artist, a fellow boarder, who is dying of tuberculosis. When his lover is evicted and the apparition stops appearing, the Narrator also leaves.

**Young Artist** The Young Artist is dying of tuberculosis, but he refuses to believe he is sick. He has intimate relations with the Narrator, and he leaves the boardinghouse when the Landlady verbally attacks him.

## FURTHER READING

Holditch, W. Kenneth. "Tennessee Williams in New Orleans," in *Magical Muse: Millennial Essays on Tennessee Williams,* edited by Ralph Voss. Tuscaloosa: University Press of Alabama, 2002, pp. 193–206.

Leverich, Lyle. *Tom: The Unknown Tennessee Williams.* New York: W. W. Norton, 1995.

# *At Liberty*

A one-act play written before 1940.

## SYNOPSIS

The play is set in Blue Mountain, Mississippi, in the modest living room of Gloria Bessie Greene and her Mother. A "glamour photo" of Gloria is prominently featured in the room. The time is two-thirty in the morning, in early autumn. The rain can be heard and seen streaming down the living-room window outside. Gloria's mother sits alone in the darkened living room. She has sat up all night waiting for Gloria to return from her date with Charlie. Upon her return, Gloria can be heard in the hallway bidding Charlie farewell. Charlie does not appear onstage but can be heard leaving Gloria reluctantly. He makes further advances, which Gloria rejects. Gloria enters the house and is in a bedraggled state. Her white satin evening dress is wet, soiled, and torn. Gloria's mother addresses her as "Bessie," interrogates her about her evening, and expresses her frustration about Gloria's choice in men. (All of her dates are men she "picks up" in hotels.)

Gloria's mother admonishes her for ruining her reputation and becoming the subject of town gossip. Mother reminds Gloria that she is recovering from tuberculosis and pleads with her to heed the doctor's advice to take bed rest. She encourages Gloria to give up her hope of fame and glamour and consider Vernon's offer of marriage. Gloria shows her mother an advertisement she has placed in *Billboard* magazine, proclaiming her skills ("singing, dancing specialties") and her immediate availability to take any role offered. Gloria's mother accuses her of falsifying her age and abilities in the advertisement. Gloria chastises her mother for trying to destroy her confidence and crush her dreams. Gloria begs her not to "stifle" her passion. She declares that she has a "cry from [her] soul" that needs to be expressed. Gloria opens the window and surveys the small town that lies before her. She recalls a former childhood love named Red Allison who died.

Gloria's mother again reminds her of her illness, but Gloria refuses to accept her limitations. She acknowledges her entrapment but does not allow it to discourage her. Gloria concedes that for the time being luck has not been on her side. She runs from the room, sobbing uncontrollably. During Gloria's absence her mother quietly admits her dissatisfaction with the state of her own life and returns to the sofa.

## COMMENTARY

Written around 1940, *At Liberty* is linked chronologically and dramaturgically to the works of Williams's early AMERICAN BLUES period. Similar to the one-act plays in the *American Blues* collection (MOONY'S KID DON'T CRY, THE DARK ROOM, THE CASE OF THE CRUSHED PETUNIAS, THE UNSATISFACTORY SUPPER, and TEN BLOCKS ON THE CAMINO REAL), *At Liberty* illustrates the working-class quest for a better and more expressive way of life. Here, as in *Moony's Kid Don't Cry*, the American dream is a dream that is repeatedly deferred.

This early work also contains many of the themes, ideas, characterization, and environment that Williams would fully develop in his later drama and fiction, particularly the theme of "the artist in isolation." Gloria, once the small-town girl with stars in her eyes, has become the showgirl past her prime. Poor health has propelled her back into the "dark, wide, spacious land" (Kozlenko, 174) of Blue Mountain, Mississippi. Blue Mountain's vast open spaces only serve to remind Gloria of the gaping void between her ambition and her reality.

Gloria Bessie Green is an engaging character study reminiscent of many of Williams's headstrong female characters, such as Heavenly Critchfield in SPRING STORM or Lady Torrance in ORPHEUS DESCENDING. She shares their gritty determination to survive against all odds, and in spite of societal expectations. She is strikingly similar in manners, appearance, and dialogue to Cassandra Whiteside in BATTLE OF ANGELS. Both possess a "feverish look" and appear in excessive makeup, dressed in white satin evening dresses that have been soiled by mud and rain. Both women are outcasts, who feel they are caged animals in their respective societies. Gloria is also similar to Alma Winemiller of SUMMER AND SMOKE (and ECCENTRICITIES OF A NIGHTINGALE), who is another passionate artist trapped in a stifling, repressed small-town environment. As do Alma and Blanche DuBois (A STREETCAR NAMED DESIRE), Gloria engages in sex with strangers as a means to combat her sense of loneliness, isolation, and restlessness.

Gloria's tale and her fate are reminiscent of those of many of the artist-characters who populate the Williams canon and find themselves trapped in a stagnant environment. Gloria has placed an ad in *Billboard* proclaiming herself "at liberty" to accept any stage role on offer, but she soon realizes that there are literally and figuratively very few "roles" open to her either onstage or within the tiny community of Blue Mountain. Her choices are either to settle down and play wife to a man she does not care for or to take on a leading role as the town's most scandalous woman.

## PRODUCTION HISTORY

*At Liberty* was first produced in New York in September 1976.

## PUBLICATION HISTORY

*At Liberty* was published in *American Scenes: A Volume of New Short Plays* in 1941.

## CHARACTERS

**Greene, Gloria Bessie** She is a thin aging "ingenue," a dancer/performer struggling for success. Her stage name is "Gloria La Greene." The poor state of her health (she suffers from tuberculosis) forces her to return to her small rural childhood home of Blue Mountain, Mississippi. Gloria refuses to follow her doctor's orders to stay in bed and insists on enjoying herself. Always an outsider in her community, Gloria, by her return and her provocative behavior, generates considerable gossip in town. Gloria's long-suffering Mother waits patiently for Gloria to return from her nightly excursions with men she meets in hotels. Similar to Alma Winemiller in SUMMER AND SMOKE (and ECCENTRICITIES OF A NIGHTINGALE), Gloria is a passionate artist trapped in a stifling, repressed small-town environment. As do Alma Winemiller and Blanche Dubois (in A STREETCAR NAMED DESIRE), Gloria engages in sex with strangers as a means to combat her sense of loneliness, isolation, and restlessness.

**Mother** She is the long-suffering mother of Gloria Bessie Greene. Gloria's mother worries constantly about her daughter's ailing state of health, unhappiness, and reputation. She fears that her daughter is headed for ruin, death, or both. This middle-aged woman does not sleep at night, knowing that her daughter is out on the town with strangers she meets in hotels. She hopes to salvage Gloria's life and reputation by encouraging her to marry Vernon, a stable local man. Unknown to her daughter, Gloria's Mother shares her daughter's sense of mortality and isolation and her longing for "good luck."

### FURTHER READING

Kozlenko, William, ed. *American Scenes: A Volume of New Short Plays.* New York: John Day, 1941, pp. 174–182.

## *Auto-Da-Fé*

A one-act play written in 1938.

### SYNOPSIS

The play is set on the front porch of an old house in the Vieux Carré section of New Orleans, Louisiana, in the late 1930s. Eloi, a young postal worker, returns home after a bad day at work. He is confronted by his mother, Madame Duvenet, who insinuates that he is hiding something from her. Eloi denies her allegations and fumes about the immorality that surrounds him in the French Quarter. He remarks that the town needs to be purified by fire. Eloi confesses that he found a lewd photograph that was being sent through the mail. Madame Duvenet suggests that she should burn the picture for him. Eloi lights a match and becomes mesmerized by the flame. He burns his finger, and his mother tells him to go inside and rinse his burn. Eloi enters the house and locks himself inside. There is an explosion and flames begin to engulf the house. Madame Duvenet stumbles down the porch stairs screaming for help.

### COMMENTARY

*Auto-Da-Fé* is a brief but intense glimpse into the strained relationship between a sexually repressed, fanatical young man and his domineering mother. The play is a dark, tragic tale of hypocrisy, guilt, and self-loathing. Eloi's conflict and ultimate tragedy center on his suppressed sexuality and his inability to acknowledge and accept his emotional and physical needs.

The term *auto-da-fé,* which literally means "act of faith," dates to the time of the Spanish Inquisition. It is the public denouncement and execution of a religious heretic or outcast by burning alive. In Williams's *Auto-Da-Fé,* Eloi becomes the executioner and the accused as the secret of his sexuality is slowly exposed. Eloi rails against what he sees as the degeneration of the French Quarter and claims that he wants to confront the immorality that surrounds him. His fanatical search for purity leads to self-condemnation. Eloi has transgressed because he has been enticed by the lewd photograph he found in the mail. Although the contents of the photograph are never fully discussed, Dean Shackelford deduces that the photograph depicts a younger and an older man together. The photograph thereby serves as a symbol of Eloi's unacknowledged sexual identity and as a catalyst for his growing self-awareness (Shackelford, 50). The photograph, as a tangible reminder of that which Eloi has tried to keep hidden from his mother and himself, must be destroyed. However, when Eloi strikes the match he has an epiphany that he must destroy himself along with the photograph. His death by fire will be the extreme act of faith that will purge and purify him of his lust.

Shackelford argues that through this play Williams was openly negotiating his own identity as a gay subject. He also believes that *Auto-Da-Fé* provides an example of how, early in his dramatic career, Williams acknowledged and dramatically explored the dilemma of self-acceptance for gay men, and as such the play foreshadows his later treatment of the gay subject in such works as SUDDENLY LAST SUMMER. Contemporary criticism by scholars such as Shackelford has prompted a new interest in this previously ignored play.

*Auto-Da-Fé* possesses several additional thematic connections with other Williams works. The rejection and denial of one's self as a sexual being, whether homosexual or heterosexual, are recurring themes in Williams's works. The conflict of the flesh versus the spirit is a dilemma faced by many of Williams's heroes and heroines (such as Alma Winemiller), and Eloi's torment foreshadows Williams's later treatment of sexual repression in such works as SUMMER AND SMOKE. In addition, as an early work in the Williams canon that exposes an unsatisfactory mother–son relationship, *Auto-Da-Fé* can be viewed as a precursor to THE GLASS MENAGERIE.

### PRODUCTION HISTORY

Michael Kahn directed the first New York production of *Auto-Da-Fé* at the Lucille Lortel Theatre in 1986, with Richard Howard as Eloi and Lisa Banes as Madame Duvenet.

### PUBLICATION HISTORY

The play was published in the one-act play collection *27* WAGONS FULL OF COTTON, AND OTHER ONE-ACT PLAYS in 1966.

### CHARACTERS

**Duvenet, Eloi** Eloi is a 30-year-old postal worker, who lives with his mother. He is outwardly very conservative and hypercritical of the world around him in the French Quarter of New Orleans. Although Eloi preaches about the immorality of his environment, his mother is suspicious of him and fears that he is hiding something from her. Eloi confesses to having found a lewd photograph while sorting the mail. He becomes obsessed with the lust that he feels when he looks at the photograph. Eloi wants to be rid of the photograph and his desire. His mother offers to burn the picture for him, but he decides to burn it himself. In an effort to purify his existence and surroundings, he finds the solution in fire, or purification through auto-da-fé or an "act of faith," by burning himself alive in the house.

**Duvenet, Madame** Madame Duvenet is the mother of Eloi. She is an elderly conservative and old-fashioned woman. She is extremely overbearing and domineering. Her son, who is in his 30s, still lives with her. She is very critical of Eloi and suspects that he is hiding something from her. When Eloi confesses that he found a lewd photograph in the mail, Madame Duvenet offers to burn it for him.

### FURTHER READING

Shackelford, Dean. "The Ghost of a Man: The Quest for Self-Acceptance in Early Williams," *The Tennessee Williams Annual Review* 4 (2001): 49–58.

## *Baby Doll*

A screenplay written in 1955.

### SYNOPSIS

The screenplay is set in a small town in rural Mississippi. The action takes place at the dilapidated homestead of Archie Lee Meighan and his wife, Baby Doll Meighan, and at various other locales in and around their home. The period of the screenplay is around 1955.

Baby Doll Meighan is asleep in a large crib in the nursery. She wears baby-doll-style pajamas and sucks her thumb. Roused from sleep by a scraping noise, she rises to discover her husband peeking at her through a hole in the wall. Baby Doll reprimands Archie for being a "peeping Tom." Baby Doll and Archie Lee discuss the terms of their marital "agreement," an arrangement made by Archie Lee and Baby Doll's father. For this agreement Archie Lee promised to "leave [Baby Doll] alone" (not attempt to consummate their marriage) until she reached the age of 20. Archie is exasperated as they are two days away from Baby Doll's 20th birthday, and he has dutifully waited more than a year.

The telephone rings, alarming Baby Doll's elderly aunt, Aunt Rose Comfort McCorkle, who is living with the couple. Aunt Rose Comfort finally answers the phone, and Archie Lee snatches it from her only to find the Ideal Pay As You Go Furniture Company on the other end threatening to repossess all of their recent acquisitions. Archie Lee warns Aunt Rose not to tell Baby Doll that the furniture company called.

Archie orders Baby Doll to accompany him to his doctor's appointment in town. He waits impatiently in his 1937 Chevy. When Baby Doll appears, she is wearing a skintight skirt and blouse. Archie Lee criticizes her clothing and refuses to get out and open the car door for her. Baby Doll announces that she will find her own way into town, walks to the end of the Meighan drive, and sticks out her thumb. A carload of teenage boys pulls over and stops for her. Archie Lee rushes down the drive and hurls gravel at the car.

On their way to the doctor's office Archie Lee admonishes Baby Doll for the "torture" she is putting him through and the "public humiliation" he has endured because of it. Baby Doll warns Archie Lee that their agreement will be canceled if their "five complete sets of furniture" are repossessed. Archie Lee changes the subject to Aunt Rose Comfort—he is weary of her "visiting." At Doctor John's office Baby Doll flirts innocently with a Young Man. Archie Lee becomes irate and the doctor prescribes sedatives for him.

An Ideal Pay As You Go Furniture Company truck passes Archie Lee and Baby Doll on the road as they return home. Sensing that they are hauling away her furniture, Baby Doll attacks Archie Lee. When they return home the furniture company removers are still working. Baby Doll jumps out of the car and attacks the workers. Baby Doll threatens to leave Archie Lee, get a job, and take up residence in the Kotton King Hotel. Archie Lee wanders out of the house and has a drink from a hidden pint. He jumps into his Chevy and drives away.

Archie Lee visits his local drinking hole, the Brite Spot, and finds it deserted. Everyone is attending the celebrations being held at the Syndicate Gin. Archie Lee ventures over to the Syndicate celebration. Shortly after his arrival, an explosion is heard, and a fire erupts in the gin. Silva Vacarro, the Syndicate Plantation manager, rushes into the burning cotton gin and retrieves an empty kerosene can.

Carroll Baker (Baby Doll Meighan) and Eli Wallach (Silva Vicarro) in *Baby Doll* *(Warner Bros., 1956)*

Archie returns home to find Aunt Rose Comfort asleep in the porch swing and Baby Doll sitting with her suitcases. Baby Doll chastises Archie Lee for leaving her behind and causing her to miss the fire. He becomes irate and physically abusive. He corrects Baby Doll and reinforces his alibi with her by squeezing her arm. Baby Doll accepts Archie Lee's alibi. Archie Lee tries to make peace and seduce Baby Doll by kissing her wounded arm. He teases her playfully and again quizzes her on his alibi. When she fails to answer correctly, he seizes her wrists sharply and sends her to bed.

The next day, Vacarro and his assistant, Rock, arrive at the Meighan home with 27 wagons of cotton. Meighan eagerly accepts the opportunity to gin Vacarro's cotton. Archie Lee introduces Baby Doll to Silva and Rock and instructs her to entertain Silva while his cotton is being ginned. Baby Doll yawns and apologizes for her bad manners, stating that she and Archie were up very late the previous night. Rock and Silva note the discrepancy between Baby Doll's statement and Archie Lee's. Archie Lee returns and shakes Silva's hand, confirming the "good neighbor policy." Silva suspects that Archie

Lee destroyed his gin. After Archie Lee and Rock have disappeared to start ginning cotton, Silva toys with Baby Doll to find out the truth. Baby Doll inadvertently lets it slip that Archie Lee left the house and did not return until after the fire at the Syndicate Plantation had started. When he questions her directly about Archie Lee's whereabouts, Baby Doll tries to retract her comments.

Silva teases and taunts Baby Doll, and seducing her becomes a means of revenge for him. Silva's advances awaken Baby Doll sexually. She is aroused and confused and runs to Archie for protection. He is infuriated by her disruption and slaps her. Frustrated by a piece of broken machinery, he vents his rage on her. Silva sends Archie Lee all over the state to fetch a new part for the machinery. Silva and Rock make arrangements to have the part delivered from their cotton gin across the road. Silva takes this opportunity to pursue Baby Doll further.

Silva hopes to obtain a confession from Baby Doll. He tries to charm her, then to scare her by telling her that her house is haunted. Silva engages Baby Doll in a game of hide-and-seek. He then terrorizes her into signing a statement verifying that Archie Lee burned down the Syndicate Gin. Baby Doll is disappointed that Silva is satisfied and wants nothing more than her signature. She invites him to stay and have a nap with her in the nursery. Silva lies in the crib and Baby Doll sings him to sleep.

Archie Lee returns to discover the gin working again. He goes to the house in search of Silva. Baby Doll descends the stairs dressed in a silk slip. Archie

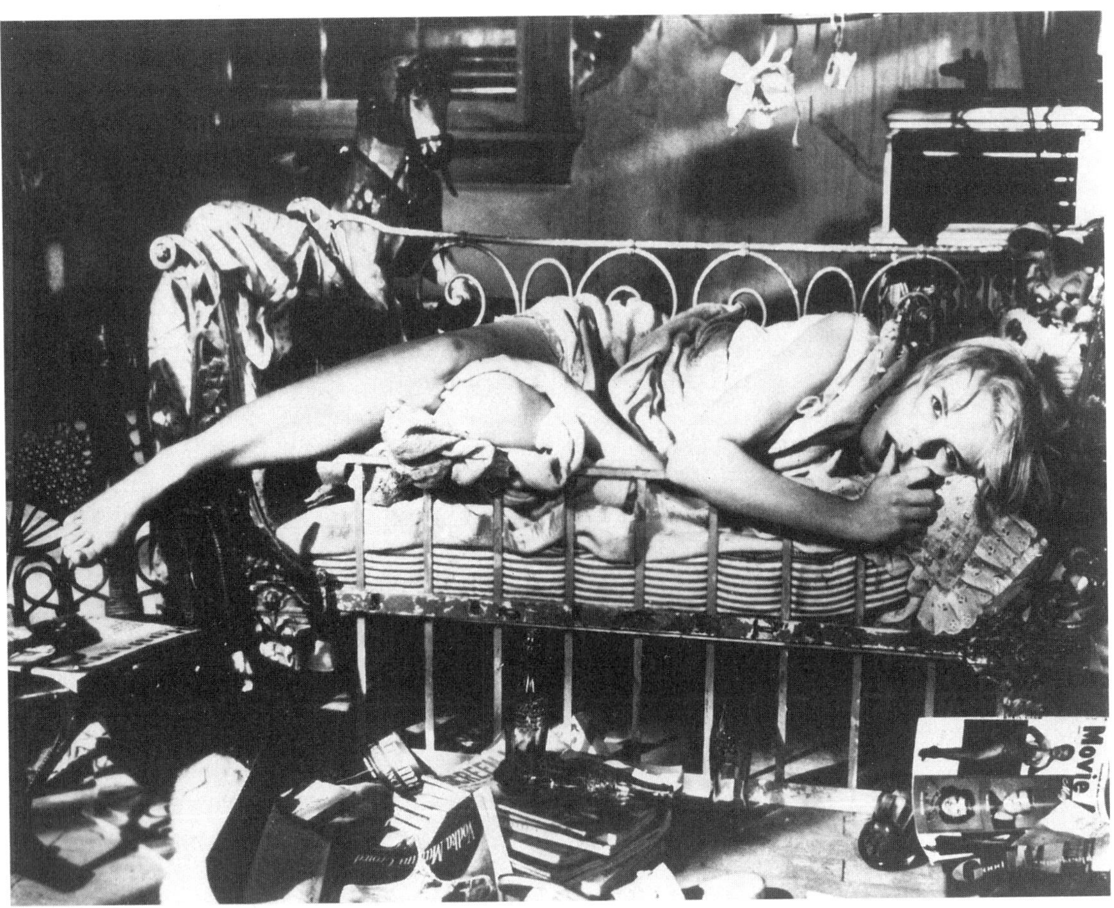


Warner Bros. promotional shot of Carroll Baker for the film *Baby Doll* (Warner Bros., 1956)

Lee shouts at her for her appearance and her uselessness and refers to "useless women." Baby Doll counters by referring to "destructive men," who "blow things up and burn things down." Archie Lee is stunned and stung by her words. Baby Doll walks out onto the porch; Archie Lee follows her and switches on the porch light. The workers from the Syndicate Gin catch a glimpse of Baby Doll and several of them call out and whistle. Archie Lee defends what is "his," and Baby Doll warns him about taking his possession of her for granted. She reminds him of the earlier episode when she sought his protection and he slapped her instead.

Archie Lee is shocked to discover Silva pumping water from the well at the side of the house. Baby Doll informs Archie Lee that Silva wants to establish a "good neighbor policy" whereby Archie Lee will gin cotton for him indefinitely. The one condition is that Baby Doll must entertain him every day. Aunt Rose Comfort calls everyone to supper. The meal is undercooked and unsatisfactory to Archie Lee. He accosts Aunt Rose Comfort and threatens her with eviction. Silva promptly offers her a job cooking for him.

Archie Lee collects his shotgun and chases Silva out of the house. Silva quickly climbs a nearby pecan tree. Baby Doll phones the police and runs out of the house to join Silva in the tree. Archie Lee runs around the yard crying out for his "Baby Doll!" The police arrive and escort Archie Lee away. As Aunt Rose Comfort sings a hymn, Silva descends from the tree and raises his arms to catch Baby Doll.

## COMMENTARY

Elia Kazan, the director who successfully realized many of Williams's dramas for stage and screen, urged the playwright to fuse two of his early one-act plays, *27 Wagons Full of Cotton* and *The Long Stay Cut Short, or the Unsatisfactory Supper* into a screenplay. These two one-acts share a rural Mississippi setting and are concerned with essentially the same characters and situations. The screenplay, which was tentatively titled *The Whip Hand* and *Mississippi Woman,* was developed throughout 1955 and released as *Baby Doll* in 1956.

Upon its release, *Baby Doll* was swiftly denounced as "salacious," "revolting," "dirty," "steamy," "lewd," "suggestive," "morally repellent," and "provocative." *Time* magazine declared it "the dirtiest American-made motion picture that has ever been legally exhibited" (Sova, 28). Reactions to the film were visceral and violent. Francis Cardinal Spellman, who was at that time the leader of the Catholic archdiocese of New York, officially denounced the film from the pulpit of New York City's Saint Patrick's Cathedral. Spellman warned, "in solicitude for the welfare of the country," that Catholics should not view the film "under pain of sin" (Kolin, 2). As a result of Spellman's declaration, Catholics picketed cinemas that dared to air the film, and some theaters received bomb threats.

Despite such substantial opposition, the film, which vividly and poignantly explores such themes as sexual repression, seduction, revenge, and human corruption, resonated with a large number of moviegoers, and the film did well at the box office. In addition, *Baby Doll* won several major international awards, such as the British Academy Awards' "Best Film" (1957) and "Most Promising Newcomer" (Eli Wallach, 1957) prizes and the Golden Globes' "Best Motion Picture Director" (Elia Kazan, 1957).

Considered by many to be "the most provocative collaborative venture" (Kolin, 2) between Williams and Kazan, *Baby Doll* was a pivotal event in Williams's artistic career. As Barton Palmer notes, whatever its artistic value—which is significant—the release and reception of *Baby Doll* prompted a surge in the overall interest in Williams's works, themes, and characters.

## PRODUCTION HISTORY

*Baby Doll* was produced by Warner Brothers as a feature film in 1956. Elia Kazan directed the film, which featured Karl Malden (Archie Lee), Carroll Baker (Baby Doll), Eli Wallach (Silva Vacarro), and Mildred Dunnock (Aunt Rose Comfort).

## PUBLICATION HISTORY

*Baby Doll* was first published in *Baby Doll: The Script for the Film by Tennessee Williams* in 1956. It was subsequently published with *Tiger Tail* in 1991.

## CHARACTERS

**Doctor John** He is the town physician. Archie Lee Meighan is one of his patients. The doctor notices that Archie Lee is nervous and high-strung and warns him that he is "not a old man, but not a young man, either." The doctor prescribes sedatives, which Archie Lee refuses to take.

**McCorkle, Aunt Rose Comfort** She is the elderly unmarried relative of Baby Doll Meighan. Aunt Rose Comfort lives with Baby Doll and her husband, Archie Lee Meighan and makes herself "useful" by cooking for the Meighans. Archie Lee has grown tired of Aunt Rose Comfort, her "simple-minded foolishness," and her poor cooking skill. When Archie Lee threatens to throw her out, the rival cotton gin operator, Silva Vacarro, offers her a job cooking for him.

**Meighan, Archie Lee** Archie Lee is a cotton gin owner in rural Mississippi. He has been down on his luck since the Syndicate Cotton Gin started to dominate the cotton-ginning business in the area. He is married to a voluptuous 19-year-old virgin, Baby Doll Meighan. Archie Lee promised Baby Doll's father that he would "leave [Baby Doll] alone" (not attempt to consummate their marriage) until she reached the age of 20. Archie is exasperated as Baby Doll's 20th birthday is two days away, and he has dutifully waited more than a year.

To improve his financial situation, he sets fire to the gin owned by his prime competitor and neighbor, the Syndicate Cotton Gin. After the fire at the Syndicate gin, Silva Vacarro, the Syndicate plantation manager, approaches Archie Lee with the prospect of ginning his 27 wagons of cotton. Archie Lee orders Baby Doll to entertain Silva while the cotton is being ginned.

**Meighan, Baby Doll** She is the voluptuous 19-year-old virgin wife of Archie Lee Meighan. Her husband is down on his luck since the Syndicate Cotton Gin began to dominate the cotton business in the area. After the fire at the Syndicate Plantation, her husband is given the opportunity to gin 27 wagons of cotton for Silva Vacarro, the Syndicate Plantation manager. Archie Lee orders Baby Doll to entertain Silva. During their visit Baby Doll accidentally contradicts Jake's alibi. She essentially confirms for Silva that Archie Lee started the fire at his gin. Silva takes his revenge on Archie Lee by persuading Baby Doll to sign a statement confirming that Archie Lee started the fire. In the midst of their heated flirtations, Baby Doll is aroused sexually for the first time and gains a sense of herself as an adult woman.

**Vaccaro, Silva** The dashing Italian manager of the Syndicate Cotton Gin in a small town in rural Mississippi. Silva's operation at the Syndicate Gin has put many local cotton gin owners out of work. His chief business rival is Archie Lee Meighan. After a fire destroys his cotton gin, Silva and his assistant, Rock, consider Archie Lee Meighan the primary suspect. When Silva takes his 27 wagons of cotton to Archie Lee to be ginned, his suspicions are confirmed. Archie Lee orders his full-figured teenage virgin wife, Baby Doll Meighan, to entertain Silva, while the cotton is being ginned. During their conversation, Baby Doll innocently and unintentionally contradicts Archie Lee's alibi. Silva then forces her to sign an affidavit swearing that Archie Lee committed arson.

**Young Man** He is a young patient, who is waiting to see Doctor John. The Young Man flirts with Baby Doll Meighan, Archie Lee Meighan's full-figured teenage wife.

### FURTHER READING

Kolin, Philip. "Civil Rights and the Black Presence in *Baby Doll*," *Literature-Film Quarterly* (January 24, 1996): 2–11.

Palmer, Barton. "*Baby Doll:* The Success of Scandal," *The Tennessee Williams Annual Review* 4 (2001): 29–38.

Sova, Dawn B. *Forbidden Films: Censorship Histories of 125 Motion Pictures.* New York: Facts On File, 2001, pp. 26–29.

## *Battle of Angels*

A play in three acts written in 1939.

### SYNOPSIS

The play is set in the rural town of Two Rivers County, Mississippi.

### *Prologue*

The action takes place in the Torrance Mercantile Store, a general goods store formerly owned and run by Jabe and Myra Torrance. The prologue presents the store as it appears at the present time, one year after the tragic events and actual action of the play. The store is no longer functional. Eva and Blanch Temple have turned the store into a museum exhibiting various souvenirs of the tragic events that occurred in the store. The Conjure Man sleeps on a chair at the rear of the store. Eva and Blanch escort a pair of middle-aged tourists, Oliver and Woman, through the store with a commentary on the events that occurred there on Good Friday of the previous year.

### *Act 1*

The scene is in the same location as the prologue; however, the time frame is a year earlier, in early February. Dolly Bland and Beulah, two local townswomen, set up a buffet table in the store and discuss the poor state of Jabe Torrance's health. Cassandra (Sandra) Whiteside visits the store in need of cartridges for her pistol, and she helps herself to them. Vee Talbot arrives accompanied by Valentine Xavier, a handsome young stranger. Vee hopes that Myra will give Val a job in the store. Val is left alone in the store with Sandra, who makes suggestive advances toward him. Myra enters the store and admires the decorations and the food the women have prepared for Jabe's return. Jabe summons Myra upstairs by pounding on the floor above. Sandra persuades Val to have a look at her car, and they leave the store. Vee Talbot tries unsuccessfully to prevent Val from leaving with Sandra; the other women mock Vee's attempt to keep Val away from Sandra. Vee attacks Dolly and Beulah for what she sees as their degraded practice of drinking and playing cards on Sundays. Dolly responds by calling Vee a "professional hypocrite," and the two women exchange more heated words until Vee flees upstairs to Myra. Blanch and Eva greedily gather the food left out for Jabe's party to take away with them.

Val returns to the store. Myra enters from the upstairs living quarters and does not notice Val sitting at the counter as she goes to the telephone box. She calls Mr. Dubinsky for sleeping pills. Val startles her, and she threatens to call the sheriff. Myra offers Val food but says that there is no work available in the store. Val amuses Myra by recounting his recent episode with Cassandra Whiteside, during which he slapped her for making a sexual advance toward him. Myra laughs and offers Val a drink and a job.

### *Act 2, Scene 1*

The time is roughly one week after act 1, in the same location, the Torrance Mercantile Store. Val works on his book and writes his ideas on the lid of a shoebox. Myra watches him curiously and teases him about his behavior and appearance. Three teenage girls enter the store to flirt with Val. They claim to be interested in purchasing a pair of shoes. Eva Temple goes to the store and plays a similar game. Eva becomes a giddy, giggling coquette as Val handles her feet.

Cassandra Whiteside returns to the store in search of a pair of dress shoes to wear to the Delta Planters' Cotillion. Dolly and Beulah enter the store discussing a card game that ended abruptly. They encourage Cassandra to share her recent exploits at the Mardi Gras festivities in New Orleans. Cassandra's enthusiasm prompts Myra to recount her own magical Mardi Gras experience many years ago. Sandra informs Val she did not come to the store for a pair of shoes: She returned to Two Rivers County to see him. Sandra reveals her various neuroses and tells Val that he should have killed her instead of merely slapping her. This, she informs him, would save her the trouble of killing herself slowly. Sandra taunts him because he is afraid to kiss her. Val grabs Sandra and attempts to kiss her. Sandra responds by kneeing him in the groin and biting his hand. Myra becomes angry at Val's potential interest in Sandra and begins to vent her frustrations by criticizing Val's work in the store.

Val takes off his clerk's jacket and offers his resignation. Myra apologizes and admits that she in fact has been very pleased with Val's work in the store. Myra confesses that she is uncomfortable with Val's interactions with the female customers, particularly Sandra Whiteside and the high school girls. Myra accuses Val of having a suggestive manner while dealing with female customers. Val shares his life story with Myra.

### *Act 2, Scene 2*

This scene occurs several hours later in the afternoon of the same day as act 2, scene 1. Val admires a large Coca-Cola poster, which features a curvaceous young woman in a yellow swimsuit. Myra's former lover, David Anderson, enters the store to purchase cartridges for his shotgun and to speak with Myra. Myra and David speak privately. She chastises David and informs him that her life is not over.

Vee Talbot enters the store with a painted canvas. Val notices that Vee needs new shoes. He decides to toy with Vee and starts to rub her foot between his hands. Vee is flabbergasted and rushes quickly out of the store. Myra and Val engage in a playful shoe fitting session. Loon, a homeless black man, stops outside the store and begins to play his guitar. Initially he plays a very solemn tune, but then he changes to a lively waltz matching Myra's transition and mood. Myra becomes enraptured by the music. She begins to sashay about the room and reminisces about her youth. Myra shares her heartbreak with Val. Val acknowledges Myra's unspoken desire to be rid of Jabe for good.

### *Act 2, Scene 3*

The scene follows the previous scene immediately with no break in the music. There is a shift in lighting to the outside of the store as Sheriff Talbot enters the scene. Sheriff Talbot accosts Loon and arrests him for vagrancy. Val intervenes and rescues Loon by giving him money and offering him a job. Pee Wee Bland and the other members of the sheriff's posse, First Man and Second Man, verbally abuse Val for sympathizing with Loon. A Third man, referred to as Pinkie, joins the squabble and spits on Val's shoes. Val responds by pushing him to the ground. Val confesses to Myra that he is a wanted man because a woman in Texas has accused him of rape. Myra asks Val to clarify what happened and he shares his side of the events surrounding the charge. Val also confesses that he wants to touch Myra but is afraid of where it might lead. Val invites Myra to go into the back room with him.

### *Act 3*

The time is two months later. It is a rainy spring day in the same location, the Torrance Mercantile Store. It is Good Friday, two days before Easter Sunday. The only significant alteration to the setting is that the confectionery area in the rear of the store has been completely redecorated to resemble a beautiful flower-filled orchard. Myra sings and chatters gleefully as Val works on his book. He is stunned by her erratic behavior and inquires about its source. Myra is giddy and confides only that she has a secret.

Sonny, a small African-American boy, enters the store to purchase snuff for his grandmother. Bennie comes in and asks whether he may give Myra a credit note for some tobacco. Myra turns on the lights in the confectionery and enjoys the brilliant spring paradise before her. She feels herself glowing and realizes that she is pregnant. The Conjure Man slips silently into the store. Myra offers him money to wash her car. Dolly rushes into the store for safety because of fear that the Conjure Man will put a curse on her unborn child. Beulah runs in with news that Cassandra Whiteside is causing another disturbance in Two Rivers County. Beulah teases Val and Myra, suggesting that they have a secret. The three women discuss Jabe's poor state of health. Myra excuses herself to administer Jabe's medicine.

Dolly and Beulah exchange knowing glances and giggle with each other. The Temple sisters rush into the store to share the news about Cassandra Whiteside's arrival in town. Vee Talbot enters the store dressed in black for Good Friday. She announces that she has at last had a vision of Jesus Christ and has painted his picture. Beulah and Dolly dismiss Vee's "vision" as a result of excessive fasting. Vee declares that the man in her vision relieved her of her torments by touching her. She illustrates his touch by placing her hand on her bosom. Dolly debases Vee's experience and implies that the man in her vision was making a sexual advance. Blanch and Beulah ask to see the painting. Vee starts to unwrap the canvas as the women hear an outburst and the sound of breaking glass above them.

Vee is forced to compete with Myra and Jabe for the townswomen's attention. Jabe loudly accuses Myra of trying to kill him. The townswomen react with disbelief and shock. As Vee reaches the dramatic climax in her story, Myra bursts through the upstairs door screaming for Val to call Jabe's doctor. Val greets Vee Talbot as he crosses her path to get to the telephone. There is a new commotion in the store over Vee's sudden hysteria. Vee orders the women to let her go, although no one is holding her. Dolly tries to examine Vee's painting; Vee grabs it from her before she can see it. Myra rushes out to find Jabe's doctor. Beulah grabs Vee's canvas and shrieks with laughter as she reveals that Val is the man depicted in the painting. Dolly taunts Vee as she runs out of the store in tears.

The Conjure Man reenters from the confectionery and asks Val whether he may spend the night in the confectionery. In a flash of lightning, Cassandra enters the store. Her hair is wet, and her white satin evening gown is spattered with mud and grass stains. Cassandra warns Val that Myra will tie him down. Val orders her to leave, but Cassandra moves closer to him with her wet evening dress clinging to her body. She flings her arms around Val and kisses him. Myra attacks Cassandra and slaps her face forcefully. Cassandra nearly faints from the blow. Val carries Cassandra up the stairs to Myra's bedroom.

Sheriff Talbot enters the store with Mrs. Regan, the woman from Waco, Texas, who is in pursuit of Val. Mrs. Regan immediately demands to see the male shop clerk who works in the store. Mrs. Regan recognizes Val from Vee Talbot's painting. Myra formulates a plan of escape for Val, one that includes her. She shares her dreams of running away and seeing the world with Val. Val immediately rejects this possibility and informs Myra that he must go alone. Myra tells Val a parable about a barren fig tree her family owned. No one believed the little fig tree could produce fruit except Myra. When the tree came into bloom, Myra celebrated its triumph by decorating it with Christmas ornaments and tinsel. Myra asks Val to place Christmas ornaments on her. Val is stunned by Myra's revelation and accuses her of feigning the pregnancy. Myra threatens that she, along with Mrs. Regan, will never let Val escape.

As the two lovers squabble, Jabe enters the upstairs landing. Myra introduces Jabe to Val. Myra and Val argue quietly as Jabe plays the pinball machine in the confectionery. Jabe threatens Myra with the news that he is going to live. She becomes hysterical and announces that she is pregnant. Val runs to the cash register, rings it open, and starts taking money out of it. Myra races to the phone box and calls the sheriff. While she is still on the phone, Jabe shoots Myra in the abdomen. Val wrestles the gun out of Jabe's hand. Jabe hobbles out of the store to get help. Myra is drawn to the "soft, spring-like radiance" of the confectionery and in her dying breath declares that the only things she ever wanted were David Anderson and "the orchard across from Moon Lake!" Myra collapses and the lights in the confectionery flicker out.

Val dashes out of the store through the confectionery. Mrs. Regan and Sheriff Talbot enter the store with a lynch mob bearing lit pine torches. The Conjure Man suddenly appears in the archway of the confectionery. He strikes a defiant pose by lifting Val's jacket in the air above his head.

***Epilogue***

The scene is the same as that of the prologue. It is a Sunday afternoon, one year after the events of the

Publicity portrait of Williams, 1959 *(Photograph courtesy of the Billy Rose Theatre Collection, New York Public Library)*

play. Eva and Blanch Temple are completing their tour of the museum with the tourists. Eva orders the Conjure Man to go to the shelf and retrieve the Cassandra Whiteside objects for the tourists to see. Blanch and Eva describe Cassandra's death to the tourists. Blanch and Eva exhibit Val's snakeskin jacket: The Conjure Man assumes his pose of act 3, with the jacket clenched in his uplifted fist. The Temple sisters report that Val was captured as he ran out of the store through the confectionery. He was stripped naked and lynched in the cottonwood tree.

To illustrate how Val was killed, Blanch takes a blowtorch from the wall. The female tourist cries out as Blanch causes the blowtorch to emit a sharp blue flame. The female tourist nearly faints and must be carried out of the store by the male tourist. The Temple sisters quickly chase the tourists to obtain their admission fee. The Conjure Man returns Val's jacket to its special place on the wall. Treating it with the respect of a sacred relic, he bows to it slightly as the melody of a Negro spiritual is heard.

## COMMENTARY

*Battle of Angels* was Williams's first professionally produced dramatic work and his first full-length dramatic treatment of life in the Deep South. Set in the fictional town of Two Rivers County in rural Mississippi, the drama exposes the repression, cruelty, hatred, hypocrisy, and brutality that lie beneath the surface of a small, upstanding Southern community.

*Battle of Angels* is one of the most neglected works in the Williams canon. However, the eminent significance of this play to Williams's development as a dramatist and to the Williams canon should not be overlooked. *Battle of Angels* served as an "important repository of images, symbols, themes, place-names, character types, and even bits of dialogue that Williams was to draw upon and develop more expertly throughout his dramatic career" (Thompson, 95–96). Themes and conflicts such as sexual repression versus sexual freedom and conformity versus nonconformity, the idea of the poet as outcast and fugitive, the insatiable quest for truth and beauty, and the image of the artist as prophet-hero permeate *Battle of Angels*.

## PRODUCTION HISTORY

*Battle of Angels* premiered at the Wilbur Theatre in Boston, Massachusetts, on December 30, 1940, under the direction of MARGARET WEBSTER with Miriam Hopkins as Myra and Wesley Addy as Val. The opening night performance was a complete disaster. More troubling than the critical reaction to the play was the moral outrage that quickly followed. The Boston City Council denounced the play and called its presentation in the city of Boston a criminal act. The council ordered an official investigation and demanded that production be shut down. The police commissioner and the city censor recommended that the play be allowed to continue with the understanding that Williams would remove certain lines from the text. None of the officials involved in the investigation had actually attended the performance. The city council based its accusations on six complaints received from members of the audience. Changes to the text were made and the production was allowed to continue but closed only 17 days after its opening. At the tender age of 24, the young playwright had launched his career explosively. Williams was shocked and devastated by the audience's reaction to the play.

Although the production proved to be his first great professional fiasco, Williams did not give up on *Battle of Angels*. He continued to develop the material, and the play was subsequently revised as *ORPHEUS DESCENDING* and produced in New York under that title in 1957. The same material was revised as a screenplay retitled *THE FUGITIVE KIND*, which was produced in 1960. Starring MARLON BRANDO and ANNA MAGNANI, it was the most successful incarnation of *Battle of Angels*.

## PUBLICATION HISTORY

*Battle of Angels* was first published by Pharos in 1945.

## CHARACTERS

**Anderson, David** David is a wealthy landowner in Two Rivers County, Mississippi. He is Myra Torrance's former lover. He visits the Torrances' store with the pretext of needing to purchase cartridges for his shotgun. He has actually gone there to see Myra and apologize for abandoning her many years ago.

**Bennie** He is an African-American workman, who is a regular customer at Jabe and Myra Torrance's general store.

**Beulah** She is a member of a group of gossiping townswomen who frequent Jabe and Myra Torrance's store. This gaggle of women includes Vee Talbot, Eva Temple, Blanch Temple, and her best friend, Dolly Bland. Although they consider themselves friends, they despise each other intensely. They unite forces against common enemies, such as Cassandra Whiteside, but turn on each other at the slightest provocation.

**Bland, Dolly** Dolly is Pee Wee Bland's wife. She is one of a group of gossiping townswomen who frequent Jabe and Myra Torrance's store. Dolly also serves a symbolic function. As the mother of six children, expecting her seventh, she is a constant reminder to Myra Torrance that she is childless.

**Bland, Pee Wee** The husband of Dolly Bland, he is the manager of the cotton gin across the road from the Torrances' Mercantile Store. Pee Wee is also the deputy of Sheriff Talbot. As is the sheriff, Pee Wee is a mean-spirited racist.

**Conjure Man** He is one of several dispossessed African-American characters in the play. As is Valentine Xavier, he is a social outcast and lives an isolated existence. With the exception of Val and Myra Torrance, the townspeople of Two Rivers County either are severely frightened by the Conjure Man or treat him disrespectfully. Figuratively, the Conjure Man represents the wild, magical, and vibrant spirit of human nature—and humanity—which cannot be suppressed.

**Dubinsky, Mr.** He is the local pharmacist in Two Rivers County. Myra Torrance calls him in the middle of the night and begs him to deliver sleeping pills to her. Even though it is very late, he obliges her request.

**First Man** He is a member of Sheriff Talbot's posse in Two Rivers County. As are the sheriff and his deputy, Pee Wee Bland, the First Man is a mean-spirited racist. The First Man along with the Second Man verbally abuse Valentine Xavier, who sympathizes with the plight of the poor African-American residents of the town.

**Girl** She is one of three schoolgirls who visit the Torrance Mercantile Store to flirt with the store's new clerk, Valentine Xavier. She tells Val that her friend, Jane, is interested in a pair of shoes. When Jane demurs, the Third Girl offers to take her place, but the Girl beats her to the chair. Val holds her foot in his hands and measures it. She wears a size 5½B.

**Jane** See Second Girl.

**Joe** He is an African-American workman at the Torrance Mercantile Store. Joe delivers a shipment of hats and carries several display signs into the store for Myra Torrance.

**Loon** He is a homeless African-American man in the town of Two Rivers County. Loon stops outside the Torrance Mercantile Store at closing time and plays his guitar. Initially, he plays a very solemn tune, but then he changes to a lively waltz. His music mirrors Myra Torrance's transition and mood within the store. Valentine Xavier intervenes on Loon's behalf when he is accosted by Sheriff Talbot.

**Oliver** He is a middle-aged tourist in Two Rivers County, who visits the Tragic Museum, formerly the Torrance Mercantile Store.

**Pinkie** See Third Man.

**Regan, Mrs.** She is a matron from Waco, Texas, who goes to Two Rivers County, Mississippi, in search of Valentine Xavier. Mrs Regan claims that Val raped her while he was traveling through Texas. Val's version of the events is significantly different. Mrs Regan pursues Val for vengeance and is only fully satisfied after his death.

**Second Girl** Also referred to as Jane, she is one of three teenage girls who are infatuated with Valentine Xavier. She is the shyest of the three.

The First Girl tells Val that the Second Girl wants to try on a new pair of shoes. Second Girl protests vehemently and tries to coerce the Third Girl to have her feet measured by Val.

**Second Man** He is a member of Sheriff Talbot's posse in Two Rivers County. As are the sheriff and his deputy, Pee Wee Bland, the Second Man is a mean-spirited racist. The Second Man and the First Man verbally abuse Valentine Xavier for sympathizing with the plight of the poor African-American residents of the town.

**Sheriff Talbot (Jim Talbot)** Sheriff Talbot is a mean-spirited and bigoted town official in Two Rivers County, Mississippi. He is married to Vee Talbot. The sheriff is a close associate of Jabe Torrance's and keeps a watchful eye on Jabe's wife, Myra Torrance, and their new shop clerk, Valentine Xavier.

**Sonny** He is a small African-American boy who visits the Torrance Mercantile Store on Good Friday afternoon. He goes to the store to purchase snuff for his bedridden grandmother. Myra Torrance gives Sonny a free bag of peanuts before he leaves the store.

**Talbot, Vee** Vee is the wife of Sheriff Talbot. She is a member of a group of gossiping townswomen who frequent Jabe and Myra Torrance's store. However, Vee is quite unlike the other women in her circle; she is a painter of some local renown. The other women, especially Dolly Bland, ridicule Vee behind her back. Vee struggles to lead a normal existence in Two Rivers County, but she, as are the other outcasts in the play, is an outsider by nature. In her eccentricity, she produces a portrait of Christ that bears a striking resemblance to the Torrances' clerk, Valentine Xavier. When she shows the painting to the other women, their howls of derision send her headlong into madness.

**Temple, Blanch** Blanch is the sister of Eva Temple and the cousin of Jabe Torrance. She and her sister are middle-aged single women who are snooping, churchgoing busybodies. Blanch is the more animated of the two. She is somewhat jumpy and clumsy and susceptible to palpitations. As Jabe's only surviving relatives, the Temple sisters will inherit his store. When Jabe kills his wife, Myra, and the townspeople burn Val Xavier alive, Blanch and Eva take over the property and convert it into the Tragic Museum. They maintain an exhibit of the memorabilia of the tragedy, such as Val's snakeskin jacket. Blanch frightens the tourists away from the museum by setting off a blowtorch similar to the one that was used to kill Val.

**Temple, Eva** She is Blanch Temple's sister and the cousin of Jabe Torrance. She is one of a pair of unmarried middle-aged women who are nosy, snooping, churchgoing busybodies. Eva is the more forthright of the two. As is her fellow townswoman, Vee Talbot, Eva is smugly pious, yet ardently attracted and physically drawn to the store's new clerk, the handsome stranger in town, Valentine Xavier. Throughout her shoe fitting session with Val, Eva is a giggling coquette. After Jabe kills his wife, Myra Torrance, and the townspeople burn Val alive, Blanch and Eva inherit the property and convert it into the Tragic Museum. They eke out a meager existence as the museum's macabre tour guides.

**Third Girl** She is one of three schoolgirls who visit the Torrances' store to flirt with Valentine Xavier. She is the most aggressive of the three in their pursuit of Val. While her companions, a Girl and Second Girl giggle and are rather coy with Val, the Third Girl is direct and actually asks Val for a date.

**Third Man** He is also referred to as Pinkie. He is the last member of Sheriff Talbot's posse. As are the Sheriff and his deputy, Pee Wee Bland, the Third Man, is a mean-spirited racist. He is the most physically aggressive of the sheriff's gang. He accosts Valentine Xavier, graphically describes to him the method he uses to kill snakes, and threatens to do the same to him.

**Torrance, Jabe** Jabe is the husband of Myra Torrance and the owner of the Torrance Mercantile

Store. He and Myra have been in an unhappy marriage for many years. Jabe is older than Myra and is dying of cancer. For more than two-thirds of the play, Jabe does not appear on stage, as he lies dying in his bedroom above the store. He repeatedly bangs on his floorboards to get Myra's attention when she is downstairs in the store. Symbolically Jabe represents death and the cancerous, oppressive nature of life in the rural Southern town of Two Rivers County, Mississippi. As do many of his fellow residents, Jabe reacts to any act of defiance or nonconformity with violence. When he discovers that Myra has been having an affair with the shop clerk, Valentine Xavier, and has become pregnant with his child, Jabe responds by horrifically shooting her in the stomach.

**Torrance, Myra** Myra is the wife of Jabe Torrance and the co-owner of the Torrance Mercantile Store. The emotional disasters of Myra's life are numerous. She was loved and left by David Anderson; however, in desperation and self-loathing she married the mean-spirited, repulsive, and terminally ill Jabe. Her marriage and her life have been barren and full of regret. Valentine Xavier saves Myra from despair by offering her love and sexual fulfillment.

**West, Jonathan** An alias used by Valentine Xavier.

**Whiteside, Cassandra (Sandra)** Cassandra is an anomaly in the rigid, repressed Southern society of Two Rivers County, Mississippi. She is of wealthy, genteel stock; however, her behavior is common and crude. The prim and pious townsfolk of the small rural town have ostracized her and branded her a scarlet woman. Cassandra finds salvation and release in sex and alcohol. Her fast-paced quest for freedom and perpetual motion is abruptly cut short, and, as Valentine Xavier does, Cassandra meets a violent end.

**Woman** She is a middle-aged tourist who visits the Tragic Museum, which was once Myra and Jabe Torrance's Mercantile Store but is now owned by Eva and Blanch Temple. The Woman is accompanied by a middle-aged male tourist named Oliver.

**Woman** See Mrs. Regan.

**Xavier, Valentine** He is a handsome young writers who drifts into Two Rivers County, Mississippi. Vee Talbot helps him find a job in the Torrance Mercantile Store, which is owned by Jabe and Myra Torrance. The presence of this sexy young stranger creates an uproar in the small, repressed community. As Williams's first tragic hero, in his first full-length treatment of life in the Deep South, Valentine Xavier offers a glimpse of various male characters who would later inhabit the Williams canon. He is a dreamy poet, as is the quintessential Williams hero, Tom Wingfield, in *THE GLASS MENAGERIE.* Myra comments that Val "talks to himself, writing poems on shoe-boxes! What a mess!" Tom Wingfield does so as well. Val also possesses a strong sexual magnetism and animal passion that would later be fully developed in the character Stanley Kowalski in *A STREETCAR NAMED DESIRE.* As is Stanley, Val is irresistible to the women who fall in love with him, and similarly he has an element of violent aggression in his relationships with women. Val's passionate nature prompts equally passionate responses by the other characters in the play. Much to the chagrin of the town bigots, he becomes the champion of disenfranchised African-American characters, such as Loon and the Conjure Man. The local women want to love him; the local men want to kill him. Ultimately, the men prevail and Val is burned to death. Symbolically, Val represents the spirit of nonconformity and freedom. His name relates to love (Saint Valentine) and Christ (Savior).

## FURTHER READING

Thompson, Judith J. *Myth and Symbol in the Plays of Tennessee Williams.* New York: Peter Lang, 1989.

# *Beauty Is the Word*

One-act play Williams submitted for the annual play contest at the UNIVERSITY OF MISSOURI in 1930. This play is considered Williams's earliest dramatic work. The biographer Lyle Leverich states the play is important "because the theme . . . was Tom's first attack upon the inhibitions of Puritanism and its persecution of the artist . . . depict[ing] the heroism of a freethinker." This form of heroism would continue to resurface in Williams's dramatic and fictive writings and would become the hallmark of his dramaturgy. *Beauty Is the Word* remains unpublished.

### FURTHER READING

Leverich, Lyle. *Tom: The Unknown Tennessee Williams.* New York: W. W. Norton, 1995.

# "Big Black: A Mississippi Idyll"

Short story written between the years 1931 and 1932.

### SYNOPSIS

Big Black is a member of a Mississippi road crew that labors in the heat of summer under the brutality of their Irish boss. Big Black does not openly rebel against his torturous conditions, but periodically he rips open his shirt and bellows out an intense "YOW-OW, YOW-OW-W-W." In the central scene, Big Black happens upon a young white girl swimming in the river. He aggressively pursues her, stopping short of rape when he realizes how bestial he has become. To escape the violent scene he has created, Big Black dives into the river and swims away. He reappears in Georgia, working on another road gang. Big Black once again lets out his savage cry.

### COMMENTARY

"Big Black: A Mississippi Idyll" is Williams's first story set in his signature American South, and the story cannot be fully appreciated without an understanding of the historical context within which it was created. This era was a particularly bleak period in American history, especially in terms of race relations in the country. A society devastated by the economic disaster of the stock market crash, which led to the Great Depression, turned in on itself. Racial animosity reached a zenith during this period and racially motivated hate crimes against African-American males escalated to an unprecedented level as social commentators warned anxious readers of the latently dangerous monsters who roamed freely within their midst. Reports of the time recounted horrific tales of "drug-crazed," violent, and depraved black supermen, who could not be stopped by conventional means and whose one goal was to defile the sanctity of white womanhood. Such was their incredible strength, law officials claimed, that these men were impervious to ordinary bullets; special ones had to be invented to kill them. The hysteria created by these reports led to a frenzied spree of lynchings throughout the troubled South.

Williams, never one to shy away from controversial topics, directly addresses this social phenomenon in this piece of short fiction. As in his plays CANDLES TO THE SUN and NOT ABOUT NIGHTINGALES, Williams approaches the inherent social conflict from the outsider's or disenfranchised group's perspective. Big Black is a literary incarnation of the much maligned and deeply feared African-American superman: As he bakes in the midday sun, he stands, like a black colossus, towering above his work-gang peers and his Irish boss; he releases the violence that lies within him as he rips his shirt and roars. Just as his clothing cannot contain his dark skin, his volatile sexuality must also find release. This leads him predictably to ardently pursue a delicate, young white girl. Big Black is a figure that Williams's contemporary readers would have immediately recognized, expected, and feared. However, as Williams often does, he takes his reader on a familiar journey and then abruptly alters the final destination. When Big Black captures the young girl, he, in a moment highly reminiscent of Shakespeare's *Othello,* notices his huge, dark hands about her alabaster face and neck. In this moment, Williams twists conventional wisdom. Big Black is struck by his own humanity and his own oppression. Instead of venting his rage at his own victimization by victimizing the young girl, he releases her. He flees the encounter and swims away.

More then merely recycling a convenient stereotype, Williams exposes the conditions and circumstances that lead Big Black down his intended path of destruction: the brutality of his Irish boss, the oppressive work conditions, and the blistering heat. These circumstances reveal that Big Black is forever shackled in a world where he is a second-class citizen. Williams's empathy for African Americans and their plight in the American South would become a prominent feature of such works as *Battle of Angels* and *Orpheus Descending*.

### PUBLICATION HISTORY

"Big Black: A Mississippi Idyll" was first published in *Collected Stories* by New Directions in 1985.

### CHARACTERS

**Big Black** Big Black works on a chain gang building roads in the heat of summer. His misery stems from his torturous work conditions as well as the oppression he feels as an African American living in the segregated South. When he happens upon a young white girl who is swimming, violent desire overtakes him, and he attacks the girl. When he sees his dark hand spanning the girl's porcelain face, he regains rationality and flees before he rapes and kills her.

## *Blue Mountain Ballads*

A collaborative project with his longtime friend Paul Bowles. Williams provided poems that largely appear in the collection *In the Winter of Cities* (1954), and Bowles composed music to create these ballads in 1946.

## *Cairo! Shanghai! Bombay!*

Williams's first performed dramatic work. This one-act comedy was first presented on July 12, 1935, by the Garden Players at Mrs. Roseboro's Rose Arbor Theater, in Memphis, Tennessee. Detailing the adventures of two sailors, the play was a modest success. With this work, however, Williams instantly became enamored of the laughter and applause he could evoke in an audience. As he wrote in his *Memoirs*, "Then and there the theatre and I found each other for better and for worse." The play remains unpublished.

### FURTHER READING

Williams, Tennessee. *Memoirs*. Garden City, N.Y.: Doubleday, 1975.

## *Camino Real*

Full-length play written in 1946. *Camino Real* is based on the one-act play *Ten Blocks on the Camino Real*. Williams added six more "blocks," or scenes, to the older work and created the frame of Don Quixote's dream.

### SYNOPSIS

The play is set in a windy, deserted town in an unspecified Latin American country.

#### *Prologue*

Don Quixote and his squire, Sancho Panza, stumble onto the scene. Two guards stop them on their way into the Siete Mares Hotel by order of its proprietor, Gutman. Tiring of Quixote's endless romantic pilgrimages, Sancho abandons him. In his desperation and loneliness, Quixote resorts to sleep, inviting his dreams to sweep him away from his dire predicament and to help him find new meanings in life.

The next morning a pageantry of boisterous townspeople commence their day. Prudence Duvernoy enters in search of her lost dog. She encounters Jacques Casanova, who charms her. Prudence tells him the story of Camille (from Dumas' *La Dame aux Camélias*) and reprimands Casanova for his idealistic notions. She informs him that on the Camino Real one must always think and act realistically. Gutman interrupts them to announce the first block on the Camino Real as he announces every subsequent block.

#### *Block 1*

Casanova advises Prudence that Camille is only a dream (or fiction). In an attempt to protect her illusion, Prudence changes the subject by remarking that Casanova is older than she thought. When she sexually objectifies Casanova, he hurriedly walks away from her. As does Quixote, Prudence resides in the world of fiction, in the blurry liminal space of imagination. Ironically, Prudence escapes the realism of the Camino Real. Olympe, Casanova's lover (another Dumas character), interrupts this conversation as Gutman announces the next block.

### Block 2

The Survivor enters and begs for water. Rosita, a prostitute, laughs at him and shoves him into the hotel. Upon seeing the stranger, Gutman whistles for the Officer, who immediately shoots the dehydrated man. The Survivor writhes in pain as Casanova enters, horrified by the violent scene. Gutman explains that the plaza happenings do not concern the characters. He claims that the Survivor was shot in an attempt to protect the water supply. When Casanova attempts to help the Survivor, the Officer stops him. The blind singer, La Madrecita, enters with the popular and beloved Dreamer. Gutman feels his power waning in the presence of the Dreamer. He pontificates on the dangers of dreamers, but the Dreamer utters the forbidden word "Brother," which miraculously restores La Madrecita's eyesight. She, in turn, unsuccessfully attempts to heal the Survivor.

When the Survivor dies, the Gypsy and her daughter, Esmeralda, and her son, Abdullah, enter to distract attention from the dead man. In a dreamlike state, Kilroy, a former champion boxer and an all-American guy, enters. Wearing his lucky boxing gloves around his neck and a ruby-encrusted belt that says, "Champ," he is considered a savior; he is also a clown.

### Block 3

Kilroy unsuccessfully searches for a Wells-Fargo bank. He tells the Officer that he is a hero and has an enlarged heart that even has forced him to leave his wife because he fears that even an intense kiss may prove fatal. When Kilroy asks where he is, the Officer purposely walks away. The Gypsy, Esmeralda, and Nursie, enter. Rosita distracts Kilroy while a pickpocket steals his wallet. The Streetcleaners collect the Survivor's body, stuffing it into a trash barrel, much to Kilroy's shock and disgust. Kilroy enters the pawnshop to cash in his belt.

### Block 4

A Frenchman in a yellow suit, Baron de Charlus, enters talking with A. Ratt. Lobo follows him. The owner of the Ritz Men Only Hotel entices him to stay at his hotel with promises of sexual escapades. Kilroy emerges from the Loan Shark's pawnshop, disappointed that the pawnbroker was interested only in his precious boxing gloves. He refuses to pawn them. Charlus flirts with Kilroy but loses interest when he notices Kilroy's too-gentle eyes. Charlus leaves and Casanova enters. A loud noise interrupts the scene, and the Streetcleaners return with Charlus's lifeless body stuffed into a barrel. Kilroy vows to avoid death in the barrel.

### Block 5

Casanova explains to Kilroy that the Streetcleaners throw the dead bodies into barrels if there is no money in the pockets. The moneyless bodies are then taken to the laboratory, where each becomes "an undistinguished member of a collectivist state." Casanova offers Kilroy a way out of the Camino Real, but Kilroy fears the unknown, so he declines the offer.

### Block 6

Exhausted, Kilroy searches for shelter. A. Ratt offers him a room at the Ritz Men Only. The Officer arrests Kilroy for vagrancy when he decides to sleep in the plaza. Gutman offers to hire him as a patsy or clown, but Kilroy tries to escape. Simultaneously, Esmeralda tries to escape from her mother. They are both apprehended, and Kilroy is forced to wear a red nose and wig.

### Block 7

Gutman describes this block as his favorite while the Dreamer sings in the background. Abdullah informs Casanova that his long-awaited remittance check has arrived. Casanova notices Kilroy, who is crouched and wearing a clown suit. Lady Mulligan asks Gutman to evict Casanova because of his radical ideas. A Hunchback Mummer somersaults across the stage, heralding a new scene. Casanova's lover, Marguerite, enters to announce that her purse has been stolen. Casanova sends Abdullah to find the papers that were in her purse. Marguerite begs Casanova to leave the Camino Real with her. Casanova confesses that he fears the outside world.

### *Block 8*

Gutman addresses Lord Byron, who is planning to leave the Camino Real for Greece because he has lost his inspiration to write. Lord Byron's thoughts wander to Shelley, and he describes Shelley's cremation. The people overhearing this graphic and gruesome story become entranced by the details. Byron misses the effect his poetry used to have on people. He admits that succumbing to earthly pleasures has been his downfall, and he is fleeing temptation. He exits through an archway that reveals the desert beyond the plaza. Kilroy begins to follow him, but his fear of the unknown makes him stop. His nose blinks as Gutman laughs at his cowardice.

### *Block 9*

Casanova and Marguerite witness the arrival of the unexpected freedom ship called the *Fugitivo*. Everyone scrambles to get on the ship, but Gutman tries to talk people into staying with him. In the midst of the chaos, Lord Mulligan declares that he is sick. The Streetcleaners appear as if they are vultures waiting to take the body. Lady Mulligan leaves her husband, ordering that his body be placed on dry ice when he dies. Marguerite fights with Casanova for the papers she needs in order to board the ship. Casanova is too afraid to go and wants her to stay with him. She is left standing on the shore as the *Fugitivo* sails out of sight.

### *Block 10*

Marguerite plans to leave Casanova. Abdullah enters selling hats for the lunar fiesta that annually reinstates Esmeralda's virginity. Marguerite gives Abdullah her sapphire ring to pawn and secure another lover for her. Marguerite is swept away by the wind.

### *Block 11*

Casanova is forced to wear deer horns and is declared "King of the Cuckolds." He defends himself by proclaiming his sexual prowess, but he is ignored because Esmeralda's long-awaited lunar fiesta is beginning. Kilroy enters and removes Jacques's antlers. In return, Casanova removes Kilroy's wig and red nose. Kilroy finally musters the courage to leave. He sells his prized gloves to the Loan Shark. Gutman enters and announces the Gypsy's ceremonial entrance. She proclaims that the Moon has restored Esmeralda's virginity. Everyone is forced to pay homage to Esmeralda as she dances on a rooftop in the plaza. Kilroy has nearly escaped when Esmeralda calls out, "Yankee," drawing attention to him. He dances with her, trying to resist her. When Esmeralda calls him "Champ," he becomes instantly smitten by her and abandons his plans.

### *Block 12*

The Gypsy prepares Esmeralda to seduce Kilroy for money. After some interrogation, the Gypsy reads tarot cards that reveal Kilroy is dying. The Streetcleaners eagerly wait outside for him. They escort him to Esmeralda, who is carried in on a couch, wearing a veil and a skirt. After some conversation, Kilroy asks to lift her veil, but she says that she wants to go to Acapulco. Kilroy criticizes her materialistic nature and asks again to lift her veil. Esmeralda does not believe Kilroy will be gentle enough. He protests and she explains that each of her lovers is the first because her virginity is always restored. Just as it appears that Kilroy is beginning to lift her veil, he stops and says that he is "tired and full of regret." He pities himself and all the other men who go to Esmeralda because of their own desperation. Penniless and trapped in the Camino again, Kilroy leaves Esmeralda.

### *Block 13*

The Streetcleaners enter and place a barrel in the middle of the stage. When Kilroy enters and sees the barrel, he tries to escape into the Siete Mares, but Gutman does not answer the door. Just as Gutman is about to evict him, Casanova enters. When Casanova opens his remittance check, he finds a note which states that payment has been discontinued. Gutman throws Casanova's suitcases out of the hotel. Kilroy decides to sleep in the plaza.

### *Block 14*

Marguerite enters with her Young Man, who takes her purse and jewelry. Marguerite does not resist. Kilroy enters and warns her that the Streetcleaners are coming for him. They sit down and hold hands. He explains that he left his wife because he could not handle the thought of such a beautiful woman being married to a "broken down champ." The Streetcleaners make their way to Kilroy, who positions himself as a boxer to fight them. Kilroy falls to his knees. Before the Streetcleaners can get to him, La Madrecita goes to his aid.

### *Block 15*

La Madrecita sits with Kilroy's body lying across her lap. A Medical Instructor stands beside an operating table at center stage. La Madrecita emotionally eulogizes Kilroy's life while the Instructor addresses students and nurses who are witnessing the removal of Kilroy's heart. Kilroy's spirit rises from his body to witness the surgery. The Instructor shouts in surprise when he discovers the heart is made of gold.

### *Block 16*

Kilroy chases the Instructor, demanding that his heart be returned. Gutman tries to stop Kilroy, claiming that the heart is the property of the state. Esmeralda and the Gypsy enter as they prepare to go to bed. Esmeralda wishes to dream about Kilroy, the hero. Kilroy tries to get her attention, but she calls him a cat. He goes to the Loan Shark to pawn his golden heart, and he returns with money. Esmeralda calls him a cat again, and Kilroy bemoans the Gypsy and her daughter.

Quixote enters. Gutman announces the knight's return and the end of his dream. Quixote goes over to the dry fountain in the middle of the plaza and water begins to flow. Kilroy watches in amazement and asks Quixote whether he knows everything is "rugged." He agrees with Kilroy but suggests that Kilroy should not pity himself. Quixote asks Kilroy to leave with him. The Street People and Marguerite enter. Casanova enters, he and Marguerite embrace, and Gutman tells the audience, "The curtain line has been spoken," ordering that the curtain be lowered as he bows as the ringmaster.

## COMMENTARY

*Camino Real* is centered on an epic journey of indefinite time and surreal happenings. In the foreword to the script, Williams writes, "This play has seemed to me like the creation of another world, a separate existence." As emphasized by the quoting of a line by Dante Alighieri in the play's epigraph, "In the middle of the journey of our life I came to myself in a dark wood where the straight way was lost" (*Inferno* Canto 1), this play is Williams's "modern inferno" (Falk, ch. 5). Kilroy is then Williams's version of a Dante figure, the archetypal American who encounters a compliant social wasteland on the Camino Real or "real way of life." The Camino Real is a parade of colors and characters: trapped romantics, drifters, and literature's archetypal lovers. Casanova, Don Quixote, Lord Byron, among fictional literary figures, have landed themselves in this timeless, ethereal place. Unlike Socrates, Plato, and Homer, who are trapped in Dante's inferno because they are afflicted with melancholy or hopelessness, Casanova, Don Quixote, and Lord Byron inhabit the Camino because they are hopeful dreamers.

Williams establishes a literary connection to the romantics by using Lord Byron as the chief heralder of hope. With graphic memories of the burning corpse of his companion, Shelley, he states the play's primary maxim when he encourages the other characters, "Make voyages! Attempt them!—there's nothing else." Despite Gutman's despotic control over the town and the Streetcleaners' frenzied lust for death, the journey still affords zeal for living.

A character in Marcel Proust's lifework, *A la Recherche du temps perdu* (Remembrance of Things Past), Baron de Charlus is a masochistic gay man who is also a marginalized character in *Camino Real.* This character, who delights in the love of men and enjoys being flogged and physically overpowered by lower-class toughs, is reminiscent of Williams's character Anthony Burns in "DESIRE AND THE BLACK MASSEUR." Charlus's cameo appearance in *Camino Real* as does Burns's in "Desire and the Black Masseur," demonstrates the ironic possibility that through his brutal sexual encounters with various men, he is able to cope with the harsh realities in life. With this notion, Williams incorporates sexuality as an escape route of its own, beyond the wasteland of the Camino Real and contextually above the oppressive and conservative mood of the McCarthy-era setting of the 1940s and 1950s, a time when "Communists and queers" were under scrutiny (Schrecker, 148).

Williams was also drawn to Proust's voluminous novel for its passage of time, "a controlled torrent of personal experience" (*Where I Live,* 125). Williams's deliberately experimental nature of time incorporated in *Camino Real* lends the play a surreal, dreamy sense of life. There is no concern with chronology, negating verisimilitude insofar as it creates unity within a script; however, emotional and universal truths are gained. Williams focuses attention on Kilroy's "psychic history—[his] love, fear, loneliness,

Production shot of Jo Van Fleet, Joseph Anthony, and other cast members, from the Broadway production of *Camino Real*, 1953 *(Alfredo Valente)*

disgust, humor, and most important of all, his forgiving perception of the reasons for the tragicomedy of human confusion" (*Where I Live*, 125). Kilroy is "the American" who dies, his oversized golden heart is stolen, and so he returns to life to reclaim it.

The themes Williams incorporates in this sociopolitical dream play are based on the friction between liberty and the state as well as between despondency and optimism. Engulfed in a very mechanical sense of authoritarianism and conformity, *Camino Real* is Williams's criticism of capitalistic society in the cold war era.

Williams enjoyed the freedom of writing an expressionistic drama and by its endless creative staging possibilities. He was always most interested in creating new theatrical forms of dramaturgy; THE GLASS MENAGERIE, with its PLASTIC THEATRE moments, is his most successful example of revolutionary staging.

## PRODUCTION HISTORY

*Camino Real* is dramaturgically similar to Williams's more experimental writings late in his career. However, it premiered after the success of *The Glass Menagerie* (1945), A STREETCAR NAMED DESIRE (1947), and THE ROSE TATTOO (1950) and before CAT ON A HOT TIN ROOF (1955) and was not well received. Audiences were either offended by his political views or bored by what they perceived as a formless play about nothing. Williams cut much of the play's political commentary for the Broadway production; however, he restored it for its first publication in 1953.

*Camino Real* premiered at the Martin Beck Theatre in New York, March 19, 1953; it closed after only 60 performances on May 9, 1953. Directed by ELIA KAZAN, the play starred Eli Wallach and JESSICA TANDY.

## PUBLICATION HISTORY

*Camino Real* was published by Dramatists Play Service in 1953. Several subsequent publications include minor revisions of the text.

## CHARACTERS

**Casanova, Jacques** Historical figure and a character in *Camino Real*. Casanova, once the notorious lover of countless women, now only has one friend, Marguerite Gautier. He is depicted as an old man, a shadow of his former self, living in the Siete Mares Hotel. In this abstract and fantastical play, he represents second chances in life.

**Charlus, Baron de** A stately Frenchman dressed in a pale yellow suit, Baron de Charlus is a literary figure and character in the play *Camino Real*. Based on the character of the same name in Marcel Proust's lifework *A la Recherche du temps perdu* (Remembrance of Things Past or, more recently, *In Search of Lost Time*), he is a masochistic gay man who enters the Camino Real. He encounters a handsome former boxer named Kilroy. Charlus is attracted to him until he realizes that Kilroy's eyes are too gentle. Charlus dies on the Camino Real and the Streetcleaners stuff his body into a barrel and take it to the laboratory for experimentation.

**Dreamer** He is a hero of the citizens of the Camino Real whose visit and mere presence challenge the authority of Gutman. When he utters the forbidden word "Brother," La Madrecita de Las Soledades's eyesight is miraculously restored.

**Duvernoy, Prudence** She befriends Jacques Casanova and tries to seduce him. Prudence relates the story of Camille in Alexandre Dumas' *La Dame aux camélias*. She reprimands Casanova for his idealistic notions and informs him that on the Camino Real one must always think and act realistically.

**Esmeralda** Esmeralda is the beautiful daughter of the Gypsy. She is a highly desirable young woman and a lover of many men. Esmeralda's virginity is restored every month during a lunar fiesta celebrating the full Moon. She seduces Kilroy, but her criticism that he is not gentle enough provokes him to leave before their interaction is consummated by the lifting of the veil she wears over her face. Esmeralda represents the regret all men feel for a desire that cannot be fulfilled. She is a part of the "rugged deal," or the unfortunate moments in Kilroy's life.

**Gautier, Marguerite** Marguerite is based on the character of that name in Alexandre Dumas' novel *La Dame aux camélias*. This elegant woman, once the best dressed, most expensive, and most successful courtesan in Paris, is now Jacques Casanova's aging lover. Hints of her former glory remain in her grand demeanor and her attire, which includes a hat heaped with violets. She abandons Jacques early in the play but ultimately returns to him. In this highly symbolic play, Marguerite represents faithfulness and companionship.

**Gutman, Mr.** He is the despotic proprietor of the Siete Mares Hotel. Gutman orders the death of people who enter the Camino Real. Mr. Gutman is sly, well dressed, and indifferent to the plight of the needy. He functions as a ringmaster of a circus, announcing the "blocks" or acts in the play as well as the conclusion. Mr. Gutman is a highly politicized character who represents the oppressive mood of the McCarthy era.

**Gypsy** She is a psychic and the mother of Esmeralda. The Gypsy procures male customers for Esmeralda after her virginity is restored at the lunar fiesta.

**Kilroy** Kilroy is an all-American guy and a former champion boxer. He has an abnormally large heart, which is said to be the size of a baby's head. Because of this medical condition, Kilroy left his wife for fear that intimacy would kill him. He becomes trapped in the Camino Real, and although he wants to leave the destitute and surreal place, he becomes too afraid to break out on his own. In the moment he is brave enough to escape, he is caught and forced to wear a red clown nose and wig. Hailed as the "Chosen Hero," Kilroy is seduced by Esmeralda. Kilroy meets Don Quixote and becomes his new squire. Together, the two leave the Camino Real.

**La Madrecita de Las Soledades** A motherly figure who goes to the aid of Kilroy. She holds him during a surreal moment when simultaneously he is cradled in her lap and has his golden heart removed by a surgeon on a cold operating table. La Madrecita de Las Soledades's name means "little mother of the lonely."

**Lord Byron (George Gordon, Lord Byron)** (1788–1824) Historical figure and character in *Camino Real.* Williams admired Byron so much that he included him among his characters. Williams was inspired by Byron's sense of freedom and poetic lyricism. In the play, Byron is a hopeful dreamer who encourages Kilroy to live and "Make voyages!" Lord Byron pontificates on the cremation of his fellow romantic poet, Percy Bysshe Shelley. He tells of his decision to travel to Athens in an attempt to find his poetic voice once more. Lord Byron encourages Kilroy to travel and live.

In addition, Lord Byron is the subject of LORD BYRON'S LOVE LETTER, a one-act play, which serves as a tribute to Byronic themes of love and romantic candor.

**Officer** He shoots the Survivor, who wanders into the Camino Real desperately in search of water. The Officer is Gutman's ruffian; he obeys orders, however brutal or unjust.

**Panza, Sancho** Sancho accompanies Don Quixote to the Camino Real; however, he abandons him there because he is tired of their lifelong travels.

**Quixote, Don** He is abandoned by his longtime squire, Sancho Panza. Lonely and desperate, he decides to commune with the characters in his dreams. He believes that he will find the answers to life's difficult questions in those dreams. Quixote's dream serves as the framework for the entire play. The Camino Real offers Quixote a new traveling companion, Kilroy.

**Streetcleaners** They are public servants who collect the dead bodies of the Camino Real. It is their decision whether a deceased body can be claimed by relatives or becomes property of the state, and they base their decision on the amount of money found in the cadaver's pockets. The Streetcleaners are fixtures in the corrupt power structure of the Camino Real. They are also manifestations of the ever-present existential and foreboding tone that permeates the Camino Real.

**Survivor** He is a drifter dying of thirst who stumbles on the Camino Real. When Gutman discovers the Survivor in the plaza, he orders the Officer to shoot him instead of offering him water. Jacques Casanova and La Madrecita de Las Soledades try to help him, but he dies.

### FURTHER READING


Atkinson, Brooks. "First Night at the Theatre: Tennessee Williams Writes a Cosmic Fantasy Entitled *Camino Real,*" *New York Times,* 20 March 1953, p. 26.

Falk, Signi. *Tennessee Williams.* New York: Twayne, 1978.

Savran, David. *Communists, Cowboys, and Queers.* Minneapolis: University of Minnesota Press, 1992.

Schrecker, Ellen. *Many Are the Crimes: McCarthyism in America.* Boston: Little, Brown, 1998.

Spoto, Donald. *The Kindness of Strangers: The Life of Tennessee Williams.* Boston: Little, Brown, 1985.

Williams, Tennessee. *Where I Live.* New York: New Directions, 1978.


# *Candles to the Sun*

Full-length play written in 1936.

### SYNOPSIS

This play is set in a coal mining camp in the Red Hill section of Alabama.

*Scene 1*

Before sunrise, Bram Pilcher barges out of the bedroom of his cabin. He stumbles into the furniture, complaining to his wife, Hester, that she has not lighted the oil lamp. Hester busily makes a breakfast of hot mush and coffee. She grumbles about Bram's refusal to use the milk sparingly. Bram laughs when Hester demands that he buy a cow. He hurries her to make his coffee before the work whistle blows. When Bram scalds his tongue on the hot coffee and yelps, Hester hushes him so that he will not wake their children, Joel and Star. Bram fusses about Joel's laziness and complains about his wasting time in school. He says that coal miners have no use for school. Hester retorts that Joel is not going to be a coal miner, but Bram reminds her that all men become coal miners in this part of the country; they have no choice. Bram does not like Hester encouraging Joel to leave the camp because they have lost contact with their oldest son, John, who left.

When Bram criticizes the newly built school, Hester calls him a "natural born slave," as he is loyal to the mining company that keeps him ignorant and poor. Bram notices a shift in Hester's attitude toward him, and he enquires as to the source. Hester produces a letter from her pocket. Tim Adams, the postmaster, told her it is from Pennsylvania, but she cannot read. They fear something has happened to John. Bram leaves the table to wake up Star to read the letter to them. Hester does not want Star to be awakened because she has only been home for a few hours. Bram is infuriated that Star has been out so late. Hester says that Star has been hanging out with rich girls in Birmingham who buy her nice things.

Bram drags Star out of her bed and into the living room. Refusing to believe her story, he demands to know how she obtained the bright red kimono she's wearing. When Star states that it is none of his business, and Bram slaps her and asks again. Star retorts that her father has never given her anything in her life and this is why she has to have friends that will help her. In her rage, Star admits that she has been going to Birmingham with Jake Walland. Bram objects to her relationship with Jake and demands that Star leave the house.

Joel enters the living room. He notices the letter that has fallen to the floor and hands it to his mother. He asks what all the shouting is about, but Hester instructs him to get ready for school and study hard. She also tells him to take the letter to school and have Mrs. Wallace read it to him.

*Scene 2*

The next evening Mrs. Wallace reads the letter to Bram and Hester. John has been killed in a Pennsylvania coal mine. His widow has written the letter informing them that she and their young son, Luke, are on their way to live with them. Bram blames Hester for encouraging John to leave home and, "them damn Yankee mines . . . where they got all them damn fool contraptions like machine loadin' and things to kill people with." Hester blames John's widow for killing him by forcing him to work in the mines.

Tim Adams approaches the cabin with a very thin woman named Fern and a small boy. He says that she came into the store looking for them. Hester is delighted to see that her grandson, Luke, looks just like John.

*Scene 3*

One early summer morning five years later, Fern washes clothes in a big wooden washtub in the middle of the cabin floor. Mrs. Abbey, the mining superintendent's wife, enters. She asks Fern about a pair of purple pajamas that were missing in the last batch of washing that she brought to Fern. Fern says that there were no pajamas in the last load. Mrs. Abbey plops down on a chair and begins to gossip about Joel, who is working at the company store rather than in the mine. She calls him weak for choosing not to go into the mines. Fern is insulted, but keeps calm. Mrs. Abbey talks about Bram's failing eyesight and how unimportant it is anyway because he works in the dark. She tells Fern about a fight that occurred at the store between Star and a red-haired woman.

Hester enters the cabin. Mrs. Abbey excitedly begins to relate the story again for Hester, but Fern interrupts and tells her good-bye. As she is leaving, Mrs. Abbey tells her to be on the lookout for Mr. Abbey's purple pajamas that may be lost among Joel's and Bram's clothes. Hester takes serious offense to this insinuation and throws the bundle of laundry at Mrs. Abbey and tells her never to return to the cabin or to utter another word about her family. Mrs. Abbey threatens to tell her husband, and Hester emphatically encourages her to do that.

After she leaves, Hester regrets her actions and remarks to Mrs. Abbey. She worries that Mrs. Abbey will have Joel fired from the store. Fern tries to comfort her. Hester encourages Fern to start looking for another husband so she won't have to wash other people's dirty laundry. She wants Fern to have a good life. Fern confesses that she feels responsible for John's death and has been saving all of her money for Luke as recompense. Fern sends Luke down the mountain to pick blueberries for lunch. Both women watch him run home, and Hester is struck by his resemblance to John.

### *Scene 4*

Five years later Star sits in her cabin with the windows open to the passing crowd on a lively Saturday. Ethel Sunter comes by to deliver dinner to Star. When Ethel comments on the cards on the table, Star says she has been telling fortunes. Ethel chastises her for such sinfulness and reminds her that only the Lord can divine the future. Ethel also apologizes for missing Jake's funeral, but says that she could not attend it because Jake would not "profess belief" on his deathbed. Ethel asks Star what she has planned for her future, and Star bluntly says there is no plan. Ethel proselytizes and leaves.

Luke visits Star. He tells her that Hester is very ill and that the doctor has prescribed a long rest for her. Luke talks about a man he met, called Birmingham Red, who is organizing a miners' strike. Luke has been reading books that Red has loaned him, and he believes a strike is in order. Star admits that she has heard Red speak, but she is puzzled as to why he never pays her any attention. Star expresses her cynical belief that nothing ever really changes, but Luke refuses to accept her point of view. He is young and hopeful that a strike will improve his family's circumstances.

Luke tells Star that Hester thinks and talks about her all the time. Star makes Luke promise that he will come and get her if Hester should take a turn for the worse. Later that evening, Red visits Star. He talks about miners' rights, the lung disease Jake contracted in the mines, and the atrocities that happen underground. Unaware of Star's family connections, he tells her that Hester Pilcher is dying of pellagra, a disease associated with malnutrition. Star is shaken by this blunt news of her mother, and Red apologizes for his candor. Red and Star go down to the spring to watch the stars. Luke returns and frantically searches for Star.

### *Scene 5*

A few months later, Bram stumbles out of his bedroom, tripping over furniture in the dark. Fern makes his breakfast in the kitchen and scolds him for being so loud and cantankerous. Bram says that Hester always had the lamp burning for him when he got up. Fern sends him out to pump a kettle of water, and Joel enters to eat breakfast. Tim Adams comes by to collect payment of a past-due bill. Bram gives him all the scrip (coal company dollars) he has, but it is not enough to cover the debt. Luke appears in the living room in mining clothes. Fern is horrified and demands that he take the clothes off and go back to bed. Joel and Bram try to reason with her, as they are proud that Luke is going underground with them. Fern is completely beside herself, but Luke says that he has to earn more money if he is going to college next fall. Fern pleads with him, but with Bram and Joel taking Luke's side, her efforts are stifled.

### *Scene 6*

Later that day Star visits Fern. She is lonely and talks about her excruciating love for Red. Star informs Fern of the impending strike. She explains that the miners are divided over the action and are forming alliances. Star and Fern lament Hester's passing, and especially how much they miss her in troubling times. At this moment, the women hear the whistle blow three times, signaling an emergency at the mine. A crowd forms in the distance, and there is shouting. Fern sends Star outside to see who has been killed, as she stands frozen in terror. Fern has a flashback of John's tragedy. Bram can see Star's outline, and he shouts to tell Fern that it is not Luke. The men approach the cabin rushing Joel inside on a plank. His head is covered with a cloth.

### *Scene 7*

Bram's cabin is swarming with miners who have come to pay their respects. Ethel enters to conduct the prayers and service in the back room where Joel's body is on display. Eventually the strike comes up in conversation. Bram begins to fight with the younger miners who believe a strike will create better conditions. Bram reminds the miners, including Luke, that the company store will shut down if there is a strike and the whole camp will starve to death. Luke suggests the miners use his mother's savings to sustain the camp. Bram refuses to allow Luke to touch Fern's money. The argument escalates when other miners enter after attending Red's strike rally. Fern attempts to contain the argument.

*Scene 8*

One or two nights later, Star paces in her cabin while Red writes something. The camp has been silent since the strike began. Star begs Red to tell her what he knows, but he refuses to involve her. Star asks Red when the provisions are going to arrive, as the whole camp is hungry. Red tells her they will arrive as soon as they can. His answer makes Star angry, and she mentions that Fern has $300. Red insists that he will get it from her, but Star tries to convince him that Fern will never part with Luke's college money. Red suggests to Star that he move out of her house because she is not safe with him there. Star confesses that she is in love with him and that she wants a home and family with him. Red is surprised by her declaration. He reminds Star that he is not "a woman's man." Red explains that their relationship cannot get in the way of his mission.

Luke enters the cabin to inform Red that a truckload of men has arrived at the camp and that they are convening in the basement of the company store. Luke has stolen his mother's savings and hands it to Red. Star is angry that Red has made a thief of Luke. Star worries about Red's safety and begs him to go into hiding. Red refuses to shrink from the superintendent's goons. Fern enters demanding her money. Red tells her that she can have it back if she can deal with the guilt of refusing to feed 1,500 of her own people. He appeals to her sentimentality and asks her to ask John what to do. Fern relents and leaves the money on the table.

*Scene 9*

Star and Red wait for the superintendent's men. Star criticizes Red for merely waiting for trouble to arrive instead of escaping and making the fight a little harder for the goons. Red asks her why Fern left the money. Star jokes that maybe she "saw the light," and Red agrees. Star says that she remembers Fern looking, "struck blind." Red says, "There's a lot of difference between looking at a candle and then looking at the sun." Star does not understand what Red means, but she begs him to take her away from the camp. Red promises her that next spring they will go north. Star again professes her love and says that she wants him all to herself. Red explains that he must fight before he loves.

A group of men assemble outside Star's cabin. Red gives Star the money and tells her to take it to the miners. Star asks what he is going to do, and he replies, "Nothing." The men break down the cabin door, grab Star, and pinion and gag her. The men shoot Red and quickly leave when they hear a militia of miners approaching. Star goes to Red, sobbing and screaming for help.

*Scene 10*

Two months later Star goes to Bram's cabin to say good-bye. She tells Fern that she is going to work in Birmingham. She also promises to send money back to pay off Red's debt, but Fern refuses repayment. The superintendent has submitted to the conditions of the strike. Now blind, Bram has also become disoriented. He believes Fern is Hester and that Luke is John. Luke leaves for work at the mines, and Fern rocks in Hester's old rocking chair.

## COMMENTARY

One of Williams's first full-length plays, *Candles to the Sun* was written to be performed by a small semiprofessional theater group in Saint Louis, Missouri, called The Mummers. The group was concerned with social issues and invited Williams to explore socially conscious themes in the plays he wrote for them. Addressing the concerns of coal-mining families, Williams drafted the play during a difficult time in U.S. history. Shortly after the Great Depression and just prior to World War II, poverty was widespread, and the struggle for survival was enormous for the poor. Coal-mining families were starving; fathers, brothers, and husbands were being killed due to unsafe conditions underground.

*Candles to the Sun* should answer questions some contemporary scholars may have about Williams's political convictions. As in his play NOT ABOUT NIGHTINGALES, Williams is wrestling with the serious social concerns of his time. *Nightingales* is informed by the Holmesburg Prison Strike of 1938, during which four inmates were killed for having participated in a hunger strike; in *Candles,* Williams refers to the coal miners' strikes of the early 20th century. The Matewan Massacre and the early Harlan County ("Bloody Harlan") strikes were some of the most brutally suppressed attempts of coal miners to unionize.

Just as Birmingham Red is killed by the superintendent's hired thugs, many miners were brutally beaten and killed in their attempt to receive fair wages, better living conditions, and safety. Some, like Bram Pilcher, felt they could mine as long as conditions were bearable, but Williams focuses on a shift in the economy that made it impossible for miners to feed their families in spite of their hard labor. There is also a generational shift among the miners themselves, with the younger miners expressing the most dissatisfaction. Luke and Joel's generation have witnessed the steady deterioration of their elders, and in Luke's case, the death of his father in the mines. Bram is blind and mentally unstable by the end of the play. Hester dies from malnutrition in the camp. Star loses all hope when Birmingham Red is killed and leaves to work in a brothel in Birmingham. Every person suffers as a result of their association with the mines. There is complete destruction—emotional, physical, social, and environmental.

*Candles to the Sun* was, and remains, Williams's poignant plea on behalf of long-suffering mining communities—an impoverished social group that has been largely ignored and brutually disenfranchised.

## PRODUCTION HISTORY

There have been no professional productions of this play.

## PUBLICATION HISTORY

*Candles to the Sun* was published by New Directions in 2004.

## CHARACTERS

**Abbey, Mrs.** The wife of the coal-mining superintendent, Mrs. Abbey spends her time gossiping and stirring up trouble among the people of the mining camp. She considers herself superior to the women in the camp.

**Adams, Tim** Tim Adams runs the company store in a coal camp in Red Hill, Alabama. He is at the mercy of the mining superintendent, who conducts business in a dishonest way. Although Tim has escaped the coal mines, his struggles are the same as the miners'.

**Birmingham Red** Leader of a group of coal miners in the Red Hill section of Alabama who are fighting for a union. Provocative in his beliefs and convincing in his speeches, Birmingham Red storms into the coal camp with the sole intention of fighting the tyrannical mining company. He realizes that he is jeopardizing his own life, but his convictions are so great that he is fearless. Birmingham Red falls in love with Star Pilcher, and he promises that together they will leave the camp the following spring; however, Red is killed by the mine superintendent's thugs.

**Pilcher, Bram** A dedicated coal miner and a profoundly simple man who believes that he should mine coal as long as he is living. Bram is the oldest man in the mines and the brunt of many cruel jokes. Though losing his eyesight, Bram refuses to stop mining, in part because he knows that his family will starve if he does. When Birmingham Red organizes a miners' strike, Bram strongly objects, believing that as long as the conditions are bearable he should never complain. Bram ages very quickly during the play, and by the end, he is mentally unstable and blind. He still believes, however, that he should be mining coal, even though his body is physically spent.

**Pilcher, Fern** The widow of John Pilcher, a miner who was killed in Pennsylvania. Fern takes her young son, Luke, to Alabama to live in a coal camp with her in-laws. She is determined that Luke should not grow up to be a miner, although his fate may be inevitable. When Luke starts mining coal with his grandfather Bram and his uncle Joel, Fern suffers her greatest disappointment. Like her mother-in-law, Hester, Fern retreats into her own world.

**Pilcher, Hester** The wife of a coal miner, Bram Pilcher. Hester struggles to live in the dismal conditions of the mining camp. Determined that her sons not become miners like their father, Hester tries to send them out into the world in the hope that they will better themselves. When her son John moves to Pennsylvania and becomes a coal miner and is killed, Hester realizes that she is waging a losing battle. Exhausted by the constant struggle to feed her family, Hester herself becomes weak and dies from a disease associated with malnutrition.

**Pilcher, Joel** A young miner and the son of a miner. Despite his mother's wishes, Joel follows his father and mines coal. He becomes involved in a strike but is killed due to unsafe conditions. His death ignites the angry miners to win the strike.

**Pilcher, Luke** He is the son of John and Fern Pilcher. His father was a coal miner who was killed when Luke was a young child. Luke grows up with his grandparents and mother in a mining camp in Alabama. He is an avid reader who dedicates himself to the idea of going to college; however, the social pressure to mine coal becomes too great, and he succumbs to it. Luke gets involved in a strike for unionization. Convinced by Birmingham Red and despite his grandfather Bram's warning, Luke aligns himself with the strike. When the strike is eventually won with the benefit of his college savings, Luke once again considers college, but puts on his work clothes and he enters the mines.

**Pilcher, Star** The daughter of a hardworking mining family, Star struggles to make a life for herself in a mining camp. She falls in love with Birmingham Red, but when he is killed during a miners' strike, Star decides to move to Birmingham to work in a brothel.

**Sunter, Ethel** The friend of Star Pilcher and the coal camp's impromptu minister. Ethel brings dinner to Star and preaches to her about her sinful ways.

**Wallace, Mrs.** She is the teacher in a mining camp school in Alabama. Mrs. Wallace is one of the few people in the camp who can read. She goes to the Pilchers' house to read a letter telling them that their son John has been killed in a Pennsylvania mine.

### FURTHER READING

Leverich, Lyle. *Tom: The Unknown Tennessee Williams.* New York: W. W. Norton & Co., 1995.

# *The Case of the Crushed Petunias*

A one-act play written around 1939.

### SYNOPSIS

The play is set in a tiny boutique called "Simple Notions" in the small New England town of Primanproper, Massachusetts. Dorothy Simple informs a Police Officer that someone with a size 11D foot has deliberately trampled all of her petunias. A Young Man enters Dorothy's shop and admits that he crushed her petunias to liberate her garden. He offers to replace Dorothy's petunias with wild roses. He also offers to liberate Dorothy from her rigid surroundings if she will meet him that night on Highway 77. The Young Man leaves the shop with a tentative promise from Dorothy.

One of Dorothy's regular customers, Mrs. Dull, enters the shop and finds Dorothy considerably transformed. Dorothy is no longer her prim and proper self. She openly ridicules Mrs. Dull, who rushes out of the boutique in a fury. Dorothy asks the Police Officer for directions to Highway 77. The policeman advises her that Highway 77 is a derelict road. He warns Dorothy that once she travels down Highway 77, she can never return to Primanproper, Massachusetts. Dorothy is exuberant in the face of this warning.

### COMMENTARY

Described by Williams as a lyrical fantasy, *The Case of the Crushed Petunias* is a delightful tale of a young woman's liberation from the mundane and conventional world she inhabits. *The Case of the Crushed*

*Petunias* was one of the three plays that launched Williams's career. In 1939, Williams submitted *The Case of the Crushed Petunias* along with MOONY'S KID DON'T CRY and THE DARK ROOM to a play competition sponsored by THE GROUP THEATRE. Williams's one-act collection won a $100 prize and drew the attention of the talent agent AUDREY WOOD. The three plays were later published together in the collection AMERICAN BLUES.

Each of the three plays in the collection illuminates the day-to-day existence of ordinary men and women and their quest for freedom and a better way of life. Unlike its companion pieces in *American Blues, The Case of the Crushed Petunias* is a comic fable with a hopeful ending. Dorothy Simple leaves her Primanproper hometown and travels on the mysterious Highway 77, metaphorically the road of life. Although the outcome is uncertain, Dorothy has taken the risk and broken free of her confined and overly protective environment. This daring young woman calls to mind many of the spirited female dreamers and chance takers who would later populate the Williams canon, such as Lady Torrance in ORPHEUS DESCENDING.

Dorothy Simple's most immediate successor is the fallen debutante Cassandra Whiteside in the play BATTLE OF ANGELS. As Dorothy does, Cassandra longs for a life fuller and more vibrant than her small-town community can offer her. One of Cassandra's most memorable sections of dialogue in *Battle of Angels,* in which she tells Valentine Xavier that her dead ancestors frequently admonish her to "Live! Live! Live!" is taken directly from Dorothy's exchange with the Young Man in *The Case of the Crushed Petunias.* This one-act play clearly served as a template for *Battle of Angels,* Williams's first full-length treatment of life in the South. Aside from sharing sections of dialogue, both plays are centered on the story of an attractive female shopkeeper liberated from her stifling environment by a charismatic and dynamic young man.

## PRODUCTION HISTORY

*The Case of the Crushed Petunias* was first produced at the Shelterhouse Theatre, in Cincinnati, Ohio, in May 1973, under the direction of Pirie MacDonald.

## PUBLICATION HISTORY

*The Case of the Crushed Petunias* was first published in the one-act collection *American Blues* in 1948.

## CHARACTERS

**Dull, Mrs.** Mrs. Dull is one of Dorothy Simple's faithful customers at her shop, Simple Notions, in Primanproper, Massachusetts. Mrs. Dull enters the shop after the Young Man has enticed Dorothy to leave her safe small-town life. Dorothy's impending escape from Primanproper allows her the freedom to speak her mind frankly. She gleefully crushes Mrs. Dull's feelings.

**Police Officer** He counsels Dorothy Simple about the dangers of traveling Highway 77. The Police Officer advises her that she should not leave the safety and security of Primanproper, Massachusetts. He warns her that if she does leave, her life will never be the same and she can never return.

**Simple, Dorothy** Dorothy is an attractive 26-year-old unmarried New England woman. She lives a sheltered and restrictive life in Primanproper, Massachusetts, behind a protective double row of petunias. She is the owner of a small boutique, Simple Notions. One evening a young drifter, referred to only as the Young Man, crushes her petunias with his size 11D foot. The next day he enters her shop and explains that his intention was to liberate Dorothy's garden from its excessively methodical and painfully rigid existence. He offers to do the same for Dorothy if she will meet him in the evening on Highway 77. Dorothy is warned by a Police Officer that if she travels down that road, she will never be able to return to life in Primanproper. Dorothy opposes her proper upbringing and conventional wisdom and meets the Young Man that night on the dark, desolate road. Although her future is uncertain, Dorothy is exuberant with her newly found freedom.

**Young Man** He is the culprit with the size 11D foot who crushes Dorothy Simple's double row of petunias. The formality and rigidity of her petunia garden enrage the Young Man, who believes that gardens and people should be wild and free. He offers to liberate her garden further by planting wild roses. Likewise, he offers to liberate Dorothy from her restricted life in Primanproper, Massachusetts.

## Cat on a Hot Tin Roof

A play in three acts written in 1955.

### SYNOPSIS

The play is set in the Pollitts' stately home, a Southern plantation in the fertile Mississippi Valley.

#### Act 1

Brick Pollitt emerges from the bathroom at the insistence of his wife, Margaret Pollitt (Maggie the Cat). With his left ankle broken, Brick hobbles around the room and dresses. He is coolly detached from his wife despite her poise and beauty. Maggie tells him that the evening's festivities will include a birthday party in honor of Brick's father, Big Daddy Pollitt. She bemoans Brick's brother, Gooper, and his wife, Mae, and the way they strategically display their children for Big Daddy. Maggie is disgusted by the children, the "no-neck monsters," who used her dress as a napkin. As it has become known that Big Daddy is dying of cancer, Maggie is competing with Gooper and Mae to secure the family estate for Brick.

A scene from the Broadway production of *Cat on a Hot Tin Roof,* starring Burl Ives as Big Daddy, Barbara Bel Geddes as Maggie the Cat, and Ben Gazzara as Brick Pollitt, 1955 *(Photograph courtesy of the Billy Rose Theatre Collection of the New York Public Library)*

Maggie criticizes Mae and her family, the Memphis Flynns. Maggie realizes that Brick is staring at her with cold contempt and she begs to know why. Maggie believes loneliness has changed her, and she prays for the day when their marriage will be rekindled. Maggie asks why Brick remains so handsome despite his alcoholism. She notes that he has not deteriorated as his friend Skipper did. The mention of Skipper's name sends Brick to the bar to make another drink. Maggie comments that she would surely kill herself if Brick chose not to make love to her anymore. When she realizes that her dramatic overture has not stirred him, she maliciously utters the name Skipper again. Brick fills his drink once more. He drops his crutch and tries to run from Maggie's pronouncements of Skipper.

Brick waits to hear "the click" in his head, the peaceful feeling he experiences when he drinks enough alcohol. Maggie's presence and constant nagging to join the party distract him and prevent him from feeling the click. Brick is angered by Maggie's persistence, and just as their argument crescendos there is a knock at their door. Mae enters with an old trophy of Maggie's from her sporting days at Mississippi University. Mae orders that this be placed high enough to be out of the reach of her children, to which Maggie replies that if they were well bred they would not be touching things that did not belong to them. Mae retorts that Maggie knows nothing of children because she has none of her own, a vicious truth. Maggie nastily asks Mae why she has given her children "dogs' names": Trixie, Buster, Sonny, and so on.

Mae storms out of the bedroom, and Brick begs Maggie not to be so catty. Maggie claims that she cannot control her temper because Brick has turned her into a cat on a hot tin roof. Brick suggests that she jump off the roof and take another lover. Maggie shows her longing affection for him, but he refuses her again. She runs to the door and locks it, turns down the shade, and crawls closer to Brick. She grabs him, and he violently shoves her away as his disgust for her increases.

Big Mama enters the bedroom. Brick runs into the bathroom to hide from his mother, and Maggie finishes getting dressed. Big Mama excitedly announces that Doc Baugh has just informed her that Big Daddy does not have cancer after all. She asks Brick to dress and join the party; otherwise, the party will join him in the bedroom (since he has a broken ankle).

When Big Mama exits, Maggie resumes her talk about their sex life, which declined abruptly. Maggie says that she maintains her figure for Brick because she knows he will return to her. She brags that other men devour her with their looks. She revels in the knowledge that she is still gorgeous.

Brick acknowledges that his father really is terminally ill and his mother is oblivious to this truth. Gooper and Mae thought it best to withhold the truth from Big Daddy and Big Mama in an attempt to put the estate in order.

Maggie returns to the topic of Skipper. Brick tries to avoid the conversation and calls out on the gallery for the party to join him upstairs. Maggie will not desist. She is determined to get to the truth about Brick and Skipper. Brick threatens to hit her with his crutch.

Angrily, Brick demands that Maggie stop trying to taint the memory of Skipper. Maggie relentlessly tells the story of two college football heroes who organized their own team, the Dixie Stars, in order to keep playing after college. Brick was injured midseason, and Skipper also did not have a successful season. Brick runs around the room trying to catch Maggie for her vulgar insinuations regarding his relationship with Skipper. Maggie confesses that Skipper had sex with her to disprove the allegation that he was gay. Maggie had made this allegation the night that Skipper plunged himself into a fatal drug-induced alcoholic coma.

At this admission, Brick falls to the floor with grief. One of the children runs into the room shooting a toy gun. When the child asks why he is on the floor, Brick responds that he tried to kill Aunt Maggie. Maggie yells at the little girl, and she answers smartly that Maggie is just jealous because she cannot have babies as her mommy can.

Maggie confides to Brick that she visited a fertility doctor who said there was no reason why they should not be able to have children. Repulsed, Brick asks how she plans to have a child with a man who cannot stand her.

### *Act 2*

The partygoers usher Big Daddy into Brick and Maggie's quarters. The Reverend Tooker converses with Gooper about memorial stained glass windows donated by certain parishioners and widowers. Mae talks about the children's vaccinations with Doc Baugh, forcing Maggie to blast the radio. Big Daddy demands that the radio be turned off, but when Big Mama enters shouting for Brick, he changes his order so as to drown out the noise.

Big Mama begs Brick to stop drinking and join the family. Big Mama tries to be close to her husband, but she is met with a cold stare of irritation. The servants and Gooper's children enter with Big Daddy's birthday cake, singing and dancing in a rehearsed act. Big Mama cries and Big Daddy quarrels with her because she is crying. Big Daddy asks whether Brick was drunk and jumping hurdles at the track field last night. Big Mama shows Big Daddy his cake in hopes of changing the subject. Infuriated by Brick's asinine actions and Big Mama's need to cover them, Big Daddy accuses her of never knowing anything in her whole life. Big Mama objects to being treated this way in front of the family, but he continues to accuse her of usurping his position. Everyone gradually leaves the room.

Big Daddy talks about being a self-made man, one of the richest plantation owners in the South. He orders Big Mama to blow out the candles and she refuses. As she leaves the room, she repeats that she always loved him. Big Daddy comments, "Wouldn't it be funny if that was true."

Big Daddy calls Brick back into the room. Maggie enters with a begrudging Brick and she kisses him on the lips as she exits to the gallery. Brick wipes off her kiss and Big Daddy asks why he would object to being kissed by such a beautiful woman. Brick informs him that Maggie and Mae are fighting over the plantation. Big Daddy responds that he intends to live another good 20 years.

They discover Mae eavesdropping on their conversation. Big Daddy threatens to move them out of the room next door because he is tired of getting reports about what goes on between Brick and Maggie every night. Brick is amused that his debacle of a marriage is so important to everyone. When questioned about his refusal to sleep with Maggie, Brick returns to the liquor cabinet. Big Daddy asks Brick to stop drinking.

Big Daddy reminisces about his travels with Big Mama to Europe and the useless things they bought. He comments that one cannot buy back life or any of the memories that have built it. Brick grows restless with these ramblings. Brick says he is not interested in talking to his father because it will turn out as all of their talks do: talking in circles and leading to nowhere in particular. He just wants to hear the quiet click and rest in peace.

Big Daddy is compelled to close the doors and confide to Brick that he was truly frightened about having cancer. He declares that he is going to live life to the fullest now that he knows he is healthy. Big Daddy confesses that he could never tolerate Big Mama, and he now thinks he will pursue women as a hobby. Big Mama crosses through the room to answer the phone. Brick is so ashamed by his father's disgust for his mother that he exits for fresh air.

Big Mama begs her husband to take back all the awful things he said to her. He responds by throwing her out of the room and locking the door. Brick aimlessly hobbles around the room. Brick says that he is waiting for the click in his brain. Big Daddy vows to cure Brick's alcoholism.

Brick knows his father's death is imminent and cannot face his father's talk of a second chance at life. He tries to leave but Big Daddy violently thrusts him back into the room by the sleeve of his shirt. They begin to fight and Big Mama rushes in to resolve the situation. Big Daddy orders her out and grabs Brick's crutch so that he is immobile. Big Daddy will not give it back to him until he can answer why he drinks. Brick cannot answer him.

Brick confesses that the "mendacity" of life is plaguing him. Big Daddy explains that mendacity is merely a part of life for everyone with false institutions such as church, government, and marriage. Brick suggests that the only true companion is alcohol. Big Daddy deduces that Brick began drinking when Skipper died. Brick's cool detachment immediately changes to defensiveness.

Brick asks his father whether he believed his relationship with Skipper was more than just a friendship. The conversation escalates as Brick rants about the insinuations about his relationship with Skipper. Big Daddy doubles over with pain.

Brick describes his friendship with Skipper and their closeness as comrades, not as lovers. Brick regains his composure and speaks frankly to Big Daddy. He admits that Maggie threatened to leave him if he did not marry her and so he did, out of obligation rather than love. She tagged along with Brick and the football team all over the country. When Brick was hospitalized following his injury, Skipper and Maggie continued on the road. Brick witnessed the closeness of their relationship from the confines of his hospital bed. Maggie accused Skipper of being in love with her husband, which provoked Skipper to sleep with Maggie to prove his heterosexuality. When he could not physically complete the act with her, he was convinced that he was gay. This realization was too much for him to handle, and led to his breakdown and subsequent death.

Big Daddy suspects that there are missing pieces of the story. Brick confesses that later that same night Skipper called him at the hospital and professed his love for him. Skipper told Brick about the situation with Maggie, and Brick hung up on him. He never spoke to Skipper again.

Big Daddy concludes that Brick never resolved the issue with Skipper. Brick questions whether anyone ever completely faces the truth, and he challenges Big Daddy about his own reality. Brick declares that there will be no more birthdays for his father. Big Daddy becomes enraged and vows to bury his drunk son before giving the plantation to him. Brick exits as Big Daddy witnesses his birthday fireworks in the evening sky.

Brick returns and tenderly explains to Big Daddy that he told him the truth about his illness because no one else had the courage to face him. Big Daddy exits, condemning his family as liars.

**Act 3**

Mae and the Reverend Tooker search for Big Daddy, who has retired to bed. Gooper gathers the family to discuss important matters while Maggie searches for Big Daddy. Big Mama basks in the news that her husband is healthy, except for a nervous condition. She calls for Brick, and Gooper quickly informs her that he is outside drinking. When Maggie exits to fetch Brick, Mae charges that Brick revealed the truth about Big Daddy's health to him. Gooper tries to delicately inform Big Mama about Big Daddy's condition.

Big Mama expresses concern for Brick's depression and his decline after Skipper's death. Brick overhears her as he enters and moves toward the liquor cabinet, silencing the family members in the room. Big Mama sobs and Maggie tries to improve the situation by forcing Brick to sit beside Big Mama; however, Brick leaves the room. Gooper and Dr. Baugh tell Big Mama that Big Daddy is terminally ill with cancer. Hysterical, Big Mama calls for Brick. Gooper goes to her, but she pushes him away and says, "You're not my real blood." Mae is astounded by her mother-in-law's hurtful remark, and she rushes over to plead with Big Mama. The Reverend Tooker quickly escapes this heated moment of family crisis.

Big Mama accuses Gooper of never liking Big Daddy. She accuses him of being happy that his father is dying so that he can finally gain control of the plantation and family assets. Maggie joins in the conversation and is met with insults from Mae, who accuses Brick of being an alcoholic. Maggie denies the charges, explaining that his current inebriation is a result of the difficult news. Big Mama calls for Brick so that she can discuss his taking over the plantation. Astounded by the thought, Gooper quickly instructs Mae to get his briefcase, insisting on handling business contracts he has readied for this occasion.

Mae criticizes Brick's lifestyle. She claims he is still living in the glory days of his high school football career. Maggie defends her husband once again, and Gooper rages toward her with his fists clenched. Big Mama sweeps Maggie to her side. Maggie tells Gooper that they plan to leave the plantation as soon as Big Daddy dies. Maggie then apologizes to Big Mama. Mae accuses Maggie of being barren, and she divulges that Brick refuses to have sex with his own wife. Gooper shouts at Mae for the plummeting conversation and demands fairness and rights to the plantation. When Brick enters the room, Gooper and Mae make fun of his petty local football stardom. Gooper produces a contract, urging Big Mama to sign it. Maggie contests the document while Brick sings and pours another drink. Big Mama demands that Gooper stop talking as if Big Daddy were already dead. She rejects the contract, demands it be put away, and coddles Brick. Big Mama asks him to have a child with Maggie before Big Daddy dies. Mae scoffs at this remark which prompts Maggie to announce that she is pregnant. Big Mama is elated because

Burl Ives (Big Daddy) and Barbara Bel Geddes (Maggie) in the Broadway production of *Cat on a Hot Tin Roof,* 1955 *(Photograph courtesy of the Billy Rose Theatre Collection, New York Public Library)*

she believes a child will sober Brick. Big Mama rushes out to tell Big Daddy the good news. Gooper makes a drink for himself while Mae accuses Maggie of lying.

A thunderous moan of pain overcomes the house. Gooper and Mae run to Big Daddy's bedroom. Maggie scolds Brick for not backing her story. Brick says that it has not happened yet, the peaceful click in his mind. He asks for a pillow from the bed in preparation for his slumber on the couch, and the peaceful click occurs with Brick's next drink. Maggie tells her husband that she used to think he was the stronger in their relationship, but now that he drinks, she has become the stronger. Maggie asks him to bed, and she explains that it is her time to conceive. Brick asks how that is possible with a man in love with his liquor. Maggie counters that she has locked the liquor away until he satisfies her. Brick grabs his crutch and attempts to get up, but Maggie steals the crutch away from him.

Big Mama rushes into the bedroom still euphoric with the news of the pregnancy. Big Daddy's groans are heard, prompting Big Mama to rush out again. Maggie states that the lie is going to become the truth. She proposes that she and Brick get drunk after they have conceived. She switches off the lamp and declares her love for him. Brick comments that it would be funny if her declaration were true.

## COMMENTARY

There are several versions of the final moments of *Cat on a Hot Tin Roof.* The ending outlined above is from Williams's first published version of the play

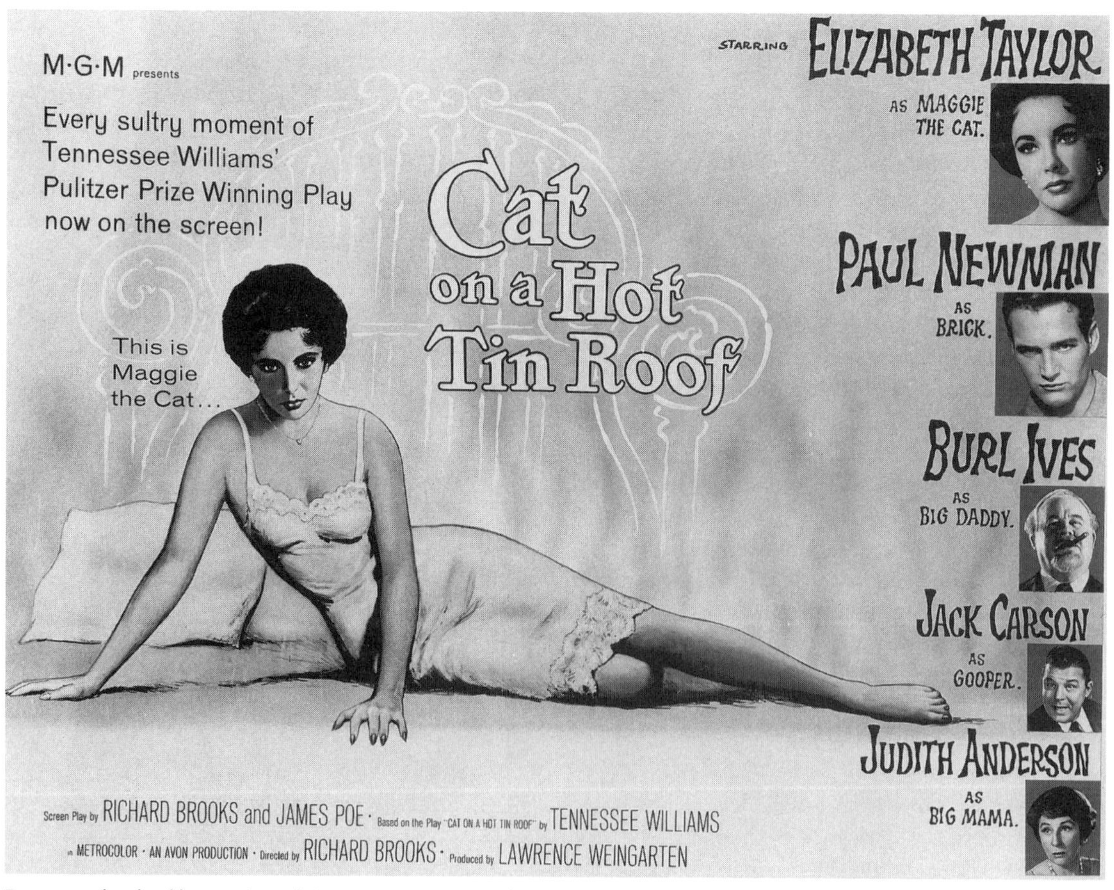


Poster art for the film version of *Cat on a Hot Tin Roof* (MGM, 1958)

(1955). The version that was created for the premiere production on Broadway (under the direction of ELIA KAZAN) in 1954 differs from this version in the manipulation of the last lines. Kazan believed the play needed a less harsh ending. In the Kazan version, after Maggie suggests she and Brick conceive a child and get drunk together, Brick states, "I admire you, Maggie." He then turns out the light, and she likens his "weak" condition to "gold you let go of." She says she is determined to give him back his life. This version of the play ends with Maggie posing the following question: "And nothing's more determined than a cat on a tin roof—is there? Is there, Baby?" This version of the script lessens Brick's tragedy, as he chooses Maggie and their marriage rather than merely surrendering to her.

A third and final version of the script, created for the 1974 Broadway revival of *Cat on a Hot Tin Roof,* starring ELIZABETH ASHLEY, is a combination of the two endings. In this version, Big Daddy reappears to tell a joke. Although the severity of Brick's tragic fate (tragic because he does not want Maggie) is not completely restored in this version, it is, however, less neatly packaged than the 1950s happy ending. Brick still comments on his admiration for Maggie, but when Maggie declares her love for him, Brick responds, "Wouldn't it be funny if that were true?"

The nuances that are created in the slight manipulation of the last lines dramatically affect the overall weight of the play. The original version's impact lies in Brick's tragic turn in his forfeiting dominance to Maggie the Cat, an ingenious shift that occurs in the final seconds of the lengthy play; the second and third versions of the script shift the play's focus to Maggie. She remains in control of the plot, and the introduction of such sudden and complete tenderness between these mismatched characters seems heavy-handed and inconsistent. In his preface or note of explanation about the changes Kazan wanted in the script, Williams stated, "The moral paralysis of Brick was a root thing in his tragedy, and to show a dramatic progression would obscure the meaning of that tragedy in him . . . because I don't believe that a conversation, however revelatory, ever effects so immediate a change in the heart or even conduct of a person in Brick's state of spiritual disrepair." Williams, however, conceded and made the change because he wanted Kazan to direct the play. Williams admired Kazan and in the same preface he defends the director: "No living playwright, that I can think of, hasn't something valuable to learn about his own work from a director so keenly perceptive as Elia Kazan."

In this play, Williams pushes the boundaries of subjects taboo at this time, such as homosexuality (particularly taboo in the South), decay, disease and death, and depression stemming from the mendacity of life. Interestingly, the play is based on the short story "THREE PLAYERS OF A SUMMER GAME," in which the character Brick Pollitt loves the company of women.

Although he is profane, violent, and gluttonous, Big Daddy is interestingly and surprisingly tolerant. He questions the source of Brick's alcoholism, implying that Brick's relationship with Skipper was more than platonic. Big Daddy explains that his plantation was previously owned by two men, and Brick and Maggie's bedroom was in fact the bedroom of the men who lovingly shared their lives together. In his stage directions to the play, Williams writes, "The room must evoke some ghosts; it is gently and poetically haunted by a relationship that must have involved a tenderness which was uncommon." Whereas Big Daddy is tolerant about this relationship, Brick rages, rails, and cannot accept the idea. Big Daddy validates Brick's loss. He also addresses his self-possessed tolerance: "Always, anyhow, lived with too much space around me to be infected by ideas of other people. One thing you can grow on a big place more important than cotton!—is tolerance!—I grown it!" At the heart of Big Daddy's unexpected act of understanding is an enlightened view of himself in relation to the world around him: his rebellious approach to living without societal pressures to conform and his uncommon belief that tolerance for human beings is more important than any cash crop. His tolerance is widely overlooked and underrated in traditional scholarship.

The core of Brick's pain stems from the phone call in which Skipper revealed to Brick his love and desire for him. Brick's guilt arises from his insensitive response to Skipper and Skipper's subsequent suicide. Big Daddy responds to this story by saying, "This disgust with mendacity is disgust with yourself. *You!*—dug the grave of your friend and kicked him in it!—before you'd face the truth with him!" Brick's only defense when cornered in such a profound way is to counter with the attack that Big Daddy is dying of cancer. His rejection of this personal truth runs so deeply, his internalized homophobia is so severe, that in this moment of rare understanding, Brick lashes out, severing the unprecedented connection with his father.

Big Daddy's dysfunctional and loathsome marriage with Big Mama is mirrored in Brick and Maggie's relationship. This is another tragic element in the play, as their marriage is destined to become more miserable and unbearable. Maggie and Big Mama are similar creatures in that they both search for the satisfaction of knowing they are admired and loved by their husbands. Brick's love for Maggie has been usurped by another: the memory of his beloved Skipper, whom Maggie exposed (Maggie "tested" his sexuality when she lured him to bed and he could not perform). Brick blames Maggie for Skipper's death. As Nancy Tischler comments, "Brick, knowing how Maggie forced this intolerable self-realization on Skipper, sees her as his enemy, while Maggie feels that this, like everything she does, was a testimony of her all-embracing love for Brick" (Tischler, 201). What is left of this marriage is a rudimentary set of assigned roles that Maggie must force upon Brick. It is revealed in the final moments of the play that she indeed proves victorious. Brick gives up and sleeps with the enemy.

Maggie is a strong woman, determined to become a wealthy plantation owner. She does love Brick, but for her it is impossible to separate the idea of Brick from his social position and potential power. Although Brick is the athlete, no one understands competition and winning more than the powerful Maggie. In the original version of the script, it is her strength and her assuming the willful characteristics of Big Daddy that finally reward her. Her trump card is her pregnancy, and upon declaring herself with child, Maggie wins the plantation, conquering Gooper and Mae and their host of "no-neck" children, as well as achieving intimacy with her handsome Brick.

## PRODUCTION HISTORY

*Cat on a Hot Tin Roof* was one of Williams's most successful plays. It premiered at the Morosco Theatre in New York on March 24, 1955, produced by the Playwright's Company, directed by Elia Kazan, and designed by JO MIELZINER. The cast included Barbara Bel Geddes (Margaret), Ben Gazzara (Brick), Mildred Dunnock (Big Mama), BURL IVES (Big Daddy), Madeleine Sherwood (Mae), and Pat Hingle (Gooper). With this play, Williams garnered the Drama Critics Circle Award and the Pulitzer Prize. Critics generally praised the cast; however, they commented negatively on what they perceived as the play's vulgarity and its treatment of homosexuality.

The play was revived in 1974, at the American Shakespeare Theatre, Stratford, Connecticut, and then at the ANTA Theatre in New York. The revival was directed by Michael Kahn; it starred Fred Gwynne (Big Daddy), Elizabeth Ashley (Margaret), and Keir Dullea (Brick). Though the 1955 premiere had shocked audiences, by 1974, audiences were no longer struck by the controversial themes.

A London revival in 1988, directed by Howard Davies and starring Lindsay Duncan (Margaret), Eric Porter (Big Daddy), and Ian Charleson (Brick), restored the original third act. The production received high praise from critics. Howard Davies also directed the 1990 New York revival of *Cat,* starring Kathleen Turner (Maggie), Daniel Hugh Kelly (Brick), and Charles Durning (Big Daddy). The original third act was again produced. As Alice Griffin commented, "It took thirty-five years to appreciate how much better Williams's original third act served the play in production" (167). A 2003 New York revival starred Ashley Judd (Maggie), Jason Patric (Brick), and Ned Beatty (Big Daddy).

The film version of *Cat on a Hot Tin Roof* was produced in 1958, directed by Richard Brooks, and starred ELIZABETH TAYLOR (Maggie), Paul Newman (Brick), and Burl Ives (Big Daddy). Maurice Yacowar writes in *Tennessee Williams and Film,* "Cat was the biggest grosser of 1958, the tenth biggest that MGM ever had, and the biggest of all the Williams adaptations." The film remains a popular classic.

## PUBLICATION HISTORY

*Cat on a Hot Tin Roof* was published by New Directions in 1955, including the two versions of the third act, accompanied by Williams's "note of explanation," which sparked some controversy as some perceived that Williams was blaming Kazan for his compromised ending.

## CHARACTERS

**Baugh, Dr.** He is the Pollitt family doctor, who delivers the news that Big Daddy is dying of cancer. He relays this awful news at Big Daddy's birthday party. Dr. Baugh stands in the shadows during heated family arguments.

**Big Daddy** A prominent Southern plantation owner and tycoon, Big Daddy is profane, gluttonous, and brutally honest. Big Daddy is terminally ill but is told by his family that his test results prove that he is healthy. In a heated argument with his alcoholic son, Brick Pollitt, regarding Brick's implied sexual relationship with his friend Skipper, Brick lashes out and tells his father that he is actually dying of cancer. Like Boss Finley of *SWEET BIRD OF YOUTH*, Big Daddy is a powerful figure in his community. Talk of his impending death ushers in a whirlwind of change in which his son, Gooper Pollitt, intends to profit.

Burl Ives (Big Daddy) and Ben Gazzara (Brick Pollitt) in the Broadway production of *Cat on a Hot Tin Roof*, 1955 *(Photograph courtesy of The Billy Rose Theatre Collection, New York Public Library)*

Burl Ives (Big Daddy) and Mildred Dunnock (Big Mama) in the 1955 Broadway production of *Cat on a Hot Tin Roof* *(Photograph courtesy of The Billy Rose Theatre Collection, New York Public Library)*

Big Daddy also shares Boss Finely's boisterous point of view and outlook on life. He is arguably Williams's most famous male character.

**Big Mama** The wife of Big Daddy. She and Big Daddy have been married nearly 40 years. Despite their years together, Big Mama still searches for ways to know she is loved by Big Daddy. Big Mama is the matriarch of a large family, including Brick and Margaret Pollitt, Gooper and Mae Pollitt, and a host of grandchildren. She is fun-loving and colorful and openly expresses her sincere love for her family. When Big Daddy is diagnosed with cancer, Big Mama refuses to believe the news because she cannot fathom a life without him. She is faced with the decision about which son will run their plantation.

**Maggie the Cat** See Pollitt, Margaret.

**Pollitt, Brick** He is the son of Big Daddy and Big Mama and husband of Margaret "Maggie the Cat" Pollitt. Brick is a jaded soul whose life is spent in an alcohol-induced haze of memories about Skipper, a friend with whom he shared a mutual attraction. When Skipper revealed his love for Brick, Brick did not acknowledge it. Skipper then committed suicide. Brick has never forgiven himself for not being honest with his friend. Brick blames Maggie for revealing the sexual tension that existed between the two men. Maggie is very unhappy because Brick refuses to be intimate with her. Brick eventually gives in to his wife's continual demands. As the play ends, Brick forfeits his own personal desires to satisfy Maggie. He succumbs to the mendacity of life.

**Pollitt, Gooper** He is married to Mae Pollitt. Gooper competes with his parents' favorite son, Brick Pollitt. This tension escalates as it is revealed that their father, Big Daddy, is dying of cancer and

Paul Newman (Brick) and Elizabeth Taylor (Maggie the Cat) in the film version of *Cat on a Hot Tin Roof* *(MGM, 1958)*

will leave behind an empire of wealth and the largest plantation in the state of Mississippi. Gooper and Mae have produced several children to please Big Daddy and Big Mama, but their obvious opportunism is scorned by the other members of the family.

**Pollitt, Mae** She is the wife of Gooper Pollitt. Mae rails against her brother-in-law and his wife, Brick and Margaret Pollitt. She competes with them by having children to be the heirs of the Pollitt wealth and plantation. Mae is ruthless about securing the rights to the estate, and when it becomes known that Big Daddy is dying of cancer, she and Gooper set up camp at their home, equipped with a contract in preparation for the final moment.

**Pollitt, Margaret (Maggie the Cat)** She is the wife of Brick Pollitt. As the title of the play suggests, Maggie is the catalyst for the plot of the play. She married the handsome Brick because she values his social standing and his money and because she loves him. Having grown up in poverty, Maggie has no doubts about the power of wealth, and so she openly competes with her brother-in-law, Gooper Pollitt, and his wife, Mae Pollitt, for the best position in the family. Brick is an alcoholic, and Maggie makes excuses for his behavior and lack of participation in family events, as well as covering up the severity of his condition. When it is revealed that Big Daddy is dying of cancer, Maggie deceives the family by announcing that she is pregnant, in a ploy to inherit the family's plantation. Despite Brick's lack of interest in the inheritance or his wife, he decides to play the game with her. Maggie proves triumphant.

**Reverend Tooker** He is the Pollitt family's minister. The Reverend Tooker attends a birthday party for Big Daddy, who donates significant amounts of money to his church. When the news breaks that Big Daddy is dying of cancer, the Reverend Tooker says a quick good-bye instead of consoling the family. His interest in the family seems fueled by financial gain.

### FURTHER READING

Griffith, Alice. *Understanding Tennessee Williams.* Columbia: University of South Carolina Press, 1995.

Tischler, Nancy. *Tennessee Williams: Rebellious Puritan.* New York: The Citadel Press, 1965.

Yacowar, Maurice. *Tennessee Williams and Film.* New York: Frederick Ungar, 1977.

# "Chronicle of a Demise"

Short story written in 1947.

### SYNOPSIS

A female religious leader known as the Saint mysteriously disappears and her followers scour the city in search of her. They find her living on the roof of her Cousin's apartment building. She sleeps on a cot and refuses anything to eat or drink except black coffee. Under her cot, she keeps a heart-shaped box called the "Possible Box" that contains the religious sect's articles of faith. A fierce thunderstorm threatens the city, and the Narrator and Agatha Doyle gather the Saint and the Possible Box and attempt to take cover inside, but the Cousin claims that his wife refuses to have the Possible Box in their home.

The Saint has a spiritual manifestation during the storm, during which she floats in the air. After the storm, the Saint delivers a sermon. Her cousin is late for the gathering and confronts the Saint about the Order's current mission. He accuses her of stalling for time because the latest expedition returned empty-handed. The Saint admits that she has kept this knowledge a secret for several weeks. The Cousin slings the Possible Box from the roof. The Saint rises from her cot and opens her chest, and leaves of thin tissue paper float out of her heart. Her eyeballs, "beautifully blue as marbles," spring out of their sockets. Her disciples try to force the tissue paper back into her heart, but it is too late: Her heart has stopped. The Saint melts into the air.

### COMMENTARY

"Chronicle of a Demise" is a satirical look at religion narrated by a former member of a religious group. The story is written as an eyewitness account of the events that changed the disciple's life and chronicles the last days of the Saint, a religious leader of a sect called "the Order." No specific details regarding the narrator, such as name or gender, are ever revealed. Presenting the narrative in the form of a report is a device which makes the story highly engaging. The brevity and objectivity of the Narrator entice the reader to want to know more.

This story is an example of Williams's engagement with fantasy and magical realism in his fiction: The Saint physically dissolves in midair; she opens her heart, revealing a vault of tissue paper leaves that blow away; and her eyes spring out of their sockets, while her body evaporates in front of her disciples. The fantastic quality of this tale is reminiscent of other Williams short stories such as "THE COMING OF SOMETHING TO WIDOW HOLLY." Similar to that comic fantasy, "Chronicle of a Demise" ends on a hopeful, if somewhat solemn, note. Just as the Saint undergoes a miraculous transfiguration, her follower (the Narrator) has been touched and transformed by his or her interaction with the Saint.

### PUBLICATION HISTORY

"Chronicle of a Demise" was first published in 1948, in a collection of short stories called *One Arm.*

### CHARACTERS

**Cousin** He is the relative of a much-revered religious figure known as the Saint. He is angered when the Saint is not completely honest with him, and, as a result, he becomes the catalyst for her death.

**Saint** She is the leader of a religious sect called the Order. When she retreats to die on a rooftop of a New York City apartment building, her disciples find her and continue their worship of her. When she dies, she opens her heart, and tissue paper leaves float from inside her. She magically disintegrates in front of her followers.

## *Clothes for a Summer Hotel*

A play in two acts written in 1980.

### SYNOPSIS

The action takes place on the grounds of Highland Hospital, Asheville, North Carolina.

#### *Act 1, Scene 1*

The time is late afternoon in early autumn. F. Scott Fitzgerald sits waiting for his wife, Zelda Fitzgerald. As he waits he converses with Sister One and Sister Two. Zelda enters wearing a tattered ballet costume. Scott tries to be affectionate, but their exchange becomes tense and bitter. Zelda begins to hallucinate and Scott calls out for a doctor. Dr. Zeller appears and speaks to Scott in German and English. Scott loses his temper and an Intern leads him into the asylum. Zelda approaches the front of the stage and speaks directly to the audience. A Nurse enters, pushing Boo-Boo in a wheelchair. Zelda greets Boo-Boo and speaks directly to the audience again.

#### *Act 1, Scene 2*

A writer's office is set downstage of the asylum facade. Scott tries to work at his desk. Zelda admires him from a distance. She calls him "pretty," and a discussion of his sexuality ensues. Scott becomes cross with Zelda's interruption and she responds by acknowledging his perpetually interrupting her work as a writer. He insists she should be happy in her role as the wife of a successful writer. Zelda finds this role "too confining." She announces she will study ballet and threatens to take a lover. A pair of dancers perform a pas de deux. Zelda returns, dressed in beach attire, followed by her lover, Edouard. Zelda and Edouard make arrangements for a romantic tryst as the dancers conclude their duet.

#### *Act 2, Scene 1*

The downstage area is set to resemble a small hotel room. Zelda and Edouard lie naked in a double bed. They exchange tokens of remembrance, dress themselves, and leave the hotel room for an evening soirée. The upstage area has been dressed to resemble a gala lawn party at Gerald and Sara Murphy's villa. Lively music is heard as assorted party guests mill about and dance. Zelda and Edouard enter from opposite sides of the stage, greet one another, and go to the dance floor. Scott enters from the asylum. He is distressed by the recent news of Joseph Conrad's death. He attacks Gerald, Sara, and Mrs. Patrick Campbell for failing to grieve properly. Zelda and Edouard reappear, dancing the tango. Scott is outraged by their behavior and calls for the doctor. Dr. Zeller praises Zelda's gifts as a writer and proclaims her a better writer than Scott. Hadley and Ernest Hemingway arrive at the party. Scott and Hemingway discuss the "duality of gender" which they share. They also explore their reluctant, though mutual, attraction to each other and the homoerotic content of Hemingway's works. Hemingway abruptly goes in search of Hadley, while Scott is left alone calling for Zelda.

### *Act 2, Scene 2*

The setting and the time are the same as in act 1, scene 1. It is early evening and sunset approaches. Scott once again waits for Zelda outside the asylum. She reappears in her distressed tutu. She and Scott address the "monumental error" that was their life together. Their confrontation concludes with Zelda's resolve to release herself from Scott's restraint. She leaves him begging her to maintain their "covenant with the past."

## COMMENTARY

*Clothes for a Summer Hotel* is loosely based on Hemingway's epic novel *A Moveable Feast.* Some have characterized this retelling of Hemingway's life and experiences in Europe with the Fitzgeralds as his "crazy memories" of those times. In his play, Williams develops Hemingway's "crazy memories" and actualizes them in a dreamlike and episodic manner that is notably reminiscent of the erratic style of Zelda Fitzgerald's paintings. The drama is, therefore, an incredible amalgamation of the styles and techniques of its famous characters.

The scholarly assessment of *Clothes for a Summer Hotel* has been surprisingly limited. Much of the commentary is focused on an oversimplified notion that Williams was writing about his sister, ROSE WILLIAMS, in the guise of Zelda Fitzgerald. This superficial reading of the play illustrates a reluctance to engage Williams's artistic license as a dramatist.

Williams defines the piece as a ghost play underscored by dreamlike passages of time. *Clothes for a Summer Hotel,* as is SOMETHING CLOUDY, SOMETHING CLEAR, is a play about reliving past events. In both works time does not move chronologically: The past and the present coexist; the dead walk among the living. As such, the play unavoidably fails when judged by conventional standards of theatrical realism. Critics who have read beyond the simplistic interpretation and have not judged the play in terms of realistic value have found quality in its content. Alice Griffin finds the play's dialogue to be "among Williams's best" (Griffin, 12). Williams's treatment of character, particularly that of Zelda Fitzgerald, also makes the play extraordinary. Although Zelda can be linked thematically to other "Tennesseean Ophelias" (Simon, 82) such as Alma Winemiller in *THE ECCENTRICITIES OF A NIGHTINGALE*, she is more akin to Williams's frustrated artist-heroes, such as Valentine Xavier in *BATTLE OF ANGELS* and Tom Wingfield in *THE GLASS MENAGERIE*. Through the character of Zelda, Williams explores the deterioration of a stifled artist driven to madness by thwarted creative ambitions. The theme of the artist in torment is prominent in Williams's work.

## PRODUCTION HISTORY

*Clothes for a Summer Hotel* was Williams's last full-length play to be presented on Broadway during his lifetime. It premiered at the Cort Theatre in New York on March 26, 1980, and was directed by Jose Quintero. The production was a critical and commercial failure.

## PUBLICATION HISTORY

*Clothes for a Summer Hotel* was published by Dramatists Play Service in 1981.

## CHARACTERS

**Becky** Becky is a patient at the Highland Hospital asylum along with Zelda Fitzgerald. She is delusional and raves about having been a celebrity hair stylist in Hollywood, California.

**Black Male Singer** He is a professional singer from the Moulin Rouge who performs at the party given by Sara and Gerald Murphy. One of the Murphy's guests, F. Scott Fitzgerald, provokes the Singer by questioning his sexuality. The Singer responds by knocking Fitzgerald to the ground.

**Boo-Boo** Boo-Boo is a mental patient at the Highland Hospital asylum. She shares a room with

Zelda Fitzgerald. A nurse wheels Boo-Boo on stage to chat with Zelda outside the asylum. Boo-Boo, who is in a catatonic state, does not speak to Zelda.

**Campbell, Mrs. Patrick** Historical figure and character in the play *Clothes for a Summer Hotel.* Mrs. Patrick Campbell is a guest at a party given by Gerald and Sara Murphy. She is scandalized by the uncouth behavior of F. Scott Fitzgerald and Ernest Hemingway.

**Edouard** Edouard is Zelda Fitzgerald's French lover. He and Zelda have a romantic tryst at a hotel and attend a party given by Gerald and Sara Murphy together. At the Murphys' party, Zelda's husband, F. Scott Fitzgerald, watches the two lovers perform a tango. Edouard's role is doubled with that of the Intern.

**Fitzgerald, F(rancis) Scott** (1896–1940) Historical figure and character in the play *Clothes for a Summer Hotel.* As a novelist he was regarded as the chronicler of the Jazz Age. He was married to the writer, dancer, and painter Zelda Sayre Fitzgerald. His major works include *Tales of the Jazz Age* (1922), *The Great Gatsby* (1925), *Tender Is the Night* (1934), and *The Last Tycoon* (1941).

In *Clothes for a Summer Hotel* Fitzgerald relives moments of his turbulent marriage with Zelda, such as her infidelity with Edouard and her repeated accusations that he stifled her creative ambitions. Their marriage is depicted as strained and unfulfilling. Fitzgerald is more moved and engaged by the death of Joseph Conrad and his intimate conversation with Ernest Hemingway than he is by Zelda. Williams developed his portrait of Fitzgerald from a variety of sources, notably the collected letters of Ernest Hemingway and his epic novel *A Moveable Feast.* Williams was drawn to Fitzgerald, as he felt they shared "the experience of early fame" and "the humiliation that follows when you fall out of fashion" (Terkel, 146).

**Fitzgerald, Zelda Sayre** (1900–1948) Historical figure and character in the play *Clothes for a Summer Hotel.* She was the wife of the renowned novelist F. Scott Fitzgerald. Zelda was also a writer and penned short stories, articles, a novel—*Save Me the Waltz* (1932)—and a play, *Scandalabra* (1932). She was a dancer and painter as well. She died in an asylum fire in 1948.

As the central character in *Clothes for a Summer Hotel,* she is depicted as an artist living in the shadow of her husband's great fame. She feels stifled and trapped by her husband's success and the limited role that success has created for her. She is not content to be merely a successful writer's wife; she has talents of her own, which her husband forces her to suppress. This torment drives her into infidelity and ultimately into madness. During the course of the play Zelda relives poignant moments in her marriage with Scott, such as her affair with Edouard, a French aviator, and her attempts to develop her talents as a dancer. Doctor Zeller praises Zelda's writing and informs Scott that she is the better writer of the two, completely crushing Scott. Madness provides Zelda with the freedom to say and do whatever she pleases. Although she is the asylum patient, she appears far more sane and rational than Scott. Williams was drawn to the Fitzgeralds' story as he felt he had "experienced all their problems" (Terkel, 146) and in Zelda's madness he saw the reflection of his sister's repression and mental collapse. Because she was greatly overshadowed by her husband and his success, Zelda Fitzgerald was largely undervalued as a writer. Williams believed that her writing often possessed a "brilliancy that Scott was unequal to" (Hicks, 322).

**Hemingway, Ernest** (1899–1961) Historical figure and character in the play *Clothes for a Summer Hotel.* Williams considered the Pulitzer and Nobel Prize–winning author to be one of the greatest American literary stylists and admired his "poet's feeling for words." Hemingway's major works include *The Sun Also Rises* (1926), *A Farewell to Arms* (1929), *To Have and Have Not* (1937), *For Whom the Bell Tolls* (1940), *The Old Man and the Sea* (1952), and *A Moveable Feast* (1964).

Williams met Hemingway in Havana, Cuba, in 1960. Hemingway is said to have been "delighted" (Tynan, 138) to meet Williams. The two writers had a "friendly conversation" (Hicks, 321), and Hemingway gave Williams a letter of introduction that enabled him to meet the Cuban leader Fidel Castro. In his letter to Castro, Hemingway characterized Williams as "the great American dramatist." Ultimately, the two writers did not develop a profound rapport, which Williams believed was the result of Hemingway's timidity and not, as many scholars have claimed, a by-product of Hemingway's supposed homophobia.

In *Clothes for a Summer Hotel,* Hemingway and his wife, Hadley Hemingway, are guests at a lavish party being given by Sara and Gerald Murphy. At the party, Hemingway is boisterous and intoxicated. He engages in an intimate conversation with F. Scott Fitzgerald. Scott and Hemingway discuss the duality of gender that they both possess. They also explore their reluctant, though mutual, attraction to each other and the homoerotic content of Hemingway's works. At the end of their conversation, Hemingway abruptly goes in search of Hadley, leaving Scott alone and calling for Zelda. Williams drew extensively from Hemingway's writing in his re-creation of the Fitzgeralds.

**Hemingway, Hadley** Historical figure and character in the play *Clothes for a Summer Hotel.* She is the wife of Ernest Hemingway and attends Sara and Gerald Murphy's party with him. At the party, Hadley confronts Ernest with the fact that he is going to leave her. Her frankness with Ernest parallels Zelda's with Scott in her assessment of their marriage.

**Intern** He is a member of the staff at the Highland Hospital asylum. He comforts Zelda Fitzgerald when she becomes upset during her conversation with her husband, F. Scott Fitzgerald. His role is doubled with Edouard.

**Murphy, Gerald** He is Sara Murphy's husband and a close friend of F. Scott Fitzgerald and his wife, Zelda Fitzgerald. Gerald and Sara visit Zelda at the asylum at Highland Hospital before Scott arrives. Gerald breaks the news to Scott that Zelda's condition has deteriorated.

**Murphy, Sara** Gerald Murphy's wife. She is a close friend of Zelda Fitzgerald and her husband, F. Scott Fitzgerald. Sara and Gerald host an evening party that is attended by the Fitzgeralds, Ernest Hemingway, and Hadley Hemingway. At the party Sara admonishes Zelda for her affair with Edouard.

**Sister One** She is one of a pair of nuns who stand guard outside the gates of Highland Hospital. She and Sister Two converse with F. Scott Fitzgerald while he waits to see his wife, Zelda Fitzgerald.

**Sister Two** She is one of a pair of nuns who stand guard outside the gates of Highland Hospital. She and Sister One converse with F. Scott Fitzgerald while he waits to see his wife, Zelda Fitzgerald.

**Zeller, Dr.** He is the German doctor who cares for Zelda Fitzgerald at Highland Hospital asylum. Dr. Zeller upsets Zelda's husband, F. Scott Fitzgerald, by declaring that Zelda's writing is better than his.

### FURTHER READING

Dundy, Elaine. *Life Itself!* London: Virago Press, 2001.

Griffin, Alice. *Understanding Tennessee Williams.* Columbia: University of South Carolina Press, 1995.

Hicks, John. "Bard of Duncan Street: Scene Four," in *Conversations with Tennessee Williams,* edited by Albert Devlin. Jackson: University Press of Mississippi, 1986, pp. 318–324.

Simon, John. "Damsels Inducing Distress," *New York Times,* April 7, 1980, pp. 82, 84.

Terkel, Studs. *The Spectator: Talk about Movies and Plays with the People Who Make Them.* New York: New Press, 1999.

Tynan, Kenneth. "Papa and the Playwright." *Playboy* 11, no. 5 (May 1964): 138–141.

## "The Coming of Something to Widow Holly"

Short story written around 1943.

### SYNOPSIS

Isabel Holly is a widow, the owner of a New Orleans rooming house. Her only tenants are Regis de Winter, and two aging spinsters, Susie Patten and Florence Domingo. The tenants are constantly fighting. During these feuds, Widow Holly's furniture, dishes, and glasses are often used as ammunition. Bill collectors also frequent the rooming house in search of the old bachelor. All of this greatly distresses Widow Holly. A business card magically appears for Widow Holly advertising the services of A. Rose, Metaphysician. Widow Holly visits A. Rose, who reveals that Widow Holly has been transplanted to Earth from another planet. She does not believe him but considers that it might provide an explanation for her discontent.

Widow Holly catches Florence carrying a box of explosives into the boardinghouse. Widow Holly narrowly escapes the great explosion. The house is destroyed, but the occupants are unharmed. A. Rose returns in this dark moment. He has been transformed into Christopher D. Cosmos. He magically restores Widow Holly's boardinghouse. Christopher D. Cosmos instructs Widow Holly to burn everything from her past life and begin again. Widow Holly and Christopher D. Cosmos become lovers and consummate their relationship as the smell of roasting apples permeates the house.

## COMMENTARY

"The Coming of Something to Widow Holly" is an example of Williams's experimentation with magical realism and ability to weave elements of the fantastical with the mundane experiences of ordinary life. In this fable of good being rewarded, Widow Holly is freed from the drudgery of her boardinghouse and its badly behaved tenants. Her life is leveled when the boardinghouse explodes, but from the dust, there is a resurrection. Her home is restored to her, better than it was before—better because now it is empty, all hers and free of troublesome tenants. In addition, she is also released from loneliness, as her savior also becomes her lover.

Widow Holly, the benevolent and hard-done-by landlady, is a striking contrast to other landlady figures demonized in Williams's other works, such as "ANGEL IN THE ALCOVE," *THE LADY OF LARKSPUR LOTION*, and *VIEUX CARRÉ*. This comic fantasy, a Cinderella story of sorts, is the basis for the play *THE REMARKABLE ROOMING-HOUSE OF MME. LE MONDE*.

## PUBLICATION HISTORY

"The Coming of Something to Widow Holly" was published in *ND Fourteen—New Directions in Prose & Poetry* and included in the short story collection *Hard Candy* in 1954.

## CHARACTERS

**Cosmos, Christopher** Initially, Cosmos appears as A. Rose, an angel who guides Isabel Holly to the explanation of her existence. Christopher D. Cosmos is A. Rose transformed into a supernatural savior who restores Widow Holly's house.

**DeWinter, Regis** He is a cantankerous old man who fights with Susie Patten and Florence Domingo in the boardinghouse of Isabel Holly.

**Domingo, Florence** She is an ill-tempered woman who fights with the other tenants in Isabel Holly's boardinghouse. Miss Domingo blows up Widow Holly's house with a box of explosives. She miraculously survives and leaves to find somewhere else to live.

**Holly, Isabel** She is an elderly widow who owns a boardinghouse in New Orleans. She is tormented by her bickering tenants who wreak havoc in her life daily. One tenant, Florence Domingo, blows up the boardinghouse with explosives. The house is completely destroyed, but its occupants survive unscathed. Christopher D. Cosmos magically restores Widow Holly's house and becomes her lover.

**Patten, Susie** She is a mean-spirited tenant who enjoys the numerous arguments which regularly occur in Isabel Holly's boardinghouse.

# "Completed"

Short story written in 1973.

## SYNOPSIS

Rosemary McCool is a pathologically shy young woman in her late teens, who has never experienced menstruation. Her mother, Miss Sally McCool, orchestrates a societal debut for Rosemary during which her daughter is completely humiliated. Rosemary takes refuge in the home of her reclusive relative, Aunt Ella, who is a "proud virgin" and a morphine addict. In the company of her aunt, Rosemary feels normal and comfortable. When she returns to her mother's house, she menstruates for the first time. She decides to move in with her Aunt Ella and, as her aunt has, resign from the world. Rosemary is secure with Aunt Ella, but she also realizes that she has fallen into a trap from which she will never escape.

## COMMENTARY

"Completed" is the final installment of Williams's "trilogy-tribute" (Spoto, 162) of short stories to his sister, ROSE ISABEL WILLIAMS. This story, along with "PORTRAIT OF A GIRL IN GLASS" and "THE RESEMBLANCE BETWEEN A VIOLIN CASE AND A COFFIN," is centered on a fragile young woman reminiscent of his sister, and each of these stories capture aspects of the events in Rose's pitiable life. Rosemary McCool's failed and humiliating societal debut mirrors Rose Williams's unfortunate experience in 1927. In his *Memoirs,* Williams recalled a formal "coming out" or debut party that had been arranged for Rose in Knoxville, Tennessee, by her father's sisters, one of whom was named Aunt Ella, as is the other principal character in "Completed." As Rosemary's mother had in the short story, Rose's aunts had very unrealistic expectations of Rose's success as a debutante and eligible young woman. Williams, who did not attend the festivities, recalled that Rose's informal presentation to society was "not exactly a howling success" (*Memoirs,* 117) and was, as were so many events in Rose's life, a traumatic fiasco.

When she returned to Saint Louis, Williams noticed that Rose had been severely shaken by the experience. It seemed to Williams that "a shadow" had fallen over his sister, and that she had had the painful realization that by the standards of her aunts and fashionable society she was "not charming" (*Memoirs,* 117). In "Completed" Williams retells Rose's story but provides his main character with a strong, comforting role model and a defiant female ally his sister never had.

## PUBLICATION HISTORY

"Completed" was published in the short story collection *EIGHT MORTAL LADIES POSSESSED* in 1974.

## CHARACTERS

**Aunt Ella** Aunt Ella is Rosemary McCool's maiden aunt, who lives as a recluse. She is a morphine addict who is perfectly content to let life pass her by. She serves as an ally and role model for her pathologically shy niece.

**McCool, Rosemary** Rosemary is a timid, socially inept 20-year-old woman. She is traumatized by her mother's efforts to have her married. Her societal debut is a humiliating disaster. She finds solace and refuge in the home of Aunt Ella.

**McCool, Sally** Miss Sally is the overbearing mother of Rosemary McCool. Her daughter is a pathologically shy young woman. Sally forces her to have a humiliating societal debut and drives her to refuge in the home of her morphine-addicted relative, Aunt Ella.

## FURTHER READING

Spoto, Donald. *The Kindness of Strangers: The Life of Tennessee Williams.* Boston: Little, Brown, 1985.

Williams, Tennessee. *Memoirs.* Garden City, N.Y.: Doubleday, 1975.

# *Confessional*

A one-act play written in 1967.

## SYNOPSIS

The play is set in a seaside bar in Southern California. The inside of the bar is dark and dingy. As the play is centered on the intimate confessions of the bar's patrons, Williams underscores this idea by utilizing an area of the stage and special lighting to evoke the sense that each character is entering a confessional and speaking privately to the audience.

***Scene 1***

The time is late evening. Leona, Violet, and Bill are in the middle of a heated argument. Leona caught Violet fondling Bill. Monk and Steve try to calm Leona. The Young Man and Bobby enter the bar, and Monk refuses to serve them because they appear to be a gay couple. Bill observes the two newcomers, goes to the confessional area of the stage, and expresses his hatred of gay men. Steve takes his place in the confessional area. He offers details of his relationship with Violet, referring to her as the scraps that life has thrown him. Leona reminisces about her brother, Haley, who died of anemia at a young age.

Doc goes into the confessional before leaving the bar to deliver a baby at a trailer park. Violet walks to the confessional area and shares her thoughts about her life. Leona converses with the Young Man and Bobby. The Young Man enters the confessional and discusses his thoughts on being a gay man. The Young Man leaves the bar and Bobby begins his confession. He is traveling by bicycle from Iowa to Mexico in search of freedom and tolerance. He leaves the confessional and exits the bar. Leona rushes after him. Monk enters the confessional area and explains his dilemmas as a bar owner. Leona observes Violet sitting between Bill and Steve. Violet is blissfully engaged in lewd activities with both Bill and Steve simultaneously.

*Scene 2*

One hour later in the same location as scene 1. Leona chastises Bill and announces that she is leaving town. Doc returns to the bar. Leona interrogates him until he admits that he no longer has a license to practice medicine. Violet, Steve, and Bill start to leave together. Leona chases Violet out of the bar. Violet reenters the bar with a bloody nose. Monk offers Doc a nightcap. A Police Officer enters the bar and has a drink. Leona, Monk, and Violet share a nightcap. Violet fondles Monk under the table. Leona speaks to the audience and leaves $20 for Monk. Monk sends Violet upstairs to shower. He sits holding one of Violet's tattered slippers and contemplates its meaning: It will be worn until there is nothing left.

## COMMENTARY

In *Confessional,* Williams provides a harsh look at the human condition and the yearning for human connection. Openly displaying dialogue and acts concerning sex and sexuality, the play explores loneliness, longing, and the need for love.

The primary theme of *Confessional* is the idea of sex and sexuality as a catalyst and remedy for social isolation. Each character in Monk's bar is there to remember, forget, or find someone or something. With the help of alcohol, sex, or flight, they temporarily ease their pain and relieve their loneliness. This one-act play, with its mixture of rough honesty and lyricism, is the foundation for the full-length play *SMALL CRAFT WARNINGS.*

## PRODUCTION HISTORY

William Hunt directed the premiere of *Confessional* at the Maine Theatre Arts Festival in Bar Harbor, Maine, in July 1971.

## PUBLICATION HISTORY

*Confessional* was published in the one-act play anthology *DRAGON COUNTRY* in 1969.

## CHARACTERS

**Bill** Bill is a regular customer at the cheap seaside bar owned by Monk. He is a ruggedly handsome male prostitute in his 20s who lives with Leona in her trailer. Leona catches Violet pleasuring Bill in the bar. Bill offers no excuse and continues to dally with Violet. Leona responds by evicting him from her trailer.

**Bobby** Bobby is a young gay man from Iowa who is cycling to Mexico. He is picked up by the Young Man and accompanies him to the beachside bar owned by Monk. The Young Man loses interest in Bobby when he discovers he is gay, because he prefers to have intimate relationships with heterosexual men. The Young Man leaves Bobby at Monk's Bar, and Leona offers Bobby a place to stay.

**Doc** Doc is a regular patron at the cheap seaside bar owned by Monk. He lost his medical license after being caught performing a procedure under the influence of alcohol. Although he no longer has a license, Doc continues to practice illegally. Leona tries to stop Doc from delivering a baby at her trailer park, but her efforts are in vain. Doc delivers the baby, but there are numerous complications. The baby is stillborn and the mother hemorrhages to death. He pays the woman's husband $50 to forget his face and name. Hoping to avoid imprisonment, Doc plans to leave town as soon as he can.

**Leona** Leona is a regular patron at cheap seaside bar owned by Monk. She is a lonely, gregarious beautician, who lives in a trailer. Lena is a kindhearted person who is often used by her friends, Bill and Violet. Leona befriends Bobby and the Young Man, two gay men who are not regulars at Monk's Place. She shares her trailer with Bill; after she evicts him because of his lewd behavior with Violet, she offers his space in her trailer to Bobby.

**Monk** Monk is the owner and bartender of a cheap beachside bar in Southern California. He sincerely cares about his regular patrons and thinks of them as his family.

**Police Officer** The Police Officer is called to Monk's bar to break up a fight. Monk offers him a drink, which he accepts although he is on duty.

**Steve** Steve is a middle-aged short-order cook who frequents the cheap seaside bar owned by Monk. He is not ambitious and is content to settle for the scraps in life. He has an affair with Violet, but he does not love her.

**Violet** Violet is a mentally unstable nymphomaniac who frequents Monk's bar. Leona tries to take care of Violet and be a good friend to her, whereas the other bar regulars, Bill, Steve, and Monk, use her sexually.

**Young Man** The Young Man is a wealthy, attractive screenwriter. He picks up Bobby on the highway and takes him to Monk's bar for a drink, in the hope of leaving him there.

# *Creve Coeur*

The initial title of the play *A LOVELY SUNDAY FOR CREVE COEUR* when it premiered at the Spoleto Festival in Charleston, South Carolina, in June 1978. The literal translation of the title is "heartbreak."

# "The Dark Room"

Short story written around 1940.

## SYNOPSIS

Miss Morgan, a social worker, pays a visit to the home of Mrs. Lucca. For nearly six months, her daughter, Tina Lucca, has locked herself in her bedroom, where she lies naked and crying in the dark. Tina has done this because her boyfriend, Sol, has married another woman. Mrs. Lucca explains that Tina only leaves her room to use the bathroom and only eats when Sol takes her food. The social worker is shocked when she realizes Mrs. Lucca allows the former lovers to be alone together. Miss Morgan insists that Tina be removed from the home. Mrs. Lucca is relieved because she can no longer tolerate her daughter's behavior.

## COMMENTARY

In his writing, Williams often utilized a two- (and sometimes three-) tiered method, with a direct line being drawn from fiction into drama. In other words, his short stories were often the first-stage drafts that would form the basis or outline for subsequent dramatization of the story as either a one-act play, full-length play, or both. (In many instances the one-act play functioned as a second-stage draft or foundation for an expanded, full-length dramatic treatment of the same material.) "The Dark Room" is a prime example of Williams's fiction-to-drama process as the text of this short story is nearly completely composed in dialogue. This work later became the one-act play *THE DARK ROOM.*

## PUBLICATION HISTORY

"The Dark Room" was first published in the anthology *Collected Stories* in 1985.

## CHARACTERS

**Lucca, Mrs.** Mrs. Lucca is a poor Italian immigrant trying to care for her children with few resources. She is the mother of Tina, a heartbroken young girl.

**Morgan, Miss** She is a social worker who visits the home of the Lucca family. She has been sent to investigate the condition of Tina Lucca, a heartbroken young woman who has resigned herself to living in a darkened room.

# *The Dark Room*

A one-act play written around 1939.

## SYNOPSIS

The play is set in a small, untidy inner-city tenement apartment owned by the Pocciottis, a family of poor Italian immigrants. Miss Morgan interrogates Mrs. Pocciotti about her husband and children. Miss Morgan probes more deeply into the whereabouts of Mrs. Pocciotti's older children and quizzes her about her daughter, Tina Pocciotti. It is revealed that Mrs. Pocciotti's teenage daughter has locked herself away and lies naked and pregnant in her darkened bedroom, awaiting nightly visits from her estranged lover. Miss Morgan is shocked and decides that the Pocciotti children should become wards of the state.

## COMMENTARY

In 1939, Williams submitted *The Dark Room* along with MOONY'S *KID DON'T CRY* and *THE CASE OF THE CRUSHED PETUNIAS* to a play competition sponsored by THE GROUP THEATRE. Williams's one-act collection won a $100 prize and drew the attention of the talent agent AUDREY WOOD. *The Dark Room* was one of the three plays that essentially launched Williams's career.

*The Dark Room* and the other plays in *AMERICAN BLUES* underscore the plight of the American working class and depict isolated individuals whose invisible life has slipped through the cracks. Felicia Hardison Londré notes that *The Dark Room* is the least successful piece of dramatic writing in *American Blues.* Compared to its companion pieces, its characters are "flat," and the play's ending "falls short of its intended shock effect" (Londré, 40).

## PRODUCTION HISTORY

*The Dark Room* was first produced in London in 1966.

## PUBLICATION HISTORY

*The Dark Room* was first published in 1948 in a one-act collection, *American Blues.*

## CHARACTERS

**Morgan, Miss** Miss Morgan is a fussy, pretentious unmarried woman working for a social service agency. She has been sent by her agency to visit the home of the poverty-stricken Pocciotti family, who are Italian immigrants. Miss Morgan's sympathetic nature during her interview with Mrs. Pocciotti can be interpreted as shallowness or arrogance. She has little patience for Mrs. Pocciotti, whose English is very limited.

**Pocciotti, Mrs.** Mrs. Pocciotti is a heavy-set Italian immigrant mother who lives in poverty with her three children. Her husband is insane, and her grown children are scattered about the country. Two of her children, Lucio and Tina, are still in her care.

**Pocciotti, Tina** Tina is Mrs. Pocciotti's only daughter. Although the plot of the play centers on Tina, she is never actually seen. Her mother, Mrs. Pocciotti, tells Miss Morgan, a social worker, the story of Tina's unrequited love.

## FURTHER READING

Londré, Felicia Hardison. *Tennessee Williams.* New York: F. Ungar, 1979.

# "Das Wasser ist kalt"

Short story written between the years of 1973 and 1979.

## SYNOPSIS

Barbara is a professor at a junior college in Georgia, whose colleagues gave her the gift of a trip to Italy. She is enjoying her adventures, trying not to think about her bad back pain. She recalls her bon voyage party, the professors who were elated to give her the trip. Barbara is lonely, but she is in paradise, so she tries to make the best of it. She meets a German man named Klaus while swimming in the cold ocean. They agree that the water is shockingly cold. He fondles her body in the water, placing his hand on her vagina. They swim to a remote cove when an angry female voice shouts for her husband. The German man returns the call, apologizes to Barbara, and swims to his wife. Several days pass, and Barbara realizes that her colleagues have purchased a one-way ticket for her: She cannot go home.

### COMMENTARY

Barbara, the protagonist of "Das Wasser ist kalt," is an example of a persistent figure in Williams's works: the troubled teacher. As do Blanche Dubois (*A Streetcar Named Desire*), Gretchen ("The Interval"), Dorothea (*A Lovely Sunday for Creve Coeur*), Jenny Starling (*All Gaul Is Divided*), the French Club Instructor (*Will Mr. Merriwether Return from Memphis?*) and Alma Winemiller (*The Eccentricities of a Nightingale*), Barbara pursues and engages in a clandestine relationship with an opportunistic and unattainable lover and ultimately suffers abandonment and isolation. Gretchen, who, as does Barbara, finds romance while on a shore vacation, is the only character in this group who develops and sustains a protracted relationship with her love interest, Jimmie. However, their relationship, too, is ultimately ill-fated. Jimmie is gay, and eventually leaves Gretchen in Iowa to pursue fame, fortune, and his boyfriend Bobby in New York City.

The tragedy and disarray of these teachers' troubled lives leads one to question, as Jane does (an artist, though not a teacher) in *Vieux Carré*, how an educated person could land themselves in such dire circumstances. The problem for each of these characters hinges on a conflict central to Williams's writings, that of the soul versus the flesh, or the spiritual versus the worldly. For all of their education and wealth of knowledge, these scholars are naive in their understanding of the world and human nature. Their tragic mistake, or hamartia, is a lack of judgment and indiscretion. Barbara and her fellow teachers are far too trusting of the kindness of strangers.

Barbara vulnerably opens herself to Klaus, and her encounter with him (which is reminiscent of the unfulfilling experience Hannah Jelkes recalls in *The Night of the Iguana*) is tentative, adolescent, awkward, and incomplete. She is left alone, disappointed, and unsatisfied. Similarly, she blindly accepted the seeming generosity of her colleagues and their gift of an Italian holiday, only to find that they had successfully maneuvered her halfway around the world. She has been abandoned, with no way to return home. The "cold water" in which Barbara finds herself serves as a symbol of the chillingly rude awakening she has about her life, her society, and human nature.

### PUBLICATION HISTORY

"Das Wasser ist kalt" was published in the journal *Antaeus* in 1982, and was included in the collection *Collected Stories*.

### CHARACTERS

**Barbara** She is a middle-aged professor at a community college in Georgia. Barbara is thrilled when her colleagues present her with a free vacation to Italy, but when she has had enough of the solitude of traveling alone, she discovers that the faculty purchased a one-way ticket for her. She realizes she is stranded and unwanted.

**Klaus** Klaus is a German tourist on vacation in Italy. At the beach, he swims with Barbara and fondles her body underwater. Barbara enjoys his attention, and they try to become more intimate but are interrupted by Klaus's wife.

## *The Demolition Downtown*

One-act play written before 1971.

### SYNOPSIS

The play is set in the homes of two upper-class families living in the suburbs of a capital city.

Mr. Kane sits in his living room nervously waiting for his wife, Mrs. Kane, to return. When she enters, he scolds her for departing unannounced and for driving the car and wasting gasoline. He suggests they run from their city, which has been overtaken by guerrilla forces. A dynamite blast rattles the pictures on the walls as they debate their next move. Mrs. Kane replies that there is nowhere to go, no way to escape the demolition, as the highways are barricaded. During this argument, Mrs. Kane notices that her husband's pants are unzipped, and she suddenly becomes aroused. She suggests they have sex on the couch, but Mr. Kane counters that he is too tense.

In the house next door, Mr. Lane notices that his wife has developed a twitch at the side of her mouth. She considers it a natural reaction to the dynamite blasts and the guerrilla takeover. She decides to go outside and rake leaves to pass the time; however, Mr. Lane objects, stating that the house should be made to look abandoned. When Mrs. Lane takes a rake from the closet, Mr. Lane snatches it from her.

Their children, Rosemary and Gladys, enter. Dirty and disheveled, they inform their parents that their boarding school was seized by guerrilla forces, and the nuns were carted away. Rosemary and Gladys escaped, but not before they were molested by a man with a black beard. Mrs. Lane glazes over their story and orders them to take a bath and go to bed.

Mr. Lane and Mrs. Lane, enter. The two couples decide to escape to the mountains. Mr. Lane and Mr. Kane decide that this is a feasible plan, and they leave to gather equipment. The women discuss a glitch in the escape plan: They must take a major highway to get to the lesser-known dirt road that leads to the mountains. Mrs. Lane shows her concern for Mrs. Kane's bronchial infection, a strange new virus that began during the guerrilla takeover.

Rosemary and Gladys are heard singing the guerrilla marching song, a variation of "The Battle Hymn of the Republic." Mrs. Lane shouts for them to stop singing, but she too becomes taken by the tune. Mrs. Kane tells Mrs. Lane that she has a plan to go to the headquarters of the general of the guerrilla army wearing only a long gray coat to offer herself to the young general. Mrs. Lane decides to join her friend, and she takes off her clothes and puts on a plain overcoat. As they exit, a large dynamite blast rattles the pictures off the walls. Mr. Lane and Mr. Kane run into the house. They hear their wives singing the marching song as they leave the neighborhood. Mr. Lane dusts the plaster off Mr. Kane's jacket, and Mr. Kane reciprocates.

## COMMENTARY

With nightmarish visions of guerrilla warfare in post–cold war America, Williams creates drama of revolution and chaos in *The Demolition Downtown.* The upper-middle-class lives of the carbon-copy citizens of the suburban dwellings are drastically reduced to survival of the fittest. While Mr. and Mrs. Lane are busying themselves with the attempt to feel normal and simultaneously planning an escape in their Jaguar or Cadillac, their daughters have been molested and brainwashed by the revolutionaries. Absurdly, Mr. Lane still addresses the car by its name brand, a sign that he is grasping for an aristocratic existence while his home is literally crumbling around him as a result of dynamite blasts. Even though Mr. Lane and Mr. Kane decide to protect themselves and their families by attempting to escape, they have already been struck by the dissidents.

The violence that obstructs their lives and homes and the propaganda of the new regime infiltrate the suburban setting through the youth culture of Rosemary and Gladys. By merely singing the marching song, Mrs. Lane becomes infected with the revolution. She and her comrade and doppelgänger, Mrs. Kane, decide to join forces with the guerrillas downtown. In their descent into the capital, the women cast off their social class and actively engage the movement. Felicia Londré states, "Late in his career, however, [Williams] began to write plays that dealt directly with problems like the threat of large-scale violence" (31). *The Demolition Downtown* is a prime example of aspects of Williams's social conscience dramaturgy and his politically astute sense of his global surroundings.

## PUBLICATION

*The Demolition Downtown* was published in *Esquire* magazine in 1971.

## CHARACTERS

**Kane, Gladys** She is the daughter of Mr. Kane and Mrs. Kane. Gladys, along with her sister, Rosemary, escape their boarding school as it is being seized by the guerrilla forces who have taken over the city. Gladys and Rosemary make their way home, where they are treated with indifference, even after they inform their parents that they have been molested.

**Kane, Mr.** Mr. Kane teams up with his neighbor, Mr. Lane, to flee their homes and city, which has been taken over by a guerrilla army. While the men gather camping equipment to live in the mountains, their wives are overcome by guerrilla propaganda, and they leave to offer themselves to the guerrilla general and his brother, the Panther.

**Kane, Mrs.** She is the neighbor of Mrs. Lane. When their city is conquered by a guerrilla army, the two women decide to offer themselves to the general and his brother, the Panther. Singing the marching song of the guerrilla army, they leave their families and husbands, Mr. Lane and Mr. Kane, who are busy making preparations for escape.

**Kane, Rosemary** She is the daughter of Mr. Kane and Mrs. Kane. Rosemary, along with her sister, Gladys, escaped their boarding school which was seized by a guerrilla army. The girls arrive at their home and are coolly greeted, despite their announcements that several of the nuns at their school were killed and that they were molested.

**Lane, Mr.** He is an upper-middle-class man who is forced to consider basic survival when the city in which he resides is taken over by a guerrilla army from the nearby mountains. Mr. Lane nervously conserves resources while debating and arguing with his wife, Mrs. Lane. When he teams up with his neighbor, Mr. Kane, and decides to escape the city under siege, he is left by his wife, who chooses to offer herself to the general of the army.

**Lane, Mrs.** She is an upper-middle-class woman whose life is turned upside down when the city in which she resides is seized by a guerrilla army from the nearby mountains. Mrs. Lane frantically tries to maintain order in her home while dynamite blasts shower plaster from her ceilings and knock her pictures off the walls. Mrs. Lane teams up with a neighbor, Mrs. Kane, and they decide to offer themselves to the general of the guerrilla army.

### FURTHER READING

Londré, Felicia. *Tennessee Williams: Life, Work, and Criticism.* Fredericton, Canada: York Press, 1989.

# "Desire and the Black Masseur"

Short story written between 1942 and 1946.

### SYNOPSIS

Anthony Burns is a small, pale, and timid warehouse worker. A coworker suggests Burns have a therapeutic massage to relieve a chronic backache. Burns becomes sexually aroused at the prospect of having a massage and privately hopes to relieve more than his back strain. One Saturday afternoon in November, Burns goes to a Turkish bath and massage parlor. He discovers that all of the masseurs are African American, and their bodies amid the billowy white backdrops appear immense, fierce, and godlike.

Burns's masseur commands that he remove his clothes, and he watches Burns as he fumbles out of them. The masseur instructs Burns to lie on the table and Burns eagerly obeys. The Black Masseur then pours alcohol all over Burns's body. The stinging sensation spreads over Burns, leaving him gasping as he tries to cover his groin. The masseur begins the massage by hitting Burns hard in the stomach. After this initial violence, Burns feels pleasure in the masseur's fists and becomes sexually aroused. The masseur is pleased at this response and continues the massage by flipping Burns over onto his belly. He pummels Burns's shoulders and buttocks, each strike more forceful than the last.

Burns frequents the Turkish bath and remains loyal to his particular masseur, who enjoys dominating the small white body that lies prostrate before him. As the winter progresses, the massages become more brutal, and on several occasions Burns is severely wounded. In one instance, he limps into work with broken ribs. During his next visit to the baths, the Black Masseur fractures his leg, and Burns cries out in anguish. His howl echoes through the building and draws the attention of the manager. When the manager discovers the numerous bruises on Burns's small, willing white frame, he promptly dismisses both of them. The Black Masseur lifts Burns from the massage table and carries him to his lodgings. Their relationship continues for several months into the spring.

There is a church in the next building, across from the Black Masseur's room. It is now the Lenten season, and a fiery sermon erupts out of the church and oozes into their room. The minister in the church bellows the Crucifixion story in gruesome and agonizing detail to admonish his congregation to repent. In the masseur's room, atonement is physically at hand as the Black Masseur administers his most violent massage yet. The minister reaches a fevered pitch and shouts, "Suffer, suffer, suffer!" (210), and his congregation becomes impassioned and delirious. They erupt in a frenzy and stream out of the church and into the streets, tearing their clothes in anguish and grief for Christ's death. Burns and the Black Masseur are similarly inflamed and consumed, to the point that Burns is nearly dead. In a whisper, he reminds the Black Masseur what he must do to complete the act. The Black Masseur gathers Burns's broken body and places him on a table and begins to feast on his flesh. This act of communion lasts 24 hours, until Burns's bones have been picked clean. The Black Masseur places Burns's bones in a bag, carries them to the pier, and drops them into the lake. He acquires a new position at another bathhouse and waits for his next Anthony Burns to appear.

## COMMENTARY

This Poe-like tale encapsulates Williams's view that the essence of life is "grotesque and gothic" (Brown, 264). In this and similar narratives, Williams uses an exaggerated form to capture the "true essence of life" and the "outrageousness of reality" (ibid.). Williams believed that truth was often more accessible when a writer was willing to "ignore realism" (ibid.).

This story also literally and metaphorically features the prominent Williams theme of otherness. The story's principal characters and their relationship are manifestations of otherness and opposition: white/black, powerlessness/powerfulness, rich/poor, master/servant, weak/strong, small/large, sacred/profane, and pain/pleasure. However, for Williams, opposing forces are always two sides of the same coin. As he often reminds his audience, desire and death are two streetcars on the same tramline. Therefore, when opposites meet in "Desire and the Black Masseur" they not only attract, but willfully collide, and their conflict produces a blissful, sacramental result.

Many critics share Ren Draya's view that this intriguing and engaging tale is not only a masterfully written work, but one of Williams's most "carefully crafted," a story that overwhelmingly "succeeds as serious, startling fiction" (Draya, 650).

## PUBLICATION HISTORY

In his *Memoirs,* Williams recalled that PAUL BOWLES wrote a short story similar to "Desire and the Black Masseur" called "The Delicate Prey." When Bowles asked Williams to read the story, Williams was surprisingly shocked by its content. Williams quickly advised Bowles not to publish it in America; likewise, Williams did not publish "Desire and the Black Masseur" openly. It was published in the short story collection *One Arm* (1948), which was issued only in private editions and was not made available to bookstores for the general public. Although it contains some of his most imaginative writing, Williams feared that its content could potentially have been damaging to his career. Now generally available, the story has received recognition as a major achievement in Williams's fiction canon.

"Desire and the Black Masseur" was published in *New Directions in Prose and Poetry 10: An Annual Exhibition Gallery of New and Divergent Trends in Literature* (1948) and in Williams's *Collected Stories* in 1985.

## PRODUCTION HISTORY

"Desire and the Black Masseur" was adapted for the screen by the French film director Claire Devers. Her adaptation *Noir et blanc* (Black and White) won the Camera d'Or prize at the Cannes Film Festival in 1988.

### CHARACTERS

**Black Masseur** He is the masseur who falls in love with Anthony Burns. The Masseur is a dark, statuesque, godlike man, in the billowing white backdrop of the Turkish baths. He administers brutal sadomasochistic massages to Burns, enjoying the domination of a white body on his table. He delights in the reversal of a master-slave relationship. The Masseur is completely infatuated by Burns and daydreams about him when the two are apart. The Masseur is happy to consume Burns, just as Burns savors being consumed.

**Burns, Anthony** Anthony Burns is a small, timid, and birdlike man, who is childlike in his appearance and actions. He finds solace from the world in his relationship with a Black Masseur who works at a local Turkish bath. Burns longingly anticipates the beatings he receives during his massages from his beautiful, large, and dark masseur. Burns harbors guilty feelings about his passions—but believes his sins are atoned for in the beatings he receives. He longs for the simultaneous pleasure and pain. Burns awakens to life through this passion; however, the massages consume him and ultimately lead to his death.

### FURTHER READING

Brown, Cecil. "Interview with Tennessee Williams," in *Conversations with Tennessee Williams,* edited by Albert Devlin. Jackson: University Press of Mississippi, 1986, pp. 251–283.

Draya, Ren. "The Fiction of Tennessee Williams," in *Tennessee Williams: A Tribute,* edited by Jac Tharpe. Jackson: University Press of Mississippi, 1977, pp. 647–662.

## *Dragon Country*

Collection of one-act plays published in 1970 by New Directions. The collection contains the following works: IN A BAR IN A TOKYO HOTEL; I RISE IN FLAME, CRIED THE PHOENIX; THE MUTILATED; I CAN'T IMAGINE TOMORROW; CONFESSIONAL; THE FROSTED GLASS COFFIN; THE GNÄDIGES FRÄULEIN; and A PERFECT ANALYSIS GIVEN BY A PARROT.

Williams defines "dragon country" as "the country of pain, an uninhabitable country which is inhabited" (Williams, *Tomorrow,* 138). The plays in this collection present a view of this brutal landscape. Each of these works offers an examination of fractured and broken individuals seeking solace from isolation and personal struggle.

### FURTHER READING

Williams, Tennessee. "Landscape with Figures: Two Mississippi Plays," in *American Scenes,* edited by William Kozlenko. New York: John Day, 1941.

## *The Eccentricities of a Nightingale*

A play in three acts written in 1951.

### SYNOPSIS

***Act 1, Scene 1***

The setting is a public square in Glorious Hill, Mississippi, during the summer of 1916. An elevated fountain dominates the stage with a stone angel called Eternity. It is evening on the Fourth of July. Alma Winemiller can be heard singing offstage. Her parents, the Reverend and Mrs. Winemiller, sit near the fountain enjoying fireworks. John Buchanan also sits near the fountain. Alma joins her parents and is flustered by John's presence. John's mother, Mrs. Buchanan, tries to hurry John away from Alma. Alma's parents depart, leaving Alma alone. John throws a lighted firecracker under Alma's bench. He sits beside her and the two discuss John's vocation as a doctor and Alma's nervous palpitations. Mrs. Buchanan returns to whisk John from Alma's side.

***Act 1, Scene 2***

The setting is the interior of the Winemillers' home, the living room of the rectory. It is Christmas Eve. The Winemillers are gathered in the living room. Alma spies on the Buchanans from the living room window and catches sight of Mrs. Buchanan in a

Santa Claus costume out delivering gifts with John. Reverend Winemiller informs Alma that there is talk of her eccentric behavior in town. He denounces her literary circle as a "collection of misfits" (33). Alma has a panic attack and rushes out of the parlor.

### Act 1, Scene 3

A few minutes later in the rectory parlor, Mrs. Buchanan and John call on the Winemillers. Alma is overwrought with nerves in the presence of John's mother. Mrs. Buchanan and Alma revel in John's accomplishments. Mrs. Winemiller joins the gathering and embarrasses Alma by sharing the sordid tale of her sister, Albertine, and her lover, Mr. Schwarzkopf, and their "Musée Mecaniqué." John persuades Alma to sing, and the two are momentarily left alone to sit by the fire. Alma invites John to attend her upcoming literary circle meeting. Mrs. Winemiller catches Alma and John holding hands.

### Act 2, Scene 1

The scene is the interior of the Buchanan home, John's bedroom. John and his mother discuss Alma. John finds beauty in her; his mother only sees peculiarity. Mrs. Buchanan revels in her visions of John's future, with an attractive, well-bred, and stable wife and many lovely, healthy children. Alma watches John from her bedroom window. She waits for his bedroom light finally to go out so that she may go to sleep.

### Act 2, Scene 2

The scene is the Winemillers' parlor on the following Monday evening. The members of the literary circle gather for their weekly meeting. The group discusses the manifesto that Vernon has written, which states the group's mission, to make Glorious Hill the "Athens of the South." Alma reads the minutes of the club's last meeting. John Buchanan arrives late and is introduced to the group. Rosemary attempts to read her paper on the poet William Blake but is stopped short by Mrs. Bassett. Alma recites Blake's poem "Love's Secret." John's mother arrives to collect John and rudely escorts him out of the meeting. Rosemary begins her paper once again as Mrs. Winemiller bursts into the room begging Alma to help her get to the Musée Mecaniqué in New Orleans. Alma runs out of the parlor in tears.

### Act 2, Scene 3

The scene is the interior of Dr. Buchanan's office. The time is late evening. Alma visits the Buchanan home to see John's father. As his father has gone to bed, John offers to assist Alma. He gives her a shot of brandy. He opens the shutters and shares his study of astronomy with Alma. He unbuttons her blouse and checks her heart with a stethoscope. He tells her that inside her chest he hears a little voice saying, "Miss Alma is lonesome." Alma vents her fury and discontent on John. She and John make arrangements for a date the next evening. Mrs. Buchanan enters the office and Alma dashes away happily.

### Act 2, Scene 4

The scene is the interior of the rectory, the following evening. It is New Year's Eve. Roger and Alma sit together viewing slides of Roger's mother's trip to Asia. Alma waits impatiently for John to arrive. Roger questions Alma's devotion to John Buchanan and surmises that she is "barking up the wrong tree." He offers Alma permanent companionship. Alma makes it clear that she wants more and tells Roger the story of her aunt, Albertine, and the man she loved, Mr. Schwarzkopf. John finally arrives, 25 minutes late for their date.

### Act 3, Scene 1

The scene is the park with the stone angel fountain, later that same evening. Alma declares her love for John and her desire to be making love with him as the clocks strike midnight. John consents and goes to find a taxi.

### Act 3, Scene 2

The scene is the interior of a small hotel room with a bed and a fireplace, a few moments after the previous scene. John tries to light the fire but the logs and the paper are damp. John compares the failing fire with their romantic endeavor: There are no sparks and no heat. The New Year arrives and as the bells chime, the couple slowly develops passion for each other as the fire miraculously begins to blaze.

### Epilogue

The scene is the public square with the stone angel fountain. It is the Fourth of July of an indefinite time. Alma sits on a park bench listening to another soprano singing with the town band. She engages a young Traveling Salesman in conversation and points out the landmarks of the town. Alma offers to take him to the part of town that has "rooms that can be rented for one hour." The traveling salesman goes to get a taxi while Alma bids farewell to the stone angel.

## COMMENTARY

As was that of its predecessor, SUMMER AND SMOKE, the plot of *The Eccentricities of a Nightingale* was derived from the short story "THE YELLOW BIRD," published in 1947. Williams considered *The Eccentricities of a Nightingale* to be a significantly different play from its predecessor, *Summer and Smoke,* and ultimately he preferred *The Eccentricities of a Nightingale.* He considered *Eccentricities* less conventional and melodramatic. This shift is due largely to the substantial paring down of the characters and content in the revision.

In *Eccentricities* Williams completely eliminates such characters as Nellie Ewell, Rosa Gonzales, and Papa Gonzales. The stabbing and shooting that occur in *Summer and Smoke* are also eliminated. The most profound difference between the two plays is the substitution of the character of John's father, Dr. Buchanan, with his mother, Mrs. Buchanan, who becomes a very active obstacle and force in keeping John and Alma apart. The addition of this inexorable character enhances the shift in Williams's treatment of John and Alma in terms of their character development. In this version of the drama, John is less depraved and unmistakably manipulated by his mother. He is actually drawn to Alma but is repeatedly pulled away by his mother and conventional wisdom. Alma appears less stridently prudish and more clearly eccentric.

In addition, Alma's dilemma becomes more compelling and more akin to that of other Williams heroines such as Heavenly Critchfield in SPRING STORM. As is Heavenly, Alma is caught between a passionate male (John Buchanan) who has very little to offer her and a sensible male (Roger Doremus) who can offer her only companionship and stability. As a result of these alterations, John and Alma are more balanced figures, and, by extension, their relationship is far more realistic. Their conflict and resolution, and the drama as a whole, are more engaging and straightforward.

## PRODUCTION HISTORY

*The Eccentricities of a Nightingale* premiered at the Tappan Zee Playhouse in Nyack, New York, in June 1964. *Eccentricities* premiered on Broadway at the Morosco Theatre on November 23, 1976, with Betsy Palmer and David Selby, respectively, playing Alma Winemiller and John Buchanan. The Broadway production had a lukewarm reception from critics and audiences and closed on December 12, 1976.

The most significant production of *The Eccentricities of a Nightingale* was created for television, presented by the Public Broadcasting Service (PBS) as part of their "Great Performances" series in June 1976. It featured Blythe Danner (Alma Winemiller) and Frank Langella (John Buchanan). Many, including the playwright himself, considered this version the play's most successful incarnation.

## PUBLICATION HISTORY

*The Eccentricities of a Nightingale* was published by New Directions in 1964.

## CHARACTERS

**Bassett, Mrs. Nancy** She is a member of the literary circle led by Alma Winemiller. Nancy is a hypocritical gossip, who talks about Alma and her mother, Mrs. Winemiller, behind their back. She is passionate about culture and cries when she reads the literary circle's manifesto written by Vernon, which declares their mission to make Glorious Hill, Mississippi, the "Athens of the whole South."

**Buchanan, John** John is the dashing, wealthy son of Mrs. Buchanan. He returns to Glorious Hill, Mississippi, as a successful doctor and very eligible bachelor. Mrs. Buchanan has lofty plans for her son, which do not include the Buchanans' eccentric, lovelorn neighbor Alma Winemiller. Against his mother's wishes, John is drawn to Alma and sees great beauty and grace in her. Although he does not love Alma, he grants her wish and has sex with her on New Year's Eve.

**Buchanan, Mrs.** Mrs. Buchanan is the snobbish, manipulative, and controlling mother of John Buchanan. She has great hopes for her handsome and accomplished son. Mrs. Buchanan wants him to marry an attractive, well-bred socialite, who will supply John and the Buchanan family with strong, sturdy, and mentally sound heirs. For this reason, she adamantly thwarts John's attempts to develop a relationship with their eccentric neighbor, Alma Winemiller. Whereas her son sees beauty and grace in the delicate songstress, Mrs. Buchanan sees Alma as only a social misfit and fears that mental instability is in her blood.

**Doremus, Roger** Roger is a member of the literary circle led by Alma Winemiller. He is Alma's only true friend. Roger is fond of Alma and offers her a marriage of companionship. Alma wants a marriage of passion with John Buchanan.

**Rosemary** A member of the literary circle led by Alma Winemiller. She resents that Alma invites her neighbor, John Buchanan, to the literary club meeting without a group vote. Rosemary has written a paper on the poet William Blake, which she attempts to read at the group's meeting.

**Traveling Salesman** The Traveling Salesman meets Alma Winemiller after she has decided to lead a licentious life. Alma eagerly escorts the Salesman to the part of town where they can rent a room for an hour.

**Vernon** Vernon is a member of the literary circle led by Alma Winemiller. He questions the mission of the group and drafts a manifesto, declaring that Glorious Hill, Mississippi, will become "the Athens of the whole South."

**Winemiller, Alma** Known as the "Nightingale of the Delta," Alma is the daughter of the Reverend Winemiller and Mrs. Winemiller. She gives singing lessons to local children and is a noted eccentric in Glorious Hill, Mississippi. Alma is hopelessly in love with her next-door neighbor, John Buchanan, but his mother, Mrs. Buchanan, forbids their connection. Williams acknowledged this ultrasensitive artist as his favorite character.

**Winemiller, Mrs.** Mrs. Winemiller is the mentally unbalanced mother of Alma Winemiller. Unlike those of her predecessor in SUMMER AND SMOKE, Mrs. Winemiller's mental problems stem from the tragic death and loss of her sister, Albertine.

**Winemiller, Reverend** The Reverend Winemiller is the Episcopalian minister in the town of Glorious Hill, Mississippi. He is the father of Alma Winemiller. He warns his daughter that she is developing an eccentric reputation.

# *Eight Mortal Ladies Possessed: A Book of Stories*

Published in 1974 by New Directions, the collection contains the short stories "HAPPY AUGUST THE TENTH," "THE INVENTORY AT FONTANA BELLA," "MISS COYNTE OF GREENE," "SABBATHA AND SOLITUDE," "COMPLETED," and "ORIFLAMME." These stories concentrate on eight women and their relationships with men, sexual desire, emotional fulfillment, and one another.

# "The Field of Blue Children"

Short story written in 1937.

## SYNOPSIS

Myra is a restless young college student. Although she is very popular, she is troubled. Writing is the only activity that settles Myra. She joins a poetry club and encounters a young man named Homer Stallcup. She is aware that Homer has been in love with her for some time, but she remains cautious because he is from a lower social class. Homer works at the college to earn his tuition, and his companion is a strange passionate girl named Hertha. In her restlessness, Myra approaches Homer. She compliments his poetry, and Homer is so honored that he stumbles down the stairs. He hands her pages of poems out of his notebook and begs her to read them.

Later that night, when Myra retires to her room, she reads his poetry. She is completely enthralled by Homer's talent. She is so captivated by the force of his words that she is knocking on his door before she realizes it. Homer is pleasantly surprised by her visit. He is completely ecstatic when Myra tells him she loves his writing, especially the poem about "the field of blue children." Homer grabs her arm and rushes to show her the field of which he writes.

In the moonlight, Myra views the huge wave of blue flowers as they dance in the wind. It is an exhilarating moment for her. Homer leads her through the flowers and they kneel in the middle of the field. He kisses her, and as he does so, she gasps and responds openly to his kiss. The couple gently "lay back against the whispering blue flowers." The next day Myra sends a note to Homer telling him that a relationship between them would be impossible. She announces that she is engaged to Kirk Abbott, but she assures Homer that what transpired between them was a beautiful memory she will always cherish.

The following fall, Myra marries Kirk. She and Kirk are relatively content. Although she ceases to write, Myra seems satisfied with her life. One evening Myra drives out once again to the field of blue flowers. She lies down in the midst of them and weeps.

## COMMENTARY

"The Field of Blue Children" is a "sensitively realized" tale (Leverich, 309) of two young college students drawn to each other by their love of poetry. The basis for this story was Williams's relationship with Hazel Kramer, who was the "great extra-familial love" of Williams's life (*Memoirs,* 15). Williams met Hazel shortly after his family moved to Saint Louis in 1918, and she became one of Williams's closest childhood friends.

His companionship with this curvaceous redhead with "great liquid brown eyes and skin of pearly translucence" (*Memoirs,* 15) blossomed into a romantic attachment for Williams. He proposed to Hazel during his first semester at the UNIVERSITY OF MISSOURI at Columbia, and she promptly but gently rejected his offer of marriage. In "The Field of Blue Children," Williams is actively coming to terms with Hazel's rejection. The work is an expression of the "imagined effects" (Leverich, 310) that her rejection could have had on Hazel.

## PUBLICATION HISTORY

"The Field of Blue Children" was first published in *Story* magazine in 1939. It was also published in *One Arm,* a collection of short stories published in 1948. It was later published in *Housewife* magazine (1952) and in *Four Elements: A Creative Approach to the Short Story* (1975). It also appears in Williams's short story collections *Three Players of a Summer Game and Other Stories* (1960), *Collected Stories* (1985), and *Night of the Iguana and Other Stories* (1995).

## PRODUCTION HISTORY

"The Field of Blue Children" was adapted for the stage by Blue Roses Productions, Inc., and produced at the Manhattan Theatre Source, under the direction of Erma Duricko, in October 2000.

## CHARACTERS

**Abbott, Kirk** Kirk is a young college student at a midwestern university, who marries Myra. Myra and Kirk have a relatively happy life together, although she remains enamored of her former beau, Homer Stallcup.

**Myra** A restless young college student who finds solace in her writing. She joins a poetry club and meets Homer Stallcup, a like-minded young man who shares her love of writing. Despite their class differences, Myra is drawn to Homer because his poetry inspires her. The two spend a romantic evening together in a field of blue flowers; however, the next day Myra ends the relationship. Myra ignores her passions and promptly marries her fiancé, Kirk Abbott. She puts aside her writing and leads a relatively contented life with Kirk. On one occasion, Myra reminisces about her passionate youth and returns to the field of blue flowers and sobs for Homer.

**Stallcup, Homer** He is a young college student who has a talent for writing poetry. Because Homer comes from a less privileged background, his peers ostracize him. However, Myra, also a poet, loves his writing. She is especially enamored of the poem he has written about the field of blue children. Late one night, Homer takes Myra to the blue flowers. They make love amid the flowers, but the next day Myra breaks his heart by sending him a note informing him that she is engaged to Kirk Abbott.

### FURTHER READING

Leverich, Lyle. *Tom: The Unknown Tennessee Williams.* New York: W. W. Norton, 1995.

Williams, Tennessee. *Memoirs.* Garden City, N.Y.: Doubleday, 1975.

## *The Frosted Glass Coffin*

A one-act play written in 1941.

### SYNOPSIS

The play is set in a retirement community in Miami, Florida. The time is early morning. Three elderly men gather outside their hotel to observe the ritual lineup at the cafeteria across the street. One expresses outrage over the cafeteria's recent price increase and shares his plans to start a petition in protest. Two and Three argue that the petition will be unnoticed if the media do not publicize it. One taunts Two, and the men launch into a heated discussion comparing their respective states of health. The three men are interrupted by the sound of shouting. They discover that an old woman has fainted while standing in line under the early morning Sun. Someone calls to the men and orders them to fetch a taxi. One laughingly disregards the request, musing, "In our age bracket, you're living in a glass coffin, a frosted coffin, you barely see light through it."

One delivers news of the recent death of Mr. Kelsey's wife. Two and Three are shocked by the news. One divulges the events surrounding Mrs. Kelsey's death. One and his wife, Mrs. One, had driven Mrs. Kelsey to the hospital (after she had complained of abdominal pain). They left Mrs. Kelsey alone at the hospital and went to retrieve Mr. Kelsey from the hotel. When they returned to the hospital, it was too late. Mr. Kelsey has been in a state of denial about his wife's death ever since. One continues to observe the traffic of the street. He and Two have a conversation about the habits of their wives. One remarks that his wife takes pleasure in knowing that she will most likely outlive him.

Mr. Kelsey joins the men on the porch; he is dazed and lethargic. Mrs. One tries to persuade Mr. Kelsey to join them at the cafeteria, but he refuses. One, Two, and Three rise to take their spots in the cafeteria line. Mr. Kelsey is left sitting alone on the porch. He utters a pained howl of grief.

### COMMENTARY

As are many of Williams's works, this one-act play is focused on the predicament of old age, aging, and impending death. These themes are apparent in such works as "SABBATHA AND SOLITUDE," *THE ROMAN SPRING OF MRS. STONE*, *SWEET BIRD OF YOUTH*, and *THE LAST OF MY SOLID GOLD WATCHES*. However, in *The Frosted Glass Coffin*, Williams approaches these subjects in an essentially comic manner. Philip Kolin notes that in the play Williams incorporates "sardonic wit with genuine pathos," which reveals "the farcical and tragic aspects of old age" (Kolin, 44).

One of the most notable characteristics of this work is the naming, or the lack of naming, of the principal characters. By labeling the three principal characters as One, Two, and Three, Williams strips the characters of any essential humanity or individuality. Only the traumatized Mr. Kelsey is set apart from the dehumanizing world that the senior citizens inhabit. Although he is isolated and motionless, Mr. Kelsey experiences grief and pain, which, ironically, make him the character who is the most individual and the most "alive." Scholars and theatrical producers have largely ignored this satirical drama. Williams, however, considered *The Frosted Glass Coffin* to be one of his finest short plays.

### PRODUCTION HISTORY

Williams himself directed the first production of *The Frosted Glass Coffin*, at the Waterfront Playhouse in Key West, Florida, in 1970.

## PUBLICATION HISTORY

The text was published in two one-act play collections: *Dragon Country* (1970) and *In the Bar of a Tokyo Hotel and Other Plays* (1981).

## CHARACTERS

**Kelsey, Mr.** Mr. Kelsey is a resident of a retirement community in Miami. He is elderly and infirm and is forced to make weekly visits to the hospital for medical attention. He and the members of his community are shocked when his wife passes away before he does. Alone and bereft, Mr. Kelsey is nearly deaf and nearly blind and is living in what another character refers to as a frosted glass coffin.

**One** One's actual name is Claude Fletcher, but he is never referred to by that name. One is a retired mayor of a small town in the Carolinas. He is a man in his 70s consumed by fear of becoming senile. One searches for meaning in his life now that he is old. He is married, but he resents his wife, Mrs. One.

**One, Mrs.** Mrs. One, whose real name is Betsy Fletcher, is married to One. She is dedicated to helping the older members in her community. Her husband accuses her of gloating about being the youngest person in the community.

**Three** Three is the companion of Two. He is an elderly man well past 80, who has a hearing impairment and is blind.

**Two** Two's real name, although never used, is Mr. Sykes. He is a man in his late 80s, who is often accompanied by his friend, One.

## FURTHER READING

Kolin, Philip C. "Williams's *The Frosted Glass Coffin*," *Explicator* 59, no. 1 (fall 2000): 44–46.

# *The Fugitive Kind*

A one-act play written between 1936 and 1938, set in a men's flophouse. In this unpublished work a criminal on the run falls in love with the adopted daughter of a man who runs the flophouse. The play's title—and nothing else about it—was borrowed for the film version of the full-length play ORPHEUS DESCENDING. Willard Holland directed the first production of this play at the Wednesday Club Auditorium, SAINT LOUIS, MISSOURI, in November 1937.

# *Garden District*

See *SOMETHING UNSPOKEN; SUDDENLY LAST SUMMER.*

# "The Gift of an Apple"

Short story written in 1936.

## SYNOPSIS

A young Hitchhiker is attempting to hitchhike from California to Kentucky. It is hot and he has spent more than an hour waiting on the road. He is not having any luck securing a ride. He continues to walk and finally spots a trailer off the road. A large, buxom, dark-haired woman named Irma sits near the trailer. She asks the Hitchhiker whether he would like to buy something she is selling. He informs her that he is broke and asks whether she might have some food to spare. Irma gives him an apple. He thanks her and sits down to eat it. It is the best apple he has ever tasted.

Irma goes back inside the trailer and returns with another apple, and the young man expects that she that will give it to him, but she eats it herself. He asks her why she is alone, and she tells him that her husband and son are out on the town getting drunk. The Hitchhiker confesses that he is still hungry. Irma moves closer to him and runs her fingers through his hair and down his neck. Irma aks him his age. When he tells her he is 19 years old, she recoils and demands he leave because he is too young. The Hitchhiker denies that he is too young for her, but Irma says he is the same age as her son. He walks away, laughing to himself and enjoying the lingering clean taste of the apple in his mouth.

## COMMENTARY

The scholarly assessment of "The Gift of an Apple" has been quite limited. However, this engaging early work is an important feature of the Williams fictive canon. As are many of the short stories and longer fiction that follow it, "The Gift of an Apple" is centered on the theme of hunger and satisfaction.

In this and other works, such as "DESIRE AND THE BLACK MASSEUR" and *THE ROMAN SPRING OF MRS. STONE*, the hunger for food is inextricably linked with the passionate hunger for sexual intimacy and fulfillment. In this tale of a handsome young drifter and a buxom, sexually deprived older woman, Williams masterfully juxtaposes the twin desires of the characters. Both Irma and the Hitchhiker personify hunger; however, both also become the "food" or object of desire of the other. The young traveler is weary from his journey, parched from the heat, and ravenous from wandering the road. The lonely Irma sits idly in the heat, longing for physical warmth. The young Hitchhiker, who has quite literally been "cooked" in the Sun, appears before her as a sexy morsel; likewise he in turn devours her greasy figure with his eyes and imagines her sprawled across her bed waiting to be being greedily consumed by her lover. The meeting of the two pits hunger against hunger, need against need.

As does the biblical character Eve, Irma offers the Hitchhiker an apple and tempts him. She also offers him a compromise: She will satisfy his hunger if he will satisfy hers. This, too, is a familiar Williams theme: the trade-offs and compromises individuals make for a few, fleeting moments of satisfaction or happiness. These ideas are explored at greater length in such works as *CONFESSIONAL* and *SMALL CRAFT WARNINGS*.

Although initially content to play the seductress, Irma is unable to follow through on the bargain she has proposed. Once she learns the Hitchhiker's age, she rejects the idea of being intimate with him. She and the Hitchhiker walk away from their meeting only partially satisfied, or half full. She must remain content with the sensation of running her fingers through his hair, just as he must pacify his hunger with the lingering taste of the apple. "The Gift of an Apple" is an example of Williams's skillful mastery of the short story genre.

## PUBLICATION HISTORY

"The Gift of an Apple" was first published in *Collected Stories* in 1985.

## CHARACTERS

**Hitchhiker** He is a young man traveling from California to Kentucky. The Hitchhiker befriends Irma, a woman who lives in a trailer beside a desolate desert highway. The young man is famished and Irma offers him an apple. He eagerly eats the apple and hopes that she will share a more substantial meal with him. She offers him more on the condition of a sexual encounter. However, when she realizes he is only 19 years old, the same age as her son, she immediately becomes uninterested. The Hitchhiker continues his journey, relishing the apple he received from her and believing it is the best apple he has ever tasted.

**Irma** Irma is a large dark woman who lives in a trailer beside a deserted road. She encounters a young Hitchhiker, who asks her for food. She offers him an apple and the possibility of more food if he will have sex with her. When Irma realizes the young man is the same age as her son, she loses her courage. She sends the Hitchhiker on his way. Irma and the Hitchhiker share a number of similarities, particularly their unsatisfied hunger and their transience.

# *The Glass Menagerie*

A full-length play in seven scenes written in 1944.

## SYNOPSIS

The setting is the Wingfield apartment in a shabby tenement building, in Saint Louis, Missouri, in the year 1937. The set has an interior living room area and an exterior fire escape.

### *Scene 1*

Tom Wingfield is in the fire-escape area outside the Wingfield apartment. He explains the concept of a memory play. He enters the interior setting, where his mother, Amanda Wingfield, and his sister, Laura Wingfield, who wears a brace on her leg, are seated at a table, waiting to eat dinner. All aspects of the meal are mimed, and as Tom seats himself, Amanda begins to instruct him on how to eat politely. Tom abruptly leaves the table to have a cigarette. Laura rises to fetch an ashtray, but Amanda tells her to stay seated, for she wishes Laura to remain fresh and pretty for her prospective gentleman callers. Amanda recalls her Sunday afternoons in Blue Mountain, Mississippi, where she received and entertained countless callers. Amanda asks Laura how many callers she expects to have, and Laura explains that she is not expecting any callers.

*Scene 2*

In the interior of the Wingfield apartment, Laura sits alone, polishing her glass figurines. Hearing her mother approach, Laura quickly hides her collection and resumes her place behind a typewriter. Amanda reveals that she has discovered that Laura has dropped out of secretarial school. Laura explains that she became ill during the first week of school and was too ashamed to return. Amanda pleads with Laura, asking her what she is going to do with her life. Amanda fears that Laura will be dependent on the charity of others for the rest of her life. Amanda warns Laura that there is no future in staying home playing with her glass collection and her father's phonograph records. She implores Laura to set her sights on marrying. Laura confesses that she had liked a boy named Jim O'Connor in high school, but she is certain that he must be married by now. Laura acknowledges her disability as her primary obstacle in forming relationships. Amanda dismisses this claim and advises Laura to cultivate aspects of her personality to compensate for her disadvantage.

*Scene 3*

The same location as scene 2. Tom addresses the audience. He explains that Amanda has become obsessed with finding a gentleman caller for Laura and has begun selling magazine subscriptions to generate extra income. Amanda has a telephone conversation with a neighbor, trying to convince her to renew her subscription to *The Homemaker's Companion.* Tom and Amanda quarrel about his habits, his writing, and his books. Amanda accuses Tom of being selfish and of engaging in immoral activities. Tom swears at his mother and bemoans his fate of working in a warehouse to support his mother and sister. In the heat of the argument, Tom accidentally crashes into Laura's glass collection, shattering it to pieces on the floor. Amanda refuses to speak to him until he apologizes. Laura and Tom collect the shattered glass from the floor.

*Scene 4*

The same location as scene 3. Tom returns home from a movie and talks with Laura. She asks him to apologize to Amanda. Amanda sends Laura out on an errand so that she may speak with Tom alone. She and Tom make peace. Amanda warns Tom of the danger in pursuing an adventurous life. Amanda raises the subject of Laura and the need for Tom to bring a nice young man home to meet Laura. Amanda promises Tom that she will let him do as he pleases and leave after he has provided for Laura's future. Amanda begs him to secure a nice man for Laura first. Tom grudgingly agrees to try to find someone. Amanda happily returns to soliciting magazine subscriptions.

*Scene 5*

On the fire escape, the exterior of the Wingfield apartment, Amanda suggests that Tom be more mindful of his appearance. She makes a wish on the new Moon. Tom tells her that he is inviting a gentleman caller for Laura to the apartment the following evening. Amanda inquires about the character of the gentleman caller. Tom describes Jim's qualities and characteristics, and Amanda determines that he is suitable to call. Tom warns Amanda not to be too excited, because Jim is unaware that he is being invited for Laura's benefit. Tom expresses concern that Amanda has unrealistic expectations of Laura. Amanda refuses to accept the reality of Laura's condition. Tom goes to a movie and Amanda calls Laura out onto the fire escape. Amanda urges Laura to make a wish on the new Moon.

*Scene 6*

On the fire escape and in the interior of the Wingfield apartment, Tom speaks directly to the audience and explains the nature of his friendship with

Jim. Tom makes Jim feel important because Tom can recall Jim's high school glory days. In the living room, Amanda and Laura prepare for the arrival of the gentleman caller. Amanda dresses Laura and discovers one of her own former gowns. At the mention of the name Jim O'Connor, Laura refuses to participate in the evening's events. Amanda chastises Laura and orders her to answer the door when the doorbell rings. Laura freezes with anxiety as Amanda forces her to welcome Tom and Jim. Laura hides in the kitchen while Amanda converses with Jim O'Connor. Tom goes to the kitchen to check on supper. Amanda summons everyone to the table. Laura maintains that she is sick and lies on the couch for the duration of the dinner.

### *Scene 7*

In the interior of the Wingfield apartment, the lights in the apartment suddenly go out. Amanda quickly lights candles, asking Jim to check the fuses. Finding that the fuses are fine, Amanda asks Tom whether he has paid the electric bill; he has not. After dinner, Amanda asks Jim to keep Laura company. She gives him a candelabrum and a glass of wine to give to Laura. Amanda forces Tom to join her in the kitchen to wash the dishes. Settling down on the floor beside Laura, Jim asks her why she is so shy, and Laura asks whether Jim remembers her. She explains that they had singing class together in high school and reminds him that she was always late because of her disability. Jim confesses that he never noticed her limp and admonishes Laura about being self-conscious. Laura takes out her high school yearbook and Jim autographs it for her.

Laura shows her glass collection to him and Jim marvels over her delicate figurines. Hearing music from the nearby dance hall, Jim asks Laura to dance. She hesitates, but Jim persuades her to join him. They stumble into the coffee table, breaking Laura's favorite figurine, a unicorn that she has had for 13 years. Jim apologizes, and Laura consoles him. Struck by Laura's charm and delicacy, Jim kisses her. He chastises himself for his hasty action and informs Laura that he is engaged. Laura gives him the glass unicorn. Amanda gleefully returns to the living room with a pitcher of cherry lemonade. Jim apologizes and announces that he has to leave to collect his fiancée at the train station.

Amanda is horrified by the news and calls Tom out of the kitchen. She accuses him of playing a cruel joke on the family, but Tom explains that he had no knowledge of Jim's engagement. Amanda again chastises Tom for selfishness and for lack of concern for his abandoned mother or his disabled sister. Tom finally leaves the Wingfield apartment for good. The lights fade on the interior setting, leaving Laura and Amanda in candlelight. Tom appears on the fire escape and offers the audience details of his departure and journey away from his family. He explains that no matter how much distance is between them, he can never forget his sister. He instructs Laura to blow out her candles, and she does.

## COMMENTARY

*The Glass Menagerie* began its life as a screenplay, *The Gentleman Caller.* This script was an adaptation of Williams's short story "PORTRAIT OF A GIRL IN GLASS." The script of "The Gentleman Caller" was submitted to METRO-GOLDWYN-MAYER (MGM) in the summer of 1943. Williams had hoped that this script would impress studio executives and ultimately relieve him from other contractual obligations at MGM such as writing what he scathingly termed a "celluloid brassiere" for the actress Lana Turner. MGM was less than amenable to Williams's idea. They declared that the popular film *Gone With the Wind* (1939) had served up enough Southern women for a decade (Spoto, 97). In an oddly ironic twist, this response and its implicit preference for fiction over reality resonated with the play's central theme.

Stylistically, *The Glass Menagerie* reflects its prehistory. The screenplay-turned-stage-script shows a number of elements more familiar, and perhaps more suited, to the cinema than to the theater. In theatrical terms, Williams's approach is Brechtian: It uses devices meant to create what the German playwright and dramaturge Bertolt Brecht, a contemporary of Williams's, called the "alienation effect." In *The Glass Menagerie,* these devices constitute a sometimes disjointed sequence of tableaux (or scenes) rather than the more conventional

Anthony Ross (Jim O'Connor), Laurette Taylor (Amanda Wingfield), Eddie Dowling (Tom Wingfield), and Julie Haydon (Laura Wingfield) in *The Glass Menagerie* *(Photograph courtesy of the Billy Rose Theatre Collection, New York Public Library)*

three-act structure; a narrator/commentator (Tom) who also is a character in the play and steps in and out of the action; Williams's scripted suggestions of legends to be projected onto gauze between the dining and front rooms, "to give accent to certain values in each scene"; the very strictly defined music, which assigns specific pieces or themes to certain scenes, especially in relation to Laura; and the lighting, "focused on selected areas or actors, sometimes in contradistinction to what is the apparent center."

For Brecht, the alienation effect served to remind the audience that what they saw on stage constituted the real world. Williams takes this concept a crucial step further, in that he turns alienation—the conscious or unconscious loss of a person's feeling of connection with his or her surroundings—into the mainstay of the play: It becomes a way of life for the characters. Brecht tries to prevent his audience from escaping into illusion. Williams forestalls his characters' conquest of "a world of reality that [they] were somehow set apart from." None of the characters is truly able to cope with the demands of everyday life; therefore, all seek refuge in their own dream world, to such an extent that illusion itself becomes subjective reality.

In this the characters are not alone. Williams declared this denial of reality symptomatic of an era during which individuals would seek out "dance halls, bars, and movies, and sex that hung in the gloom like a chandelier and flooded the world with brief, deceptive rainbows," in order briefly to forget about their lives and their troubles. But the diversion cannot last, and the conflict between fact and fiction, reality and make-believe, remains irreconcilable. This is the central theme of *The Glass Menagerie.* From it emerge two related themes: the impossibility of escape and the trap of memory—or of the past in general.

The play is memory in more than one sense. As is much of Williams's work, *The Glass Menagerie* is poignantly autobiographical. However, this is by far his most autobiographical work. In July 1918, Williams's father, CORNELIUS COFFIN WILLIAMS, exchanged his job as a traveling salesman for a managerial post with the International Shoe Company in SAINT LOUIS, MISSOURI. Cornelius, his wife (EDWINA DAKIN WILLIAMS), and their two children, ROSE ISABEL WILLIAMS and Tom, left Clarksdale, Mississippi, to take up residence in what then was the fourth-largest city in the United States and a major industrial center.

From their initial quarters at a boardinghouse they moved into and out of a succession of apartments, including one at 4633 Winchester Place in downtown Saint Louis. The apartment had "two small windows, in the front and rear rooms, and a fire escape [that] blocked the smoky light from a back alley" (Spoto, 16). The wording may be less poetic than Williams's stage directions for *The Glass Menagerie,* but it accurately describes the Wingfield home, and the Williams's tenement at 4633 Winchester Place in Saint Louis later became known as the "Glass Menagerie Apartments."

For Rose and Tom, both delicate and accustomed to the rural gentility of Mississippi and the relative stability their maternal grandparents had helped to provide, the relocation and its effects on their home life proved traumatic. Tom was seven years old at the time of the move, old enough to recognize that "there were two kinds of people, the rich and the poor, and that [the Williams family] belonged more to the latter" (Tynan, 456)—with all the ostracism this entailed. Although the play's references to the Spanish civil war and the bombing of Guernica in April 1937 set *The Glass Menagerie* nearly two decades later, during the depression, the social and economic context and its bleak inescapability are virtually the same.

The family's reduced circumstances were due to Cornelius Williams's compulsive drinking and gambling, and the domestic situation was worsened by a string of illnesses and operations Edwina Williams had after the birth of the Williams's youngest son, DAKIN WILLIAMS. Caught between a volatile father and an infirm mother, Rose and Tom each found their own ways of escaping into safer fantasy worlds. Tom fled into literature, at first reading voraciously (much to his father's distaste), but when his mother gave him a typewriter, he started to write poetry. The consequences for Rose, however, were far bleaker. By the early 1920s mental illness began to manifest itself through psychosomatic stomach problems and an inability to sustain any social contact, which turned her enrollment at Rubicam's Business College into a debacle. Her condition worsened over the next 15 years, until, in 1937, her parents agreed to a prefrontal lobotomy, which left Rose in a state of childlike, almost autistic detachment. Tom, studying at the State University of Iowa by then, was informed only after the disastrous procedure. From that point on, the spirit of his sister "haunted his life" (Spoto, 60).

It also haunts *The Glass Menagerie.* Though physically rather than mentally disabled, Laura Wingfield is painfully shy and socially inept, and she wears her physical difference as a stifling protective cloak. Nicknamed "Blue Roses" in a clear reference to Williams's sister, she has stomach pain caused by nervous self-consciousness when exposed to strangers, and she visits the penguins at the zoo instead of attending classes at Rubicam's Business College. The focus of her life, to the exclusion of everything else, is her collection of glass animals, which serves as a symbol of her (and Rose's) fragility. When Jim O'Connor accidentally breaks her glass unicorn, the loss of the horn offers a subtle but nonetheless striking reminder of Rose's lobotomy. As Laura states, her unicorn "had an operation" to make it "less freakish."

Rose is not the only member of the Williams family to appear in *The Glass Menagerie.* With the exception of Dakin, all of the Williamses are cast. Williams himself infuses his namesake Tom, the trapped poet-narrator, who hides in a closet to write and dreams of joining the merchant marine. Tom is a warehouse worker for Continental Shoemakers, and his job fills him with the same desperate frustration that caused Williams to suffer a nervous breakdown after his father withdrew him from college and forced him to work at the International Shoe Company between 1932 and 1935. Cornelius Williams, an alcoholic and a former telephone company employee, is clearly identifiable as the absent head of the Wingfield household, "a telephone man who fell in love with long distances."

A more oblique and more sinister reference, which plays on Cornelius's middle name, illustrates Tom's/Williams's attempts to break away from the presence of the father. Recounting his nightly exploits to Laura, Tom launches into the tale of Malvolio the Stage Magician and a coffin trick, "the wonderfullest trick of all. . . . We nailed him into a coffin and he got out of the coffin without removing one nail." For Williams, his father, Cornelius Coffin Williams, was a flesh-and-blood opponent; for the character, Tom Wingfield, he is a photograph over the mantel and the mirror his mother relentlessly holds up to him. This disembodied specter is all the more oppressive because it cannot be fought or escaped. Condemned to stay at home because his father ran away, Tom looks for vicarious adventure, always fancies himself on the brink of moving, but has no idea when or where. When he finally does make a break, it is at the expense of taking the past with him. True escape is as impossible for him as it was for Williams: Laura/Rose constantly haunts him.

Completing the family analogies, Tom and Laura's mother, Amanda, is a replica of Edwina Dakin Williams. Both have pretensions to be Southern belles, both claim to have been pursued by countless gentleman callers only to marry "this boy," both are capable of prattling incessantly, and neither can cook or bake anything apart from angel food cake. They also share a dangerously tenuous grasp on reality that materializes in their aspirations for Laura and Rose, respectively. Both mothers are convinced that their daughter's problem—be it lameness or schizophrenia—will dissolve if only she finds the right man. In the autumn of 1933, Edwina invited a family friend, "the very handsome Jim O'Connor" (Spoto, 43), as a prospective suitor for Rose. The experiment concluded in only one brief visit, which apparently upset Rose greatly. In the same vein, Amanda badgers Tom into inviting his shoe company colleague, and former high school basketball hero Jim O'Connor, as a gentleman caller for Laura. This attempt leads to an equally devastating result. Jim, brimming with self-satisfied optimism and bent on self-improvement, has nothing in common with Laura. He has genuine affection for her and does manage to draw her out, but the relationship cannot go further, because he is engaged to someone else. This revelation occurs just as Laura is beginning to believe that her high school crush on Jim could be fulfilled. In other words, the Gentleman Caller breaks her illusions and her spirit as easily and as casually as he has broken her glass unicorn.

*The Glass Menagerie* is Tom's recollection of the events culminating in the visit of the Gentleman Caller. Everything in the play happens in and from memory. Insight and perspective are counterpoised by that peculiar trick of memory that diminishes some things and enlarges others, according to their importance. Such distortion always serves to sharpen and explain. Likewise, Tom's account, always slightly unreal, always slightly over the top, veers between caricature and canonization.

Reminiscent of the brittle translucency of glass, Laura is imbued with a "pristine clarity" similar to that found in "early religious portraits of female saints or madonnas." In stark contrast to Laura's otherworldliness, Amanda and her idealized Southern girlhood—grotesquely laden with jonquils and suitors—clash with the everyday contingencies of cold-calling, mastication, a disabled daughter, and an absconded husband in a way that is both painfully comical and brutally revealing. Even Jim cannot escape from the exaggeration of memory. Having failed "to arrive at nothing short of the White House by the time he was thirty" (53), he is shown to wallow in the sweet smell of former basketball glory, yearbook pictures, and the admiration of a shy, lonely girl. "Try and you will succeed" is the futile battle cry Jim and Amanda share in the face of stagnation.

Publicity photo of Williams *(Photograph courtesy of the Billy Rose Theatre Collection, New York Public Library)*

Because he is an outsider and inhabits the real world, Jim is raised to a symbol of hope, "the long-delayed but always expected something that we live for." For Amanda expectation does not stop here. Roger B. Stein makes a convincing case that Jim has been cast as a Christ-like savior figure or, at the very least, as Moses about to lead the Wingfield family to the promised land of harmony and happiness (Stein, 141–153). There is no such land, of course, and only Amanda has promised it. The pivotal scene between Jim, the flawed suitor, and Laura exposes this fallacy. "Unicorns, aren't they extinct in the modern world?" he asks when Laura shows him her favorite glass animal. The unicorn is a mythical animal and an alien even in the unreal world of Laura's glass menagerie. In fact, it is so strange that Jim cannot recognize it as what it is without being prompted, just as he is unaware of the real reason why he has been invited to dinner. At this point the unicorn stands for the Wingfields' combined dreams of escape: Amanda's hope of the miracle cure of marriage for Laura, Tom's longing for adventure and motion, and Laura's tentative, naive, and unformed dream of love. The shattering of the glass unicorn heralds the collapse of those dreams as much as it heralds the personal shattering of Laura. Unicorns are extinct in the modern world, Jim is engaged, and escape from reality is impossible. Tom's last monologue underscores this fact. His own break from home has only succeeded in setting him adrift and the sole guilty resting point he has left are his memories. Ironically, it is precisely those memories that prevent his true escape, because they forever tie him to the past.

With *The Glass Menagerie,* Williams set out to create a new kind of "PLASTIC THEATRE," a highly expressionistic language of the stage that would replace what he saw as the stale conventions of realism. He succeeded, thereby revolutionizing American theater. Within two weeks of opening on Broadway in 1945, the play won the New York Drama Critics Circle Award. CLAUDIA CASSIDY, present at the Chicago premiere, had predicted *The Glass Menagerie*'s success: "It was not only the quality of the work as something so delicate, so fragile. It was also indestructible and you knew right then" (Terkel, 144). Cassidy was correct about the play's indestructibility, although for a long time, critics either failed to see or attempted to marginalize the play's achievement. For some, the lyricism of language and expressiveness of theatrical devices obstructed the action. This response was due to the fact that the critics were married to an American theater tradition that demanded realism, which is precisely what Williams denounced in the production notes for the play. Instead of scientific photographic likeness, Williams attempted and conveyed spiritual and emotional truth.

The acid test of audience reception bears this out. Not tied to ideologies and convictions, audiences understood and responded immediately and favorably to *The Glass Menagerie.* A generation after its Chicago premiere, critical attitudes and opinions had shifted markedly. Many acknowledge *The Glass Menagerie* as possibly Williams's greatest achievement because of the breadth of its cataclysmic vision, a vision "not only of individuals who fail to communicate with one another, nor a society temporarily adrift in a depression, but of man abandoned in the universe" (Stein, 153). This is the explanation for the play's enduring appeal. As are all great works of art, it is not limited by time and space but manages to transcend both by touching on matters shared and universal. Spoto surmised that nothing Williams wrote after *The Glass Menagerie* possesses the "wholeness of sentiment," its "breadth of spirit," or its "quiet voice about the great reach of small lives" (Spoto, 116).

## PRODUCTION HISTORY

*The Glass Menagerie* was completed in the summer of 1944. Williams's agent, AUDREY WOOD, submitted the play to the actor-producer EDDIE DOWLING, who decided to direct the play (with MARGO JONES as codirector, at Williams's insistence). Dowling also secured the role of Tom Wingfield for himself. Jo Mielziner created the design (omitting the projection device), and PAUL BOWLES composed the incidental music. Julie Haydon was cast as Laura Wingfield, with Anthony Ross playing Jim O'Connor. The part of Amanda Wingfield went to the veteran theater star LAURETTE TAYLOR. The 60-year-old Taylor, who had recently retired from the stage after the death of her husband, was a calculated risk. After a rehearsal period dogged by problems, not least due to Taylor and her bouts of alcoholism, *The Glass Menagerie* opened for a trial run at the Civic Theatre in Chicago, Illinois, on December 26, 1944.

Neither the date (the day after Christmas) nor the raging blizzard that hit Chicago that night was conducive to attracting audiences. By the afternoon of December 27, the box office had taken in only $400 and the producers had begun to prepare a closing notice. What rescued *The Glass Menagerie* were the reviews it received from the press. CLAUDIA CASSIDY, drama and music critic of the *Chicago Tribune* and one of the most influential critical voices outside New York, called *The Glass Menagerie* "a dream in the dusk and a tough little play [that] reaches out tentacles, first tentative, then gripping, and you are caught in its spell" (Cassidy, 1944). Cassidy and her colleague Ashton Stevens, critic for the *Chicago Herald Examiner*, actively promoted the play; the management of the Civic Theatre persuaded the mayor of Chicago to sanction a 50 percent ticket subsidy for municipal employees; word spread, and by mid-January 1945 *The Glass Menagerie* was playing to sold-out houses.

On March 31, 1945, the evening before Easter, the same production opened at the Playhouse Theatre in New York to an extraordinary 25 curtain calls and shouts for the author to appear on stage. By the following Monday theatergoers were lining the streets for tickets. New York reviews were slightly more restrained than Chicago's, quibbling with Williams's style and theatrical language, but they were unanimous in their extolling of Laurette Taylor's performance and their appreciation of the impact of the play. Less than two weeks after opening on Broadway, *The Glass Menagerie* won the New York Drama Critics Circle Award.

## PUBLICATION HISTORY

There are three distinct versions of *The Glass Menagerie* text: the Reading Edition, the Acting Edition, and the London Edition. These textual variations are due to Williams's practice of extensively reworking scripts even after they had gone into production. The earliest in-print version of the play is the Reading Edition, published in 1945 by Random House. The Acting Edition, published by Dramatists Play Service, containing some 1,100 revisions, all introduced by Williams himself, followed in 1948. In the same year, John Lehmann published the London Edition, which reflects the minor textual alterations made for John Gielgud's production at the Haymarket Theatre, London. The version most widely known and used today is the Reading Edition, which also most closely corresponds to Williams's original script.

## CHARACTERS

**O'Connor, Jim** Jim is a former hero of the high school Tom and Laura Wingfield attended. He is also a colleague of Tom's at the International Shoe Company. Tom invites Jim for dinner at the Wingfields' apartment. Jim does not realize that Tom's mother, Amanda Wingfield, has the ulterior motive of presenting him as a gentleman caller and prospective suitor for Laura. The plan fails, as Jim is already engaged. The character of Jim is based on an actual Jim O'Connor, who was one of Williams's fellow students at the UNIVERSITY OF MISSOURI at Columbia. On one occasion he was invited to the Williams home with the goal that he would become better acquainted with Williams's sister, ROSE WILLIAMS.

**Wingfield, Amanda** She is the mother of Tom and Laura Wingfield. Living in a dingy, Saint Louis apartment and struggling to make ends meet by selling magazine subscriptions, Amanda finds solace in the romantic memories of her girlhood. Her concern about her children's future prompts her to bully them to live her ideal life, that of Southern gentility. Her inappropriate sense of propriety makes Tom and Laura miserable. As does Esmeralda Critchfield in *SPRING STORM*, Amanda places importance on the need to have Laura marry a socially suitable young man. This goal causes an unhappy tension in the household and bitter friction, especially between Amanda and Tom. At her insistence, Tom invites Jim O'Connor, a fellow shoe factory worker, to visit the Wingfield home as a prospective gentleman caller for Laura. Amanda Wingfield is based on Williams's mother, EDWINA ESTELLE DAKIN WILLIAMS. Mrs. Williams acknowledged the similarity and recalled that in her youth she was always "the belle of the ball," who proudly "made [her] debut in Vicksburg twice" (Brown, 119). Mrs. Williams also said that she greatly enjoyed the character of Amanda, especially when she was played by LAURETTE TAYLOR, a "real genius," who adequately captured the "pathos" of the character (Brown, 115–116).

**Wingfield, Laura** Laura is the daughter of Amanda Wingfield and older sister of Tom Wingfield. A childhood illness has left her with a shortened leg, for which she has to wear a brace. Laura's self-consciousness about her disability renders her unable to attend business college, and she seeks refuge in her collection of glass animals, the eponymous glass menagerie. Her encounter with Jim O'Connor, with whom she has been secretly infatuated since high school, proves traumatic when she finds out that he is engaged. Laura Wingfield is based on Williams's sister, ROSE ISABEL WILLIAMS.

**Wingfield, Tom** Tom is the narrator and simultaneously a character in the play. He has ambitions to be a poet, but he is forced to work at a shoe factory warehouse to support his mother, Amanda Wingfield, and his sister, Laura Wingfield. His home life in their Saint Louis apartment is miserable. His mother repeatedly accuses him of being selfish and regularly looks through his possessions. Dreaming of adventure and escape from his depressing job and home life, Tom spends most of his evenings at movies. He becomes a reluctant accomplice in his mother's plan to secure a gentleman caller for Laura. He invites his workmate and former high school associate Jim O'Connor to the Wingfield apartment for dinner. The evening is a disaster, and his mother blames the negative turn of events on Tom. As a result, he leaves home, abandoning Amanda and Laura to their own resources. Tom is forever haunted by memories of his sister, and the play is his account of events surrounding his departure. Tom Wingfield is Williams's most autobiographical character. Tom's leave-taking mirrors Williams's own departure from his family's SAINT LOUIS, MISSOURI, apartment and from his emotionally unstable sister, ROSE ISABEL WILLIAMS.

## FURTHER READING

Brown, Dennis. *Shoptalk: Conversations about Theatre and Film with Twelve Writers, One Producer—and Tennessee Williams's Mother.* New York: Newmarket Press, 1992).

Cassidy, Claudia. "Fragile Drama Holds Theatre in Tight Spell," *Chicago Daily Theater Tribune*, December 27, 1944, p. 11.

Spoto, Donald. *The Kindness of Strangers: The Life of Tennessee Williams*. Boston: Little, Brown, 1985.

Stein, Roger B. "*The Glass Menagerie* Revisited: Catastrophe without Violence," *Western Humanities Review* 18, no. 2 (spring 1964): 141–153.

Terkel, Studs. *The Spectator: Talk about Movies and Plays with the People Who Make Them*. New York: New Press, 1999.

Tynan, Kenneth. "Valentine to Tennessee Williams," in *Drama and the Modern World: Plays and Essays*, edited by Samuel Weiss. Lexington, Mass.: D. C. Heath, 1964, pp. 455–461.

# *The Gnädiges Fräulein*

A one-act play written around 1965.

## SYNOPSIS

The play is set in a seaside landscape called Cocaloony Key. The action of the play takes place on the porches and the areas surrounding the rooming houses owned by Polly and Molly.

### *Prologue*

Polly speaks directly to the audience and offers the history of Cocaloony Key. She warns the audience of the island's inhabitants, the cocaloony birds. As she speaks, several of these birds swoop in, causing Polly to duck and dodge them. Polly introduces herself and her neighbor, Molly, who is mopping her porch next door.

### *Scene 1*

Molly and Polly engage in light banter about the niceties of mopping a porch. They sit down in their rocking chairs and "synchronize their rockers." Molly reveals that she is actually cleaning blood from her porch, shed by the Gnädiges Fräulein earlier that morning. Quickly changing the subject, Molly pleads with Polly, who is also the society editor of the *Cocaloony Gazette,* to place an advertisement in her column for her.

The Permanent Transient, a local drunkard, diverts Polly's attention. Polly inquires about his condition and discovers that Molly rents out "Standing Room Only" vacancies on the weekends to transients who cannot afford a bed. The Gnädiges Fräulein's voice is suddenly heard, asking to come out to the porch. Molly explains that the Fräulein has lost "porch and kitchen privileges" until she can deliver food to Molly. Polly wants to interview the Fräulein, so she is permitted to leave the house. When the Fräulein appears, she has only one eye, with a bandage wrapped around the other empty socket.

The Fräulein asks Polly to choose a selection from her playbill—she intends to sing for Polly. After the selection is made, the Fräulein begins to sing. She is interrupted by a violent attack by the Cocaloony Bird, which forces her back into the house. Lighting on the porch, the large bird frightens Polly and Molly, until Indian Joe, another tenant, appears to shoo it away.

After Joe disappears back into the house, the women resume their banter. Polly reveals that she is infatuated with Joe, while Molly relays how the Fräulein lost her eye to the birds. A fish-boat whistle is heard in the distance, and the Fräulein dashes out of the house, armed with a tin bucket. She races to the docks to retrieve the fish the vendors reject. To accomplish this, the Fräulein is forced to compete with the Cocaloony Bird.

When the Fräulein returns, she is being viciously attacked by the Bird once again. The Bird chases her into the house and emerges triumphantly with the fish the Fräulein had caught. The Fräulein slowly emerges minutes later, now completely blinded, and begins to rifle through an old scrapbook filled with old clippings from her performing days. She begins to recite from them.

Polly prompts Molly to reveal the Fräulein's entire history, but, before she can begin, a boat whistle is heard again and the Fräulein dashes off, bucket in hand.

Indian Joe reappears from the house, proclaiming that he "feels like a bull," and a lovelorn Polly immediately starts to "moo" and follows him back into the boardinghouse.

### *Scene 2*

The location is the same as in scene 1. The time is several hours later. Polly reappears on the porch in her underwear, "giggling and gasping." Molly takes a photograph of her in this condition to ensure that Polly will run the advertisement in the *Cocaloony Gazette* for her. The two women synchronize their rocking chairs, and Molly relates to Polly the history of the Gnädiges Fräulein's downfall.

When she was younger, the Fräulein performed in a trio with a "Viennese dandy" and a seal. The Fräulein was forced to take second place to the performing talents of the seal and the dandy. She felt the need to prove her worth to the dandy, who nightly gave her an "insincere smile" during the performance. On one occasion, the dandy threw the Fräulein an insincere smile as he threw the seal a fish. The Fräulein, in a bout of spontaneity, jumped into the air and, intercepting the seal, caught the fish between her teeth.

The audience loved her stunt, and as a result the Fräulein received rave reviews and became the prominent member of the trio. The seal and the dandy were not happy with this new arrangement. The seal took revenge by whacking the Fräulein across the face and knocking out her teeth. After this, the Fräulein drifted from place to place until she ended up at Molly's rooming house.

As Molly completes the Fräulein's history, the Fräulein appears, battle-wounded, but with a bucket full of fish. The Fräulein marches into the kitchen and begins to fry the fish for dinner. She appears at the door, calling out, "Toivo?"—which, Molly explains, was the name of the Viennese dandy.

Indian Joe appears, and he, Molly, and Polly sit down to eat. Another fish-boat whistle is heard, and the Fräulein once again dashes toward the docks, bucket in hand.

## COMMENTARY

*The Gnädiges Fräulein* is a powerfully symbolic tale. As are many of Williams's later works, *Fräulein* is a black comedy centered on destitute social outcasts and their fierce fight for survival, dignity, and self-respect.

The wounded and embattled Fräulein, the one-time European singing sensation, is in many ways a victim of her own ambition. Her rise to fame enraged her performing associates (the seal and Toivo, the dandy). To gain Toivo's (and the seal's) respect, the Fräulein jumped for fish; this cycle continues as she is now forced to run for fish to retain her place at Molly's rooming house and, by extension, to impress Polly, the local art critic. Every performer must, on some level, face seemingly insurmountable obstacles to achieve success; the obstacles in the Fräulein's path are literally inhuman. However, she does ultimately defeat the Cocaloony Bird and returns proudly to the rooming house with a bucket full of fish. Her triumphant "Tovio?" at the end of the play is a declaration of independence. She calls to him in an acknowledgment of her victory and survival, as she goes to battle the birds once more. Although she has lost both eyes, she has not lost her voice, her dignity, or her pride.

*The Gnädiges Fräulein* is solidly aligned with other dramas of the THEATER OF THE ABSURD, a quality it shares with numerous later Williams works, such as *THE REMARKABLE ROOMING-HOUSE OF MME. LE MONDE. The Gnädiges Fräulein,* as many works of this dramatic genre do, features grotesque humor and larger-than-life characters who are living in fantastical conditions. The locale of the play, Cocaloony Key, is a horrific landscape where overgrown vicious pelicanlike birds regularly attack the human inhabitants. The set design that Williams calls for is meant to be rendered exclusively in gray-scale coloring, promoting its surreal nightmarish quality. The costumes of all characters, with the exception of the Fräulein, are also meant to be rendered in this "colorless" palette. *The Gnädiges Fräulein* is a highly evocative and imaginative drama. It was Williams's favorite drama of his later period.

## PRODUCTION HISTORY

*The Gnädiges Fräulein* premiered in tandem with THE MUTILATED. The two short plays were produced together under the title *Slapstick Tragedy.* Alan Schneider directed the premiere production in New York in 1966 at the Longacre Theatre.

## PUBLICATION HISTORY

*The Gnädiges Fräulein* was first published in *Esquire* magazine in 1965.

## CHARACTERS

**Cocaloony Bird** The Cocaloony Bird is a vicious creature that torments Molly and Polly and steals fish from the Gnädiges Fräulein.

**Gnädiges Fräulein** The Fräulein is a once-famous European performer who has fallen on hard times. After being attacked by a jealous member of her performing trio, the Fräulein has drifted around the world and has landed at the rooming house owned by Molly. To earn her keep, the Fräulein is forced to compete with the Cocaloony Bird for the fish rejected by the fishing boats. The bird and his fellows viciously and repeatedly attack the Fräulein.

Although they succeed in pecking out her eyes, she continues to return to Molly's house with buckets full of fish.

**Indian Joe** He is a lodger at the boardinghouse owned by Polly. Contrary to the image his name suggests, he has blond hair and blue eyes. He is shapely and athletic, and he rescues Polly and Molly from an attack by the Cocaloony Bird. Indian Joe earns his keep by having a clandestine affair with his lovelorn landlady.

**Molly** She is the landlady of a boardinghouse in Cocaloony Key. Her principal tenant is the Gnädiges Fräulein, a former European singing sensation who has fallen on hard times. Although she admires the Fräulein's tenacity, Molly has little tolerance for free-loaders. She denies the Fräulein "porch and kitchen privileges" and forces her to earn her keep by competing with the Cocaloony Bird for fish rejected by the fishing boats. The Fräulein is reinstated when she successfully takes home a bucket full of fish.

**Permanent Transient** He is a local drunk who resides in the boardinghouse owned by Molly. Because he, and other transients, cannot afford a room with a bed, Molly rents them "Standing Room Only" space in her boardinghouse on weekends.

**Polly** As is her best friend and next-door neighbor, Molly, Polly is the landlady of a boardinghouse in Cocaloony Key. She is also the society page editor of the *Cocaloony Gazette*, and she would very much like to interview Molly's principal tenant, the Gnädiges Fräulein. Polly is smitten with her virile young tenant Indian Joe. Molly uses her knowledge of Polly's clandestine affair with Indian Joe to secure a free advertisement in Polly's column.

# "Grand"

A short piece of nonfiction written around 1964.

## SYNOPSIS

This account chronicles the last days of Williams's beloved maternal grandmother, ROSINA OTTE DAKIN, who died of tuberculosis in 1944. Williams's grandmother, affectionately called Grand, was a selfless, beautiful woman, whom Williams referred to as "a living poem." Throughout his life, Williams credited all of his good qualities to his Grand. He appreciated her constant sacrifices for her husband, WALTER EDWIN DAKIN, and for her family at large.

Although she was an elderly woman, suffering from tuberculosis, she regularly cared for her daughter's young family by cooking and cleaning and was doing so minutes before she died. At the moment of her death, she tried unsuccessfully to communicate to her daughter, EDWINA DAKIN WILLIAMS, that there was money hidden in one of her corsets in her bureau. The piece is focused on Grand's tragic end and the realization of her greatest fear, that of being forced—because of her husband's folly—to live with her daughter's family.

## COMMENTARY

Although published as a short story, "Grand" is technically not a short story. However, regardless of its classification, this biographical account of his grandmother's final days is vibrantly and movingly written. Williams said he wrote the piece "in partial recompense for that immeasurable gift of the spirit that she had so persistently and unsparingly . . . pressed into my hands when I came to her in need" (Leverich, 533–534).

Williams was severely traumatized by his grandmother's fight with tuberculosis. He wrestles with the disease in a number of his works, such as "THE ANGEL IN THE ALCOVE," "ORIFLAMME," and "THE KINGDOM OF EARTH." In several instances the disease itself functions as a menacing or engulfing character. Although many of the characters suffering from the disease ultimately die of it, Williams often romanticizes their deaths, which become ethereal and prove oddly empowering.

## PUBLICATION HISTORY

"Grand" was first published privately by House of Books in 1964. It then appeared in *Esquire* magazine in November 1966. It was subsequently published in two short story collections, *The Knightly Quest and Other Stories* (1966) and *Collected Stories* (1985).

### CHARACTERS

**Grand** Modeled after Williams's grandmother, ROSINA OTTE DAKIN, Grand is the principal subject of this work, which chronicles the tragic death of his beloved grandmother.

### FURTHER READING

Leverich, Lyle. *Tom: The Unknown Tennessee Williams.* New York: W. W. Norton, 1995.

## "Happy August the Tenth"

Short story written in 1970.

### SYNOPSIS

Elphinstone and Horne are best friends, who have shared a small brownstone in New York City for the past 10 years. Horne awakens Elphinstone by shouting, "Happy August the Tenth!" As Elphinstone has not slept well, she is irritated by Horne's playful, yet insensitive intrusion.

The two women bicker all morning about Horne's new "destructive" friends. Horne defends her need to have her own group of friends apart from Elphinstone. Elphinstone feels sorry for herself because her only friends are the women with whom she attended Sarah Lawrence College. Horne implies that Elphinstone thinks she is "too good" to socialize with her new friends. She begs Elphinstone to spend the evening with her and her friends.

As the argument escalates, Horne accidentally spills coffee on Elphinstone's antique white satin love seat. Elphinstone is enraged by the way in which Horne carelessly rubs the delicate material with a wet, rough towel. When she attacks Horne as sloppy and thoughtless, Horne loses her temper: She announces that she can no longer live with Elphinstone and her precious antique furniture. Horne abruptly decides to move out.

Later that afternoon, Elphinstone calls Horne at work. Both apologize for the fight. Elphinstone goes to her therapist and tells him about the fight. He admonishes her to accept that her relationship with Horne has ended. Elphinstone cries, and the doctor concludes their session early. On the way back to their apartment, Elphinstone becomes angry with Horne all over again. She forgets their reconciliation, and when she enters the apartment, she begins to pack the rest of Horne's possessions. She then packs a bag for herself and leaves for Shadow Glade, her mother's country home. She plans to stay at her mother's until Horne has moved out completely.

When Elphinstone arrives at her mother's home, she finds her mother suffering from cardiac asthma. A nurse assists her mother, but Elphinstone fears that her mother is going to die. In this moment, she thinks about her mother's will and speculates that everything will go to her sister. She feels guilty for thinking such thoughts. When her mother recovers from the episode, she and Elphinstone discuss Horne and their fight. Elphinstone's mother questions her daughter's relationship with Horne. Elphinstone quickly dismisses her attachment to Horne. She states that they are merely two professional women sharing a home in the city, and nothing more.

As her mother falls asleep, Elphinstone continues to ponder her mother's question and has a sudden change of heart. She quickly returns to the city in the hope of surprising Horne and her bohemian friends. When Elphinstone enters the apartment, she does not find any visitors, or mayhem, just Horne asleep on the love seat. Elphinstone realizes fully that she is indeed in love with Horne and loves her very much. Elphinstone crouches down and places her head on Horne's slender knees. Elphinstone hugs Horne's legs and whispers, "Happy August the Eleventh."

### COMMENTARY

"Happy August the Tenth" is one of Williams's finest pieces of short fiction. It is also his most candid treatment of same-sex attraction and desire between women. Unlike his rather explicit and often graphic treatment of other romantic relationships, his depiction of lesbian desire is presented tenderly and with very limited physical expressions of love. However subdued their physical expression may be, Elphinstone and Horne's emotional connection and romantic attachment are solidly evident in this beautifully written story.

Although their relationship is presented without the steamy sensuality of others in the Williams canon, Elphinstone and Horne's relationship is notably one of the few featured in Williams's work that is nurturing and loving and ends happily. Love between women is also at the center of the play SOMETHING UNSPOKEN and a feature of A LOVELY SUNDAY FOR CREVE COEUR. Donald Spoto believes that the two lovers in "Happy August the Tenth" were modeled on Williams and his partner, FRANK MERLO.

Donald Spoto sees the "hard and somewhat bitter" Elphinstone as a "stand-in" for Williams and the slightly "emotionally distant" Horne as a variation of Frank (Spoto, 294). Spoto declares the story a "gentle tribute" (ibid.) to Williams's relationship with Merlo.

### PUBLICATION HISTORY

"Happy August the Tenth" was first published in *Antaeus* in 1971. It was reprinted in *The Best American Short Stories of 1973* and *Esquire* magazine (1973). It was included in a collection of short stories called *EIGHT MORTAL LADIES POSSESSED* (1974).

### CHARACTERS

**Elphinstone** Elphinstone is Horne's best friend and roommate. She and Horne have shared a brownstone apartment in Manhattan for 10 years. A graduate of Sarah Lawrence College, Elphinstone is a genealogist. She is obsessed with antiques, her mother's china, and her genealogical study. Fighting depression because she is sleep-deprived, Elphinstone is irritable and relies on Horne for emotional stability. The two women bicker constantly, until they realize they are in love with one another and need each other for comfort and support.

**Horne** Horne is an intellectual young woman who shares an apartment in Manhattan with Elphinstone. When Horne befriends a group of bohemians, Elphinstone feels excluded and becomes jealous. The two women argue over this issue ferociously, and Horne decides to move out. She returns to the apartment to collect her possessions and discovers that she cannot leave Elphinstone behind. Through their argument the two women discover that they are actually in love and depend on each other immensely.

### FURTHER READING

Spoto, Donald. *The Kindness of Strangers: The Life of Tennessee Williams*. Boston: Little, Brown, 1985.

## "Hard Candy"

Short story written in 1953.

### SYNOPSIS

Mr. Krupper is an elderly man living in a seaport town in the U.S. South. He is the owner of a sweet shop; when he retires, he subleases his business to a distant relative and his family. The Cousin has an overweight 12-year-old daughter, whom Mr. Krupper refers to as the "Complete Little Citizen of the World." Mr. Krupper visits the sweet shop every morning, and the cousin and his family detest these visits. During his visits, Mr. Krupper helps himself freely to the candy stock. He loads his pockets with candy, which he says is for feeding birds. The cousin, who is struggling to make a living from the little shop, resents the old man's frivolity. Unknown to his relatives, Mr. Krupper is leading a double life. Every day after his routine visit to the sweet shop, he rides a streetcar to a nearby town, dons dark sunglasses, and enters a dilapidated old cinema called the Joy Rio. He wearily climbs the large stairwell to the second balcony and has sexual relations with anonymous homeless young men. Mr. Krupper entices the young men to join him by offering them candy and a handful of quarters.

On this particular day, Mr. Krupper discovers a beautiful Spanish youth in the balcony. He is the most handsome of all of the young men waiting in the balcony. In the flashing shadows of the movie screen, Mr. Krupper finds monumental pleasure with this youth. Several hours pass and when the lights finally go up in the theater, Mr. Krupper's body is discovered in the balcony alone. He has died, his body in a kneeling position, with sticky candy wrappers clinging to his pants and shirt. When his obituary appears in the newspaper, his cousins are elated. Mr. Krupper's anonymous activities are not disclosed in the death notice; however, the candy wrappers are mentioned in the newspaper. The Complete Little Citizen of the World delightedly comments, "Just think, Papa, the old man choked to death on our hard candy!"

## COMMENTARY

"Hard Candy" is considered by many to be one of Williams's most accomplished pieces of fiction. It is a revision of an earlier short story, "THE MYSTERIES OF THE JOY RIO," and as is its predecessor, it is focused on a defeated individual battling loneliness and isolation. In both stories, Williams illustrates the perpetual quest and fundamental need for compassion and companionship.

Although Williams retains the "bleak landscape" (Sklepowich, 531) of the Joy Rio movie house as a setting, and both stories conclude with the death of their respective protagonists, his narrative style differs considerably in the two stories. In "Hard Candy" Williams withholds the Gothic and fantastical elements found in "The Mysteries of the Joy Rio" and incorporates a more realistic and naturalistic tone. Although "Hard Candy" has been largely dismissed as merely a reworking of "The Mysteries of the Joy Rio," in many ways that story surpasses its predecessor as a "more controlled, realistic and aesthetically effective" narrative (Sklepowich, 532).

Williams's greatest achievements in this story lie in his skill for investing "the sordid with the meaningful, even with a touch of the transcendent or compensatory" (Sklepowich, 531), and his ability to humanize Mr. Krupper, "a character who could easily be sensationalized or caricatured" (Summers, 148). Recent critical reevaluation has validated "Hard Candy," "The Mysteries of the Joy Rio," and "TWO ON A PARTY," previously shunned as torrid tales, as "strong and healthy contributions to the literature of compassion" and as examples of "the most significant gay fictions of their time" (Summers, 133–134).

## PUBLICATION HISTORY

"Hard Candy" was first published in the short story collection *Hard Candy: A Book of Stories* in 1954, and subsequently in short story collections: *The Kingdom of Earth with Hard Candy,* (1954) and *Collected Stories* (1985).

## CHARACTERS

**Complete Little Citizen of the World** The Complete Little Citizen is the 12-year-old daughter of a sweet shop owner, who is continually taunted by her distant relative, Mr. Krupper. She is overweight and becoming larger. Mr. Krupper, a grouchy 70-year-old man, gives her this nickname because she is overweight. The young girl cannot stop eating the hard candy in her parents' shop, and when she is punished for eating it, she finds ways to smuggle the candy out and eat it when no one is looking. The Complete Little Citizen of the World is happy when she sees Mr. Krupper's obituary in the newspaper.

**Cousins** They are the relatives of Mr. Krupper and the heirs to his sweet shop.

**Krupper, Mr.** Mr. Krupper is a 70-year-old man who is emotionally remote from his family. He is unable to relinquish control of the sweet shop he ran for nearly 50 years, even after he has sublet the business to distant relatives. Mr. Krupper's secret passion is to commune with young male prostitutes in the dark balcony of the Joy Rio, a dilapidated cinema in a nearby town. Mr. Krupper dies there and is eventually found in a kneeling position with candy wrappers stuck to his pants and shirt. The distant relatives, including The Complete Little Citizen of the World, are relieved and elated the old man has finally died. They presume he choked on a piece of hard candy that he stole from their shop.

## FURTHER READING

Sklepowich, Edward A. "In Pursuit of the Lyric Quarry: The Image of the Homosexual in Tennessee Williams's Prose Fiction," in *Tennessee Williams: A Tribute*, edited by Jac Tharpe. Jackson: University Press of Mississippi, 1977, pp. 525–544.

Summer, Claude J. *Gay Fictions: Wilde to Stonewall—Studies in a Male Homosexual Literary Tradition.* New York: Continuum, 1990.

# *Hello from Bertha*

One-act play written in 1941.

## SYNOPSIS

The play takes place in a shabby room in a cheap Saint Louis brothel. Bertha, a large blonde prostitute, lies on her bed. She is deathly ill and intoxicated. Her landlady, Goldie, urges her either to seek help from her former lover, Charlie, or go to a convent. Goldie is tired of Bertha and wants her out of the brothel. Goldie suggests that Bertha write a letter to Charlie, but Bertha replies that she would only send him a postcard saying, "Hello from Bertha to Charlie, with all her love." The two women argue and Goldie threatens to call an ambulance. Bertha threatens to call the police, as she believes Goldie has been stealing money from her. Goldie leaves Bertha alone in her room. Bertha talks to herself in private and cries about her ailing health, her life, her fading looks, and the loss of Charlie.

Lena enters Bertha's room and tries to console her. Lena helps Bertha pack a few of her belongings before Goldie returns. There is an ambulance waiting outside for her, and Bertha reluctantly agrees to go. She asks Lena to write to Charlie for her, requesting his help. Bertha quickly changes her mind; she instructs Lena to send him a postcard instead, saying, "Hello from Bertha, with all her love." Lena is called for and leaves Bertha alone; Bertha repeats, "With all her love."

## COMMENTARY

As are many of Williams's early one-act plays, *Hello from Bertha* is a "lyrical revelation of character and situation" (Boxhill, 59). The painful solitude of Bertha's swansong is bittersweet. There is an obvious similarity between Bertha and Blanche Dubois of *A STREETCAR NAMED DESIRE* as two aging beauties who reminisce and lament that which has passed. Bertha is, however, an engaging study in her own right. There is something noble in her resolve and acceptance of her fate. Instead of giving in to the repeated suggestion that she plead with Charlie to rescue her, Bertha accepts responsibility for her life and the choices she has made.

Although some view Williams's one-act plays, particularly his earlier efforts, as merely short studies for the major characters and themes he would later develop, these brief sketches should not be so quickly dismissed. These plays hold a significant place in the Williams canon and feature the same dramatic force that can be found in his longer dramas. Williams's one-act plays reveal him as a master of precision and economy.

## PRODUCTION HISTORY

*Hello from Bertha* was produced for television on the PBS-TV program "Play of the Week: Four Plays by Tennessee" in 1961.

## PUBLICATION HISTORY

The play was published in the one-act-play collection *27 WAGONS FULL OF COTTON AND OTHER ONE ACT PLAYS* in 1953.

## CHARACTERS

**Bertha** She is a prostitute who has an unstated illness and is being sent to a hospital. Bertha strives to be completely independent. However, she laments the loss of her old lover, Charlie.

**Girl** She is Bertha's friend, who cares for her when she is sick. She enters late in the play and serves as a symbol of lost childhood.

**Goldie** Goldie is Bertha's landlady. She runs the brothel where Bertha lives. Goldie cares for Bertha when she is sick. Bertha accuses her of stealing money from her, but it is not confirmed that Goldie does. Eager to have Bertha situated elsewhere, Goldie pressures Bertha to call her former lover, Charlie, or go to a convent.

**Lena** Lena is a fellow prostitute and a friend of Bertha. She tries to support Bertha through her illness. Lena helps Bertha to pack her belongings before she goes to the hospital. Before she leaves, Bertha asks Lena to write a letter to her former lover, Charlie.

### FURTHER READING

Boxhill, Roger. *Tennessee Williams.* New York: Macmillan, 1988.

## *Hot Milk at Three in the Morning*

A one-act play written around 1930. Written while Williams was a student at the UNIVERSITY OF MISSOURI, Columbia, the play was a submission for the 1931–32 university play competition. Williams won an honorable mention for the work. The play, about a discontented factory worker, his wife, and their month-old child, was subsequently revised and retitled *MOONY'S KID DON'T CRY.*

## *I Can't Imagine Tomorrow*

A one-act play written in 1966.

### SYNOPSIS

The action of the play takes place in the home of One, a middle-aged woman. Her home is not realistically presented. The actors mime action involving doors and windows. The location and the period are not specified.

One, and her male friend, Two, repeat a scene that they relive each day. One watches from a window as Two arrives at her door. He stands before the door and raises his arm as if he will knock. He knocks, and One opens the door. She states, "Oh, it's you." He responds "Yes, it's me." This is a part of the ritual they perform. One has grown weary of this senseless, empty daily routine. Although she demands a change in their relationship ("Something or nothing"), their situation remains unaltered. One and Two bicker and try unsuccessfully to invent new forms of communication and connection for themselves. They try writing messages to each other rather then speaking, but this also proves unfulfilling.

Two professes his love for One. One expresses her frustration and disdain ("I don't have the strength anymore to try to make you try to save yourself from your paralyzing—depression! Why don't you stop looking like a middle-aged lost little boy?"). One tries to end the visit; Two begs her to let him stay on her sofa. They try to complete a game of cards.

### COMMENTARY

About his dramaturgy Williams once stated: "A somber play has to be very spare and angular . . . you must keep the lines sharp and clean—tragedy is austere" (*Remember Me to Tom,* 134). This comment is an adequate assessment of his gripping late play *I Can't Imagine Tomorrow:* Sharp, spare, angular, and austere, it is a tragedy of the human condition that bears "a nod towards Absurdism with its depiction of [human] inability to communicate" (Grecco, 586).

Reminiscent of many later Williams dramas (such as *FROSTED GLASS COFFIN* and *NOW THE CATS WITH JEWELLED CLAWS*) and other works of the THEATER OF THE ABSURD, this play features two unnamed protagonists who grapple in a desolate void to form some semblance of human connection. They perform their mindless daily ritual to avoid the "intolerable silence" that surrounds them. Their disjointed dialogue is a verbal manifestation of their helplessness and isolation. In this play Williams uses the "dialogue of pathos" (Cohn, 45) to expose "the bruised individual soul and its life of 'quiet desperation'" (ibid).

### PRODUCTION HISTORY

*I Can't Imagine Tomorrow* was first produced for television in 1970. Glenn Jordan directed Kim Stanley as One and William Redfield as Two for PBS-TV. The first stage production was in Bar Harbor, Maine, in 1971.

### PUBLICATION HISTORY

*I Can't Imagine Tomorrow* was first published in *Esquire* magazine (March 1966).

### CHARACTERS

**One** She is a middle-aged woman who lives alone. Her only friend and companion is a middle-aged man, named Two. He visits her daily and they engage in routine conversation and card games. One is desperate for change. She has grown weary of the senseless, empty ritual they perform.

**Two** He is a pathologically shy middle-aged schoolteacher. His only friend and companion is a middle-aged woman, One, whom he visits daily. She is the only person with whom he can speak. However, even with her, his speech is severely impaired and disjointed.

### FURTHER READING

Cohn, Ruby. "The Garrulous Grotesques of Tennessee Williams," in *Tennessee Williams—a Collection of Critical Essays,* edited by Stephen Stanton. Englewood Cliffs, N.J.: Prentice-Hall, 1977, pp. 45–60.

Grecco, Stephen. "World Literature in Review: English," *World Literature Today* 69, no. 3 (summer 1995): 586–591.

Williams, Edwina Dakin, with Lucy Freeman. *Remember Me to Tom.* New York: G. P. Putnam's Sons, 1964, p. 134.

## "The Important Thing"

Short story written in 1945.

### SYNOPSIS

A young writer, John, attends the spring dance given by the Baptist College for Women. When he becomes bored and tries to leave the dance, he is stopped by one of the teachers, referred to as "the Harpy." The teacher forces him to dance with Flora. Flora recognizes that both she and John are uncomfortable in the environment of the dance. John suggests they venture outside. They go outside and smoke cigarettes in the oak grove. They sneak into the college chapel and talk about religion, agnosticism, and the concept of guilt. They delightedly discover that they are both writers.

They discuss the craft of writing and Flora stresses the supremacy of honesty and personal integrity over style. John and Flora return to the gymnasium where the dance is being held but do not venture back inside. They remain outside watching the dance and the dancers through the windows. Flora declares that she is seeking "the important thing," in life and that writing is the means by which she will find it.

John encounters Flora again at the start of the new school year. She has transferred from the Baptist College to State University, where John is also a student. While speaking together, John is embarrassed, as he notices other girls making funny of Flora. Their mockery enrages John but is unnoticed by Flora. She proudly acknowledges that she is different from the other students and refuses to compromise or conform. She declares herself a "barbarian," and John is inspired by her defiance. He is happy to have found a kindred spirit. Flora encourages him to submit the play he has just written to a competition. Over the next several months the two become inseparable. They both write for the university literary journal and join the Poetry Club, the French Club, and the Young Communists League. John becomes a zealous radical and is nearly expelled from the university for protesting fraternities and academic conservatism. Although John and Flora seem to be soul mates, they find that there is uneasiness between them, awkwardness in the lulls of conversations.

By the spring, John's life changes dramatically. Conforming more to his environment, he joins a fraternity, buys a car, and starts to become perturbed by Flora's reluctance to adapt. She has developed a reputation on the campus as an odd and eccentric character. John's fraternity brothers ridicule him for his relationship with such a "queer" person as Flora. John begins to resent that Flora does not attempt to modify her behavior or make herself more socially acceptable. Flora and John frequently picnic in the country and spend afternoons studying and discussing civilization, art, and literature.

On one such occasion, John brings wine, although he knows that Flora does not drink. As they study for their upcoming French examination, John drinks the wine, while Flora quizzes him. John becomes intoxicated as the sun beats down upon them. Flora becomes agitated that John is inebriated; her reaction and the look on her face remind John of a child he once knew in grammar school, named Peekie. Peekie was an effeminate little boy who was regularly mistreated by the older boys at John's school. John recalled that something in Peekie's demeanor caused the bigger boys to mock him and feel the need to abuse him physically. In that moment, John feels a similar urge to harm

Flora. He suddenly grabs her thighs, but she rejects his advances and pushes him away. John becomes more aggressive, and a violent struggle ensues. They claw at each other and wrestle in the grass "like two wild animals." Flora fights to free herself, but John knees her in the stomach to make her lie still. He overpowers her and forces himself on her.

Flora whimpers when John tells her that he is finished and that he will not hurt her again. John stands and observes the university town in the distance. His face is bleeding where Flora has scratched him. He becomes angry and confused. He imagines the happy couples dancing, laughing, and whispering at the parties that are taking place all over town. These are the "natural celebrations of youth," but John realizes that he and Flora are each destined for "something else . . . outside the common experience." John declares that he and Flora were only deluding themselves to think that they were a couple, as the others are. John observes Flora, looking at her as if for the first time, and sees that she is completely unattractive. He ponders her intensity, her strangeness, her "anonymous" gender and realizes how much of an outsider she truly is. As he speaks her name and helps her to her feet, the fear and awkwardness between them have subsided. However, their intimacy has also revealed to them the important knowledge that each of them shall remain an outsider in the world, individual and alone.

## COMMENTARY

As is the short story "THE FIELD OF BLUE CHILDREN," "The Important Thing" is centered on the struggle against convention and the plight of the writer. Both stories involve two college students at a midwestern university, who are writers in search of artistic and personal fulfillment. Both stories also focus on the act of writing and the intensely passionate, though solitary nature of the craft.

In "The Field of Blue Children" Myra dallies with nonconformity and unconventional possibilities but ultimately chooses to conform to societal expectations, although she fondly regrets the bohemian life she could have led with Homer Stallcup. In "The Important Thing" the battle against conformity takes on new dimensions. Flora, whose name means "flower" and is a reference to nature, is the embodiment of nonconformity. Her passionate, eccentric demeanor and her "queerness" are what made her initially attractive to John. However, as Myra does in "The Field of Blue Children," John chooses conformity over difference. Unlike Myra's, his choice is reluctant. He is nudged by his society to be more like his fellows. The primary signifier of his acquiescence is his sudden membership in a fraternity, the traditional brotherhood he had previously vehemently disdained and openly fought.

Once John modifies his behavior, Flora begins to represent something wild that must be physically subdued and tamed. In "taming" Flora, John uncovers a part of himself that cannot be tamed or suppressed—his attraction to and desire for other men. His sexual orientation is implied throughout the piece, as is Flora's. Repeatedly John refers to her as "queer," and after his sexual assault of her, John is immediately cognizant of Flora's sexual ambiguity, or her "gender anonymity." John sees himself and his own "nature" reflected in Flora. She becomes a "repository of certain repellent qualities which [John] would like to disavow" (Haskell, 244). John projects onto Flora all that he fears is developing and surfacing inside himself, particularly his sexuality, eccentricity, and marginalization. John's lust for Flora is laced with self-hatred and fear of self-exposure. John uses Flora to relieve his isolation and sexual confusion. He tries to build a bridge to conformity through their physical act.

Conformity within this context is an issue of a heterosexual mandate that is vividly illustrated at the beginning of the story when the Harpy physically coerces John to dance with Flora. His violent attempt at conforming to heterosexual expectation leaves John feeling empty, enraged, and disgusted. His isolation and his true nature remain. John's assault on Flora, as that of Stanley Kowalski against Blanche Dubois in *A STREETCAR NAMED DESIRE*, can be viewed as "the ravishment of the tender, the sensitive, the delicate, by the savage and brutal forces of modern society" (Haskell, 230). The rape serves as a brutal awakening for both Flora and John. Although it relieves the physical tension that existed between them, it shatters the delicate bond of their friendship and serves only to isolate them further as individuals. This violent episode is a crucial moment in their development.

Unlike John, Flora had completely accepted her sexual identity and embraced her (and John's) "difference" from others in regard to "human relationships." The values she holds dear are honesty and personal integrity. The "important thing" that they have each discovered is the acceptance of one's true nature and marginality. "The Important Thing" is one of Williams's most engaging and complex works of fiction.

## PUBLICATION HISTORY

"The Important Thing" was first published in the collection of short stories *One Arm* in 1948. It is also included in *Collected Stories,* published in 1985.

## PRODUCTION HISTORY

"The Important Thing" was adapted for the screen by Anne Borin for Anne Borin Productions in 1980. Borin directed and produced the film, which featured Mark Kaplan and Jackie Jacobus as John and Flora.

## CHARACTERS

**Flora** Flora is an intelligent young woman who is attending an all-female Baptist college. As she is extremely bored by her education, writing and the philosophy of writing dominates her thoughts. Flora prides herself on being a freethinker, and a woman uninhibited by religious moral codes or gender roles. She is radical in her beliefs and finds a companion in John, a like-minded young man. Her relationship with John is intense and awkward. He, too, is a writer and an intellectual. They spend many hours together talking. Flora is overwhelmed by John's sexual longings. There is an altercation while they are alone on a picnic. John sexually assaults her, and she claws and fights to free herself. Her dedicated pursuit of the "important thing" in life comes full circle as she realizes there is no kind of intimacy that will make her feel less of a stranger in the world.

**John** John is a college student at a midwestern university. He is a young writer who is absorbed by his writing and the philosophy of writing. John meets and befriends Flora, another young writer, at a college dance. He is overwhelmed by Flora's radical thoughts and eccentric behavior. Although initially drawn to Flora because of her uniqueness, John grows weary of her unwillingness to conform. In her nonconformity John sees his own difference and natural tendencies, which he hopes to suppress. During a picnic in the country with Flora, John acts on his frustrations and rapes her. Afterward, John and Flora are left in quiet desperation with the knowledge that they are equally isolated from society.

## FURTHER READING

Haskell, Molly. *From Reverence to Rape: The Treatment of Women in the Movies.* Chicago: University of Chicago Press, 1987.

# "In Memory of an Aristocrat"

Short story written in 1940.

## SYNOPSIS

The Narrator and his friend, Carl, are penniless and living in New Orleans. They visit their artist friend, Irene, who sustains herself by prostitution. The three of them lie on a bed together, talk, and smoke cigarettes. Carl is passionately attracted to Irene, but he has no money to pay her for sex. While they fight, the Narrator helps himself to a bowl of stew. When Carl and Irene make up, she tells the two men they have to leave because she has to work.

A couple of weeks later, there is the Annual Spring Display of Paintings in New Orleans. It is a highly exclusive event, to which Irene anxiously submits 10 of her best paintings. When she is informed that her paintings have been rejected and are going to be burned by the police for their indecent themes, she becomes enraged. At the exhibit, Irene collects her paintings from the storeroom. She starts a riot in the gallery and is arrested.

The Narrator and another friend leave New Orleans for Hollywood. The Narrator begins to write screenplays, and runs into Carl, who says

Irene left New Orleans, too. However, he has no idea where she resides.

## COMMENTARY

As are Tom Wingfield in *THE GLASS MENAGERIE*, Sebastian Venable in *SUDDENLY LAST SUMMER*, and Matilda Rockley in *YOU TOUCHED ME!*, the Narrator in this story is a struggling writer. He attaches himself to colorful (and shady) characters in order to feed his imagination. As is Irene, the Narrator is an ambitious artist.

"In Memory of an Aristocrat" details the difficult and often tragic existence of the artist. Irene's artwork is rejected because she supplements her creative endeavors and supports herself with prostitution. Her New Orleans peers are hypocritical, as they participate in the debauchery of Mardi Gras but do not accept innovative paintings from a "whore." Irene's story is open-ended, as neither the Narrator nor Carl know what has become of her. In his introduction to CARSON MCCULLERS's novel *Reflections in a Golden Eye* (1950), Williams writes, "Of course there are those who are not practicing artists and those who have not been committed to asylums, but who have enough of one or both magical elements, lunacy and vision, to permit them also to slip sufficiently apart from 'this so-called world of ours.'" Irene is one such example of the artist who dares to slip through the liminal space of social margins to live in order to create. She loses her composure when her artistic vision collides with censorship.

## PUBLICATION HISTORY

"In Memory of an Aristocrat" was published in *Collected Stories*, in 1985.

## CHARACTERS

**Carl** He is a professional thief operating in the French Quarter of New Orleans. Carl is the friend of the Narrator and Irene. He has a crush on Irene, a prostitute, but does not have money to pay her for sex.

**Irene** Irene is a painter who supplements her income by engaging in prostitution. She has had a very rough life, which has included severe physical abuse. Irene left New York City in search of a new start in New Orleans.

**Narrator** He is the friend of Carl, a thief, and Irene, an artist who is also prostitute. The Narrator is an observant young man whose life becomes a bohemian adventure with Carl and Irene. He exemplifies the plight of the artist living in New Orleans.

# "The Interval"

A short story written in 1945.

## SYNOPSIS

Two Iowa schoolteachers, Gretchen and Augusta, take a summer road trip to Hollywood, California. Augusta bullies Gretchen into covering all of their vacation expenses. Gretchen is too polite to complain. Instead, she remains silent and sulks. Augusta chastises Gretchen for being moody and miserable, thus pushing her further into silence. Gretchen plots ways to get away from her friend, until Augusta meets Carl Zerbst. Carl claims he knows Cary Grant and can introduce the young women to various Hollywood stars. Carl turns out to be a liar, and instead of meeting stars, he and Augusta drive around in a borrowed flashy convertible roadster. Carl and Augusta abandon Gretchen to sit alone on the beach or in the rented tourist cabin. On the few occasions when Gretchen encounters Augusta, Augusta uses the situation as an opportunity to degrade Gretchen. Gretchen is left feeling unwanted, unattractive, and undesirable.

One day on the beach, Gretchen meets Jimmie, a handsome young actor. Jimmie spies Gretchen walking alone on the beach and starts a conversation with her. Gretchen is delighted to have found companionship, and her self-confidence begins to flourish because of Jimmie's attention. Jimmie is uncertain and uncomfortable around women but feels safe with Gretchen. The two swim together and find their bodies entwined as popular love songs play on a nearby radio.

The couple marry and remain in Hollywood. Gretchen works as a private tutor for Hollywood children, while Jimmie continues to pursue his acting career. Jimmie loses interest in Gretchen and has an affair with Bobby, a fellow film actor and a rising star. When their affair becomes public, Bobby and Jimmie are dismissed from the studio; both men are disgraced and never work in Hollywood again. Gretchen ignores the incident and does not question Jimmie about it. Bobby is forced to move in with Jimmie and Gretchen when he is evicted from the Beverly Wilshire Hotel. Gretchen is so enamored of Jimmie that she welcomes Bobby into their apartment and occasionally into their bed.

Just as World War II begins, Jimmie and Gretchen leave California and move to Dubuque, Iowa. Jimmie avoids the draft because of his temperament and gets a job at a defense plant. Jimmie and Gretchen hold on to their faith that he has talent and will one day be a famous actor. Jimmie becomes disheartened by his life at the defense plant, where his coworkers call him "Piggy." Jimmie is rescued by a telegram from Bobby summoning him to New York. Jimmie packs and leaves immediately without Gretchen. He telegrams her frequently.

Gretchen discovers she is pregnant but has no way of contacting her husband. She receives another enthusiastic telegram and promptly packs her bags, anticipating her summons to New York. The next telegram she receives presents a grim outlook and delays her departure indefinitely. Gretchen travels to New York despite the telegram. Jimmie meets her at the train station, and they cry together joyfully when Gretchen gives him the news of her pregnancy. Bobby is very accommodating and gives the couple his apartment. He moves into the apartment next door with a bachelor friend. Gretchen is impressed by Bobby's apartment and Jimmie's "up-and-coming" Broadway friends.

Late one evening, during Gretchen's second week in New York, Bobby's friend the bachelor barges into the apartment calling out to her and making accusations about Jimmie and Bobby. Bobby and Jimmie physically restrain the bachelor and remove him from the apartment. Gretchen is stunned but refuses to believe the bachelor's claims. Jimmie, Bobby, and Gretchen discuss the situation and decide it would be best for her to return to Iowa and have the baby there. Gretchen returns to Iowa, has the child, and returns to teaching. She leads a very quiet life but hopes for more. She maintains her faith in Jimmie, trusting in his innate goodness. Gretchen romanticizes her memories of him and hopes that her beautiful son will be just like his father. Jimmie sends Gretchen a final, apologetic postcard advising her to forget him.

## COMMENTARY

In this engaging short story, Williams masterfully explores many of his principal themes: the sadness of defeated relationships, the deceptions of love and sexuality, homosexuality and the pressures of heterosexual society, the shattering of dreams, the indefatigable specter of old age, and the loss of youthful beauty.

At the center of this tale is another compelling female Williams character. Gretchen, the loyal, naive schoolteacher, is a kindred spirit of fellow teachers Jenny Starling (*ALL GAUL IS DIVIDED*), Dorothea Galloway (*A LOVELY SUNDAY FOR CREVE COEUR*), and Blanche Dubois (*A STREETCAR NAMED DESIRE*). Gretchen is also an early prototype of the "abused wife" (Kolin, 26) who appears throughout the Williams canon, such as Stella Kowalski in *A Streetcar Named Desire*.

Gretchen is also reminiscent of the character Nina Leeds in EUGENE O'NEILL's play *Strange Interlude*. As Nina does, Gretchen drifts mindlessly into a marriage of convenience and finds happiness in submission to her husband's wishes and to the fulfillment of his dreams. Gretchen's interval or "strange interlude" with Jimmie is an awakening, which leaves her with a "hunger for more than a routine comfort." Although she has experienced the dazzling, romantic glamour of Hollywood and New York with Jimmie, Gretchen is left, as are Amanda Wingfield and so many of Williams's women, with only her memories of the beautiful boy who deserted her. All that remains are the final resignation and acceptance of the life that is available to her.

Scholars and critics have unjustly neglected "The Interval." This work demonstrates Williams's ability as a writer to reveal "the secrets of the human race, and deepest truths about ourselves" (Burnett, 4). This sensitivity permeates Williams's work as his art originates in such an intimate and deeply personal place. Philip Kolin reads "The Interval" as a self-reflective "fictional record" of Williams's "dreams, fears and defeats in the world of 'terrible glamour'" (Kolin, 21).

## PUBLICATION HISTORY

"The Interval" was first published by New Direction in 1985 in the short story anthology *Collected Stories.*

## CHARACTERS

**Augusta** Augusta is an exuberant and adventuresome schoolteacher from Iowa. She travels to Hollywood, California, with her friend, Gretchen, a naive fellow teacher. Augusta dominates the friendship with Gretchen. She bullies her into covering their expenses during their vacation, and she cruelly shatters Gretchen's self-esteem. When Augusta meets the flashy, smooth-talking Carl Zerbst, she quickly abandons Gretchen. Carl convinces the star-struck Augusta that he can introduce her to Cary Grant and other glamorous Hollywood stars.

**Bobby** Bobby is a Hollywood film actor who becomes romantically involved with Jimmie, a fellow actor. When their affair is publicly exposed, Bobby is fired by the studio and loses his "near-royalty of Hollywood" status. He is never again offered roles in motion pictures. He takes to drinking and is evicted from his apartment in the Beverly Wilshire Hotel. After the eviction, Bobby moves in with Jimmie and his wife, Gretchen. Because Gretchen is so enamored of Jimmie, she tolerates Bobby's presence in their apartment. She feels only "sorrow and perplexity" toward him. Bobby moves to pursue his acting career in New York City. He sends Jimmie a telegram inviting him to join him in New York. Jimmie leaves Gretchen and follows Bobby to New York to become an actor on Broadway.

**Gretchen** Gretchen is a naive schoolteacher from Iowa. She is a quiet, contemplative young woman, who is easily manipulated by her friend, Augusta. When she and Augusta travel to Hollywood, California, Augusta intimidates Gretchen to cover all of their expenses. Gretchen fulfills Augusta's needs until she can find something better. Augusta is easily impressed by Carl Zerbst, a smooth-talking local man who says he can introduce Augusta and Gretchen to various Hollywood stars. Having found Carl, Augusta abandons Gretchen. Gretchen meets Jimmie, a hopeful actor, and the two marry. When Jimmie's acting career and male lover, Bobby, take him away from her, Gretchen remains loyal to him.

**Jimmie** Jimmie is a young actor living in California, pursuing his dream of a Hollywood film career. He regularly has small roles in films. When he is not acting, he spends much of his time on the beach. Jimmie meets Gretchen on the beach, immediately feels comfortable around her. Ignoring the fact that he is gay, Jimmie and Gretchen marry. When his sexuality becomes public knowledge, Jimmie is shut out of the film industry and he and Gretchen move to Iowa. Ultimately, he becomes discontented with his life in Iowa. He abandons Gretchen for a career on Broadway and a life with his lover, Bobby.

## FURTHER READING


Burnett, Hallie. *On Writing the Short Story.* New York: Harper & Row, 1983.

Kolin, Philip. "Tennessee Williams's 'Interval': MGM and Beyond," *The Southern Quarterly* 38, no. 1 (fall 1999): 21–27.


# *In the Bar of a Tokyo Hotel*

A one-act play in two parts written in the mid- to late 1960s.

## SYNOPSIS

The action of the play takes place in the bar of a Japanese hotel.

### *Part 1*

Miriam Conley sits at the bar making friendly conversation with the young Barman. She flirts with him and he graciously tries to avoid her attention. Miriam drafts a telegram to Leonard Frisbie demanding that he fly to Tokyo immediately to assist her with her husband, Mark Conley. Mark enters the bar, dazed, disheveled, and incoherent.

He tries to discuss his art and painting with Miriam, but she orders him to return to his room. Miriam reveals that she wants a separation and advises Mark to fly back to New York. Their tempers flare and a heated argument ensues. Mark physically attacks Miriam and throws her out of the bar.

*Part 2*

In the same location as part 1, Miriam flirts with the Barman. The Hawaiian Lady enters the bar and Miriam makes a joke about her. As Miriam tries to order a drink, the Barman informs her that the bar is closed. She strikes up a conversation with him about sightseeing in Kyoto in order to keep him engaged.

Leonard arrives at the bar, and he and Miriam argue about Mark. Mark appears and Leonard observes that he has cut his face shaving. Miriam tries to convince Leonard to take Mark back to New York. Mark interrupts their discussion; he is breathless and on the verge of collapse. He confronts Miriam about her intention to ship him off and she admits that she would like him to leave. Mark accuses her of adultery and announces that he is very tired. Shortly thereafter, Mark collapses and dies. The Barman and Leonard remove Mark's body from the bar. Miriam expresses her relief and feeling of being released by Mark's death. Leonard attacks her and warns her not to show any happiness. He questions Miriam about her future plans, and she reveals that she has none. Miriam suddenly becomes distraught and throws her bracelets to the floor.

## COMMENTARY

*In the Bar of a Tokyo Hotel* is possibly the most misinterpreted of all of Williams's dramatic works. The initial critical reception of the play was overwhelmingly and scathingly negative. In his review of the play, Clive Barnes labeled it as Williams's "sad bird of loneliness" (Barnes, 54). Henry Hewes viewed the play as an expression of "Williams's agony both at the difficult process of artistic creation and at the specter of old age, waning sexual magnetism, and death" (Hewes, 18).

Because the play was written in the mid- to late 1960s, critics assumed that it was largely autobiographical and reflective of Williams's own artistic frustrations and his personal struggles with depression and chemical dependency. Critics failed to see that the artist at the center of the play, Mark Conley, was not a Williams self-portrait, but rather a sketch of the legendary American artist, JACKSON POLLOCK.

Mark Conley shares many aspects of Pollock's tormented life, such as his frustrated genius, alcoholism, sexual anxieties, sensitivity, rage, and slow descent into madness. Mark and Miriam's volatile relationship in many ways mirrors Pollock's turbulent, and often abusive, marriage to fellow-artist Lee Krasner. Mark's interactive painting technique of being physically engaged with a horizontal canvas is the most revealing signifier that he is Pollock. Williams places himself in the drama within the character of Leonard Frisbie, the art dealer who understands and cares for Mark in a way that Miriam cannot. The triangle of Leonard, Mark, and Miriam is a heightened variation on Williams's relationship with Pollock and Krasner. Williams and Pollock shared a bond as kindred spirits and had a playful friendship. Krasner deeply resented Pollock and Williams's relationship. On one occasion she barred Williams from her studio.

Williams greatly admired Pollock and believed that he could "paint ecstasy as it could not be written" (*Memoirs*, 250). In many ways the play serves as a projection of what Williams may have believed would have transpired if Pollock had not died, in his prime, in a car accident in 1956.

## PRODUCTION HISTORY

*In the Bar of a Tokyo Hotel* was first performed in New York in 1969 at the Eastside Playhouse. Herbert Machiz directed Donald Madden and Anne Meacham as Mark and Miriam.

## PUBLICATION HISTORY

The play was first published by Dramatists Play Service in 1969.

## CHARACTERS

**Barman** The nameless bartender of the hotel bar, the Barman is a young, attractive Asian man. He becomes the focus of the seductive tactics of Miriam

Conley. Although very articulate, he serves as a bystander and witness of much of the play's action.

**Conley, Mark** Mark is a famous American painter at the end of his career. He and his wife, Miriam, are traveling abroad together. The change of location has irritated rather than improved their stormy relationship. Mark is slowly, but steadily, being driven into madness by his work and is deathly ill as a result of alcoholism. Mark is a portrait of the great American abstract painter JACKSON POLLOCK. As does Pollock, Mark paints in a highly physical and interactive style; he appears in the play with his clothes covered in paint and has a highly volatile relationship with his wife.

**Conley, Miriam** She is an attractive, impatient American tourist. Miriam is married to Mark Conley, a famous painter on the brink of a complete nervous breakdown. She is restless and hungry for love. She feels trapped in her relationship with Mark and wants to have him committed to a mental institution. Her promiscuity and infidelity are hinted at by her pursuit of the attractive young hotel Barman. Miriam's turbulent relationship with Mark is reminiscent of the relationship between the artist JACKSON POLLOCK and his long-suffering wife, Lee Krasner. Miriam is a complex blending of the supportive Krasner and Pollock's provocative patron, Peggy Guggenheim.

**Frisbie, Leonard** He is an art dealer and Mark Conley's publicist. Mark's wife, Miriam Conley, seeks Leonard's help in an attempt to place Mark in an asylum. Leonard, who loves and respects Mark deeply, goes to Tokyo and is infuriated by Miriam's request, behavior, and negligence toward Mark.

**Hawaiian Lady** She is a tourist on vacation and a guest at the hotel. She appears in the hotel bar for brief moments throughout the play. She is the focus of Miriam Conley's jokes with the Barman.

### FURTHER READING

Barnes, Clive. "Theatre: *In the Bar of a Tokyo Hotel,*" *New York Times,* May 12, 1969, p. 54.

Hewes, Henry. "Tennessee's Quest." *Saturday Review,* 52 (May 31, 1969), 18.

Naifeh, Steven, and Gregory White Smith. *Jackson Pollock: An American Saga.* New York: C. N. Potter, 1988.

Williams, Tennessee. *Memoirs.* Garden City, N.Y.: Doubleday, 1975.

# In the Winter of Cities

A collection of poetry published in 1954. An honest and intensely private portrait of Williams's inner thoughts, this collection of poetry, along with his other collection, ANDROGYNE, MON AMOUR, serves as the fullest account of Williams's desires and fears. Williams presented merely his public persona in his MEMOIRS; his poetry is the truest testament of the actual man. Although this collection of poetry is an early publication, it already details the conflicts Williams would wrestle with his entire life—sexuality and religion, self-loathing and desire, death and isolation—as well as representations and images of those people closest to him. Just as in his plays, Williams creates powerful images in his poetry that invoke a severe sense of melancholy and isolation as well as moments of spectacle and oddity.

Williams would, however, be continually conflicted about his need to write poetry and about the public's refusal to accept him as a poet/dramatist. Williams writes in an unfinished preface to this collection,

> When some of these poems first appeared, eleven years ago, in a book called *Five Young American Poets 1944,* they were fallen upon and torn couplet from couplet with that special cold-blooded ferocity which is peculiar to the tiger shark and saw-toothed barracuda and the poet-critics that hiss and spit in the groves of academe (qtd. in Roessel, 2002, xi).

Williams would be discouraged by his peers from pursuing a career writing poetry as well as writing for the theater, because these forms of expression seemed impossible to maintain simultaneously on a professional level. Committed to his craft, Williams never stopped writing poetry; in fact, he stated: "I am a poet. And then I put poetry in the drama. I put it in the short stories, and I put it in the plays. Poetry's poetry. It doesn't have to be called a poem, you know" (Radar, 98). Furthermore, Williams traverses these mediums with the ease of a poet whose verse does in fact become the action of the stage. William E. Taylor claims that "as one reads Williams's poems, the mind constantly flashes to characters, situations, themes, and symbols in the plays and the fiction" (Taylor, 624).

Because *In the Winter of Cities* was not enthusiastically received, Williams believed it would be his sole volume of published verse. However, *Androgyne, Mon Amour* would be published more than 20 years later.

## FURTHER READING

Adler, Thomas P. "Tennessee Williams's Poetry: Intertext and Metatext," *Tennessee Williams Annual Review* 1 (1998): 63–72.

Radar, Dotson. "Interview with Tennessee Williams," in *Playwrights at Work: The Paris Review Interviews*, edited by George Plimpton. New York: Modern Library, 2000.

Roessel, David, and Nicholas Moschovakis, eds. *The Collected Poems of Tennessee Williams*. New York: New Directions, 2002.

Taylor, William E. "Tennessee Williams: The Playwright as Poet," in *Tennessee Williams: A Tribute*, edited by Jac Tharpe. Jackson: University Press of Mississippi, 1977, pp. 609–624.

# "The Inventory at Fontana Bella"

Short story written in 1972.

## SYNOPSIS

This narrative is centered on Principessa Lisabetta Von Hohenzalt-Casalinghi. At 102 years old, she has become senile, and her sight and hearing are failing. Her most vivid memory is that of her last lover and husband, Sebastiano. When Lisabetta thinks of him, she hits herself in the groin violently with her fist to recall their lovemaking. One night, after dreaming of Sebastiano, she awakens, rises from her bed, and summons her doctor and servants to her chamber. She announces they will accompany her to her other estate, Fontana Bella, on the north shore of Lago Maggio. She requires her entire retinue of servants, including her lawyer, bookkeepers, and curator, as she plans an official appraisal of her belongings and treasure at Fontana Bella.

As they journey to Fontana Bella by boat, the servants amuse themselves as the old woman talks to herself. A lawyer cavorts with a chambermaid and there is much merrymaking around Lisabetta. When the party arrives at Fontana Bella, Lisabetta is taken to bed immediately. During the night, she awakens and demands that the inventory commence. Lisabetta imagines that her servants and chambermaids are dressing her and rushing busily about her heeding her orders. Unknown to Lisabetta, her entourage has left her in the palace unattended and have all ventured out to a nearby casino. Naked and alone, Lisabetta goes outside and conducts the appraisal with imaginary courtiers and a flock of storks who are nearby. Lisabetta strides about the terrace grandly giving orders and making demands. A female stork trying to protect her young suddenly attacks her. The stork pecks at the old woman's arms, breasts, and stomach. Lisabetta fights with the stork and grabs its beak and forces it into her vagina. In her delirium, Lisabetta believes that she is having sex with Sebastiano. Her servants return to find Lisabetta on the terrace physically engaged with the stork. Her doctor intervenes and frees the bird, but it has suffocated inside her.

Lisabetta's servants convince her to leave Fontana Bella. They lie to her and make her believe that a party is being given in her honor on a nearby island. On the return boat ride home the old woman reclines on a mound of pillows, as her servants once again amuse themselves. Lisabetta is delirious and dreams of her lover. She suddenly awakens from her slumber and pounds her groin with her fist once again. Her doctor attempts to restrain her to prevent serious injury. Lisabetta dies in ecstasy and her servants are relieved.

## COMMENTARY

"The Inventory at Fontana Bella" is more than merely a short story about an old woman who "gets her jollies in a very peculiar fashion" (Peden, 82). The story is a prime example of Williams's use of sexuality as a metaphor for life. In this story haunted by death, the elderly Lisabetta clings to her passionate memories of Sebastiano, and they become her life force. The memories of this once-lived intense physical passion propel her into action and keep her alive. Unlike her health, her sight, and her hearing, her passion remains constant and unchanged. It is an essential part of her that will not age or decay. In the end Lisabetta succumbs willingly and violently to her passion. She dies in ecstasy as her spirit is released upon the water.

In this grotesque tale Williams combines "poetic delicacy with primal violence" (Hassan, 142) and "fuses images of uncontrollable sexual urges with the fact of death" (Spoto, 301) to acknowledge the frailty of the body and to celebrate the passionate power of the sensuous spirit. In this, and similar narratives, Williams uses exaggeration as an art form to "catch the outrageousness of reality," as he found the very essence of life to be "grotesque and gothic" (Brown, 264).

## PUBLICATION HISTORY

"The Inventory at Fontana Bella" was first published in *Playboy* magazine in 1973. It was included in the short story collections EIGHT MORTAL LADIES POSSESSED (1974) and *Collected Stories* (1985).

## CHARACTER

**Hohenzalt-Casalinghi, Principessa Lisabetta von** She is an exceedingly wealthy old noblewoman. At the age of 102, Lisabetta is remarkably agile and alert, although her sight and hearing are rapidly failing. She is obsessed by her strong, visceral memories of her fifth and final husband, Sebastiano, and their passionate lovemaking. Lisabetta is also obsessed by her wealth and power. She orders her retinue of secretaries, lawyers, curators, bookkeepers, and chambermaids to attend her as she takes an inventory of her palace at Fontana Bella on the north shore of Lago Maggio. While her servants secretly enjoy themselves at a nearby casino, Lisabetta conducts an inventory at midnight outside the palace with a gaggle of storks. Lisabetta does not realize that she is naked and holding court with the birds. Her followers return and discover her on the portico, where she has mistaken one of the birds for her dead husband, Sebastiano. Her servants induce her to forgo the inventory by telling her that a great party is being held in her honor on a nearby island. During the boat ride home, the Principessa has one final, forceful memory of her passionate husband and dies in ecstasy.

## FURTHER READING

Brown, Cecil. "Interview with Tennessee Williams," in *Conversations with Tennessee Williams*, edited by Albert Devlin. Jackson: University Press of Mississippi, 1986, pp. 251–283.

Hassan, Ihab. *Contemporary American Literature: 1945–1972*. New York: Frederick Ungar, 1973.

Peden, Williams. *The American Short Story*. Boston: Houghton Mifflin, 1975.

Spoto, Donald. *The Kindness of Strangers: The Life of Tennessee Williams*. Boston: Little, Brown, 1985.

# *I Rise in Flame, Cried the Phoenix*

One-act play written between the years 1939 and 1941.

## SYNOPSIS

The play is set in the French Riviera. Dying of tuberculosis, the famous writer D. H. Lawrence rests on the sun porch of a home overlooking the ocean. A banner of a phoenix in a nest of flames hangs on the wall behind him. Frieda Lawrence enters to deliver a package for Lawrence from a female admirer. The package's sender provokes Lawrence to question the nature of woman and God and to express bitter hatred for Frieda. Lawrence makes her promise that she will not touch him or allow any other woman to touch him during the act of his death. When Frieda agrees to his request, he continues to criticize her. He is interrupted by the arrival of Bertha, who has just returned from London with news regarding Lawrence's latest work—an exhibition of his paintings. When Bertha tells him that the collection was not well received, Lawrence responds with anticipated pessimism. He explains that only he can truly understand his paintings.

Lawrence dives into yet another tirade about women and their shortcomings as the Sun sets. Watching the Sun fall in the sky, Lawrence pontificates on the similarity of light and darkness to women and men. He proclaims himself a prophet of things to come. Frieda and Bertha witness Lawrence's death throes. True to her promise, Frieda restrains herself and Bertha as Lawrence expires savagely and alone.

## COMMENTARY

Williams admired D. H. Lawrence for the freedom he assumed to write about taboo subjects such as sexual conduct and sensuality. He also admired Lawrence "for his spirit . . . his understanding of sexuality, of life in general" (Rader, 153). Williams would become the premier playwright of decay and decline of the human spirit as well as the body, so it is no surprise that he would decide to pen the last days in the life of D. H. Lawrence. *I Rise in Flame, Cried the Phoenix* is an example of the anguished dying male and the gaggle of women who never psychologically "touched" him in life and, therefore, are not privileged to hold him physically during his passing. In the note to the limited edition (New Directions, 1951), Frieda Lawrence writes that the central theme is "the eternal antagonism and attraction between man and woman" (8).

Overwrought with the desire to model a savage creature at the time of his death, with the image of the classical phoenix rising from the ashes, Lawrence becomes a timeless and legendary creature when he dies.

## PRODUCTION HISTORY

*I Rise in Flame, Cried the Phoenix* premiered at the Theatre de Lys on April 14, 1959, starring Alfred Ryder as Lawrence, Viveca Lindfors as Frieda, and Nan Martin as Bertha. This production was well received and thought to be "Williams's purest piece of dramatic writing" by the critic Henry Hewes.

## PUBLICATION HISTORY

In 1951 New Directions published a limited edition of this play with a note by Frieda Lawrence. An acting version of the script was also published that year by Dramatists Play Service. The two versions have slightly different endings, but the impact is immense: In the New Directions version, Frieda agrees to allow Lawrence to die alone and untouched, but when the moment occurs, he calls for her and she rushes to his side. In the acting version of the script (the one used for this synopsis), Frieda and Bertha refrain from going to Lawrence.

## CHARACTERS

**Bertha** She is a young English gentlewoman. An admirer of D. H. Lawrence, she is sent to London to oversee the opening of his exhibition of paintings.

**Lawrence, D. H.** (1885–1930) Historical figure and character in *I Rise in Flame, Cried the Phoenix*. In the play he is a controversial 20th-century writer who succumbs to tuberculosis and hopes to leave the world as a phoenix rising from the ashes of life. Williams chronicles the last days of Lawrence with his wife, Frieda, and his friend and admirer, Bertha. D. H. Lawrence was one of Williams's favorite writers because Lawrence challenged the puritanical order of society with his candid exploration of the sensual and sexual dynamics between men and women. In this one-act play, Lawrence is a frustrated and caged animal who wishes to be alone during his death throes.

**Lawrence, Frieda** She is the wife of the writer D. H. Lawrence, and a patient admirer of her husband's intellect and energy. Frieda suffers the ranting of Lawrence and calms his rage. She fulfills her promise not to go to her husband when he finally succumbs to tuberculosis, demonstrating extreme courage and restraint. Frieda holds Bertha as they witness Lawrence's tormented death.

## FURTHER READING

Hewes, Henry. "Off Broadway," in *The Best Plays of 1958–1959*. New York: Dodd, Mead, 1959, p. 50.

Rader, Dotson. "The Art of Theatre. V.: Tennessee Williams," *Paris Review* 81 (fall 1981): 145–185.
Williams, Tennessee. *I Rise in Flame, Cried the Phoenix,* limited ed. Norfolk, Conn.: New Directions, 1956, p. 16.

# "It Happened the Day the Sun Rose"

A short story written before 1981.

## SYNOPSIS

Set in Tangier, Morocco during the summer.

### *Part I*

Madame La Sorcière, a woman of considerable age and sexual prowess as well as supernatural powers, resides at the Grand Hotel des Souhks. Known for her escapades with young, handsome hotel employees, Madame La Sorcière desires Ahmed, the evening barman.

Late one evening, the Narrator follows Madame and a young man to Madame's room. After a few minutes he overhears her protestations over the man's inhibited approach to sexual positions. She administers an aphrodisiac of camel dung to him, and soon after the Narrator hears a wild ruckus coming from the suite. The next morning, the Narrator dines on the patio below Madame's suite window. He witnesses a crow fly out of the suite, and he does not see the young man for several days. When the young man resurfaces at the hotel, he sporadically makes winglike gestures with his arms.

Princess Fatima sits next to Madame at El Bar. She challenges Madame's assertion that Ahmed has no body hair and charges that Madame has not been intimate with him. Madame summons the four-piece orchestra to her table. As they play a seductive melody, she unzips the caftan she is wearing, exposing herself below the waist to Ahmed. Madame's powerful stare transfixes Ahmed. Feeling as though she is losing the argument, Princess Fatima counters Madame's actions by loudly asking her age; however, Madame is not distracted by the question. She simply answers that she was born on a day when the sun rose. Princess Fatima is perturbed by the coolness of Madame's avoidance of the question. Madame baits the princess further by questioning her social status. Enraged by this slight, the princess states that she is second in the line of succession to the throne of the country of Kughwana. Madame retorts that she has never heard of such a place.

Madame positions her chair to expose her vagina to Princess Fatima, who is stunned by its beauty. She does not believe it is real, but Madame suggests they retire to the bathroom so that the princess may investigate its authenticity. The two women agree to end their argument, though as enemies, and agree to avoid any future contact. Before Princess Fatima exits, she asks Madame the exact date of her birth, and Madame repeats her previous answer. Again, Madame questions the importance of Princess Fatima's country. Insulted and furious, Princess Fatima instructs Madame to take a closer look at the gold jewelry adorning her body. Madame deems the ornaments nothing more than brass or copper. Madame coolly purrs and disengages from the tiresome Princess Fatima. Disgusted by Madame's actions, Princess Fatima quickly rises from her table, overturning a carafe of chilled wine on her two guard-eunuchs. One eunuch yelps with pain, as his castration is recent. Madame goes to this eunuch, wipes his tears, and propositions him with a night in her suite. He questions her choosing him, but she assures him that she can still give him pleasure.

### *Part II*

One night in July of the same summer, Lady Abhfendierocker docks her yacht at the port in Tangier. Banned from most ports in the Mediterranean because of previous lascivious behavior with a high-ranking official, Lady Abhfendierocker is accompanied by a set of notorious jewel thieves who have paid for their passage with a fake emerald and sexual favors. During their passage from Nice, one of the thieves suffered a moment of impotence, which made Lady Abhfendierocker suspicious of the emerald. Upon appraisal in a port, she learns the emerald is not real. She forces the thieves to board a slowly deflating raft in the middle of the ocean in an act of revenge. The thieves, however, manage to survive, make their way to shore, and room with Madame at the Grand Hotel des Soukhs.

Ahmed proposes to spend a night with Madame. Madame however rejects him because she knows he is only interested in garnering a passport to Argentina. Ahmed becomes angry, cursing Madame as she exits the bar. In response to this humiliation, Ahmed phones the front desk and alerts them to the jewel thieves in Madame's suite. Ahmed's blunder results in his own dismissal from the hotel.

Now unemployed, Ahmed submits to being seduced by a wealthy older man, Lord Buggersmythe, who has courted him for many months. Lord Buggersmythe arranges a trust fund for Ahmed from the earnings of his five-star restaurant. This fund will forever be available to Ahmed on the condition that Ahmed never strays for a single night from their bed. Ahmed happily agrees to this condition.

One evening nearly one month later, Madame enters the restaurant of Lord Buggersmythe. She requests that Ahmed serve her. Ahmed apprehensively acquiesces. Madame coos with delight when she sees him. She congratulates him for his new occupation as Lord Buggersmythe's kept boy. Despite the voluble orchestra, Ahmed faintly hears crows cawing from under Madame's chair. Madame's dinner date whispers that Madame is afflicted by crows, five of which have entered her person. The man explains that Madame has an extra orifice, much like the pouch of a kangaroo. Madame interrupts to say that the crows are pecking away at her abdomen because their sedation has worn off. She is able to release them, but not without a type of magic practiced with camel manure and the bottle of elixir in her purse.

Ahmed tells her that he cannot bring camel manure to her table. Furthermore, there are no camels for miles and miles. Madame replies that she only needs a tiny amount of manure, and produces a small box for Ahmed to gather it in. She begs him to hurry before her screams blow the roof off the building.

The chef presents a platter of manure to Madame within minutes. She immediately recognizes the manure to be human, not camel. Angered and insulted, Madame hurls the manure at the chef and Ahmed. Chaos breaks out in the restaurant, and five crows begin to circle overhead. Pleased that the crows are released in spite of the lack of ingredients for the elixir, she thanks Ahmed. Madame invites him to share a bottle of champagne in celebration. He hesitantly walks to her and is transformed into the sixth crow circling the ceiling.

Time passes. In the moonlight of Lord Buggersmythe's bedroom, a 12-year-old Balinese boy and a physician tend to the dying old man. Lord Buggersmythe calls out to Ahmed, the crow. He accuses Ahmed of escaping his cage when he sleeps. Lord Buggersmythe wishes he could have sex with Ahmed. The cries of women and men and the barking of dogs throughout Tangier interrupt this sentimental moment. Miraculously, Ahmed's human body is reinstated. Madame appears in the room and throws a brilliant gem at Ahmed's feet. Another gem is discarded at the threshold of the room. She calls out her suite number and disappears. Lord Buggersmythe dies.

The moral of the story is, "truth is all that we know of right in this world, and therefore its absence is all that we know of wrong. In other words, it is not good, it is God."

## COMMENTARY

Williams investigates the power of feminine sexuality in this story. He pushes the boundaries that he created in such archetypal women as Maggie the Cat Pollitt (*Cat on a Hot Tin Roof*), Blanche DuBois (*A Streetcar Named Desire*), and Miss Valerie Coynte ("Miss Coynte of Greene"). Like Blanche who "avoids adult sexual relationships but actively seeks affairs with adolescents" (McGlinn, 513), Madame La Sorcière seeks sexual encounters with considerably younger men, but her actions, combined with supernatural powers, literally transform her conquests if they do not satisfy her sexual appetite.

Wielding their sexuality as weapons to conquer their male counterparts and manipulate situations, Williams's overtly sexual female characters "seem to have been conceived by their creator, if not as representatives of a sort of salvation, then at least as attractive earth goddesses whose salvation is their own sexuality" (Jones, 211). Madame's power is her beautiful vagina. Men and women alike are enamored of it. Williams presses the boundaries of feminine sexuality to involve the physical organ, and what was merely (yet powerfully) the essence of feminine sexuality in past characters such as Blanche and Maggie is now physically manifest. Madame La Sorcière's earthiness is exemplified when she states that she was "born the day the sun rose," revealing a wraithlike and ancient soul.

In the short story "Miss Coynte of Greene," Williams portrays another earthy woman who is sexually liberated and profoundly concentrated on sexual fulfillment. Miss Coynte is also a character who is centrifugal to the cycle of life. Her daughter, Michele Moon, carries on the sexual liberation in her affair with twin lovers. Michele Moon and Miss Coynte are also unconventional as they publicly celebrate their African-American lovers in a racially segregated setting. Their fearless love, desire, and wants supersede any human-based laws or social, religious, or political mores.

Ahmed the barman does not escape Madame's wrath, as his invitation to have sex is not sincere desire but rather a means to garner a passport. The all-knowing Madame is aware of Ahmed's deceit. His downfall is that he underestimates her psychic powers. Ahmed also attempts to trick Madame into believing that he has delivered the required camel dung for her case of crows. His punishment for this misdeed is that he, too, becomes a crow. And while Ahmed does not succumb to Madame's seduction, he suffers the same punishment because he rejects her sexually. In this instance, Madame's sexual power is an inescapable trap.

Characters such as Madame La Sorcière are most often found in Williams's fiction rather than his dramatic works. Jürgen C. Wolter writes in his essay, "Tennessee Williams's Fiction," "Since fiction allows space for undramatic reflections and digressions and since the breaking of taboos can be much more radical in a text that is written for the private closet of the individual reader than in a script for the 'public theatre,' a story can be a more spontaneous reaction." This is also evident in Williams's treatment of gay issues and themes. His short stories and fiction detail and celebrate gay characters and situations, and in no way has he shied away from this topic, which was generally considered taboo during his lifetime. Williams provides a subplot in this story that involves a relationship between Ahmed and Lord Buggersmythe, who becomes Ahmed's savior after he is fired from the hotel. Even after Ahmed has been turned into a crow, Lord Buggersmythe desires him.

Tennessee Williams visited Tangier in the summer of 1973. This visit is chronicled in the book *Tennessee Williams in Tangier,* by Muhammad Shukri. Williams was struggling to write *THE RED DEVIL BATTERY SIGN.* According to Gavin Lambert, in his introduction to the book, Williams was very restless and having terrible luck in his travels that summer. What proved, however, to be an unplanned success was the relationship between Shukri and Williams: two men who seemed to have very little in common. During their chance encounters in cafes, on the streets, or at PAUL BOWLES's apartment, Shukri became very interested in Williams as a writer. Williams was very pleased with the book, calling it "gently humorous and discreet with a reticent sympathy implicit" (Shukri, Epilogue), and Williams was relieved and surprised that he was chronicled in such a positive light after years of suffering a waning public image.

## PUBLICATION HISTORY

"It Happened the Day the Sun Rose" was published in *It Happened the Day the Sun Rose and Other Stories* by Sylvester & Orphanos in 1981.

## CHARACTERS

**Ahmed** A handsome young Moroccan barman who works at the Grand Hotel des Souhks. Ahmed's life changes when he encounters Madame La Sorcière, a woman with supernatural powers and a robust sexual appetite. Ahmed coolly keeps his distance from her. When Ahmed proposes to spend a night with Madame La Sorcière in hopes of securing an Argentine passport from her, she rejects him. When Ahmed tries to trick Madame La Sorcière a second time, she turns him into a crow. Ahmed is restored in the final moments of the story when Madame La Sorcière returns and turns him back into a man. She also reinstates the invitation to her suite.

**Lady Abhfendierocker** A wealthy woman who docks her yacht in Tangier. She is accompanied by a gang of notorious jewel thieves who have paid her for their passage with a fake emerald. When Lady Abhfendierocker has the emerald appraised at the port and learns that it is counterfeit, she forces the thieves to board a slowly deflating raft in the middle of the ocean in an act of revenge.

**Lord Buggersmythe** An aging wealthy bachelor who, smitten by Ahmed, supports him financially on the condition that Ahmed never stray a single night from their bed. Lord Buggersmythe desires Ahmed even after he is turned into a crow.

**Madame La Sorcière** A wealthy and powerful woman who lives at the Grand Hotel des Souhks in Tangier, Morocco. Endowed with supernatural powers and psychic intelligence, Madame La Sorcière has an insatiable sexual appetite. She is also in the habit of turning her young lovers into crows if they do not meet her expectations. Equipped with an extra pouchlike orifice around her stomach, she carries these crows inside her, calming them with a magic elixir when they become restless. Madame La Sorcière fancies Ahmed, the barman at the hotel, but when he attempts to trick her, she turns him into a crow. She does return after some time and reinstates his human form, rewards him with two precious gems, and leaves an open invitation to tryst in her suite.

**Princess Fatima** Madame La Sorcière's rival, Princess Fatima is second in succession to the throne of Kughwana. Madame La Sorcière questions the importance of her country, insulting Princess Fatima and causing her to retire to her room with her eunuch-guards, but not before she tries to embarrass Madame LaSorcière by asking her age. Madame La Sorcière ripostes by displaying her youthful and extraordinary vagina for Princess Fatima to envy.

## FURTHER READING


Jones, Robert Emmet. "Tennessee Williams's Early Heroines." *Modern Drama* 2 (1959): 211–219.

McGlinn, Jeanne M. "Tennessee Williams's Women: Illusion and Reality, Sexuality and Love." In *Tennessee Williams: A Tribute,* edited by Jac Tharpe. Jackson: University of Mississippi Press, 1977.

Shukri, Muhammad. (Mohamed Choukri). *Tennessee Williams in Tangier.* Santa Barbara, Calif.: Cadmus Editions, 1979.

Wolter, Jürgen C. "Tennessee Williams's Fiction." In *Tennessee Williams: A Guide to Research and Performance* by Philip C. Kolin. Westport, Conn.: Greenwood Press, 1998, pp. 220–228.


# "The Killer Chicken and the Closet Queen"

Short story written in 1977.

## SYNOPSIS

Stephen Ashe is a successful lawyer on the brink of becoming partner at a prominent Wall Street law firm. Stephen hides the fact that he is gay in an attempt to protect and preserve his career and reputation at work. The other partners in the firm are supporting his promotion and the retirement of a senior member, Nat Webster.

One afternoon at the gym and while receiving massages at adjoining tables, a colleague, Jerry Smythe, gossips about Nat's brother-in-law, who has been in jail for "lewd vagrancy" or male prostitution. The brother-in-law was staying with Nat and his wife until Nat found out. Stephen is uncomfortable with the topic of conversation and changes the subject.

Several weeks pass and Stephen receives a call from Nat's teenage wife, Maude. She tells him that her brother, Clove, has been renting a room at the Young Men's Christian Association (YMCA) and she would like him to stay with Stephen. She worries about him at the Y because they are "overrun with wolves out for chickens." Maude does not give him a chance to object before she hangs up the phone. Stephen has a dilemma, as his mother will soon be visiting him from Palm Beach, and he has only one guest bedroom.

Concerned about what to tell his mother about Clove and contemplating how to handle her constant reminders that she wants to meet his girlfriend, Stephen invites his colleagues for Sunday brunch. During a limousine ride to the airport to collect his mother and after indulging in the backseat bar, Stephen has a drunken tryst with the driver. Stephen has a moment of sobriety and rejects the previously welcomed advances of the driver. The driver becomes angry and calls Stephen a "closet queen." Stephen's mother is delayed in Palm Springs and does not arrive when she is scheduled, so he returns home.

The next morning, Stephen wakes up with a hangover. He stumbles out of bed and realizes that it is Sunday, and Clove and Maude are on their way to his apartment. When they arrive, Stephen is immediately smitten with Clove. Stephen asks Clove to pretend to be his teenage son, the product of a love affair with a socialite, Miss Sue Coffin of Nantucket Island. Stephen goes back to bed and wakes up nearly an hour later with Clove. Nat Webster enters the apartment, realizes what has transpired between the two men, and demands Stephen's resignation Monday morning. Stephen returns to bed and is awakened by his mother's exclamation upon meeting her supposed teenage grandson. After taking a quaalude tablet and drinking a Bloody Mary, Stephen's mother is calmed. Clove also gives Stephen a quaalude tablet and sends him out to face his mother. Stephen and Clove send his mother to a hotel. After several days, she leaves for Palm Beach.

Stephen and Clove board a train for Miami, accompanied by a French pug puppy. Clove feeds Stephen more quaaludes while he plans to partake in his "grandmother's" money. Clove urges Stephen to stop living his life in the closet.

## COMMENTARY

"The Killer Chicken and the Closet Queen" is a "wonderfully crazed" tale in which Williams displays his gift for storytelling (Vidal, xxv). Written late in Williams's life, the story is an intense examination of such themes as the conflict of success and sexuality, social acceptance, and familial relations. These are all topics that Williams continually traversed both in his works and in his life.

The story immediately calls to mind such works as AUTO-DA-FÉ and STEPS MUST BE GENTLE, which also feature a mother and a son caught in a cat-and-mouse game centered on the son's sexual orientation. There are also overtones of SUDDENLY LAST SUMMER, which also depicts a mother concerned by her son's sexuality, but more important, the two works share the prevailing idea of a young man's sexuality threatening his future success and reputation.

Structurally "The Killer Chicken and the Closet Queen" exhibits a wonderful, playful absurdist view more often associated with Williams's later dramas, rather than his fiction. This concept is chiefly illustrated in the character Clove. As his name suggests, Clove adds much needed spice to Stephen's bland existence. Clove is a liberating force for Stephen and literally personifies Stephen's hidden sexuality and repressed nature. Crude, crass, and sensual, Clove storms into Stephen's stiff and refined life, throwing the doors of his emotional closet wide open. Clove is also a trickster character, like the mischievous sprite Puck in Shakespeare's *A Midsummer Night's Dream.* As does Puck, Clove casts a spell upon Stephen and his mother with his magical potions (quaaludes and Bloody Marys). He offers them a new way of seeing the world and ultimately transforms their sense of reality and way of life. Clove also calls to mind his namesake, Clov, from SAMUEL BECKETT's *Endgame.* Both Clove and Clov serve an enlightening function in their respective plays. In *Endgame,* Clov actively and literally reveals what is hidden or unseen to his audience, and provides vision for the blind character, Hamm. In much the same way, Clove uncovers and exposes Stephen's repressed sexuality both to Stephen and to his "audience," or onlooker, Nat Webster. "The Killer Chicken and the Closet Queen" also shares a common theme with *Endgame,* which is the idea that "a new path out of the old ruts might lead, if one has the courage to walk it, to a new vision and a new life" (Webb, 57).

## PUBLICATION HISTORY

"The Killer Chicken and the Closet Queen" was published in *Christopher Street* in 1978. It was subsequently published in *Collected Stories,* in 1985.

## CHARACTERS

**Ashe, Stephen** A closeted gay man who hides his sexuality for the advancement of his law career. He anticipates partnership at a prominent Wall Street law firm but is forced to resign when it becomes known that he is gay. He meets his teenage lover, Clove, in the midst of this fiasco through the teenage wife of his boss.

**Clove** He is a handsome young man of 16 who is jailed for being a male prostitute in Arkansas. When Clove moves to New York City as the ward of his sister, he lives with Stephen Ashe, a successful lawyer.

**Smythe, Jimmie** A young lawyer at a prominent Wall Street law firm, Smythe is a colleague of Stephen Ashe. Jimmie and Stephen often exercise at the gym together. On one occasion at the gym, Jimmie shares with Stephen the company gossip that a senior partner's brother-in-law has been arrested for lewd vagrancy, or prostitution.

**Webster, Maude** She is the teenage wife of Nat Webster, a senior partner at a prominent Wall Street law firm. Maude calls upon one of her husband's younger colleagues, Stephen Ashe, to do her a favor. She asks Stephen to allow her delinquent brother Clove to stay at his apartment while Clove is visiting New York City. Stephen begrudgingly complies with Maude's request because he is anxious to gain a promotion and needs Nat's support.

**Webster, Nat** He is an elderly senior partner at a prominent Wall Street law firm, with a teenage wife named Maude. Nat demands the resignation of his younger colleague, Stephen Ashe, when he discovers that Stephen has become intimately involved with his wife's delinquent brother, Clove.

## FURTHER READING

Vidal, Gore. "Introduction" in *Collected Stories*. New York: New Directions, 1985.

Webb, Eugene. *The Plays of Samuel Beckett*. University of Washington Press: Seattle, 1974.

# "The Kingdom of Earth"

Short story written in 1942.

## SYNOPSIS

A young man named Chicken leaves his family's farm when he learns that the homestead has been bequeathed, at the death of his father, to his half brother, Lot. Chicken is quickly summoned back when Lot becomes terminally ill of tuberculosis. Chicken returns on the condition that the property will be his when Lot dies. When Lot returns home with a new bride, Myrtle, Chicken rejects Myrtle because he fears she will usurp his claim to the farm. Although Chicken is sexually attracted to Myrtle, he is suspicious of Lot's reasons for marrying her and her interest in a dying man.

Chicken's suspicion stems from the fact that he has been mistreated his entire life because he is part Cherokee and illegitimate. Myrtle is not aware that Lot is dying, so she tries to find ways of making him desire her sexually. While Lot grows weaker, Myrtle and Chicken become increasingly attracted to each other. Finally, they succumb to their attraction while Lot suffers one final and violent coughing attack. Lot calls for help, but Chicken and Myrtle ignore his pleas as they are enrapt in vigorous lovemaking. The next morning, they find Lot dead on the floor in a pool of blood. Myrtle and Chicken marry. When Myrtle becomes pregnant, she and Chicken decide that they will name their child after Lot.

## COMMENTARY

In this provocative and explicit tale, Williams uses passionate sexuality as an expression of life and liberation. Myrtle and Chicken's energetic lovemaking provides a vision of life, which contrasts sharply with the resounding death throes of the dying Lot. The oppressed Chicken is an outcast who has spent his life fighting for his right to his family's farm. He has been repeatedly mistreated, and when the opportunity to gain a better life presents itself, he takes it. This opportunity is embodied by Myrtle. Through her, Chicken gains his inheritance, material wealth, status, and love. In the act of consummating his relationship with Myrtle, Chicken triumphs over the oppression he has faced as a racial and social minority.

Chicken is reminiscent of Stanley Kowalski in *A STREETCAR NAMED DESIRE*. Both characters possess an animalistic sexuality and a brutish disposition. They also share an obsession for inheritance, legacy, and what they believe to be their "right," what is owed to them. Whereas Stanley is unable to realize his claim, Chicken is rewarded for his patience and hard work. Chicken calls himself a lustful creature and acknowledges his indifference to the kingdom of heaven. He is more concerned with the kingdom of Earth, a place of pleasure and carnal living that is finally accessible to him.

"The Kingdom of Earth" is considered by some to be one of Williams's lesser works of fiction. However, this powerful short story is an engaging study in character and contains some of Williams's most vivid writing.

## PRODUCTION HISTORY

"The Kingdom of Earth" is the basis for the one-act play of the same title and the full-length play *THE KINGDOM OF EARTH, OR THE SEVEN DESCENTS OF MYRTLE*. A film version of this story, *THE LAST OF THE MOBILE HOT SHOTS*, was released in 1969. GORE VIDAL wrote the screenplay for the film, which was directed by Sidney Lumet and featured Lynn Redgrave as Myrtle, James Coburn as the Lot character called Jeb, and Robert Hooks as Chicken.

## PUBLICATION HISTORY

Because of its provocative content, Williams was advised not to include "The Kingdom of Earth" in his short story collection *Hard Candy* (1954). Instead, the story was published privately in an unbound edition in 1954 and eventually published in the short story collection *The Knightly Quest* (1966). "The Kingdom of Earth" also appears in *Collected Stories* (1985).

## CHARACTERS

**Chicken** He is the half brother of Lot. He is a young part-Cherokee farmer who fears that he will not inherit the family farm, although he spends his life working on it. Chicken experiences complete satisfaction when he inherits not only the farm, but his deceased half brother's wife, Myrtle.

**Lot** Lot is the son of wealthy landowners and heir to a farm on the Mississippi Delta. Handsome and blond, he has debonair good looks that belie his terminal illness and impotence. Lot is slowly dying of tuberculosis. He marries Myrtle, a former prostitute, and loses her and his farm to his despised illegitimate half brother, Chicken. Lot dies crying out for help, but neither Myrtle nor Chicken goes to his aid.

**Myrtle** A former prostitute who marries Lot, a handsome man who is dying of tuberculosis. Lot takes Myrtle to his family homestead, a farm on the Mississippi Delta. When Myrtle meets his half brother, Chicken, she is immediately drawn to his sexy, brutish disposition. She gives in to her sexual desires and abandons her husband as he dies.

# *The Kingdom of Earth*

One-act play written in 1967.

## SYNOPSIS

The setting is a Mississippi Delta farmhouse during a flood. A voice calls out to a young man in rubber hip boots called Chicken. The voice belongs to a neighbor who is leaving his farm to escape the flood. He tells Chicken that he would give him a ride, but he does not have the room in his car. Chicken proudly states that he would never leave his house. He says that he will climb onto the roof if the water level rises. Chicken explains that is how he got his name—he sat on the rooftop with the chickens during a flood nearly 18 years ago. The neighbors drive away, and Chicken returns to his kitchen to make coffee. Another car approaches the farmhouse. Chicken peers out of the window, recognizing that his brother, Lot, has returned. He is shocked to see that there is a woman with him.

Lot calls out to Chicken. Registering Lot's frail condition, Chicken is surprised that he has been released from the Memphis hospital. Lot introduces the woman as his wife, Myrtle, whom he met three days ago. Lot orders Chicken to carry their bags into the house. Lot follows them to tell Myrtle that the house will soon be completely flooded in an attempt to scare them back to Memphis. Lot says he does not have the strength to make the trip again, as he goes to rest. Chicken goes to the kitchen, where he talks with Myrtle. She admits that she did not know Lot had just been released from the hospital. Chicken assures her that the flood will occur and that she will be at his mercy to climb up to the roof. Myrtle runs a plate of french fries upstairs to Lot, but she quickly returns. She tells Chicken that Lot is panting heavily and believes that Chicken thinks he is dying. Chicken confirms that Lot is dying of tuberculosis and that the hospital released him to die in his home. Myrtle says that she has been deceived by her new husband, knowing nothing of his failing health.

Chicken informs Myrtle that when Lot dies, he is to inherit everything. He explains that he is Lot's half brother: Their father had an affair with a Cherokee woman, Lot's mother. For this reason, Chicken has been discriminated against not only within the family, but in town. Chicken threatens to allow the flood to get Myrtle because she could take the farm. Myrtle pleads that she despises the country and would never want to live there. Chicken demands that Myrtle give him the marriage license. She goes upstairs and gets the document. Chicken orders her to destroy the paper, and she complies.

Myrtle says her marriage to Lot is already over, and she feels as though he is already dead. She begins to talk about her "maternal cord," and how Lot took advantage of that part of her nature. Chicken blames his dark complexion on working on his own farm, "like a field hand." Chicken tells her the story of a girl he dated for three years. When they broke up, she spread rumors around town that he was mulatto, not Cherokee. Now no white women will have anything to do with him. Chicken talks about his spiritual conversion, which did not "stick." He had to return to his lustful ways. Myrtle says that she is the same way. Lot shouts for Myrtle, but she ignores him. Chicken continues to talk about the carnality in his nature and his efforts to read books to "shut the gates" on such thoughts. He gave up and returned to thinking about "drinking and screwing, and trying . . . to make something out of the place." Lot calls for Myrtle once again. In agitation, she demands that he "shut up."

Lot is heard coughing and gagging. Myrtle decides to check on him, but she remains seated with Chicken. She confesses that she does not want to witness Lot's suffering. She says she has had a bad life, working since she was 15 years old. She talks about being sexually harassed at her jobs. Lot calls for her once again, and she shouts that she is on her way. Chicken suggests that she allow him to keep screaming, to strengthen his lungs. Myrtle says that her boss raped her in his office, and she immediately fell in love with him. She stayed with him for a long time, until he grew tired of her. Myrtle left Biloxi and traveled around everywhere working at odd jobs. Myrtle confesses that life just happens to her: She does not plan anything. When Lot asked her to marry him the morning after she met him, she saw no reason she shouldn't.

Myrtle finally tends to lot. She is angry when she returns because he has accused her of being Chicken's whore. Chicken responds to the statement by philosophizing on the most perfect thing in the whole "kingdom of earth": "what's able to happen between a man and a woman." Lot calls and Myrtle goes to him. She returns panicking because Lot is fighting to breathe. She fumbles to find the doctor's phone number on the wall. Chicken sits on the stoop coolly admiring the evening. They hear Lot crawling down the hallway. Myrtle begs Chicken to put him back into bed, but Chicken says he has no respect for the weak. He grabs Myrtle and kisses her. She falls to her knees as Lot's movements cease. Chicken picks up Lot's lifeless body and instructs Myrtle to go upstairs and change the sheets on the bed. Chicken goes outside and surveys his kingdom.

## COMMENTARY

This one-act play is part of an evolution that culminates in the much more seedy and severe full-length play of the same title. This version of Chicken's story has not fully matured to the level of dramatic action Williams's other plays possess. Chicken and Myrtle are streamlined characters, less volatile and less sexually engrossed. Here, Lot has very little actual stage time, and becomes merely a voice from backstage. His persistent pleas for Myrtle and her dismissal of them set up a very different dynamic from that of the full-length play. In this version, Myrtle expresses her maternal instinct toward Lot; however, the ironic twist is that she wants nothing to do with him when she realizes that he cannot provide for her. Myrtle will become a more rounded character who does in fact act on her need to be needed by caring for her dying husband. In this one-act play, Lot and Myrtle's relationship is not fully established, as Lot leaves the action as soon as they enter the farmhouse.

The theme of sexual and personal fulfillment is prominent in this play. Myrtle is somewhat like Blanche Dubois in *A STREETCAR NAMED DESIRE;* however, she is less refined in the one-act version. Myrtle is a sexually uninhibited woman whose femininity has shaped her life. Her sensual nature can be better aligned with that of "Maggie the Cat" Pollitt in *CAT ON A HOT TIN ROOF,* whose sexual prowess is a celebrated aspect of her personality. Myrtle admits to Chicken that she has always enjoyed sex. She does not have a puritanical morality; rather, she focuses on survival. She does not find much happiness in life, viewing it as "killing time, no change except time going."

In the full-length *KINGDOM OF EARTH, OR THE SEVEN DESCENTS OF MYRTLE,* Williams changes Chicken's ethnicity from Cherokee to African American. With this change he creates a topical social commentary rooted in the injustices of racism in the American South. Chicken garners much more sympathy as a marginalized man in his own family and society, and despite his crude disposition, there is a more defined sense of retribution at the end of the full-length play, Chicken's existence is finally validated, and he is worthy of his father's farm.

## PRODUCTION HISTORY

There is no production history for this version of "The Kingdom of Earth." Williams expanded it to the full-length play shortly thereafter.

## PUBLICATION HISTORY

*The Kingdom of Earth* was published in *Esquire* magazine, February 1967.

## CHARACTERS

**Chicken** Chicken is a young man of Cherokee descent, whose life's sole intent is to gain the farm of his white father. Nicknamed Chicken after a previous flood had forced him to stay on the rooftop with the chickens, he prepares for another flood of similar magnitude. Chicken is a simple man who has faced racism and has become isolated in life. He does find temporary redemption when he converts to Christianity, but he gives up this pursuit when he cannot rid his life of lustful thoughts. Chicken is angered by his tuberculous brother, Lot's, recent marriage to a stranger named Myrtle. Chicken's baseness and primal behavior earn him the position of authority when Myrtle realizes that Lot is dying. Chicken immediately gains a wife who will follow his orders as well as the farm, when by the end of the play, Lot dies.

**Lot** Lot is a pallid young blond man who is dying of tuberculosis. He meets Myrtle at a Memphis drugstore after his release from a nearby hospital. Lot takes her home to the farm during a great flood and loses her to his hedonistic brother, Chicken. Lot dies shouting for Myrtle, who has become the property of Chicken. He crawls for help but dies before he is aided by either of them.

**Myrtle** A cynical woman who has only known intimacy through one-night stands and rape. When Myrtle meets Lot and he proposes to her, she is relieved to be released from a life fueled by the goal of survival. Myrtle returns to Lot's farm and meets his virile brother, Chicken. When he tells her that Lot is dying of tuberculosis, she immediately clings to Chicken to provide for her.

# *The Kingdom of Earth, or The Seven Descents of Myrtle*

A play in seven scenes written in 1967.

## SYNOPSIS

The action of this play takes places in a farmhouse on the Mississippi Delta, during the flooding season in early spring. The lower level of the interior of the farmhouse consists of an ornate living room/parlor and a kitchen. There is a master bedroom on the upper level of the farmhouse set.

### *Scene 1*

A car is heard approaching, and it stops near the farm of Chicken. A man and woman shout salutations to Chicken and inform him they are leaving their homes as the floodwaters continue to swell. The unseen couple warn Chicken to escape while he can. Chicken refuses and is determined to guard his home. The couple drive away. Another car approaches; Chicken's half brother, Lot, and his new wife, Myrtle, have arrived. Chicken panics, runs inside, and locks himself in the kitchen. Lot and Myrtle enter the house and go directly to the ornate parlor. Myrtle investigates her new home with excitement. She approves of her surroundings while Lot explains that the house belonged to his mother and everything has been preserved as she left it when she died. Chicken eavesdrops on Lot and Myrtle's conversation through the kitchen door. Lot continues to romanticize his mother, and Myrtle becomes disgusted and accuses him of having a "mother complex." She intends to cure him of this disorder. Lot does not allow Myrtle to sit on his mother's furniture. Myrtle is hurt by his rudeness but does not allow it to darken her mood.

Myrtle discovers that the kitchen door is locked. Lot confesses that his half brother, Chicken, is hiding in the kitchen. Myrtle becomes angry that Lot did not tell her about Chicken before they were married. Lot has a violent coughing spasm that leaves him exhausted. Myrtle promises to nurse Lot back to health. Lot apologizes for his disappointing sexual performance the previous night. Lot makes Myrtle promise that if Chicken asks her whether he is a good lover, she will say that he is. Myrtle tells Lot that he does satisfy her, even if they have not yet consummated their marriage. Lot reveals that the family farm belongs to him, and to Myrtle by extension.

Chicken enters the parlor and asks Lot about his health. Lot refuses to discuss it in Myrtle's presence. He tells Chicken he has been cured of his ailment; Chicken does not believe him. Lot introduces Myrtle. She becomes frightened by their talk of the flood. Myrtle suggests that she and Lot escape while they can; however, Lot is determined to stay and protect his home. Chicken reminds Lot of their former agreement concerning the farm. Lot disavows the agreement now that he is married. Lot, Myrtle, and Chicken go into the kitchen for coffee. Chicken assumes that Myrtle is Lot's nurse, and his assumption upsets Myrtle. Lot defends Myrtle and tells his half brother that Myrtle once had a career in show business. Myrtle seizes this opportunity to tell her history. Chicken accuses Myrtle of being a stripper, and she is offended. She rushes out to the car to rescue her electrical appliances from the flood. Chicken informs Lot that he knows Lot does not have long to live. Chicken again reminds Lot about the contract he signed. The men begin to fight. When Myrtle returns, she finds Lot on the floor. Lot and Myrtle retire to their bedroom, and Lot tells her he is dying.

### *Scene 2*

The time is two hours later. Lot sits in a rocking chair smoking a cigarette with his mother's ivory cigarette holder. Myrtle is very upset by Lot's news and expresses her feelings of betrayal. Lot confesses that he kept the information about his health and his half brother secret because he feared her reaction. In the kitchen Chicken busily carves a lewd drawing into the breakfast table. When Myrtle enters for dinner, she notices the carving. Stunned and offended by it, she becomes uncomfortable with Chicken and exits with the plate of food he prepared for her. Chicken watches Myrtle as she ascends the stairs. Unnerved by Chicken, Myrtle drops her plate.

### *Scene 3*

Myrtle returns to Lot's bedroom. She tells Lot about the lewd picture Chicken carved into the table and Lot laughs hysterically. Myrtle threatens to call the police. Lot urges Myrtle to return downstairs, find Chicken's wallet, and steal his contract. Lot instructs her to get Chicken drunk and steal the contract when Chicken passes out.

### *Scene 4*

Myrtle returns to the kitchen with her laundry. Chicken sits at the kitchen table. She apologizes to

Chicken for abruptly leaving earlier and confesses to him that she is worried about Lot. Chicken is indifferent to his brother's illness. Myrtle asks for a drink, and Chicken obliges. They both drink while Myrtle hangs her underwear to dry on a clothesline that has been strung up in the kitchen. Lot calls for Myrtle, but she remains in the kitchen talking with Chicken. Myrtle and Chicken sing and drink.

### *Scene 5*

When Myrtle returns to the bedroom she finds Lot smoking a cigarette in the dark. He tells her that he hates his half brother and admits that he cannot tolerate the thought of Chicken's having his mother's home, an estate worth more than $50,000. Myrtle dresses in one of her theatrical costumes, determined to get the contract from Chicken. Lot accuses her of being physically attracted to Chicken.

Myrtle returns to the kitchen, and she and Chicken discuss Lot's condition. Chicken compares Myrtle's predicament to buying a used car and finding out it is a lemon. Myrtle cries and Chicken tells her his family's history. He explains that his father was not married to his mother when he was born, and 10 years later he married Lot's mother, Miss Lottie. Lot is therefore the legitimate heir. Miss Lottie made Chicken leave the farm shortly before she died. Chicken was asked to return when Lot became too ill to manage without him, and Chicken returned on the condition that he would own the farm after Lot died. When Myrtle becomes frightened by Chicken's passionate tirade she pretends that she is not legally married to Lot. She claims it was just a joke. Chicken therefore demands to see the marriage license. Myrtle goes to the bedroom to find the license. Lot calls Myrtle a whore and she is shocked by his terrible temper. Nervously fumbling to find the marriage license, Myrtle leaves Lot, vowing not to return until he apologizes.

### *Scene 6*

Myrtle enters the kitchen with the license. Chicken inspects the document. He forces Myrtle to draft a contract that states she will give the farm to him when Lot dies. Chicken brutishly kisses Myrtle and she is aroused by his strong body and calloused hands. Chicken blows out the kitchen lamp. Lot notices that the house is completely dark. He reconciles himself to the fact he has brought home a woman for Chicken. He considers Myrtle his last gift to Chicken.

### *Scene 7*

The lights return in the kitchen. As a result of their intimacy, Chicken confides that his mother was a mulatto. He relates stories of prejudice and abuse. Myrtle advises him to simply deny his identity. Chicken also confides that Lot is a transvestite, who often wears a wig and his mother's lingerie and mimics her in the parlor. In the bedroom, Lot struggles out of his rocking chair. He dresses himself in one of his mother's white summer gowns and descends the stairs. Lot appears in the hallway, and Myrtle is horrified by his appearance. Chicken restrains her as Lot walks into the parlor and performs his "Miss Lottie" act one final time. When Lot collapses on the parlor floor, Chicken picks up his limp body and places him on the couch. Myrtle becomes hysterical in the kitchen. Chicken enters the kitchen and asks her to have his children. Myrtle tells him she has already had five children, who had to be given up for adoption because she was too poor to keep them. Chicken exits to monitor the flood. He calls out to Myrtle, informing her it is time to climb onto the roof.

## COMMENTARY

*The Kingdom of Earth, or The Seven Descents of Myrtle* is based on the short story "THE KINGDOM OF EARTH" written in 1954 and is an expansion of the one-act play *THE KINGDOM OF EARTH* written in 1967. The result of this re-writing is a suspenseful tale of three ambitious outcasts struggling for survival. In this version of the Lot-Chicken-Myrtle story Williams heightens the contrast and tension between Lot and Chicken. They remain half brothers, though their racial and sexual differences are far more dramatic.

Chicken, who is described as "part-Cherokee" in the short story, becomes the son of an African-African woman in the full-length play. Lot, who is sexually "disappointing" in the short story, takes to cross-dressing and imitating his deceased mother. Lot's transvestitism is a notable feature of this provocative work, as his final moments are rendered with a delicacy reminiscent of the character Blanche Dubois in *A STREETCAR NAMED DESIRE.*

*The Kingdom of Earth* has suffered critically from scholarly comparisons made between this play and Williams's masterwork *A Streetcar Named Desire.* The similarities are numerous and persist even with the shifts in gender. Lot is often viewed as a revision of the fading beauty Blanche Dubois; the virile Chicken fills Stanley Kowalski's role, and Myrtle that of Stella Kowalski. The plays also share concerns with inheritance and legacy. Similar connections can be made between *The Kingdom of Earth* and *BATTLE OF ANGELS* and its subsequent revision, *ORPHEUS DESCENDING.* These three plays depict a love triangle consisting of a dying man, his sexually unfulfilled wife, and an able-bodied young man. Myrtle, Myra Torrance (*Battle of Angels*), and Lady Torrance (*Orpheus Descending*) share the occupation of traversing up and down a set of stairs, literally and figuratively traveling between the world of the dying (the kingdom of heaven) and the world of the living (the kingdom of Earth).

## PRODUCTION HISTORY

*The Kingdom of Earth* was retitled *The Seven Descents of Myrtle* for its Broadway premiere. The production, directed by Jose Quintero, opened at the Ethel Barrymore Theatre in March 1968 with Estelle Parsons as Myrtle, Harry Guardino as Chicken, and Brian Bedford as Lot. The production received very poor reviews and closed after 29 performances. A film version, *THE LAST OF THE MOBILE HOT SHOTS,* was released in 1969. GORE VIDAL wrote the screenplay for the film, which was directed by Sidney Lumet and featured Lynn Redgrave as Myrtle, James Coburn as the Lot character called Jeb, and Robert Hooks as Chicken.

## PUBLICATION HISTORY

*The Kingdom of Earth* was first published by New Directions with the title *The Seven Descents of Myrtle* in 1968. It was subsequently revised and published with the former title reinstated in 1976.

## CHARACTERS

**Chicken** He is a young farmer, the half brother of Lot. Because Chicken is a mulatto man living in a small Mississippi Delta town during the 1940s, he is mistreated and regarded as inferior by his community. Because of this ill treatment he has become callous and resentful. Chicken also feels he is an outcast in his own home. He suffers the wrath of his stepmother, an upper-class, genteel white woman. She throws him off the farm after his father dies. Chicken wants to own the family farm to prove that he is worthy of something more than work as a field hand. He finds some sort of happiness when Myrtle arrives with Lot. Chicken considers his intimate encounters with Myrtle the only truly happy and worthwhile moments in his life. Chicken has a tumultuous relationship with Lot; their bitterness stems from competition, and from Chicken's low-class upbringing as well as his dark skin. In the end, Chicken inherits Lot's farm and his wife.

**Lot** Lot is the son of wealthy landowners and heir to a farm on the Mississippi Delta. Handsome and blond, Lot has dashing good looks that belie his terminal illness and impotence. He is slowly dying of tuberculosis. Lot lives with his half brother, Chicken, and has spent his adult life pining for his deceased mother, Miss Lottie. When he takes home his new bride, Myrtle, he is disappointed that she is not like his mother. Because he is dying, Lot quickly marries Myrtle to ensure that his property will not be owned by Chicken. Lot despises his half brother because he is from a lower class, is insensitive, and is racially mixed. As the play progresses, it makes clear that Lot is a transvestite and a homosexual. Lot blames his sexual impotence on his terminal illness and Myrtle believes him. Chicken reveals his secret sexual identity to Myrtle. He tells Myrtle that Lot dresses in his mother's clothing and impersonates her in the parlor. Lot is a complex character, frustrated by his social status, sexuality, and health. He becomes a stranger in his own body. Lot loses his wife and his inheritance to the socially inferior Chicken. In many ways he is reminiscent of "fading beauties" in the Williams canon, such as Amanda Wingfield in *THE GLASS MENAGERIE* and Blanche DuBois in *A STREETCAR NAMED DESIRE.*

**Myrtle** The newlywed wife of Lot. Myrtle is a vivacious and gregarious woman, who once had a career in show business. She returns to her new husband's homestead, a farm on the Mississippi Delta, and is content to care for him and nurse him back to health. Lot has not been completely honest with Myrtle; he has failed to mention that he is slowly dying of tuberculosis and that he shares his home with his illegitimate half brother, Chicken. Myrtle is stunned by Chicken's crass behavior but is simultaneously attracted to his rugged physique. She subsequently realizes that she is faced with an impossible situation with Lot: He is dying and he is impotent. Myrtle pursues a relationship with Chicken initially to obtain his deed to the family property; however, as she wants nothing more out of life than to be a loving and fulfilled wife and mother, she decides to try to create this sort of life with Chicken.

# *The Knightly Quest*

A novella written before 1968.

## SYNOPSIS

After years of travel and the drug death of his tutor and traveling companion Dr. Horace Greaves in Manhattan, Gewinner Pearce returns to his hometown of Gewinner. He is met at the airport by his sister-in-law, Mrs. Violet Pearce. During the years of his absence the town of Gewinner has changed; the most prominent evidence of this change is The Project, which people shy away from discussing in public.

On the drive back to the Pearce residence it turns out Gewinner's brother, Braden Pearce, has transformed their father's business, the Red Devil Battery plant, into The Project—a bomb factory. Gewinner's questions are unanswered and are cut short when Violet informs him the car is bugged. Over the coming days, he is able to piece together more information and notes that The Project has attracted scientists and workmen to the town of Gewinner, which has grown since he left. The newcomers live in a new development called Sunshine Houses. Overall, the town of Gewinner seems to have prospered from the changes; however, its namesake, Gewinner Pearce, is shocked by the loss of tradition and heritage, as symbolized by a drive-in built on what used to be Pearce family land.

The story flashes back to events in the recent past: While undergoing her daily Vibra-Wonder treatment, Gewinner's newly widowed mother, Nelly Pearce, dictates a letter to a society friend, Boo, in which she describes a weekend visit of President Stew Hammersmith and his family to the Pearce mansion. Braden and the president formally discuss the problems in Ghu-Ghok-Shu. Babe, the president's daughter, has designs on Braden Pearce, an attraction that their mothers decide to encourage. After all, Braden's wife, Violet, is a social upstart and not suited to the position she currently holds.

A further flashback reveals that Gewinner began his travels at the age of 16 in the company of Dr. Greaves, who contracted a nervous condition and collapsed. While Dr. Greaves is hospitalized, Gewinner enlists in the navy, but his service lasts a mere 10 days before he is dismissed and all his records are destroyed. His return home is not only prompted by the death of Dr. Greaves, but also by the fact that his late father has left the Pearce estate to Mother Pearce and Braden. Gewinner has returned in order to convince Braden that their continued financial support of his travels would be in the best interest of all parties involved.

Gewinner and his younger brother, Braden, are opposites: Gewinner is slight and youthful-looking and tries to hold himself apart from the family, whereas Braden is robust, bullish, and energetic and practically controls the town. The energy extends to his sexual drive, and his and Violet's marital pursuits even disrupt a bridge match with the neighbors, Mrs. Fisher and her son. As Nelly Pearce goes upstairs to quiet them, Gewinner starts making seemingly random conversation and proceeds to win the game. The end of the bridge game is marked by a cessation of the noise, the return of Mother Pearce, and the arrival of an order from Laughing Boy Drive-In. It is Braden and Violet's postcoital snack, which is delivered to the bedroom by Billy Spangler, the drive-in's proprietor, who usually stays for a nightcap with Braden. Billy and Braden go a long way back, and they spend these occasions reminiscing about their racist pranks as boys. Braden intimates that come Halloween, there will be an event at The Project that will ensure a "white Christmas."

Two weeks after his return home, Gewinner has his first personal encounter with Billy. Curious about Braden's boyhood chum, he visits the detested drive-in. Recognizing the car as Violet's, Billy emerges from the shop, and the two men appraise each other. Gewinner is not fooled by Billy's innocent good looks, ignores him, and strikes up a conversation with the girl carhop. Still not knowing who his customer is, Billy begins praising the merits of the business location and the wisdom of Braden Pearce. Gewinner is too angry to reply and drives off abruptly, slightly injuring Billy.

Billy complains to Braden, who confronts Gewinner that same evening. When Gewinner suggests that the problem could be solved by Braden and Mother Pearce's restoring, or better yet, increasing, his traveling allowance, Braden warns him that new arrivals in town are vetted and if they do not fit in, they run the risk of being interned in order to safeguard The Project. In order to prevent problems, he urges Gewinner to go to the drive-in the next day and apologize to Billy. Gewinner points out that restoring his travel allowance would spare Braden the embarrassment of having a brother in "isolation." However, despite his overtly material motives, Gewinner becomes increasingly aware of a moral responsibility to oppose The Project.

Morality of a different sort is displayed by Billy Spangler. He is proud of the fact that his drive-in contributes to The Project in a small way, and he lets customers know that he loses money by making sure that the guards at The Project have a steady supply of coffee. This evening he is alone in the drive-in with Big Edna, the carhop, who still is shaken up over her conversation with Gewinner earlier in the day. He wonders whether he should let her go home, because he does not expect to have much business. The Project, which governs the life of the people in the town of Gewinner as a quasi religion, encourages early bedtimes and punishes those who frivolously stay out late. But instead of sending Edna home, he rapes her in the gents' toilet. His own interpretation is that he has been seduced by her, and the following morning he fires her because she is a bad woman.

While Billy places an ad for a new carhop, Gewinner enters the drive-in and takes a seat at the counter. He has been dropped off by Braden, who is waiting in his limousine outside, escorted by two motorcycle cops. Aware that Braden has forced Gewinner to apologize, Billy orders some coffee for him and explains that apologies are not necessary. All Gewinner has to do is drink the coffee and leave a dime tip for Little Edna, the carhop. Gewinner's response is to spit in the coffee and leave a $100 tip before going back home. Called out by Braden, Billy walks over to the limousine unable to tell Braden the truth.

As Gewinner returns to the Pearce mansion, he expects a renewed confrontation but finds that Braden and Mother Pearce have flown to the state capital by helicopter to attend the deathbed of the governor, who has been shot by an assassin. Only Violet is at home, mixing drinks in the game room. It is, as she informs her brother-in-law, the only room in the house that is not bugged. Their conversation is briefly interrupted by the arrival of a carrier pigeon and the exchange of messages with Violet's childhood friend, Gladys. After the pigeon has flown, Violet resumes the conversation. She is fully aware of Mother Pearce's attempts to bring Braden and Babe together, and she approves of it, wanting to be rid of Braden's sexual demands as well as of their child, who makes a brief, startling appearance. She also confides that she is aware of Braden's plans to achieve world domination through the Project. Together, Violet and Gewinner decide to thwart Braden's plans.

The town of Gewinner is subject to constant suspicions about spies. Outside mail and the inhabitants are rigorously screened, and the town is rife with undercover detectives. Project employees live in a perpetual state of anxiety, which they do not dare to admit. Anyone who is diagnosed as unbalanced is removed from the town and sent to Camp Tranquility for readjustment. People who go there are not heard of again; allegedly they transfer to Rancho Allegro when their condition improves. Fear of *the spy* prevents workers at The Project from forming close relationships, as there is a constant awareness that anything said or done may be reported to the authorities.

Billy Spangler is extremely conscious of this spy threat, and so he carefully screens the applicants for the carhop vacancy. In the interviews he asks two key questions, the first of which regards the applicant's opinion of Gloria Butterfield, a famous spy at The Project, who has been caught by The Eye. It is widely assumed that Billy knows more about the disappearance of Gloria and her associates than anyone else. The second question is "How do you feel about love?" Billy expects a clean-minded, open-hearted attitude on the subject. So far the interviews have not been going well. The girls all share the same bland looks, with only one exception, an exceptionally attractive young woman. However, her answer to the Gloria Butterfield question reveals that she is aware of how the spy and her associates were killed, information Billy had thought only he and Braden had. Her answer to the question about love—"I have not had much experience with it but I think the idea is great!"—is equally unsettling. Torn between unease and attraction, Billy tells her to wait while he interviews the other applicants, none of whom meets his expectations. Her figure and smile eventually overcome his reservations and he hires her.

In early February there is a sudden outbreak of crime in the town of Gewinner. Policemen and Project workers on the night shift are beaten unconscious and robbed by offenders who become known as the Black Cat Gang. Measures imposed to protect the population are unable to stop the crime wave, until the investigating committee discloses that the chief perpetrator is the Chief of Police himself. The entire police force is sent to Camp Tranquility and replaced by government agents.

Every night between midnight and dawn Gewinner carefully prepares himself for his nocturnal wanderings. Initially he has been stopped by the odd patrolman, but now the authorities are sufficiently familiar with him and Violet's car not to interfere. His nightly journeys always follow the same pattern and frequently end at the high school stadium to pick up a lover for a brief, wordless affair.

After an uneasy night, Billy puts Gladys, the new carhop, to work the next morning, determined not to let her attractiveness affect him. By midafternoon she has proved herself to such an extent that he feels comfortable with expressing his appreciation. However, matters become fraught with tension when Big Edna's old uniform is delivered from the tailor's and is slightly too tight for Gladys. Billy orders her to wear it anyway, and come closing time, he sends home the two other women and asks Gladys to stay.

In a long explanatory passage, Gewinner is likened to Don Quixote, his nightly cruising a crusade to rediscover Sancho Panza. Crucially, he is a romantic, who believes in the transforming power of vision.

Gewinner and Violet, the two conspirators, are carrying on a secret correspondence by carrier pigeon with Gladys the carhop, who is Violet's childhood friend. Within days of starting to work at the drive-in, she tells Billy that she is an undercover agent for The Project, but that even Braden is not to know about this. Billy, completely influenced by lust, agrees to keep it a secret but soon develops doubts, as Gladys' counterespionage methods seem less than subtle. On the occasion of a tryst in his office, she explains to him that their overt counterespionage efforts are purposeful to make the spies think she and her associates are stupid.

On Saturday, March 19, Braden Pearce arranges a dinner at the Pearce mansion in celebration of his and Violet's seventh—and last—wedding anniversary. Also invited are the Catholic and Methodist ministers, Father Acheson and the Reverend Dr. Peters, whom Braden has bribed to create a truce. During dinner, Violet becomes embarrassingly drunk and is carried off to her room by two attendants. Gewinner follows to look after her, while Mother Pearce converses about flowers, as though nothing has happened. Eventually Braden cuts in and delivers an incoherent political diatribe, occasionally interrupted by Mother Pearce, who announces that the First Family, including Babe, is due for another visit the following weekend. After coffee, she excuses herself and visits her aviary in the conservatory, where she finds Gewinner and Violet, the latter unaccountably sober now and carrying a flight bag. According to Gewinner, he and Violet have been invited to an event at the drive-in. Mother Pearce, although slightly bemused, lets them go, hoping she will be rid of both for good.

Billy meanwhile has received an order for a quart of coffee and a dozen barbecue sandwiches from The Project. The order is to be delivered by him, not to the guards but to the Golden Room in the administration building; he interprets the instruction as a huge promotion of his standing within The Project. Miraculously, Gladys presents him with the ready-made sandwiches, and the transport problem is solved, too, when a conciliatory Gewinner pulls up with Violet. Both Billy and Gladys get in, and the four speed off to the plant. En route, Billy believes he hears a ticking sound, but Gewinner reassures him that it is merely the engine, which needs service. The guard at the gate lets them through when Violet tells him that her husband, Mr. Braden Pearce, is expecting them. Insistent electronic beeping is heard from several different areas of the plant. Billy gets out of the car, and as it drives off, he realizes that something must be seriously wrong at the plant. Alarm lights are flashing and klaxons blaring, people running around. Despite this, he decides to fulfill his mission, which is to deliver his famous coffee. Suddenly silence falls, only broken by a loudspeaker announcement, but Billy has heard the ticking sound again. He examines the coffee container and finds a bomb, which detonates while he is looking at it.

Moments before the detonation, Gewinner, Violet, and Gladys escape on a spaceship. The spaceship is piloted by three astronauts, and in the course of their journey to an unknown destination, Gewinner befriends the Navigator, who eventually informs him that he will be allowed to land with them.

## COMMENTARY

> Of course, America, and particularly the Southern states, is the embodiment of an originally romantic gesture. It was discovered and established by the eternal Don Quixote in the human flux. Then, of course, the businessmen took over and Don Quixote was an exile at home: at least he became one when the frontiers had been exhausted. (Williams, 74)

This, in Tennessee Williams's own words, is the central dilemma of his 1966 novella *The Knightly Quest.* It also is the thread that unifies a sometimes disjointed narrative and the multilayered imagery typical of his later work. Thematic strands appear to develop and mutate as the story unfolds—the novella has variously been read as an "antiwar satire" (Spoto, 265), dealing with cold war issues, or "a Kafkaesque parable set in a secret weapons factory" (Price, *New York Times,* Dec. 1, 1985). It is all of these, and a few more: a scathing indictment of 1950s small-town morality, an equally scathing verdict on McCarthyism, a uniquely Williamsesque version of *Brave New World,* an unlikely piece of chivalric romance, and a rite of passage for an even more unlikely hero. Signally, the hero is an outsider, and with this, the core theme of *The Knightly Quest* can be distilled in Williams's recurring subject of the outcast's struggle against a society intolerant of divergence.

The novella's title is a none too subtle pointer. As the subversive Gladys points out, "the term 'knightly quest' instead of 'nightly quest' is not just a verbal conceit but a thing of the highest significance in every part of creation, wherever a man in the prison of his body can remember his spirit." The knight errant Gewinner Pearce takes some time remembering, and for a protagonist he remains strangely reactive throughout most of the story. The German word *Gewinner* means "winner," specifically of a contest or competition. His name, too, has significance, suggesting that he will emerge victorious at the end. For his namesake town Gewinner, on the other hand, the word is ironic: Having won in material terms, the town has lost its spirit.

As many of Williams's characters are, Gewinner Pearce is at least in part an incarnation of his author and trapped in the familiar idealized vision of a Southern past. Remembering his hometown as "a romantic ballet setting," he at first instinctively wants to reboard the plane when confronted with the vulgar reality of the town of Gewinner. However, the past cannot have been as idyllic as Gewinner Pearce's memory would have it. As outrageous an eyesore and earache as the Laughing Boy Drive-In may be, the Pearce family home—"Pearce's Folly," as he refers to it—is a mock-medieval castle with an imitation drawbridge, hardly in better taste. The name recurs in the 1975 play *The Red Devil*

*Battery Sign,* which also deals with cold war issues. His father's Red Devil Battery Plant has been converted into The Project, an indication that the forces shaping the town of Gewinner may not have been as concentrated in the past but surely have been at work for a long time. However intensely Gewinner may cling to a supposedly romantic childhood, evidence suggests that it is a distortion of memory rather than genuine. His sister-in-law, Violet, fellow outsider because of her unsatisfactory social background, calls him a changeling, "something else, not of this world," implying that he is an alien within his own family; Gewinner's estrangement is underlined by his taking up residence in the secluded tower of the family mansion.

Distance and discretion constitute a modus vivendi that allows for coexistence at least, and it is an established pattern. Rather than enforce conformity, his parents were quick to ship off 16-year-old Gewinner—and the problem—to Europe once it was obvious that his tutor, Dr. Horace Greaves, was teaching the boy more than humanities. Whereas Braden and Violet's marital cavorting and the attendant decibel levels are tolerated (qua heterosexual) and Billy Spangler's predatory sexual aggression can be explained away (qua misogyny), Gewinner's lonely cruising must take place under cover of night and be couched in rituals and secret signals recognizable only to the initiated. The reason for the secrecy is obvious: "New legislation is being pushed through at high speed for the isolation of all you don't-fit-inners."

The "don't-fit-inners," sexual and otherwise, are sent to Camp Tranquility and Rancho Allegro, both of which undoubtedly are ironic references to Williams's own periods of hospitalization, but beyond that they also hold a far more sinister connotation. Nobody ever returns from these places; the last life sign of an internee usually consists of a single postcard. In other words, the victims' fate is not unlike that of the South American *desparecidos.* As in any totalitarian system, The Project and its proponents will insist that this method is necessary for there "is too much at stake, too much pending, on a world-wide scale."

The Project's specific intent is never fully spelled out. There are several hints, most of them unsavory, such as the "white Christmas" and "white-hot snow," which Braden promises, blanket images for both ethnic holocaust and nuclear winter. It seems equally clear, however, that "bomb factory" is merely one function of The Project. It variously takes on the guises of corporate giant, quasi religion, and new world order, as defined by Billy, a global community of "friendly Caucasians . . . dedicated to a Great New Thing." The sponginess of purpose is driven home in Braden's memorably muddled after-dinner speech, a superb travesty of political utterances past and present. In one respect, however, The Project's effects are perfectly obvious. Aided and abetted by the national government, it succeeds in creating a totalitarian state within a state whose absolute ruler is Braden Pearce and whose citizens are intimidated and equalized to the point of facelessness. The job applicants screened at the Laughing Boy Drive-In bear witness to it; they are all daughters of Project workers, and there is "a sameness about them, a blank kind of neatness and trimness which made you feel a bit let down somehow." The smells and sounds of The Project permeate the entire town, and Gewinner, the changeling, feels "a vibration in himself like a counter-vibration to the one that [comes] from The Project."

Beyond being a moral imperative, resistance thus becomes an inevitable physical instinct for Gewinner, a logical development within the context of prohibited sexuality. He finds a coconspirator in Violet, who, having an abusive husband and unwanted child, is as trapped as he. As the conspiracy gains momentum, the objectives change. Initially the goal is to cut the little wire that connects a button to the doomsday machine, which will either blow the planet or put it "under the absolute dominion of the Project." But disabling this mechanism, though likely to be beneficial to the world, can hardly amount to more than an act of personal revenge against Braden. "Yes, I would love to be there when he pressed the little button and it dawned on his sensitive mind that someone had cut the little wire," says Violet. In the end it emerges that the plan has grown significantly beyond the cutting of wires. With their dupe Billy Spangler carrying in a bomb, Gewinner, Violet, and Gladys destroy the doomsday machine, The Project, and—one would infer—the world, while the trio of conspirators escape in a conveniently available spaceship.

The implicit verdict is that there exists no small town, no state, and no nation on this planet that will accept divergence from the—usually arbitrary—norm. The only recourse for the oppressed must be to do as the oppressor would, blow up the exhausted frontiers, and find an entirely new one. Such an ultimate escape is, of course, both disillusioned and disillusioning, but it promises release for the hero at least. Romantic to the core, Gewinner reacts with quiet surprise when the spaceship's Navigator informs him that he has been cleared to land on the new planet:

> . . . the possibility that he might not be
> accepted had never occurred.
> But what, he asked, about this? . . .
> Will this be admitted with me?

*This* refers to his silk scarf, a token of homosexuality that Gewinner wears as a knight would wear the token of his lady. The Navigator sees it differently, merely as a "highly valued . . . historical item in our Museum of Sad Enchantments in Galaxies Drifting Away." At that moment the champagne corks begin popping, reinforcing the message that where Gewinner is going, the quest may be conducted in broad daylight and without secrecy. The exile is over.

## PUBLICATION HISTORY

*The Knightly Quest* was first published by New Directions in 1966 in a volume with four short stories. It was published again in 1968 by Secker & Warburg, in a volume that included 12 short stories.

## CHARACTERS

**Big Edna** She is a carhop at Billy Spangler's Laughing Boy Drive-In. Edna is raped by Billy in the bathroom of the restaurant. Afterward, he fires her and sends her home.

**Butterfield, Gloria** She has been a spy at the Project, who has been caught passing on information. She and her associates have been killed.

**Gladys** She is the school friend and carrier pigeon correspondent of Violet Pearce. Gladys is a spy, who takes a job as carhop at Billy Spangler's drive-in.

**Greaves, Horace** He is the former tutor and traveling companion of Gewinner Pearce. He suffers from a nervous disorder and dies in consequence of a drug overdose, leaving Gewinner to return to his hometown.

**Pearce, Braden** Braden is the younger brother of Gewinner Pearce. He is the creator of the Project, a military weapon factory. A white supremacist, he practically controls the town of Gewinner.

**Pearce, Gewinner** Gewinner returns to his hometown; he has traveled since the death of his mentor, Dr. Horace Greeves. Gewinner finds that many conditions have changed for the worse, namely, a bomb warehouse called the Project. Gewinner returns to convince his family that funding his travels and thus keeping him out of their way is in the best interest of everyone, but he is warned by his brother, Braden Pearce, that outsiders or those who oppose the Project are not tolerated. With his sister-in-law, Violet Pearce, Gewinner blows up the bomb factory, and they escape on a spaceship.

**Pearce, Nelly** She is the mother of the protagonist, Gewinner Pearce. Generally referred to as "Mother Pearce," she is a society lady and friend of the First Family.

**Pearce, Violet** Violet is the sister-in-law of the protagonist, Gewinner Pearce. She is married to the brutish Braden Pearce and tries to drown her problems in alcohol. Together with Gewinner, Violet blows up the bomb factory as a protest against the unwanted changes in the town. She then escapes with him on a spaceship.

**Spangler, Billy** He is a former amateur wrestler and old friend of Braden's. Billy is the owner of the Laughing Boy Drive-In and sexually harasses his employees. He rapes Big Edna and then fires her.

## FURTHER READING

Price, Reynolds. "His Battle Cry Was 'Valor'!" *New York Times,* Dec. 1, 1985, Sunday, Late City Final Edition. Section 7, Page 11, Column 1.

Spoto, Donald. *The Kindness of Strangers.* Boston: Da Capo, 1997.

Williams, Tennessee. "The Knightly Quest." In *The Knightly Quest: A Novella and Twelve Short Stories.* London: Secker & Warburg, 1968.

# *The Lady of Larkspur Lotion*

A one-act play written before 1942.

## SYNOPSIS

The play is set in a shabby rooming house in New Orleans. Mrs. Hardwicke-Moore sits on her bed as her landlady, Mrs. Wire, knocks at her door and demands the rent. Mrs. Hardwicke-Moore admits Mrs. Wire and complains to her about the poor conditions of the boardinghouse. Mrs. Wire suggests that Mrs. Hardwicke-Moore find another place to live. Mrs. Hardwicke-Moore makes excuses for being unable to pay her rent. She explains that she is expecting money from her rubber plantation in Brazil. Mrs. Wire does not believe money is in transit and accuses Mrs. Hardwicke-Moore of being a prostitute and an alcoholic.

The Writer enters the room and tries to end the argument. Mrs. Wire attacks him, calls him an alcoholic, and condemns all the "[French] Quarter rats, half-breeds, drunkards, degenerates, who try to get by on promises, lies, delusions!" She harasses Mrs. Hardwicke-Moore by calling her "the lady of larkspur lotion," again implying that she is a prostitute. Mrs. Wire quizzes The Writer about his rent payment and when his great masterpiece will be finished. The Writer becomes sullen as he realizes his book may never be finished. He has lied to his landlady about promises of commission checks. The Writer shoves Mrs. Wire out of the room. She threatens to evict them. The Writer inquires about Mrs. Hardwicke-Moore's Brazilian rubber plantation. She launches into a series of reminiscences about her life on the plantation. She thanks The Writer for his kindness, and when she asks his name, he tells her he is Anton Pavlovich Chekhov.

## COMMENTARY

Larkspur lotion is used in a treatment for body vermin. Mrs. Hardwicke-Moore's possession of this ointment identifies her as a prostitute, but she has created a fictitious existence in an attempt to salvage some dignity for herself. The Writer is equally given to fantasy and delusion. He struggles to write in the hope that someday he will be as famous as his favorite writer, ANTON CHEKHOV. Since he has not reached that point in his life, he takes on the Russian writer's identity, at least in the presence of Mrs. Hardwicke-Moore. These two companions in misery allow each other to dream and live out their fantasies as a means of escaping their wretched life in their separate rented rooms.

*The Lady of Larkspur Lotion* is reminiscent of Williams's experiences as a young artist living in the French Quarter of New Orleans, in the late 1930s. Williams moved to New Orleans in 1938, and this vibrant environment became a major influence in his development as a writer. This bohemian locale introduced Williams to a community of fellow artisans and liberated him socially, artistically, and sexually. Williams would later describe New Orleans as "the paradise of his youth" (Holditch, 194). It was a paradise of young, ambitious, and poverty-stricken artists living in shabby conditions presided over by suspicious, unstable, and often violent landladies. One such landlady, Mrs. Louise Wire, who owned and ran the boardinghouse Williams lived in at 722 Toulouse Street, became the inspiration for her namesake in the play and for other landlady characters in such works as "THE ANGEL IN THE ALCOVE" and *VIEUX CARRÉ.*

## PRODUCTION HISTORY

*The Lady of Larkspur Lotion* was first produced at the Monceau Theatre, Paris, France, in 1948. It premiered in New York at Lolly's Theatre Club in 1963.

## PUBLICATION HISTORY

*The Lady of Larkspur Lotion* was first published in the collection *27 WAGONS FULL OF COTTON AND OTHER ONE-ACT PLAYS.*

### CHARACTERS

**Hardwicke-Moore, Mrs.** She is a middle-aged prostitute and a tenant in the boardinghouse owned by Mrs. Wire. While she has fantastic dreams of owning a Brazilian plantation, she fights to survive and avoid eviction from her dreary rented room. Mrs. Wire feels an obligation to remind Mrs. Hardwicke-Moore of the reality that she is only a prostitute. Mrs. Hardwicke-Moore encounters another tenant in the boardinghouse, the Writer, and discovers a fellow dreamer who chooses to deny reality.

**Wire, Mrs.** Mrs. Wire is the landlady of a pair of deadbeat tenants, Mrs. Hardwicke-Moore and the Writer, whom she despises. Mrs. Wire must harass them for rent and mocks their fantastic excuses.

**Writer** He is an aspiring writer who dreams of fame and acceptance. He befriends another tenant, Mrs. Hardwicke-Moore, and the pair indulge each other in their fantasies of fame and fortune. The Writer fantasizes about being ANTON CHEKHOV, while Mrs. Hardwicke-Moore dreams of owning her own Brazilian rubber plantation. Both are threatened with eviction.

### FURTHER READING

Holditch, W. Kenneth. "Tennessee Williams in New Orleans," in *Magical Muse: Millennial Essays on Tennessee Williams*, edited by Ralph Voss. Tuscaloosa: University of Alabama Press, 2002, pp. 183–206.

# "The Lady's Beaded Bag"

A short story written in 1930.

### SYNOPSIS

One cold November morning, The Rag Picker discovers a splendid lady's beaded bag in a dumpster. He is cautious as he removes the purse from its mauve box, afraid that someone on the street will see him take it. The Rag Picker quickly grabs the purse and stuffs it into his pocket. Upon further inspection, he finds that it is stuffed with money. As The Rag Picker walks to the end of the alley, he sees a chauffeur standing guard. They make eye contact and the trash picker becomes alarmed, imagining that the police have been called.

He begins to wonder what the authorities will think if they find the beaded bag in his possession. The trash picker thinks he must rectify the situation by returning the bag to its original owner. He bolts out of the alley and follows the street until he faces an extravagant gray stone house. He rings the doorbell and a maid answers. Unable to face her directly, he holds his head down and raises up his arm to hand her the bag, which he tells her he found in the trash. The maid takes the bag, realizing she accidentally threw it away when she discarded the milliner's box. Without thanking or rewarding the Rag Picker, she informs its owner, Mrs. Ferrabye, that she found it lying on the piano.

Mrs. Ferrabye is dressing for dinner and is annoyed by the maid's interruption. She orders the maid to put away the bag. A few minutes pass and a parcel arrives for Mrs. Ferrabye. It is a glistening white evening wrap. She investigates it, proclaims the item ridiculous, and throws it onto the bed as if it were a rag. Mrs. Ferrabye returns to the business of dressing for dinner.

### COMMENTARY

"The Lady's Beaded Bag," one of Williams's earliest works of fiction, was written when Williams was a freshman at the UNIVERSITY OF MISSOURI. The story's protagonist, the Rag Picker, is the first of Williams's fugitive kind. He is a poverty-stricken individual with no hope of bettering his life. The American dream has failed the Rag Picker, and for 15 years he has been rummaging through dumpsters in search of treasure. His survival depends on absentminded behavior of someone richer than he.

"The Lady's Beaded Bag" is social commentary on the class structure of the modern-day America. Williams demonstrates the vast division between the rich and the poor and examines the question of morality. The trash picker finds the beaded bag and returns it because he fears he may appear to be a thief, although it is clearly his ticket out of dire poverty. He feels guilty just for finding the beaded bag. The trash picker upholds moral order, whereas Mrs. Ferrabye is rude, wasteful, and unappreciative of the luxuries she possesses. The equation of criminality and poverty is clearly established, as the Trash Picker knows if he is caught with the bag, he will never be able to prove his innocence.

The plight of the poor and invisibility of the working class are recurring themes in Williams's early work. Williams illustrates their predicament in a number of ways in "The Lady's Beaded Bag." For instance, the protagonist, the Rag Picker, remains nameless. He and the other members of the working class in the story, such as the chauffeur and the maid, are identified exclusively by the functions they fulfill in society. Their existence is defined by their relationship to the upper classes whom they serve. They are without an essential humanity and individuality that the privileged, such as Mrs. Ferrabye, possess. In an ironic twist, which underscores the insignificance of the poor, once Mrs. Ferrabye's character is introduced, the Rag Picker is forgotten. His welfare is inconsequential, and he is not rewarded for doing the right thing. He is left to continue his rummaging through rubbish, while Mrs. Ferrabye grows richer with very little effort. "The Lady's Beaded Bag" is a prime example of the significant social commentary found in many of Williams's works.

### PUBLICATION HISTORY

"The Lady's Beaded Bag" was first published by the University of Missouri's English Club in 1930. It was subsequently published in the short story collection *Collected Stories* in 1985.

### CHARACTERS

**Ferrabye, Mrs.** She is a wealthy aristocrat who owns so many priceless possessions that she dismisses the beaded bag that is returned to her by the Rag Picker.

**Rag Picker** He is an impoverished street dweller who during his routine dumpster sifting discovers a lady's beaded bag. The Rag Picker's imagination whirls as his daily routine has finally paid off. He then becomes fearful and imagines that he will go to prison if he is found with such an exquisite item. The Rag Picker returns the purse to the nearest mansion. The maid quickly snatches it, without any thanks or compensation for the Rag Picker.

## *The Last of the Mobile Hot Shots*

A film version of *The Kingdom of Earth, or The Seven Descents of Myrtle* produced by Warner Brothers in 1969. Sidney Lumet directed the film, which featured Lynn Redgrave (Myrtle) James Coburn (Lot), and Robert Hooks (Chicken).

## *The Last of My Solid Gold Watches*

A one-act play written before 1946.

### SYNOPSIS

The play is set in a hotel room in a Mississippi Delta town. The room is rundown but has vestiges of its former coziness, now faded with time. The room is filled with luggage and top-quality shoes. Charlie Colton is a traveling shoe salesman, who hopes to sell a selection of shoes to Harper. Harper is bored by the talk of leather shoes. He pulls a comic book out of his back pocket and starts to read. Mr. Colton is frustrated by Harper's lack of interest and respect. Charlie reprimands Harper and launches into a speech about the "world of illusion" Harper now inhabits. Charlie acknowledges the numerous gold watches he has collected over the years as the top salesman. He realizes that he is now surviving on the last of his solid gold watches but still deserves respect from the younger generation. Harper leaves the senior salesman alone to reminisce.

### COMMENTARY

Charlie Colton struggles with growing old and reaching the end of his career as a traveling shoe salesman. He is left alone in a shabby hotel room, reliving his former glory and success. Mr. Colton is enraged that he is being replaced by a younger generation who do not appreciate the art of selling shoes. Old age, dying, and the frivolity and brevity of youth are recurring themes in Williams's writing and are a prominent feature in such works as *SWEET BIRD OF YOUTH* and "THE INTERVAL."

The narrative of this one-act play was drawn from aspects of Williams's life. His father, CORNELIUS COFFIN WILLIAMS, was a traveling shoe salesman for the INTERNATIONAL SHOE COMPANY. Cornelius forced Williams to work for the company after his poor academic performance at the UNIVERSITY OF MISSOURI. The young Williams hated the job and documented his experiences at International Shoe in such works as *STAIRS TO THE ROOF* and *THE GLASS MENAGERIE*. The uninterested Harper, who cares more for fantasy and reading, resembles the youthful Williams.

## PRODUCTION HISTORY

*The Last of My Solid Gold Watches* was first produced at Laboratory Theatre, Los Angeles, California, in 1948. It was also produced by MARGO JONES at Theatre '48 in Dallas, Texas, 1948. In 1958 this play was turned into a television movie directed by Sidney Lumet.

## PUBLICATION HISTORY

*The Last of My Solid Gold Watches* was published in *Best One-Act Plays of 1942* and in *27 WAGONS FULL OF COTTON AND OTHER ONE-ACT PLAYS* (1966).

## CHARACTERS

**Colton, Mr. Charlie** Charlie is a traveling salesman who has won numerous gold watches for being the top salesperson. He realizes that he is losing his competitive edge and will probably not receive another gold watch. Mr. Colton grapples to recover the remains of his reputation and nourish the remnants of his better days. Failing to sell his wares, he is faced with the reality that his era has passed.

**Harper, Bob** Bob is a young shoe salesman, who is completely indifferent to his occupation. He encounters Charlie Colton, a proud older salesman, and is bored by Charlie's tales of the antics of the older generation.

# *Life Boat Drill*

A one-act play written around 1970.

## SYNOPSIS

An elderly couple, E. Long Taske and his wife, Ella Taske, a pair of ailing nonagenarians, are sailing together on the *Queen Elizabeth II* (*QEII*), a luxury ocean liner. They occupy twin beds in their stateroom cabin. The frail couple bicker fiercely, and Ella suggests they contemplate legal separation. In the midst of their wrangling they entertain the idea of attending the ship's daily "lifeboat drill."

Ella and Long are joined in their stateroom by two members of the ship's staff. The Steward and Stewardess serve the couple breakfast and tell them that the lifeboat drill has been canceled. At the sound of the lifeboat drill whistle, the staff members depart. The Steward lets slip that the lifeboat drill is occurring that day.

Mr. and Mrs. Taske fall into a panic as they realize they will miss the drill and have been left to their own devices. Mr. Taske makes a frantic search through their cabin for their life-preserver jackets. In the process, he breaks his glasses and upsets Ella in her bed. He eventually finds the two jackets under the beds. With great effort, Ella and Long struggle to don their jackets. Alone and unsure, the elderly couple cling to their beds and each other in desperation.

## COMMENTARY

*Life Boat Drill* is a short, grotesque comedy that explores the panic, isolation, confusion, and sense of abandonment that often accompany old age. Mr. and Mrs. Taske are set adrift in their stateroom, attempting to settle past grievances and grappling for survival. Beyond the slapstick humor of Mr. Taske's breaking his glasses and crawling under the twin beds to retrieve their life jackets and Mrs. Taske's swatting him away with her life jacket, there is a sober and a desperate sense of helplessness in their tale. Mrs. Taske's fight for dignity and respect in the midst of the impersonal treatment the couple receives from the condescendingly cheerful staff members is poignantly depicted.

In many ways the nautical *Life Boat Drill* is reminiscent of two other Williams seaside dramas: SMALL

CRAFT WARNINGS and CONFESSIONAL. In each of these plays the characters search for a means of survival and life preservation in whatever form. There is a sense of lives set adrift, lost at sea and clinging desperately to those around for safety and security. *Life Boat Drill* is also similar in theme and tone to THE FROSTED GLASS COFFIN. Both of these plays portray the pain and bewilderment of aging and the fear of impending death.

## PRODUCTION HISTORY

There have been no major documented productions of *Life Boat Drill.*

## PUBLICATION HISTORY

*Life Boat Drill* was published in *The Theatre of Tennessee Williams,* volume VII, by New Directions in 1970.

## CHARACTERS

**Steward** He is a member of the crew of the *QEII* luxury ocean liner. Along with his fellow staff member, the Stewardess, he is responsible for attending to a pair of elderly passengers, Mr. E. Long Taske and his wife, Mrs. Ella Taske. He is irritated by the ailing, demanding couple and greets them with a "bright, icy smile." After delivering their breakfast, the Steward lies to Mr. and Mrs. Taske telling them that the ship's daily lifeboat drill has been canceled. Just before he leaves their cabin, the Steward lets slip that the drill is occurring.

**Stewardess** She is a giggly, condescending member of the crew of the *QEII* luxury ocean liner. Along with her fellow staff member, the Steward, she is responsible for attending to a pair of elderly passengers, Mr. E. Long Taske and his wife, Mrs. Ella Taske. She is annoyed by the ailing, demanding nonagenerians. The Stewardess conspires with her colleague to lie about the time of the daily lifeboat drill.

**Taske, Mr. E. Long** An ailing, elderly man in his nineties, Mr. Taske is the husband of Mrs. Ella Taske. Mr. Taske and his wife are passengers on the *QEII* luxury ocean liner. The couple are confined to their stateroom cabin and remain in their twin beds for much of their journey. Mr. Taske's existence at this stage in his life is not a happy one. He has a strained relationship with his argumentative and physically abusive wife, who enjoys chronicling her husband's faults and shortcomings. He suffers her wrath, as well as the condescending treatment of the ship's staff. When it becomes apparent that the Steward and the Stewardess are not going to assist the couple in preparing for the lifeboat drill, Mr. Taske takes it upon himself to make provisions for himself and his wife. He frantically searches their room for their life-preserver jackets and eventually finds them under their twin beds.

**Taske, Mrs. Ella** An ailing elderly woman in her 90s, Mrs. Taske is the wife of Mr. E. Long Taske. Mrs. Taske and her husband are passengers on the *QEII* luxury ocean liner. The couple remain in their stateroom cabin and keep to their twin beds for much of their journey. At this stage in her life, Mrs. Taske has found her voice and is very frank about her feelings. She will no longer remain silent about her husband's faults and shortcomings, particularly his dalliances with other women. These past deeds have led Ella to become argumentative and physically abusive with her husband. She demands that Long agree to a legal separation. Ella also feels she has been violated and treated with disrespect by the condescending ship's staff. She struggles to maintain her dignity against the "advances" of the young Steward. When it becomes apparent that the Steward and his fellow staff member, the Stewardess, are not going to assist the couple in preparing for the lifeboat drill, Mrs. Taske panics and urges her husband to take action.

# *The Long Goodbye*

A one-act play written in 1940.

## SYNOPSIS

Joe and his friend, Silva, clear out Joe's family's apartment. As the movers take out the furniture, Joe is bombarded with memories of his Mother and his sister, Myra. Joe explains to Silva that his mother suffered from cancer and took her own life so that her children could collect the insurance money. In a flashback, Myra enters the room with her boyfriend, Bill, whom Joe despises. Bill is rich and arrogant and treats Myra disrespectfully. The couple leave the apartment as the movers enter, and Joe returns to the present time.

Hearing children playing outside, Joe asks Silva about the games he played as a child. Joe stiffens as another flashback emerges. His mother asks him to keep an eye on Myra. She urges Joe to warn Myra about Bill. His mother informs him that her cancer is in remission. She and Joe reminisce about his father. She reassures Joe that she will not abandon her children, as their father did. As the flashback ends, Joe's mother tells him where her insurance policy can be found. The movers return once again.

Silva suggests that he and Joe have a drink, but Joe does not want to disengage from his memories. One of the movers asks what to do with the perfume bottles. The smell of perfume propels Joe into a flashback of Myra and Bill fighting. Bill pressures Myra to have sex with him, and Joe ejects him from the apartment. Their mother screams in her bedroom as she dies. Joe returns to the present moment.

Silva notices a picture of Myra and inquires as to her whereabouts. Silva's question prompts another flashback for Joe: Myra appears wearing a negligee. Joe and Myra have an argument, during which Myra threatens to throw Joe out of the apartment. The flashback ends and Joe says he received a postcard from Myra but still has not heard from his father. As he looks around the apartment a final time, Joe realizes that life is merely one "long goodbye."

## COMMENTARY

*The Long Goodbye* is a companion piece and an early template for THE GLASS MENAGERIE. As is its successor, *The Long Goodbye* is a memory play that depicts the unfortunate life of an abandoned mother and her two children. By contrast, *The Long Goodbye* features a reversal of the brother-sister dynamic found in *The Glass Menagerie*. Here it is the female sibling, Myra, who is determined to live her own life and actively pursues a means of escape. Joe is the one left behind.

He, as is Tom Wingfield in *The Glass Menagerie*, is a narrator-protagonist who moves fluidly between the past and the present. Williams's treatment of time, whereby the past and the present coexist, is a prominent feature in many of his works, such as CLOTHES FOR A SUMMER HOTEL and SOMETHING CLOUDY, SOMETHING CLEAR, another highly autobiographical work.

## PRODUCTION HISTORY

*The Long Goodbye* was first produced at the New School for Social Research in 1940. It was subsequently produced at the Straight Wharf Theatre, Nantucket, Massachusetts, in 1946.

## PUBLICATION HISTORY

*The Long Goodbye* was published in the collection 27 WAGONS FULL OF COTTON AND OTHER ONE-ACT PLAYS (1966).

## CHARACTERS

**Bill** Bill is Myra's new boyfriend. Myra's brother, Joe, dislikes Bill and tries to dissuade Myra from dating him. Bill is rich, arrogant, and aggressive. He treats Myra disrespectfully and pressures her to have sex with him. Myra and Joe's Mother are very concerned about the situation and urge Joe to talk with Myra about Bill. Bill appears with Myra in Joe's flashbacks.

**Joe** Joe is a 23-year-old man who is moving out of his family's apartment. As the movers clear out his belongings, Joe has flashbacks of the time he has spent in the apartment with his Mother and his sister, Myra. Joe feels utterly alone in the world. His life has been a litany of loss. His father abandoned him, his mother committed suicide, and his sister communicates with him only through occasional postcards. With the help of his friend Silva, Joe leaves the apartment to start a new life. As Tom Wingfield is in THE GLASS MENAGERIE, Joe is the narrator-protagonist of the play.

**Mother** The mother of Joe and Myra. When she discovers she has cancer, she decides to commit suicide so that Joe and Myra can collect the insurance money. Mother is very concerned about her daughter and is not happy that she is dating Bill. She pleads with Joe to take care of his sister. Joe's Mother appears to him in flashbacks on the day he moves out of their apartment.

**Myra** As is Tom Wingfield in *THE GLASS MENAGERIE*, Myra is restless and wants more out of life. She is unhappy living in her family's shabby apartment with her overly protective Mother and brother, Joe. Her Mother and brother are concerned about her because she is dating Bill, who is rich, arrogant, and aggressive. Bill treats Myra disrespectfully and pressures her to have sex. When Myra leaves home she communicates only with Joe, through postcards.

**Silva** Silva is Joe's friend, who helps Joe move out of his family's apartment. Silva's presence serves to trigger Joe's flashbacks of his family before their tragic decline.

# *The Long Stay Cut Short, or The Unsatisfactory Supper*

A one-act play written before 1945.

## SYNOPSIS

The setting is a small, rundown cottage in Blue Mountain, Mississippi.

Sucking his teeth, Archie Lee Bowman complains to his wife about the undercooked dinner of collard greens and salt pork that Aunt Rose prepared. Aunt Rose enters and walks to the rosebush, announcing that she needs fresh roses in the house on Sundays. Aunt Rose pontificates on the joys of cooking for relatives, but not for others. Archie Lee reminds his wife, Baby Doll, that Aunt Rose has overstayed her welcome in their home.

Aunt Rose creeps around the rosebush, singing, "Rock of Ages, cleft for me / Let me hide myself in thee!" Archie Lee orders Baby Doll to tell her aunt that she has to leave. Aunt Rose becomes hysterical when Baby Doll asks whether she has made other living arrangements. Aunt Rose says that an old maid does not give much thought to the future because she will soon die as do the roses that drift away in the wind. Archie Lee informs Aunt Rose that he will drive her to someone else's house in the morning. Considering the matter settled, Archie Lee slams the screen door shut as he disappears into the house. After a long pause, Aunt Rose remarks, "I thought you children were satisfied with my cooking."

As a blue dusk settles over the cottage, a faint strain of music is heard, followed by a tornado. Archie Lee and Baby Doll beg Aunt Rose to come inside as the storm roars, but she is resolute as the fierce wind lashes her dress. Aunt Rose sinks to her knees and thinks of her life as if "she had always carried an armful of roses that no one had ever offered a vase to receive." With a mighty gust, the storm carries Aunt Rose away.

## COMMENTARY

*The Long Stay Cut Short* or *The Unsatisfactory Supper* is a tribute to Williams's maternal grandmother, ROSINA DAKIN (whom he affectionately called "Grand"). During the autumn of 1943, Rosina Dakin and her husband, Williams's grandfather, WALTER EDWIN DAKIN, moved in with Williams's immediate family. Grand was dying of tuberculosis; however, she insisted on performing her usual domestic duties. Her efforts did not appease Williams's father, CORNELIUS COFFIN WILLIAMS, who, as does Archie Lee, resented the elderly couple's living in his home. This tension was very painful for Williams, who had a deep, reverential love for his grandmother. He retells this traumatic episode in several works, such as "The Man in the Overstuffed Chair" and "GRAND." There are also overtones of Grand's death in "ORIFLAMME" and "THE ANGEL IN THE ALCOVE."

## PRODUCTION HISTORY

*The Long Stay Cut Short, or The Unsatisfactory Supper* was produced in London in 1971. Most importantly, this one-act play served as the basis for Williams's most controversial work, *BABY DOLL*.

## PUBLICATION HISTORY

*The Long Stay Cut Short, or The Unsatisfactory Supper* was published as *The Unsatisfactory Supper* in *Best One-Act Plays of 1945* and as *The Long Stay*

*Cut Short* in AMERICAN BLUES (1948). With this collection of one-act plays, Williams caught the attention of Molly Day Thacher of the Group Theatre, who awarded him $100 for the plays. She also directed his writings to the woman who would become his longtime agent, AUDREY WOOD.

### CHARACTERS

**Aunt Rose** She is Baby Doll Bowman's aunt. Aunt Rose takes refuge at the Bowman house. She is an elderly woman who "resembles a delicate white-headed monkey." Aunt Rose does not realize that she has become a nuisance to the Bowman family. Her absentmindedness infuriates Baby Doll's husband, Archie Lee. Her aggravating laughter and naïveté prompt the Bowmans to ask her to find somewhere else to live. Aunt Rose is emotionally crushed by her family's insensitivity.

**Bowman, Archie Lee** Archie Lee is Baby Doll Bowman's husband. He resents his wife's relative, Aunt Rose, who lives with them. He is insensitive and becomes impatient with the elderly woman. Eventually, Archie Lee forces Baby Doll to tell Aunt Rose she must leave their home.

**Bowman, Baby Doll** Baby Doll is Archie Lee Bowman's wife. She feels an obligation to care for her elderly relative, Aunt Rose, and has allowed her to stay in the Bowman home. Archie Lee is displeased with this arrangement and does not want the old woman in his home. He presses Baby Doll to evict Aunt Rose, and she eventually obeys.

## *Lord Byron's Love Letter*

A one-act play written before 1946.

### SYNOPSIS

This play is set in the parlor of an old mansion in the French Quarter of New Orleans, Louisiana. The time is the late 19th century, during Mardi Gras. Sounds of the annual Mardi Gras festivities are heard in the distance, as the Spinster (Ariadne) and the Old Woman (Irenée) sit in their parlor. The Spinster is sewing. The doorbell rings. The Old Woman hides behind a curtain and watches what transpires from this location. The Spinster opens the door and admits the Matron (Mrs. Tutwiler), who is interested in viewing Lord Byron's love letter. The Spinster and the Old Woman discuss the details of the infamous letter's history. The Matron drags her husband, Winston Tutwiler, into the parlor to hear the story, but he falls asleep instantly.

From behind the curtain, the Old Woman explains that the letter's recipient met Lord Byron on the steps of the Acropolis in Athens, Greece. The Spinster reads aloud from a diary, recounting the romantic encounter at the Acropolis. The Old Woman repeatedly and strictly instructs the Spinster to "remember where to stop" in the diary. The two women then allow the Matron to view the actual letter. The Spinster reveals that upon Lord Byron's death, her grandmother became a recluse. She reads the sonnet that her grandmother wrote for Byron, the poem "Enchantment." The Old Woman recites it from behind the curtain, along with the Spinster. The Old Woman recites the very last lines of the poem by herself.

A Mardis Gras parade marches past the house, rousing the husband from his slumber. He rushes out of the parlor to see the parade. The Matron starts to follow him, and the Spinster and the Old Woman beg her for a donation. The Matron becomes preoccupied with finding her husband, who has disappeared in the crowd. The Spinster pursues the Matron and confetti is thrown in her face. The Old Woman is furious that customers have left without paying. She chastises the Spinster for dropping her grandfather's letter on the floor.

### COMMENTARY

*Lord Byron's Love Letter* is a Williams theatrical miniature that possesses all the "rueful poetry and theatrical dexterity that characterizes [his] best work" (Atkinson, 1955). The Spinster (Ariadne) and her grandmother (Irenée) are reminiscent of many of Williams's heroines, who are left watching the parades of life pass them by and time march on without them. In this delicate tale of long lost love,

Williams also pays homage to one of his favorite poets, George Gordon, Lord Byron, who appears as a character in Williams's play CAMINO REAL.

## PRODUCTION HISTORY

There is no record of a professional theatrical premiere of *Lord Byron's Love Letter.* However, Williams collaborated with Raffaello de Banfield on an operatic version of the play that was produced at Tulane University in New Orleans, Louisiana, in January 1955. The opera was subsequently performed at the Lyric Theatre in Chicago, Illinois, in November 1955.

## PUBLICATION HISTORY

*Lord Byron's Love Letter* was published in the collection *27 WAGONS FULL OF COTTON AND OTHER ONE-ACT PLAYS* (1966) and *The Best American One-Act Plays* (1964).

## CHARACTERS

**Husband** Also known as Winston Tutwiler, the Husband is a tourist on vacation in New Orleans with his wife, the Matron. His wife is interested in seeing the famous letter owned by the Old Woman and the Spinster; Winston is more concerned with seeing the Mardi Gras parade. He is in a celebratory mood and has been drinking heavily. His wife forces him to sit down and listen as the two women recount the story of the love letter written by Lord Byron; however, Winston cannot stay awake. He is revived by the sound of the marching bands and rushes into the street to join the festivities.

**Matron** She is a middle-aged woman on vacation in New Orleans with her Husband, Winston Tutwiler. She visits the home of the Spinster and the Old Woman to see the infamous love letter written by Lord Byron. After viewing the letter the Matron leaves without giving the two women a donation.

**Old Woman** She is the grandmother of the Spinster. Her name is Irenée Margúerite de Poitevent. The Old Woman claims to have had a love affair with Lord Byron when she was a young woman. She reads the letter from Byron to tourists in New Orleans as a means of making a living.

**Spinster** Also known as Ariadne, she is a woman of 40 who lives in poverty with her grandmother, the Old Woman. Together they eke out a meager living by displaying a love letter her grandmother received from Lord Byron.

## FURTHER READING

Atkinson, Brooks. "Theatre: 2 by Williams," *New York Times,* January 19, 1955, p. 23.

# *The Loss of a Teardrop Diamond*

Screenplay written during the 1950s.

## SYNOPSIS

Fisher Willow returns from a party in Memphis that lasted until the early morning hours. She drives to Jimmy Dobyne's house and proposes that he be her escort to the debutante parties through the season. Jimmy is uncomfortable in the presence of Fisher, a strong and extremely wealthy young woman. Fisher has become an outcast in her hometown in Mississippi because of her father's disastrous decision to blow up a levee, which resulted in several deaths and in destruction to farms below their plantation. As a result, Fisher is forced to bribe Jimmy with new suits and exposure because she is no longer highly regarded. She has also been summoned home by Aunt Cornelia, who dangles a large inheritance before Fisher in exchange for following her orders. Fisher is not happy to conform to Southern protocol.

Jimmy visits his mother in an asylum, where she has become violent and no longer recognizes him. Jimmy has been left to care for his alcoholic father. Although Jimmy is the grandson of the former governor of the state, his family has been ruined by accusations of theft. The allegations were false, but Jimmy's family served as the scapegoats for a wealthier family.

Fisher and Jimmy attend a soirée at the home of an old friend, Julie. Before they arrive, Fisher tells Jimmy to take a detour to the river. She tries to seduce Jimmy, but he ignores her advances. Upset by this rejection, Fisher jumps out of the car before it stops, and she loses a valuable teardrop diamond earring. Sifting through the gravel, Julie, Jimmy, Fisher, and several other partygoers finish empty-handed. Angered by Jimmy's indifference to her and his attention to Vinnie McCorkle, a beautiful young woman at the party, Fisher publicly accuses Jimmy of stealing the earring. Deeply insulted by this remark, Jimmy announces that he has been paid to be Fisher's date and demands to be searched for the earring.

Fisher pays her respects to Julie's Aunt Addie, who has suffered a stroke and is bedridden. Addie relates to Fisher and her desire for exotic travel. She lived in Hong Kong most of her life and after a stroke became dependent on opium to relieve her pain and deterioration. Addie asks Fisher to help her "go on her travels" once again by overdose. Fisher complies, giving her several pills and promising to return to administer the final dose. Fisher leaves her other teardrop diamond earring on Addie's mantle as she exits.

Fisher discovers that Jimmy has furthered his acquaintance with Vinnie. They disappear to have sex in Jimmy's car. Vinnie confides that she did indeed find Fisher's missing earring but has kept it because although she is pretty, she does not have enough money to marry a man who has social standing. Jimmy is horrified by her dishonesty. He demands she return the earring.

Jimmy and Fisher leave together. Fisher asks Jimmy to take a detour to the river. She suggests that she could have his mother placed in a better care facility if they marry.

## COMMENTARY

Fisher Willow is a combination of two characters in the Williams canon: Heavenly Critchfield and Dick Miles, both from SPRING STORM. As does Heavenly, Fisher finds her Southern society too restrictive and narrowly focused. As Heavenly is hopelessly in love with Dick Miles, Fisher is enamored of Jimmy Dobyne, a fallen aristocrat and socialite. Fisher does not know how to handle this attraction, as she has never been attracted to one particular person. Heavenly desperately tries to rein in Dick, but she is left alone, and, as Fisher Willow subconsciously fears, a spinster.

Fisher suffocates under the rules of proper Southern society. Although she is undeniably wealthy, she is living as a part of an outcast family, because of her father's dastardly actions against his neighbors. Fisher suffers from his actions, and she is a target of ridicule of a society that has eagerly awaited an opportunity to disown her. Fisher has been pulled back to Mississippi and to Memphis as a dutiful heir; however, she is misunderstood by even her powerful and wealthy aunt, whose approach to life mirrors Fisher's. Although Aunt Cornelia and Fisher are very similar creatures, with only age separating their life experiences, Aunt Cornelia is often bewildered by her protégé's actions. This, more than any other element in the screenplay, is the most realistic.

Fisher's love of the river, symbol of freedom, is much like that of Dick Miles. She restlessly attends social events with an uncontrollable desire to be free and wild. Fisher finds other young women childish and foolish in their pursuit of the opposite sex. As Fisher has been educated in Europe and spent a great deal of time there, she lives in a divide of cultures, not quite European and certainly intolerant of the ways of her Southern community.

## PRODUCTION HISTORY

*The Loss of a Teardrop Diamond* has never been produced.

## PUBLICATION HISTORY

This screenplay was published by New Directions in 1984.

## CHARACTERS

**Aunt Addie** She is a wealthy woman who has suffered a stroke that has left her bedridden. Living in Hong Kong most of her adult life, Addie has had a stroke that has led her to use opium to curb her anxieties about her poor health. She is taken back to her home in Mississippi, where she urges Fisher Willow to help her overdose and end her misery.

**Dobyne, Jimmy** He is a handsome young man who is pressured to be Fisher Willow's seasonal escort to social events. Jimmy's family, once a prominent Southern clan, has been ruined by untrue allegations of theft. Jimmy feels uncomfortable around Fisher, but he also pities her position as another type of social outcast.

**Fisher, Aunt Cornelia** She is a wealthy woman who orders her niece, Fisher Willow, to return from Europe. Ever dissatisfied with Fisher's behavior, Aunt Cornelia struggles to teach her protégée grace and etiquette.

**Julie** Julie is an old friend of Fisher Willow and Jimmy Dobyne. She hosts a grand debutante party at her home that Fisher and Jimmy attend. When Fisher loses one of her diamond earrings at the party, Julie and other partygoers try to help her find it.

**McCorkle, Vinnie** A partygoer who catches the eye of Jimmy Dobyne. Vinnie is a simple, yet elegant girl who, after being intimate with Jimmy, reveals that she has stolen a teardrop diamond earring belonging to Fisher Willow. Vinnie views the earring as her ticket to a good life. Because of her dishonesty, she loses Jimmy, but she returns the earring.

**Willow, Fisher** She is a socialite whose family has become a source of ridicule because of her father's dastardly deeds. Fisher returns from Europe at the wish of Aunt Cornelia to attend the social events of the season. Fisher only agrees to do so in order to remain her aunt's heir. Fisher falls in love with a man of a lower class, Jimmy Dobyne, who rejects her but eventually succumbs to her money and aggressive pursuit.

# *A Lovely Sunday for Creve Coeur*

A play in two scenes written in 1976.

## SYNOPSIS

The action of the play takes place on a summer Sunday morning in June in SAINT LOUIS, MISSOURI, during the mid- to late 1930s.

### *Scene 1*

The setting is the interior of a modest middle-class efficiency apartment in an urban housing complex. Dorothea performs her morning exercise routine in her bedroom. Bodey enters the apartment carrying a copy of the Sunday *St. Louis Post-Dispatch* newspaper. Just as she makes her way to the sofa, which stands in the center of the living room, the telephone begins to ring. Bodey, who has a hearing disability, ignores the phone, sits on the sofa, and becomes engrossed in her newspaper. At the sound of the telephone's ringing, Dorothea falls into a panic and is so struck with emotion she cannot make herself move. She waits for Bodey to answer the phone; when the phone stops ringing Dorothea storms out of her bedroom to attack Bodey. Bodey rises quickly in response to Dorothea's outcry. Dorothea has been waiting all morning for a call from Ralph Ellis, the principal of Blewett High School, where Dorothea teaches civics. He is also the object of Dorothea's romantic affections, and he has promised her that he would call her before noon to tell her something very important. Bodey responds indifferently to Dorothea's rage. She tries to turn Dorothea's attention to other matters, such as their regular Sunday outing, a picnic at Creve Coeur amusement park, and Bodey's twin brother, Buddy. Dorothea demands that Bodey use her hearing aid. Bodey expresses her concern about Dorothea's attachment to Ralph Ellis and suggests that her brother might be a better choice. A squabble ensues over whether Ralph Ellis is actually interested in Dorothea or Dorothea is merely infatuated by him. Dorothea shares the intimate details of this love affair with Bodey. Dorothea's story infuriates Bodey, who threatens to report Ralph to the board of education. Dorothea insists unashamedly that she must have romance, passion, and sex in her life.

Dorothea's rich and pretentious friend, Helena Brooksmire, stops by the apartment to speak with her. She surveys the squalor of Dorothea and Bodey's apartment. Dorothea and Bodey's upstairs neighbor, Sophie Gluck, opens the apartment door and peeks inside. At the sight of Helena, Sophie is alarmed and hides behind the door. Helena rushes to the door, slams it shut, and bolts it locked, leaving Sophie crying outside. The telephone rings once again and Helena answers it. Helena announces she is going to see Dorothea and marches directly into her bedroom. Bodey follows quickly behind. Dorothea is surprised and embarrassed to see Helena. Helena promptly shuts the door behind her so that they may have a private conversation regarding the arrangement they have made to share a plush apartment on the fashionable side of Saint Louis.

Bodey drags Helena out of Dorothea's bedroom and attacks her for being cruel to Sophie. She also accuses Helena of trying to sponge money from Dorothea. Helena clarifies that, on the contrary, she is here to rescue Dorothea. While Bodey and Helena are engaged in their verbal volley, Sophie stalks Dorothea around the living room. Dorothea has a panic attack and collapses behind the sofa. Helena, Bodey, and Sophie are momentarily confused. Bodey and Helena carry Dorothea into her bedroom. Bodey comforts Sophie, who is grieving for her deceased mother.

Bodey tries to escort Sophie back upstairs to her apartment, leaving Helena alone in the apartment living room momentarily. She is drawn downstage to the center of the living room. Her shallow mask of superiority has dropped and she reveals her own fear of being alone. She needs Dorothea's permanent companionship to avoid loneliness and the attentions of "vulgar old maids." As Sophie and Bodey return to the apartment, Sophie screams and clutches her abdomen. She is struck by severe diarrhea. She dashes into Dorothea's bathroom. Bodey returns to the living room to keep an eye on Helena. There is a sudden crash; Sophie has flooded the bathroom. Bodey rushes around to collect a mop. She returns, pushing Helena out of her way as she goes through the bedroom to take the mop to Sophie. Dorothea accuses Bodey of intercepting her telephone call from Ralph and of lying to her. Helena looks out of a window and catches sight of a solitary pigeon, the only sign of life she can see in this urban landscape. She remarks that although the bird is capable of obtaining its freedom, it has chosen to remain perched for a moment in this desolate place.

### *Scene 2*

The setting is the same as that in the previous scene, the time a few minutes after a previous action. Dorothea sits at her dressing table drinking from a sherry bottle. As she drinks she soliloquizes about the time she wasted with her former love, Hathaway James. Although gifted as a musician, Hathaway was not a skillful lover. She laments that Hathaway had a chronic case of premature ejaculation and her doctor advised her to let him go. Sophie shoves the mop out the bathroom door. Helena is shocked to discover that Dorothea is talking to herself so loudly. She rushes to the bedroom door to hear what is being said. Bodey searches frantically through the newspaper for a particular item. Helena knows what Bodey has been hiding and advises Bodey that hiding the truth from Dorothea is pointless. Bodey finds the page she has been looking for and quickly tears out the offensive item and throws it away.

Bodey and Helena divulge their respective plans for Dorothea's future. Bodey will offer Dorothea her brother, Buddy. Helena can offer Dorothea a civilized and stylish life, away from the squalor she resides in currently. While Bodey and Helena debate Dorothea's future, Sophie walks out of the bathroom and falls onto Dorothea's bed. Dorothea cries out for help and Bodey rushes from the kitchenette into the bedroom. As Bodey plunges into the bedroom, Dorothea rushes out. Helena informs Dorothea that she has shared their plans with Bodey and suggests that Bodey has already found a suitable replacement in Sophie. Helena and Dorothea discuss their financial arrangements. Dorothea informs Helena that she will not be residing with her at Westmoreland Place very long. Sophie creeps back into the living room. Helena sees her and warns Dorothea that bridge parties, an elegant foreign car, and a stylish address are the only safeguards against a life such as Sophie's. Sophie responds by splashing the contents of her water glass in Helena's face.

Dorothea explains to Helena that what she seeks is marriage, and particularly marriage with Ralph Ellis. Bodey begins to sing nervously in the kitchen. Dorothea is perturbed that Helena and Bodey are both so adamantly opposed to her relationship with Ralph Ellis. She tells Bodey for the last time that she is not going anywhere until she has received her call from Ralph Ellis and that she is not interested in Buddy. Bodey begins to cry and offers Dorothea the streetcar schedule in the event she changes her mind. Helena suggests that Dorothea should have a look at the society page in today's newspaper.

Dorothea searches and finds the newspaper but is unable to locate the society page. Bodey explains that she used that portion of the newspaper to wrap her fried chicken. Dorothea goes into the kitchen and unwraps the greasy newspaper only to find that Bodey has torn an article from the page.

Dorothea finds the torn section of the newspaper in the trash and reads that Ralph Ellis has become engaged to another woman. Dorothea ferociously forces Bodey out of the apartment. Helena comforts Dorothea and urges her to solidify their plans together. Dorothea announces that she has changed her mind about moving in with Helena and affirms that she would find a life with Bodey, Buddy, and Sophie less disappointing than a life with Helena. Helena is hurt but elegant as she takes her leave of Dorothea, her only prospect for companionship and happiness. Dorothea makes a dash for the telephone and calls the Creve Coeur train station. She asks the station worker to deliver a message to Bodey and Buddy, asking them to wait for her. Dorothea pulls Sophie into an embrace and the two weep together. Dorothea collects her hat, gloves, and handbag and rushes out of the apartment.

## COMMENTARY

*Creve Coeur* in the title is French, for "heartbreak." The name also refers to an amusement park of the same name outside the city of Saint Louis in the 1930s. The heartbreak at the center of *A Lovely Sunday for Creve Coeur* is the pain of rejection and isolation. Loneliness, and the fear of being left alone, are the primary themes of the play. Each character has a need and constant yearning for love and human connection. Thematically, the play is not unusual in the Williams canon, particularly among his later works, which avidly address issues of seclusion, aging, and death. As a study of impending spinsterhood, *A Lovely Sunday for Creve Coeur* is also reminiscent of other Williams works such as THE GLASS MENAGERIE, SPRING STORM, and A STREETCAR NAMED DESIRE.

However, the female characters who inhabit the exclusively female world of this play (there are no male characters present) make the play truly exceptional. Williams's treatment of the unmarried schoolteacher, Dorothea Gallaway, sets the play apart significantly. Unlike her fellow "aged Southern belles," such as Blanche DuBois and Alma Winemiller, Dorothea accepts her lover's rejection with resolve. She has loved and lost, given herself too quickly, but she wastes little time on regret. She is a hopeful, strong-willed survivor. When she finds she is unable to have what she wants, she is momentarily crestfallen but promptly seizes the nearest available, if unattractive, option. Scholars have generally found the play to be sparse in terms of plot, but highly intriguing in terms of character study. The plot does suffer from the lack of any real dramatic tension beyond Helena and Bodey's battle of words and wills. Yet, the four female characters are notably fascinating, particularly the elegantly catty and "quasi-lesbian" Helena (Bilowit, 17), who fights ardently in her tug-of-war with Bodey for possession and love of Dorothea.

## PRODUCTION HISTORY

The play premiered at the Spoleto Festival in Charleston, South Carolina, in June 1978, under the title *Creve Coeur.* Keith Hack directed the production and Shirley Knight played Dorothea. *Creve Coeur* ran for 36 performances and was unanimously praised in the press and well received by audiences. The play premiered in New York under its new title, *A Lovely Sunday for Creve Coeur,* at the Hudson Guild Theatre on January 10, 1979. It was directed again by Keith Hack, with Shirley Knight as Dorothea, Peg Murray as Bodey, Charlotte Moore as Helena, and Jane Lowry as Sophie.

## PUBLICATION HISTORY

*A Lovely Sunday for Creve Coeur* was published by New Directions in 1980. Some of the characters and dialogue from *A Lovely Sunday for Creve Coeur* also appear in the screenplay ALL GAUL IS DIVIDED.

## CHARACTERS

**Bodenhafer, Bodey** Bodey is Dorothea Gallaway's roommate and Sophie Gluck's neighbor. Bodey is a homely, plump, middle-aged working-class German woman. She is single and has devoted her life to caring for and promoting the happiness of others. She is very mothering to Sophie, who speaks very little English and has recently lost her mother. Bodey's primary goal is to secure Dorothea for her twin brother, Buddy. Their union would provide nieces and nephews to compensate for the children she never had. Bodey tries unsuccessfully to protect Dorothea from the news that her sweetheart, Ralph Ellis, has recently become engaged to another woman. She also tries to guard Dorothea from the advances of Helena Brooksmire. Bodey has a hearing impairment that requires she wear a hearing aid. The hearing device, which she detests, is a source of humor throughout the play.

**Brooksmire, Helena** Helena is Dorothea Gallaway's best friend. As is Dorothea, Helena is a teacher at Blewett High School. Helena is an art historian and cares only for the finer things in life. As are the other characters in the play, Helena is yearning for love, companionship, and human connection. She tries desperately to lure Dorothea away from Bodey's shabby apartment in downtown Saint Louis. She hopes to convince Dorothea to share an upscale apartment with her in an exclusive neighborhood in another part of the city. Helena's attachment to Dorothea is more than a platonic need for companionship. However, she is as misguided in her devotion and attraction to Dorothea as Dorothea is in her attachment to the philandering Ralph Ellis. Both women receive harsh rejections from the object of their affection. Helena's cool, elegant, and often sarcastic exterior belies a delicate, frightened interior.

**Gallaway, Dorothea** Dorothea is a 30ish single high school civics teacher. She shares a shabby apartment with her roommate, Bodey. Dorothea has a romantic notion that her boss, Ralph Ellis, the principal of Blewett High School, is going to marry her. She has been engaged in a clandestine affair with Ralph and is awaiting his marriage proposal. He has promised to phone her on Sunday morning before noon. Bodey and Dorothea's best friend, Helena Brooksmire, knows that Dorothea is waiting in vain. The action of the play is driven by Dorothea's eagerly anticipated telephone call, which never occurs. Although reminiscent of other Williams "jilted spinsters," such as Heavenly Critchfield, Blanche Dubois, and Alma Winemiller, Dorothea is unique in that she accepts her rejection with resolve. She is a hopeful, strong-willed survivor. When she finds she is unable to have what she truly wants, she is only momentarily crestfallen. She promptly seizes the nearest available—if somewhat distasteful—option in the form of Bodey's beer-swilling twin brother, Buddy.

**Gluck, Sophie** Sophie is Bodey and Dorothea Gallaway's upstairs neighbor. She is the most isolated character in the play. Dorothea detests the very sight of Sophie; Bodey pities her and tries to care for her. Bodey and Sophie are both German; however, Sophie speaks very little English. In addition to the language barrier, Sophie suffers from hysterical depression as a result of her mother's recent death. Throughout the play, she assails Bodey and Dorothea, sobbing, weeping, and howling uncontrollably in their apartment.

### FURTHER READING

Bilowit, Ira J. "Tennessee Williams (Playwright), Craig Anderson (Producer/Director) Talk with T. E. Kalem (Theater Critic) about *Creve Coeur.*" *New York Theatre Review,* March 1979, 14–18.

## *The Magic Tower*

An early one-act play written around 1935. Williams hurriedly sketched the play for the Webster Groves Theatre Guild. It centers on a relationship between a young artist named Jim and a vaudeville actress named Linda and their studio apartment, which becomes a magic tower for them. The Guild produced the work in 1939, and the *St. Louis News-Times* called the play "a poignant little tragedy with a touch of warm fantasy."

## "The Malediction"

Short story published in 1945.

## SYNOPSIS

A nervous man named Lucio befriends a homeless cat while inspecting a room for rent. The Landlady of the boardinghouse explains that the cat (whose name is Nitchevo) belonged to a previous boarder. The former tenant had a special arrangement with her: In order to accommodate the cat the man would help her with chores her husband can no longer do. Lucio agrees to have sex with the Landlady in order to keep Nitchevo.

The Landlady secures a job for Lucio at the local factory. He hates the mundane work. Lucio writes to his brother, Silva, who is in prison. In this letter, he creatively exaggerates about his great life, but in reality Lucio is miserable. Lucio encloses three dollars to Silva; however, he soon receives a notice that Silva was shot dead in an attempted jailbreak.

Several days later, as Lucio is returning home from work, he encounters a man who claims to be God. He thinks the man is drunk or insane, but a little part of him entertains the idea that maybe the man is telling the truth. Soon after this incident, Lucio is fired from his job, and he encounters the man again. Carrying empty beer bottles, the man speaks maledictions of the factory, the workers, and the lies in the world. He drops his beer bottles and Lucio, when he helps him gather them, becomes ill and faints. The police appear to collect Lucio. The man protests that Lucio is not a drunk, but they ignore him.

When Lucio gains consciousness, he is disoriented and panicked. He searches for Nitchevo. When the police ask him questions, he answers, "Nitchevo." One week later, he is released from jail. Lucio returns to the boardinghouse to find his cat. The Landlady does not let him enter his old room because she has rented it to someone else and has ejected the cat. Lucio finds Nitchevo in a dark alleyway around the house. Nitchevo has been wounded. Lucio picks her up, realizing that she will not live much longer. He feels they both deserve to be released from pain. Holding Nitchevo, he walks out into the river, disappearing forever.

## COMMENTARY

Lucio is another example of Williams's fugitive kind, the lost traveler without a history or an identity who often appears in his works. As does the Hitchhiker in the short story "THE GIFT OF AN APPLE," Lucio wanders through his life without a sense of vocation or purpose. Ren Draya explains that for these characters, their "lack of purpose in life is the sad corollary to lack of identity." Lucio is a stranger, even by the resolution of the story. The role of victim becomes his sole identity, and even this role is indeterminate, as it is dependent upon external factors. His one true human connection, with his brother, Silva, is tragically severed by Silva's violent death. The sexual intimacy in his life is the condition of a deal with his Landlady. It is a mercenary, passionless act which instead of providing solace, merely serves to alienate Lucio further. Lucio's only source of connection is with the cat. Nitchevo and the odd transient who believes he is a divine spirit. Lucio's arrest leads to the victimization of Nitchevo, his only true source of companionship. Lucio and Nitchevo are similar creatures: They are both victims at the mercy of a cruel industrial town.

As does that of Anthony Burns in "DESIRE AND THE BLACK MASSEUR," Lucio's psyche functions on violence. Even his encounter with "God" is one of maledictions and physical harm. The message of the corruption of the world and the lies people tell is related to Lucio's way of life: The lies he writes his brother, and the affair with his landlady, are artificial means by which Lucio strives to survive. However, this encounter with God leads Lucio to imprisonment and to the realization that his life is at its end. Williams establishes the mystical experience as a culminating religious impulse that catapults Lucio to action; the action, however, is dark and unheavenly.

"The Malediction" is the groundwork for the one-act play *THE STRANGEST KIND OF ROMANCE.*

## PUBLICATION HISTORY

"The Malediction" was published in *One Arm* (1948), *Three Players of a Summer Game and Other Stories* (1960), and *Collected Stories* (1985).

## CHARACTERS

**Landlady** She is a large blonde woman, who has sexual relations with her male tenants, including Lucio. She is mystified by his affection for his cat, Nitchevo. She finds their relationship very peculiar.

**Lucio** Similar to the character Musso in *THE STRANGEST KIND OF ROMANCE,* Lucio is a desperately lonely and frail man, who befriends a cat called Nitchevo. The Landlady rents him a room in her boardinghouse and allows him to keep Nitchevo there. Lucio has an affair with his landlady, but he is emotionally connected to Nitchevo, the cat. The Landlady becomes jealous and condemns him for his love for the cat.

# "Mama's Old Stucco House"

Short story written before 1965.

## SYNOPSIS

At noon Jimmy Krenning wakes up, stumbles into his kitchen, and drinks coffee. His maid, Brinda, is a young, attractive African-American woman who is filling in for her ailing mother. Brinda is apprehensive about her work because Jimmy and his friends have reckless parties while his mother, Mrs. Krenning, lies in a coma in her upstairs bedroom.

Mrs. Krenning has had five different nurses, but all have quit because Jimmie's parties made them feel unsafe during the night. When Mrs. Krenning dies, Jimmy is devastated. He finds it ironic that when his mother was living, she refused to give him a key to her old stucco house, and now he owns all of the keys.

The minister and friends arrive to pay their respects. Brinda's Mother makes sandwiches and coffee and sets the dining room table while Jimmy sits on the back porch drinking whiskey. Brinda's Mother has become very weak, so Jimmy drives them home. Brinda's Mother asks Jimmy what has happened to him, why he has stopped painting, but he cannot answer her. Brinda's Mother says she is going to die. She reminds Brinda and Jimmy to take care of each other and tells Jimmy to take Brinda home with him. Jimmy drives Brinda back with him, and they retire inside Mama's old stucco house.

## COMMENTARY

Jimmy Krenning is a failed painter who lashes out in life because he is so miserable. The one person he respects is Brinda's Mother, who serves as his maternal figure. She encourages his talent, motivates him, and reprimands him for his bad behavior. As is Quentin in *Small Craft Warnings,* Jimmy is a closeted gay man who picks up strange men for pleasure. He lives a reckless life, enjoying the newness of every man he takes home. Jimmy is in search of something that will cancel out his severe depression and loneliness. Brinda will live a life of servitude in the Krenning household just as her mother did through the years. She does not have the resources or courage to leave. Instead, she will take care of Jimmy in his self-destructiveness. The results will be nothing short of tragic for both of them.

## PUBLICATION HISTORY

"Mama's Old Stucco House" was published in *Mademoiselle* (1959), *Esquire* (1965), *The Knightly Quest: A Novella and Four Short Stories* (1966), and *Collected Stories* (1985).

## CHARACTERS

**Brinda** Brinda works as a maid for Jimmy Krenning and his dying mother. She becomes the Krennings' maid when her mother becomes too ill to continue working for them. When Mrs. Krenning dies, Brinda helps Jimmy cope with his loss. Brinda's Mother is very fond of Jimmy and has a sense of maternal affection for him. Brinda and her mother try to help Jimmy come to terms with life and his craft as a painter.

**Brinda's Mother** She is an old African-American woman who has worked as a maid for Jimmy Krenning and his family her entire life. When Jimmy's mother dies, Brinda's mother goes to his aid. Even though she is deathly ill herself, she musters the last bit of strength she has to cook and receive the mourners in the Krenning home. Brinda's mother loves and understands Jimmy. She pleads with him to stop drinking, live his life, and develop his talent as a painter.

**Krenning, Jimmy** Jimmy is a reckless young man and a failed painter. He spends his nights drinking and carousing with strange men. When his mother dies, he finally feels free. He believes his mother has been a terrible parent, and he revels in the fact that he now owns her house and all of her belongings. He also finds solace in the elderly African-American woman who has served his family as a maid all of his life. She advises him to clean up his life and take care of himself and her daughter, Brinda.

# "Man Bring This Up Road"

Short story written in 1953.

## SYNOPSIS

Mrs. Flora Goforth is a rich woman in her 70s. She owns three seaside villas on the Amalfi coast, where she hosts artists. Giulio, one of her many servants, delivers a book of poetry and says, "Man bring this up road!" Flora sends him to fetch the poet as she watches from her mountaintop view. The man, whose name is Jimmy, is taken to the villa and ushered to a guest bedroom, where he collapses with exhaustion. Mrs. Goforth phones her friends to find out the gossip about Jimmy. She learns that he lived in New York with a rich woman and, socializing in prominent social circles, he was known as the ski instructor/poet. The woman who took him to New York published his poetry, gaining him considerable notoriety, but he soon stopped writing. Now in his mid-30s and no longer a handsome gigolo, Jimmy resorts to making mobiles to earn money to eat.

When Jimmy wakes up, he joins Mrs. Goforth in her breakfast room. He is starving, but she informs him that only black coffee is served for breakfast in her home. He tries to remain polite and focused on her, but he is starving. Mrs. Goforth cruelly interrogates him. When she ushers him into the library to continue talking, Mrs. Goforth removes her clothes. Jimmy is scandalized and she is terribly insulted. He pleads with her for a second chance, and she agrees to let him stay for dinner. He is elated as he returns to his room to sleep until the evening. Jimmy receives a phone call, informing him that he must leave because a large party of friends is on the way to the villa, and there will be no spare rooms. Jimmy collects his knapsack and heads out into the hot sun.

## COMMENTARY

In "Man Bring This Up Road" Williams develops themes, ideas, and situations similar to those found in an earlier short story, "THE GIFT OF AN APPLE" (1936). Both these stories are centered on the concepts of hunger and satisfaction. In these two pieces of fiction, and other works, such as "DESIRE AND THE BLACK MASSEUR" and *THE ROMAN SPRING OF MRS. STONE*, the hunger for food is inextricably linked and paralleled with the passionate hunger for sexual intimacy and ultimately for life itself.

Mrs. Goforth and Jimmy are both in search of fulfillment and satisfaction. Their joint quest to be fed (physically and emotionally) is matched by their similar struggle against aging and isolation.

Jimmy has lived a wonderful life as a gigolo to the elite widows of the world, and now that he is no longer in his 20s, he is left to commune quite literally with the scraps of life in his business of mobile making. Although she is at the end of her life, Mrs. Goforth remains a sexual creature; however, she has ceased to be sexually attractive. She is desperate to have a male companion, someone to be ordered around and to please her (to feed her ego), but she is never satisfied with her options. When she removes her clothes, Jimmy is too busy fighting his hunger for food to play the game, so he expresses a genuine response to Mrs. Goforth's body. As a result, both characters are left to starve as they refuse to satisfy each other.

This story is the basis for *THE MILK TRAIN DOESN'T STOP HERE ANYMORE* and the screenplay *Boom!*

## PUBLICATION HISTORY

"Man Bring This Up Road" was published in *The London Magazine* (1965), *The Knightly Quest: A Novella and Four Short Stories* (1966), and *Collected Stories* (1985).

## CHARACTERS

**Dobyne, Jimmy** He is an escort and the kept man of rich older women. As he begins to age, Jimmy realizes that his charms are fading. He pursues Mrs. Flora Goforth, but she does not keep him. Jimmy is left penniless and is forced to move on, walking from town to town.

**Giulio** He is the son of Flora Goforth's gardener. Giulio introduces Mrs. Goforth to Jimmy Dobyne, a young escort.

**Goforth, Mrs. Flora** She is a wealthy woman in her 70s whose pastime is socializing with exciting young artists. She owns several villas in Italy, on the Amalfi coast, and she entertains her friends and acquaintances there. When Jimmy Dobyne visits her, hoping to stay with her, she is too embittered to realize that she is starving for male attention. She sends him on his way and remains lonely.

# "The Mattress by the Tomato Patch"

Short story written in 1953.

## SYNOPSIS

Olga Kedrova runs a seedy hotel in Santa Monica, California. She tends a garden of tomatoes and lounges on a ragged mattress at the edge of her yard. The Narrator reckons the mattress was tossed into the garden because it was ruined by excessive lovemaking. Her primary worry is that a guest will fall asleep with a lit cigarette and burn down her hotel. Ernie, her husband, helps her remove the mattress from an upstairs room. The immense joy of daydreaming fills her leisure moments, and the mattress has taken on a new life, even after it has been discarded.

## COMMENTARY

Olga appears to be earthen as she lies in the tomato patch. Like a sensuous statue, she reclines on her mattress and revels in her existence as a goddess of love in this woman-made garden of Eden. She enjoys her life, listening to all types of human response around her. She is content to provide unmarried lovers with a place in which to make love. Passion and romance are central to Olga's existence and nature. She stays with Ernie because he needs her, but she sleeps with anyone she chooses.

Williams is the Narrator of this largely autobiographical story. In a letter to Donald Windham, Williams describes his encounter with a landlady who inspired the creation of Olga. Her name was Zola, and she "[was] a wonderful character . . . she sleeps with any man in the house who will have her. . . . There is a tremendous short story in the place . . . [about] the woman on the raggedy mattress . . . with the great rocking days of California weaving in and out while she ages and laps up life with the tongue of a female bull." Zola also inspired Williams's Maxine in *The Night of the Iguana*. Williams enjoyed detailing the idiosyncrasies of life at the Santa Monica hotel, and he adored Olga's—and Zola's—liberated and passionate views on life.

## PUBLICATION HISTORY

"The Mattress by the Tomato Patch" was published in *Hard Candy* (1954), *The Kingdom of Earth with Hard Candy* (1954), *The London Magazine* (1954), *American Short Stories Since 1945* (1968), *Collected Stories* (1985), and *Writing Los Angeles: A Literary Anthology* (2002).

## CHARACTERS

**Kedrova, Ernie** Ernie is the owner of a hotel in Santa Monica, California. He suffers from a diseased intestine and is perpetually miserable. While his wife, Olga, suns herself on the mattress by the tomato patch, he undertakes the housekeeping.

**Kedrova, Olga** Olga is Ernie Kedrova's wife. She and her husband own and run a hotel in Santa Monica, California. Unlike her husband, who is always miserable, Olga greatly enjoys her life. She is especially proud of the tomatoes she grows in her garden. Olga spends her days sunbathing and daydreaming on an old mattress near her beloved tomato patch.

## FURTHER READING

Windham, Donald, *Tennessee Williams: Letters to Donald Windham, 1940–1965*. Athens: University of Georgia Press, 1977.

# *Me, Vashya!*

Written for the Washington University Playwriting Competition while Williams was a senior there in 1937. The play is about a munitions mogul who wins in a love triangle by having his rival shipped to the front line. Williams was furious when he learned that the play only placed fourth in the competition.

# *The Migrants*

A screenplay written around 1973. The screenplay was a dramatization of the epic poem *The Migrants,* written by the U.S. poet Clark Mills. Mills, a literary associate of Williams's, met Williams while they were both students at Washington University in ST. LOUIS, MISSOURI. He published *The Migrants* in 1941 and dedicated the book-length poem to Williams.

*The Migrants* is the story of a simple family of migrant farmers who worked the fields, loved each other, and dreamed of seeing their hard work rewarded. Williams's screenplay was never published, but it was adapted for film in 1973. Tom Gries directed the film, which featured Ron Howard, Sissy Spacek, and Cloris Leachman.

## FURTHER READING

Mills, Clark. *The Migrants: A Poem.* Prairie City, Ill.: James A. Decker, 1941.

# *The Milk Train Doesn't Stop Here Anymore*

Full-length play written between 1959 and 1962.

## SYNOPSIS

The setting is a magnificent mountain estate owned by Mrs. Flora Goforth. The estate is situated on Italy's Divina Costiera.

### *Prologue*

A pair of stage assistants, named One and Two, serve as Japanese Kabuki characters. One announces the flag-raising ceremony on Mrs. Goforth's mountain. They place the banner with a golden griffin into its stand. They introduce themselves and explain their function as stagehands who shift props and furniture throughout the play. They are also characters (when they appear in costume).

The elderly Mrs. Goforth's morning laments can be heard, although it is already noon.

### *Scene 1*

Mrs. Goforth dictates her memoir to her always-exhausted secretary, Blackie. She speaks lovingly of a former young lover with Romanov blood who recklessly drove a red "demon" sports car. Blackie becomes frustrated because the memoir, as Mrs. Goforth is establishing it, is confusing and randomly structured. Mrs. Goforth explains that her first marriage was to a tycoon named Harlon Goforth. She then becomes infuriated by Blackie, shouting insults and explaining that she has been talking about her fourth husband, "the last one" (although she has had six husbands), who drove his sports car off the Grande Corniche and died. Mrs. Goforth believes that her heart died with him.

Mrs. Goforth blames her condition on the medication she is taking. Blackie suggests that they take a break. Mrs. Goforth does not care that Blackie gets little sleep due to caring for Mrs. Goforth night and day. The elderly woman has nightmares and shouts through the night. While Mrs. Goforth is talking on the phone with her stockbroker, Doctor Lullo enters pushing an X-ray machine into the room to examine Mrs. Goforth, who has lung cancer. The aging woman vehemently objects to the machine, and she shoves it out the door and over the cliff. Mrs. Goforth confesses to Blackie that she fears she will die this summer.

Insisting on getting back to the memoir, she talks about Alex, her last husband. She describes his beauty and loving grace. In this moment, the watchdogs are heard attacking someone outside. The servants shout in Italian for Rudy, the overseer. Mrs. Goforth is annoyed that her wonderful recollections have once again been interrupted. A young man named Chris Flanders stumbles onto the terrace. His pants are ripped and he is weak. Blackie runs out to meet him, and she offers to get the doctor for him. Chris is concerned only with seeing Mrs. Goforth. Blackie helps him sit down while she fetches her boss. Mrs. Goforth is worried that the visitor will sue her for the attack. Chris calls out for Mrs. Goforth. Rudy admits that he set the dogs on Chris because he was trespassing from the highway. Mrs. Goforth instructs him to add "Beware of the Dogs" to the "Private Property" sign that stands at the bottom of the mountain.

Chris sends his book of poetry to Mrs. Goforth via the gardener's son. She uses binoculars to see him before meeting him. Mrs. Goforth is not pleased to have a visitor, as she is tired of being bombarded by houseguests who have no intention of leaving. She says the island has been overrun by beatniks with little money, and a list of rich older women to call on for accommodations and food. She sends Blackie out to tell Chris that she will not be used. Mrs. Goforth becomes interested in Chris when she notices that the lederhosen he is wearing resembles the ones Alex wore. She orders Blackie to interrogate Chris, and if he answers to her satisfaction, he will be in the pink *villino* to bathe and rest. Blackie shows Chris to the small villa.

### *Scene 2*

Blackie escorts Chris to the pink villino, which is decorated with cupids. She is concerned about the dog bites on his legs, but he assures her he is fine. Blackie explains that she is helping Mrs. Goforth with her memoir. A servant draws a bath for Chris. Blackie rummages through Chris's rucksack and finds metalsmith tools and mobiles. Chris catches her and explains that he was once a poet, but now he makes mobiles. They smoke a cigarette together, and Chris asks whether Mrs. Goforth remembers him. Blackie indicates that Mrs. Goforth did like his looks. Blackie advises Chris that if he handles the situation correctly, he will be able to stay with Mrs. Goforth for a long time. Blackie calls her employer a "dying monster." Blackie explains that Mrs. Goforth eats nothing but pills, suffers nightmares, and hysterically raves into a tape recorder for Blackie to transcribe. She tells Chris that Mrs. Goforth has "demented memoirs," which are recollections of her position as an international beauty. Chris says that he has had experience with dying women who refuse to admit that they are. He gives a mobile entitled "The Earth Is a Wheel in a Great Big Gambling Casino" to Blackie to give to Mrs. Goforth. He gives Blackie a copy of his book of poetry. He asks to make a phone call to another elderly woman in Sicily. Blackie orders food for Chris to eat when he awakens.

Mrs Goforth sits on the terrace. She shouts at the Italian servants, who do not understand her pigeon Italian. Blackie chastises her for her hateful disposition toward them. Mrs. Goforth asks about Chris. Blackie gives her the mobile and tells her its title. Mrs. Goforth is too cranky to acknowledge the gift and orders Blackie to help her up to escape the Sun; they return to the library. Mrs. Goforth decides she needs a lover to combat her depression. Mrs. Goforth sends for Chris's rucksack. She begins dictation again, but Blackie leisurely smokes a cigarette. Mrs. Goforth talks about the season of '24 and the costume ball at Cannes. She went as Lady Godiva, entirely gilded except for a green velvet fig leaf. She recalls the year 1929, the year the mad parties ended.

Mrs. Goforth searches through Chris's rucksack, finding metalsmith tools and metal. She is impressed that he has been hauling such a heavy load. She also finds his address book and fumbles through its contents. She learns that he is 35 years old when she finds his passport. Mrs. Goforth asks how he looked in the bathtub, as she finds a samurai warrior's robe that once belonged to Alex. She tells Blackie to take it to Chris to wear while his clothes are being repaired. Mrs. Goforth orders Blackie to call the Witch of Capri and invite her to dinner.

### *Scene 3*

Later that evening Mrs. Goforth dresses in a kimono and wig. Blackie announces that the Witch of Capri's boat has arrived. Mrs. Goforth greets her and they sit down for dinner. After several minutes of conversation, Mrs. Goforth inquires about Chris Flanders. The Witch knows his entire history: He has an affinity for dying old women. At an elite party in Texas, he was christened with champagne "Christopher Flanders, the Angel of Death." Mrs. Goforth says that she has met him somewhere before. The Witch recounts that Chris was a ski instructor and a poet in Nevada. Sally Ferguson found him there the season she broke her hip. Chris carried her back to the ski lodge and stayed with her for several years. She had her hip repaired but broke it again on a cruise. Sally's friends blamed Chris for allowing Sally to fall again. Sally kept Chris until she died; after her family contested her will, Chris left empty-handed.

### *Scene 4*

Rudy hears an intruder on the terrace in the middle of the night. He discovers Chris, searching for food. Rudy beats him with his stick. Blackie runs onto the terrace and stops Rudy. Chris tries to catch his breath and confesses that he has not eaten in five days. Blackie tells him that she had food sent to his room. He answers that nothing was delivered. Blackie deduces that Mrs. Goforth intercepted her order. She says he will have to wait until morning to eat because Mrs. Goforth locks the kitchen. Mrs. Goforth calls Blackie on the intercom to dictate. When Blackie enters her bedroom, she begins the story of the death of her first husband, Harlon, who became deathly ill during their lovemaking. Mrs. Goforth guiltily confesses that she let him die alone. She runs onto the terrace, stopping at the edge of the cliff. Blackie pleads with her to stand still. She sways and Blackie runs to grab her. Mrs. Goforth begs her to stay with her.

### *Scene 5*

The next morning Mrs. Goforth and Blackie are seated on the terrace. Mrs. Goforth begins the dictation, pondering the meaning of life. Chris enters and stands at the edge of the terrace. Blackie sees him and motions for him to stay out of Mrs. Goforth's sight for a moment. One and Two enter and play a game of ball, elaborating on Mrs. Goforth's ideas. When they exit, Blackie introduces Chris in the samurai robe. Mrs. Goforth beckons him to her. She addresses the dog attack, and Chris apologizes for disturbing her. Mrs. Goforth calls the vicious dogs necessary, as she possesses very rare jewels and furniture. She asks whether he read the "Beware of the Dogs" sign. Blackie becomes angry and states that the sign was put up after his attack. Mrs. Goforth asks Chris to sign a statement releasing her from responsibility of the attack. Chris is happy to oblige her.

Mrs. Goforth compliments Chris on his beautiful teeth. She calls him a Trojan Horse because he arrived without invitation. Chris asks whether she remembers their meeting a few years ago and her invitation to visit. Mrs. Goforth retorts that invitations expire. Chris asks her how it feels to be legendary. She replies that she was blessed with a beautiful face and body. She was born "between a swamp and the wrong side of the tracks" in Georgia. She started in show business at age 15, became famous, and married a tycoon. She says that lately she has been a little run down. Mrs. Goforth asks Chris how he feels about being a legend. He is dumbfounded by the question.

Chris suggests they picnic on the beach and have a wonderful late night dinner on the terrace "with the sea still booming." He tells her that he has lost his sense of reality lately and this summer's travels have made him realize that he is treated as a leper. Mrs. Goforth calls him a professional houseguest. She addresses him by his nickname, Angel of Death, and informs him that she is not superstitious. Chris tells Mrs. Goforth that he just needs someone to care for. The Witch enters. She missed her boat to Capri the previous night. Mrs. Goforth immediately calls for another boat to take her home. The Witch tries to embarrass Chris by mentioning his nickname. She asks him to go to Capri with her. Mrs. Goforth ushers the Witch off the veranda and suffers a coughing fit.

Chris asks about the numerous villas Mrs. Goforth owns on the mountain. She tells him about the smallest of them, "the Oubliette," by the ocean. Mrs. Goforth says she has been bombarded with guests claiming to be famous people. When she inspects their passports, she learns their true identity and places them in the Oubliette, or "the place where people are put to be forgotten." Blackie enters with a plate of long-awaited food for Chris. Mrs. Goforth detests the smell of food and orders that the plate be removed. Famished and weak, Chris watches the food disappear from sight. He reaches for a cigarette, but Mrs. Goforth will not let him have one unless he kisses her. He does not oblige her. He takes her hand in his. She admits that she has been very lonely this summer. Mrs. Goforth talks about Mrs. Ferguson and Chris's freeloading relationship with her. Chris defends his position by stating that he made her walk again, and in return, she published his book of poetry. Chris goes on to tell Mrs. Goforth that she is suffering from unnecessary loneliness.

Mrs. Goforth produces a letter she recently received from her publishers praising her unfinished memoirs as equal to Marcel Proust's *Remembrance of Things Past.* Chris believes the publisher is "snowing" her, and Mrs. Goforth grows livid at this remark. Chris is entertained by her ire. He reiterates his belief that she needs companionship. Mrs. Goforth orders Chris to remove the sword belt he has been wearing to keep the samurai robe shut. When he obeys, she gives him the scarf from around her neck to use as a belt. Blackie interrupts with a call for Chris. The call is from Madelyn, the daughter of an elderly admirer, who reveals that her mother has died. Mrs. Goforth is unnerved by the call.

Chris returns to Mrs. Goforth. He gazes out at the ocean and imagines a time when Roman triremes rowed ashore. Chris grabs her diamond-studded cigarette lighter. When he refuses to put it down, she rings a bell for Rudy. Chris takes the bell out of her hand and says that he was only joking; Mrs. Goforth is not amused. Blackie enters and asks why Mrs. Goforth has dismissed the kitchen staff. Mrs. Goforth explains that they were stealing valuables. Blackie reminds her that the items she mentions are in storage. Mrs. Goforth is offended by Blackie's outburst in front of a guest. She demands that Blackie go to her desk, write a check for herself, and leave. Blackie is happy to do so. As Blackie leaves, Chris shouts that Mrs. Goforth is coughing blood. The doctor in Rome is called.

### *Scene 6*

Later that evening Blackie sits on the terrace writing lists of things to do before she leaves. One and Two are ready to lower Mrs. Goforth's banner. One suggests contacting Mrs. Goforth's daughter to inform her that her mother is dying. One and Two discuss a death celebration. One states that Rudy is pillaging the library safe for jewels. Chris enters wearing his repaired clothes. Blackie tells him that the doctor gave Mrs. Goforth a shot of adrenaline, which made her frantic and fearful that someone would steal her jewels. Blackie continues compiling her list. She tells Chris that she has placed a bottle of milk in his rucksack. He should drink it now and dine with her later. Chris asks whether he can stay in the Oubliette. Blackie says he would never be discovered down there. He says he would like to stay by the beach and make a mobile entitled "Boom."

Mrs. Goforth calls for Chris but asks him to stand by the door until she is ready to receive him. She believes working on her memoir has made her ill. She decides to stop the dictation for a while. Chris agrees that this is a good idea. He is embarrassed when he enters her quarters and discovers that she is nude. He compliments her beautiful body. Mrs. Goforth hopes that he will stay at the villa with her. Chris hangs a mobile and prepares to leave. Mrs. Goforth orders a huge feast be prepared for Chris in an attempt to persuade him to stay. Chris says good-bye. Mrs. Goforth says he is the first man who ever refused an invitation to her bedroom. He apologizes, and she says, "Man bring this up road, huh?" showing him his book of poetry. She makes him take back the book because she is sure he is running short of copies and she is certain she would not enjoy it.

Chris calls Mrs. Goforth a fool for not understanding that everyone eventually needs someone to care for them at the end. Chris tells her about his relationship with Mrs. Ferguson: about the drowning man he saved and the Swami who told him that this would be his vocation in life. The Swami taught him how to live and die in a dignified way, without fear. Mrs. Goforth acknowledges that Chris is the Angel of Death. Mrs. Goforth stubbornly rejects his comfort. She tells him that he will get nothing from her, and that "this milk train doesn't stop here anymore."

Mrs. Goforth coughs blood into a tissue. She calls it a paper rose and hands it to him. She begs him not to leave her alone. Chris says he never leaves until the end. He holds her hand, removing the rings on her fingers. She tells him to be present when she wakes up.

One lowers the flag on Mrs. Goforth's mountain. Chris enters the forestage to meet Blackie. Blackie inquires as to what transpired. Chris relates Mrs. Goforth's order and tells Blackie that he placed Mrs. Goforth's rings under her pillow, "like a Pharaoh's breakfast waiting for the Pharaoh to wake up hungry." Blackie comments on the sound of the sea, and Chris says, "Boom."

## COMMENTARY

In his *Memoirs,* Williams writes that *The Milk Train Doesn't Stop Here Anymore* was a work which "reflected so painfully the deepening shadows of my life as a man and artist." During this period of his life, Williams's life partner of 16 years, FRANK MERLO, died of cancer and the dramatist began his downward spiral into depression and drugs. Williams experienced severe loneliness and traveled as a means of alleviating his pain and running from the shadows of bad reviews. As Williams believed, "The very root-necessity of all creative work is to express those things most involved in one's particular experience" (*Too Personal?,* 157), *Milk Train* is no exception, as it reflects the impact of Merlo's death and the end of a creatively fruitful and socially exciting era in the writer's life. The character Mrs. Goforth is dying of cancer, and as Williams witnessed in the protracted illness of Merlo, Mrs. Goforth battles death, refusing to yield to the inevitable.

In *Milk Train* Williams wrestles with mortality. He addresses life's larger questions through Mrs. Goforth. Her intensely materialistic and narcissistic life has placed her in a very lonely and vulnerable position as an ailing elderly woman because, as Blanche must, she must depend on the "kindness of strangers." Chris Flanders is the one person who cares for her, and even he is questionable in his role as the Angel of Death reserved only for rich old women.

Creative and good-looking, Chris Flanders has breezed through life on his charm and sex appeal; now he is an aging playboy, like Chance Wayne (*SWEET BIRD OF YOUTH*) who undergoes a life crisis because aging has made him less desirable. Unlike other playboy characters, such as the Comte Paolo Di Leo (*THE ROMAN SPRING OF MRS. STONE*), Chris is unique in that he, like The Poet in the short story of the same name, has a spiritual duty to the drama's protagonist. He is an otherworldly character who knows his higher calling is to serve humanity in a spiritual capacity. His presence as the Angel of Death is at once alarming and soothing to Mrs. Goforth, whose glory days are filled with handsome men by her side.

Hunger is another dominant theme in the play. Chris is starving for sustenance while Mrs. Goforth's desperation manifests itself through her need to be desired and to have sexual intercourse. She cannot accept Chris as a friend who has entered to see her through death. Mrs. Goforth is too jaded for that. She must have him physically in order to consider her relationship with him legitimate. Chris rejects that intimacy. His prolonged physical hunger results. The quest for life is also central to the play, as Mrs. Goforth struggles to find a life-sustaining power through retelling her memories. In a desperate attempt to immortalize herself, Mrs. Goforth rushes to deliver all of her memories—and those memories are of lovers and great passion.

As is the griffin on her flag, Mrs. Goforth is a monster at the end of her life. She is callous and cruel, but in moments of deep contemplation, her fear of death is revealed. In these moments, Mrs. Goforth becomes sincere and childlike. Nothing has prepared her for this moment, the time when she dies a violent and painful death.

*The Milk Train Doesn't Stop Here Anymore* is based on the short story "MAN BRING THIS UP ROAD" (1953). After an extended trip to Japan, where Williams met the famous novelist Yukio Mishima, he was influenced by Eastern philosophy. After he had expanded this short story into the play and revised the play several times, those influences can be traced through the use of the Kabuki characters as well as the philosophies regarding death.

## PRODUCTION HISTORY

*Milk Train* premiered at the Festival of Two Worlds in Spoleto, Italy, July 11, 1962. It was produced on Broadway on January 16, 1963, directed by Herbert Machiz and starring Hermione Baddeley. The play was not well received. Williams blamed the poor reception on the newspaper strike in New York City at the time. Williams advocated another run, for which he revised the script one year later. This second New York production included Kabuki characters and starred TALLULAH BANKHEAD. One review of the production stated, "The saddest thing of all, however, is that time runs out on the play and all the gimmicks fail, one after another, one hears Mr. Williams more and more frequently rattling the dry bones of old speeches from old plays together to try to strike a spark" (West, 40). Despite its American failure, *Milk Train* premiered in London in 1968, where critics responded with fervent praise.

*Milk Train* was adapted into a screenplay entitled *Boom!* The 1968 film starred Elizabeth Taylor, Richard Burton, and Noel Coward. Despite the remarkable cast the film was not a success.

## PUBLICATION HISTORY

The *Milk Train Doesn't Stop Here Anymore* was published in *The Best Plays of 1962–1963* by Dodd, Mead. It was subsequently published by New Directions in 1964.

## CHARACTERS

**Blackie** She is the abused secretary of Mrs. Flora Goforth. Blackie is in charge of transcribing Mrs. Goforth's memoirs. Blackie serves as her companion, taking care of the dying woman through her morphine nightmares. Blackie is finally released when the woman dies. Blackie befriends a wanderer, Chris Flanders, at the estate.

**Flanders, Chris** He is another of Williams's fugitive kind, a wanderer of the world. Chris has made a career of attaching himself to wealthy aging women who admire his charm and good looks. As Chris has himself aged, he has reached a desperate point in his life in which he is no longer in demand. He arrives at Mrs. Flora Goforth's Italian estate in hopes of securing food and accommodations. Chris also claims to have a spiritual duty, to help women die peacefully, gaining him the nickname the Angel of Death. Mrs. Goforth does not immediately welcome him; however, Chris fulfills his obligation and stays with her until she dies.

**Goforth, Mrs. Flora** She is an angry aging woman who is dying of lung cancer. Mrs. Goforth has long tired of the social life of the elite. She fights death by living in the domain of memory. She frantically writes her memoir, detailing the sexual escapades of bohemian parties of the 1920s. When she is interrupted by a visitor, a "beatnik" or "professional house guest," as she calls Chris Flanders, Mrs. Goforth does not warm to him immediately. She does, however, ask him to be by her side when she dies.

**Lullo, Dr.** He is Flora Goforth's doctor. Lullo tries to care for Mrs. Goforth, who has cancer, but the elderly woman adamantly resists his efforts.

**One** Inspired by the conventions of Kabuki drama, Williams created this character and his cohort, Two, to serve as stage assistants in the play. One and Two introduce themselves to the audience at the start of the play and explain their function as stagehands.

**Rudy** He is a rough and drunken guard at the estate of Mrs. Flora Goforth. Rudy is willful and untrustworthy. As Mrs. Goforth lies dying, he empties her jewelry vault.

**Two** Two is one of a pair of stage assistants in the play. A convention taken from Kabuki drama, these stagehands complete their tasks of shifting properties and moving furniture and scenery in full view of the audience.

**Witch of Capri** She is a contemporary of Mrs. Flora Goforth's. The Witch is one of a number of wealthy aging women who compete for the attention of young men. The Witch dines with Mrs. Goforth and tries to convince her guest, Chris Flanders, to go home with her.

## FURTHER READING

Paller, Michael. "*The Day on Which a Woman Dies: The Milk Train Doesn't Stop Here Anymore* and Noh Theatre," in *The Undiscovered Country: The Later Plays of Tennessee Williams,* edited by Philip Kolin. New York: Peter Lang, 2002, pp. 25–39.

West, Anthony. "One Milk Train, One Scandal." *Show* 3, no. 4 (April 1963): 40–41.

Williams, Tennessee. *Memoirs.* Garden City: N.Y.: Doubleday, 1975.

———. "Too Personal?" In *Where I Live.* New York: New Directions, 1978.

# "Miss Coynte of Greene"

Short story written in 1972.

## SYNOPSIS

Valerie Coynte, a 30-year-old single woman, has dutifully cared for her cruel, bedridden, incontinent grandmother, Mère, for the past 10 years. On a particularly stressful day, the old woman adamantly requests a bowl of sherbet. Valerie makes a crude remark and slams the door as she leaves the old woman's room. Mère becomes enraged and literally screams herself to death in her bedroom. Valerie lies on the couch and fantasizes about her future and the freedom she will have now that her grandmother is dead. One week after Mère's death, Valerie uses her inherited money to open an antiques store.

Jack Jones, a handsome young mulatto man, visits the store. After several minutes of conversation, the two engage in Miss Coynte's first sexual experience. Their affair continues over an extended period of time until Jack suffers a heart attack caused by overexertion. Miss Coynte visits him in the hospital and has sex with him as he dies. Miss Coynte's next sexual partner is Sonny Bowles, a large African-American man who works as a deliveryman in her shop. When Sonny becomes unresponsive to Valerie's sexual advances, she sends him on a vacation. Sonny returns to discover that a set of African-American twins, Mike and Moon, have replaced him. Mike and Moon take Valerie out dancing at various African-American clubs and show her a world she has never seen. She thoroughly enjoys her newly found freedom, and her bliss is complete when an angel descends to inform her that she is pregnant. Miss Coynte gives birth to a daughter, Michele Moon.

Twenty years pass, and Michele Moon is pregnant with Miss Coynte's grandchild. Miss Coynte is dying, and the two women visit the grave of Jack Jones, Valerie's first lover. Valerie spreads roses over Jack's grave as Michele Moon has a sexual encounter with a cemetery caretaker. Miss Coynte dies on Jack's grave, completely satisfied with her legacy.

## COMMENTARY

A survey of the very limited commentary on "Miss Coynte of Greene" reveals highly superficial analyses of the story that largely dismiss it as "shallow" and "trite" (Vannatta, 69, 115). However, beneath the surface of this tale of sexual excess, Williams is making a powerful political declaration. Valerie Coynte wages a personal crusade for racial, sexual, and social equality. The excessively judgmental stance some critics have taken toward the story and the characters in it reveals much about the prejudices and social mores that Williams actively confronted, challenged, and flouted throughout his work—particularly the societal constraints regarding sexual freedom, women's liberation, and civil rights. Harry Rasky acknowledges that Williams felt a real sense of kinship with African Americans. As a gay man, Williams was intimately aware of what it meant to be an "outcast" in U.S. society. "Miss Coynte of Greene" illustrates Williams's concern with the social injustices faced by African Americans, and he offers a vivid vision of the future in which there is racial harmony, with the races blending completely, symbolized by a genteel Southern white woman who happily leaves a legacy of mulatto children.

## PUBLICATION HISTORY

"Miss Coynte of Greene" was first published in *Playboy* magazine, in 1973. It was subsequently included in the short story collection *Eight Mortal Ladies Possessed* in 1974 and the Williams short story anthology *Collected Stories* in 1985.

## CHARACTERS

**Bowles, Sonny** Sonny works as a deliveryman for a short time in the small-town antique shop owned by Valerie Coynte. He and Miss Coynte become lovers, and they frequently engage in sexual activity in her shop. Sonny is one of several local African-American men who become romantically involved with Miss Coynte.

**Coynte, Miss Valerie** She is a woman who dedicates 10 years of her youth to her mean-spirited and bedridden grandmother, Mère. When Mère dies, Miss Coynte is free to live as she chooses, and she chooses to live without regard to her Southern society's codes of conduct. She engages in affairs with various local African-American men, such as Jack Jones, Sonny Bowles, and the twins, Mike and

Moon. She becomes pregnant and has a biracial daughter, whom she names Michele Moon.

**Jones, Jack** Jack is a young handsome mulatto man who becomes Valerie Coynte's first lover. Valerie has lived as a repressed virgin, caring for her cruel bedridden grandmother. At Mere's death, Valerie is liberated to live as she pleases. Jack opens a world of sexual freedom to Valerie. Their wild affair is the first of several in Valerie's life, but it is the one she treasures most.

**Mère** Mère is the spiteful bedridden grandmother of Valerie Coynte. It is suspected that Mère may not actually be unwell, that she is pretending in order to force Valerie to devote her life to taking care of her. Valerie literally shocks Mère to death by responding crudely to her request for sherbet.

**Michele Moon** The mulatto daughter of Valerie Coynte and her twin African-American lovers Mike and Moon. As is her mother, she is a passionate woman. When Miss Coynte dies, Michele Moon is left to carry on her mother's passionate legacy.

**Mike and Moon** They are handsome African-American twins. They work in the store owned by Valerie Coynte, and both become romantically involved with her. Miss Coynte becomes pregnant by one of the twins but is uncertain as to which. She names their female love child Michelle Moon after each of them.

## FURTHER READING

Rasky, Harry. *Tennessee Williams: A Portrait in Laughter and Lamentation.* Oakville, Canada: Mosaic Press, 2000.

Vannatta, Dennis. *Tennessee Williams: A Study of the Short Fiction.* New York: G. K. Hall, 1988.

# *Moise and the World of Reason*

Novel published in 1975.

## SYNOPSIS

### *Part 1*

The Narrator lives in a squalid walled-off section of an abandoned warehouse near the South Hudson Docks, together with his lover, 25-year-old Charlie. He is a writer in his 30s from a small town in the South. He has "inherited" his present abode from his first lover, Lance, an African-American ice skater.

The Narrator and Charlie visit Moise, an artist-friend, who is preparing to host a party later that night. When they arrive, they find the apartment open, but Moise nowhere in sight. They see wine, some snacks, and a nearly empty port bottle, indicating that she is already drunk. A painter himself, Charlie mocks Moise's painting that stands in the corner. Two well-dressed young men enter the room and begin taking photographs with old-fashioned box cameras. Moise appears from a door halfway down the hall, wearing a see-through dress and refusing to wear anything underneath. She poses for the photographers.

Later that night, Moise admits to the Narrator that her patron has recently died, leaving her destitute. She says that her last resource is Tony Smith in South Orange, New Jersey, and his wife, Janie. The Narrator notices that Moise's voice is failing and recommends she make her announcement now, so the guests will be listening. Moise whispers that conditions have become untenable in her world. The statement is not heard, and the Narrator repeats it, shouting. With the exception of the Actress Invicta, the guests listen uncomprehendingly as Moise tells them about her depleted paint supplies and her patron and client, an 87-year-old gentleman, recently deceased. In exchange for his financial assistance, she regularly provided sexual favors for him. A new guest, Big Lot, arrives, and when Charlie shows an interest in him, the Narrator declares the party over. Big Lot invites Charlie to join him for chili, and a brief argument ensues, which is broken up by Moise.

The Narrator has a flashback about being notified of Lance's death and about spending the night with Moise, not for sex but for comfort. The Actress Invicta rises and puts on her cloak to leave. At that moment, several newcomers arrive, led by Moise's rival, Miriam Skates. The Narrator is dismayed and unable to believe that Moise has invited Skates, but Moise greets her and repeats her announcement. The sole candle illuminating the room dies, and the guests stumble over each other, frantic to get out the door. Skates strikes a match as her entourage drag her through the corridor and out into the street. Moise says that she has to pray and sends the Narrator home.

Leaving the aftermath of the party and suspecting betrayal, the Narrator goes in search of Charlie and Big Lot. He comes across a speed freak, who is abusing his dog, and shouts at him to stop. The man threatens to beat the Narrator and scares him across the street and into the brightly lit area outside the Truck and Warehouse, an off-off-Broadway theater. There is a public rehearsal or performance going on, and the pavement is obstructed by a bum, who asks the Narrator for change. He refuses, and suddenly the door flies open, and a man in a fur coat storms out, complaining loudly. It emerges that he is a playwright, author of the play rehearsing inside, and he left in a huff when the leading lady insulted him. Then he realizes that he has met the Narrator, at a party at Moise's. The playwright asks about Moise, saying that he has not seen her since that party, and requests that the Narrator walk him to the corner. The Narrator realizes that the man is neither drunk nor drugged, but ill. They go to a corner bar, with the intention of calling a cab. Instead, the playwright orders a bottle of wine and two glasses and punches the same song on the jukebox three times. The playwright, as is the Narrator, is originally from the South. The Narrator admits that Charlie has left him, and the playwright counsels against an attempt to win him back. They catch a cab, and the playwright turns amorous, but they reach the Narrator's home, a dockside warehouse. Seeing the warehouse, the playwright feels he has found a kindred soul: Only a dead person could live in a place like that, and he had thought he was the only one: "The only tenant of the great ebony tower!" At that moment the cab whisks the playwright away.

### *Part 2*

The Narrator is back home and alone with his Blue Jay notebook. Thirty years old, he still feels he is on the run from the truant officer of his hometown of Thelma, Alabama, and from his mother, who has had no contact with him for years. He imagines her in a rocker in the day room of a care facility. The Blue Jay notebook is nearly full, and in an effort to conserve the remaining pages, he begins writing on rejection slips from publishers. The notebook is an extension of him, and he and the Blue Jay are alone with the clock now. The clock is the subject of Charlie's most recent painting, which attempts to be more precise than the actual object but falls short of it. The Narrator places Charlie's portrait of the clock in the same place as the clock itself.

He attempts a chronological account of his life. He was thrown out of his home by his father at age 15 and went to New York City, where he met Lance and Moise at the San Remo bar in Greenwich Village. He recalls his first night together with Lance at Moise's apartment, leading to a love affair that lasted 13 years, and his mother's pleading letters to return home. The Narrator remembers his mother's visit to the city to collect him and her collapse on the street and subsequent arrest for public drunkenness.

The Narrator has never known a writer to say that he cannot write alone, but he himself prefers company. He has fallen into the habit while living with Lance, and it is one of the reasons for using the Blue Jay notebooks, as the noise of a typewriter would be too distracting. However, at the moment his only companion is the clock. At 4:10 A.M. he waits for Charlie.

The Narrator moves to the boarded-off living area, saying out loud a snatch of lyrics he has heard once, "Boys are fox-teeth in the heart." For the third time in his life, he contemplates committing suicide. The first time was during his stay at a sanatorium, Governor's Island, and the second time after Lance had given him gonorrhea for the first time.

During his confinement on Governor's Island, the Narrator is interviewed once a week by a student psychiatrist. On the last visit, the student tells him that he considers the Narrator a sexual deviant and asks whether he has ever had a "normal" sexual experience. The Narrator recounts an exaggerated childhood memory of a summer afternoon in Thelma when he was seduced to perform cunnilingus by a 13-year-old playmate. The psychiatrist calls him a "pervert," but the Narrator points out the psychiatrist's erection. The psychiatrist ejaculates, confirming to the Narrator his ability to excite with words. The psychiatrist's verdict on his patient is "Arrested at puberty. *Hopeless.*"

The Narrator recalls the time when he went on a tour with Lance, which resulted in "a crescendo of disasters." The tour manager was horrified by the thought of desegregation, so Lance told him that the Narrator was an albino and threatened to leave the tour unless the manager acquiesced. Lance and the Narrator shared a hotel room with another skater and his dog. One night, drugged by a pill that was supposed to prevent him from talking in his sleep, the Narrator became lost on his way back from the bathroom and was repeatedly bitten by the dog. Insufficiently treated, the bites on his ankles became severely infected; one night in Sheboygan, the Narrator was rushed to a hospital, where he nearly died.

The Narrator explains about "Bon Ami," a crate he uses as a work desk. Lance resented Bon Ami, because it diverted the Narrator's attention from him. Occasionally, Lance's interruptions would force the Narrator to leave the warehouse and continue writing in a nearby bar. On these occasions Lance would follow him to the bar and, in the end, physically carry him home.

Shoving away Bon Ami, the Narrator begins to root around inside the crate, finding more rejection slips, some of them preprinted, others containing messages accusing him of sexual hysteria or suggesting confinement at a monastery. He searches for ways of dealing with his "chronically inflamed libido" now that his youth has gone and he is determined not to stoop to the indignity of haunting the baths. Without noticing, he has taken his penis out and is holding it. Putting it back into his pants, he wonders about where one lives when alone, possibly in a corner of the day room in the asylum.

The Narrator writes to combat his loneliness. He remembers a time when Lance inquired about his self-education in Thelma. The Narrator told him that he went to the public library every night. At the library he had access to all the classics, from the Greeks to the works of Rimbaud, whom he thinks he resembles. The identification with Rimbaud was so strong that he tore his picture from a library book. Lance doubted that this qualified him for pursuing a writing career in New York and preferred that he pursue his literary ambitions while he was on tour.

The impoverished Reverend and Mrs. Lakeland also lived in Thelma, Alabama, in the house next door, and their audible conversation would revolve around the failing health of Mrs. Lakeland. Occasionally anonymous gifts of food would be placed at their door, and, too proud to accept them, they would pass them on to an old African-American man. His grandmother told the Narrator that the Lakelands had received an intolerable insult from the bishop of the diocese and the town. They protested the insult by making themselves ever present on their porch. The Narrator's mother forbade the grandmother to reveal the nature of the insult. It piqued his curiosity, and he persuaded a lady named Pinkie Sales to tell him the story. The Lakelands had a daughter who was in the habit of screaming out the window, and on one occasion she threw a chicken leg at the bishop. The bishop gave an ultimatum to the Reverend Lakeland, to have his daughter committed and publicly recant his heretical opinions about the Bible. The Reverend Lakeland did neither. Subsequently he was dismissed without a pension and his daughter ran off. A few days before the Narrator himself left Thelma, Mrs. Lakeland died, and the same night the Lakelands' house burned down, cremating both her and the Reverend Lakeland. Both were buried in unhallowed ground.

The Narrator goes into the bathroom to look at his face and assure himself that he is real. While there, he hears footsteps on the staircase and assumes that it is Charlie returning home. The arrival speaks out, and the voice is not Charlie's, but the playwright's. He sits on the bed, leafing through the Narrator's notebooks. The playwright says that he could not make himself enter his hotel room alone. Studying the playwright, the Narrator realizes that the man's loneliness must correspond in magnitude to his effrontery. He seriously contemplates whether he is enough of a hustler to accept this invitation, but decides he is not. He takes a deep breath, tells the playwright that he is not for sale, and, looking at the man, is struck by a vision of a Dorian Gray–like portrait of himself. The Narrator accuses the man of being egocentric, and the accusation is turned back at him. They argue briefly; then the Narrator tells him to be gone by the time he returns. He leaves the living area, seeing without looking, that the playwright begins scribbling on a piece of hotel stationery.

The Narrator walks up a long flight of stairs to the roof of the building, six floors above where he and Charlie live. It is light enough to write now, and he sits on a ledge, waiting for his heartbeat to stabilize. He believes that the irregularity is due to one of the childhood diseases he suffered, which were misdiagnosed. As his heartbeat steadies, he wonders about the point of lingering on in life.

Sitting on the ledge in clothes that are too light for the cold temperature, he shivers but does not feel cold. The warmth he feels is that of fever and drugs. He returns his attention to the light from street lamps, a few windows, and a cloudy sky. The rooftop feels mystical to him, a place of purification. The play of light and dark reminds him of Moise's painting style and her attention to "plastic space," space that is alive.

The Narrator considers the "absolutes of existence" and from there contemplates the sky and the memory of Moise's retirement from the world of reason. A violent fit of shivers sends him back down the stairs and to the living area. As he arrives, he hears a cab honking outside the warehouse and wonders whether it is Charlie. A female voice calls his name, and he runs down to street level, where he finds the Actress Invicta. She is looking for Big Lot but the Narrator only comments that Big Lot is with Charlie. The Narrator returns to the living area, contemplating that "love is demolition."

At first he is not aware that there is something missing from the room and sits down in front of Bon Ami. Then he realizes that the one-legged clock has stopped. He reenters the warehouse to look out the window again and realizes that it has become morning. Sneezing and noticing his fever, he thinks he will not survive it. At this moment Charlie returns. He is nonchalantly unrepentant, wishes to sleep alone, and declares that his infidelities are not confined to the present. His remarks recall thoughts of Lance, his constant search for beauty, and his eventual overdose.

The Narrator asks Charlie where he has been, and Charlie admits he has been with the poet La Langa. The admission makes the Narrator realize that their relationship is over, and he decides to visit Moise. Charlie informs him that he probably will not get in, as there was some kind of riot after they left. Moise bolted the door and will not open it until Tony from South Orange arrives. Miriam Skates also claims that she killed Moise. The Narrator doubts the latter and Charlie looks at him contemptuously and tells him that he has no concept of reality or truth. The Narrator counters that having sex with a poet will inject neither Charlie nor Skates with talent. Charlie tells him to leave, and as the Narrator staggers down the steps, he realizes that Moise, although she has locked out the world of reason, cannot lock him out, because he is not part of that world. He walks east, down to Bleecker Street, holding Lance's photograph as if it is a cross above him.

### *Part 3*

As the narrator approaches Moise's apartment, policemen stop him. When they harass the Narrator for being gay, the Narrator provokes them to further brutalization. Moise appears, claiming she is well connected and has phoned police headquarters. The Narrator loses the picture of Lance during this beating, and Moise refuses to tell him how she knew what was going on.

### *Part 4*

The absence of a watch or clock tends to accentuate the Narrator's obsession with the passage of time. He keeps looking at the frosted window in Moise's back wall to figure out what time it is. Despite Moise's calm he feels anxious and not ready to drift out of existence. Attempts to make conversation with Moise fall flat. The Narrator is persistent in his efforts to draw out Moise. She breaks her silence to accuse him of substituting words for authentic emotion. He tells her that he does not recognize her, and she replies that is because she is not thinking but reflecting on the profusion of crones in the city. Feigning ignorance, the Narrator asks about the meaning of *crone,* and she advises him to look it up in the dictionary. Instead of a dictionary, he finds an edition of *Who's Who* for 1952. The Narrator finds a candle and matches, places them on the table, and sits by Moise. She launches into an explanation of what she means by "crone" and finally reveals that, according to a letter from a friend of hers, her mother has turned into a "scavenger crone," jiggling pay phones for change and eating at a cheap diner. The friend blames Moise and suggests she should either have her mother stay with her or move back to Midtown and provide for her mother. Moise admits that she fears Moppet is dead, and it transpires that Moppet is a dog who had turned into a scavenger crone, foraging for food in garbage pails despite being well fed. Moise fears that her mother has assumed the character of Moppet. The Narrator points out that this idea might be a little unreasonable, and that Moise by her own account left home 15 years ago because her mother threw a piece of luggage at her. Moise claims not to understand and explains that her mother blocked the door when she said she was leaving for good. Possessed with superhuman powers, Moise flung the door open, her mother fell, and Moppet tried to follow her into the street.

Portrait of Tennessee Williams, taken in the mid-to-late 1970s *(photographer: Vandamm Studio)*

The room is ice-cold, and the Narrator takes Moise's hand, telling her that her story parallels his leaving Thelma and fleeing from his mother. Moise concedes the parallel but feels that he has alternatives and will not stay with her long: His nature is evanescent. He takes up a Blue Jay and begins to write. When he stops writing, the atmosphere in the room has gone colder and darker.

Moise continues talking, saying that she ought to get an animal for a companion, because the Narrator will remain with her only temporarily and she does not want to repeat her accurate analysis of his nature. When he points out that nothing in the world is totally accurate, she retorts that this may apply to his world, but her world is more simplistic now. The Narrator offers to find her a kitten for company and warmth, but Moise does not believe him, because the living always lie to the dying. She then touches his face, finds that he is unshaven, and admonishes him not to let his appearance slip. He says he did not bring a razor, and Moise tells him she once had one to shave her pubic hair. She confesses to a certain vanity about her vaginal area and says that although she has performed fellatio, she never has had vaginal sex because she refuses to contribute to the worldwide population problem. The Narrator drifts into ruminations about Edgar Allan Poe.

Moise lights a candle and after a while remarks that the handwriting on the piece of hotel stationery she has picked up with his papers is not the Narrator's. He takes a look at the sheet and realizes that it is the one the playwright has used during the night. Under the hotel's letterhead is a poem, and Moise orders the Narrator to copy it into his Blue Jay. Disliking the poem as much as its author, he obeys reluctantly. Moise asks about the playwright, concludes that he is the Narrator grown old, and warns the Narrator to stay away from him, because "Monsters of loneliness receive and offer no mercy." Moise suffers a seizure and the Narrator tends to her. Then there is loud banging on the door.

A delivery of painting materials arrives from the Smiths in South Orange, who have been alerted to Moise's appeal by the Actress Invicta. There is also a note promising a weekly delivery of food until Moise feels strong enough to have a small exhibition at Hunter. She suffers another seizure and declines the "invitation to join the Symbionese Liberation Army as their Field Marshal's mate," in favor of painting.

The Narrator records her declaration in the notebook and is interrupted when she approaches him on her knees, washes his feet, and dries them with her hair. He helps her to rise, and she turns to her easel and a painting she has already begun. Submerged again in the notebook, the Narrator is vaguely aware of the two men with the box cameras Moise has admitted into the room. The younger one shyly flirts with him, and he reciprocates his interest. Moise announces that they all belong in this room and begins undressing the older of the men, just as the younger man turns to the Narrator. With this the last Blue Jay is completed.

## COMMENTARY

Williams's second novel, *Moise and the World of Reason,* was published in 1975, the same year as his *Memoirs.* In many respects it poses a riddle, and, in order to be at least partly solved, it requires the "unencrypted" companion piece of the *Memoirs.* Parts of the novel are clearly autobiographical, "linking [the author's] Greenwich Village life in the early 1940s with his difficult time during SMALL CRAFT WARNINGS" (Spoto, 311)—the play that was to provide a theatrical comeback for him at the Truck and Warehouse Theatre on East Fourth Street in 1972. The eponymous Moise, a struggling artist, is based on Williams's friend, the promiscuous painter, Olive Leonard and named after one of his fraternity brothers, Matt H. Moise, pictured in the University of Missouri yearbook of 1932. Other friends, such as his fellow writer CHRISTOPHER ISHERWOOD; Isherwood's partner, the painter Don Bachardy; and the artist/designer Tony Smith and his wife, the actor Jane Lawrence (faithful supporters of Olive Leonard), are featured with their real names and identities. The sense of the autobiographic is heightened by the unnamed first-person Narrator, suggesting that the author himself is speaking. However, if anything, this complicates—perhaps intentionally—the interpretation of the novel.

*Moise and the World of Reason* is divided into four parts, the second part the longest, and the third the shortest. The division is less arbitrary than it appears. Its criteria are defined by events and their chronology rather than by structural considerations. The first part deals with what happens before, during, and immediately after Moise's party. In the second part, the Narrator waits for Charlie to return home, writing the night away. His escape from the warehouse and Charlie makes up the brief third part; the fourth part consists of his conversation with Moise. Overall, however, the novel's "narrative structure mirrors the complexity of a post-modern world and contradicts traditional assumptions about sequence, logic, order, and completion" (Bray, 62). Narration and occasionally language are fractured throughout, and there are frequent, seemingly random interjections of memories and metatextual stylistic comments by the author-Narrator.

The critical response to the work ranged from speechlessness to bewilderment. In an attempt to apply quantifiable terms of interpretation, critics fastened on to the autobiographical content and, given that the novel is more explicitly and more openly gay than any of Williams's previous work, on personal sexual enfranchisement. The latter, according to David Savran, accounts for the work's often frustratingly incoherent style, for "finally empowered to speak directly after so many years of (self-)censorship, [Williams] could only stutter, only hammer out broken and lacerated speech" (137). Heavily drawing on Savran and on deconstructionist theory, as well as D. W. Winnicott's study of transitional phenomena, Matt Di Cintio sees the Narrator's writing as an "object" intended to allow his transition from internal to external world. The development as outlined by Di Cintio necessitates the destruction of the object in order to complete this transition—hence the fragmentation language. However, in *Moise,* the much-cited incomplete sentences amount to 24 over 190 pages: frequent enough to constitute a dent, but hardly indicative of destruction. Above all, sense remains and therefore language (and writing) must be considered functional. Ultimately any linguistic peculiarities can, perhaps more cogently, be explained as a function of character and theme.

In the most detailed and most illuminating study of *Moise* to date, Robert Bray points out that the "connections between character, situation, and biography are so obvious in this novel that one discerns the imprimatur of Williams's life on virtually every page" (67). Bray correctly perceives the Narrator, Moise, and the playwright—the Narrator's aging future self, who hopes to make a comeback with a production at the Truck and Warehouse Theatre—to form "a composite of the author himself" (67). There is a good case for assuming a fourth "persona" that constitutes an integral part of the composite: the French rebel poet Arthur Rimbaud. This is far from surprising given that Rimbaud had become an icon of the sixties and particularly of the gay movement. In *Moise,* Rimbaud is a member of that heady group of writers and painters who feature among the novel's slew of incidental characters. But unlike the collection of other artists referred to, Rimbaud does not remain incidental. He is the one with whom the Narrator identifies.

As has Rimbaud, the Narrator escaped an oppressive home life to flee to a cultural metropolis while still a child. As did Mme. Rimbaud, the Narrator's mother bombards him with letters and sets the authorities on him. The 15-year-old Arthur Rimbaud meets and seduces the married poet Paul Verlaine; the 15-year-old Narrator meets Lance, who at the time is living with Moise, and seduces him into his first submissive sexual experience. Both Rimbaud and the Narrator read voraciously and start writing at a very young age (as does Williams). Both Rimbaud and the Narrator prefer notebooks as their medium; both attach sexual connotations to their writing; both write on any scrap of paper available, for the sake of continuing to write. As does the Narrator's future self—the Playwright—Rimbaud travels obsessively, to a list of countries that includes Indonesia and Ethiopia. The Narrator, at 30, calls himself a "failed, distinguished writer" (much as Williams is at the same age) (Bray, 63). Rimbaud, in his early 20s, has abolished writing—"the impossible telling of things"—altogether.

However, above and beyond these biographical similarities between fictional and real characters, there exists a striking thematic link that proves helpful in the reading of *Moise.* The novel is "a self-conscious testimony to the act of writing. It contains numerous musings about fragmented language and the ineffable nature of words" (Bray, 61). Indeed, fragmentation and ineffability are unavoidable because true communication is a function of the world of reason, which has been left behind in Part 1. In Part 2, the Narrator's wake is filled with an endless, frequently incoherent string of memories, fever- and drug-induced hallucinations that turn out to be real, and absurd snippets of reality that in their recursiveness often feel more distorted than ostensibly "unreal" images—in short, compounded unreason. Parts 3 and 4 introduce dawn and with it the prospect of new beginnings, unknown as yet but no longer tied to reason or unreason—or any stable rule of society—and possibly containing renewed human contact and thus the demolition of a terrifyingly solipsistic vision. This takes the main theme of *Moise and the World of Reason* beyond a chronicle of the act of writing, to encompass the journey of the writer.

## PUBLICATION HISTORY

*Moise and the World of Reason* was published by Simon and Schuster in 1975.

## CHARACTERS

**Actress Invicta** She is a partygoer at Moise's apartment. Appearing dramatically in a cape, Invicta searches for Big Lot, but he is interested in spending the night with the Narrator's lover, Charlie.

**Big Lot** He is a partygoer at the apartment of his artist friend Moise. Big Lot becomes interested in the Narrator.

**Charlie** He is the Narrator's lover. A painter himself, Charlie scoffs at Moise's artwork. When they attend a party hosted by Moise, Charlie leaves with Big Lot. Charlie returns to his destitute apartment, where the Narrator has waited all night for him. Charlie evicts the Narrator out onto the street.

**Lance** He is the former lover of the Narrator. Lance is a professional ice skater whose life of touring shows affords him a life of promiscuity. When Lance dies the Narrator recollects on the many times they spent together.

**Moise** She is a struggling artist who fancies herself as a socialite of the artist subculture in New York City. Moise delights in promiscuity and enjoys using drugs and being the center of attention. Gathering all of her friends (and enemies), Moise announces that her art patron and financial supporter, an elderly man, has died. She is left wondering how she will survive through this winter in the city. Moise often bolts herself into her apartment to paint because she refuses to be interrupted until her work is completed. When Moise locks herself in after the announcement, her friends worry that she will hurt herself. Moise is said to live outside the world of reason, as she is consumed by her art through the concentration she finds when she is intoxicated.

**Narrator** He is a struggling writer in his 30s who records the life of his artist-friend Moise. The Narrator is hopelessly in love with a now-deceased former lover, Lance. He spends his time recollecting those days spent with him and angrily waits for his present lover, Charlie, to return from an evening of sex with Big Lot. The Narrator ponders his writing and Moise's paintings, and falls into a state of depression. He is accosted by police officers, and Moise saves him from further brutality.

**Skates, Miriam** She is the archrival of Moise. Miriam and Moise are visual artists, and Miriam is jealous of the praise Moise received from a teacher years ago.

## FURTHER READING


Bray, Robert. "Moise and the Man in the Fur Coat," *The Southern Quarterly* 38, no. 1 (fall 1999): 58–70.

Di Cintio, Matt. "Ordered Anarchy: Writing as Transitional Object in *Moise and the World of Reason.*" *The Tennessee Williams Annual Review,* available online, URL: http://www.tennesseewilliamsstudies.org/archives/2002/4dicintio.htm. Accessed January 18, 2004.

Korda, Michael. "That's It, Baby," *The New Yorker,* 22 March 1999, 60–68.

Savran, David, *Communists, Cowboys, and Queers: The Politics of Masculinity in the Work of Arthur Miller and Tennessee Williams.* Minneapolis: University of Minnesota Press, 1992, p. 137.

Spoto, Donald, *The Kindness of Strangers.* Boston: Da Capo, 1985.


# *Moony's Kid Don't Cry*

A one-act play written in 1930.

## SYNOPSIS

The setting is the kitchen of a small three-room apartment. It is cheaply furnished and shabbily unkempt. An old table that has a small artificial Christmas tree on it occupies much of the kitchen space. Over the stove hangs a sign that reads, "Keep Smiling." At center stage stands an extravagantly expensive rocking horse—it seems out of place in the cheap surroundings. Soft, blue lights illuminate the stage, and a clothesline is stretched across an upstage corner of the set. Jane enters the kitchen to make Moony a cup of hot milk. Moony follows her into the kitchen, complaining that it is four o'clock in the morning and he will have to go to work soon.

He paces restlessly, mumbling about the small size of their apartment. He reminisces about his former life in the open air as a lumberjack. Jane ignores Moony's reverie. When he spills milk on the floor, she scolds him. She ridicules his dreams and reminds him that she, too, has sacrificed a better life to be with him. Moony suggests that he should follow in his father's footsteps and leave Jane and their baby behind. Jane physically attacks Moony, and he retaliates by choking her and throwing her against a wall. Jane crawls to Moony and begs him not to abandon her. Moony flings a few coins at her. She responds by flinging the baby into his arms, telling him that he needs to take the child with him. The baby begins to cry and Moony tries to soothe him. He reassures the child that he is not going to desert them.

## COMMENTARY

Written in 1930, *Moony's Kid Don't Cry* was initially titled *Hot Milk at Three in the Morning.* In 1939,

Williams submitted this play along with *THE DARK ROOM* and *THE CASE OF THE CRUSHED PETUNIAS* to a play competition sponsored by THE GROUP THEATRE. *Moony's Kid Don't Cry,* as well as the other plays in this collection, underscores the plight of the American working class and their quest for freedom and a better existence. Williams's one-act collection won a $100 prize and drew the attention of the talent agent AUDREY WOOD. *Moony's Kid Don't Cry* was one of the three plays that essentially launched Williams's career.

### PRODUCTION HISTORY

*Moony's Kid Don't Cry* was first produced in 1946 at the Straight Wharf Theatre in Nantucket, Massachusetts. It was filmed for NBC Television's *Kraft Theater* along with *THIS PROPERTY IS CONDEMNED* and *THE LAST OF MY SOLID GOLD WATCHES* in 1958.

### PUBLICATION HISTORY

*Moony's Kid Don't Cry* was first published in *Best Plays of 1940.* It was subsequently published in the one-act collection *AMERICAN BLUES* in 1948.

### CHARACTERS

**Jane** She is Moony's frail and sickly wife and mother of Moony's Kid. Although she is only in her mid-20s, there is a weariness about her that makes her seem much older. She has a caustic attitude toward her husband and his dreams of escape and freedom. She, too, dreams of a better life, yet she acknowledges the reality of their menial existence and accepts her fate.

**Moony** He is Jane's husband and father of a child referred to only as Moony's Kid. As his name suggests, Moony is a dreamer. He works in a factory but dreams of returning to his life as a lumberjack. He feels trapped by city life, cramped in the concrete jungle of his slum apartment and factory job. He expresses his desire to escape to his wife, who ridicules him for his fantasies and ambitions. Moony's struggle and longings suggest that he may have been an early prototype for Tom Wingfield in *THE GLASS MENAGERIE.* His bulk, physicality, and aggressiveness to Jane link him with Stanley Kowalski in *A STREETCAR NAMED DESIRE.*

**Moony's Kid** Moony's Kid is the month-old child of Moony and Jane. The child appears only in the final moments of the play. He is the one thing that keeps Moony from leaving. As Moony prepares to walk out on his family, Jane presents him with the baby. Moony remains, cradles the child, and rocks him to sleep.

## "Mother Yaws"

Short story written before 1977.

### SYNOPSIS

Barle McCorkle is a woman married to a cruel, abusive man named Tom McCorkle. He treats her as the servant to their three disrespectful, unloving children. Barle notices that a strange sore is forming on her face. When Tom sees the sore, he makes fun of it, harasses her about the condition, and demands she stay out of the kitchen until it heals.

Barle becomes very sick. Tom forces her to take the train to the city and see the doctor. He says that if she is contagious, she cannot return home. At the doctor's office, Barle is quarantined in the heat of the midday sun, and she faints. The doctor examines Barle and admits her to the hospital. After a few days, he diagnoses her condition as yaws, a rare African disease. Barle returns home to her malevolent family, who make her sleep on a palette in the storeroom until the morning when she can go to her father's house.

The next morning, Barle journeys to her father's house; however, she finds a sign in his front yard that states, "BARLE, YOU CANNOT ENTER." She has no other option than to go into the woods to find shade and water. Barle climbs Cat's Back Mountain to live. When she encounters baby wildcats, she is attacked and killed by their mother.

### COMMENTARY

This macabre tale, written in a style reminiscent of Edgar Allan Poe, is an example of the Southern Gothic tradition. "Mother Yaws" deals with the very grotesque nature of human decay and degeneration. In this mode of writing, the grotesque leads to alienation, and Barle's physical condition leads to ridicule and rejection. Barle could be redeemed by being cured, but she is forced to live in the wild and is killed by those elements. By rejecting her, the McCorkle family sentence Barle to death. "Mother Yaws" is a prime example of Williams's Gothic style, and it is stylistically and thematically aligned with "DESIRE AND THE BLACK MASSEUR," an important work of fiction in the Williams canon.

## PUBLICATION HISTORY

"Mother Yaws" was first published in *Esquire* (1977) and in *Collected Stories* in 1985.

## CHARACTERS

**Gatlinburg Doctor** He is the physician who cares for Barle when an unusual growth develops on her face. The Gatlinburg Doctor runs clinical tests on Barle, and his diagnosis is that she has mysteriously contracted "yaws," a rare African disease. He coldly informs Barle that there is nothing he can do to help her.

**McCorkle, Barle** Barle is a weak and submissive woman who is married to a barbaric man, Tom McCorkle. When Barle becomes ill and develops a large, unusual sore on her face, she becomes a social outcast. Tom sends her to the doctor and warns her that if she is contagious, she cannot return home. She is mistreated at the doctor's office by being forced to wait outside in the blazing sun. Barle's father reacts in a similarly inhumane fashion: He forbids her to enter his home. Barle is a pathetic figure, who is ultimately attacked and killed by a wildcat, when she tries to pet its cubs.

**McCorkle, Tom** Tom is the cruel and insensitive husband of Barle McCorkle. He enjoys mistreating his wife. When she becomes ill with yaws, a rare African disease that causes sores to develop on her body, Tom forbids her to live in their home.

## FURTHER READING

Flora, Joseph M., Lucinda Hardwick MacKethan, Todd W. Taylor. *The Companion to Southern Literature.* Baton Rouge: Louisiana State University Press, 2002, pp. 311–316.

# The Mutilated

A play in seven scenes written in 1965.

## SYNOPSIS

The play is set in the French Quarter of New Orleans, Louisiana. The action of the play takes place in and around the Silver Dollar Hotel, during the Christmas holiday.

### *Scene 1*

A group of Carollers are heard singing verses of songs that pertain to the theme of the play. They sing about the residents of the French Quarter and the loneliness that surrounds them during the festive Christmas season. The Carollers also sing about "the mutilated being touched by hands that nearly heal."

Celeste and her brother, Henry, arrive at the Silver Dollar Hotel. Celeste has just been released from jail and has returned to reclaim her belongings and her old room. Henry reprimands Celeste and abandons her at the hotel. Maxie and the Bird-Girl come along the street. Maxie invites spectators to pay to see the Bird Girl, a "freak of nature." Celeste chastises Maxie and the two begin to fight in the street. A Cop breaks up their fight. Celeste goes to find her old friend and fellow tenant, Trinket Dugan, Trinket accuses Celeste of manipulating her for money and turns Celeste away. Celeste declares that she will get even with Trinket. In the lobby of the hotel, Celeste meets Bernie, the desk clerk, and tries to persuade him to allow her back into her old room. Bernie refuses and informs Celeste that all her belongings have been locked away. Celeste tries to offer Bernie sexual favors in exchange for a room. Trinket calls for Bernie to see what "some vicious person has scratched on the wall." Trinket knows that Celeste has scrawled the "vicious lie" about her on the wall, and, as she leaves, Celeste threatens to do it again. As Celeste leaves, she calls out, "So long, Agnes Jones!"

### *Scene 2*

This scene is set on a bench in Jackson Park, near the Silver Dollar Hotel. Trinket is alone. She talks to herself and recounts the shock of seeing Celeste once again, and the history of their friendship. Trinket reveals that she has been mutilated. One of her breasts has been surgically removed, and Celeste is the only person who knows about it. While undergoing her mastectomy, Trinket used the alias "Agnes Jones." Trinket tries to exorcise this name from her memory throughout the scene, shouting, "Out out out! Agnes Jones, out!"

Because of her mutilation and the memories surrounding her friendship with Celeste, Trinket has spent the past three years with no one to love. Trinket swears that a miracle will happen, and that she will meet a man this Christmas night at the Café Boheme. As Trinket exits the park, the Carollers reappear. They sing another round of verses, touching upon the theme of love and the miracle of finding it.

### *Scene 3*

This scene is set in the interior of the Café Boheme. Tiger, the owner of the bar, is conversing with two bar patrons, Woman at the Bar and the Pious Queen, as Trinket enters. The three discuss a recent death and Tiger announces that drinks are on the house in memory of the deceased. Trinket orders an absinthe frappe and learns that the person they are referring to died in the bar.

Two sailors on leave, Slim and Bruno, arrive at the bar, and Trinket immediately takes a liking to Slim. Bruno arranges for Trinket to take Slim home with her.

### *Scene 4*

This scene takes place outside the Café Boheme. Trinket covers for Slim and Bruno when the Shore Police arrive. She claims that Bruno is her brother and she is about to take him to the candlelight Christmas service at the chapel. As they leave, Trinket confides in Bruno about her relationship with Celeste. Suddenly, Bruno tries to grope Trinket. Trinket becomes frightened and yells for Slim. Celeste reappears, drunkenly singing "Jingle Bells." Trinket decides to take Slim back to her hotel room and departs with him, hurling insults and abuse at Celeste.

As she calls for a taxi, Trinket threatens to have Celeste committed to the State Hospital for the Criminally Insane. Celeste snatches Trinket's purse, but Trinket has hidden her money and Celeste gets away with only Trinket's empty purse. The Carollers return and sing about forgiveness.

### *Scene 5*

This scene takes place in Trinket's room at the Silver Dollar Hotel. Slim debates whether or not he wants to spend the night with Trinket. When he finally learns of Trinket's mutilation, he demands that Trinket pay him for his company. She agrees. Celeste is heard howling insults under Trinket's window. She shouts for "Agnes Jones!" A screaming match between the two women ensues at Trinket's window. Trinket calls for Bernie and Celeste retreats. She takes rosary beads out of Trinket's purse and starts to confess her sins, as Trinket resumes her encounter with Slim. Celeste mutters to herself about Trinket's being mutilated, while Trinket mutters about Celeste's being alone. The Carollers reappear, singing verses about the lonely and misfit finding homes, warmth, comfort, and mercy.

### *Scene 6*

This scene takes place in the interior and exterior of the Silver Dollar Hotel. Celeste wakes from sleep on the hotel lobby couch, as Trinket wakes in her room, beside Slim. Slim searches for his wallet and accuses Trinket of stealing it. Trinket becomes hysterical and starts to scream. Bruno collects Slim from the hotel, while Trinket cries, whimpering that the pain in her chest has returned. The Carollers enter and the lead singer tunes his pitch pipe, but no one starts to sing. Instead, Jack in Black enters. He is dressed in a black cowboy outfit that has diamond detailing on the pockets and holster and on the edges of his hat. The Carollers sing with Jack about measured time, the tolling of a final bell, and denial.

### *Scene 7*

This scene takes place in the interior and exterior of the Silver Dollar Hotel. Trinket inquires whether Celeste is still in the lobby. Trinket gives Bernie a message for Celeste, instructing him to tell her that she is ready to "bury the hatchet." Celeste tries to pretend that she is indifferent to Trinket's message, but she reveals her true feelings by racing up the stairs to Trinket's room.

Celeste informs Trinket that her friendship is "not for sale." Trinket entices Celeste into the room with the promise of wine and Nabisco wafers. After sitting down and snacking together, Celeste decides to forgive Trinket. She begins making plans for them for the week. Celeste relates a prophecy that an old nun once told her. True to the prophecy, Celeste senses an invisible presence in the room with them. Celeste smells roses, candles, and incense. Celeste hears a tolling bell and realizes that she is being visited by the Virgin Mary.

Falling to her knees, Celeste reaches out and touches the robes of the Virgin Mother. She begs Trinket to do the same. Together, they witness a miraculous visitation and Trinket's pain is healed. As they cry together, "A miracle! A miracle!" Jack in Black appears. He smiles as he begins the Carollers' final verses. They sing about a miracle and the halting of death. In their song they admonish the audience to forget about Jack in Black for a little while.

## COMMENTARY

*The Mutilated,* as is its companion piece, THE GNÄDIGES FRÄULEIN, is a powerfully symbolic tale, another example of a Williams's black comedy centered on destitute social outcasts and their quest for love, acceptance, survival, and self-respect.

The two women at the center of *The Mutilated,* Trinket and Celeste, are damaged and stigmatized. Because of her mastectomy, Trinket is perceived as "less of a woman," and after her time in prison, Celeste is treated as "less of a person." Williams often uses physical deformity as a badge or outward expression of social isolation and loneliness. This technique is a feature in such works as ONE ARM, *The Gnädiges Fräulein,* and THE GLASS MENAGERIE.

With its fantastical conclusion—a visitation from the Virgin Mary—*The Mutilated* shares the theme of extraordinary events occurring in squalid places with other "boardinghouse dramas" such as THE REMARKABLE ROOMING-HOUSE OF MME. LEMONDE, THE COMING OF SOMETHING TO WIDOW HOLLY, and the short story "ANGEL IN THE ALCOVE." In these works Williams often depicts elements of the magical or divine interceding into the lives of those who are forgotten or abandoned. The characters in these works may be destitute and forlorn, yet they are not without hope or comfort.

## PRODUCTION HISTORY

*The Mutilated* premiered in tandem with *The Gnädiges Fräulein.* The two short plays were produced together under the title *Slapstick Tragedy.* Alan Schneider directed the premiere production of *Slapstick Tragedy* in New York in 1966 at the Longacre Theatre.

## PUBLICATION HISTORY

*The Mutilated* was first published by Dramatists Play Service in 1967, then revised for inclusion in DRAGON COUNTRY, published by New Directions in 1970.

## CHARACTERS

**Bernie** He is the desk clerk at the Silver Dollar Hotel. Bernie is very loyal to his tenants and answers to an unseen manager called Katz.

**Bird Girl** A hooded, pigeon-toed creature who appears briefly in the play. Labeled a "freak of nature," the Bird Girl is the play's ultimate outcast. Her deformity, otherness, and isolation provide financial sustenance for Maxie, a low-life con artist. Their working arrangement is indicative of the mercantile nature of all of the relationships in the play.

**Bruno** Bruno is Slim's friend. He is an old sailor on leave, who talks to Trinket in the bar.

**Carollers** The Carollers resemble a Greek chorus in that they weave in and out of every scene of the play, either opening or closing it with verses filled with thematic elements important to the story.

**Celeste** Celeste is a tiny, plump woman in her 50s. She is a shoplifter who dresses provocatively in the clothes she has stolen. Celeste is mentally unstable and possesses the emotional and mental consciousness of a child.

**Cop** He is the police officer who breaks up the fight between Maxie and Celeste.

**Dugan, Trinket** Trinket is a lonely tenant of the Silver Dollar Hotel, in the French Quarter of New Orleans. The mutilation she has suffered is the result of a recent mastectomy. Trinket spends her days alone in her room, writing in her diary. Although she is wealthy (her father left her three oil wells), Trinket chooses a squalid existence in a cheap, run-down hotel with bottles of California wine. While in the hospital for her operation, Trinket used the alias "Agnes Jones." Trinket is threatened by the return of her friend, Celeste, who is the only other person who knows about her mutilation.

**Henry** Henry is the brother of Celeste. He is a financially stable family man, with very little respect for his delinquent sister. Celeste has become a burden for Henry. After retrieving her from jail, Henry discards her at the Silver Dollar Hotel and wishes her good luck.

**Jack in Black** He is a mystical figure who appears toward the end of the play wearing a black cowboy outfit that is encrusted with diamonds. Jack in Black is an ominous presence who symbolizes death. Trinket Dugan, a breast cancer survivor, fears death when the pain in her chest returns. The Virgin Mary miraculously appears to heal Trinket, and Jack in Black is kept at bay.

**Jones, Agnes** An alias used by Trinket Dugan when she enters the hospital to have a mastectomy.

**Maxie** Maxie is a small-time con artist in the French Quarter of New Orleans, who makes money selling a view of a "freak of nature" called the Bird-Girl. He gets into a fight on the street outside the Silver Dollar Hotel with Celeste.

**Slim** Slim is a young sailor on leave in New Orleans. He and his friend, Bruno, meet Trinket Dugan in a bar called the Café Boheme. Trinket takes Slim home for a romantic encounter. When Slim discovers that Trinket has had one of her breasts removed, he agrees to be intimate with her only if she pays him. Trinket is so desperate for affection that she agrees to Slim's terms.

**Tiger** Tiger is the owner and proprietor of a bar in the French Quarter of New Orleans, Louisiana, called the Cafe Boheme. In his 50s, he is a former boxer and seaman.

# "The Mysteries of the Joy Rio"

Short story written in 1941.

## SYNOPSIS

Pablo Gonzales is the 19-year-old apprentice of an elderly watch repairman, Emiel Kroger. The men are also lovers. When Emiel dies of old age, Pablo takes over the business. Just as Emiel frequented the Joy Rio Theater, Pablo frequents this cinema to find sexual pleasure with young male prostitutes in the darkness of the balcony.

When Pablo is an old man, he accidentally interrupts an usher having sex with a young woman in the theater bathroom. An argument ensues and Pablo escapes this altercation to be visited by vivid memories of Emiel. As he is caressed in the darkness of the theater, Pablo is soothed by his lover's voice. He dies in the arms of his beloved deceased Emiel.

## COMMENTARY

In "The Mysteries of The Joy Rio" Williams explores the universal theme of loneliness. The tale is centered on Pablo's battle with grief and his quest to overcome his loss and isolation. He finds temporary relief in anonymous sexual acts in a shabby, darkened movie theater, but these futile attempts at intimacy and human connection never eradicate his feeling of emptiness and loss. As Pablo ages and faces his own mortality, his need for compassion and companionship is heightened. He finally finds solace in the arms of his deceased lover, who returns to guide Pablo into death.

"The Mysteries of the Joy Rio" is the basis for the short story "Hard Candy," considered by many to be Williams's most accomplished piece of fiction. "The Mysteries of the Joy Rio" and "Hard Candy," along with "TWO ON A PARTY," are considered "strong and healthy contributions to the literature of compassion," and prime examples of "the most significant gay fictions of their time" (Summers, 133–134).

### PUBLICATION HISTORY

"The Mysteries of the Joy Rio" was published in the collections *Hard Candy* (1954), *The Kingdom of Earth with Hard Candy* (1954), *Collected Stories* (1985), and *The Omnibus of 20th Century Ghost Stories* (1989).

### CHARACTERS

**George** George is an usher who works at the Joy Rio Theater. He is in love with Gladys.

**Gladys** Gladys is a young girl who lingers at the Joy Rio Theatre every afternoon to spend time with George.

**Gonzales, Pablo** Pablo is an apprentice at the watch shop owned by Emiel Kroger. During his apprenticeship, he and Emiel become lovers. When Emiel dies, Pablo takes over the watch shop. He finds solace from his grief and loneliness in the darkness of the Joy Rio Theater.

**Kroger, Emiel** He is an aging watch repairman who lives with his apprentice and lover, Pablo Gonzales. Emiel loves Pablo deeply and bequeaths his home and his business to him when he dies.

### FURTHER READING

Summer, Claude J. *Gay Fictions: Wilde to Stonewall—Studies in a Male Homosexual Literary Tradition.* New York: Continuum, 1990.

## "The Night of the Iguana"

Short story written between 1946 and 1948.

### SYNOPSIS

Miss Edith Jelkes is staying in a Mexican pension called Costa Verde. She is a painter and art teacher who suffered a nervous breakdown and has resigned herself to drifting through the world. Remarkably lonely, Edith tries to connect with the only other guests at Costa Verde: two handsome men (the younger is named Mike) who concentrate on their writing and each other. The two writers converse in low tones, intensifying Edith's curiosity. Getting to know them becomes a challenge, and she remains at the pension to penetrate their world.

Edith places her easel near the writers' veranda to demonstrate that she is a member of the artistic community. When they respond with indifference, she complains to the Patrona that their radio keeps her up at night. Edith resorts to stalking the couple, discarding her daily routines to align herself with their schedule. Edith overhears just enough of their conversations to fuel her imagination. Edith eventually recognizes that one of them is a famous writer.

The Patrona's son catches an iguana and ties it to the post of Edith's veranda. She discovers it when she hears a strange scratching sound outside her door. She screams and runs to the two writers, who are drinking and lying in hammocks. They are finally cornered and forced to converse with her. To distance herself from the restrained animal, Edith moves into the room next door to the two writers. She delights in eavesdropping on them, but when she overhears the couple mocking her and laughing, she is deeply offended.

She falls asleep and wakes a few hours before dawn. The writers are still awake. When they hear her stirring, they quickly turn off the lights for privacy as the walls have cracks in them. They begin talking about her once again. One writer says that the Patrona is eager to get rid of Edith, going so far as to order the cook to oversalt her food. Edith jumps to her feet and knocks on their door.

When she enters, Mike shoves her to the floor and storms out of the room. The old writer remains in the room as Edith begins to cry. He grabs Edith and attempts to rape her. Edith panics, fights to free herself, and escapes to her original room. Crying, she discovers that the iguana has also freed itself. Although it was horrific at the time, Edith becomes aroused by this sexual encounter. "Ah, Life," she ponders.

### COMMENTARY

"The Night of the Iguana" is the basis for Williams's later creation, the full-length play of the same name. Edith Jelkes becomes Hannah Jelkes, with the addition of an elderly poet grandfather for her to look after and dote upon. The Patrona becomes a more fully developed character named Maxine Faulk, and Williams adds another central character, the Reverend T. Lawrence Shannon, a defrocked minister who leads tours through Mexico.

The short story version of this plot hinges on the iguana as a symbol for Edith's life. Edith is similar to this subdued and restrained creature in that she is an aging, lonely unmarried woman trapped and isolated in a world that finds her undesirable. She is freed during a violent sexual encounter and finds satisfaction in the interconnectedness she feels with the world as a result of sexual assault. By contrast, the play focuses on several characters for whom the iguana becomes a metaphor for the oppressive state of their lives.

### PUBLICATION HISTORY

"The Night of the Iguana" was published in the collections *One Arm* (1948), *Collected Stories* (1985), and *Escape to Mexico* (2002).

### CHARACTERS

**Jelkes, Miss Edith** Edith is a traveling painter staying at a resort in Mexico. She actively seeks the attention of two vacationing writers, who are also guests at the resort. Edith becomes bored at the Costa Verde, and instead of moving on to the next adventure, she stays to eavesdrop on the other guests.

**Older Writer** He is an accomplished writer who vacations with his lover, Mike, at the Costa Verde Hotel in Mexico. Another guest at the villa, Edith Jelkes, harasses and stalks them out of curiosity and boredom. There is a confrontation among the Older Writer, Mike, and Edith that culminates in the Older Writer sexually assaulting Edith.

## *The Night of the Iguana*

Full-length play written in 1962.

### SYNOPSIS

The play is set on the west coast of Mexico, a town called Puerto Barrio, in the Costa Verde Hotel. It is the summer of 1940.

#### *Act 1*

Maxine Faulk owns the Costa Verde Hotel in Puerto Barrio, where the Reverend T. Lawrence Shannon has taken his tour group of begrudging Baptist travelers from Texas, including a young love-struck woman named Charlotte Goodall and her overbearing chaperone, Miss Judith Fellowes. Stumbling onto the porch of the hotel, Shannon greets Maxine and falls into a hammock, breathing heavily. Calling for help with baggage, Maxine offers Shannon a drink, which he refuses, instead asking to speak with Maxine's husband, Fred (who died two weeks before Shannon's arrival). Shannon calls for Hank to lead the ladies up from the bus, while he complains about his tour bus full of women to Maxine; he is on the verge of a nervous breakdown, for he has engaged in sexual relations with Charlotte (one of the tourists), who is not of legal age. Frau Herzkopf and Herr Herzkopf enter and troop down toward the beach, and Maxine explains their presence as favored guests in her hotel. Hank appears, complaining that the women on the bus will not walk up to the hotel because they have found out about Charlotte's seduction and are in an uproar about it.

Miss Fellowes charges in and demands that Shannon hand over the bus key. She is dissatisfied with the conditions of the trip and demands that Maxine let her use a phone. Hannah Jelkes appears, looking for the hotel manager. A vagabond artist, accompanying her elderly grandfather poet, Hannah asks for a vacancy; securing two rooms, she disappears to fetch her grandfather, Nonno. Miss Fellowes accuses Shannon of cheating the women of their hard-earned money. She also chastises him for being a defrocked minister. Shannon loses his cool and chokes out the command, "Don't! Break! Human! Pride!" Miss Fellowes charges back to the bus to try to stop the porters, who are collecting the luggage.

Nonno and Hannah enter. Hannah tries sweetly to persuade Maxine to let them entertain the other hotel guests in exchange for accommodations.

Nonno interrupts the negotiations with incoherent and random phrases. Hannah explains, due to a recent stroke, Nonno falls victim to narcoleptic episodes. Maxine begrudgingly grants them a room, promising to find them another hotel in the morning; she leaves to tend to the luggage dilemma. Shannon heads to the beach "for a swim," and Nonno pipes up again with a few verses from his poem, which describe the nondespairing attitude of a skyward-tilting orange branch.

### Act 2

Several hours later, Maxine and Hannah appear on the veranda to set the tables for supper. Maxine refuses to let Hannah stay at her hotel on credit, even after Hannah offers her jade jewelry for payment. Shannon and the German tourists appear from the beach, calling for beer. Maxine goes to fetch the beer and Charlotte enters, calling for Shannon. He quickly ducks into his cubicle, but Charlotte hears him and demands that he marry her, as she is in love with him. Shannon refuses, saying that his "emotional bank account [is] overdrawn" and that he does not love her. Miss Fellowes approaches, scolds Charlotte for conversing with Shannon, and forbids her to be near him. She happily boasts that a warrant for his arrest has been issued in Texas.

Hanna fetches Nonno for supper and Shannon reappears from his cubicle, dressed in a clerical robe to prove that he has not been defrocked. Hannah begins to sketch his profile as Shannon reminisces about his life: An Episcopal minister, Shannon had a nervous breakdown after he was seduced by a young Sunday school teacher. He gave a blasphemous sermon that angered his congregation, who then locked him out of the church. Shannon spent time in an asylum and gave up the ministry to become a tour guide. He now spends his time searching for a personal idea of God. When he asks to see his portrait, Hannah asks him to promise that he will give gentle sermons if he ever returns to the church. She believes people need someone to guide them beside "still waters."

Maxine enters with her porters, who have caught an iguana. Hearing a crash in Nonno's room, Shannon goes to help the old man down to supper. Nonno embarrasses Hannah by asking her how much money she has made selling her paintings. Shannon gives Nonno five pesos to calm him. Hannah laments the "dimming out of the mind" that accompanies old age. Maxine offers everyone cocktails. She then bickers with Shannon, and turns on Hannah, warning her to stay away from Shannon. Hannah is surprised (and amused) that Maxine considers her a threat. She assures Maxine that she has no interest in Shannon. Shannon returns, and offers Hannah a smoke, as a rainstorm approaches. Reaching shelter under the porch, Shannon watches the storm and bathes his face in the downpour.

### Act 3

A few hours later, Shannon and Hannah sit on the veranda—Hannah reading a book and Shannon writing a letter to his bishop. Maxine criticizes Shannon for being rooted in his guilt concerning his masturbatory pleasures. (Maxine once overheard a conversation about the source of Shannon's mental instability: His mother once paddled him for masturbating as a little boy and told him the paddling was better than what God had in store for him.) Maxine says that since that incident, Shannon has been subliminally spiting his mother (and God) by seducing young girls and preaching blasphemous sermons. Jake Latta, a tour guide for Blake Tours and Shannon's boss, arrives. Fiercely reluctant, Shannon hands over the bus key. Shannon demands his severance pay, to which Miss Fellowes objects. She informs him that she has made certain that he will be "blacklisted from now on at every travel agency in the States." Delirious with rage, Shannon runs down the hill and urinates on the ladies' luggage.

When Shannon returns, Maxine orders her porters to tie Shannon in a hammock, while she goes to fetch the bill for the tourists. The German tourists enter, tormenting Shannon, who is panicking in the hammock. Hannah shoos them away, and Shannon asks her to untie him; Hannah refuses to do so until he has calmed down. Brewing poppy tea for him, Hannah surmises that Shannon enjoys his panic attacks as they are easier than a crucifixion. Shannon tries viciously to wrench himself free from the hammock, and Hannah calls for Maxine, who sits on him and threatens him with a trip to the asylum. Shannon calmly sips his tea. He escapes from his prison and makes himself a "rum-coco" cocktail.

Hannah reveals the story of her life: how she herself had a nervous breakdown, how she is accustomed to traveling alone with her grandfather, and how she feels about being a spinster. Noticing a scuffling sound under the veranda, Hannah inquires about it. Shannon tells her that it is an iguana, tied up and "trying to go on past the end of its . . . rope." Hannah begs Shannon to untie the animal; he refuses, at Maxine's request. Nonno suddenly calls from his room, requesting that Hannah record his finally finished poem. Maxine enters, ready for a swim, and finds that Shannon has escaped the hammock. Shannon appears from below the veranda and tells Maxine that he has set the iguana free. Maxine invites Shannon for a swim and asks him to stay and help manage the hotel with her. Exiting to the beach, they discuss their plans for renovating the hotel. Alone with Nonno, Hannah speaks to the sky, asking God to let her stop where she is. Nonno's head drops and Hannah knows he has died. She hugs him.

## COMMENTARY

"Flight could be called Tennessee Williams's natural existence" (Leverich, 370), and the escape Williams made to Mexico in the summer of 1940 was intended as an antidote to the difficult ending of his relationship with the Canadian dancer Kip Kiernan. Expecting, as did his character, the defrocked minister, T. Lawrence Shannon, "to be dead before the summer was over" (Spoto, 82), he stayed at the Hotel Costa Verde—real-life model for the hotel in *The Night of the Iguana*—which was inhabited by people "of two classes, those who are waiting for something to happen or those who believe that everything has happened already" (Leverich, 377). During his stay there, Williams began a creative process that extended over two decades, took his subject matter through several formal permutations (including letters, an essay, a short story, and a one-act version), and at last culminated in a full-length play.

*The Night of the Iguana* which premiered in 1961 was Williams's last critical and commercial success. With remarkable synchronicity, the play's thematic links and the accolades it received appear to close a circle, back to his breakthrough play, *The Glass Menagerie,* and "its breadth of spirit and [. . .] unangry, quiet voice about the great reach of small lives" (Spoto, 116). Donald Spoto's observation chimes uncannily with the closing remark of Howard Taubman's review, which attributes to *The Night of the Iguana* "a vibrant eloquence in declaring its respect for those who have to fight for their bit of decency" (Taubman, *New York Times,* 1961).

Though nearly 30 years apart, both plays share a preoccupation with the notion of escape and the conflict between reality and fantasy. Self-absorbed to the point of ignoring the world at large and its events—be they the bombings of Guernica or of London—the characters in both plays seem to be kissing cousins in their garrulous speechlessness. The barely concealed casting of family members is a prominent feature of the autobiographical *Glass Menagerie,* and Williams does it again in *Night of the Iguana,* when he bases Nonno (the Italian word for grandfather) on his maternal grandfather, the Reverend Walter Edwin Dakin, who had been a surrogate father to young Tom and his sister, Rose. Although Jonathan "Nonno" Coffin, grandfather of Hannah, "ninety-seven years *young*" and "the oldest living and practicing poet," shares part of his name with Tennessee's father, Cornelius Coffin Williams, all of his spirit and frailties are those of Walter Dakin. Other family members have made their way into *Night of the Iguana* via the Wingfield family of *The Glass Menagerie.* The resemblance is most conspicuous in the case of Hannah Jelkes, whose description echoes almost verbatim that of Laura Wingfield: She is "ethereal, almost ghostly. She suggests a Gothic cathedral image of a medieval saint, but animated" (*Iguana,* preface). Whereas Laura embodies Williams's sister, Rose, on a near-realistic level, Hannah is "a projection of what might have become of Rose" (Leverich, 376)—or Laura. She is not the only one who has matured in this fashion. Shannon, a latter-day Tom Wingfield, appears always to teeter on the brink of leaving—the church, Blake Tours, life. Forever on the move, he consistently fails to move on, aware of and "spooked" by the impossibility of escape. Finally, Maxine

Faulks's abrasiveness, pragmatism, and behavioral malaprops call to mind Amanda Wingfield, as does her tendency to smother people she cares about. In terms of setting, resemblances between *The Glass Menagerie* and *Night of the Iguana* are less readily apparent, but their locales, too, share telltale elements of mood and function. Atmospherically, the Saint Louis tenement is surprisingly close to the jungle-locked hotel on the Mexican coast and its ramshackle veranda: Heat and confinement render both places womblike, simultaneously both shelter and prison. Given these parallels, it is easy to see how *The Night of the Iguana* could be perceived as "somewhat aimless and self-derivative . . . [lacking] an organizing principle, though it covers familiar terrain" (Brustein, 26). However, the play is a natural progression, a "grown up" *Glass Menagerie* and not merely because its protagonists—and its author—are older and, in some cases, wiser.

In *The Night of the Iguana,* there is an overriding clash of the physical and spiritual. As far as Shannon is concerned, body and soul are as irreconcilable as matter and antimatter, one necessarily annihilating the other. Early on, Williams offers a subtle hint at this mutually destructive potential when Maxine comments on Shannon's letter of contrition to his bishop, "If this is the letter, baby, you've sweated through it, so the older bugger couldn't read it even if you mailed it to him this time."

The physical—sweat, in this instance—has blotted out spiritual meaning. Shannon has been caught in the middle of this explosive conflict, and it shows. The first metaphoric squalls of the "gathering storm" that is the mood throughout most of acts 1 and 2 (Belden, 33) blow a "panting, sweating, and wild-eyed" Shannon before them, and he certainly appears to have been subjected to this mode of travel over a long distance and for a long time. In fact, the defrocked priest, locked out of his church in (the suggestively named) Pleasant Valley for committing statutory rape and heresy, is about to lost his secular flock of tourists for the same offenses. The description of his Gladstone bag—"beat-up [and] covered with travel stickers from all over the world"—seems equally suited to the man himself, "who has cracked up before and is going to crack up again—perhaps repeatedly."

Shannon has fled to the Costa Verde Hotel, fully expecting to find Maxine's husband, Fred, who "knew when [Shannon] was spooked" and was privy to "how [his] problems first started." Ironically, the hotel and its owners have since been encroached upon by the presumptive safety barrier. The jungle is, of course, the very epitome of natural eros and its rampant cycle of life, and as such it is both fertile and destructive. Its climate has made the cabin roofs leak, and "old Freddie the Fisherman is feeding the fish—fishes' revenge on old Freddie." Gifted, as is the jungle itself, with an earthly sensuality that cannot be satisfied by her young Mexican men alone, the widowed Maxine is looking for someone literally to fill Fred's shoes—and bed. Shannon, by his very presence, has won and resists her advances in the way he invariably weathers events that leave him unsettled: by resorting to socially unacceptable behavior. Lindy Levin concisely diagnoses this as a result of the "anarchy of the unconscious and the emotional costs of denying the tension of opposites that one is asked to endure" (Levin, 88).

A different but equally threatening reality intrudes in the shape of the women of the Baptist Female College—and the not-quite-17-year-old Charlotte Goodall, and her chaperone, Judith Fellowes. The intrusion is one Shannon has precipitated himself, by withholding the bus keys in an act of tourism "heresy" that mimics his agnostic outburst on the chancel of Pleasant Valley church. Both instances were preceded by sexual transgression, and if the latter was a refusal of spiritual guidance, the first is a refusal of secular guidance. The results are the same: Shannon will be ousted from Blake Tours just as he has been ousted from his church. Williams reinforces the parallel through Judith Fellowes's constant reminders of Shannon's disgrace and, somewhat more obscurely, by Shannon's reference to the two women as "the teen-age Medea and the older Medea." According to Greek mythology, the sorceress Medea, wife of Jason the Argonaut, had a penchant for killing in rather unsavory ways people who offended her. The murder that stands out is that of Glauce, Jason's second wife, whom Medea gave a wedding robe of poisoned cloth. Unable to remove the robe once she had put it on, Glauce was burned alive by the poison. Shannon, professing to be wedded to the cloth, also cannot take off his figurative robes, burning—with despair and fever—as both "Medeas" make a point of driving home his sexual and social offenses.

With the arrival of Hannah Jelkes and Nonno, yet another ingredient is thrown into the already volatile mix. Shannon immediately warms to the old poet. One can hardly avoid suspecting that Nonno is intended to be a much older, future version of Shannon, who still refuses to take his charges where they expect to be taken, who still has visions of impending death (albeit with reason now), and who still—as a result of actual rather than psychological blindness—refuses to recognize the people around him as who and what they are. This parallel is supported by the remarkably similar, if more antagonistic, relationship between the Narrator and the playwright Williams sets up in his 1975 novel, *MOISE AND THE WORLD OF REASON.* Almost inevitably, Hannah, who is Nonno's guardian angel, becomes that of Shannon as well, and her spirituality constitutes a counterpoise to Maxine's sensuality. With Shannon a—quite literally—captive audience in the hammock and Nonno giving a George Burns–type impersonation of the Almighty in this not-so-medieval morality play, the allegorical fight between the two opposing forces unfolds on the veranda, and it is, in the truest sense, a fight for Shannon's soul.

The rivalry between the two women is apparent from the beginning, but what is equally obvious is that it is one-sided in terms of claims of ownership. Unlike Maxine, who—squatter-fashion—affirms her right of possession by physically sitting on Shannon, Hannah, the "New England spinster who is pushing forty," has no sexual designs on Shannon. She wants to help, but "ethereal, almost ghostly" as she is, physical touch is not for her. Her and Shannon's kinship is of a different type, grounded in a familiarity with demons that each recognizes in the other. What "the spook" is to Shannon, "the blue devil" is to Hannah, and in both cases the conflict is the same, namely, that of reality and fantasy. In order to straddle the gap, they both play their part—Shannon that of the ascetic, Hannah that of the artist—and their dressing-up for dinner in act 2 offers a foreshadowing of the predictable outcome of their shared drama:

> For a moment they both face front, adjusting their two outfits. They are like two actors in a play which is about to fold on the road, preparing gravely for a performance which may be the last one.

The fundamental difference between them is that Hannah has learned to endure the conflict between what is and what ought to be, whereas Shannon persists in fighting it. "Endurance is something that spooks and blue devils respect," she says. The truth of this remains doubtful. As Shannon flings coco shells into the bushes to drive away the spook, she takes a few deep breaths. Neither action is likely to bring about change. All that has truly changed is that their respective performances are about to end: Shannon will lose his job and be left with nowhere to go, and Hannah's hard-selling artist act will become unnecessary with the death of Nonno, irrespective of whether she decides to go on as before. Spooks and blue devils remain, however.

> See? The iguana? At the end of its rope? Trying to go on past the end of its goddamn rope. Like *you!* Like *me!* Like Grampa with his last poem!

The iguana remains trapped at the end of its tether. As it is tied, it would indeed have to chew off its head to get away. The only one who—figuratively speaking—masters that trick is Nonno. For everyone else a higher power is required to effect the escape.

The central symbol of the captured iguana, only unraveled at the end of the play, serves as a profoundly evocative illustration of Shannon's plight, as everything that happens to him finds its echo in the fate of the lizard. Pursuit, capture, escape, and recapture are mirrored, and as the iguana is tied to a post underneath the veranda to be poked and prodded by the Mexican boys, so Shannon is tied into the hammock to be poked and prodded by the Fahrenkopfs. When Shannon, playing God, frees the iguana, the message clearly seems to be that he is, after all, the "god" capable of freeing himself. Though obvious and blunt on the surface, the image has another, less apparent but highly suggestive layer, and it casts into doubt the play's qualified happy ending.

When Shannon at last accepts Maxine's offer, he appears to have reached a compromise with himself, some form of a bearable modus vivendi. What remains unanswered, however, is the question of whether this iguana has been set free or whether he has merely found some more rope to stretch. The purpose of capturing an iguana is to fatten and eat it. And, as Shannon observes, "Mrs. Faulks wants to eat it. I've got to please Mrs. Faulks. I am at her mercy. I am at her disposal." With this perspective, escape truly is impossible.

## PRODUCTION HISTORY

*The Night of the Iguana* was Williams's last major theatrical success. The play, produced by Charles Bowden and Viola Rubber and designed by Oliver Smith, made it to Broadway and opened at the Royale Theatre on December 28, 1961. Critics, possibly expecting a sequel to *SWEET BIRD OF YOUTH,* were somewhat bewildered by what *Time* magazine called "much the best new American play of the season [and] the wisest play he has ever written" (Spoto, 248). But "leashed violence" and "sensitive, restrained writing" were by no means unwelcome, and the reception was relatively friendly.

As with *The Glass Menagerie,* the main accolades followed the muted initial reception in New York. On April 10, 1962, the *The Night of the Iguana* won the New York Drama Critics Circle Award—one week after Bette Davis had left the production of her own choice and was replaced by Shelley Winters. Margaret Leighton won a Tony for her portrayal of Hannah Jelkes. *The Night of the Iguana* also was nominated in the Best Play category, as was Viola Rubber as Best Producer of a Play.

Almost inevitably after a sell-out Broadway production, the motion picture followed in 1964. It is considered to be the best film version of any of Tennessee Williams's works. Directed by John Huston, its cast list reads as a *Who's Who* of early sixties cinema: Richard Burton (Shannon), Ava Gardner (Maxine), Deborah Kerr (Hannah), and Sue Lyons, of *Lolita* fame, as Charlotte Goodall. The star-studded cast undoubtedly helped to secure the film's virtually instant (and lasting) popular and critical success. *The Night of the Iguana* garnered five Golden Globe nominations (including Best Picture and Best Director) and four Academy Award nominations. In 2001 another screen version was produced by Ray Stark. Directed by the Bosnian filmmaker Predrag "Gaga" Antonijevic, it starred Jeremy Irons, Thora Birch, and Kirk Douglas, who played the Gentleman Caller in the 1950 film version of *The Glass Menagerie.*

## PUBLICATION HISTORY

*The Night of the Iguana* was first published in 1962 by New Directions, New York.

## CHARACTERS

**Faulk, Maxine** The owner and proprietor of the Costa Verde Hotel, Maxine loves Shannon and is jealous of his acquaintance with Hannah Jelkes. Maxine wages war against Hannah for Shannon's attention. In the end, she is permitted to keep Shannon at the Costa Verde Hotel.

**Fellowes, Miss Judith** She is a beastly Baptist matron from Texas. The chaperone of Charlotte Goodall, Miss Fellowes wages a campaign against Shannon, whom she accuses of seducing and robbing the young woman.

**Goodall, Charlotte** She is a young tourist who is seduced by the defrocked Reverend T. Lawrence Shannon, who is now a tour guide in Mexico. She thinks she is in love with Shannon and professes her love publicly, causing a major upset within the touring party of prudish Baptist women.

**Jelkes, Hannah** She is an ageless vagabond artist who travels the world with her grandfather, Nonno, selling her paintings and Nonno's oral recitations of his famed poems. She is Shannon's saving grace. Deeply sensitive and wholly dedicated to those in need, Hannah has courage and strength that are guideposts in her own life. Hannah has a peaceful melancholy that is not present in many Williams characters. She is a paragon of spiritual harmony despite the difficulties she has faced during her life.

**Nonno** Jonathan Coffin is Hannah Jelkes's aging grandfather. At 97 years, Nonno is composing a new poem, which is presenting some difficulty, given his failing memory. However, the recitations Nonno gives throughout the play provide a metaphoric background for Shannon's psychological problems.

**Shannon, the Reverend T. Lawrence** In his mid-30s, Shannon is a "black Irish" Episcopal minister who denies that he has been defrocked and now leads tropical tours for Blake Tours. On the verge of a nervous breakdown, Shannon seeks refuge from his problems at the Costa Verde Hotel. When he becomes involved with a young tourist named Charlotte Goodall, he is fired from Blake Tours and harassed by the group of Baptist women with whom Charlotte travels. Shannon meets Hannah Jelkes at the Costa Verde Hotel, during a time when he is questioning his existence and place in the universe. Having struggled and endured many disappointments, Shannon learns to accept his life as a defrocked minister, and with Hannah's help, he finds answers to questions that have plagued his life.

## FURTHER READING


Adler, Jacob H. "*Night of the Iguana:* A New Tennessee Williams?" *Ramparts* 1, no. 3 (1962): 59–68.

Brustein, Robert. "Revisited Plays, Revised Opinions." *New Republic,* June 17, 1996.

Leverich, Lyle, *Tom: The Unknown Tennessee Williams.* New York: W. W. Norton, 1995.

Levin, Lindy. "Shadow into Light: A Jungian Analysis of *The Night of the Iguana,*" *The Tennessee Williams Annual Review* 2 (1999): 87–98.

Parker, Brian. "Introduction to a One-Act Version of *The Night of the Iguana,*" *Tennessee Williams Annual Review* 4 (2001): URL: www.tennesseewilliams studies.org/archives/2001/index.htm

Spoto, Donald, *The Kindness of Strangers.* Boston: Da Capo, 1997.

Taubman, Howard. "Theatre: *Night of the Iguana* Opens," *New York Times,* December 29, 1961. p. 10.

Thompson, Judith J. *Tennessee Williams's Plays: Memory, Myth, and Symbol.* New York: Lang, 1987.


# *Not About Nightingales*

Full-length play written in 1938.

## SYNOPSIS

The action takes place in a large U.S. prison in the summer of 1938. *The Lorelei,* a sightseeing cruise ship, circles around the prison island. A loudspeaker announces the city's skyline, the prison, its inmate statistics, and the evening's entertainment on the upper deck.

### *Act 1, Episode 1*

An Announcer broadcasts the title of each episode, or scene.

Announcer: *"Miss Crane Applies for a Job."*

Eva Crane nervously arrives at the prison's office, hoping to secure a secretarial position. She waits for Mr. Whalen, the Warden, along with Mrs. Bristol (also known as Mrs. B.), an inmate's mother. Mrs. B. has traveled from Wisconsin to check on her son. Mrs. B.'s concern has been prompted by her son's progressively more hysterical letters, which tell of the "Klondike," where it is "hot as hell." Mrs. B. is surprised to learn that Eva is interviewing at such an atrocious place, but Eva assures her that this is "a model institution," where psychology and sociology are used to rehabilitate prisoners.

Jim Canary walks by the two women, and Eva jumps up to ask to see the Warden. Mrs. B. asks about her son, a sailor named Jack. Jim says the Warden has not returned from "inspections," or his daily jaunt to the bar. Eva makes her way into the office, where Jim is filing papers. In idle conversation, Jim reveals that he is a reformed prisoner, a model for the institution, who is allowed to work in the office and perform clerical duties for the Warden. Mrs. B. enters the office to ask again about her son. Jim is not at liberty to divulge information, but when she exits, he tells Eva that Jack has recently become insane. Eva is stunned to learn that the articles she has read about the prison have been just propaganda and that the conditions are actually unbearable. The Warden finally enters. He is coarse and large, and he greets Eva warmly. Eva discusses her qualifications for the job. The Warden points to the window in the office and tells Eva that it is called "the quick way out," because it is the only window without bars. Jumping out of it would lead to a violent death on the rocks and ocean far below. The Warden hires Eva and gloats about her curvaceous figure.

***Act 1, Episode 2***

Announcer: "*Sailor Jack.*"

In a prison cell, Jack mumbles quietly to himself. The guard, Schultz, announces lights out while Butch, Queen, and Joe complain and converse. Queen finds out that he has syphilis. Jack does not stop talking after the lights are out, and Butch complains to Schultz about him. Butch informs the other inmates that Jack became insane in the Klondike. The inmates grumble about the terrible food. Butch requests that Jack be moved elsewhere. Mac, another one of the guards, puts Jack in isolation while Jim is escorted back to a cell. The inmates harass Jim because they think he is a traitor and a spy for working in the Warden's. The men hear *The Lorelei* steamer and its band playing on the deck. It reminds Butch of a former girlfriend named Goldie. He reminisces about life before prison. Queen searches for his manicure set, which has been stolen, and Joe starts a conversation about escaping through the "quick way out" window. Queen says that he has always been persecuted (because his manicure set is missing), while Butch discusses Jack's letters from his mother, which he has read.

***Act 1, Episode 3***

Announcer: "*The Prognosis.*"

As Eva arrives for her first day of work, Mr. Whalen studies a racing form. Mrs. B. enters the office to ask about Jack. The Warden makes Jim look for Jack's file. It is revealed that Jack was sentenced to three years for larceny, slacked on his work, and was sent to the Klondike, the torturous steam room, for three days. The Warden becomes angry when Jim offers too much information. Jim reads that Jack was transferred to the psychopathic ward for violence and delusions. Mrs B. grows hysterical with disbelief. Jim escorts her out of the office.

***Act 1, Episode 4***

Announcer: "*Conversations at Midnight.*"

Ollie and Butch talk between their two prison cells. Ollie kneels praying for his six children and pregnant wife. He is an African-American man who has been sentenced for stealing a case of canned vegetables for his starving family. Relaxing and smoking, Butch chastises Ollie for believing in prayer. Jim comforts Ollie. Butch cruelly taunts Jim about being a canary and "singing" to the Warden. Jim defends himself.

Another cruise ship circles around the island, disrupting the conversation with its lights and music. Joe has become ill from the spoiled meatballs he had for dinner. Butch decides the inmates should go on a hunger strike for better food. Joe warns that they would be put in the Klondike. Butch has suffered the Klondike and persuades everyone that it can be survived. Butch recalls that it is like "breathin' fire in yer lungs . . . the floor is so hot you can't stand on it, but there's no place else to stand."

***Act 1, Episode 5***

Announcer: "*Band Music!*"

Jim sits in the office as Eva enters. Jim explains that the woman who previously had her job had intimate relations with the Warden and died during "an operation" a few months afterward. The Warden bought his wife a mink coat as a result. Eva becomes worried by this information, but she is desperate to keep her job. Jim confides in her that the inmates are actually being starved because the food is terrible and spoiled. The prison band is heard practicing in the distance. Eva does not want to believe the horrible realities of the place. Jim spontaneously embraces Eva, and she pushes him away.

***Act 1, Episode 6***

Announcer: "*Mister Olympics.*"

A new inmate is admitted to Hall C, where Joe, Butch, and Queen reside. Swifty, an Olympic runner who "likes to kill distance," is the newest member of the cell, convicted of stealing money. Swifty claims that he did not receive a fair trial, and his lawyers are appealing the verdict. Joe predicts that Swifty will end up like Jack. Butch explains to Swifty that inmates are not considered human, and guards have "god complexes."

***Act 1, Episode 7***

Announcer: "*A Rubber Duck for the Baby!*"

The Warden shows Eva a rubber duck, which he has purchased for his baby daughter. Jim informs the Warden of the inmates' escalating complaints about the food. Jim relates the seven recent cases of food poisoning. The Warden accuses Jim of exaggerating the truth because Eva is present. The Warden reminisces about beating Jim and he recalls Jim having a high threshold for pain. The Warden proudly laughs about Jim's stamina and the scars on his back. This act was an initiation into the clerical position Jim now holds. Eva starts to faint. Jim catches her and the Warden instructs him to leave. The Warden tries to explain away his brutality, assuring Eva that running a prison requires such extreme actions. Eva is not convinced.

*Act 1, Episode 8*
Announcer: *"Explosion!"*

Joe, Butch, Swifty, and Queen sit in their cell. They debate the hunger strike. Butch thinks it will work; the other men fear the Klondike. Jim steps inside the cell to warn Butch not to go through with the strike. Jim informs the others that he will have a parole hearing next month and if he gets parole, he will tell the public about the terrible conditions of the prison. Jim's goal is to have the Warden stripped of his position. Butch is not interested in waiting a month or relying on Jim. Joe is engrossed with Jim's plan; however, Butch squelches his hope.

*Act 1, Episode 9*
Announcer: *"Hunger Strike!"*

Eva enters the office. The Warden offers her dinner and apologizes for making her work overtime. He fears the strike will attract public attention and expects Eva to organize the files in case there is an investigation. Eva inquires about the "bad discrepancies" in the financial records. He quickly advises her to manipulate the books and calls for Jim to help her. The Warden compliments Eva on her figure, particularly her breasts. He licks his lips as he moves closer to her. The Warden asks her to go into an inner office with him, but she refuses. He grabs her roughly as he exits the office. Jim interrupts them and asks the Warden to reconsider improving the quality of the food. He warns that the hunger strike may happen tonight. The Warden talks of the Klondike and says the pipes are being prepared.

Jim notices that Eva is pale and upset. She shows him a bruise on her arm the Warden caused. Jim pleads with Eva to quit the job and to tell the world how the prisoners are suffering. Eva refuses to leave because jobs are scarce. They discuss the romantic feelings they have for each other. Eva urges Jim to think about his parole. The Warden enters, prepared to inspect the prisoners. A group of inmates enter. They are bloody and delirious because they have been severely beaten. The Warden gloats about the way the men look, and he is excited to send them back to the others who are thinking about striking. Swifty is one of them. He has been in a straitjacket for five days. Ollie pleads with the Warden not to make them go to the Klondike another night.

Eva witnesses the whole scene, and she sinks into a chair in shock. The men are escorted back to the Klondike. Several minutes later, outcries of protest are heard. Jim rushes into the office with the news that Ollie has died. The Warden orders Eva to complete a death certificate for Ollie. She is instructed to list the cause of death as stomach ulcers and severe hemorrhage. Jim reminds him that that is the information he supplied for the man who died the previous week. The Warden changes the cause to complications of a bad cold.

In the cells, the men rebel because Ollie has been killed. Shouts of "Ollie's dead! They killed Ollie!" are heard. Butch announces that the hunger strike is in effect. The scene shifts to a Newsboy on the street, who is shouting the headlines about the hunger strike. Several voices from the Associated Press announce the strike.

*Act 2, Episode 1*
Announcer: *"Not about Nightingales!"*

Eva answers phone calls from several newspapers about the recent hunger strike. The Chaplain nervously pleads with the Warden to agree to the prisoners' demands. Jim enters with a bloody arm, caused by walking too closely to the cells. Eva bandages his arm while he urges her to leave the prison. She returns to typing while Jim angrily grabs a book of poetry, rips out pages, and denounces John Keats's "Ode to a Nightingale." Eva says that Keats was like Jim, because he had a lot to say but not enough time to say it. She turns to the poem "When I Have Fears That I May Cease to Be" and reads aloud. Eva tells Jim that Keats wrote about beauty as a means of escaping reality. Jim replies that his form of escape is destruction.

Eva and Jim converse about love and sex. Jim confesses that being without women for so many years has forced him to imagine them, and he cannot believe Eva is real. He embraces her as the Warden enters the office. The Chaplain enters, but the Warden is not happy to see him. The Chaplain asks about the Ollie's death, as he believes it could have been prevented. The Warden is affronted by this statement, and he accuses the Chaplain of leaking information to the press that instigated the current uprising. The Chaplain states that he is a "conscientious steward of Christ," and the Warden fires him. The Chaplain is not fazed; he claims that he will take memories of the torture with him. He also says he will make sure the prison is shut down. The Chaplain exits, as the Warden calls another chaplain to replace him.

### Act 2, Episode 2

Announcer: "*Sunday Morning in Hall C!*"

In the cell Joe, Queen, and Swifty read the society section in the Sunday paper.

### Act 2, Episode 3

Announcer: "*Mr. Whalen Interviews the New Chaplain!*"

The Warden interviews a Chaplain. He asks the Chaplain to deliver a sermon to the prisoners that will incorporate the three words *food, heat,* and *Klondike.* The Chaplain is puzzled, but he creatively includes the words. The inmates respond by stomping their feet and shouting.

### Act 2, Episode 4

Announcer: "*Zero Hour!*"

Back at the Warden's office, Eva frantically welcomes Jim's return from the cell. Jim again begs Eva to leave the prison and tell the world what is happening on the island. The Klondike is prepared for the inmates in Hall C. The Warden enters the room with the expectation that the strike will be broken tonight when the inmates learn of the Klondike. The Warden tells Eva that she will have to return to the prison after dinner. Jim asks about his parole. The Warden is so offended that Jim would be thinking about his parole at a time such as this that he threatens to put him in the Klondike as well.

### Act 2, Episode 5

Announcer: "*Hall C!*"

In the cell Butch sings and tells Joe about his former girlfriend, Goldie. Queen is disturbed that his fingernails are in such terrible condition. The men talk about the Klondike, and Butch details his experience there. Schultz returns the tortured men to their cells. A chorus of men ask for Ollie. Butch instigates a ruckus while Queen comforts Swifty. The prisoners are told that if they do not eat their dinner tonight, they will be put in Klondike. Another prisoner, Mex, begins to pray fervently. Schultz exits, and Butch rallies the prisoners to stand firm on the strike.

### Act 2, Episode 6

Announcer: "*Definition of Life!*"

Jim is depressed. He believes that his parole will be refused. He is angry with himself for mentioning it to the Warden. Eva tells Jim that she loves him, but Jim's mind is dominated by the thought that he will never escape. Eva kisses him. Eva says that she is going to the newspaper offices at City Hall the next morning, because she has realized that saving the life of the inmates in the Klondike is more important than keeping her job. The Warden enters to tell Jim to deliver the order to start the Klondike. When he exits, the Warden informs Eva that she will not be permitted to leave the prison until the following day. Eva refuses, grabbing the phone to call for help. She learns that the phone line has been disconnected for the night. The Warden triumphantly offers her a shot of whiskey. Eva panics because her plan for saving the inmates has been sabotaged, as she cannot leave the island. She admits she is afraid as the Warden makes advances toward her. She becomes aroused by his groping and upset by her own reaction when he is called out of the office. She screams for Jim, who runs to her. She begs to leave the prison. Jim refers to *The Lorelei*'s music, and this soothes her nerves. Eva tells Jim that she too is a prisoner now. She confesses that the Warden's touches mesmerized her to the point of immobility. Jim vows to escape with her. They devise a plan to meet in the dark southwest corner of the yard.

### Act 3, Episode 1

Announcer: "*Morning of August 15!*"

The Warden asks for an update on the Klondike and instructs Schultz to set the temperature at 130 degrees Fahrenheit. The scene shifts to the men inside the Klondike. They are breathing heavily and are shiny with sweat. Butch tries to talk to Joe and Swifty through the ordeal, but Swifty can only beg for water. They have been in the boiler room for eight hours. Queen becomes faint with heat exhaustion. They talk to make the time pass more quickly, but tension builds as they fight to survive. Butch initiates a sing-along, but none of the men is well enough to join him. Queen hysterically prays to be released as he falls on the floor. They fight over the small air vent that keeps them alive. Butch tries to maintain order as the men lift Swifty's unconscious body to the vent. It is too late; Swifty is dead.

### *Act 3, Episode 2*

Announcer: "*Evening of August 15!*"

The Warden receives the puzzling report that the men in the Klondike are singing. He orders the guards to increase the temperature. The scene shifts to the men in the Klondike. The men's voices are hoarse and they are becoming dehydrated. Queen sobs while another inmate, Shapiro, mumbles in Yiddish. Butch extracts a razor from his belt and shows it to Joe. Butch plans to kill the Warden when he visits them. They hear the bell that indicates they have now been locked up for 24 hours. Queen staggers into the steam and scalds himself. He screams and falls to the floor. Butch grabs his head and slams it on the floor, killing him. Joe is shocked, but Butch responds that he was only putting him out of his misery.

The scene shifts back to the office, where the Warden calls on Schultz for a Klondike update. He orders him to increase the temperature to 150 degrees. The scene shifts to the Klondike, where Joe pleads with Butch to use the razor on him. Butch tries to convince Joe that they are going to survive the torture. Butch angrily shouts to turn off the steam. He staggers and rages toward the radiators, where he scalds his hands.

### *Act 3, Episode 3*

Announcer: "*The Southwest Corner of the Yards!*"

In the darkness of the prison yard, Eva whispers for Jim, who has been waiting for her there. Eva explains that she will be alone with the Warden if she goes back to the office. Jim quiets her for fear of being caught. The searchlight moves around the yard and over them. There is a pause and Eva and Jim sigh with relief. Eva asks Jim to tell her that he loves her. Jim does, and the light scans the yard again. This time it circles lower and closer to them. They quickly try to crawl away from the light, but it suddenly stops on Eva's face. The sirens sound.

The scene shifts to the office, where the Warden berates Jim and Eva. The Warden grabs the rubber hose and demands Jim take off his coat. Eva implores him to refrain from beating Jim. She claims that the incident is her fault. She threatens to tell the public about the Klondike. The Warden orders the guard to remove Eva. Jim fights to free her, and the Warden orders Jim to the Klondike.

The Warden and Eva are alone in the office. The Warden tries to explain his behavior and comforts her by pouring drinks. He implies that he will not record the incident in Jim's files if she has sex with him. Eva says she will do whatever he wants if he will approve Jim's parole. The Warden signs the parole form and calls the guard to put it in the mailbox. He ushers Eva into the inner room.

### *Act 3, Episode 4*

Announcer: "*The Showdown.*"

In the Klondike Butch lies near the air vent as the bodies of the deceased inmates are heaped in the center of the room. Schultz and another guard enter with Jim. Butch hides, and when Schultz enters, he attacks him. Jim attacks the other guard, steals his gun, and holds the guards at gunpoint. Butch steals Schultz's keys and they lock the guards in the Klondike.

The screaming sirens lure the Warden out of the inner room. Jim enters the office. He is wild-eyed and his clothes are bloodied from the Warden's beating. Jim announces that the inmates have broken out of the Klondike. The Warden tries to sound another alarm for help, but the prison has become chaotic with revolt. Holding the gun, Jim asks for Eva. The Warden claims she left the prison. Eva appears and pleads with Jim not to harm the Warden because he has sent the parole approval. The

Warden agrees that he did send the letter because Eva agreed to have sex with him.

Jim opens the door to the eager inmates, who are waiting to attack the Warden. The Warden tries to negotiate with Butch. The sound of boats with sirens approaching the island is heard. The inmates douse the prison with gasoline. Butch kills the Warden by throwing him out the window. Jim decides to jump out the window instead of fighting the police. Eva cries when Jim tells her that he has to risk everything to escape. He hopes to swim to *The Lorelei.* They say good-bye. Jim leaps out the window as several men enter the office and find Eva holding Jim's shoes. Over the loudspeaker, someone announces statistics about the prison.

## COMMENTARY

Williams was inspired to write *Not About Nightingales* when he read of the Holmesburg Prison Strike of 1938. Four men were steamed to death in the "klondike," or a large furnace room, for their participation in a strike for better food rations. As in *Candles to the Sun,* Williams addresses the social evils of the Great Depression before World War II.

*Not About Nightingales* was a play strongly influenced by the Federal Theatre Project, a grassroots depression-era program that supported the writing of new plays and their regional performances in the United States. Williams was a young playwriting student at the University of Iowa when he wrote this play as a class assignment. Using the project's emphasis on the "living newspaper" form (socially poignant plays based on factual information), Williams's early dramaturgy focuses on the social injustices experienced by impoverished and disenfranchised people. As is *Candles to the Sun* (about a miner's strike), *Not About Nightingales* is Williams's bitter expression of the inequalities throughout American society.

A dominant feature of the living newspaper style of playwriting is the use of announcements, which seam together the scenes and acts. *Not About Nightingales* functions in this manner. Williams pushes the boundaries of traditional staging to incorporate expressionistic moments in sudden and numerous scene shifts from the inmates' cells to the Warden's office, choral responses at the death of Ollie and the strike itself, and "Announcements . . . extended to offstage reporting: shouted newspaper headlines, voices of broadcasters, sirens" (Hale, xvii).

*Not About Nightingales* was never performed or published in Williams's lifetime. Williams makes a single reference to its existence in the essay that he published during the 1957 Broadway premiere of ORPHEUS DESCENDING. He states in the essay *The Past, the Present, and Perhaps,* "I have never written anything since then that could compete with it in violence and horror." Williams attributed the dramatic heft of the play to the fact that the hunger strikes and torture of the Klondike, a large room of radiators heated to their maximum levels, actually happened. The Pennsylvania hunger strike and the literal roasting of several convicts exposed the horrific conditions in the U.S. prison system.

Williams followed the story to its unjust resolution as the police tried to say that the victims had killed each other. When the coroner rejected this explanation, the men involved in the case refused to talk, and the coroner called their action "a conspiracy of silence." According to VANESSA REDGRAVE, who discovered the manuscript, Williams originally entitled this play *The Rest Is Silence* and dedicated it to the memory of those victims.

Williams changed the title to *Not About Nightingales* in reference to the Keats poem (that Jim mentions in act 2, episode 1). This title juxtaposes the romantic notions that Eva has about the prison as a conscientious environment of rehabilitation with the hellish realities of torture. Canary Jim emphatically rejects Keats's poetry, ripping pages out of the book in frustration at its sentimentality: the unrealistic propaganda that allows one to escape life. Eva reads the sonnet "When I Have Fears That I May Cease to Be" to prove to Jim that Keats was dealing with strong emotions related to death as well as love. This notion causes Jim to reach a breaking point. His form of escape involves "blowing things wide open!" Jim embraces destruction in the midst of the prison nightmare as a last resort for coping with the physical torture and confinement.

Canary Jim is caught between two worlds, himself rejecting—and simultaneously being rejected by—both versions of reality. He is despised by Butch, the cell boss, and he despises the Warden, with whom he spends most of his time. In his more philosophical moments, Jim clearly becomes the playwright's mouthpiece. When he ponders the cages in which all human beings reside, he becomes the young Williams, who was forced to work at the INTERNATIONAL SHOE COMPANY and Ben Murphy in *STAIRS TO THE ROOF,* who responds to factory life by escaping to the rooftop to write. Jim is also like Kilroy of *CAMINO REAL,* who wants only to find a way out of the maze. The "real way" for Jim can be nothing but destruction and revenge after years of physical abuse and oppression.

Eva is representative of the Great Depression of the 1930s. Her moral values are sacrificed as she waits too long to reveal the truth about the Klondike because the threat of losing her job means losing the survival game. She has, as the inmates have, been suffering from hunger and the bitter economic climate. With no one to depend on, Eva accepts a nightmarish job, as hunger is worse than what she witnesses at the prison. The Great Depression heavily influenced this play as well as Williams's other major dramatic works, such as *THE GLASS MENAGERIE.* "The Depression was a controlling factor in Tom Williams's life. It forced him to quit the University of Missouri, where he had already won notice in a literary contest, to work in a St. Louis shoe factory" (Hale, xiii). Similarly Eva is forced to work in a less than amiable environment to meet her financial needs. Eva is forced to suffer the conditions of the prison and exist as a prisoner, although she is not a criminal. Eva has a change of heart and decides to forfeit the job for the sake of humanity, but she unfortunately makes her decision too late. Because she loves Jim, she chooses the moral high road. In the end, however, she loses Jim (who, it may be assumed, dies after jumping out of the window) and maintains her position in the prison system, although much of it has crumbled around her.

The violence of the Klondike story clearly resonated with the young Williams. Ironically, the principal resonance can be found in his own work. The severity of the Klondike is reminiscent of Williams's earliest published short story, "THE VENGEANCE OF NITOCRIS" (1928), in which a banquet hall serves as an inescapable vault or mass grave. The claustrophobic atmosphere surrounding the entrapment parallels the Klondike's misery. Both devices give their victims time to be cognizant of the horror that awaits them.

## PRODUCTION HISTORY

In his essays, interviews, and autobiography, Williams fondly recalls a semiprofessional theater troupe called THE MUMMERS. While at the University of Iowa, Williams befriended this socially active group of theater radicals, who staged his early plays *Candles to the Sun* and *Headlines.* The Mummers anticipated producing *Not About Nightingales,* as it was appropriate for their mission of performing plays that had strong social commentary. Unfortunately, the troupe was forced to disband because they could not survive the depression years. The play was abandoned (although Williams reworked it for the next 30 years).

In 1991, renowned British actor and activist Vanessa Redgrave discovered the script of *Not About Nightingales* in the Williams archives at the University of Texas at Austin. On March 5, 1998, the play premiered at the Royal National Theatre, London, England, coproduced by Moving Theatre and in association with the Alley Theatre of Houston, Texas. Directed by Trevor Nunn, the cast included Corin Redgrave (Boss Whalen or The Warden), Finbar Lynch (Canary Jim), James Black (Butch O'Fallon), and Sherri Parker Lee (Eva Crane). The performance was met with stellar reviews. Some critics went so far as to hail the play as the most poignant in the Williams canon. Benedict Nightingale in the *New York Times* wrote, "Isn't it ungrateful to admonish a bolt of lightning . . . for not being subtle and measured enough?" (AR3).

## PUBLICATION HISTORY

*Not About Nightingales* was published by New Directions in 1998.

## CHARACTERS

**Boss Whalen** The sadistic warden of a prison, Boss Whalen embezzles the government-issued funds to the run the prison, and the inmates suffer from spoiled food and beatings. Boss Whalen hires Eva Crane, a curvaceous young woman, as a secretary. Canary Jim, an inmate, falls in love with Eva and tries to escape with her during a prison revolt. When the plot fails, Boss Whalen beats him with a rubber hose. As his name suggests, Boss Whalen enjoys administering pain to the inmates. Boss Whalen shoves Jim into the Klondike, a human oven. Jim and another prisoner, Butch O'Fallon, escape the Klondike and kill the guards. Butch kills Boss Whalen.

**Bristol, Mrs.** The concerned mother of Sailor Jack, a young inmate. Mrs. Bristol travels from Wisconsin to the prison to inquire about the status of her son's health. After receiving strange and nonsensical letters from him, she learns through Canary Jim that Jack has been placed in the Klondike and has lost his mind as a result.

**Canary Jim** He is a prisoner who has suffered at the hands of Boss Whalen, or the Warden. Jim has spent many years in the prison and has graduated to the position of an office secretary for the Warden. He is despised by his fellow inmates because it is believed that, as his name suggests, he spies on them to "sing" to Boss Whalen. Jim writes a prison newspaper and becomes the model prisoner in an attempt to gain parole. He is at his wit's end when Eva Crane joins the prison staff. Jim falls in love with Eva but is tragically aware that he cannot be with her. Jim plays an intricate role in an inmate revolt after men are placed in a furnace called the Klondike. This revolt leads to the death of the Warden and several guards. Jim bids Eva farewell and jumps out the window to the ocean below to avoid being incarcerated for these additional crimes. As does Kilroy in *CAMINO REAL*, Jim constantly thinks of escape and philosophizes on the caged human condition while searching for a way out of the roughness of his life.

**Chaplain** The Chaplain disapproves of Boss Whalen's torturous punishments, and during a hunger strike, he sides with the prisoners and cooperates with the newspaper to make the abuse public knowledge. Boss Whalen fires him when he protests and pleads with him to stop the use of the Klondike.

**Crane, Eva** She is a destitute, though educated young woman who is forced to take a job as a prison secretary. Eva is extremely naive about her new position; she believes the propaganda that the prison is a state-of-the-art center for rehabilitation. Eva soon witnesses the torture that occurs in the domain of Boss Whalen, or the Warden. She falls in love with an inmate, Canary Jim, who works in the office with her. Although she loves Jim, she admits that she becomes excited when the Warden makes sexual advances to her. Eventually she does have sex with the Warden so that he will grant Jim his parole. The conditions worsen when the Klondike is reinstituted, and inmates are literally baked alive. Eva could have prevented the atrocity by making the authorities publicly aware of the plan if she had been willing to sacrifice her job. Eva decides to reveal the information too late: She is trapped at the prison. Eva subsequently loses Jim when he commits suicide to avoid another prison sentence after an inmate revolt.

**Joe** He is an inmate who suffers the wrath of the prison warden, Boss Whalen. Joe dies in the Klondike during punishment administered to squelch a hunger strike.

**O'Fallon, Butch** A prison inmate, Butch despises the Warden for his beatings and the Klondike. He is driven to survive these episodes so that he may seek revenge and kill Boss Whalen. Butch's archenemy is Canary Jim, who, he believes, spies on the inmates for the Warden. Butch dreams about his former days of freedom and his girlfriend, Goldie. He initiates a hunger strike, which leads to a prison revolt. Butch finally gets his wish when, ironically with the help of Canary Jim and after serving days in the Klondike, he kills Boss Whalen.

**Ollie** He is an African-American man who has been incarcerated for stealing a crate of canned food for his starving family. His sole hope is to get out of prison to help his wife and children. Ollie is placed in the Klondike as an example to the other inmates; he does not survive.

**Queen** He is a gay inmate who was incarcerated for selling marijuana. The Queen spends his time in prison giving himself manicures. He suffers the wrath of Boss Whalen during a prison strike, when he is placed in the torturous Klondike, a human oven and dies there.

**Reverend** He replaces the Chaplain, who quits his job at the prison because Boss Whalen administers unjust torturous punishments to the inmates. The Reverend agrees to ignore what goes on in the prison. When he gives a speech to the prison body, he is met by a frightening mob of inmates, who throw hymnals at him.

**Sailor Jack** He is a young inmate at the prison run by Boss Whalen. Sailor Jack suffers the Klondike, a human oven, and becomes insane.

**Schultz** He is a prison guard who follows the orders of Boss Whalen, the Warden. As does his boss, Schultz enjoys terrorizing the inmates. He is forcibly locked in the Klondike, a human oven, when he tries to place Canary Jim, another inmate, in the oven.

**Swifty** He is a marathon runner and Olympic hopeful who is imprisoned for stealing money. Swifty suffers the Klondike, or the human oven, as an example to the other inmates who are on strike. Swifty dies in the Klondike at the orders of Boss Whalen.

**Warden** See Boss Whalen.

## FURTHER READING

Hale, Allean. "Introduction: A Call for Justice." In *Not About Nightingales.* New York: New Directions, 1998.

Nightingale, Benedict. "The Redgraves' 'Nightingales' Sings Grandly." *New York Times,* April 5, 1998, p. AR3, 30.

# *The Notebook of Trigorin*

A free adaptation of ANTON CHEKHOV's *The Seagull* written between 1981 and 1983.

## SYNOPSIS

The play is set on the estate of Sorin in the Russian countryside.

### *Act 1*

A platform stage obscures the otherwise beautiful view of the lake. It is sunset and several servants are completing the stage for an evening performance of a play written by Constantine.

Masha and Medvedenko take a walk by the lake. They discuss Masha's life, their relationship, and Masha's unrequited love for Constantine. Masha admits that she sympathizes with Constantine because his mother, Arkadina, a famous and aging actress, mistreats him. Medvedenko proposes marriage, and Masha rejects the proposal with contempt.

Constantine appears on the makeshift stage, and Masha is captivated by his presence. Sorin joins Constantine on stage. Sorin expresses his desire to live in the city. Masha and Medvedenko discuss Arkadina's relationship with Trigorin, her famous playwright companion. With childlike excitement, Constantine anticipates his mother's reaction to his play, as it is an experimental form of theater. Constantine informs Sorin that his mother does not support him because she is a miser and because he is a depressing reminder that she is no longer young.

Sorin and Constantine discuss the importance of theater, and Constantine describes his vision of a new theatrical aesthetic. Trigorin interrupts their conversation and invites Constantine to join him for a swim. Constantine declines as he is waiting for Nina to arrive. From a distance, Arkadina calls for Trigorin; he leaves to join her.

Sorin advises Constantine to love his mother despite her faults. Nina arrives. She is distressed, as she fears that she is late for the performance. She accepted a carriage ride from a stranger, who alarmed her so much that she jumped from the moving carriage and ruined her dress. Sorin tells Nina that Constantine is in love with her. Embarrassed and unable to reciprocate the sentiment, Nina makes light of the moment while Constantine cowers in humiliation.

Constantine quickly calls his audience to their seats. For a moment, Nina and Constantine are alone. Nina reports that her father has forbidden her to come to the estate because he believes Constantine's family is too bohemian. Constantine declares his love to her, but she silences him.

Constantine's play is a disaster. Nina forgets her lines and suffers a sneezing fit. She is embarrassed to be performing such an esoteric and unusual script. Constantine helps her through the performance, whispering directions to her. Arkadina grows impatient, interrupting the experimental play to recite her own favorite monologues. Constantine rages at his mother's behavior.

Trigorin and Arkadina debate new forms of theater as Nina joins them. She is awestruck to be in their presence. Arkadina quickly orders a carriage to take Nina home. Sorin demands that Arkadina make peace with her son. She concedes but retorts that she will always be truthful about his lack of talent as a writer. Trigorin leaves to find Nina. Dorn, Sorin's doctor and an old family friend, attempts to comfort Constantine. Trigorin tries to reassure Constantine that he is a promising writer. Masha informs Constantine that his mother would like to see him. Trigorin acknowledges that Masha is in love with Constantine.

*Act 2*

In the garden of Sorin's estate, Arkadina and Masha picnic while Dorn reads aloud to them. Arkadina becomes bored and orders Masha to stand beside her, so that they may compare their figures. She orders Dorn to decide which appears to be the elder. Dorn winks at Masha and asks Arkadina her age. Dorn flirts with Masha while he criticizes Arkadina for her attempts to fight inevitable aging. Masha scolds Dorn for his flirtations because her mother, Polina, is in love with him. Arkadina becomes angry and seizes Dorn's book and begins to read aloud. Sorin and Nina join them in the garden. Sorin announces Nina will be staying at the estate for three days while her parents are on holiday. He complains about his aches and pains. Arkadina begs Dorn to write a prescription that will help Sorin, but Dorn coldly responds that nothing can be done about old age. Masha's parents, Shamrayev, the estate manager, and his wife, Polina, hurry into the garden. He and Arkadina argue about the horses she requires for a trip into town. Shamrayev refuses to provide her with horses. Arkadina decides to end her stay in the country.

Dorn and Polina are left alone in the garden. Polina begs Dorn to run away with her. Dorn is not interested in settling down with one woman. Nina returns to the garden and gives Dorn a bouquet of flowers she has picked. Polina destroys the flowers. Constantine enters the garden and asks to be left alone with Nina.

Constantine killed a seagull and brings it to Nina. Constantine leaves as he sees Trigorin approaching. Trigorin informs Nina he is leaving the estate today. Nina begs him to stay. Trigorin asks Nina to take care of Constantine, and she declares that she does not love Constantine. Trigorin confesses that he would trade his success to be truly loved by Nina. He notices the dead seagull on the ground. When Nina tells him that Constantine killed it, Trigorin writes this information in his writer's notebook. Arkadina calls out to Trigorin and announces that they are not leaving. Nina talks to Trigorin about her dream of becoming an actress.

*Act 3*

In the dining room of Sorin's estate, Trigorin and Masha sit drinking vodka together. Masha confesses she could not have gone on living if Constantine had fatally wounded himself. Masha announces that she is going to stop loving Constantine and marry Medvedenko. Masha bids Trigorin farewell and requests a signed copy of his latest book.

Nina seeks Trigorin's advice about whether she should pursue an acting career. Trigorin has reservations about helping her with such a huge decision. Nina gives him a medallion by which to remember her. Arkadina calls for Trigorin. Nina requests a few minutes alone with him before he departs.

Arkadina becomes jealous when she realizes that Nina has been alone with Trigorin. Sorin and Arkadina argue and discuss how Arkadina could be a better mother. During their argument, Sorin becomes dizzy and staggers. Arkadina calls out for help; Constantine runs in to assist his uncle. Constantine pleads with his mother to take better care of her brother. Arkadina suggests that Constantine give up writing and become an actor. Constantine asks his mother to put fresh bandages on his gunshot wound. Arkadina lectures him about hurting himself and makes him promise never to do it again. Constantine questions her about Trigorin's promiscuous behavior. Constantine informs Arkadina that Trigorin has been engaging in sexual activities with various male servants.

Trigorin returns to the dining room, expressing a wish to stay in the country longer. Arkadina refuses. Trigorin pleads with her that an affair with Nina could be the most important thing in his life and for his writing. He asks Arkadina to release him. She reminds him that she launched his literary career and has taken care of him his entire adult life. They exchange insults. Arkadina kneels and begs him to stay with her. Arkadina blackmails him, explaining that she possesses a photograph of a young Italian man with an intimate inscription on the back. Trigorin proudly confesses he has had many male and female lovers before and during his relationship with Arkadina. She threatens to make this photograph public if he does not continue his life with her. Trigorin concedes and the two embrace. Trigorin runs to meet Nina by the lake.

Constantine eavesdrops in a nearby bush as Trigorin and Nina make plans to meet in Moscow. Trigorin stuffs extra money into the front of Nina's bodice. The two lovers kiss passionately.

### Act 4

Two years have passed. The drawing room of the estate is now Constantine's study. A violent thunderstorm brews in the distance.

Masha and Medvedenko are in search of Constantine. Masha prepares a bed for Sorin on the sofa. Medvedenko urges Masha to have intimate relations with Constantine. He advises her to undress and reveal her beautiful white skin to him. Masha is offended by Medvedenko's plan.

Medvedenko announces that it is time for them to go home and take care of their baby, but Masha refuses to leave Sorin's estate. Medvedenko tells Polina of Masha's insolence, but Polina ignores his whimpering. Constantine enters the study and Medvedenko exits. Polina congratulates him on his literary success. Masha steps out onto the veranda, and Polina asks him to be more cordial to her daughter. When Masha returns, Constantine storms out of the study. Polina holds Masha while she cries about her life with Medvedenko.

Medvedenko wheels Sorin into the study, and Dorn follows them. Masha is frustrated that her husband has not gone home. Sorin is awaiting the arrival of Arkadina. Dorn broadcasts the latest gossip regarding Nina: She chased Trigorin, she had a child by him, and then Trigorin cast her out of his life. Now Nina is back in the area, but her father has disowned her. Constantine challenges Dorn to a duel in the garden for spreading such vicious lies. Masha and Polina try to calm him.

Dorn also shares details of Arkadina's latest theatrical failure. Constantine demands that Dorn be thrown off the estate. Arkadina arrives and Dorn asks her about her latest performance. She hides the truth, declaring that it was a spectacular success. Trigorin greets Constantine with news of admirers. Polina sets up a card table and they play lotto. Everyone leaves Constantine in the study when supper is served. Nina peers in through the French doors.

Constantine quickly takes her inside. They converse about his recent fame, and Nina expresses a desire to go on living even though life has been cruel. She entreats Constantine to do the same. Nina begins to cry. Constantine asks about her child. Nina confides that an American family adopted her baby. Nina admits she still loves Trigorin, more than ever. Nina leaves. Constantine destroys his manuscripts and goes into the garden.

The dinner party reconvenes in the study. As Trigorin and Arkadina bicker, a gunshot is heard in the distance. Arkadina panics and Dorn comforts her by explaining that the sound must have been a bottle of ether exploding in his medicine bag. He goes to investigate. Polina and Masha rush to the garden, the direction from which the shot rang, while Arkadina sits frozen with fear. Dorn asks her about the bows she took at her most recent performance, urging her to demonstrate. As she does, Constantine's lifeless body is carried into the study.

## COMMENTARY

As an adaptation of Anton Chekhov's *The Seagull* (1896), *The Notebook of Trigorin* is the successful blending of two master voices. *Notebook* was Williams's last dramatic work; to date little scholarship about this work exists. Scholars have extensively explored Williams's affinity with Chekhov. Most of the scholarship in this area is focused on Chekhov as a primary literary influence for Williams and the relationship between THE GLASS MENAGERIE and *The Seagull* and A STREETCAR NAMED DESIRE and *The Cherry Orchard* (1904). Only a handful of scholars have focused their studies on *Notebook* and Williams's adaptation process.

Throughout his life, Tennessee Williams studied and admired the works of Chekhov. Williams aspired to create plays in the vein of Chekhov's naturalistic dramatic mode. Chekhov's genius lay in his extraordinary ability to depict human beings with all of their flaws, foibles, and bad behavior. Williams was enamored of this focus in Chekhov's work, particularly in *The Seagull.* He embraced this Chekhov masterwork, pushed it beyond its subtle sphere, and recast it in a new "PLASTIC THEATRE" aesthetic. As does the young playwright at the center of *The Seagull,* Williams believed that "all unconventional techniques in drama have only one valid aim, and that is a closer approach to truth" (*The Glass Menagerie,* xix).

Under Williams's pen, Chekhov's text becomes a different, though familiar, story. The characters change, the action is rerouted, the culture shifts, and the end product is reminiscent of Chekhov, yet simultaneously and stunningly Williams. In *The Notebook of Trigorin,* Williams fleshes out Chekhov's textual subtleties to create more dramatic conflict and direct action, as well as heightening the emphasis on the morose and tangled existence of Chekhov's characters.

One of the most intriguing shifts is that of the character Trigorin, the famous writer. In Williams's version he is defiantly bisexual and succumbs to Arkadina when she threatens to expose his sexuality. Love, in this new version of Chekhov's story, has a hefty price. Here, as in so many of Williams's works, intimate relationships become tainted commercial exchanges, and those who refuse to barter or who seek something more ethereal are left behind, abandoned or betrayed.

Williams has quite appropriately been called the "American Chekhov." As did his favorite writer, Williams repeatedly explored issues of loss and longing, social stagnation, deterioration of genteel society, and social revolution. These concerns permeate Williams's dramaturgy. Both playwrights advocated a new theater form to speak to a progressive society as it reinvented itself.

There is little doubt that the young Tom Williams eagerly and immediately identified with Chekhov's young playwright protagonist, Constantine, and his many artistic and personal battles. Returning to this work toward the end of his life took Williams back to his starting point. *The Notebook of Trigorin* was an appropriate finale for America's greatest dramatist.

## PRODUCTION HISTORY

*The Notebook of Trigorin* premiered at the Cincinnati Playhouse in the Park, in Cincinnati, Ohio, on September 11, 1996—commemorating the 100th anniversary of *The Seagull*'s first performance in Saint Petersburg, Russia, in 1896. The production, directed by Stephen Hollis, featured Lynn Redgrave as Arkadina.

## PUBLICATION HISTORY

*The Notebook of Trigorin* was published by New Directions in 1997.

## CHARACTERS

**Arkadina** Based on the principal female character in Anton Chekhov's *The Seagull,* Arkadina (whose full name is Irina Nikolayevna Arkadina) is a famous aging actress who fears growing old and goes to great lengths to remain youthful. Arkadina is extremely manipulative, very insecure, and self-deceiving. She has spent her life focusing on her career instead of her family, particularly her son, Constantine. Arkadina brutally opposes her son's desire to become a writer. Constantine feels overshadowed by his mother's career. Arkadina's lover, Trigorin, a famous writer, is repeatedly unfaithful to her. His affairs with women and men are public knowledge and aggravate her extreme jealousy and codependence. Arkadina's steady deterioration is apparent as the play progresses. By the end, even her most devoted admirer, Dorn, is making fun of her increasingly disastrous performances. Arkadina has traits similar to those of other Williams women, particularly Amanda Wingfield of THE GLASS MENAGERIE. The two women suffer the same unhealthy need to be the center of attention, to be admired and adored for their legendary beauty and exquisite presence. Their self-centeredness blinds them to the reality of their life and those of their children. Both women dismiss the writing talent of their son and his need for freedom and creative expression. Arkadina is as oblivious to Constantine's discontent as Amanda is to Tom Wingfield's restless unhappiness; as a result both women ultimately lose their son.

**Constantine** Based on a character of the same name in Anton Chekhov's play *The Seagull,* Constantine, whose full name is Constantine Gavrilovich Treplev, is the son of Arkadina and the nephew of Sorin. Constantine is an aspiring young playwright with dreams of creating new forms of theater. His desires are fueled by his mother's negative criticism and his uncle's faith that he will someday be recognized for his talent. He lives a simple and poor life although his mother is the most famous actress in Russia. Constantine is content to spend his days writing by the lake. He is not obsessed with fame as his mother is, but he does become frustrated when his beloved Nina falls in love with Trigorin, a famous writer who is also Arkadina's lover. Constantine becomes extremely depressed because Trigorin is making his mother look foolish and has taken Nina away from him. Although he does become an accomplished writer, he laments the loss of Nina, as she has moved to the city to be an actress and to follow Trigorin. Constantine is reunited with Nina eventually, but her feelings for Trigorin have not changed. This pain is more than Constantine can take and he commits suicide.

**Dorn** Based on the character in Anton Chekhov's *The Seagull,* Dorn, who is also known as Yevgeny, is a country doctor. He is a friend of Sorin and his family, who visits the family estate every day. Although he is aging, Dorn prides himself on being a bachelor. He loves women and does not want to have only one. Dorn can be cruel, and his sense of humor is quite dry. Sorin's nephew, Constantine, loathes the doctor because he is so matter-of-fact and rude. Because of his failing health, Sorin likes having the doctor around. Dorn always assures Sorin that he is incurable and there is nothing to do to help him. Polina, the wife of Sorin's estate manager, is deeply in love with Dorn. Their encounters are always histrionic because Polina wants to run away with him. Dorn no longer wants Polina because he can have younger women. He is quick to remind Polina that he will never be hers.

**Masha** Based on the character Masha in Anton Chekhov's play *The Seagull,* Masha is the daughter of Polina and Shamrayev. As the daughter of an estate manager, Masha has been raised around wealthy and famous people although she is of the lower classes. Masha is bored and discontented with her life. She has a very melancholic nature and always wears black as an expression of her discontent. Masha is in love with Constantine, the estate owner's nephew. Masha is very intelligent, and she is trapped in a society that does not afford many options to women. She finds solace in vodka and takes pleasure in her conversations with the writer, Trigorin. After many years of being pressured by his requests, Masha relents and marries Medvedenko, a simple schoolteacher. She does not love him, but she knows she will never have Constantine. Even after she is married and has a child, Masha remains devoted to Constantine. She often stays away from her husband and child as she resents being someone's wife and mother. Masha relies on her mother, Polina, for emotional support. The two women share the same fate.

**Medvedenko** Based on the character in Anton Chekhov's *The Seagull,* Medvedenko (whose full name is Semyon Semyonovich Medvedenko) is an impoverished schoolteacher who lives near the estate of Sorin. Williams's Medevedenko is a man hopelessly in love with the idea of marriage and family; he is much more aggressive than Chekhov's character. He demonstrates frustration with his impoverished life by being condescending and patronizing to Masha, the woman whom he wishes to marry. Medvedenko's aggressive declarations of love to Masha serve only to alienate him further from his gentrified peers. He does wear Masha down, and she marries him; however, she despises him. Medvedenko sees his dream of marriage reach fruition, but Masha refuses to cooperate and be his loving, dutiful wife. When she decides to devote her time to Constantine, the man she loves, Medvedenko is left to take care of their infant. Medvedenko worries about finances and about supporting his unmarried sister, widowed mother, and unloving wife.

**Nina** Based on the character in Anton Chekhov's *The Seagull* (also known as Nina Mikhailovna Zarechnaya), she is the daughter of an estate owner. Nina lives in the Russian countryside and dreams of becoming a famous stage actress. Her family's estate is adjacent to the family homestead of Russia's most famous actress, Arkadina. Nina's childhood friend, Constantine, is Arkadina's son, and through this association, she meets and begins a clandestine courtship with Arkadina's longtime lover, Trigorin. She crushes Constantine's relentless declarations of love by following Trigorin to Moscow to become his mistress and an actress. When Nina becomes pregnant with Trigorin's child, she gives it to an American couple for adoption. She returns to the province only to be shunned by her family. While she has been gone, Constantine has become a literary success; however, he still desperately pines for her. Nina urges him to forget her and to persevere. Determined to succeed, she returns to Moscow.

Williams's Nina searches for a way to become a successful actress. Her affair with Trigorin seems to be fueled more by this need than by the love that Chekhov creates between the characters. In Williams's version, Nina is willing to do whatever it takes to become famous. She cruelly criticizes Constantine's play, an action that Chekhov's Nina does not take. When she first appears in *The Notebook of Trigorin,* Nina is recovering from being accosted by a man who offered her a carriage ride to the estate. As do so many female characters Williams created, Nina becomes a victim from her first appearance; however, Williams also imbues Nina with strength that propels her to action. In *The Seagull,* Nina does love Constantine; however, she falls head over heels in love with Trigorin because he is charming, powerful, and famous. She gladly accepts this affair, whereas Williams creates a Nina who does not love Constantine and only reluctantly loves Trigorin.

**Polina** Based on the character in Anton Chekhov's *The Seagull,* Polina (also known as Polina Andreyevna) is the wife of an estate manager, Shamrayev, and the mother of Masha. Polina is an older woman who has suffered the wrath of a cruel and indifferent husband. Polina has always been in love with the bachelor doctor Dorn. She had an affair with him when she was younger but refused to leave her husband and young daughter to be with him. This has been her life's regret. Now that Masha is an adult, Polina is ready to leave Shamrayev, but Dorn does not want her. Polina continues to pursue Dorn. She is miserable and consumed by jealousy of the women who enjoy Dorn. Polina witnesses her life's mistakes repeated when Masha suffers unrequited love and marries Medvedenko, a man she detests.

**Shamrayev** Based on the character in Anton Chekhov's *The Seagull,* Shamrayev (whose full name is Ilya Afanasyevich Shamrayev) runs Sorin's estate with harsh authority. He is unhappily married to Polina. While she seeks the attentions of Dorn, Shamrayev seeks the favor of Arkadina, Sorin's sister, a famous actress. He cares for his daughter, Masha, but he cannot understand her melancholy disposition.

**Sorin** Based on the character in Anton Chekhov's *The Seagull,* Sorin (who is also known as Pytor Nikolayevich Sorin) is an elderly estate owner. Williams's creation is a willful man who is more assertive, less feeble and fumbling than Chekhov's. Sorin is the brother of Arkadina, a famous Russian actress. He regrets the simple bachelor life he has led. He mourns that he has never married and has never had a family of his own. Sorin's nephew, Constantine, lives with him in the large house on the lake. Sorin hates the bucolic setting and longs to be in the city, where the atmosphere is buzzing with life. He begs to be taken to the city. As Sorin's health declines during the course of the play, he becomes less and less responsive to the action, often sleeping through difficult conversations. By the end of the play, it is clear that Sorin is going to die. The family calls Arkadina home during a critical point in Sorin's illness.

**Trigorin** Based on the character in Anton Chekhov's play *The Seagull,* Trigorin (whose full name is Boris Alekseyevich Trigorin) is a famous writer and the companion of Arkadina. In *The Notebook of Trigorin,* as in Chekhov's *The Seagull,* Trigorin is a writer who is absorbed by his need to write. He carries a notebook and jots down his thoughts about interesting moments that occur in his life. He is middle-aged and has many lovers. In Williams's adaptation, Trigorin is bisexual, although he is emotionally devoted to Arkadina. Trigorin takes a fancy to Nina, a young girl from a neighboring estate. His conquest of Nina is tumultuous because Arkadina's son, Constantine, is in love with Nina as well. The two men become rivals, and Trigorin wins Nina. Trigorin says he despises Arkadina's petty games; however, he cannot live without her. He refuses to leave because he cannot handle the thought that another man will take his place. At one point in the play, Trigorin wants to be free of his obligations to Arkadina so that he may live with Nina. Arkadina threatens to blackmail him with a licentious photograph she found of a young Italian man. Trigorin buckles under this pressure; he gives up his plan and wholeheartedly accepts his fate of being Arkadina's possession.

**Yakov** Yakov is a servant on the estate of Sorin. Yakov is also the clandestine lover of Trigorin, a famous writer who accompanies Arkadina when she visits her brother and the family estate.

# *Now the Cats with Jewelled Claws*

A one-act play written in 1981.

## SYNOPSIS

The play takes place in a restaurant in New York City.

### *Scene 1*

Madge sits at a table awaiting the arrival of her luncheon companion, Bea. Bea arrives after a frantic shopping trip to Guffel's, a department store near the restaurant. She carries a large costume rabbit head. Finishing each other's sentences, Bea and Madge discuss the chaos during Guffel's after-Christmas sale. A pregnant Waitress with a blackened eye takes their order. The restaurant Manager, "an aging queen," who wears a white carnation in his lapel, teases the Waitress about being unwed.

A hunched figure dressed in black appears outside the restaurant window wearing a sandwich board on which is written "Trivialities." Bea and Madge try to ignore the man outside the window. They perform a dance as the Manager sings a beautiful, doleful tune of love found too late. Bea and Madge discuss their respective vacation plans, and in anticipation of the warm Florida weather, Bea lifts her skirts and reveals her thighs. The Manager chastises her for her indecent behavior and is prompted to perform an outlandish "Dionysian and vulgar" dance around their table. Bea and Madge respond by performing a dance of their own in the style of "acid rock." They return to their table and discuss traffic and Madge's night class at New York University.

A handsome young couple, the First Young Man and the Second Young Man, enter the restaurant wearing pink leather jackets that bear the insignia "The Mystic Rose." The lights fade on Madge and Bea as a table and chairs are taken out and arranged for the young men. As they wait to be served, the First Young Man shares his sense of isolation with his lover. He is estranged from his family and resents the Second Young Man's repeated infidelity. He tries to make his partner understand that only he can truly love him. As he pleads with the Second Young Man ("I love you and I'm scared. You're my life. I'm scared."), the hunched figure again appears outside the window, this time with a placard reading "Mr. Black." The First Young Man rises from his seat and begins to panic. He orders Bea, Madge, the Waitress, and the Manager to acknowledge the "Mr. Black" outside the window, but they all deny that they can see him. The Second Young Man tries to calm his boyfriend, but he too becomes frightened by the mysterious presence.

The Second Young Man sends a note to the Manager, inviting him for a tryst in the lavatory. The First Young Man pleads with The Second Young man to be faithful. Left alone as his boyfriend goes to meet the Manager in the restroom, the First Young Man performs a lonely dance. He resumes his place at their table as the Second Young Man returns from the restroom. Aroused by his encounter with the Manager, the Second Young Man is eager to leave the restaurant and go home with the First Young Man. The Waitress arrives with their order, and the Second Young Man instructs her to give their bill to the Manager, who complies.

### *Scene 2*

The Waitress delivers Bea and Madge's lunches. As she serves them, the two women converse with one another. Their dialogue is sung in the style of a Gregorian chant. Bea confesses that her husband, Phillip, is impotent. She inquires whether she can take legal action against him because of his dysfunction. Madge advises her that Phillip's condition is the result of repeated infidelity or Bea's failing in the "art of seduction." Bea becomes outraged at the suggestion that Phillip is having an affair. Madge insists that she is right and orders Bea to hire a private detective to follow her husband. Madge has learned from experience with her husband, Hugh, the importance of hiring a "professional shadow" to "provide an account of all of his activities." The two women then criticize the Waitress for her blackened eye.

The shattering sounds of a traffic accident are heard outside the restaurant. Madge and Bea rush to the window and discover that the handsome young couple in the restaurant earlier have been involved in a horrific crash. One of the young men has been mortally wounded in the accident, and Madge describes in graphic detail what she can see outside the window. The First Young Man staggers back into the restaurant. A table and chair are taken out for him. Madge and Bea confusedly pick up their belongings and abruptly leave the restaurant. The Waitress informs the Manager that she is quitting her job and walks out of the restaurant. The First Young Man becomes nauseous and rushes into the lavatory. The Manager faces the audience and shares a brief, tender song. The Waitress, Bea, and Madge sing along with him as they stand outside the restaurant window. The Manager knocks on the lavatory door and the First Young Man tentatively steps out of it. The First Young Man closes his eyes as the Manager leads him out of the restaurant.

## COMMENTARY

*Now the Cats with Jewelled Claws* is an extraordinarily complex work. It is another enigmatic example of Williams's engagement with the conventions of the THEATER OF THE ABSURD. *Jewelled Claws*, as do such works as *THE REMARKABLE ROOMING-HOUSE OF MME. LE MONDE*, depicts exaggerated, satirical, and nearly puppetlike characters, "bewildered beings in an incomprehensible universe" (Harmon and Holman, 2), who barely communicate with one another through often irrational and illogical dialogue. Within this surreal reflection on the fleeting nature of life and love and the uncertain inevitability of human fate, Williams juxtaposes the social isolation that can result from personal choices or individual circumstances (by the pregnant waitress) and old age (embodied by Madge and Bea), which are often experienced by gays and lesbians (personified by the nameless First Young Man and his beloved, the Second Young Man).

Notably, the play also contains two of Williams's most dimensional and poignantly drawn gay characters. Although they initially seem to be merely cliché caricatures of gay men (they enter in scene 2 wearing bright pink leather jackets), The First Young Man and his partner, the Second Young Man, are fully developed, multifaceted characters. They are confident, open, and vocal about their sexuality and their relationship. As Madge and Bea's does, their conversation hinges on the question of fidelity. The First Young Man wants his relationship with the Second Young Man to be centered on love, security, and permanence. As Bea does, he believes that infidelity is a crime against love. For him, love is the only source of meaning in a senseless universe underpinned and overwhelmed by "Instant. Oblivion." For his partner it is merely a game that human beings play as they attempt to outdistance or ignore "Mr. Black," the apparition symbolizing death who hovers outside the restaurant window.

In many ways these young lovers mirror an earlier Williams couple, Alma Winemiller and John

Buchanan of SUMMER AND SMOKE. Alma Winemiller and the First Young Man share the view that the human quest for love is for something greater than carnal gratification. The Second Young Man and John Buchanan are passion-filled creatures who strive to live in the moment, and seize from life what they can, as long as they can. The First Young Man's fate also mirrors Alma's, as they both must face the future alone and without the object of their affection. Ultimately, they both seek solace, however fleeting, in the arms of strangers.

## PRODUCTION HISTORY

No professional productions of *Now the Cats with Jewelled Claws* have been recorded to date.

## PUBLICATION HISTORY

*Now the Cats with Jewelled Claws* was first published by New Directions in *The Theatre of Tennessee Williams,* volume 7, in 1981.

## CHARACTERS

**Bea** She is a nearly middle-aged woman who is joining her friend, Madge, at a restaurant near Guffel's department store in New York City. Bea arrives for lunch with a giant costume rabbit head that she has just purchased at Guffel's to entertain another friend's "mongoloid child." Bea and Madge exchange "trivialities" about after-Christmas shopping at Guffel's and their winter vacation plans. The two women also make sport of harassing the lethargic pregnant Waitress. Bea confesses that her husband, Phillip, is impotent and is scandalized when Madge suggests that Phillip's condition is the result of repeated infidelity or Bea's failure in the "art of seduction." Madge encourages Bea to hire a private detective to follow her husband.

**First Young Man** He is the partner of the Second Young Man and accompanies him to a restaurant near Guffel's department store in New York City. A young man in his 20s, he describes himself as a "social alien." He and his partner are members of a motorcycle group, the Mystic Roses. The First Young Man loves the Second Young Man deeply and pleads with him to be faithful. When the Second Young Man has a romantic tryst with the restaurant Manager in the men's lavatory, the First Young Man performs a lonely dance to express his sorrow. Upon leaving the restaurant the young couple are involved in a traffic accident on their motorcycle. The Second Young Man is killed in the collision. The First Young Man returns to the restaurant and is consoled by the Manager.

**Madge** A nearly middle-aged woman who is having lunch with her friend, Bea, at a restaurant near Guffel's department store in New York City. Madge and Bea exchange "trivialities" about after-Christmas shopping at Guffel's and their winter vacation plans. They also make sport of harassing the lethargic pregnant Waitress. When Bea confesses that her husband, Phillip, is impotent, Madge advises her that his condition is probably the result of his repeated infidelity or Bea's failure in the "art of seduction." Madge encourages her to hire a private detective to follow her husband. She has learned from experience with her own husband, Hugh, the importance of hiring a "professional shadow" to "provide an account of all of his activities."

**Manager** He is the manager of a restaurant near Guffel's department store in New York City. The Manager, described as "an aging queen," wears a white carnation in the lapel of his elegant suit. During lunch he patronizes Bea and Madge, teases the Waitress for being unwed and pregnant, and flirts with the young gay couple who come in. The Manager has a romantic tryst with the Second Young Man in the men's lavatory. Upon leaving the restaurant, the young couple is involved in a traffic accident on their motorcycle. The Second Young Man is killed in the collision. The First Young Man returns to the restaurant and the Manager consoles him.

**Second Young Man** He is the handsome temperamental lover of the First Young Man. The men are members of a motorcycle group called "the Mystic Roses." They stop for lunch at a restaurant near Guffel's department store in New York City. While waiting to be served by the Waitress, the First Young Man professes his love and pleads with the Second Young Man to honor their love and remain faithful.

The Second Young Man dismisses his lover's sentimentality and proceeds to have a romantic tryst with the restaurant Manager in the men's lavatory. On leaving the restaurant the couple is involved in a traffic accident on their motorcycle. The Second Young Man is killed in the collision.

**Waitress** The Waitress works at a restaurant near Guffel's department store in New York City. She is in the last trimester of her pregnancy and has a severely blackened eye. She suffers the ridicule of her boss, the Manager, and the restaurant customers Bea and Madge, because she is a battered, unwed mother.

### FURTHER READING

Harmon, William, and C. Hugh Holman, eds. *A Handbook to Literature.* Upper Saddle River, N.J.: Prentice-Hall, 1996.

## "One Arm"

Short story written between the years 1942 and 1945.

### SYNOPSIS

A handsome blond farm boy named Oliver Winemiller joins the navy and becomes the light heavyweight champion boxer of the Pacific Fleet. Oliver's dreams of being a champion boxer are destroyed when he loses an arm in a car accident. He becomes a male prostitute. One night, in a fit of rage, he murders a man who paid him to perform in a pornographic film.

Oliver is arrested, tried, and sentenced to die in the electric chair. During his time on death row, he is bombarded with letters of appreciation from former clients. Oliver is transformed by these letters, which prompt him to forge a connection with a Minister who talks with him before his execution. Oliver reaches out to him the only way he knows, sexually, but his advance is rejected. Oliver is executed the following day.

### COMMENTARY

Compared to "a broken statue of Apollo," Oliver is a prime example of the mutilated characters found in the Williams canon. As Trinket has in *THE MUTILATED,* Oliver has locked himself outside love because he has suffered dismemberment. Trinket alienates herself from sexual intimacy to avoid revealing that she has had a mastectomy. She confesses, "Oh, but not daring to expose the mutilation has made me go without love for three years now, and it's the lack of what I need most that makes me speak to myself with the bitter-old, winter-cold voice." Her static response to dismemberment creates the same self-loathing that spurs Oliver to sell his body. His frenetic self-destruction fuels his anger and rage, and ultimately it drives him to commit murder.

Oliver is an ANTIHERO, who becomes a complete human being after he has killed and is awaiting his death. His redemption is brought about by his clients' letters, and their words of thanks and love. Oliver awakens to the human connections he has made and the positive impact he has had on these men's lives. He begins to understand his own emotional strength, and personal worth exclusive of his "mutilation."

### PUBLICATION HISTORY

"One Arm" was first published in the short story collections *One Arm* (1948) and later in *Collected Stories* (1985).

### CHARACTERS

**Minister** While trying to comfort and counsel Oliver Winemiller, a murderer on death row, the Minister fends off Oliver's sexual advances.

**Winemiller, Oliver** He is a champion boxer who loses his arm in a car accident. He becomes a male prostitute and, manifesting his repressed anger about the car accident, commits murder. He becomes a celebrity on death row, and through his fan mail, he realizes that he actually made a difference in the lives of his clients.

### FURTHER READING

Summers, Claude J. *Gay Fictions: Wilde to Stonewall: Studies in a Male Homosexual Literary Tradition.* New York: Continuum, 1990.

## *One Arm*

Screenplay written in the 1960s.

### SYNOPSIS

The setting is New Orleans.

Ollie is a male hustler who was once a champion boxer. After a car crash left him without one arm, he is forced into a life of selling his still-beautiful body, likened to an ancient statue of Apollo with a broken arm. Ollie now lives his life on the streets, advising other hustlers. Incredibly lonely, with his dreams of being an athlete gone, Ollie disregards human connections and focuses only on survival.

It is revealed during a flashback that he killed a wealthy client who refused to allow him to leave during the filming of a sex video. Unwilling to "perform" with a young woman on camera, Ollie exploded in pent-up anger and murderous rage. He then ran away from the scene. A few years pass, and Ollie is finally arrested. He pleads guilty to the murder charge and is sentenced to death. His case is publicized in the national press. Ollie's former clients, some of whom are prominent men, write him letters of gratitude for the fleeting pleasure he granted them. Ollie enjoys the letters, pleased that he would even be remembered.

A Young Divinity Student follows Ollie's story in the press, and he is drawn to visit him. When he does meet Ollie, he is taken aback by his beauty and spends the visit listening to him. When the Young Divinity Student becomes sexually tempted by Ollie, he calls for the guard to release him.

The next morning Ollie is escorted to the electric chair. He carries his letters with him, holding some of them between his legs and placing the others where he can see them. When he dies, his body is released to a medical college. The students there admire his sculpted body and remark that he resembles a broken ancient statue.

### COMMENTARY

Williams prefaced this screenplay with the explanation that the work is a "dark poem whose theme is the prevalence of mutilations among us all, and their possible transcendence." Although Ollie considers his life ruined, he remains beautiful, transcending his mutilation. His anger and deep self-hatred fuel him to ultimate violence. He tells the Young Divinity Student,

> I seemed to go through a change which I can't account for except I stopped caring what happened to me. That is to say I lost my self-respect. I went all over the country without any plans except to keep on moving. I picked up strangers in every city I went to. I had experiences with them that only meant money to me and a place to shack up for the night—liquor, liquor—food.

It is through the act of murder that Ollie is redeemed. During his imprisonment, Ollie awakens to the real human connections he has made and the incredible impact he has had on the men and women he encountered as a hustler. This is his spiritual conversion. He realizes and accepts his own humanity and worth. To him his encounters were fleeting moments for survival's sake after his boxing career ended. To others they were acts of charity, beauty, and love. The change in Ollie's character is great; although he never fully sheds his rough edges, he transcends his mutilation.

### PRODUCTION HISTORY

*One Arm* has not been produced.

### CHARACTER

**Ollie** He is a beautiful young man who loses his arm in a car accident. Ollie becomes a hustler and dreams of his days as a champion boxer. Because of his beauty, he is compared to a broken statue of Apollo. While entertaining a client, Ollie becomes violently angry when his wishes are ignored, and he kills the wealthy man. Ollie is arrested a few years later, and sentenced to death row. He is executed in prison gripping a collection of letters he received from former clients.

## "Oriflamme"

Short story written in 1944.

## SYNOPSIS

Anna Kimball is dying of tuberculosis. She interprets her illness as "a natural anarchy of the heart." On this particular day, Anna cannot decide what to wear. When she takes off her nightgown, she is forced to acknowledge the sickly image of her frail, nearly transparent body in a nearby mirror.

The reflection prompts Anna to buy a flowing red silk dress. She imagines that she is a flag; her legs are the two trailing points billowing in the wind. She feels she is leaving the world behind, rising and moving without direction. As Anna glides over the streets of Saint Louis, she thinks back on her life. She recalls two men: Mr. Mason, a coworker she dated once, and a young boy in high school with whom she danced and kissed. Anna becomes disoriented. She enters a park and walks toward a statue of a soldier on a horse, deliriously avoiding the path. Acknowledging the green park and the vivid blue sky, Anna rests to regain her breath and pause to allow the pain to subside. Blood seeps across her lips, and a flag of the colors green, blue, and red forms in her final dying moments.

## COMMENTARY

Anna Kimball provides an intriguing example of Williams's solitary strangers. Her life has not been fulfilled, and she will die at a very young age without the experience of romantic relationships or human connection. During her suffering, Anna reminisces about her fleeting encounters. Anna's simplistic approach to her own illness becomes a sublime experience of bittersweet tragedy. Intellectually, Anna understands she is dying a violent death, but emotionally, she still sees her world in terms of poetic wonder.

Williams's vivid imagery is masterfully woven through the poetic language of this short story. Although considered a largely marginal work, this delicate tale possesses beauty that is reminiscent of "Baudelaire, Rimbaud, and their colleagues" (Vannatta, 38) and an aesthetic that is rooted in the theater. The narrative reads as a scene for the stage. Williams devotes much attention to the marriage between Anna Kimball and her surroundings. The vibrant colors and images detail the psychological state of this dying woman. As she is presented in a near-spirit form, her ethereal existence communes with the setting, evoking a sense of beauty and a blending with nature.

## PUBLICATION HISTORY

"Oriflamme" was published in the short story collections EIGHT MORTAL LADIES POSSESSED (1974) and in *Collected Stories* (1985).

## FURTHER READING

Vannatta, Dennis. *Tennessee Williams: A Study of the Short Fiction.* Boston: Twayne, 1988.

# *Orpheus Descending*

A play in three acts written in 1957. It is a revision of the play BATTLE OF ANGELS.

## SYNOPSIS

The play is set in Two Rivers County, Mississippi. The action takes place in the Torrance Mercantile Store, owned and run by Jabe and Lady Torrance. It is a two-story building with the store in the lower portion and the Torrance living quarters upstairs.

### *Prologue*

The time is late afternoon in late winter or early spring. Dog Hamma and Pee Wee Binnings are in the confectionery, playing pinball. Their wives, Dolly Hamma and Beulah Binnings, set up a buffet table in the store. Dolly and Beulah discuss the severity of Jabe Torrance's illness. Beulah gossips (and directly addresses the audience) about Lady's father, Papa Romano, who was a bootlegger during Prohibition. He owned a clandestine wine garden where lovers drank and made love during the dark summer nights. Beulah nostalgically recalls frequenting the wine garden, but she also remembers the night the Ku Klux Klan burned it down because Papa Romano also served African-American clientele. After the Klan set fire to the garden, the fire department refused to put out the flames. Papa Romano burned to death trying to fight the fire single-handedly. Beulah also relates the story of

Lady's wild courtship with David Cutrere. She was devastated when he left her to marry a "society girl," and that is when she married Jabe, never knowing that he helped start the fire that destroyed the wine garden and killed her father.

### *Act 1, Scene 1*

Carol Cutrere enters the store through the confectionery. She carries a gun and a pint of bourbon. Dolly and Beulah and two townswomen, Eva and Sister Temple, are scandalized by Carol's presence. Carol's brother, David, has paid her to stay away from Two Rivers County, and Carol is preparing for her departure. She helps herself to the store's cash box and several bullet cartridges for her gun. The Conjure Man (Uncle Pleasant) enters. Carol asks to hear his Choctaw cry, and when the loud sound subsides, Valentine Xavier, a handsome young stranger, enters with Vee Talbot. Val is a musician who was passing through town when his car broke down, and Vee is a townsperson who paints her religious "visions." Carol is immediately drawn to Val; she asks him for a date, but he ignores her offer. Carol recognizes Val from a nightclub in New Orleans; however, he adamantly denies that they were previously introduced.

Lady enters with Jabe, who has just been released from the hospital. He has undergone experimental surgery to remedy cancer. The townswomen converge on him with feigned joy and mock tears. Jabe immediately goes to bed. The women flock around Lady seeking details of Jabe's impending death. Lady escapes upstairs while the women gossip about the "death sweat" on Jabe. Vee attacks Dolly and Beulah for being corrupt, hosting drinking parties, and playing cards on Sundays. Dolly responds by calling Vee a "professional hypocrite." Carol tells Val about how she acquired a bad reputation by using her inheritance money on projects for the African-American population. She is forced to leave the store when the gossipers turn their attention to her.

### *Act 1, Scene 2*

A few hours pass, and Val returns to the store in the hope of securing a job. Lady descends the stairs to find him in her store. She asks about his background, and Val asks her nationality. She tells him the story of her immigrant father and the wine garden. Val says that his most prized possession is his guitar. Signed by many famous people, it is the only thing important to him. Lady entertains the idea of hiring Val by quizzing him about shoe sales. Val and Lady have a lengthy exchange about the human condition: People are bought and sold as are cattle, and one is either the buyer or the bought. Lady gives Val money to have dinner at the diner and tells him to report to work the next morning.

### *Act 2, Scene 1*

Several weeks later Lady receives a complaint from a female customer, who claims that Val "got familiar" with her. Lady confronts him, and he decides to quit. She begs him to stay because she has not yet had the chance to get to know him. Val believes no one ever truly knows another person. He talks about his severe loneliness, growing up in the solitary world of Witches Bayou. He was abandoned and forced to care of himself. When he finally made contact with another human being, a young beautiful woman, he thought he had found the meaning of life; however, after he made love to her, he became bored and ran away.

Beulah, Dolly, and a Woman rush into the store to telephone David. Carol is causing a scene after being denied service at the Red Crown Service Station. Beulah urges Lady to refuse to serve Carol if she enters the store. Dolly phones Mr. Dubinsky at the pharmacy, advising him to refuse to serve her as well. In the meantime, Carol has entered the store, and she overhears Dolly's instructions. Wild-eyed and feverish, Carol sits down while Lady tries to help her. Beulah, Dolly, and the Woman whisper in the background. When Lady realizes that David is on his way to collect his sister, she angrily announces that she will not allow him in her store. Beulah happily gossips that David was Lady's lover. Lady forces Dolly, Beulah, and the Woman to leave. Carol says she has arrived to deliver a private message to Val. Lady obliges her request for privacy, but she warns Carol that she will have to leave "like a shot from a pistol" when David arrives.

Carol expresses her need for affection to Val. She is wild with passion to touch him. Val responds by exclaiming that she is too fragile: She could not withstand a man's body on top of her. Carol recognizes the Rolex watch Val is wearing as her cousin's. Val confesses that he stole the watch, and that at that moment he decided to stop running with the wild nightclub crowd. He advises her to clean up her life as well. Carol warns Val that he is in danger if he remains in Two Rivers County. Carol's brother arrives in his blue Cadillac, and Lady shouts for Carol, who has collapsed in tears at the table inside the confectionery. David enters, grabs his sister, and walks toward the door. Sharply, Lady orders David to wait. She asks Val for privacy while David tells Carol to wait in the car.

Lady reminds David that he is not welcome in the store. For the first time, she bitterly confesses that she was pregnant with his child the summer he left her to marry a rich, well-established young woman. She admits she had an abortion, and her heart was removed as well. This was also the summer Lady's father died in a raging fire that consumed the wine garden. She says that they have both been bought and sold in marriage, and he is to blame for their mutually unhappy lives. Lady proudly declares that she was the best thing that ever happened to him. Stunned, David walks toward the door, admitting that she is right. Lady reiterates that under no circumstance is he to enter her store again.

### Act 2, Scene 2

Several hours later and at sunset, Vee Talbot takes a painting to the store for Jabe. She discusses her art and her visions with Val. Her husband, Sheriff Talbot, catches Val kissing Vee's hand, and he becomes suspicious.

### Act 2, Scene 3

Val plays his guitar while he and Lady converse about the day's explosive events: his encounter with Carol and her encounter with David. The sound of chain-gang dogs chasing a convict is heard, and one gunshot is fired. Lady does not want Val to leave, so she offers to let him use the store's back room as living quarters. While she fetches linens from upstairs, Val takes money from the cash box and leaves with his guitar.

### Act 2, Scene 4

Later that night, Val returns to the store and replaces the money from a large wad of cash. Lady walks down the stairs, accusing him of stealing. He explains that he took less than the amount she owes him and he was very lucky at blackjack. Lady says she left the money in the cash box to test Val's integrity. Val accuses her of wanting him as her "stud." Lady vehemently denies any sexual interest in Val but pleads, "No, no, don't go . . . I need you!!! To live. . . . To go on living!!!" Val exits to the back room, and Lady follows.

### Act 3, Scene 1

It is early morning, the Saturday before Easter and the opening of the Torrance confectionery. Lady rushes down the stairs to warn Val that Jabe is about to inspect the inventory. Val frantically dresses as Jabe does not know that Val lives with them. Accompanied by Nurse Porter, Jabe meets Val and peruses the new confectionery. With its trees, arbors, and lights, it reminds Jabe of the "Wop's" wine garden he burned down. Lady is traumatized by the information that she married the man who killed her father. A Clown enters announcing the gala opening. The Nurse rushes to call Dr. Buchanan as Jabe has started to hemorrhage.

### Act 3, Scene 2

At sunset, Vee Talbott enters the store dazed and fumbling. She has experienced a vision of her "Savior" and has been struck blind by the brilliance of his blazing eyes. Val places a compress to soothe her eyes, but at his touch, she is struck again with the eyes of Christ. Violently she falls to her knees, wrapping her arms around his legs. Sheriff Talbott rushes in to apprehend Vee, but she clings to Val. The Sheriff and his posse attack Val for accosting Vee. He demands that Val leave Two Rivers County by sunrise the following morning.

### Act 3, Scene 3

Half an hour later, Dolly, Beulah, Eva, and Sister gather in the store to discuss Jabe's sudden turn for the worse and Lady's indifferent absence. Lady returns from the beauty salon ready for the gala opening of the confectionery. Carol Cutrere enters looking for Val, followed by the Conjure Man. Dolly and Beulah run out of the store in fear. Dog and Pee Wee remove the Conjure Man from the store. When Val enters, Lady asks him to wear a

Williams and Anna Magnani. Williams wrote the role of Lady Torrance in *Orpheus Descending* for Magnani. *(Photograph courtesy of the Billy Rose Theatre Collection, New York Public Library)*

white waiter's jacket for the opening, as a means of reinventing the wine garden while Jabe is alive. Val puts on his snakeskin jacket. He has returned to tell Lady that he loves her and will wait for her at the edge of the county. She does not want to leave until Jabe dies, but he has to escape Sheriff Talbot. Nurse Porter argues with Lady, and Lady admits that she is pregnant with Val's baby. The Nurse leaves to report this news. Fearing for Val's life, Lady urges him to leave; she will follow him. Now that he knows she is carrying his child, Val refuses to leave her behind.

Jabe descends the stairs with a revolver. Lady shields Val as Jabe fires the gun and shoots her twice. Jabe then runs out of the store calling for help and claiming that Val shot Lady and robbed the store. Lady dies in the confectionery. As Val tries to escape through the confectionery, Sheriff Talbott's posse rushes into the store. Val is caught (the action happens offstage), and grabbing a blowtorch from the store's shelf, the posse directs its flames toward Val and the confectionery. Screams are heard, and finally Carol and the Conjure Man enter from the confectionery. The Conjure Man finds Val's snakeskin jacket and gives it to Carol. Sheriff Talbot tries to prevent Carol from leaving the store. She brushes past him triumphantly, wearing Val's snakeskin jacket.

## COMMENTARY

*Orpheus Descending* is a revision of Williams's earlier, first professionally produced work, *Battle of Angels.* Over a period of 17 years Williams revised this tale of sexual liberation and repression in a bigoted rural Southern town. Although much of the play remains the same, this version of the events in Two Rivers County is significantly pared down and the drama is more focused. The most significant alteration is the shift in the principal female character. Myra Torrance transforms from a "retiring Southern housewife" (Brustein, 25) into Lady Torrance, passionate daughter of an Italian immigrant. This change adds dimension to Lady's isolation and otherness and heightens the sense that she is caught between the "bright angels of sexual freedom and the dark angels of Southern repression" (Brustein, 25). As is Val, she is an outcast in a strange land. She is here more clearly a Eurydicean figure in need of a liberating Orpheus.

In *Battle,* there is no wine garden, and Myra allows herself to be taken advantage of by the townswomen. Carol Cutrere was Cassandra Whiteside in *Battle of Angels,* where Williams focuses on her wealth and her mythological namesake. Carol retains Cassandra-like qualities: She prophesies disaster to Val, who ignores her warnings.

Williams cleverly uses the Orpheus myth to depict the South of the 1950s. He changes Val from a poet to a musician, following the story of the ancient lyre player who could charm the gods with his performance. Orpheus's beloved Eurydice dies of a snakebite soon after their wedding. He is so brokenhearted that he pursues her in the underworld. His lyre playing is so entrancing that Hades and Persephone release Eurydice on the condition that Orpheus not look back at Eurydice until they have left the underworld. Nearing the end of their journey back to the world above, Orpheus accidentally turns and faces his wife. In that moment, she dies a second time. Orpheus withdraws to the mountains, where he lives as a recluse for three years. He shuns the love of women. Bacchic women discover Orpheus in the woods. Enraged by his rejection of women, they tear his body to shreds in their trance.

As does Orpheus, Val encounters death in the character of Jabe, as he holds the key to release Lady from her death/marriage. Orpheus journeys through the underworld for the chance to regain Eurydice, and he makes a simple mistake that costs him everything. Val's descent is his entrance into the world of this volatile town, which ostracizes prophets and ridicules mystics. Nurse Porter serves as a catalyst similar to the serpent that bit Eurydice: Without her, Lady and Val could have escaped without harm. Lady is ultimately lost in the underworld of the Torrance Mercantile Store, and Val suffers a hideous, violent death in the name of love. He is destroyed by the mob of townspeople who function as the Bacchic women in the Orpheus myth.

## PRODUCTION HISTORY

HAROLD CLURMAN directed the first New York production of *Orpheus Descending* in March 1957 at the Martin Beck Theatre. MAUREEN STAPLETON played Lady Torrance and Cliff Robertson played Valentine Xavier. Critics generally dismissed the play on the premise that Williams had overextended himself. The consensus was that *Orpheus* was overwrought with symbols and biblical and mythological references. Critics felt that *Orpheus* signaled a decline in Williams's playwriting; however, it was a huge success in Russia, where it had a solid seven-year run.

Williams was shattered by the poor critical reception of *Orpheus.* The negative reactions and rejection pushed him into psychoanalysis. Williams believed *Orpheus* contained some of his best writing, but he acknowledged that for some the play might seem "overloaded" (Brown, 108). Williams felt that a part of the negative reaction toward the play was the direct result of an inability of audiences and critics of the time to accept the levels of violence presented in the play. Williams believed that this was a testament to his visionary writing.

The play was subsequently adapted for the screen and retitled *THE FUGITIVE KIND.* It was produced as a feature film in 1960 starring ANNA MAGNANI as Lady and MARLON BRANDO as Val. The film *The Fugitive Kind* was the most successful incarnation of both *Orpheus Descending* and *Battle of Angels.* Over the years, the film has garnered the status of a cult classic.

## PUBLICATION HISTORY

*Orpheus Descending* was published by New Directions in 1958.

## CHARACTERS

**Binnings, Beulah** Beulah is one of a collection of gossiping, spiteful townswomen who frequent Jabe and Lady Torrance's store. She is married to Pee Wee Binnings and is Dolly Hamma's best friend.

**Binnings, Pee Wee** Pee Wee is a local townsman in Two Rivers County, Mississippi. He is married to Beulah Binnings and is a member of Sheriff Talbot's posse.

**Clown** He is hired by Lady Torrance to announce the gala opening of her confectionery.

**Conjure Man** He is an old African-American man who sells magic charms and serves as a supernatural force in the play. Also known as Uncle Pleasant, the Conjure Man is a reworking of the character the Conjure Man in the play *BATTLE OF ANGELS.*

**Cutrere, Carol** She is the daughter of the oldest, wealthiest, and most distinguished family in the Delta. Described as "an odd, fugitive beauty," Carol is a reckless, eccentric aristocrat. Although she has been banned from the town of Two Rivers County, she returns to warn Valentine Xavier that he is in danger. She is a reworking of the character Cassandra Whiteside in the play *BATTLE OF ANGELS.*

**Cutrere, David** He is Carol Cutrere's brother and Lady Torrance's former lover. David abandoned Lady to marry a wealthy socialite. He encounters Lady for the first time in several years when he arrives to collect Carol at the Torrance Mercantile Store. David learns that Lady was pregnant with his child the summer he abandoned her.

**Dubinsky, Mr.** Mr. Dubinsky is the pharmacist in Two Rivers County. He takes Lady Torrance sleeping pills in the middle of the night after she phones him.

**Hamma, Dolly** Dolly is Dog Hamma's wife. She is one of the gossiping, spiteful townswomen in Two Rivers County. This gaggle of women includes Vee Talbot, Eva, Sister Temple, and her best friend, Beulah Binnings.

**Hamma, Dog** Dog is a member of Sheriff Talbot's posse and is married to Dolly Hamma. He is a reworking of the character Pee Wee Bland in the play *BATTLE OF ANGELS.*

**Nurse Porter** Nurse Porter cares for the dying Jabe Torrance in his convalescence after unsuccessful surgery. She is shocked by what she perceives as cold indifference from Jabe's wife, Lady Torrance. Nurse Porter suspects that Lady is having an affair with the Torrances' handsome shop clerk, Valentine Xavier. She confirms that Lady has become pregnant, informs Jabe, and serves as the catalyst for the violent ending of the play.

**Talbot, Sheriff** Sheriff Talbot is married to Vee Talbot and is a close associate of Jabe Torrance's. He attacks the Torrances' shop clerk Valentine Xavier and accuses him of accosting his wife. He is a revision of the character Sheriff Talbot in the play *BATTLE OF ANGELS.*

**Talbot, Vee** Vee is the tormented wife of Sheriff Talbot. She is a member of a group of gossiping townswomen who frequent Jabe and Lady Torrance's store. Vee is quite unlike the other women in her circle as she is a passionate painter of some local renown. Vee Talbot is a reworking of the character Vee Talbot in the play *BATTLE OF ANGELS.*

**Temple, Eva** Eva is Jabe Torrance's cousin and Sister Temple's sister. Eva and Sister are two of a group of gossiping, spiteful townswomen who frequent Jabe and Lady Torrance's store.

**Temple, Sister** Sister is Jabe Torrance's cousin and Eva Temple's sister. Sister and Eva are two of a collection of gossiping, spiteful townswomen who frequent Jabe and Lady Torrance's store.

**Torrance, Jabe** Jabe is married to Lady and is the owner of the Torrance Mercantile Store in Two Rivers County, Mississippi. A mean and spiteful man, Jabe led the Klu Klux Klan on a raid of Lady's father's wine garden. Lady's father died in the fires they set that night. Jabe is dying of cancer.

**Torrance, Lady** An elegant Italian woman, Lady is a troubled beauty who has suffered tragic events in her past. She witnessed the death of her father during a Ku Klux Klan raid when she was a teenager. Unknowingly, she marries the wretched man, Jabe Torrance, who instigated the raid. Lady finds life, passion, and release with her lover, Valentine Xavier. Her character is a reworking of the character Myra Torrance in the play *BATTLE OF ANGELS.*

**Uncle Pleasant** Uncle Pleasant is an elderly African-American man who sells magic charms and tokens. He is also known as the Conjure Man.

**Woman** She is one of a collection of gossiping, spiteful townswomen in Two Rivers County. She heads the crusade to ostracize Carol Cutrere.

**Xavier, Valentine** Val is a handsome young guitar player who drifts into Two Rivers County, Mississippi. Vee Talbot helps him find a job in the Torrance Mercantile Store, which is owned by Jabe and Lady Torrance. The presence of this sexy young stranger creates an uproar in the small repressed community. Val has an affair with Lady, who becomes pregnant. Val is a reworking of the character Valentine Xavier in the play *BATTLE OF ANGELS.*

## FURTHER READING

Brown, Dennis. *Shoptalk: Conversations about Theatre and Film with Twelve Writers, One Producer—and Tennessee Williams's Mother.* New York: Newmarket Press, 1992.

Brustein, Robert. "Robert Brustein on Theatre: Orpheus Condescending." *The New Republic,* 30 October 1998, 25–27.

Wallace, Jack E. "The Image of Theatre in Tennessee Williams's *Orpheus Descending.*" *Modern Drama* 27, no. 3 (September 1984): 324–353.

# *Out Cry*

A play in two parts was produced in 1973.

## SYNOPSIS

The actual play is set in an unspecified locale, in a theater during the evening of the performance. Within the play, the actors set the scene for New Bethesda (in the South) on a warm summer afternoon.

### *Part 1*

The curtain opens on Felice, an actor in a troupe whose company, except his fellow actor, his sister, Clare, has deserted him. A colossal dark statue overpowers the stage. Felice wrestles with how to get rid of it when Clare enters, seemingly indifferent. Felice explains their predicament: The theater company has left them, their manager has deserted them, taken their money, and a large statue obstructs their performance space. Clare argues with him about how they are supposed to perform under the circumstances. She insists they cancel the show; however, Felice begs her to persevere. He tells her that their production of "The Two Character Play" will be performed with never-before-seen flair. As the play commences, the "Two Character Play" plot unfolds: Clare and Felice are trapped in a house in which their parents were killed. (Their mentally unstable father shot their mother and immediately killed himself.) Clare witnessed the event, which drove her mad. The brother and sister have not left the house since the accident. Throughout their lines, they strike piano keys to emphasize certain statements.

Felice comments on the large sunflower that grows in the front yard, and Clare suddenly hears an insistent rapping on the door; when it ceases, she finds a flyer for help from "Citizen's Relief." (Because their father's life insurance was revoked, Clare and Felice have been living on a line of credit graciously set aside through Grossman's Grocery.) Announcing that she would like to look into Citizen's Relief, Clare argues with Felice about leaving the house. Felice refuses to leave, and Clare calls the Reverend Wiley and manically talks about the predicament of her life. Felice quickly hangs up the phone, instructing whoever is on the other end please to forget what Clare has mentioned. Fearing that the Reverend Wiley will call someone to have them institutionalized, Felice warns Clare to keep her mouth shut, and especially not to use the word *confined.* Taunting him, Clare romps about calling out, "Confined! Confined!" and Felice tries to muffle her with a pillow.

Clare points out to the audience and proclaims that there is a gunman among them. Felice quickly calls for a 10-minute intermission as he drags Clare offstage, apologizing for her sickness, and the house lights go up.

### *Part 2*

After the 10-minute interval, Clare and Felice reenter, arguing about their financial difficulties. Felice says they must visit the grocer's to convince him that the life insurance will be paid in full to him in September. Felice is prepared to lie and Clare is appalled. Clare reveals that both Felice and her dead father have been institutionalized in "State Haven" for a period and she fears that Felice has been psychologically damaged by his stay. Felice shoves Clare out the door and they stand, gathering courage to go to talk to the grocer, who is a block away from their house. Clare stalls, insists her nerves are shot, and rushes back into the house. Felice angrily attempts to go to the grocer's, but he is equally afraid. He retreats back inside, and they do not look at each other for some time.

Both realize that the house has become a prison and they embrace each other in defeat. The embrace carries a hint of sexual desire, which is quickly dispelled when Felice abruptly pulls away. Clare proceeds to call for welfare relief, but the phone is dead. Felice reveals that he is going to insert some new lines into the play, and he pulls a hidden revolver out of the piano and loads the bullets. As he sits with Clare, reminiscing about their life, she abruptly "drops character" and informs Felice that the audience has left the theater. Clare surmises that their performance has become too personal and regrets that their lives are indistinguishable from those of their characters.

Clare inquires about the ending of their play and Felice informs her that it is unconventional because it ends when they deem it to be over. He leaves the stage to procure hotel reservations for the evening but quickly returns, having discovered that they are locked in the theater. Clare becomes hysterical, and frantically searches for an escape. It quickly becomes apparent that she and Felice are trapped. Recognizing a chill spreading throughout their bodies, Felice suggests that they return to the world of the play and re-create the summery atmosphere. Losing themselves again within their dialogue, Clare and Felice discover a way to end their play: As Felice gazes at the tall sunflower in their yard, Clare finds the gun hidden behind a sofa pillow. She joins Felice by the "window," and both watch the house lights dim as Felice explains, "Magic is the habit of [their] existence."

## COMMENTARY

*Out Cry* is a revised version of THE TWO CHARACTER PLAY, which Williams began writing in 1966. It was first published by New Directions in 1969. As *Out Cry,* the play was published by New Directions in 1973. Williams extensively revised the work again, under the original title *The Two Character Play.* This version, considered definitive, was published by New Directions in 1975.

Similar to Luigi Pirandello's existential drama, *Six Characters in Search of an Author,* Williams's *Out Cry* is a play about the theater and the theater of life, or rather the performative nature of human existence. It reveals a vision of the human condition whereby "the real and [the] role overlap" (Cohn, 338). Felice and Clare, a brother and sister acting duo, perform for an unresponsive audience and wrestle with philosophical questions of life and death, family estrangement, abandonment, and protracted endings. A feeling of parallelism permeates the performances, as both actors become lost in a play-within-a-play that has become too personal for either of them to handle sanely. Ironically, their distressing circumstances are of their own making. Felice and Clare are locked in their lives and in their roles in a play that has been created by Felice.

Notably, Felice is the first of only three playwright characters in the Williams canon. (The others are August in SOMETHING CLOUDY, SOMETHING CLEAR) and Constantine in THE NOTEBOOK OF TRIGORIN. As do his fellow dramatists, Felice wrestles the ghosts of the past while struggling to envision an appropriate "ending" of future. *Out Cry,* and its predecessor, *The Two Character Play,* are also instances of Williams's making use of the play-within-a-play convention.

### PRODUCTION HISTORY

*Out Cry* premiered in Chicago at the Ivanhoe Theatre in July 1971. The production was directed by George Keathley and featured Donald Madden and Eileen Herlie as Felice and Clare.

### PUBLICATION HISTORY

*Out Cry* was published by New Directions in 1973.

### CHARACTERS

**Devoto, Clare** She is Felice Devoto's sister and fellow actor. Clare struggles alongside her brother to find meaning and purpose in the bleak landscape that is at once the empty theater they inhabit and their broken lives.

**Devoto, Felice** Felice is Clare Devoto's brother and fellow actor. He is the young playwright who has created "The Two Character Play," a play that he and Clare are trying to perform. Although he and Clare have been orphaned and subsequently abandoned by their theater company, they struggle to continue their lives and their performance.

### FURTHER READING

Cohn, Ruby. "Late Tennessee Williams." *Modern Drama* 27, no. 3 (September 1984): 336–344.

## *A Perfect Analysis Given by a Parrot*

A one-act play written in 1971.

### SYNOPSIS

The action of the play takes place in a seedy Saint Louis tavern. The period is unspecified but seems to be roughly 1939–40. Two middle-aged tourists from Memphis, Flora Merriweather and Bessie Higginbotham, are barhopping while following a Sons of Mars convention in Saint Louis. Having lost their party, Flora and Bessie have ventured out on their own.

Their money is running low and they are more than a little frazzled. Both women are garishly dressed in outlandish hats and excessive costume jewelry. The Waiter provides them with two beers served in large fishbowls. The Waiter informs them that they have just missed their fellow conventioneers, who had been drinking there earlier.

Flora and Bessie reminisce about previous conventions and all the fun they had during them. Flora says that earlier in the day she had her fortune told by a parrot. The parrot informed Flora that she has a "sensitive nature" and that she is "frequently misunderstood" by her close companions. Flora deems the parrot's analysis perfect.

Bessie admonishes Flora for not keeping up with her "beauty treatments." Flora retaliates by criticizing Bessie's weight. Bessie counters by advising Flora that men prefer "rockers" to "straight-back chairs." The two bicker and Bessie decides that they should part ways. She then drinks too much beer in one gulp and belches it onto the table. The two try to make amends, suggesting that they have both equally "let themselves go." Just as they seem on the brink of literally crying in their beers, Two Sons of Mars burst in through the tavern door. Bearing toy bugles, these two strapping young men leapfrog over one another until they reach Flora and Bessie's table. Once they arrive at the table they blow their bugles and offer each woman an elbow. The Two Sons of Mars escort Flora and Bessie from the tavern.

### COMMENTARY

For all the festivities and frivolity present in *A Perfect Analysis Given by a Parrot,* fear is the play's overriding emotion and theme. Bessie and Flora are terrified of leaving their youth, losing their looks, and ultimately being left alone. Although these concerns are not openly discussed, they are hinted at in the desperate conversation of two women clinging to remnants of the past. Adorned with an excessive amount of faux jewelry and heavily laden with enormous hats and other accessories, Bessie and Flora are "parodies of human beings, grotesque puppets" (Grecco, 586).

They are reminiscent of other reluctantly aging characters in the Williams canon who have become dismal portraits of once-beautiful people now well past their physical and emotional prime. Ironically, when the Two Sons of Mars arrive at the bar to whisk Bessie and Flora away, these gallant young men serenade them with an off-color World War II ditty ("Mademoiselle de Armentières") about a young French prostitute who had "four chins, her knees would knock, / And her face would stop a cuckoo clock."

Flora Merriweather and Bessie Higginbotham—or rather a younger and slightly less outlandish version of them—appear in act 1, scene 5, of *THE ROSE TATTOO.* They are featured only briefly in that full-length play, in which they are up to their same tricks. In *The Rose Tattoo,* Flora and Bessie are chasing men and are in a hurry to catch a train that will take them to another convention party town. *Perfect Analysis* is a continuation of their story. This half of their story suggests that they have perhaps gained a better understanding of Serafina Delle Rose—whom they ridiculed—and the fate she suffered as the wife of an unfaithful husband. Bessie states that she has had "rotten luck with men. Not once, but always!" She reminds Flora that she too has had her "disappointments." Older, but none the wiser, the two continue in their search for the next soirée.

## PRODUCTION HISTORY

*A Perfect Analysis Given by a Parrot* was first produced at the Waterfront Playhouse, in Key West, Florida, in May 1970. Williams himself directed this premiere production. The first New York production was at the Quaigh Lunchtime Theatre in June 1976.

## PUBLICATION HISTORY

*A Perfect Analysis Given by a Parrot* was first published in *Esquire* magazine, October 1958. It also appears in *DRAGON COUNTRY* and in *The Theatre of Tennessee Williams,* volume 7.

## CHARACTERS

**Higginbotham, Bessie** She is a middle-aged tourist attending the Sons of Mars convention in Saint Louis, Missouri. She is following the Sons convention with her best friend, Flora Merriweather. Bessie and Flora have lost their convention group and are in search of fun on their own. Flora is near the "point of emaciation." Bessie, who is full-figured, taunts the sickly, thin Flora about her appearance, stating that men prefer a "rocker" to a "straight-back chair."

**Merriweather, Flora** She is a middle-aged tourist attending the Sons of Mars convention in Saint Louis. She is following this convention with her best friend, Bessie Higginbotham. Bessie and Flora have lost track of their convention group and are in search of fun on their own. Flora is sickly thin "to the point of emaciation." Bessie, who is full-figured, taunts Flora about her appearance, stating that men prefer a "rocker" to a "straight-back chair."

**Two Sons of Mars** These two young men are members of a fraternity, the Sons of Mars. The name is that of an actual Southern fraternity, also known as the Sons of Confederate Veterans. They are the descendants of men who fought for the Confederacy during the U.S. Civil War. The Sons of Confederate Veterans was established in 1896 for the purpose of "preserving and defending the history, heritage, and principles of the Old South." While attending a Sons of Mars convention in Saint Louis, these two Southern gentlemen engage in some rather puerile and ungentlemanly behavior. They are said to have thrown water balloons from their hotel windows, and when they arrive to whisk Bessie and Flora from the tavern they serenade them with an off-color World War II ditty ("Mademoiselle de Armentieres") about a young French prostitute who had "four chins, her knees would knock, / And her face would stop a cuckoo clock." Flora describes this fun-loving duo as "Just great—big—overgrown Boys!"

**Waiter** He is a waiter at a shabby tavern in Saint Louis, who serves Flora Merriwether and Bessie Higginbotham beer in large fish bowls.

## FURTHER READING

Grecco, Stephen. "World Literature in Review: English," *World Literature Today* 69, no. 3 (summer 1995): 586–591.

# *Period of Adjustment; or High Point over a Cavern, A Serious Comedy*

Full-length play written in 1957.

## SYNOPSIS

The play is set in Memphis, Tennessee, on Christmas Eve at Ralph Bates's home. His house in High Point is built over a subterranean cavern into which the house is slowly sinking a few inches per year.

### Act 1

George and Isabel Haverstick arrive at the house of Ralph Bates on Christmas Eve. Welcoming the newlyweds, Ralph invites Isabel in while George unpacks the car. Leaving one of Isabel's bags in the car, George hastily speeds away without telling anyone where he is going. Isabel assumes that George has gone to the drugstore and accepts Ralph's invitation to go inside.

As they wait for George's return and subsequent explanation, Ralph and Isabel chat about their marriages. Isabel reveals that she and George are not on speaking terms. Ralph, who is a war hero and fighter pilot, has become disenchanted with his "grounded" life with his wife, Dorothy Bates. Their marital problems peaked when Ralph sent a discourteous postcard of resignation to Dorothy's father at the family's dairy chain. Ralph is now unemployed but relieved to be out of a dead-end job.

Dorothy's parents' servant, Susie, arrives with instructions to collect the Christmas presents from under the tree. Ralph refuses to let her take them, and he gives his present for Dorothy, a $700 fur coat, to Isabel as a wedding present. Isabel is delighted, albeit cautious about receiving the coat.

Feeling more comfortable with Ralph, Isabel explains that she is a virgin, even after her wedding, which was the previous day. George became drunk on their honeymoon night and tried to force himself on her. Ralph comforts Isabel with the assurance that this is simply a "period of adjustment." Sensing her distress, Ralph advises Isabel to rest in his wife's bed until George returns. Ralph tucks her in bed and returns to the living room cursing the Christmas holiday.

### Act 2

George returns with a bottle of champagne, claiming that he forgot to get a gift for Ralph. Isabel joins them in the living room, and George ignores her presence. Wounded by this treatment, Isabel insists that she will check into a downtown hotel to be alone. She then decides to take Ralph's dog for a walk. In her absence, George seeks advice from Ralph about his marital problems. George invites Ralph to escape with him to West Texas where they can raise longhorn cattle for use in motion pictures. Ralph thinks George's plan is preposterous and George sulks. In the meantime, Isabel becomes lost; finally finding the house where a Lady Caroller is singing, she calls for a cab. Isabel cannot remember Ralph's address, so she cancels the cab and prays for divine help out of her misery.

### Act 3

Ralph and George drink champagne while they discuss sex and women. George nervously admits that he knows nothing about sex. Ralph advises George to be "tender," a term that seems foreign to him.

From the bedroom, Isabel overhears their conversation. She appears in the living room and again insists that she check into a hotel. Dorothy's parents, Mr. and Mrs. McGillicuddy, a Police Officer, and Susie enter to collect Dorothy's belongings. Ralph argues with them about what they can and cannot take. Ralph accuses Mr. McGillicuddy, who is also his employer, of forcing his daughter on him. Ralph says that Mr. McGillicuddy pressured him to marry Dorothy with the promise of inheriting his empire.

Ralph confesses that he has grown to love Dorothy but feels that the McGillicuddys need to stay out of their marriage and out of Dorothy's life. Dorothy suddenly arrives. She and Ralph argue until she learns that he has spent a considerable amount of money on her Christmas gift—she takes it as a sign that he really loves her. Forgiving him, Dorothy orders her parents out and invites the Haversticks (who still harbor animosity toward each other) to stay with them Christmas Eve. She and Ralph go to their bedroom as Isabel and George are left to discuss their problems. Encouraged by Dorothy and Ralph's reunion, George and

Isabel slowly attempt to reconcile and each begins to understand what the other needs. As both couples retire for the night, snow falls softly outside.

## COMMENTARY

*Period of Adjustment* has been dismissed by some critics and scholars as a shallow, trite comedy. However, the play's "shallowness" is a dramatic device that serves as a critical commentary on modern American society.

Centering on the marital adjustments of two quintessentially American couples, Williams explores sexual prowess and virginal encounters that escalate into failure, frustration, and dissolution. Unlike the infamous characters Williams creates in his best known works, the characters of *Period of Adjustment* are flat representations of a younger generation of men and women:

> There is an almost intolerable neatness about *Period of Adjustment* which never quite allows the audience to enter into the situation Williams has created. Rather, we seem to be watching a chess game with characters being manipulated carefully and precisely . . . but too often the hand of the mover obtrudes. (Nelson, 280)

The play's subtitle, *High Point over a Cavern*, suggests a ubiquitous suburb made up of identical homes, such as in development communities throughout the United States. It conjures an overt symbol of these communities as destined for failure. Like a home sinking into a natural pit, Ralph and Dorothy's marriage has no solid foundation. Their marriage—and their reconciliation—is a business transaction. Dorothy's father feared that his daughter would never marry; therefore, he devises a solution. Mr. McGillicuddy promises Ralph that he will inherit the McGillicuddy dairy empire if he marries Dorothy. In the same way, Ralph wins back Dorothy after their argument by giving her an expensive mink coat. A low point in High Point is that "love" is a commodity that can be bought, sold, bartered, and traded. The high point of the play, the reconciliation between Ralph and Dorothy, rings false.

The other marriage explored in the play, that of George and Isabel, also lacks a firm grounding. As do Ralph and Dorothy, George and Isabel do not have a real emotional connection to one another. As a result, their attempts at physical intimacy are anxious, brutish, disastrous, and disappointing. Ironically, it is the friendship of the two men that serves as a point of reference for real human connection. Theirs is the most fulfilling relationship in the play. The two embrace and speak openly and honestly to one another about their fears and anxieties. Theirs is a "marriage" of likeness—a mutually respectful and gratifying interdependence.

Although the play is considered a comedy, the subtext and social commentary are sharp. In its exploration of the mercenary aspect of human interactions, the play is thematically aligned with other Williams dramas such as SOMETHING CLOUDY, SOMETHING CLEAR. Williams believed this play to be "about as dark as ORPHEUS DESCENDING, except that there [is] more tenderness, less physical violence" (Funke, 72).

## PRODUCTION HISTORY

*Period of Adjustment* was first produced at the Coconut Grove Playhouse, Miami, Florida, on December 29, 1958. It was codirected by Williams and Owen Phillips. The first New York production was at the Helen Hayes Theatre on November 10, 1960. Directed by George Roy Hill, this production starred James Daly (Ralph Bates), Barbara Baxley (Isabel Haverstick), and Robert Webber (George Haverstick).

The MGM film version was produced in 1962. Directed by George Roy Hill, the cast included Tony Franciosa (Ralph Bates), Jane Fonda (Isabel Haverstick), Jim Hutton (George Haverstick), and Lois Nettleton (Dorothy Bates).

## PUBLICATION HISTORY

This play was first published in *Esquire*, December 1960. It was also published by New Directions in 1960.

## CHARACTERS

**Bates, Dorothy** She is the wife of Ralph Bates. Dorothy deserts her husband on Christmas Eve, when he informs her that he has left his job at her father's office. Leaving with their child, Dorothy sends her parents, Mr. and Mrs. McGillicuddy, a police officer, and their servant Susie to collect the Christmas presents. When Ralph accuses her parents of meddling and standing in the way of their marriage, Dorothy has a change of heart and they reconcile and resolve their differences.

**Bates, Ralph** The husband of Dorothy Bates. Ralph is employed by Dorothy's father, Mr. McGillicuddy, and their marriage falls apart when Ralph announces that he no longer wants to work for his father-in-law. Dorothy and Ralph reconcile after Ralph defends his wife to her father.

**Haverstick, George** He is recently married to Isabel Haverstick. After becoming drunk and forcing himself on his wife during their honeymoon, George finds that his marriage is already disintegrating. He struggles to find a way to be gentle with Isabel, as he knows nothing about women. He seeks the advice of his longtime friend, Ralph Bates. George and Isabel begin to reconcile their differences with the encouragement of Ralph and Dorothy (Bates).

**Haverstick, Isabel** She is the newlywed wife of George Haverstick. When George tries to force himself on her during their honeymoon, Isabel stops speaking to him. On a visit to their friends, Ralph and Dorothy Bates, Isabel decides to forgive George and the two reconcile their marriage.

**McGillicuddy, Mr.** He is the father of Dorothy Bates and employer of Dorothy's husband, Ralph Bates. Mr. McGillicuddy faces Ralph when he arrives to collect his daughter's Christmas gifts. He is accused of meddling in their failed marriage.

**McGillicuddy, Mrs.** She is the mother of Dorothy Bates. Mrs. McGillicuddy, accompanied by Mr. McGillicuddy, and Susie, collected Dorothy's belongings during Dorothy's estrangement from her husband, Ralph Bates.

**Susie** She is the African-American servant who is sent to collect Christmas presents from Dorothy Bates's estranged husband, Ralph Bates. Susie is forced into the middle of the Bates's marital battle.

### FURTHER READING

Funke, Lewis, and John E. Booth. "Williams on Williams." *Theatre Arts*, January 1962, 72.

Nelson, Benjamin. *Tennessee Williams: The Man and His Work*. New York: Ivan Obolensky, 1961.

# "The Poet"

Short story written before 1948.

### SYNOPSIS

The Poet is a beautiful tall blond man who chooses to be homeless, drink his homemade liquor, and to recite his poetry on the streets. He routinely drinks until he passes out. He is often sexually accosted in dark alleyways and awakens to ripped clothes, bruises, and a coin by his side. He always brushes himself off and continues his travels.

The Poet discovers a makeshift shack on the beach. He stays there for 10 months, keeping all of his poems stored in his memory. He cultivates a small following of young people who enjoy his recitals by the sea. He becomes sick with fever; blood spurts out of his nose and mouth. The Poet knows he is going to die so he builds a fire to call his followers together. They are instantly inspired by the poet's life story, jumping wildly among the waves of the sea, frolicking around him all day and all night. When parents find their children by The Poet's side, they drive him out of their village. Initially he accedes to their demands, but as he says good-bye to the sea, he changes his mind and remains. The children find his body later, his skeleton riding the waves in perpetual motion. They find his liquor, drink it, and are warmed by a transforming poetic vision. In the meantime, two ships battle in the distance. One ship is sunk, and dead soldiers wash up on the beach.

### COMMENTARY

"The Poet" is a visionary tale in which Williams eulogizes the figure of the solitary poet often disdained by others. As with other poets in Williams's works, such as Valentine Xavier (*BATTLE OF*

ANGELS), Ben Murphy (STAIRS TO THE ROOF), Flora ("THE IMPORTANT THING"), Homer Stallcup ("THE FIELD OF BLUE CHILDREN"), and Tom Wingfield (THE GLASS MENAGERIE), The Poet is marginalized and ostracized. All of Williams's poets feel the strain of uncertainty and the pressure of being an artist in an urbanized world. They share a need for passion, love, and acceptance and search ceaselessly for meaningful human connections and transcendent relationships. The Poet, more than any other in Williams's work, most severely lacks family, home, and security. Williams underscores his isolation by making him a nameless artisan and placing him in temporary lodgings by the sea, literally on the margin of the earth.

His namelessness, or being identified only by his vocation, endows The Poet with an epic quality. Like the "Everyman" of medieval drama, the Poet becomes every-poet, the definitive poet or the personification of the poetic spirit. As such, the "beautiful, tall, blonde" poet is clearly a tribute to Williams's favorite poet, and one of his chief artistic influences, Hart Crane, who appears as a character in STEPS MUST BE GENTLE. A major theme in Crane's works was the concept of the artist as an outcast from the landscape of the modern, industrialized city. This thematic concern greatly inspired Williams, as did Crane's vocation to create a powerful, symbolic literature by which to uncover the spiritual meaning of human existence and endeavor. Williams's primal poet shares Crane's concern, encouraging his young followers to leave their material world and join him by the sea. There The Poet and his disciples return to nature and an elemental existence amid fire, water, earth, and air. The Poet's demise at sea is also similar to that of Crane, who leaped to his death from a ship off the coast of Florida. (In death, Crane became one with his principal poetic symbol.) Here, in Williams's reimagining of Crane, he lives on; his essence and poetic spirit are eternal and ever-present, riding the waves in perpetual motion.

### PUBLICATION HISTORY

"The Poet" was published in the collections *One Arm* (1948) and *Collected Stories* (1985).

### CHARACTER

**Poet** He is a very handsome young drifter, an anarchist who needs nothing but his poetry. The Poet chooses to be homeless and wanders from town to town, an evangelist of his poetry. This young writer always has a following of young people who receive his message and are inspired by his views.

## "Portrait of a Girl in Glass"

Short story written in 1942.

### SYNOPSIS

Tom Wingfield is a young poet who is forced to work in a warehouse to support his Mother and his sister, Laura. Mother enrolls Laura in business school; however, Laura secretly hides in the park every weekday instead of attending. When she becomes bedridden with a cold, Mother calls the school to explain Laura's absence. She is informed that Laura stopped attending school some time ago. Laura sits in her room and plays with her glass figurines, listening to her estranged father's old phonograph records.

Mother suggests Tom invite a friend to dinner to meet Laura. Nervously, he invites Jim Delaney. Laura is very shy and awkward around this new acquaintance. After dinner, Jim persuades her to dance with him. Laura enjoys his attention very much, but Jim mentions his fiancée, Betty. Mother is upset that Tom has introduced his sister to an unavailable young man. Not long after this incident, Tom is fired from the warehouse. He leaves Saint Louis, forgetting home, but never his sister's sweet face.

### COMMENTARY

"Portrait of a Girl in Glass" is the basis for the full-length play THE GLASS MENAGERIE. It is considered one of Williams's best short stories, and the plot is virtually unchanged in the play version. Tom Wingfield is a poet whose fate as the breadwinner is sealed when his father leaves the family. Tom is forced to take care of his mother and sister, and he can either be destroyed by this pressure or escape. Just as Tom lives for the few hours after work when he can write, Laura escapes into the phonograph records that had belonged to her father and her glass menagerie. Mother forces adulthood on Laura by briefly introducing a young man into her life, but Laura is too vulnerable and is pathologically shy. In *The Glass Menagerie,* she has a disability that forces her to walk with a severe limp. In both versions of this story, Mother (who becomes Amanda Wingfield in *Glass*) lives in a bygone fantasy world in which it is vital for a young woman to marry a young man of good social standing. Tom feels the need to protect and preserve the spirit of his sister. He does not want the world to change or hurt her. He is her protector; Laura is his emotional support. She calms his nerves after a long day at the wretched factory. As is "THE RESEMBLANCE BETWEEN A VIOLIN CASE AND A COFFIN," "Portrait of a Girl in Glass" is a short story that chronicles biographical aspects of ROSE ISABEL WILLIAMS's life. Williams writes of his sister in the guise of Laura. "I think the petals of her mind had simply closed through fear." Rose's life is also reflected in "COMPLETED" and *The Glass Menagerie.*

### PUBLICATION HISTORY

This short story was published in the collections *One Arm* (1948), *Porträtt Av En Glasflicka* (1955), *Moderne Amerikanische Prosa* (1967), *Collected Stories* (1985), and *The Art of the Story: An International Anthology of Contemporary Short Stories* (1999).

### CHARACTERS

**Delaney, Jim** Jim is a friend of Tom Wingfield's who is invited to the Wingfield home for dinner. He is an ambitious young man, who dreams of a bright future beyond the factory job he presently holds.

**Mother** An overbearing woman, who wants her daughter, Laura, to be married. An earlier version of Amanda Wingfield in *THE GLASS MENAGERIE,* she is very talkative and controlling.

**Wingfield, Laura** She is a young woman who enjoys contemplating her glass figurines and listening to records on her father's old Victrola. She has difficulty becoming assimilated in social circles, and her reclusive nature prohibits her from attending business college. When her mother, Amanda Wingfield, forces her to entertain a suitor, Jim Delaney, Laura is infatuated with Jim and enjoys his company. However, she is devastated to learn that he has a fiancée. Laura resorts to her glass menagerie and life in the world of her imagination. Williams based this character on his emotionally unstable sister, ROSE ISABEL WILLIAMS.

**Wingfield, Tom** Tom is an aspiring poet trapped in a mundane life of factory work. He is forced to work to support his mother and his sister, Laura Wingfield. Tom protects his sister from the world, but he also depends on her for emotional support.

## *Portrait of a Madonna*

One-act play written before 1946.

### SYNOPSIS

The setting is the living room of a nice, yet neglected city apartment.

A middle-aged unmarried woman, Miss Lucretia Collins, enters wearing an old negligee and Shirley Temple curls in her hair. She rushes to phone the manager, Mr. Abrams, to inform him that there is a man in her apartment. She tells him that this man enters night after night and "indulg[es] his senses with her." She orders Mr. Abrams to remove him, as he refuses to leave her bedroom. She describes the intruder as someone from a prominent family whose character has been ruined by a woman.

The Porter enters her apartment accompanied by the Elevator Boy. The Porter calls for Miss Collins, who has fled back into her bedroom. They can hear her talking to the intruder. Surveying the apartment, they agree that it has not been cleaned in 20 years. The Porter says Miss Collins never permits anyone to visit her; nor does she ever leave the apartment. They overhear Miss Collins apologizing for calling the police. The Porter says a doctor is on his way to take her to the state asylum.

The Porter sympathizes with Miss Collins. He pities her condition.

Miss Collins enters, referring to her deceased mother as if she were still living. She does not remember calling for help, and she does not recognize the men. The Porter explains that he has been sent to check on her by Mr. Abrams. Miss Collins says the man is gone now; he escaped through the bedroom window. Miss Collins refers to a photograph of a young man on her mantle. She recounts the memory of a young woman who stole the attention of this man. The Elevator Boy makes fun of Miss Collins, and the Porter reprimands him, as he considers Miss Collins a lady, who should be respected. Miss Collins is concerned that the disturbance will create scandal at the church. She does not want the intrusion to be made public for fear that people will talk. Miss Collins says that she grew up in the shadows of the Episcopal church; her father was a rector in Mississippi.

Miss Collins recalls another painful memory of passing by the young man's home when she walked home from church on Sundays. She felt self-conscious when walking by the young man sitting on the porch with the woman (now his wife) who stole him. Miss Collins felt suffocated and ran when the couple called out to her. The Porter suggests she forget about the humiliating encounter. Miss Collins recalls the pain she felt when she saw the woman's pregnant belly. She announces that she too is pregnant with this man's child. The Doctor and a Nurse arrive to take Miss Collins to the asylum. She is willing to go with them, but she insists on writing a letter to Richard, the intruder, in case he returns before she does.

## COMMENTARY

Lucretia Collins has led a desperate single life, deprived of sexual fulfillment and companionship. She is often compared to and viewed as a precursor of Blanche DuBois in A STREETCAR NAMED DESIRE. Although both characters experience mental deterioration and fall victim to harsh realities in their lives, Lucretia's repressed sexuality is very different from Blanche's history of numerous beaus and subsequent prostitution for survival's sake. Miss Collins pales in comparison to Blanche, as Blanche has a wealth of sexual experience. Miss Collins possesses an extreme innocence, whereas Blanche has a crushed maturity about her. However, both characters share the pain and regret of lost love. Again, the difference is in physical reality. While Blanche did in fact marry her sweetheart, Allen Gray, and enjoyed him for a time, Lucretia's prior claim to Richard seems wholly unfounded and artifical. In addition, Blanche's mental condition deteriorates throughout *A Streetcar Named Desire,* while Miss Collins seems to have been mentally ill for quite some time; it is only because of "the kindness of strangers" that she can still reside in her own environment.

Furthermore, Blanche's struggle is a conscious endeavor, and when she is raped, she shuts down mentally. In Miss Collins's delusions, rape is equated with love and desire. She is content with Richard's "intrusions" and the fact that he "indulg[es] his senses" with her and leaves. Miss Collins becomes somewhat afraid, and she calls Mr. Abrams for help, but she does not blame these episodes on a "dangerous" man. Her acceptance of rape and her defense of Richard are in stark contrast to Blanche's reaction to Stanley Kowalski's sexual violence.

Miss Collins explains that she's "literally grown up right in the very shadow of the Episcopal church." This conditioning has placed Lucretia in a very lonely predicament. She lost Richard to a young woman who welcomed sexual pleasure, an act that Miss Collins can only imagine as an aggressive situation now. Resigning herself to the role of recluse after her mother's death, Miss Collins refuses to accept that her sole familial connection is gone. Blanche witnessed the protracted suffering and death of her parents. Miss Collins was not as strong as Blanche: She could not persevere beyond the loss of her mother. This may have been the moment she lost touch with reality. Miss Collins's savior and oppressor has been the Episcopal church. These "shadows" have kept her desiring and dreaming of Richard, and yet it is now the church that pays her rent and protects her from homelessness and further ruin. Although Miss Collins has not left her apartment in 15 years, she believes that she attends Sunday church services: a sign of the powerful psychological connection she has with the church.

Miss Collins associates herself with the Holy Madonna, the Virgin Mother, in her announcement that she is pregnant. In a skewing of her religious and delusional beliefs, Lucretia imagines that she too has been impregnated by miraculous means. To justify her claim, she endows her supposed lover, Richard, with godlike qualities. As does the god Cupid, in the myth of Cupid and Psyche, Richard visits Lucretia under cover of darkness, unseen and undetected by others. After seducing Lucretia, he escapes her room by flying from her window. Lucretia's sad delusions lead to the play's dramatic climax and her removal to an asylum.

## PRODUCTION HISTORY

*Portrait of a Madonna* premiered at the Actors' Laboratory Theatre, Los Angeles, California, in 1946–47. It was directed by Hume Cronyn and starred JESSICA TANDY as Lucretia Collins. (Tandy's portrayal of Lucretia Collins led to her selection for the role of Blanche DuBois in the premiere production of A Streetcar Named Desire.) The play was produced in New York at the Playhouse Theatre, April 15, 1959. It was again directed by Hume Cronyn and starred Jessica Tandy. The New York production was met with warm reviews but was largely overshadowed by Lucretia's likeness to Blanche DuBois.

## PUBLICATION HISTORY

*Portrait of a Madonna* was first published in *27 WAGONS FULL OF COTTON AND OTHER ONE-ACT PLAYS* in 1966 by New Directions.

## CHARACTERS

**Collins, Miss Lucretia** A reclusive spinster who has become insane. Miss Collins lives in an apartment financially supported by the Episcopal Church, of which she is a long-standing member. Miss Collins believes she is visited by Richard, a boy she fell in love with as a young woman. In this episode, Richard enters her room and rapes her. She calls the front desk for help, but when they arrive she defends this invisible aggressor. Miss Collins is taken to an asylum at the end of the play, when she announces that she is pregnant with Richard's baby.

**Elevator Boy** He is a young man who deals unsympathetically with a tenant, Miss Lucretia Collins, when she calls for help against an intruder. The Elevator Boy accompanies The Porter and disrespectfully comments on the disheveled condition of Miss Collins's apartment as well as the mental condition of this distressed woman.

**Porter** He is a sympathetic ally of Miss Lucretia Collins. The Porter systematically answers Miss Collins's distress calls. He sits with her and respectfully allows her to talk and act as though there was a real intruder in her apartment, although the intruder is a figment of her imagination.

## FURTHER READING

Spoto, Donald. *The Kindness of Strangers: The Life of Tennessee Williams.* Boston: Little, Brown, 1985.

# *The Purification*

A one-act play written in 1940.

## SYNOPSIS

The action takes place in a sparse courtroom in a small American town in the Southwest.

### *Scene 1*

The Judge addresses the courtroom with the details of the case concerning Elena. He mentions that the rains have long been absent, fueling the rage of the two parties involved—the Casa Blanca family and the Rancher from Casa Roja. Rosalio (also called the Son) tells the court about his sister, Elena. While he talks, Luisa murmurs repeatedly, "The tainted spring is bubbling." The Father tries to silence the Son, but the Judge presses him to continue. The Son is startled by the ghost of Elena in her guise of "Elena of the Springs." She is dressed in white, carries white flowers, and stands in the archway. Luisa declares that Elena is the tainted water of which she speaks. Elena disappears from the doorway and the Son lunges furiously at Luisa.

Luisa reveals the Casa Blanca family's dark secret: Elena and the Son were incestuous lovers. The Son blames the hot August nights, the rancheros' guitar playing, and the drought for their actions. The Judge calls for a recess and leaves the courtroom. The Guitar Player strums melodically.

*Scene 2*

The Judge informs the courtroom that rain clouds are gathering. The trial proceeds, and the Son tells the court that the Rancher longed for Elena and killed her with an ax. Luisa mumbles again about the tainted spring, and the Son accuses her of being involved in the murder. The Rancher tells his side of the story. The Chorus repeats the words both men say. Their words recount events of the murder: The Rancher discovered Elena and her brother having sex in the barn and he struck Elena with an ax. At the word *struck,* thunder rumbles in the distance.

The Rancher says Elena drove him mad by rejecting his marriage proposal. He "burned" for her, but she was "water sealed under the rock." The Guitar Player strikes a chord, and the ghost of Elena appears as "Desert Elena," covered in dry, coarse material and carrying a wreath of dry flowers and a wooden cross. Desert Elena tells the Rancher that he must let her go; he will never possess her. Lightning flashes and the Guitar Player strikes another chord. The Rancher covers his face with his hands, and the Judge orders the Guitar Player to play a song that will produce rain. He instructs the Chorus to perform a rain dance. The Rancher begs Elena for forgiveness.

*Scene 3*

The Rancher confesses he tore the lovers apart with the ax. The Son rises to defend Elena's name. Clouds gather again and lightning flashes. Elena of the Springs reappears. In this moment, the Son pulls a knife from his pocket and stabs himself. He demands that the court witness his act of purification. A voice in the distance calls out, "Rain!" An Indian youth rushes in, joyfully flinging water from his sombrero. He stops when he sees the Son's dead body. The Mother, kneeling by her Son, orders that the knife be handed to the Rancher. The Rancher goes outside to taste the rain and stabs himself. Luisa screams, and the Guitar Player tosses his hat into the middle of the floor.

## COMMENTARY

Written in verse form, *The Purification* was inspired by the works of FEDRICO GARCÍA LORCA. With its rhythmical language, ritualized actions, chorus of women, and music, Williams effectively utilizes devices García Lorca mastered in such works as *Blood Wedding.* The symbols that are used throughout the play, such as water, blood, and earth, are also heavily reminiscent of elements of García Lorca's works.

Inspiration for this poetic tragedy also came from Williams's own life, particularly his early travels in the American Southwest and the tragedy that befell his beloved sister, ROSE ISABEL WILLIAMS. Toward the play's conclusion, the overwrought Son declares: "Weave back my sister's image . . . She's lost, snared as she rose . . . irretrievably lost . . . too far to pursue . . . For nothing contains you now, no, nothing contains you, lost little girl, my sister." While critical attention has primarily focused on sibling incest as the play's central interest, the true concern of this work is Williams's thinly veiled anguish at the demise of his sister. As Donald Spoto notes, the play is "a shout of outrage about the Williams family madness, a cry of hatred against his parents for what they had done to Rose" (Spoto, 83).

In the late 1930s, following accusations that her father, CORNELIUS COFFIN WILLIAMS had sexually abused her, Rose had been admitted to a state asylum in Farmington, Missouri, and diagnosed as suffering from schizophrenia. Rose remained at Farmington, where, with her parents' consent, she received a prefrontal lobotomy in November 1937. The controversial procedure, which left her practically autistic and in need of permanent institutionalization, was performed without her brother's knowledge. Williams was only made aware of the situation when he returned home from the UNIVERSITY OF IOWA for the Christmas holidays. He found his beloved sister permanently changed, resigned to a life that proved to be little more than a "living death" (Londré, 7). The surgery had left Rose bereft of her personality and any sense of identity. Williams alternately blamed his mother and himself for not having prevented the surgery. His protest against his father's boorish behavior and possible assault of Rose is clearly depicted in the Son's attack on the Rancher: "You shall not defame her, nor shall you defile her, this quicksilver girl . . . I think she always knew that she would be lost . . ."

Williams carried the guilt of not averting his sister's fate for the rest of his life. Through the character of the Son, who wields a large knife and performs an irreversible surgery upon himself, one can see a self-martyring Williams uniting himself with his sister. The Son views his own death and sacrifice of himself as an act of purification or atonement. As does Eloi Duvenet in *AUTO-DA-FÉ*, the Son sees himself as a redeemer. He is a Christ-figure; his death, an act of ultimate love, cleanses the desolate village of sin. Eloi purifies his world with fire; the Son's self-sacrifice renders life-giving rain.

## PRODUCTION HISTORY

MARGO JONES directed the premiere of *The Purification* in 1944.

## PUBLICATION HISTORY

*The Purification* was published in *27 WAGONS FULL OF COTTON AND OTHER ONE-ACT PLAYS* (1966).

## CHARACTERS

**Elena** Elena is also called "Elena of the Springs" and "Elena of the Desert." She is the daughter of the Casa Blanca family. The Rancher from Casa Roja murders her with an ax. Her ghost appears in the beginning of the trial (as Elena of the Springs), and near the end of the trial (as Elena of the Desert). Elena of the Springs is silent, whereas Elena of the Desert converses briefly with the Rancher. Elena of the Springs is visible only to the Son and to the Guitar Player.

**Father** He is the owner of Casa Blanca ranch and Elena's father. The Father seeks justice and revenge for his daughter's murder. He also considers it important to keep his family's secrets hidden.

**Guitar Player** He plays his guitar at pivotal moments throughout the play. His presence is parallel to that of the Guitar Player in *TEN BLOCKS ON THE CAMINO REAL*.

**Judge** The Judge is a wealthy and well-respected rancher. He is nominated by the townspeople to preside over a court case pertaining to the murder of Elena.

**Luisa** Luisa is a servant to the Casa Blanca family. She is an Indian with what is described as "savage blood." She condemns Rosalio by calling him a "tainted spring," because she knows he had a sexual relationship with his sister, Elena. Luisa seeks the truth and aids the court in uncovering the secrets of the family.

**Mother** She is the mother of Elena. A proud pure-blooded Castilian woman, she has a regal presence. She appears richly clad in her mourning clothes for her daughter.

**Rancher from Casa Roja** He is a lonely, dignified, powerful, and violent man. The Rancher murders his true love, Elena, when he discovers her having sex with her brother. When he is tried for killing Elena, he commits suicide outside the courtroom in an act of atonement.

**Rosalio** See Son.

**Son** Also known as Rosalio, the Son is a ruggedly handsome 20-year-old man. He speaks emotively about his deceased sister, Elena, during the trial of her murder. In the trial, he confesses that he had an incestuous relationship with Elena and commits suicide in an act of contrition.

## FURTHER READING

Londré, Felicia. *Tennessee Williams*. Fredericton, Canada: York Press, 1989.

Spoto, Donald. *The Kindness of Strangers: The Life of Tennessee Williams*. New York: Ballantine Books, 1985.

# "A Recluse and His Guest"

Short story written during the early 1970s.

## SYNOPSIS

A tall, ghostly woman named Nevrika walks into the town of Staad. She has traveled from Vladnik through the icy Midnight Forest in search of food and shelter. Nevrika approaches a Baker, who gives her bread and tells her that there is an old recluse, Klaus, who would have extra room for a guest. Nevrika goes to Klaus's home, and Klaus allows her to stay with him. The local men gossip in the pub about this newcomer. They are very surprised the recluse has let her stay with him.

The townspeople notice changes made to Klaus's home. Nevrika removes the boards from the windows, washes them, and hangs a clothesline for Klaus. Nevrika receives an invitation to return to her former dwelling place, but she is content to stay with him.

Under Nevrika's influence, Klaus becomes sociable. They attend a carnival; however, on the way home, Klaus is struck on the head by a falling roof tile. He demands to return to his former way of living. He blames her for his recent injury. Klaus orders Nevrika to float out to sea on a piece of ice, and she obeys him.

### COMMENTARY

The recluse, or individual living in willful isolation, is a recurring character in the Williams canon. As have the Spinster and the Old Woman in *LORD BYRON'S LOVE LETTER* and Rosemary McCool and Aunt Ella in "COMPLETED," the protagonist of this short story has found living in the world too much to bear and has cut himself off from it. Klaus is, however, the most reclusive of Williams's recluses.

As Dorothy Simple does in *THE CASE OF THE CRUSHED PETUNIAS*, Klaus shields himself behind a tangible barrier. For Dorothy it is her double row of prim petunias. For Klaus it is a doubly protective layer of snow and wooden boards that surround his house. Nevrika, as the Young Man in *The Case of the Crushed Petunias* and Amada in "RUBIO Y MORENA," enters Klaus's life to liberate and revive him. Whereas the isolated figures in "Rubio y Morena" (Kamrowski) and *The Case of the Crushed Petunias* end their narratives with a reawakened awareness of life and love, this mystical tale ends with the reinstatement of the protagonist's self-imposed exile.

### PUBLICATION HISTORY

"A Recluse and His Guest" was originally published in *Playboy* magazine (1970) and *Weird Show* (1971). It was included in *Collected Stories* (1985).

### CHARACTERS

**Baker** He is a baker in the fictional town of Staat. The Baker leads a traveler, Nevrika, to the recluse Klaus.

**Klaus** Klaus is an old recluse who accepts a woman, Nevrika, into his home. He enjoys her company and cooking but then grows tired of her presence. Klaus subsequently tells Nevrika she has to leave and orders her to drift out to sea on a piece of ice.

**Nevrika** She is a weary traveler who stays in the home of Klaus. Nevrika becomes very fond of Klaus and wants to live with him for the rest of her life; however, when he chooses to resume his reclusive existence, he insists that she drift out to sea. Nevrika has nothing left in the world, so she submits to his forceful suggestion of suicide.

## *The Red Devil Battery Sign*

Full-length play written in 1975–76.

### SYNOPSIS

*Act 1, Scene 1*

The settings is the lounge of a downtown Dallas hotel called the Yellow Rose, littered with drunks, businessmen, hookers, and a traditional mariachi band called the King's Men in full regalia.

A woman enters the lounge unescorted. She is distinctively dressed in an iridescent gown of gold. She is the Woman Downtown. Mr. Griffin quickly notices her and is surprised by her presence. She seems disoriented as to which hotel she is in and when she checked in. Mr. Griffin rushes over to the Woman Downtown and assures her that she is to have total anonymity while at the Yellow Rose, as specified in the instructions of her guardian, Judge Collister.

The Woman Downtown coyly accuses the manager of interfering with her anonymity and demands to check out immediately. She becomes visibly distraught when a young man known as Crewcut enters the room. She demands to know why he has been following her every move. His response is that he is trying to keep away certain persons related to the highly suspicious Paradise Meadows Nursing Home, those who held the Woman Downtown captive and administered electric shock therapy. Mr. Griffin also informs the Woman Downtown that the Judge has been in the hospital since the night he deposited her at the hotel. She responds by immediately summoning a car.

There is a break from this main action as the Woman Downtown overhears a conversation between two drunks who discuss the Vietnam War and the countless draft dodgers who are plaguing the country. The Woman Downtown becomes infuriated, and she bitingly refers to the irony that these gentlemen, so nobly preaching on their barstools, are above draft age and would never have the obligation forced on them. Her entry into the talk of war spurs some sexual innuendos by the two drunks.

Just then King Del Rey, a Mexican man, bulldozes his way into the lounge. He is surrounded by the mariachis, who welcome him with a song. He is drawn to the Woman Downtown, they strike up a conversation, and it is established that she speaks Spanish. This revelation leads the drunk into another sexual comment, and King Del Rey knocks him off his barstool. This act of chivalry induces the Woman Downtown to flirt with King Del Rey. She playfully sprays her perfume Vol de Nuit (Night Flight) on his shirt.

King is cajoled by the mariachis to sing a song with them. As he begins to leave his barstool, the Woman Downtown dramatically clutches his arm and begs him not to leave her side. She is desperate to keep him nearby, as she has eyed Crewcut making his way to her. King is unable to understand her agitation and decides now more than ever that a song is in order, any song that she would like. It is his first performance since San Antone and without La Niña.

Crewcut reaches the Woman Downtown and announces that the car has arrived. She stumbles to the door and King catches her delicate body, which is overcome by dizziness and excitement. She breaks free and asks King not to leave the hotel until she returns. She exits to the car and within seconds returns wild with tales of possessed taxi drivers wanting to take her away.

She falls to the ground and is comforted by King, who is angered by her hysterics. Charlie, the barman, warns him to stay away and begins to dial for the "doctor." Charlie then confesses that the Woman Downtown is under surveillance because of her mental state. As the Woman Downtown is being carried off the stage, Mr. Griffin returns to establish order in the lounge.

### *Scene 2*

The Woman Downtown asks King whether he thinks she is crazy. She explains to him that she is being held captive. The Woman Downtown claims Crewcut is still outside, an ever-present mystery haunting her doorway. King investigates and returns with the news that he has left.

The Woman Downtown is very grateful for her temporary freedom, but she is again troubled about King's opinion of her. He talks about his Mexican heritage and insists that he is not like the ridiculous stereotype that so many have attributed to his people. She agrees and decides to test his intentions. She requests that her suitcases be taken off her bed so that she may relax. As King picks up the suitcase it slips from his hands and the contents explode onto the floor. Papers swirl in the air. The Woman Downtown frantically protects them by hurling herself onto the floor to hide them. She laughs at the scene. King thinks she is laughing at him. To show her appreciation for his company she kisses him. The Woman Downtown tells him stories from her past. She was hospitalized and sentenced to an eternity of electric shock therapy treatments until the Judge saved her.

They order room service. The so-called doctor tries to enter the room to "treat" the woman. King assures all that she is in good hands and calmer since the episode downstairs. The Woman Downtown sprawls on the bed in a sensuous pose. King cautiously recommends that she remove her beautiful dress so that it will not be ruined. She is more than happy to oblige and slips out of her dress. She takes a step and collapses in his arms. As he begins to caress her, she pulls away screaming, "Human!" She speaks about her inhumanity and tells him that she was a hostage of the Red Devil Battery monsters. She is so agitated that King embraces her to devour her fear: "Calmate. We're human together."

*Scene 3*

The Woman Downtown and King become sexually intimate. King is disturbed by her behavior in bed: her screams of pain and cat scratches. The Woman Downtown insists they were cries of rebirth, of coming to life. King is worried about what his wife, Perla, will say about these scratches on his body. He is indebted to Perla since they found a brain tumor or as he calls it, "an accident in his head." The Woman Downtown simply replies that the she-wolf gave them to him.

*Scene 4*

The setting is the outskirts of the city in what is known as the Wasteland.

King hesitates outside his small home. Perla is in the house talking on the phone to her daughter, La Niña (who is partially lit upstage naked with a man in bed). Perla accuses her daughter of being a whore. She hangs up and refuses to call her back when King asks to speak to La Niña. He confesses that he knows his daughter and Perla have been secretly corresponding since the accident. She concurs and reasons that women, mothers and daughters, need different channels of communication than men. She stops abruptly and smells the air. Perla interrogates King as to why he smells of perfume. He tells her that she is a brave woman. Retiring to the bedroom, King catches a whiff of his shirt: "Night Flight."

*Act 2, Scene 1*

The setting is the lounge about a month later.

There is a group of conventioneers at the bar wearing the Red Devil insignia. The Woman Downtown enters cautiously. She is agitated by the presence of these battery men and asks the barman whether any messages from Mr. Del Rey have been delivered.

King Del Rey enters to the same adulation he received before. The Woman Downtown desperately vies for his company and draws him near while everyone watches. He pushes her away, explaining that Perla is on to them. She tries to change the subject by ordering him a beer. King cracks under the pressure of the affair and his unhealthy state. Just then a new mariachi enters the lounge and takes his place onstage. King seethes as a new song begins. He is doubly offended that he has been replaced in his own band, which includes his daughter.

King climbs onto the stage and throws the drummer off, reclaiming control of his men. His anger irritates his brain tumor. King rubs his eyes and sways from side to side. In order to cover his behavior, he announces that La Niña is returning to his home tomorrow. This good news also coincides with the doctor's approving that he perform again. King staggers out of the bar as Mr. Griffin enters with the drummer, demanding that he be placed onstage at once.

*Scene 2*

The Woman Downtown enters the penthouse carrying a vase full of yellow roses with King trailing behind her at a significantly slower pace. By reminding King of their "human" connection, she hopes to calm him. She takes off her clothing and lies on the bed. When King asks her name, the Woman Downtown senses that this is their last night together. Instead of answering the question, she says that she was born into a rich Texan family, to a life of political and economic secrets. She breaks down and admits that she does not have enough breath. King throws himself onto the floor and clutches her knees, imploring her to open up to him. She tells him about the ranch where she lived, her father's mistress, and the illegitimate child who followed. The Woman Downtown admits that she was constantly told she was a "disturbed" child. She was therefore sent to special schools her whole life, running from the secrets. She believed she was afflicted until she became human with King. Her secrets deal with a conspiracy surrounding the Vietnam War. She explains that genocide was practiced to protect investments. She was privy to these plans when she lived with her husband.

King pulls away from her to leave. He says that his daughter is returning home and he must stop their affair. The woman confesses that she must also leave for a secret trip to Washington for a special session of Congress. The papers have been decoded, and she is going to testify against all the secret bearers who have plagued her life.

The noise of the convention downstairs infiltrates the scene. The Woman Downtown goes to the window, and we can see the Red Devil Battery sign blinking red in the distance. He closes the blinds and she begins to evolve into the she-wolf. King initially refuses to have sex with her but cannot resist her advances. (Lights dim momentarily and then we return to the scene.) King opens the shade, and glaring red light envelops the room. He makes a vulgar gesture at the sign.

### *Act 3, Scene 1*

The setting is the Wasteland with the Dallas skyline in the background. The only visible change is the large blinking sign atop the tallest skyscraper. The Red Devil Battery sign pulses through the darkness of the night.

King secretly speaks on the phone to the Woman Downtown while he waits for Perla to return home. The woman says that Judge Collister is dead and her life is in danger. Perla enters and he hangs up the phone. Perla tells him that La Niña has been away so long because she is ashamed to show her face. La Niña met a married man and has been living with him for several months. He has come with her today to receive King's blessing, and he intends to get what he wants even it if means using his gun.

La Niña enters with her boyfriend, Terrance McCabe. He extends his hands to King and affectionately calls him "Pop." King furiously grabs a kitchen knife and points it at McCabe's groin. He must surrender his gun or leave his house. La Niña begins to sing to them, hoping to defuse the dangerous situation. Her song is magical and enchants both men, who put down their weapons momentarily. Perla interrupts her beautiful song and summons her to the kitchen to help prepare dinner.

McCabe talks to King about La Niña's depression since she lost the child they were expecting. King strikes McCabe in response to this news, but McCabe is unmoved. The men step outside, and King begs McCabe to get him some Demerol from the medicine chest. Inside La Niña is upset to learn that her father is very ill.

McCabe returns to King with the pills and a six-pack of beer. McCabe begins the conversation by describing the first moment he saw La Niña onstage. His life was empty before La Niña. He was nothing more than a computer programmed not to be human. That first night they spent together she just held him so tenderly that he never wanted to let go of her and now she is pregnant again. King accuses McCabe of stealing La Niña's glory for his own comfort: so his seed will live on. King accepts McCabe and his weapon and stumbles out of the yard toward downtown. McCabe runs into the house with excitement as he announces that King has accepted him. Perla nervously asks him where the gun is and McCabe admits that he gave it to King. They run after him.

### *Scene 2*

At the lounge the sleazy Drummer speaks to the Woman Downtown. The phone rings at the bar and it is King calling to say good-bye. She implores him to come downtown. She tells him that she has changed rooms at the Yellow Rose so that no Red Devils can come grinning into their sanctuary. He hangs up, and the Woman Downtown staggers out of the bar. As she exits, the Drummer grabs her and brutally gropes her. He snaps an incriminating photo of the woman in her disheveled state. The Woman Downtown frees herself by scratching his face as she hails a cab.

### *Scene 3*

The setting is the local pharmacy, where King has collapsed. The Woman Downtown enters, as the King's Men appear to King one last time. He places the Woman Downtown in a chair and sits opposite her. With his eyes fixed on hers, he lifts the gun toward his head just as the Drummer enters, flashing another photo. The Drummer dashes with his prize toward the door and King shoots and kills him. The Woman Downtown screams and King falls to the floor. She tries to comfort the dying King.

The delinquents of the hollowed-out Wasteland enter, and there is a break from reality. They invade the scene with their barbaric appearance. The leader has the word *Wolf* on his shirt and has circled around his prey: the Woman Downtown. She joins their ranks and becomes the mother of all the demented outcasts. They call her "Sister of Wolf."

## COMMENTARY

In *The Red Devil Battery Sign*, every character is trapped by a societal, political, physical, or emotional construct. The Woman Downtown's raw nature has been constantly suppressed by "civilities" that have held her captive. King is trapped by his physical illness and therefore by his wife, Perla, who has been forced to support him. Their daughter, La Niña, is trapped in her father's expectations for fame. This vicious cycle has drawn her to men very much like her father. Her lover, Terrence McCabe, is emotionally withdrawn from the world because he has been forced to join the humdrum technological computer world. The theme of entrapment even carries over as a metaphor for the entire nation, which after many political fallouts has been trapped in the "new world order." The characters are emotionally devoid and search for feeling: to be human again.

The Woman Downtown was born into the quintessential political family. Her tyrannical father and everything that he represented suppressed her passionate nature from a young age; she was even told that her spirit had killed her mother at birth. She grew up as a socialite attending all of the required events while dying on the inside. She tried to find freedom through marriage; however, she fell into a similar trap: Not only had she been entangled with the political suppressors, now she was caught up with the corporate suppressors, the new enemies of state. The Woman Downtown becomes the sole owner of official documents containing conspiracy secrets. The knowledge of these documents traps her in a moral dilemma: to reveal the truth. She has felt the wrath of her world too many times and now more than ever needs to share with the world the horrors of political machination.

The Woman Downtown finds peace only when she is allowed to be her animalistic self. She finds solace with King del Rey, who has a human and base quality to which the Woman Downtown is attracted. But even with King she is not totally honest until the end, when she confesses to him about her life of lies and deception. Her proper name is never revealed because she is so far removed from life that she verges on the absurd; the culmination is her induction into the Wasteland gang at the end of the play. She needs no name because she has let go of all societal trappings and become the she-wolf.

King del Rey is also trapped by his wife, Perla. She is a strong oppressive force in his life that evokes disgust and respect simultaneously in him. Since his accident the traditional roles of husband and wife have been reversed and Perla has been forced to join the workforce and support King. She also orchestrated sending their daughter, La Niña, on tour to make money for the family. Perla is such a strong force that throughout her life she has gravitated to the weak in order to "fix" them. This is a quality shared by La Niña, who hopes to fix Terrence McCabe.

La Niña is trapped in her father's dream of stardom; in the lounge scene she nomadically travels from city to city. Her father pressures her to maintain this lifestyle, which he considers the only way a Mexican can "make it" in the United States. La Niña is drawn to men like her father and finds comfort in Terrence McCabe. She is further trapped by pregnancy and is therefore stuck in this relationship. McCabe is a married man who had been ensnared by the burgeoning technological world. McCabe feels that La Niña restored him through her zest for life and through her music. La Niña and her father have been broken, but they intoxicate others with their music.

Scholars have treated *The Red Devil Battery Sign* with severe criticism. Some have implied that Williams's chemical dependencies were transcribed onto this play as the name 'Red Devil' is actually slang for a powerful prescriptive sedative at the time, and they point out that the play ends with the death of King in a drugstore. Others have concentrated on the political implications of the play and called its topics of conspiracies and wars outdated. However, the play's significance and contemporary relevance is undeniable. It deals with materialist military–industrial culture, which seems now more than ever to turn the wheels of the modern world. Williams was visionary in his understanding that these forces can be paralyzing to human expressiveness. Williams also stated that the play was an artistic response to the assassination of U.S. president John F. Kennedy. Williams believed *The Red Devil Battery Sign* was comparable to any of his major works. Contemporary criticism and reevaluation may bear this out.

## PRODUCTION HISTORY

*The Red Devil Battery Sign* premiered at the Schubert Theatre, Boston, Massachusetts, on June 18, 1976. Directed by Edwin Sherin, the production starred Anthony Quinn as King del Rey and Claire Bloom as the Woman Downtown.

## PUBLICATION HISTORY

*The Red Devil Battery Sign* was first published in 1988 by New Directions.

## CHARACTERS

**Crewcut** He stalks the Woman Downtown in an attempt to protect her from being abducted and returned to Paradise Meadows Nursing Home, where she has been an electric shock treatment patient. The Crewcut has been hired by the woman's guardian, Judge Collister.

**Griffin, Mr.** He is the manager of the exclusive Dallas, Texas, hotel the Yellow Rose. Mr. Griffin tries to appease a guest, the Woman Downtown, who demands anonymity, despite the memorable scenes she creates in the lobby and hotel bar.

**Judge Collister** He is the guardian of the Woman Downtown. He rescued her from electric shock therapy treatments at Paradise Meadows Nursing Home. After Judge Collister becomes hospitalized, his hired man, the Crewcut, protects The Woman Downtown.

**King del Rey** He is a Mexican leader of a Mariachi band called the King's Men. He is a confident Latino whose chivalrous, intoxicating spirit captures the attention of the Woman Downtown. Diagnosed with a brain tumor, King is forced to quit his profession. Through the course of the play, he mentally deteriorates. He is self-conscious about his ethnicity and tries hard to break free of stereotypes that bind him in life. He is married to Perla, who financially supports him.

**La Niña** She is the daughter of King del Rey and Perla. Gifted with a beautiful singing voice, she has also found a gift to heal. No one can relieve King Del Rey's pain as his daughter can. La Niña has fallen in love with a man whose love feels more like entrapment. She becomes pregnant and returns to her parents' home in order to see her father. La Niña is amazed at the extent of his deterioration and realizes that he is beyond help.

**McCabe, Terrence** He is a married man who wins La Niña's heart. He recalls the first time he met La Niña and cried in her arms. He had lived a life of computers and technology and had lost all sensation until he met her. She has given him new life and now his life is going to live on through their child.

**Perla** She is a strong Latina who has been forced to return to the workforce now that her husband, King del Rey, is incapacitated. She is like her namesake, strong and indestructible. She has also sent her daughter on the lounge circuit across the country to make money as well. She is aware of King's affair with the Woman Downtown but forces herself to ignore it and hope that he will return to her. When Perla becomes the breadwinner, the role reversal becomes too much for King to handle.

**Woman Downtown** She is a nameless woman who is being held captive at the Yellow Rose Hotel on the instructions of her friend Judge Collister. The Woman Downtown grew up in a political household and was forced to live a high-society life; however, her spirit has always tried to break free of these constraints. Running from the political world, she marries into the corporate world and finds herself even more suppressed. She is the keeper of certain obscure documents, which have information about a huge American political-military conspiracy. The Woman Downtown finds solace in the arms of King del Rey, who through his primal energy restores her life and allows her to be her animalistic self. In the end the animal within wins and she destroys all trappings of society to live the life she desires.

## FURTHER READING

Gross, Robert F. "The Gnostic Politics of *The Red Devil Battery Sign*," in *The Undiscovered Country:*

*The Later Plays of Tennessee Williams,* edited by Philip C. Kolin. New York: Peter Lang, 2002.

## The Remarkable Rooming-House of Mme. Le Monde

A one-act play published in 1984. The date of composition is uncertain.

### SYNOPSIS

The action of the play takes place in London, England, in a boardinghouse owned by Madame Le Monde. One of her tenants, Mint, lives alone in an attic room that is "a rectangle with hooks." Mint, who is paralyzed from the waist down, hangs suspended on the hooks. His only means of mobility is to make his way about the room by clinging to the hooks and swinging from them.

As Mint hangs in midair on his hooks, Madame Le Monde's son, the Boy, appears in Mint's doorway. He seizes Mint from his hooks and carries him into an adjacent alcove in the room and sexually assaults him. When the Boy has finished, Mint begs him to return him to his place on the hooks, but the Boy refuses and leaves Mint on the floor. Mint's former school friend, Hall, arrives for tea. Mint greets Hall by singing an old school song and pleads with him to assist him back onto his hooks. Hall does not assist Mint; instead he insults him for his "susceptibility" to "afflictions and accidents." Hall eventually lifts Mint from the floor and places him on the hook farthest from the tea table. Hall commences tea without Mint and devours all of Mint's biscuits. Mint struggles to swing to the tea table and tries to discuss his financial troubles with Hall: He has been threatened with eviction and needs financial assistance. Mint suddenly slips from his hooks and tries to crawl to the tea table to join Hall. Hall calls down to Madame Le Monde for more tea and biscuits. Madame Le Monde answers Hall, but with no indication that she will fulfill his request.

Hall replaces Mint on his hooks, again as far as possible from the tea table. Hall then gives explicit details of a recent sexual encounter with a prostitute named Rosie O'Toole. Mint again explains his financial needs to Hall, who ignores him and stamps his feet on the floor to demand more tea from Madame Le Monde. Hall leaves the attic in pursuit of Madame Le Monde and more tea. In his absence, the Boy returns to assault Mint again in the alcove. Hall returns to the attic with Madame Le Monde. Mint crawls out of the alcove to defend himself and his actions with the Boy to Madame Le Monde. Hall and Madame Le Monde announce that they have struck a beneficial financial deal between themselves. Madame Le Monde's son walks out of the alcove adjusting his clothing. Madame Le Monde seizes Mint and throws him across the room. Realizing that Mint has been killed as a result of the blow, Hall congratulates Madame Le Monde on her successful "removal of the redundant." Hall quickly tries to escape the attic. As he rushes down the stairs, Madame Le Monde pulls a lever rigged to the stairway. The stairs are flattened and Hall can be heard screaming as he slides to his death. In a final act of vengeance, Madame Le Monde kills her insolent son with a fatal karate chop.

### COMMENTARY

*The Remarkable Rooming-House of Mme. Le Monde* can best be understood as an example of absurdist drama. The plays of the THEATER OF THE ABSURD strive to expose the absurdity of the human condition. Dramas of this kind present a view of human perplexity and spiritual anguish through a series of connected incidents and patterns of images that present human beings as "bewildered beings in an incomprehensible universe" (Harmon and Holman, 2). Although Williams is not acknowledged as a principal writer within this literary genre, many of the works in his dramatic canon—particularly those of his late period—feature absurdist qualities. Similar to the more established absurdist plays of SAMUEL BECKETT, Eugene Ionesco, and HAROLD PINTER, *The Remarkable Rooming-House of Mme. Le Monde* is an exploration of human creatures living in "meaningless isolation in an alien environment" (Harmon and Holman, 2). As does Pinter's *The Birthday Party*, Williams's play "speaks plainly of the Individual's pathetic search for security" (Esslin, 241).

Pinter's works notably depict characters alone in their rooms "confronted with the basic problem of being." In this context the "room" for Pinter, as well as for Williams, becomes a symbol of the characters' individual place in the world and therefore becomes a "territory to be conquered and defended" (Esslin, 247, 258). Mint, as do many absurdist antiheroes, literally and metaphorically clings onto the tenterhooks of his precarious position in the world. Through the character of Mint, who lives suspended in midair in a room full of hooks, Williams physically substantiates the absurdist theory that human beings exist in a state of suspense (or suspension) and strain caused by uncertainty.

The principal source of Mint's discomfiture and uncertainty is his landlady, Madame Le Monde; the name *Le Monde* literally means "the world." This "large and rather globular" woman is an embodiment of the brutal, hostile world. A fiery, vengeful, and devouring mother goddess, she also represents life itself as she reigns over her domain and dispenses life and death on a whim—or the flick of a switch. Hall, whose name contains the word *all,* is the personification of greed, avarice, and gluttony. A completely sensuous creature, he is driven by appetite, and his conversation centers on food, sex, and money. Mint's name is also connected to all-consuming appetites. In ancient herbal folklore, mint (*Mentha* species) was known for its aphrodisiac quality and was said to arouse lust, which the character clearly does, as witnessed by the Boy's insatiable ardor for Mint. "Mint" is also a modern-day slang term for money.

In many ways *Rooming-House* can be seen as an absurdist revision of THE GLASS MENAGERIE. Mme. Le Monde can be seen as a literal and figurative larger-than-life version of the character Amanda Wingfield. Mme. Le Monde is a perversely domineering mother figure, who must be the center of attention and who is violently suspicious of her son's behavior and interactions with others. Her son, the Boy, is a Tom Wingfield of sorts, eager to escape his mother's control. Mint consequently becomes a more fully physically disabled Laura Wingfield. He is, however, far more proactive in relieving his isolation than his *Glass Menagerie* counterpart. Mint invites Hall, "an emissary from another world," to tea in the hope that he will provide him with much needed security and protection. But as is Laura's Gentleman Caller, Jim O'Connor, who is engaged to another girl, Hall is "not in the position to do the right thing" by Mint. He cannot rescue Mint because he is homophobic and financially unstable. Hall's insensitivity also parallels Jim O'Connor's charming oafishness. As Jim shatters Laura's quietude by breaking her favorite glass ornament and kissing her, Hall torments Mint by thoughtlessly ignoring his cries for help, absentmindedly eating and drinking all of Mint's provisions and recounting disturbing details of his sordid sexual encounters. Hall's extended and fantastical monologue about his lascivious dealings with a prostitute serves as a distancing technique to solidify Hall's claim to a heterosexual orientation, as well as to alienate, isolate, and oppress Mint further. Ironically, Hall's escapade, which takes place in the back of a London taxi cab, also calls to mind another Pinter play, *The Homecoming,* with its shockingly casual talk of prostitution and Old Sam's dying revelation that his nephew's mother committed adultery with another man in the back of his cab.

*The Remarkable Rooming-House of Mme. Le Monde* is a fascinating work that has been largely ignored or flatly rejected by scholars who have attempted to judge the play by standards of conventional, realistic drama or who have been put off by the play's sexual context. This work is, however, one of Williams's most remarkable, and it encapsulates his engagement with the theater of the absurd.

## PRODUCTION HISTORY

No professional productions of *The Remarkable Rooming-House of Mme. Le Monde* have been recorded to date.

## PUBLICATION HISTORY

*The Remarkable Rooming-House of Mme. Le Monde* was published in a limited edition by Alboncani Press in 1984.

## CHARACTERS

**Boy** He is the son of Madame Le Monde. As does his mother, the Boy takes great pleasure in having sex and tormenting others. The subject of his violent abuse is Mint, his mother's frail and disabled tenant. The Boy secretly and repeatedly assaults Mint in the alcove of his attic room. His actions are discovered by his jealous mother, who kills him with a single karate chop.

**Hall** Hall visits the rooming house owned by Madame Le Monde to have tea with his former school chum, Mint. Although Mint considers him a friend, Hall is very cruel to Mint. He regularly insults Mint, refuses to help him physically or financially, and greedily eats all of his food. Hall uses his visit to Mint's room to his own advantage: He receives a free meal, has sex with Madame Le Monde, and strikes a major financial deal with her. His great scheme backfires when he ends up on the wrong side of Madame Le Monde and suffers her wrath.

**Le Monde, Madame** Madame Le Monde is the owner of a boardinghouse in London, England. In many ways she is a larger-than-life caricature of Williams's ruthless landlady figure. As are several of the other landlady characters in the Williams canon (in such works as "THE ANGEL IN THE ALCOVE," *THE LADY OF LARKSPUR LOTION, and VIEUX CARRÉ*), Madame Le Monde is money-hungry, homophobic, spiteful, and cruel. She repeatedly threatens her disabled tenant, Mint, with eviction. Madame Le Monde cares little about Mint's basic needs and becomes jealous of his interactions with her son, The Boy. When Mint's former school friend, Hall, visits, Madame Le Monde seduces him, and the two strike an important financial deal. However, in the end, Madame Le Monde's rage gets the better of her and she kills Mint, Hall, and her son.

**Mint** He is a tenant living in the attic of a boardinghouse owned by Madame Le Monde. Mint is a fragile childlike man who is paralyzed from the waist down. The walls of his attic room are covered with hooks, and Mint's only means of mobility is swinging from one hook to another. Mint quite literally and metaphorically clings on the tenterhooks of his precarious position in the world. Through the character of Mint, Williams physically substantiates the theory that human beings exist in a state of suspense (or suspension) and strain because of uncertainty, a primary tenet of the THEATER OF THE ABSURD.

## FURTHER READING

Esslin, Martin. *Theater of the Absurd.* London: Penguin Books, 1961.

Harmon, William, and C. Hugh Holman, eds. *A Handbook to Literature.* Upper Saddle River, N.J.: Prentice-Hall, 1996.

# "The Resemblance Between a Violin Case and a Coffin"

Short story written in 1949.

## SYNOPSIS

The Narrator, a young boy, does not understand the changes Sister undergoes during puberty. He is confused by her loss of interest in him and in childhood games. Her only interest is in practicing for her piano recital. Their grandmother, who is called Grand, pampers the Sister, showing her more attention than usual. The neighborhood children tease and harass him, so the Narrator stays inside and mopes.

Miss Aehle, Sister's piano teacher, assigns her to a duet with a handsome young violin student, Richard Miles, as part of a recital. The Sister is excited and nervous about the prospect, as she has developed a crush on Richard. Her brother also has a crush on the young man. The Sister struggles with the assigned music. She plays flawlessly when she is alone, but in Richard's presence she makes mistakes and succumbs to nervous fits of crying. Despite these problems, Miss Aehle assures her that her nervousness will subside with practice. The piano teacher decides to cut several of the Sister's solos from the recital and fears that the young girl will not be able to play the duet with Richard.

The evening of performance the Sister is distraught. When she arrives at the concert hall, she pleads not to perform, but she is pressured to do so. The duet is a disaster. Richard plays wonderfully, and he patiently tries to mask all of her mistakes. At one point, the Sister simply stops playing, but Richard patiently helps to get her back on track. When the catastrophic duet is over, Richard holds the Sister near him, and they bow together, receiving a standing ovation.

After that night, the Sister refuses to play piano ever again. The family is forced to move north when the father is transferred to a job. They learn through mutual friends that Richard died of pneumonia. The Narrator recalls the similarity in Richard's violin case and a coffin.

## COMMENTARY

"The Resemblance Between a Violin Case and a Coffin" is the second narrative in a trilogy of short stories centered on autobiographical material related to Williams's sister, ROSE WILLIAMS. The Sister in this story has very deep feelings and love interests, but she is never capable of having an intimate relationship with a man. Rose suffers many humiliating experiences such as the recital, and she becomes increasingly withdrawn from the world. As the Sister has in this story, Rose has a severe nervous condition that impedes social grace in the company of the opposite sex. A similar story, "PORTRAIT OF A GIRL IN GLASS," gives another impression of Rose, as a woman caught in a childlike state of existence. A more fully developed Rose is manifested in Laura Wingfield in *THE GLASS MENAGERIE.*

## PUBLICATION HISTORY

This short story was published in *Flair* magazine (1950), *Best American Short Stories of 1951* (1952), *Hard Candy* (1954), *Collected Stories* (1985), and *The Best American Short Stories of the Century* (1999).

## CHARACTERS

**Aehle, Miss** The enthusiastic music teacher who teaches Rose to play the piano, Miss Aehle has confidence in Rose's musical ability and encourages her to perform at a recital.

**Grand** Grand is the grandmother of Rose and the Narrator. She is compassionate and supportive of Rose as she encounters emotional difficulties during puberty. Grand is reminiscent of Williams's maternal grandmother, ROSINA OTTE DAKIN, who was affectionately called "Grand."

**Miles, Richard** Richard is a handsome young violinist with whom Rose performs a disastrous duet. Richard remains patient and loving toward Rose.

**Narrator** He is a young boy whose best friend is his older sister, Rose. The Narrator feels abandoned when Rose reaches puberty and is no longer interested in childhood games. When his sister's love interest, Richard Miles, is introduced, the Narrator discovers his own sexual urges.

**Sister** The sister of the Narrator, this young woman struggles with puberty. She is nervous and awkward and suffers from low self-esteem. She experiences an embarrassing piano recital with the young, handsome Richard Miles. She fancies Richard because he is gentle and patient with her, but the humiliation of the traumatic duet leaves her devastated and emotionally wounded.

# *The Roman Spring of Mrs. Stone*

A novel written around 1950.

## SYNOPSIS

### *Part 1: "Cold Sun"*

#### *Chapter 1*

On an early evening in March in Rome, Italy, unemployed people loiter on the Spanish Steps, shifting up toward the top, step by step, as the Sun sinks. Street vendors and urchins have moved to the Via Veneto to prey on American tourists. Among the people remaining on the stairs is a nameless attractive Young Man in tattered clothing. He has been standing there, watching and waiting, for a considerable amount of time. His gaze is fixed on a terrace, five stories up from the piazza, where two women in fur coats appear. He is also aware of an American tourist near an obelisk on the piazza. The tourist reaches into his pocket to offer a cigarette to the Young Man, who recognizes the gesture as an invitation for a tryst, which would provide him with food and money for a while.

Assessing the tourist's camera, jewelry, and clothes, the Young Man declines the offer and returns to watching the women on the terrace, who seem to hold out a more lucrative opportunity.

### Chapter 2

The two women on the terrace are Karen Stone, a retired actress in her early 50s recently widowed and living in Rome, and her childhood friend, Meg Bishop, an author and journalist. They have met accidentally in the banking department of American Express that morning, and Mrs. Stone has invited Miss Bishop to her home for the afternoon. As their relationship has been strained since a fleeting lesbian encounter at college, Karen has also invited a number of Italian friends, to avoid any confidential exchanges with Meg. Miss Bishop has, however, forced a private conversation on the terrace. The conversation is centered on Karen's retirement from the stage, which was due to her failure in the part of Juliet, for which she was too old. Mrs. Stone tries to evade further discussion of the subject by calling one of her Italian guests, the Conte Paolo Di Leo, out onto the terrace. He stays only briefly, observing that he does not like "a cold sun." Meg picks up on the connotations of the remark and upbraids Karen for the company she keeps and her various liaisons with vastly younger men, which have sparked vicious gossip. Unwilling to continue the conversation, Karen returns indoors. She ignores her other party guests and retreats into her bathroom. She washes her face and then retires to her bedroom to reflect on her situation. Once her guests have left, she goes back out onto the terrace; looking down on the piazza, she spots the waiting Young Man, who made an obscene sign at her the previous day.

### Chapter 3

The story returns to Meg Bishop's point of view, from the moment Mrs. Stone has fled the terrace. Meg admits to herself that she has sought—and achieved—revenge for Karen's rejection of her in college, although she finds that the scene has disturbed her. Pacing on the terrace, she ends up outside Karen's bedroom and watches her through the French windows. When she finds the windows locked, Meg returns to the terrace, where she observes the Young Man in the piazza relieving himself against the wall below the balustrade. Shocked and repelled, Miss Bishop decides to return inside. Meg tries to find Karen, without success. Left alone in the living room, Meg discovers a glass-covered French clock on the mantel. Beneath the clock she finds a photograph of a woman with a message on the back stating, "This is how I look now!" Before Meg can read the accompanying note and determine the meaning of the picture, she is notified that the elevator has arrived.

### Chapter 4

On an afternoon late in April, Paolo is attending his daily appointment at Renato's barber's shop. For Paolo's visits, Renato turns his barber's chair toward the window, so that they both can watch and discuss the people going by in the Via Veneto. The virtually exclusive topic of their conversation is Paolo's sexual exploits with wealthy tourists. He recalls his previous conquests: Signora Coogan, the Baron Waldheim, and Mrs. Jamison Walker. He explains that he has been attempting to make Mrs. Stone his "protector." So far, Karen Stone has proved impervious to his attentions.

At this juncture, the point of view shifts to that of Karen Stone and an explanation of her ostensible reluctance to become involved with Paolo. He has been introduced to her by the Contessa, and in the early stages of their acquaintance Karen has identified Paolo with one of the weak, young actors she was able to control and manipulate on- and offstage. Although she has gradually recognized her attraction to him and accepted his attentions, she still is unwilling to reciprocate, as her idea of courtship tactics requires that she display reserve.

This state of affairs is confusing and economically challenging for Paolo, who relies on his "protectors'" financial support. He has complained about this to the Contessa, who has advised patience and pointed out that the prize is worth the effort.

While sitting in Renato's barber shop that afternoon, Paolo sees Mrs. Stone get out of her car and for a moment is disturbed by the possibility of her entering the shop. Renato remarks that the lady is not one of the shop's patrons, goading Paolo to reveal her name. The revelation causes a stir in the shop, and the attention of Renato, the customers, and the shop attendants is riveted on Mrs. Stone, who is passing outside. Everyone appears to be impressed by her poise, until Paolo makes a bawdy remark that implies that he is her lover. At that moment he determines that he will turn the lie into truth.

Mrs. Stone hears the laughter from the barber's shop and realizes that it is aimed at her. Flustered by this derision, she sets off in the direction opposite from her intended path. The nameless Young Man follows her. The spectacle of the pursuit amuses Renato, but Paolo finds it embarrassingly similar to what he intends and reacts with annoyance.

### *Chapter 5*

Confused by the situation and the bright sunlight, Mrs. Stone drifts along the street aimlessly. She reflects on how this present action resembles the aimlessness of her life in general and her relationship with Paolo in particular. She rummages in her handbag for a pair of sunglasses but cannot find them. Eager for shade, she turns off the main thoroughfare and into a dim side street. She still cannot explain where she is going or what she is doing and eventually pauses in front of the window of a leather goods shop to compose herself. Gazing into the window, she notices the reflection of the Young Man and initially confuses him with Paolo. She does not turn to look at him but hears that he is urinating against the shop window. Mrs. Stone walks away hastily and seeks refuge in a small hotel, troubled by the fact that the Young Man has tried to catch her attention on several occasions.

### *Chapter 6*

This chapter begins by providing a portion of Karen Stone's background history. In the course of three years she has retired from the stage, lost her husband, and begun menopause. This sequence of events initially caused her to cut herself off from old acquaintances and lead a solitary existence in Rome. After two years, she has resumed socializing. The first social contact she initiates is with the Contessa, whom she and her late husband met before the war. Karen maintains this association, although she quickly realizes that the Contessa is, for all intents and purposes, a madam. The Contessa has introduced Mrs. Stone to three boys, none of whom becomes more than a casual companion. All three relationships end when the boys request loans of considerable amounts of money from her. Although Mrs. Stone grants the financial requests, she subsequently breaks off her association with each of them. (The money the young men have obtained from her is divided with the Contessa.) Paolo is the fourth such suitor, and the Contessa is not pleased with his current progress. She suspects that he has become Karen Stone's lover and is cheating her of her share. Paolo assures her that it is only a matter of time and points out that Mrs. Stone, a great lady, requires circumspect handling. Unimpressed with Paolo's excuses, the Contessa accuses him of behaving as a common prostitute does. When Paolo fights back, she literally hits him below the belt.

### *Chapter 7*

The Contessa encounters Mrs. Stone at a luncheon given by a Hollywood producer working in Rome. She uses the occasion to take revenge on Paolo by warning Mrs. Stone against him. She informs Karen that Paolo is a *marchetta*—a male prostitute—and tells her about Signora Coogan, one of Paolo's former clients, who was so disgraced by his refusal to become physically intimate with her that she contracted eczema and fled to Africa. Mrs. Stone finds the story disturbing. The Contessa also informs Karen that Paolo is going to ask her for a large sum of money under the pretext of helping out a dear friend whom a dishonest priest has swindled. Mrs. Stone shrugs off the Contessa's warning and explains that she is too savvy for this ploy.

### *Chapter 8*

Later that afternoon, Mrs. Stone and Paolo are on the terrace of her apartment. Paolo is moody and feigns a headache. He launches into a tale about his friend Fabio, who has been speculating on the black market and has been cheated of 10 million lire by a dishonest priest. Paolo explains that he is troubled because he fears that Fabio will commit suicide. Mrs. Stone, who has barely been listening, points out that it is "usually more than friendship" when such a sum is involved. She also mentions Signora Coogan and, by implication, reveals that she is aware of Paolo's agenda. Leaving him to ponder the situation, she retreats to her bedroom, anxiously listening for whether or not Paolo will join her. She finally acknowledges to herself her desire for Paolo. She believes that sex with Paolo will relieve her restlessness and loss of direction. Karen takes a belladonna tablet, undresses and lies down on her bed. She hears Paolo approach the bedroom door and warns him not to enter because she is naked. Paolo enters the room, sits down on the bed, and asks why she wanted to know when "Fabio" needed the money. Mrs. Stone's reply indicates that she is afraid of running out of time. Paolo consents, and they kiss.

### *Chapter 9*

It is late spring, and Mrs. Stone and Paolo have been romantically involved for some time. The weather is warm enough for her to sunbathe on the terrace in the mornings, shielded by a roofless canvas tent. Occasionally Paolo joins her in the tent, and Mrs. Stone cannot bear to look at him, dreading the comparison between his youthful and her aging body. On one of those occasions they have an argument, sparked by Mrs. Stone's complaint about the clouds and the chilly shadows they cast. Paolo accuses her of thinking that she—as do all the rich Americans—owns Rome. Karen asks Paolo whether he was a fascist. Instead of answering the question, Paolo skirts it by pointing out that he is an aristocrat and, at age 15, was a pilot in the war and commander of a flying club called the Doves. By now familiar with his heroic daydreams, Mrs. Stone does not believe him, but Paolo carries on describing the fate of one of the Doves who was caught streetwalking. He was put on trial by the other Doves and was given the choice of various methods of suicide, of which he chose the leap from a tower. Paolo, engrossed in his story, jumps up to illustrate the action, stumbles, and falls, pulling down the tent with him. Although she knows that Paolo hates being made fun of, Mrs. Stone laughs at him. He counters that she is ridiculous herself, imagining that he loves her. He explains that the only person he has ever loved is his cousin, who was raped by U.S. soldiers and placed in a convent. Mrs. Stone tries to change the topic, asking whether it is true that the swifts stay in the air all the time because they do not have legs. Paolo explains that the birds do not want to mix with American tourists.

He continues to be hostile to her until, later that afternoon when they have gone for cocktails at the Hotel Excelsior, Mrs. Stone proposes a visit to an expensive tailor's shop to buy him some new clothes. Paolo feigns resistance to the idea and tells Karen that he rejected the gift of a car from Signora Coogan. He felt unable to accept it because he did not love her. Mrs. Stone reminds Paolo that earlier he has told her he does not love her either. He claims only to have said that in anger. Mrs. Stone starts to cry, with relief and happiness, although she is secretly unsure of her own feelings.

## *Part 2*

### *Chapter 1*

Karen is unable to determine whether what she occasionally experiences with Paolo is in fact happiness, because she has had nothing comparable in her previous life. A further flashback to her history explains this. Elation is measured by professional success and, beyond that, by the professional failure of colleagues. She is jealous of other actors and not above using her influence to have them fired if they threaten her position. She never has the time to examine herself and her motives because she is completely wrapped up in her career and social life. Her failure as Juliet has been a grave shock, forcing her, for the first time, to admit that age and time are working against her. Her reaction is to announce her retirement from the stage, supposedly on the grounds of her husband's ill health and her need to accompany him to Europe.

Tom Stone has been suffering from attacks of faintness, which they both have disregarded in order to pursue their social schedule. Her husband's illness is only taken seriously when it becomes a convenient excuse for her retirement. When the doctor informs her, a week before their departure for Europe, that Mr. Stone's heart disease is so severe that he would not survive the journey, she is outraged and refuses to face facts, claiming that rest is all her husband needs. However, when they board the *Queen Mary,* Karen has a feeling that death has boarded the ocean liner with them. Mr. Stone shares this feeling, although he will not admit to it. The sense of impending doom drives home her attachment to and dependence on her husband, who has been her only real companion and confidant. Their marriage almost failed in its initial stages because of her sexual coldness and his virtual impotence but was saved by Mr. Stone's breakdown one night, which, in her eyes, turned him into an adult child for her. When, 10 years later, she had a fleeting affair with another actor, Tom forgave her without question, thus turning dependency into codependency. By virtue of being based on a surrogate and interchangeable mother-child relationship, the marriage is lonely, however, and the voyage to Europe unmasks that loneliness. The doctor's predictions were correct, and Tom suffers a heart attack in Paris, which requires him to stay in a clinic for several days. After this, Mr. and Mrs. Stone decide to settle down in Rome for some time, and there his condition improves. During their stay they visit an expensive tailor's shop and have new suits made for Tom.

### Chapter 2

Mrs. Stone now returns to this same tailor with Paolo. The tailor selects a bolt of dove-gray flannel to show to his customers, and Mrs. Stone recalls that her husband had had a suit made from this same material and wore it when he died. Another flashback relates how Mr. Stone was taken ill on the flight to Athens, three hours before landing. Mrs. Stone looks out of her window and spots a small island beneath them. She pleads with the flight attendant and demands that the pilot land on the island. Tom tries to speak to Karen, but she cannot hear him. The flight attendant stands between Mrs. Stone and her husband. He dies during these moments, unheard and unseen by Karen. Mrs. Stone attacks the flight attendant and tries to fight her way to the cockpit. A young man in a gray uniform explains to Karen that the plane is unable to land on the island.

### Chapter 3

Paolo orders a dove-gray flannel suit, a blue tuxedo, and a silk suit. Mrs. Stone watches his childlike excitement for a while and then retreats to a dark, quiet corner of the room to reflect on what has brought her to this point. She believes that there should be some traceable development that has led her from her Virginia girlhood to the stage, marriage, and finally Paolo. She feels that she is slipping into emotional anarchy.

### Chapter 4

Mrs. Stone looks up from her gloves and notices that Paolo and the tailor have moved into another display room. At this moment she spots the Young Man, who has been stalking her, standing outside the shop window and rapping against the pane with a metal object. Although she cannot see his face properly, she recognizes him by his posture. Suddenly he parts his coat and reveals that he is nude underneath. Mrs. Stone immediately rises from her chair and faces some glass cabinets at the back of the room. The rapping stops, and in the reflection of the glass cabinets, she sees the Young Man depart. Then she calls Paolo and the other men in the shop, but when they arrive, she is too ashamed to admit what has happened.

## Part 3

### Chapter 1

This chapter opens with further exploration of Karen Stone's background. Her parents separated when she was 10, and she was sent to a boarding school. A quiet, observant girl, she was bullied there and in reaction became a tomboy. She became champion at a winter game called "King on the Mountain," which involved reaching the top of a steep, iced-over slope and defending the position against all others. In retrospect she realizes that she has played this game throughout her career, not biting and scratching anymore, but manipulating and occasionally backstabbing. Everything she did, every birthday card she sent, and every hospital visit she made was calculated to secure her position and further her career and lacked emotional engagement. She even went as far as pretending not to remember her lines in rehearsal, so that she could study other actors and pinpoint potential threats. However, these mechanisms only worked efficiently as long as her youth and beauty could disguise them.

As she remembers names and faces of people she has mentally filed away as being potentially useful, they strike her as objects lined up on shelves around an empty room. She recognizes this emptiness as an inevitable ingredient of her lifestyle and that of many of her acquaintances. The only reason she has not been sucked into this void is that she has kept constantly busy and on the move. The journey to Europe put an end to the activity, and Mrs. Stone knows that she has begun to slide toward the center of emptiness.

One afternoon late in spring, she realizes that those names and faces are all but forgotten. Getting out of her car on the Via Veneto, she is greeted by a woman whose name and face she does not recall. Finally, Mrs. Stone remembers the woman as a friend of hers and her late husband's. The woman, Julia McIlhenny, is with a Companion, whom Mrs. Stone also does not recall. She is unnerved by this lapse of memory, takes Julia aside, and tells her that she is suffering from cancer. The lie yields a sense of liberation that reminds Mrs. Stone of some of her more successful moments on stage. After this exchange, Karen has her driver take her around the streets of the Villa Borghese, and she understands that she has at last reached the center of the void.

### *Chapter 2*

Because she possessed such remarkable beauty, Karen Stone had always expected to die early. At this point in her life, she has accepted the reality that she will not die early, and she has not made proper provisions for her future. She is feeling restless and her days are occupied mostly with waiting for Paolo.

She attempts to conceal her age by applying makeup, dyeing her hair, and wearing wide-brimmed hats and elaborate designer clothes. One of these is a golden taffeta gown, which she is trying on in her bedroom when Paolo storms in, dressed in the newly completed dove-gray flannel suit. Preoccupied with his own appearance, he takes no notice of her new dress and shoves her aside, so he can admire himself in the mirror. Mrs. Stone starts laughing, and he instantly becomes angry, says that he is not accustomed to wearing such fine clothes, and retreats to the bathroom, where there is another mirror.

Regretting her behavior, Mrs. Stone mixes drinks for them and waits for him on the terrace. When he returns, Paolo ignores the drink and instead stares down at the piazza, where he spots the Young Man. Paolo asks Mrs. Stone about the Young Man and accuses her of making a spectacle of herself. She deflects his accusation by pointing out that people have been staring at him. Paolo claims that the previous week he had to challenge a man to a duel because of a disgusting remark he made about them. When Mrs. Stone shows her disbelief, he tells her that women like her are often found murdered in their bed and cites the case of a middle-aged lady who was killed on the French Riviera. She asks whether he means that he is going to kill her and then tries to smooth over the disagreement by offering him the drink. Still annoyed, he swipes her hand away, and the drink spills down the front of her new gown. Mrs. Stone bursts into tears and flees to the bedroom. Paolo follows her to apologize. They kiss, but before matters can go further, he claims he has to take off his grandmother's locket; Mrs Stone refrains from asking why.

The mood does not improve when they meet some of his friends for cocktails later that evening. Mrs. Stone does not know any of them and feels their laughter is partly directed at her. She does not participate in the conversation. Nor does Paolo, until a girl at the table finally draws him out with persistent flirting. The girl puts a cocktail cherry in his mouth, and Paolo bites her finger, which she leaves in his mouth. Unable to take any more, Mrs. Stone gets up from the table and leaves the bar unnoticed. Trying to compose herself outside, she once more remembers her failure in the role of Juliet, a part for which she was far too old. She hears a metallic tapping sound and notices the persistent Young Man. She confronts him without looking at him and demands he look at her face. The Young Man retreats, murmurs something, walks away, and stops a little farther on, expecting her to follow.

Paolo comes out of the bar. They take Mrs. Stone's car to drive through the Villa Borghese to Alfredo's Restaurant, and she calms somewhat and takes a belladonna tablet. Paolo remains cold but allows her to touch him without reciprocating. At the restaurant they have hardly begun to eat when Paolo breaks his silence to tell her that the Contessa and some friends will be at the apartment shortly. He has invited them to watch some home movies, and he and Mrs. Stone have to leave straightaway to get back in time. She starts to protest, but Paolo gets up from the table, leaving her to pay the bill. On the way to her apartment, Mrs. Stone remembers the undignified fate of the Signora Coogan. She also recalls a recent occasion when she had taken out a collection of newspaper clippings, theater programs, and stage photographs her husband had compiled and set them on the table in the living room, where Paolo would have been bound to notice them. However, the moment the doorbell rang, she returned the collection to the storeroom. A few pictures were dropped and remained on the floor, directly in the path of Paolo, who picked them up and tossed them on the table with barely a glance. The memory affirms her resolution not to lose her dignity.

Paolo brushes a kiss on her cheek, and she clasps his face in both hands and tells him that she is not like Signora Coogan. Unsettled by the outburst, Paolo pretends not to know what she is talking about. Karen claims that she is still sought after in the fashionable world. By way of proof, she offers to show him her collection of theatrical mementos. As soon as the words are out, she realizes that she has lost her dignity. Paolo points out that he has been photographed and painted. He also acknowledges that one of his former American associates, Mrs. Jamison Walker, has also appeared in various fashion magazines.

When they arrive at the apartment, the Contessa, who on the previous day has managed to settle her disagreement with Paolo, is already waiting in the sitting room. With her are three younger women, among them Miss Thompson, a young Hollywood starlet. The Contessa has invited Miss Thompson as bait for Paolo. The Contessa feels she has been driven to this by Mrs. Stone's refusal to lend her $1,000.

While waiting for Mrs. Stone and Paolo to arrive, the Contessa has had some brandy and has become inebriated. She begins gossiping about Karen's scandalous conduct. She does not realize that Mrs. Stone and Paolo have gone to the bedroom immediately after their arrival. Standing silently before separate mirrors, they both freshen up, hearing the conversation in the living room without intending to listen. Eventually, Karen starts paying attention and is shocked at what is being said. Paolo, too, has started to overhear the gossip, and once his consternation wears off, he declares that he does not approve of eavesdropping. He brushes past Karen and enters the living room. He greets the Contessa and her friends. Karen remains standing in the doorway in full view of everyone. The Contessa tries to cover her discomfiture by having another sip of brandy but finds her glass empty. This prompts Karen to enter, arrange for a refill, and greet her guests. Finally she invites the Contessa to continue her story.

The Contessa remarks that she was only telling the others about "the Signora Coogan's spectacular season at Capri," and Paolo uses this as an opportunity to ask Miss Thompson to accompany him to the terrace. Mrs. Stone stays behind with the other ladies. After her butler has set up the movie projector and screen (for the gathered assembly to watch some home movies of Paolo and Karen), she goes outside to the terrace to fetch him and Miss Thompson. Karen finds Paolo on the terrace alone. When asked where the young actress has gone, Paolo replies that he advised her to leave. The couple fall into a violent argument. Paolo accuses Karen of denying him the 10 million lire she promised to give him for his friend Fabio. As a final blow, Paolo makes Karen admit her age. Their argument continues as they return to the living room, producing an ugly public scene, which is prolonged by the Contessa's alcohol-induced inability to rise from her seat.

### *Chapter 3*

Mrs. Stone is alone in her apartment. She wanders aimlessly through the rooms and eventually goes out onto the terrace. She notices that the Young Man is still standing on the piazza, her attention attracted by the observation that he is not moving while everything else, her included, seems to be drifting. Returning to the living room, she retrieves a letter, a call card, and a photograph from under the clock on the mantel. The photograph and letter are from an old friend of hers; the call card contains the name and address of a plastic surgeon who has created the masklike face on the photograph. The striking of the clock on the mantel recalls the passing of time, and she continues to wander through the apartment, attempting to escape from the nothingness Paolo has left behind. At last she returns to the terrace and signals to the Young Man. Then she wraps the keys to the apartment into the handkerchief and tosses them down to him. He picks them up, nods, and disappears toward the front door. Mrs. Stone knows that something will shortly fill the nothingness that surrounds her.

## COMMENTARY

When *The Roman Spring of Mrs. Stone,* Williams's first novel, was published in 1950, it was met with a barrage of negative criticism. A large portion of its critical rejection was due to the level of prudery endemic in a decade that glorified middle-class values. Representative of many reviewers, the *New York Times* critic Orville Prescott complained that the novel was nothing but "an erotic and depressing study of the crack-up of a brittle and shallow character. The subject is distasteful; its atmosphere is drenched from beginning to end in sexual decadence" (Prescott, 25). However, this reaction is not confined exclusively to contemporary voices of that era. Even current discussions of the novel, which claim to address openly previously ignored issues such as gender and sexuality, seem to shy away from certain topics, such as the failed romantic relationship between Karen Stone and Meg Bishop. Prudery, however, cannot account for all unfavorable reactions to the work; nor can it explain the lack of serious attention accorded to the novel by literary critics. Part of the difficulty Williams faced was a recurring reluctance by critics to accept any literary experimentation or departure from his previous literary standard and form. (This critical view dogged much of Williams's dramatic work and plagued him greatly toward the end of his career.)

*The Roman Spring of Mrs. Stone* was chiefly an experiment for Williams. He was not enamored of the form. For him, novels seemed "purely esthetic, not *living* as plays are," but he conceded that "the temptation to wallow in words may some day compel [him] to write one" (Leverich, 313). When he finally did so, his need to infuse the "esthetic" with the "living" induced him to create a work that, formally, occupies something of an obscure area. On the surface the plot is unassuming, a very simple and straightforward tale of a woman in her 50s who makes a belated—and disastrous—bid at passion. However, this is coupled with considerable structural and narrative complexity.

Divided into three books (or acts), "Cold Sun," "Island, Island!," and "The Drift"—each title illustrative of a particular stage in the heroine's journey, each book subdivided into several chapters (or scenes)—*The Roman Spring of Mrs. Stone* is a novel that shows the structural dynamics of a three-act play. Conversely, it abounds with literary devices—such as flashbacks, sudden shifts in the narrative point of view, and extensive descriptive passages and interior monologues—that are typical of the novel form. The couching of character development in travel, physical, mental, and emotional, places *The Roman Spring of Mrs. Stone* in the vicinity of the picaresque novel. The chronological sequence of events is frequently broken up, reflecting the bewildering mirror cabinet of experiences to which the heroine finds herself subjected. Needless to say, none of this contributes to making the work easily accessible. In fact, its complexity, coupled with sometimes clichéd but extremely complex imagery, conceals much of the psychological and metaphoric depth, thus fostering a critical tendency to fasten on the obvious, as in the comment "Mrs. Stone is followed around by an exhibitionist with a penchant for urinating on walls" (Johns, 333) and to neglect the novel's meaning.

DONALD WINDHAM described the work as Williams's "first fictionalized self-portrait after his success," which "displays a hair-raising degree of self-knowledge" (Spoto, 167). Born of that self-knowledge, Mrs. Stone is the incarnation of her creator's "enduring reservation and hope that beyond promiscuity there must be something or someone beyond shame whom he could love unreservedly" (Leverich, 371). Or, as Williams himself stated, "I shall have to go through the world giving myself to people until somebody will take me" (Leverich, 366).

The quest for love is the central theme of the novel. Of course the quest for love through promiscuity is destined to fail, and Karen Stone, singularly ill equipped to identify love even if she can find it, becomes a case in point. Not through talent but through political maneuvering and relentless ambition, she has carved out for herself a stellar acting career that ends dismally with her failure in the role of Juliet. Without doubt, Juliet—epitome of true love—is everything Karen Stone is not, and Karen Stone, by her own admission, is too mediocre a talent to compensate for her personal deficiencies.

Meg Bishop observes that it was also an obvious mistake for Karen "to play Juliet at the age of Mrs. Alving." The comparison with Mrs. Alving is telling aside from its inference of middle age. The tragic flaw of Mrs. Alving (a principal character in Henrik Ibsen's play *Ghosts*) lies in her inability to place personal happiness above her need to be approved by society and in the web of lies she sustains to safeguard that approval. Similarly, Karen Stone admits that she has represented "Various parts! But never ever myself!" Since girlhood, when she transformed herself from a little Southern princess into a tomboy to become "King on the Mountain"—the winner in a violent game—and throughout her professional career, Karen Stone has made choices designed to court adulation and success, to the exclusion of everything else. Significantly, this exclusion includes children. Karen perceives fertility as a threat in herself and in others; this is illustrated most dramatically when she attacks the flight attendant, who is trying to assist the dying Mr. Stone. Mrs. Stone physically assaults precisely those parts of the young woman's body that manifest fertility: her breasts and belly. Determined not to bear children, Karen Stone has "married in order to avoid copulation." Her husband, the millionaire Tom Stone, "a plump little man that looked like an Easter bunny," admired Karen from afar for a great deal of time. These traits marked him as a suitable groom. Conveniently for Karen, he also is impotent, and his disability saves their marriage by allowing "them both to discover what they both really wanted, she an adult child and he a living and young and adorable mother."

The Stones' relationship evolves into companionship, close and fond, but passionless. The libido, however, does not remain suppressed, as Karen Stone discovers when she engages in a one-night dressing room affair. For this occasion, too, Williams has cast her in a theatrical role that illustrates the events. At the time of her affair, Karen was portraying Rosalind (*As You Like It*), one of Shakespeare's best-known gender-switching heroines. Appropriately, Karen adopts a stereotypically male role in her tryst with the young actor playing Orlando: She initiates aggressive sex with him, rejects him, and ultimately humiliates him personally and professionally. It all contributes not so much to a sense of blurred gender divides, but to the image of a woman who—for the sake of pursuing her ambition with the hunting instincts of a raptor—assumes more businesslike rigidity (or masculinity, in the eyes of her contemporaries) than even the strident Meg Bishop, memorably described as "the burly commander of a gunboat . . . presented . . . in the disguise of a wealthy clubwoman."

At the point of attack of the novel, all this has changed. Karen Stone has left the acting profession, lost her husband, and begun menopause. Once the initial grief has worn off, these events are perceived as liberating: She no longer has "to bother with pretension and effort of any kind," she is her own agent, the dread of fertility is withdrawn, and what is left is "desire without the old, implicit distraction of danger." This liberation may well have been nursed by the sultry atmosphere of a Rome that Williams imbues with all the languid sensuality Karen Stone has been lacking for most of her life. Roma Aeterna, in Williams's terms, becomes the eternal woman: "Domes of ancient churches, swelling above the angular roofs like the breasts of recumbent giant women." Rome's buoyancy and youthfulness are dangerously seductive, and, after two years of mourning in seclusion for career, husband, and youth, Karen Stone is ready at last to encounter a passion not readily available to her. What also has become evident, however, is a sense of aimlessness and emptiness—an absence of identity—that she calls "the drift" and from which she desperately tries to escape.

Passion—and with it escape—appears in the guise of the Conte Paolo Di Leo, the fourth in a series of gigolos the Contessa, "stately witch" and purveyor of "epicene dandies," parades past Karen Stone. He is the male counterpart to Rome itself: languid, attractive, predatory, and sensuous. That the indiscriminate center of his being is his groin is fortuitous, as it allows him to service an array of wealthy tourists profitably and, for his personal pleasure, to enjoy "the ministrations of the long, cool fingers" of his friend and barber Renato. Although she knows what Paolo is—a *rondino,* a swift, who will fly perpetually and never land with her—Karen Stone feels increasingly attracted to him, and this is a clear indicator of the magnitude of the change she has undergone. In her previous life, everything she did "was directed by the head as distinguished from the heart." Now, and in reaction to decades of emotional drought, she is slipping into what she calls "emotional anarchy," but for a while it remains tempered by an intellect that will not allow her to fool herself completely. "Americans aren't as romantic as their motion pictures," she says when the Contessa vengefully informs her of Paolo's profession and agenda.

But rationality and the determination to hold on to her dignity only last long enough for Karen Stone to denounce Paolo's subterfuge of the friend in desperate need of 10 million lire. She denies his request for money and retreats to her bedroom, listening for Paolo, hoping against reason that he will stay. While she is waiting, she takes a tablet of belladonna—a natural herbal sedative also known as "nightshade." The choice of this drug is deliberate and has a twofold significance. First, the herb derives its name from the Italian *bella donna* (beautiful woman) because, according to superstition, nightshade sometimes takes the shape of an enchantress of supreme beauty. Second, the active component in belladonna—atropine—has the effect of dilating the pupils, thereby impairing the eyes' ability to focus and see clearly. Karen's regular use of this potentially lethal relaxant signals a blurring of her inhibitions and a conscious denial of the facts of age and fading beauty and desirability—of missed opportunity. She does not want to see what she knows to be the truth, and as she looks at herself, "Her face in the mirror . . . [becomes] continually more indistinct and lovely," distorted by the magic of belladonna. Lying naked on her bed, she finally hears Paolo approach, and her warning "Don't come inside, I'm not dressed" is not a warning as much as it is a poorly disguised invitation. Paolo accepts, too experienced not to realize that payment has merely been deferred.

This peculiar dialectic of acuity of vision and self-deceit, rationality and need, permeates the entire novel, its characters, and its locale. The metaphorical voluptuous woman Rome serves as a giant mirror for Karen Stone. Highly polished windows and an abundance of water throw back bright sunlight, and they throw back unsettling truths. Karen Stone shuns brightness as she shuns her true mirror image, terrified one day to discover the face of the Signora Coogan, "a wretched old fool of a woman with five hairs and two teeth in her head and nothing but money to give [Paolo]." Selective blindness becomes an obsession, inducing her to sunbathe in a tent and to hide behind makeup, wide-brimmed hats, and designer clothes. However, the signs are there, not only in Paolo's sullenness and hostility. When she tries to rekindle his affections by buying him new clothes, he chooses to have a suit made of dove-gray flannel: The same suit and the same material that Mr. Stone was wearing when he died. The color gray is associated inextricably with death. In this context, death is equated with the end of a relationship. Paolo wears this suit on the evening when he calls in Karen's outstanding debt (the money for Fabio) and drops her for Miss Thompson, a young Hollywood star. The confrontation, a painfully ugly scene, precipitated by the Contessa, finally holds up an inescapable mirror that is beyond even the powers of belladonna to mitigate: "Rome is three thousand years old, and how old are you? Fifty?"

It is at this point that reality and distorted images merge at last. Alone in her apartment after Paolo, the Contessa, and their entourage have deserted her, Karen Stone turns to the one reflection that has remained curiously constant throughout: the nameless Young Man who has been stalking her. Repeatedly glimpsed in or through shop windows, ever-present on the piazza, beside the unsubtly phallic obelisk, he has been watching her every step, his posture suggesting that he is "continually upon the verge of raising his voice or arm in some kind of urgent call or salutation." He is the coarse Romeo who urinates under a deficient Juliet's balcony instead of climbing it, as a dog marks his territory, staking his claim. There is a strange complementarity between the handsome, impoverished stranger and Karen Stone. Watchful and tense as she is, he seems to be the "token, however cryptic, some inconspicuous signpost" that she is looking for and that will explain how she has ended up in her predicament. He has his own agenda: His body is for sale, but unlike Paolo, he is discriminate, and in his philosophy he resembles Karen Stone (and Mrs. Alving): "When a man [or a woman] has an appointment with grandeur, he [or she] dares not stoop for comfort." Her one "solid" and immediate encounter with him indicates that she at least suspects the kinship. She challenges him to look at her face, without looking at him: "Why do you follow me, can't you see my face?" It almost appears she cannot even glance at him without seeing herself, and at the same time she tries to point out the consequences of following in her footsteps.

Desolate and restless after the scene with Paolo, Karen summons him to her bed—to stop "the drift." The invitation is mechanical and all but involuntary, a subconscious admission that this will not be the human contact she wants. Watching this enigmatic Romeo, whom she has referred to as "it" throughout the novel, pick up the keys and make his way to the balcony, she is relieved that "the awful vacancy would be entered by something." What exactly the something is remains unclear: the fleeting purchase of passion or perhaps, if Paolo's vicious cautionary tale of the murdered middle-aged woman is to be believed, death. At best it will be a collision of two voids, and with this the quest for love has hopelessly foundered.

## PUBLICATION HISTORY

*The Roman Spring of Mrs. Stone* was first published by New Directions in 1950.

## PRODUCTION HISTORY

*The Roman Spring of Mrs. Stone* was first adapted for film in 1961. Jose Quintero directed the film, which featured VIVIEN LEIGH as Karen Stone and Warren Beatty as Paolo. Both Leigh's and Beatty's performances in the film were highly commended, although the film overall received "a barrage of obtusely unfair reviews" (Quirk, 181). Beatty's portrayal of Paolo is considered by many to be his best work on film. Equally, critics found Mrs. Stone one of Vivien Leigh's finest performances.

*The Roman Spring of Mrs. Stone* was most recently adapted for film in 2003. Robert Allan Ackerman directed this version for the U.S. cable television network Showtime. The renowned British actress Helen Mirren assayed the role of Karen Stone. The most notable alteration in Ackerman's version was the inventive addition of a character called "Christopher," a gregarious Southern playwright-socialite who is clearly a fictional treatment of the novel's creator.

## CHARACTERS

**Bishop, Meg** Meg Bishop is an American journalist and old college friend of Karen Stone's. Karen and Meg's friendship was strained after the two had an awkward romantic encounter in college. Meg has been following Karen's career and life over the years. The two women meet accidentally in Rome, many years later, and Karen invites Meg to her apartment. During her visit Meg questions Karen about the rumors she has heard regarding Karen's recent liaisons with various young Italian men.

Meg Bishop, the savvy and strident American journalist living abroad, is reminiscent of the renowned American journalist and essayist Janet Flanner. Internationally known by her pen name Genet, Flanner described her experiences living in Europe with U.S. readers in her column "Letter from Paris" in the *New Yorker* magazine. Williams met Flanner and her partner, Solita Salerno, in Rome in 1945.

**Companion** He is a male friend of Julia McIlhenny's. The Companion was also a former financial backer of Karen Stone's theatrical productions.

**Contessa** The Contessa is an impoverished Italian countess living in Rome. She survives and earns her living by supplying *marchetta*—young Italian male prostitutes—to wealthy tourists. She had met

Karen and Tom Stone before World War II and their association has continued since. After Tom's death, the Contessa comforts Karen by introducing her to a variety of attractive young Italian men. Her most successful *marchetta* is Conte Paolo di Leo. The Contessa introduces Paolo to Mrs. Stone and encourages their relationship.

**Di Leo, Conte Paolo** An impoverished Italian aristocrat, Paolo is one of the Contessa's best and most dashing *marchettas* (attractive young Italian men who make themselves sexually available to wealthy tourists). At the prompting of the Contessa, Paolo becomes Karen Stone's lover. His relationship with Karen is completely mercenary, and Mrs. Stone proves to be a willing victim. True to form, he drops Mrs. Stone for Miss Thompson, an up-and-coming Hollywood starlet, who appears to be a better financial prospect.

**McIlhenny, Julia** One of Karen Stone's former friends. Julia, along with her Companion, encounters Karen in Rome late one spring afternoon. Karen is so embarrassed that she cannot recall Julia's or the Companion's name that she panics and lies to Julia, telling her that she has cancer.

**Renato** Renato is an Italian barber in Rome. He savors the exploits of his favorite regular customer, Comte Paolo Di Leo, a handsome Italian gigolo. Renato is Paolo's confidant and admirer. There is a homoerotic undercurrent to their attachment.

**Stone, Karen** Mrs. Stone is a retired actress in her 50s, who settles in Rome after the death of her husband, Tom Stone. Wealthy and vulnerable, she is singled out as a potential victim by the Contessa, who introduces her to a series of *marchetta* (attractive young Italian men who make themselves available to wealthy tourists). Because her husband had a heart condition, the Stones' marriage was sexually unfulfilling for Karen. Freed by Tom's death, she explores her suppressed sexuality with younger men in Rome. She enjoys the passion she discovers with Conte Paolo Di Leo and falls in love with him. Paolo enters into a relationship with Karen for entirely mercenary reasons. Karen takes care of him financially and socially. She takes him to the most expensive tailor in Rome and purchases elegant clothing for him. His true motives surface when he pleads with Karen to give him 10 million lire for a friend of his who has been swindled by a corrupt priest. Paolo eventually ends their relationship and abandons Karen in favor of Miss Thompson, an up-and-coming Hollywood starlet. Miss Thompson, who represents everything that Karen is not (a young, glamorous, wealthy film star), is a much more lucrative prospect for Paolo.

Karen Stone is a kindred spirit of Sabbatha Veyne Duff-Collick, the aging poetess-protagonist of the short story "SABBATHA AND SOLITUDE." Sabbatha and Karen share a love of Rome and the Italian landscape, but more importantly they both try to ease their fading beauty, celebrity, and social standing in the arms of dashing young Italian men. Although both women suffer from the infidelity and cruelty of their lovers, Sabbatha's "kept man," Giovanni, returns to her, repents, and remains; Karen is completely abandoned by Paolo. Reminiscent of Blanche DuBois in *A STREETCAR NAMED DESIRE,* Karen Stone is haunted by the specter of old age and death and wishes to live in the illusion of her former youth, beauty, and glory. Karen and Blanche both dislike being viewed in direct harsh lighting, The two characters also share the same cruel fate of trusting the hoped-for kindness of strangers.

**Stone, Tom** A former millionaire wax paper manufacturer, he is the deceased husband of Karen Stone. Before they married, Tom was a longtime admirer of Karen's work as a theater actress. Suffering from chronic heart disease, he died on the European journey they took together after her retirement from the stage.

**Thompson, Miss** She is a glamorous up-and-coming Hollywood starlet. Miss Thompson is "between marriages" and visiting Rome alone. She encounters the Contessa, who takes her to Karen Stone's apartment and introduces her to Conte Paolo Di Leo. Miss Thompson becomes Paolo's next victim. Miss Thompson represents everything that Karen Stone no longer has, is, or can be. She is young and vivacious; Karen no longer is. She is a popular performer; Karen is a retired performer. Miss Thompson also represents the future, as she is a film starlet, performing in a dazzling new medium, whereas Karen acted only on the stage.

**Young Man** Nameless and mute, this poor and homeless Young Man spends his days watching and following Karen Stone. He stalks her through the streets of Rome for reasons that are implied but never completely explained. After her lover, Conte Paolo Di Leo, leaves her for Miss Thompson, a younger, wealthier woman, Karen invites the Young Man into her apartment to become her new lover.

### FURTHER READING

Fisher, James. "An Almost Posthumous Existence: Performance, Gender and Sexuality in *The Roman Spring of Mrs. Stone,*" *Southern Quarterly* 38, no. 1 (fall 1999): 46–51.

Leverich, Lyle. *Tom: The Unknown Tennessee Williams.* New York: W. W. Norton, 1995.

Quirk, Lawrence J. *The Great Romantic Films.* Secaucus, N.J.: Citadel Press, 1974.

Spoto, Donald. *The Kindness of Strangers: The Life of Tennessee Williams.* Boston: Little, Brown, 1985.

# *The Rose Tattoo*

A play in three acts written in 1950.

### SYNOPSIS

The action of the play takes place in the Italian community of a small Gulf Coast town. The setting is the home of Rosario and Serafina Delle Rose. As Serafina is a seamstress, the set includes mannequins, fabric, and various types of sewing equipment.

#### *Act 1, Scene 1*

The play begins at *prima sera,* or the beginning of dusk. With a rose in her hair, Serafina Delle Rose patiently awaits the arrival of her beloved husband, Rosario, a truck driver. Assunta, a *fattuchiere,* or herbal medicine doctor, visits Serafina to sell her potions. Serafina confirms Assunta's premonition that she is pregnant with her second child. She knew the night she became pregnant, as a rose tattoo identical to that of her husband appeared on her breast. Assunta teases Serafina about being so proud of her husband, a Sicilian baron turned fruit truck driver. Serafina defends her husband, explaining that he hauls more important things for the Romano Brothers. Serafina daydreams about her husband's rose-oiled hair, whose scent permeates their bedroom at night, and rejoices in her pregnancy.

Estelle Hohengarten visits the Delle Rose home. As she waits in the parlor, she rummages about the room until she discovers a photograph of Rosario. Serafina informs her that the man in the photo is her husband. Estelle commissions Serafina to make a rose-colored silk shirt for her lover. Serafina is amused that the fabric is so effeminate, but Estelle clarifies that her man is "wild like a gypsy." There is a commotion as the Strega's (witch's) black goat is loose in the neighborhood. Serafina's daughter, Rosa, yells for her, and Serafina runs out and directs the chase. Left alone in the house, Estelle steals the photo of Rosario. The goat is captured, and a boy leads it out of the yard.

#### *Act 1, Scene 2*

It is just before dawn the next day; Serafina is worried sick because Rosario has not returned home. Father De Leo and several women stand outside her house. She hears them murmuring and realizes that Rosario is dead. Serafina stands motionless and facing the crowd through a window. She gasps for air, stumbling amid her sewing mannequins. She yells, "Don't speak!" as Assunta enters the house, catches her as she falls to the floor, and wraps her in her gray shawl.

#### *Act 1, Scene 3*

The doctor and Father De Leo argue about Serafina's plans to have Rosario's body cremated. Serafina has miscarried her baby. Estelle Hohengarten enters the house bearing flowers. The neighborhood women recognize her as Rosario's mistress and force her to leave.

#### *Act 1, Scene 4*

Three years have passed, and it is the day of high school graduation. The neighborhood women convene in Serafina's yard, angrily demanding the graduation dresses she was commissioned to make. One woman begins to gossip about Rosa's sailor boyfriend, Jack Hunter. Serafina has forbidden Rosa to see him, and to ensure that, she has locked up all of Rosa's clothes. Because Rosa cannot leave her house, she missed her high school exit examinations.

Serafina stumbles out onto the porch wearing a dirty pink slip. She yells for help and rushes back into the house. Miss Yorke, a high school teacher, notices the chaos. Serafina screams that Rosa has cut her wrists. Miss Yorke runs into the house to discover a naked Rosa with a tiny, insignificant cut on her wrist. Miss Yorke persuades Serafina to unlock Rosa's closet. Serafina blames Miss Yorke for allowing sailors to attend school dances. Miss Yorke says she knows Jack and believes he is a respectable young man. Rosa dresses for graduation, and she leaves with Miss Yorke for the commencement exercises. Serafina follows them, shouting at Miss Yorke. The neighborhood women irately surround Serafina. Assunta enters and begs her to give them the dresses. Serafina finally accedes.

### *Act 1, Scene 5*

Serafina hastily dresses for Rosa's graduation because she can hear the band playing in the distance. Flora and Bessie enter to collect an order. Flora spies the unfinished blouse on the sewing machine and demands Serafina finish it immediately. She threatens to report Serafina to the Chamber of Commerce if she does not comply. Serafina tells Flora and Bessie that if she is late for Rosa's graduation, they will regret it. Flora whispers that Serafina used to be pretty, but she now has big hips.

Maliciously, Flora tells Serafina about Rosario's mistress. Serafina is stunned by this information. Flora divulges intimate details about Rosario and Estelle's relationship, explaining that Estelle has the same rose tattoo as Rosario. Bessie knows Serafina can be dangerously violent so she pleads with Flora to leave. Serafina grabs a broom and chases them out of her house. Serafina bolts the front door, fastens the shutters, and paces around the room like a wild animal. She realizes she was commissioned to make a rose silk shirt for her own husband as a gift from his lover. Serafina grieves and desperately begs for a sign from the Virgin Mary.

### *Act 1, Scene 6*

Two hours later, Serafina's house is dark except for the candle glowing on her shrine to the Virgin Mary. Rosa returns home from graduation, excited to introduce Jack to her mother. When they enter the dark house, they find Serafina in a catatonic state. Emerging from her delirium, Serafina interrogates Jack. She questions his motives regarding Rosa and makes him kneel in front of the shrine of the Virgin Mary. She forces him to vow to preserve Rosa's innocence.

### *Act 2, Scene 1*

Two hours later, Serafina drinks to ease her heartache. Father De Leo pays a visit and scolds Serafina for her wild behavior and appearance. The priest's presence has created a stir in the neighborhood, and two women stand near the house to eavesdrop. When she sees them, Serafina quickly stands, ready to fight them. Father De Leo reminds her that she has no friends because she is so hostile. She is stubbornly indifferent to his opinions. Father De Leo asks her to become respectable for Rosa's sake.

Serafina asks Father De Leo whether her husband ever confessed to having a mistress, and he remains silent. She grabs his arm and refuses to let go until he answers. Serafina threatens to smash Rosario's urn if he does not tell her the truth. The neighborhood women rescue Father De Leo, who quickly exits.

Serafina collapses on the porch steps, crying and rocking, begging for a sign from the Virgin Mary. A fat and sweaty Salesman enters, followed by Alvaro Mangiacavallo, a handsome truck driver. The men fight outside Serafina's house. The Salesman threatens to report Alvaro to his boss at the fruit company. Serafina notices Alvaro's jacket is ripped, and she insists on mending it. All at once, she is struck by Alvaro's resemblance to Rosario. The two converse about family and the old country while they drink wine to ease their awkwardness. Serafina tells him about the rose tattoo on her husband's chest and mentions the lies that are circulating about her late husband.

Alvaro calls his boss at the Southern Fruit Company. He learns that the Salesman did report him, and he has been fired. Serafina instructs Alvaro to put on the rose-colored silk shirt while she mends his own shirt. Serafina apologizes for her appearance and tells Alvaro she has had a bad day. Alvaro asks when he may return the shirt.

### *Act 3, Scene 1*

Later in the evening, Serafina waits for Alvaro. She is beautifully dressed and has a rose in her hair. Alvaro admires her. She immediately notices that he is wearing rose oil in his curly black hair. Alvaro reveals his new rose tattoo on his chest.

Serafina asks Alvaro to take her to see Estelle. He refuses but agrees to call her. Estelle confirms her affair with Rosario. Serafina throws the urn of Rosario's ashes across the room. She invites Alvaro to spend the night with her.

### *Act 3, Scene 2*

Just before sunrise, Rosa returns home with Jack. They overhear Serafina moaning from inside the house. Jack is startled by the sounds, but Rosa explains that it is just her mother's dreaming about making love to her father. Jack expresses guilt for breaking his promise to the Virgin Mary and Serafina. Rosa suggests that she and Jack marry.

### *Act 3, Scene 3*

Three hours later, Rosa is asleep on the couch. Alvaro stumbles from the bedroom and leaps onto Rosa. She screams, jumping to her feet and knocking him to the floor. Serafina rushes in, grabs a broom, and beats Alvaro. He explains that he was dreaming and mistook Rosa for Serafina. Serafina treats Alvaro as an intruder. Rosa mocks her flimsy denial, calling her a liar and hypocrite. Serafina bends under these accusations and urges her daughter to go to Jack. Rosa excitedly gathers her belongings and leaves for New Orleans.

Assunta enters, and Serafina says Rosario's ashes have been swept away by the wind. Alvaro's voice is heard outside as he has returned to her. Serafina finds the rose-colored silk shirt and runs out to meet him. She feels another burning rose on her breast.

## COMMENTARY

*The Rose Tattoo* is saturated with religious mores and superstitious overtones. Serafina prays and begs for signs from the Holy Virgin, and she believes that on the night she conceived she felt a rose tattoo form on her left breast. This stigma is the same rose as Rosario's tattoo. The burning sensation of the tattoo awakened her and made her realize she was blessed. The Strega, or witch, is another character who evokes religious and superstitious symbols. Serafina responds to her by gesturing devil's horns and forces her out of her yard because she is a bearer of bad omens. Assunta, Serafina's friend, dabbles in love potions and aphrodisiacs and can prophesy the future. When Serafina learns of her husband's infidelity, she attacks her religion, blaming the Madonna for ignoring her and forcing her to wait so long for a sign. Serafina rejects her connection with the Virgin Mary and casts off her obligations as a mourning widow when she takes Alvaro into her bed. Serafina has been miserable without sexual fulfillment. When she is finally able to release herself from her duties as widow, she becomes closer to being whole.

Symbolism also abounds in *The Rose Tattoo.* The rose is used repeatedly to express love, desire, and perfection. Serafina wears a rose in her hair and Rosario, her mate, has a rose tattoo on his breast. Serafina creates a rose-colored silk shirt for Rosario. Alvaro has a rose tattooed on his chest, hoping that Serafina will perceive it as the sign for which she has been waiting. The rose becomes a signifier of passion and female sexuality. Images of fire and heat permeate the play: The scorching summer heat forces blood to boil, and the women of the town argue and fight with Serafina. The nights are long and exhausting because of the heat. Desire and dreams overtake Serafina as she remembers making love to Rosario. Sensual red candlelight flickers on the shrine of the Madonna, and in this instance, love and religion combine as Serafina searches for a sign. She desperately prays for someone to love or for something to end her depression. The Strega's goat appears in the play as a symbol of lust. Its appearance flags the desires and sexual energy of the protagonist. Alice Griffin sees a direct link between *The Rose Tattoo* and FEDERICO GARCÍA LORCA's play *Yerma.* Serafina's all-consuming love for her husband and the barrenness after his death resemble the isolation and existential tone of *Yerma. The Rose Tattoo* also possesses echoes of the influences of D. H. Lawrence, who appears as a character in *I RISE IN FLAME, CRIED THE PHOENIX*. The power of passion and sex prevails in

Serafina's life. Without sexual release, Serafina behaves irrationally. She talks incessantly about the times she made love with Rosario.

This play is considered Williams's most positive creation, and in *Memoirs,* Williams calls it his "love-play to the world." While writing *The Rose Tattoo,* Williams was at the happiest point in his life. He had begun his long-term relationship with his partner, FRANK MERLO, who was Sicilian. In *The Rose Tattoo* Williams celebrates Sicilian culture, and with remarkable ease the play flows in and out of English and Italian. Set in the South, somewhere between New Orleans and Montgomery, Alabama, the play focuses on a small hamlet inhabited by Sicilian immigrants. This community has a strong need to maintain their Sicilian identity within the setting of the American South. *The Rose Tattoo* is a tribute to Frank Merlo's culture, and Williams dedicated it to his lover.

Anna Magnani, who starred as Serafina Delle Rose in the film version of *The Rose Tattoo,* 1955 *(Don Pinder)*

## PRODUCTION HISTORY

*The Rose Tattoo* opened at the Erlanger Theatre in Chicago in 1950, and at the Martin Beck Theatre in New York City the following year. Williams was well known as a playwright of dark and serious drama, famous for *THE GLASS MENAGERIE* (1944–45), *A STREETCAR NAMED DESIRE* (1947), and *SUMMER AND SMOKE* (1948). Audiences were not prepared for the positive, lighter side of Williams. Hence, the productions received mixed reviews. Serafina Delle Rose seems to have been a far too complex character for audiences to appreciate in the moral and cultural context of American society of the 1950s. Some considered her emotion exaggerated and compared her neurotic behavior with that of previous Williams women such as Maggie the Cat Pollitt and Amanda Wingfield. Some critics, for example, Brooks Atkinson, were delighted to see Williams shift in tone and break out of his "formula" (Atkinson, 19). Williams received the Antoinette Perry (Tony) Award for best play for *The Rose Tattoo.*

It was public knowledge Williams intended that the famous Italian actress ANNA MAGNANI play the role of Serafina Delle Rose; however, MAUREEN STAPLETON played the role in the Broadway production. Knowing she was not the first choice, critics often judged Stapleton's performance by the one Magnani might have given had she played the part. Regardless of the critical comparisons, Stapleton won a Tony for her performance as Serafina. Anna Magnani fulfilled Williams's wish by playing Serafina in the film version (1955). Her performance was also an award-winning one, garnering an Academy Award (Oscar). The film as a whole, however, received mixed reviews. The sexuality in the play was scaled down and heavily censored. Significant changes were made in the plot and dialogue to make the story line adhere more closely to conventional morality. When the film version ends, Serafina is not pregnant with Alvaro's child. The film does not suggest that Serafina and Alvaro ever consummate their relationship. Such extensive revision drastically changed the dramatic tone of the play and substantially diminished Serafina's extreme change of heart, her reversal of fortune and rejuvenation.

## PUBLICATION HISTORY

*The Rose Tattoo* was first published by New Directions in 1951.

## CHARACTERS

**Assunta** Assunta is the friend of Serafina Delle Rose. She is a *fattuchiere* (an herbal medicine doctor), who peddles her remedies and potions around the neighborhood. She is the solitary voice of reason in the play. Assunta has maternal affection for Serafina and maintains respect for her, despite her contemptuous behavior. Assunta is also a highly superstitious woman and retains a strong sense of cosmic culture. Her spirituality is based on nature, signs, and miracles. She accurately predicts that Serafina will wear a black veil. However, Assunta is a calming force in Serafina's life, and she enters the play in moments of despair to comfort and pull Serafina back from the brink of insanity.

**Bessie** Bessie is a young woman who goes to the home of Serafina Delle Rose with her friend, Flora. Serafina has been commissioned to make a blouse for Flora. Bessie and Flora are on their way to a party in New Orleans when they stop by to collect the blouse. Bessie enrages Serafina by being disrespectful in the presence of Serafina's late husband's ashes. As a result, Serafina chases Bessie and Flora out of her house with a broom, but the young women have their revenge when they publicly humiliate her by announcing that her late husband, Rosario Delle Rose, had a mistress, Estelle Hohengarten.

**De Leo, Father** Father De Leo is an aging Roman Catholic priest serving an Italian community in a small Gulf Coast town. He is growing weary of one of his particularly needy parishioners, Serafina Delle Rose. He is meek and tries to be the voice of reason and comfort for Serafina, but he is intimidated by her energy, womanliness, and passion. Father De Leo visits Serafina and her daughter, Rosa, from time to time, solely out of duty. He finds Serafina foul, sinful, and indulgent in her excessive grief. He considers her to be a bad Catholic because she never attends confession. He reaches out to her when she calls for him, but he is overwhelmed by her misery and stubbornness.

**Delle Rose, Rosa** Rosa is the teenage daughter of Rosario and Serafina Delle Rose. She is determined to escape her mother's madness and the oppressive memory of her deceased father. Rosa is very intelligent and is a good student, although she has had to fight her mother to attend high school. Rosa has been her mother's caretaker since her father's death, but the task has become overwhelming and too difficult for her to continue. She is enraged by her mother's selfish decision to remain in mourning for three years. Serafina is unpredictable and willful and her decisions are rash and inflexible. Rosa has suffered the consequences of her mother's extreme behavior and her anxieties about living without Rosario. She is often reminded she is like her father when she behaves passionately. Ironically, Serafina never sees herself as responsible for this particular character trait. Rosa searches for a way out of her mother's house and finds it at age 15 when she meets a sailor, Jack Hunter, at a high school dance. Contrary to her mother's commands, Rosa falls in love with Jack and secretly dates him. In the end, she runs away to New Orleans to be with him.

**Delle Rose, Rosario** He is a Sicilian immigrant who lives somewhere on the Gulf Coast between New Orleans, Louisiana, and Mobile, Alabama, with his wife, Serafina Delle Rose, and daughter, Rosa Delle Rose. To earn his living, he hauls illegal goods for the Mafia disguised as truckloads of bananas. Driving goods for the Mafia proves a deadly game and Rosario is killed. When she hears the news of Rosario's death, Serafina miscarries a child, Rosario's son. *The Rose Tattoo* is the story of Serafina and Rosa's lives after Rosario has died. The memory of Rosario looms darkly over the play and its characters.

**Delle Rose, Serafina** Serafina is an Italian immigrant in her 30s, living in the Italian section of a small Gulf Coast town. Upon hearing that her husband, Rosario Delle Rose, has died in an accident, Serafina miscarries her unborn son. The death of her beloved husband and the loss of her baby propel Serafina to become a bitter, angry, and grief-stricken harpy. Once a pristine, elegant Italian woman, she has allowed her appearance to become slovenly and unkempt. Serafina lived to love

Rosario, and now that he is dead, she perpetually mourns and honors his memory. She constantly prays for signs from the Holy Mother, seeking relief from the pain in which she resides.

Serafina is a complex character who functions through extreme moods of passion and panic. She is spiteful and lyrical, violent and meek, physically strong and emotionally crippled. Serafina is another member of Williams's fugitive kind. She is ostracized by her society because she is emotionally explosive and dedicated to a marriage that was a fraud and a husband who is deceased. As a working-class Italian immigrant, she faces racial and social discrimination. However, she is also misunderstood by her peers and cannot find solace even among her own people. Searching for a way to proceed in life, Serafina confines herself to her home, where the memories of her once-perfect life and love permeate in the candlelight of her shrine to the Virgin Mary.

Serafina is a prime example of Williams's dynamic and enthralling female characters: women who exist in a world of strict moral codes but who cannot adhere to such artificial concepts. They are passionate, relying upon sex and their sexuality to help them maneuver through life and to enable them to feel alive in an otherwise dreary, mundane world. As do Stella Kowalski, Cassandra Whiteside, Rosa Gonzales, Maggie Pollitt, and Myra Torrance, Serafina finds fulfillment through romance, passion, and sex. The physical need to engage with the opposite sex overrides any puritanical code that could ever exist, however strong or strictly enforced. Serafina challenges this chaste code wholeheartedly. She retains the wild and burning desire to love and be loved completely.

**Flora** Flora is a young townswoman who commissions Serafina Delle Rose to make a blouse for her. She becomes irritated when she and her friend Bessie go to collect the blouse and it is not ready. Flora and Bessie are in a hurry to catch a train to New Orleans. The two are rude and disrespectful to Serafina. Although they harass her, they are shocked by her violent reaction to them. As the situation escalates, Serafina chases them out of her house with a broom. They retaliate by informing Serafina that her deceased husband, Rosario Delle Rose, had a mistress, Estelle Hohengarten.

**Hohengarten, Estelle** She is Rosario Delle Rose's mistress. She works at the Square Roof bar, where she met Rosario one year before the action of the play. To prove her devotion to Rosario, Estelle has a red rose tattooed in the center of her chest, an exact replica of Rosario's tattoo. She also commissions Rosario's wife, Serafina Delle Rose, to make a rose-colored silk shirt for him. While placing her order with Serafina in the Delle Roses' home, Estelle steals a framed portrait of Rosario. Serafina has no way of knowing that Estelle is her husband's lover, so she constructs the shirt. Three years later, Serafina confronts Estelle when she hears rumors of their affair. Estelle proudly tells Serafina that she did love this "wild" man and that the shirt was indeed for him. Serafina is emotionally crushed by this information. Serafina struggles to reconcile her extremely romanticized memories of her husband with the harsh reality that Rosario was less than perfect.

**Hunter, Jack** Jack is a young sailor who is on leave and visiting his family in a Gulf Coast town. Jack attends a high school dance with his sister and meets Rosa Delle Rose. He is immediately smitten with her, but realizing she is only 15 years old, he is hesitant to act on his feelings. Rosa, however, passionately pursues him. When Rosa's mother, Serafina Delle Rose, finds out that Rosa is dating a sailor, she forbids the relationship. Serafina blames the high school for corrupting her daughter. She believes that the school has alienated Rosa from her reserved Sicilian upbringing and turned her into a loose American girl. Serafina confronts Jack and interrogates him. She forces him to swear before her shrine of the Virgin Mary that he will not have intercourse with Rosa. Rosa desperately wants to be physically intimate with Jack, but he has sworn before God and Serafina that he will resist. Before Jack goes back to the navy, Rosa announces she wants to be his wife and the two young lovers meet in a hotel in New Orleans to consummate their engagement before he sets sail. Jack is an innocent and genuine young man reminiscent of Jim O'Connor in *THE GLASS MENAGERIE*.

**Mangiacavallo, Alvaro** He is a truck driver and the lover of Serafina Delle Rose. Alvaro is a clownish-looking man, a Sicilian immigrant living somewhere between New Orleans and Mobile, Alabama. Alvaro works to support his mother, father, and unmarried sister. He is dedicated to their well-being, but frustrated by their gambling and drinking habits. He is stout in appearance with black curls all over his head. Serafina is attracted to Alvaro as he resembles her deceased husband, Rosario Delle Rose. Alvaro meets Serafina when a traveling Salesman on the highway harasses him. The Salesman happens to stop at Serafina's home and Alvaro argues and fights with him in her yard. Alvaro has had his fill of derogatory names such as "spaghetti" and "Wop" and confronts the salesman about his name calling. Alvaro is extremely emotional and cries after he has fought the Salesman. He is passionate about love and desperately searches for an older, wiser, and fertile woman with whom he can share his life. He finds such a mate in Serafina. Alvaro pursues her, but he is troubled by her devotion to a husband who has been dead for three years. To prove his love for her, he has a red rose tattooed on his chest, an exact replica of Rosario's. Serafina does not trust men, and she accuses Alvaro of wanting only to have sex with her. As the plot unfolds, Serafina accepts this new lover and he finds happiness in her arms.

**Salesman** He is a traveling salesman, who approaches Serafina Delle Rose. The Salesman is sweaty and overweight, and he has been shouting ethnic slurs at Alvaro Mangiacavallo. They have a fistfight in Serafina's yard. The Salesman memorizes Alvaro's license plate number and files a complaint with Alvaro's boss. Alvaro loses his job as a result of this incident.

**Yorke, Miss** She is a teacher at the local high school and Rosa Delle Rose's mentor. Miss Yorke visits the Delle Rose home when Rosa stops attending school. She begs Serafina Delle Rose to allow her daughter, Rosa, to attend graduation. Unlike the other characters in the play, Miss Yorke is not afraid of Serafina's rage.

### FURTHER READING

Atkinson, Brooks. "At the Theatre," *New York Times*, February 5, 1951, p. 19.

Griffin, Alice. *Understanding Tennessee Williams*. Columbia: University of South Carolina Press, 1995.

Kolin, Philip C., ed. *American Playwrights since 1945: A Guide to Scholarship, Criticism, and Performance*. New York: Greenwood, 1989.

———, ed. *Tennessee Williams: A Guide to Research and Performance*. Westport, Conn.: Greenwood Press, 1998.

## "Rubio y Morena"

Short story written before 1948.

### SYNOPSIS

A lonely but famous writer named Kamrowski is returning from a trip to Mexico when he is detained at the border. He is forced to stay in Laredo until he is permitted into the United States. He checks into a second-rate hotel. Just as he falls asleep, a young woman, Amada, enters his bed. She climbs on top of him, but he initially objects as he is not attracted to women. Amada ignores his apprehension and seduces Kamrowski. He is so happy that he has found the one woman who excites him that he takes her as his companion. The next day they leave Laredo together.

Several months pass, and the couple travel through the southern states. Amada rarely speaks, but she is satisfied to be with the writer. Kamrowski falls in love with Amada because he feels comfortable around her. When they make love, Amada calls him Rubio, or "blond one," and he calls her Morena, or "dark." When Kamrowski eventually grows restless in this monogamous relationship and has sex with other women, he falls in love with a fellow writer named Ida. Amada is frustrated by his indifference; many times she packs her bags but never has the heart to leave.

Kamrowski discovers Amada has been stealing money from him. When the writer finally confronts Amada, she sobs with guilt. He forgives her. Amada resists the temptation to take his money for a few weeks then resorts to stealing again. Kamrowski accepts her dishonesty because he feels guilty about his sexual infidelities. Amada contracts a kidney disease that keeps her in constant agony. At the same time, Kamrowski begins to treat her as his servant. When Amada leaves him, Kamrowski pines for her. He realizes that he does not love anyone else in the world. He travels back to Laredo and finds her in her family's shack in the desert. Amada is weak and dying. Kamrowski tries to force her to take more money, but she refuses. The next morning when he arrives at the house he finds that Amada died in the night. As he holds her hand and cries, the women in the house demand Amada's money. He does not understand them. One woman hands him old telegrams from Amada, promising the money that she stole from him. He is chased away by the women.

## COMMENTARY

"Rubio y Morena" is autobiographical, as it details the frustrations of a young male writer trying to come to terms with his lack of interest in women (as the story begins). The fictional writer gains literary notoriety, falls for another writer, and reconciles the severe unhappiness in his life. These are all aspects of Williams's life. Other examples of Williams's semiautobiographical fiction include "RESEMBLANCE BETWEEN A VIOLIN CASE AND A COFFIN," "THE ANGEL IN THE ALCOVE," "PORTRAIT OF A GIRL IN GLASS," and *THE GLASS MENAGERIE*. The biography by Donald Spoto also suggests that "Rubio y Morena" is a "heterosexualized and much sentimentalized account of Williams's travels and relationship with" his first long-term love, Pancho Rodriguez Gonzalez.

## PUBLICATION HISTORY

"Rubio y Morena" was published in *Partisan Review* (1948), *New Directions in Prose and Poetry 11* (1949), *Hard Candy* (1954), and *Collected Stories* (1985).

## CHARACTERS

**Amada** She is a young Mexican woman who meets Kamrowski, a successful American writer, in a hotel in Laredo, Texas. She slips into his darkened hotel room one evening and seduces him. The two become companions and travel together for several months. Amada, whose name means "loved one" in Spanish. Amada's love for Kamrowski bolsters his self-confidence and enables him to overcome his shyness with women. His revived self-esteem prompts him to be unfaithful, thereby ruining their relationship. Amada contracts kidney disease, leaves Kamrowski, and returns to her family in Laredo. Kamrowski pursues her and finds Amada on her deathbed.

**Ida** Ida is a young writer and an intellectual socialite. Her affair with Kamrowski, a fellow writer, brings about the demise of his relationship with Amada.

**Kamrowski** Kamrowski is a successful young writer who struggles to form lasting relationships with women. He is uncomfortable and somewhat frightened around women and has difficulty being physically intimate with them, as he is intimidated by female passion. He finds more fulfillment in his writing. On a trip through Mexico, he is detained in Laredo, Texas, and spends the night at the Texas Star Hotel. Amada, a sultry Mexican woman, sneaks into his hotel room one evening and seduces him. The two fall in love and travel the American South together. Amada affectionately calls Kamrowski Rubio, which means "blond," and he calls Amada Morena ("dark"). Kamrowski's romantic success with Amada bolsters his sexual confidence and prompts him to have multiple affairs with other women. He grows especially fond of Ida, a beautiful blonde writer and urban socialite. Amada contracts kidney disease and leaves him. Only then does he discover that he truly loves her. Kamrowski searches for her and finds her back in Laredo on her deathbed.

# "Sabbatha and Solitude"

A short story written in 1973.

## SYNOPSIS

This story chronicles the midlife crisis of Sabbatha Veyne Duff-Collick, a reclusive middle-aged poet who in her prime was considered a renegade and hailed as "the most profligate artist since Isadora

Duncan." A passionate and sensual writer, Sabbatha garnered more press and attention from her extensive international travels than from her poetry. This interest was due to her often outlandish behavior and her entourage of young attractive men, with whom she engaged in very public and passionate affairs.

Seeking refuge from the spotlight, Sabbatha retreats to a small village in Maine. In this locale she has become a legend, and whenever she enters her favorite French restaurant, L'Escargot Fou, "a few moments of hush would descend" on the place. In her heyday the restaurant proudly placed a bronze nameplate on her favorite chair, at her favorite corner table.

Sabbatha encounters a group of young poets on what proves to be her final visit to L'Escargot Fou. When she arrives with her entourage, she is shocked to find her table occupied by a "scrubby and bearded" young man and two other poets. She complains to the Maitre, who warns her that the young men will make a scene if they are asked to give up the table. Sabbatha is outraged by the "obscene barbarians" who have usurped her place. She then demands that she be given the chair with the bronze plate bearing her name, only to be told that it "collapsed and couldn't be repaired." The chair and its "old piece of metal on the back" has been sent to the junkyard. Sabbatha launches into a dramatic tirade to which the young poets respond with "howls of derision."

Sabbatha is immediately ushered out of the restaurant by her companions, but the scene has been too much for her and she faints once she is outside. When she revives, only one of her young male companions remains by her side. The two begin to cry together as the young man says to her, "Oh Sabbatha, didn't God tell you that things turn out this way?"

Sabbatha finds similar distress in her personal life. For comfort, amusement, and physical pleasure, Sabbatha establishes a relationship with Giovanni, a dark young Italian. Maintaining Giovanni as a "kept boy" makes Sabbatha appear and feel youthful and vibrant for a time. However, the relationship deteriorates, as it has clearly been based on illusion and pretense: Sabbatha is not youthful, and Giovanni is not heterosexual. They fight frequently, as Sabbatha battles her ongoing depression. Giovanni has become weary of the routine and of living in isolation with Sabbatha in their "birdhouse" in rural Maine.

Giovanni eagerly escapes and disappears to find male companionship in the nearby town of Bangor. Sabbatha does not hear from him until she receives a phone call informing her that he has been brutally raped and hospitalized. Giovanni returns to her, weak and broken, and finds her in the same state. The story concludes with the two troubled souls comforting each other.

## COMMENTARY

Sabbatha and her fate have often been viewed as an autobiographical sketch of Williams's own later life. Sabbatha's story is filled with the anguish of an aging writer facing lack of appreciation for her later works and the loss of her poetic skills, her lovers, and ultimately her life. Sabbatha's latest collection of sonnets is trashed by her editor; her youthful lover yearns to be unfaithful; her table is usurped by a younger, ascendant poet; she suffers from arthritis; and her future obituary, shown to her by a journalist friend, is scant and inaccurate. Many of the painful circumstances that she faces were surely faced, or at least feared, by Williams. The complexity of the characters and themes invites a contemplation of Sabbatha and her fate—and ultimately Williams's. In both cases, one hopes that despite the desolate circumstances, the author has a sense of acceptance, survival, and endurance at the conclusion.

This beautifully crafted story has many companion pieces throughout the Williams canon. Sabbatha is a kindred spirit of many aging artists, trying in vain to retain their youthful vigor and youthful lovers, such as Karen Stone in the novel *THE ROMAN SPRING OF MRS. STONE* and Vieux in the short play *THE TRAVELLING COMPANION*. Each work ends with a compromise: Sabbatha, Karen, and Vieux strike a bargain with the young men they love and settle for relationships that are established on mercenary terms.

## PUBLICATION HISTORY

"Sabbatha and Solitude" was first published in *Playgirl* magazine in 1973. It was subsequently published in the short story collection *EIGHT MORTAL LADIES POSSESSED* (1974) and in *Collected Stories* (1985).

### CHARACTERS

**Duff-Collick, Sabbatha Veyne** Sabbatha is a reclusive middle-aged poet. In her prime she was considered a rebel and was known for her romantic liaisons as for her poetry. Settling into middle age has not been easy for Sabbatha. Her popularity as a poet has waned, as have her looks. She tries desperately to hold on to her young Italian lover, Giovanni, who only remains with Sabbatha because she provides a luxurious lifestyle.

**Giovanni** He is Sabbatha Veyne Duff-Collick's Italian lover. Giovanni is younger than Sabbatha, and although he enjoys being kept by her, he is bored living with her in a rural area of Maine. This is not only because Sabbatha is regularly depressed and temperamental, but also because Giovanni actually prefers intimate relations with men. He often does so and has clandestine affairs. On one occasion he slips away to a bar in Bangor, Maine. There, events take a sour turn and he is hospitalized after being brutally raped. He returns to Sabbatha, and they comfort and console each other.

**Maitre** He is the head waiter at a posh restaurant called L'Escargot Fou. When the temperamental writer Sabbatha Veyne Duff-Collick finds her table usurped by younger poets, she demands that the Maitre eject them. He explains to her that the poets are very important people and refuses to move them. Sabbatha informs the young man that the restaurant dedicated a chair with a bronze nameplate to her. The Maitre coldly remarks that an old chair with a bit of metal has recently been thrown out. His words are blunt and harsh reminders to Sabbatha that her time in the spotlight has passed.

## "Sand"

Short story written in 1936.

### SYNOPSIS

Emiel and Rose are an elderly couple. Emiel has suffered a stroke and is no longer able to care for himself. He depends on Rose for his well-being, and she in return is terrified that he will die. Rose lies in bed at night and reminisces about their youthful love.

While working in the kitchen, Rose hears a loud crash in the nearby room. Fearing the worst, she panics and runs in to find that Emiel has merely dropped their old photo album on the floor.

### COMMENTARY

According to biographer Lyle Leverich, "Sand" is based on the grandparents of Williams's girlfriend Hazel Kramer. Concerned with nostalgia and former dreams, Williams wrote, "a poignant character study of the plight of an elderly couple who can look in only one direction: back to their early years together" (Leverich, 166).

### PUBLICATION HISTORY

"Sand" was published in *Collected Stories* by New Directions in 1985.

### CHARACTERS

**Emiel** An elderly man who, after suffering a stroke, must rely on the care of his wife, Rose. Emiel reminisces about their youthful love by perusing their earliest photo album.

**Rose** An elderly woman who cares for her beloved husband, Emiel, after he suffers a stroke. Rose dreams about the days when their love was young and carefree.

### FURTHER READING

Leverich, Lyle. *Tom: The Unknown Tennessee Williams.* New York: W. W. Norton & Co., 1995.

## *Senso, or The Wanton Countess*

A screenplay written in 1953. Williams drafted the screenplay for this film directed by Luchino Visconti. Set in 1855, during the Austrian occupation of Italy, the film tells the story of an Italian countess

(Livia Serpieri), who falls in love with an Austrian lieutenant (Franz Mahler). Livia betrays her country by stealing funds collected to aid the resistance and giving them to Franz so that he can bribe his way out of military service. She later discovers that the man she has helped is actually a drunken, ungrateful rogue who has used her for her money. Her revenge is swift, decisive, and severe. Williams did not publish the screenplay manuscript, and after viewing Visconti's film, he stated that only one scene had truly retained what he had written.

# *The Seven Descents of Myrtle*

The title given to the full-length play *THE KINGDOM OF EARTH, OR THE SEVEN DESCENTS OF MYRTLE* before its Broadway premiere in 1968.

# *Slapstick Tragedy*

Name under which the two short plays *THE GNÄDIGES FRÄULEIN* and *THE MUTILATED* appeared together on stage in New York in 1966.

# *Small Craft Warnings*

A play in two acts written around 1971.

## SYNOPSIS

The play is set in a seaside bar in Southern California. The idea of the characters' entering a confessional is suggested by a designated area of the stage isolated by light. Each of the characters takes a turn entering the confessional to speak directly to the audience. The time is late evening.

### *Act 1*

Leona, Violet, and Bill McCorkle are having a heated argument because Leona caught Violet fondling Bill's genitals. Monk and Steve try to calm Leona. Quentin and Bobby enter the bar, and Monk refuses to serve them as they appear to be a gay couple. Bill observes the two newcomers, goes to the confessional area of the stage, and expresses his hatred of gay men. Steve takes his place in the confessional area. He offers details of his relationship with Violet, referring to her as the scraps that life has thrown him. Leona reminisces about her younger brother, Haley, who died of anemia. Doc enters the confessional before leaving the bar to deliver a baby at a trailer park. Violet goes to the confessional area and expresses her thoughts about her life. Quentin explains that he is no longer interested in Bobby because he prefers relationships with heterosexual men. Quentin enters the confessional and describes his thoughts about being a gay man. When he leaves the bar, Bobby begins his confession. He is traveling by bicycle from Iowa to Mexico in search of freedom and tolerance. When he finishes his confession, he leaves the bar without saying good-bye. Leona chases him; she finds a kinship with him as he reminds her of Haley. Monk enters the confessional area to detail his life as a bar owner. When Leona returns, she finds Violet again engaged in lewd activities with Bill and Steve. As the scene concludes, a dim light is shone on Violet's weepy and dazed face.

### *Act 2*

One hour later in the bar, Leona chastises Bill and threatens to leave town. When Doc returns to the bar, Leona makes him confess that he no longer has a license to practice medicine. Violet, Steve, and Bill leave together. Leona chases them, and Violet returns with a bloody nose. During his nightcap, Doc reveals that the baby he delivered was stillborn, and the mother hemorrhaged to death. Doc says he has to leave town. Sirens are heard in the distance, and Leona rushes in to hide. Tony, the policeman, enters and has a drink. Leona, Monk, and Violet share a nightcap while Violet fondles Monk below the table. Leona addresses the audience and leaves $20 for Monk. He sends Violet upstairs to shower and picks up one of her tattered slippers. Contemplating it, he says the slipper will be worn until there is nothing left.

## COMMENTARY

*Small Craft Warnings* is an expanded version of the one-act play CONFESSIONAL. Williams was prompted to develop *Confessional* into a longer play by a highly regarded production of it at the Maine Theatre Arts Festival in 1971. As is its predecessor, *Small Craft Warnings* is a series of self-reflections rendered by the patrons of Monk's bar, who are navigating life through the fog of loneliness, alcohol, and despair. Williams feared that *Small Craft Warnings* would be misunderstood as "a sordid piece of writing" or "a play about groping." The play does deal explicitly with sex and sexuality, but through this stark examination of the human condition, Williams probes issues of loneliness, longing, and the need for human connection. *Small Craft Warnings* holds a unique place in the Williams canon, as Williams believed he had much at stake in this play: He feared that it would be his last work to be staged in New York and was striving to write another play as successful as *THE GLASS MENAGERIE* or *A STREETCAR NAMED DESIRE*. Although the production received only lukewarm responses from critics, it had a lengthy performance run (200 performances in total) and was considered a commercial success.

## PRODUCTION HISTORY

*Small Craft Warnings* premiered in New York at the Truck and Warehouse Theatre, April 2, 1972. This production then transferred to the New Theatre on June 1972, when Williams made his acting debut in the role of Doc. He played the part for the first five performances. It was his first and only professional appearance in a production.

## PUBLICATION HISTORY

*Small Craft Warnings* was published by New Directions in 1972.

## CHARACTERS

**Bobby** Bobby is a young gay man from Iowa who is traveling the California coast on his bicycle. He is picked up by Quentin and accompanies him to a beachside bar owned by Monk. Quentin makes a pass at Bobby but becomes uninterested in him when he discovers he is gay because he prefers sexual encounters with heterosexual men. Leona Dawson offers Bobby a place to stay when Quentin leaves him at the bar. Bobby decides to keep traveling alone.

**Dawson, Leona** Leona is a regular patron of the cheap seaside bar owned by Monk. She is a beautician who lives in a trailer, which she shares with her sometime boyfriend, Bill McCorkle. Leona visits Monk's bar to commemorate the anniversary of her younger brother's death. She becomes drunk and fights with her friend, Violet, whom she catches performing lewd acts with Bill in the bar. Leona is a caring person who tries to help others as much as she can. She befriends Bobby and Quentin, two gay men who are not regulars at Monk's bar. She tries to stop Doc from delivering a baby at her trailer park, as he is intoxicated and has lost his medical license. She tries to phone the trailer park and warn them of Doc's condition. Unlike the other characters in the play, Leona refuses merely to survive on whatever scraps life has to offer. She leaves the bar and her circle of friends for good, in search of a better life.

**Doc** Doc is a regular patron of the dingy seaside bar owned by Monk. Although he lost his medical license for operating on a patient while under the influence of alcohol, he continues to practice medicine illegally. During his "confession" Doc philosophizes about the close proximity of life and death. Leona Dawson tries unsuccessfully to prevent him from delivering a baby at her trailer park. Monk phones the trailer park and urges them to allow Doc to perform the delivery. Doc delivers the baby, but there are numerous complications. The baby is stillborn and the mother hemorrhages to death. Doc places the baby into a shoebox, drops the shoebox into the ocean, and pays the woman's husband $50 to forget his face and name. Monk advises Doc to leave town as quickly as he can. Doc is the one role that Williams actually performed on stage, in the first five performances of the 1972 production of *Small Craft Warnings* at the New Theatre in New York.

**McCorkle, Bill** Bill is a male prostitute who frequents the cheap seaside bar owned by Monk. At the bar he fights with Leona Dawson and plays sexual games with Violet.

**Monk** Monk is the owner and bartender of a dingy beachside bar in Southern California. He cares for his regular customers and thinks of them as his family. As his name suggests, he listens to the confessions of his patrons in a priestlike fashion.

**Quentin** Quentin is a lonely young scriptwriter who gives Bobby a ride. He makes a pass at Bobby but then rejects him when he discovers that Bobby is gay.

**Steve** Steve is a middle-aged short-order cook who frequents the dingy beachside bar owned by Monk. As are Bill McCorkle and Monk, he is having an affair with Violet.

**Tony** Tony is the police officer who is called to Monk's bar to break up a fight. Monk offers Tony a drink, which he accepts although he is on duty.

**Violet** Violet is a mentally unstable nymphomaniac who frequents the cheap seaside bar owned by Monk. Leona Dawson befriends Violet; the other bar regulars, Monk, Steve, and Bill McCorkle, take advantage of her sexually.

# "Something About Him"

Short story written before 1946.

## SYNOPSIS

Haskell is an overzealous grocery store clerk. The people of his Mississippi community regard him with suspicion, as they believe he is too eager to please. Every Saturday Haskell goes to the public library, where he routinely finds an out-of-the-way chair, cleans his glasses well, and reads modern poetry all day. Miss Rose, the assistant librarian, is fascinated by him.

On one particular Saturday, Haskell suffers from a terrible cold. When Miss Rose inquires about his health, he blames his sickness on the drafty room he rents. Miss Rose excitedly tells him of an available room in her apartment building. She gives him the phone number of the landlady, and he calls right away.

Haskell moves into the same building as Miss Rose. They often see each other in the hallway. They meet to discuss poetry, and Haskell walks her to work every day. They enjoy their newfound companionship. As Haskell's happiness increases, the grocery store customers become more wary of him. They tell his manager that there "is something about him" they do not like. Although he is a hard worker, Haskell is fired because of the customers' complaints. He goes to the library to return a book and to say good-bye to Miss Rose before leaving town. She is devastated by her loss and she returns to her previous mundane life.

## COMMENTARY

Williams explores themes of alienation, loneliness and acceptance in "Something About Him." Although Miss Rose is an accepted member of this Mississippi community, she leads a miserable life because of her emotional seclusion. Haskell is her opposite as he is outgoing, but this trait leads to social discrimination. Miss Rose finally has a glimpse of happiness and the prospect of marriage, but because Haskell is different, he is forced out of the town, punished for his kindness and generosity.

The Rose character in this short story, as are the other "Rose characters" in the Williams canon ("COMPLETED," *THE GLASS MENAGERIE*, "RESEMBLANCE BETWEEN A VIOLIN CASE AND A COFFIN," and *THE LONG STAY CUT SHORT*), is a tribute to his sister, ROSE ISABEL WILLIAMS.

## PUBLICATION HISTORY

"Something About Him" was originally published in 1946 in *Mademoiselle* magazine. It was not reprinted until 1985, when it was included in *Collected Stories*.

## CHARACTERS

**Haskell** Haskell is a young clerk in a grocery store. In his attempts to assist the store's customers, Haskell comes under suspicion for being too nice. Although he sincerely tries to be helpful, he is regularly perceived to be an impostor. He is punished for his goodwill when he is fired from his job at the store. His manager explains that he is being dismissed because he is generally perceived as untrustworthy.

**Rose, Miss** Miss Rose is a librarian at a public library. She leads a mundane life until a love interest, Haskell, inspires her to dress prettily and enjoy life. Miss Rose's happiness is cut short when Haskell is fired from his job and leaves town because people find him suspicious, as he is "too nice." Haskell, who is always helpful and happy, is punished for his disposition. Miss Rose has one glimpse of contentment, which quickly disappears with the departure of Haskell.

# "Something by Tolstoi"

A short story written in the years 1930–31.

## SYNOPSIS

A young man searching for a job stumbles upon a bookstore with a "clerk wanted" sign in the window. He goes in to inquire about the position and is hired. The young man assists the owner, Mr. Brodzky, an aging Russian Jew, with the daily work of running the bookshop and also witnesses the life of the Brodzky family.

Mr. Brodzky has a son, called Jacob. Jacob attends college to avoid the obligation of running the family business. Jacob is also in love with his childhood friend, Lila, but Mr. Brodzky does not want his son to marry a "Gentile," so he is relieved to send Jacob away.

Lila is Jacob's opposite. Whereas he is quiet and contemplative, Lila is boisterous and outgoing. Jacob is very attracted to her because she has an unrestrained spirit. Theirs is an endearing relationship. Only two months after Jacob leaves, Mr. Brodzky becomes ill and dies. Jacob returns home to the bookstore, and in less than one month, Jacob and Lila are married. Lila quickly grows restless with their life as shopkeepers. She dreams of becoming a rich and famous vaudeville star. Lila begs Jacob to sell the shop, but he is very happy and cannot relate to her restlessness.

Lila encounters a vaudeville agent and sings for him. The agent loves her voice and hires her to tour in his show. Jacob loves Lila more than anything—she is "the core of his life"—but she leaves him for her pursuit of fame. When she tries to give him her key to the bookshop, he tells her to keep the key because she will return someday and he will be waiting for her.

Months go by and the Narrator tries to help Jacob out of his depression. Jacob does not sleep; instead, he reads and clumsily stumbles through his days. Fifteen years pass and Jacob remains in this state. Lila returns to the small bookshop one dark December evening. The shop is closed, but Jacob is in the back, sitting at his desk reading. Lila unlocks the door with her key and confronts Jacob. She is shocked when she realizes that he does not recognize her. She pretends to be searching for a book whose title she cannot remember; she knows only that it is a familiar tragic love story. Jacob unwittingly remarks that the work must be something by Tolstoi.

## COMMENTARY

In this story, as in the short story "IN MEMORY OF AN ARISTOCRAT," Williams experiments with a second-person narrator. A young shop assistant witnesses the action of the story and relates these happenings. The narrator is not omniscient, and he is not involved in the action. He is simply a witness to the plot.

## PUBLICATION HISTORY

"Something by Tolstoi" was published in *Collected Stories* by New Directions in 1985.

## CHARACTERS

**Brodzky, Jacob** Jacob is an intelligent and well-educated young man who marries Lila Brodzky and takes over his father's, Mr. Brodzky's, bookshop when he dies. Jacob enjoys the solemn life of reading and living among the dusty shelves of books; however, Lila dreams of becoming a vaudeville star and touring the world. When she is offered a role in a touring show, she leaves Jacob to his books. Jacob becomes depressed and suffers a mental breakdown from which he does not recover. After 15 years, Lila returns to him a star. She is saddened by his mental state and shocked that he does not recognize her.

**Brodzky, Lila** Lila is a young, beautiful woman who dreams of a life as a vaudeville star. She marries a bookshop owner, Jacob Brodzky, and very quickly grows restless in that slow-paced environment. Lila leaves Jacob to be a star, and when she returns to visit him 15 years later, she is astonished that he does not remember her nor recognize their tragic love story as she relates it.

**Brodzky, Mr.** Mr. Brodzky is an elderly shopkeeper who sends his son, Jacob Brodzky, away to college to prevent him from marrying Lila. Mr. Brodzky dies, and Jacob takes over the shop and marries his beloved Lila.

# *Something Cloudy, Something Clear*

A play in two parts written in 1979.

## SYNOPSIS

The action takes place on a beach near Provincetown, Massachusetts.

### *Part 1*

Clare and Kip visit August, a young aspiring writer who inhabits a weathered shack on the beach. Clare teases August for his staring at Kip during the previous evening's party, "like a bird dog at a—quail" while Kip dances outside. Clare is dying of diabetes and wants August to support Kip, who is dying of a brain tumor. August plays Ravel's *Pavane* on his Victrola, while he and Clare slip into a 1980-present dialogue recollecting their time spent together in 1940. After an extended pause, Clare and August return to the 1940 present. Clare calls Kip into the shack and reintroduces him to August. Kip responds indifferently and exits for a swim. Ghostly figures of a Nurse with Frank Merlo in a wheelchair, from the 1980 present, appear on a sand dune. August relives his last days with Frank as he lay dying in a hospital.

When Frank and the Nurse disappear, August returns to the 1940 present. Hazel, a figure from an earlier time in August's life, appears on the dunes. They converse about their ill-fated relationship. August confesses his attraction to boys, and she admits her love for girls. Hazel leaves and August returns to the 1940 present. Clare begs August to take care of Kip for the winter. August is thrilled, but apprehensive. When Clare suddenly leaves, Kip and August awkwardly talk about the impending arrangement. A drunken Merchant Seaman interrupts the men to collect payment from August for a sexual encounter. August pays him five dollars. Meanwhile, a telegram arrives, informing August that his producers, Maurice and Celeste Fiddler, are planning to visit him.

The Fiddlers appear on the dunes with an actress, Caroline Wales. They criticize August's poverty, his play, and his ego. Celeste pursues August about his revisions, and he counters with a plea for more funding. While Maurice and August renegotiate the terms of their agreement, Clare returns, followed by Bugsy Brodsky, her former boss and lover. August retreats to his shack because Bugsy is violently homophobic. During a fight on the dunes, Bugsy knocks Clare to the ground. After he stalks away, August rushes out of the shack to help her. The drunken Merchant Seaman appears again to procure money for sex from August.

### *Part 2, Scene 1*

The setting is the same as in part 1, on the following day. Tallulah Bankhead appears on the dunes. She angrily calls for August, who exits his shack to argue with her. Kip appears to discuss the parameters of their impending relationship. He is shy about the issue of intimacy with August, but August lovingly comforts him.

### *Part 2, Scene 2*

The next evening Clare returns with food and picnic supplies. Although she brought Kip and August together, she is outraged when she finds out they have consummated their relationship. As she corners Kip, she berates August by explaining the facts of Kip's illness. She delivers a telegram to August from the Fiddlers, who have accepted his script and have guaranteed a production. Kip has a small seizure. Clare orders August to swim while she nurses Kip to health. Later that evening during dinner, Clare expresses her fear of being unattractive and unloved. August and Kip kiss her repeatedly. August writes himself a note to capture the events of this summer, as Kip traces the trajectory of a falling star with his finger.

## COMMENTARY

At the center of *Something Cloudy, Something Clear* is Williams: "the artist and his art, the man and his theatrical persona, immediacy and retrospect, time stopped and time flowing" (Adamson, vii). August is the young Williams, who spent a summer living and writing on a beach near Provincetown, Massachusetts, in 1940. Williams has described that summer of 1940 as "a summer of discovery" ("Williams, *Where I Live,* 137). This period was a coming of age for Williams, when he came to terms with his vocation as an artist and explored his sexuality. However, the play does not present only a recollection of that pivotal summer; that time coexists with the perspective of the mature artist of 1980. In this, his most autobiographical work after THE GLASS MENAGERIE, Williams incorporates a dual perspective to underscore the idea of double exposure in the play: August, as Tom Wingfield does in *The Glass Menagerie,* stands inside and outside the drama, commenting on the action while taking part. Here is the mature playwright self, from a vantage point of 40 years, seeing distinctly all that was cloudy and vague to the naive, younger self.

The influence of August Strindberg is clearly evident in *Something Cloudy, Something Clear,* the most obvious reference to which is the name of Williams's protagonist. In his expressionistic *A Dream Play* (1901), Strindberg created a fantastical drama in which chronological time is inconsequential. In his foreword to that play, Strindberg explains that he "attempted to imitate . . . the logical shape of a dream . . . the imagination spins, weaving new patterns; a mixture of memories, experiences, free fancies, incongruities and improvisations. The characters split, double, multiply, evaporate, condense, disperse, assemble" (1). In a similar fashion, *Something Cloudy, Something Clear* is an autobiographical meshing of people from different moments of Williams's life, and his characters weave in and out of the drama, without entrances and exits. Simply "appearing" to August, they form a plot that rejects the traditional conventions of realism. The characters possess an ethereal existence, literally materializing on the sand dunes, which become essentially the landscape of Williams's memories or dreams. Williams notes that Clare is "apparitionally beautiful" (Williams, 1), while the Nurse and Frank Merlo appear as ghostly figures, reminiscent of characters in Strindberg's *Ghost Sonata.* In 1907 Strindberg created a haunted play which featured a "ghost dinner." In *Something Cloudy, Something Clear* Williams creates another ghost dinner in the last scene of the play: Clare is dying of diabetes, Kip is dying of a brain tumor, and August (as does Strindberg's Young Lady) communes with characters whose lives are escaping.

Williams, as did Strindberg, searched continually for new modes of expression through his dramaturgy. Toward the end of their life and career, both playwrights concentrated on death, apparitions, dreams, and reliving (or reimagining) the past. *Something Cloudy, Something Clear* is a highly evocative example of Williams's autobiographical contemplation of his past loves and experiences.

## PRODUCTION HISTORY

Eve Adamson directed the premiere of *Something Cloudy, Something Clear* for the Jean Cocteau Repertory at the Bouwerie Lane Theatre, August 24, 1981.

## PUBLICATION HISTORY

The play was withheld from publication by Williams's executrix, MARIA ST. JUST. Lady St. Just feared that the play's content would call attention to Williams's sexuality and have a detrimental effect on his public image. As a result, *Something Cloudy, Something Clear* did not appear in print until after Lady St. Just's death. It was published by New Directions in 1995.

## CHARACTERS

**August** August is a young playwright living in a shack on a beach near Provincetown, Massachusetts. He is spending the summer revising his first work to be optioned by a professional theater. He is under pressure to appease his producers Maurice and Celeste Fiddler and their star actress, Caroline Wales. He is frequently interrupted by visits from the Merchant Seaman and his two newly acquired companions, Kip and Clare. August is Williams's most autobiographical portrait after Tom Wingfield in THE GLASS MENAGERIE. As does Tom, August stands inside and outside the drama, commenting upon action and simultaneously taking part.

**Brodsky, Bugsy** He is Clare's abusive, homophobic, and violent former boss and lover. Clare tries to end her relationship with him, and he pursues her at August's beach house. He confronts Clare and when she refuses to leave with him knocks her to the ground.

**Clare** She is Kip's traveling companion, a young, destitute dancer who suffers from diabetes. Clare and Kip meet August one summer evening in Provincetown, Massachusetts. She pretends that she and Kip are siblings. August is immediately smitten with Kip and she encourages his infatuation. She forces the two men together in the hope that August will provide shelter and solace for Kip during the coming winter. However, she becomes irate when the two actually become lovers. Clare is the only principal character in the play who is not based on an actual historical figure in Williams's life. August refers to Clare, whose name is an anagram of the word *clear,* as his conscience.

**Fiddler, Celeste** She is the curt and impatient wife of the New York producer Maurice Fiddler. Although she greatly dislikes August, she accompanies her husband to August's beach house near Provincetown, Massachusetts. Celeste is meant to be a representation of Armina Marshall of the Theatre Guild, who coproduced Williams's first professionally staged work, *BATTLE OF ANGELS,* in Boston in 1940.

**Fiddler, Maurice** He is an important New York producer who is interested in producing August's play. He visits August at the beach accompanied by his wife, Celeste Fiddler, and the actress Caroline Wales. August withholds the revised script until Maurice agrees to increase his monthly stipend and gives him a $100 cash advance. He is meant to be a representation of Lawrence Langner of the Theatre Guild, who coproduced Williams's first professionally staged work, *BATTLE OF ANGELS,* in Boston in 1940.

**Frank** He is August's former lover and companion. Frank is terminally ill and appears in a wheelchair on the sand dunes near August's beach house, accompanied by a Nurse. He and August relive the last few days of his life. Frank is a portrait of Williams's partner, FRANK MERLO, who died of cancer in 1960.

**Hazel** She is August's childhood sweetheart. She is described as a tall girl, with golden-red hair. She appears to August on the sand dunes near his beach house. He apologizes for hurting her and confesses that during the time of their relationship, he was secretly enamored of boys. She admits that she was aware of his feelings and confides that she loved girls. Hazel is a portrait of Williams's childhood sweetheart, Hazel Kramer.

**Kip** He is a poor young Canadian dancer who is living in the United States illegally. He and his destitute traveling companion, Clare, meet August one summer evening in Provincetown, Massachusetts. August is immediately smitten with Kip and Clare encourages his infatuation. She forces the men together in the hope that August will provide shelter and solace for Kip during the coming winter. Although initially hesitant to have a sexual encounter with August, Kip is drawn to the young playwright. Kip is a portrait of Kip Keirnan, a young Canadian dancer whom Williams met and loved in Provincetown during the summer of 1940.

**Merchant Seaman** A drunken sailor who frequents the beach where August lives. He repeatedly takes advantage of August's loneliness by offering to have sex with him for money. He also takes advantage of Clare's extreme poverty by offering her money in exchange for sex.

**Tallulah** She is an arrogant actress who accosts August at his beachhouse for demeaning her performance in his play. Tallulah is a portrait of the actress TALLULAH BANKHEAD.

**Wales, Caroline** She is the Hollywood film star whom Maurice and Celeste Fiddler have secured to perform in August's play. She likes the young playwright and accompanies the Fiddlers on their visit to his shack on the beach near Provincetown, Massachusetts. Caroline is a portrait of the film star Miriam Hopkins, who played Myra Torrance in

Williams's first professional production, BATTLE OF ANGELS, in Boston in 1940.

### FURTHER READING

Adamson, Eve. "Introduction," in *Something Cloudy, Something Clear.* New York: New Directions, 1995.

Isaac, Dan. "Tennessee Revisited." *Other Stages,* December 17, 1981, p. 8.

Strindberg, August. *A Dream Play,* translated by Michael Meyer. New York: Dial Press, 1973.

Williams, Tennessee. *Where I Live: Selected Essays,* edited by Christine R. Day and Bob Woods. New York: New Directions, 1978.

## *Something Unspoken*

A one-act play written before 1953.

### SYNOPSIS

The action of the play takes place in the living room of Cornelia Scott, a regal, elderly Southern woman. There is a single rose in a vase beside Cornelia's telephone.

Cornelia places a phone call to the Confederate Daughters Society, announcing her consent to be nominated for the head office of regent. Her secretary, Grace Lancaster, enters the room. Cornelia asks Grace whether she has noticed the rose on the table, which, she explains, signifies an anniversary of their time together. She informs Grace that there are 14 more roses waiting for her in her office, one for each year that Grace has been her secretary and companion.

Grace attempts to change the subject by playing some phonograph records, and Cornelia chooses not to expose the unspoken reason behind the tension. Cornelia is distracted by a phone call from a member of the society, who informs Cornelia that she has been nominated for Vice Regent. Cornelia refuses the nomination and hangs up the phone.

Cornelia inquires why Grace has never expressed her feelings toward her. Grace admits that she has been too frightened to address the issue. She protests that she is "not strong enough [or] bold enough" to break down the "wall" that has built up between them. Cornelia receives another telephone call and becomes infuriated on learning that another (younger) member of the Confederate Daughters Society has been elected to the head office. Cornelia orders Grace to draft a letter of resignation for her to submit to the society. Allowing their personal situation to hang, Grace goes into her office to retrieve paper and pen. She calls out to Cornelia, commenting on the beautiful roses in her office.

### COMMENTARY

In *Something Unspoken* Williams masterfully weaves a brief but poignant tale of unspoken, and seemingly unspeakable, desire and the animosity that arises from it. For Grace, a prim single Southern woman (and for so many of Williams's heroines) appearance and social standing—and particularly Cornelia's social standing—are of the utmost importance. For her, it is vital that their romantic feelings for each other remain unspoken and unseen. For Cornelia, the forthright matron, this polite silence can only breed bitterness. Her feelings for Grace run deep, as she acknowledges and commemorates the 15th year of their relationship in a highly romantic fashion. In the end, Grace's attempts to protect Cornelia's reputation are unsuccessful. The outside world has already detected what she has attempted to conceal, and Cornelia is ostracized by her women's group. *Something Unspoken* bears a striking resemblance to the short story "HAPPY AUGUST THE TENTH," in which two younger women live in strife until an acknowledgment of their love for each other rises to the surface.

### PRODUCTION HISTORY

*Something Unspoken* was first produced at the Lakeside Summer Theatre, in Lake Hopatcong, New Jersey, in June 1955. Herbert Machiz directed Patricia Ripley and Hortense Alden as Cornelia and Grace. Machiz also directed the first New York production of the play in February 1958 at the York Theatre, with Patricia Ripley and Hortense Alden again playing Cornelia and Grace.

### PUBLICATION HISTORY

*Something Unspoken* was first published along with SUDDENLY LAST SUMMER under the title *Garden District* in 1959.

## CHARACTERS

**Lancaster, Grace** Grace is Cornelia Scott's live-in secretary. She is in her late 40s and has been Cornelia's personal assistant and companion for 15 years. There is a romantic dimension to their relationship, which Grace hopes to keep hidden, or unspoken.

**Scott, Cornelia** Cornelia is a wealthy unmarried Southern woman in her 60s. She has a regal presence and belongs to a number of prestigious societies within her community. She commemorates her 15-year relationship with her secretary, Grace Lancaster, by giving her two dozen roses.

# *Spring Storm*

Full-length play written in the years 1937 and 1938.

## SYNOPSIS

The play is set in Port Tyler, a small Mississippi town, in 1937.

### *Act 1*

Dick Miles and his lover, Heavenly Critchfield, stand on Lover's Leap, a mountain overlooking the Mississippi River. Farther down the mountain a church fete is going on. The couple have an argument. As a storm begins to brew, Arthur Shannon and Hertha Neilson climb to the lookout.

### *Act 2, Scene 1*

In the interior of the Critchfield home several days later, a messenger delivers flowers to Heavenly. Mrs. Critchfield excitedly accepts them as she wants Heavenly to marry Arthur, but Lila, Heavenly's unmarried aunt, believes Heavenly should marry someone she loves. Heavenly enters, soaking wet from the storm. Mrs. Critchfield confronts Heavenly about her relationship with Dick. She begs Heavenly to consider Arthur. Heavenly proudly admits that she belongs to Dick because she has already consummated her relationship with him. Her mother nearly faints, calling Heavenly "horrible, shameless, and ungrateful." She demands that Heavenly apologize to the portrait of her grandfather, Colonel Wayne. Heavenly refuses.

### *Act 2, Scene 2*

Later that evening at the dinner table, Mr. Critchfield talks of cotton prices and his day at work. Mrs. Critchfield interrupts to inform him that the whole town is talking about Heavenly's loose behavior. Arthur Shannon arrives to collect Heavenly for a date. Heavenly pretends to be less intelligent than she is in an attempt to repel Arthur.

### *Act 2, Scene 3*

Later that evening, Heavenly returns to the living room to apologize to the portrait of her grandfather. Her father joins her, and they have a whiskey together and discuss Heavenly's interest in Dick Miles. Mr. Critchfield believes she is being unrealistic because Dick will never settle down.

### *Act 3, Scene 1*

Several nights later at a friend's lawn party, Arthur and Heavenly dance. Several women gossip about Heavenly's intimate relations with Dick. Arthur proposes marriage to Heavenly. Before she can respond, Dick arrives at the party uninvited. He tells Heavenly that he has been offered a job with the government levee project on the river. Dick also proposes to Heavenly and urges her to leave with him the next day. Heavenly does not want to live on the river; she wants a proper home and life. Arthur and Dick fight.

### *Act 3, Scene 2*

The next day, Arthur drunkenly visits the library to see Hertha. Arthur confesses his unrequited love for Heavenly. He pulls Hertha to him and kisses her forcefully. Hertha rejects him initially, but she ultimately submits. She declares her love for him and begs him to take her to a place where they can be alone. He rejects Hertha, who falls to her knees in anguish.

### *Act 3, Scene 3*

The following morning, Heavenly is burdened because she must choose between Arthur and Dick. She is surrounded by flowers Arthur has sent, and more flowers keep arriving.

Arthur visits Heavenly. Tragic news that Hertha was killed in the freight yard the night before causes Lila to be suspicious of Arthur. Lila demands that Arthur leave the Critchfield home. Before he goes, Arthur confesses to Heavenly that in a drunken rage he did in fact kill Hertha. Heavenly panics and makes him promise never to tell anyone else. She demands that he remain with her, but Arthur says he must leave town. Dick has also left Port Tyler. Heavenly is left suitorless, destined not to marry.

## COMMENTARY

The fear of spinsterhood is at the center of *Spring Storm.* Heavenly Critchfield tries desperately to become someone's wife. Her downfall is that she is deeply in love with the free-spirited Dick Miles. Although she appreciates his wild and passionate love for life and freedom, she does not want to live an unsettled life. Heavenly possesses Dick's love, but she can never harness his spirit in order to live a respectable life together. Heavenly's love for Dick violates convention: She has premarital sex with him because her desires overcome her proper Southern upbringing; however, in this act, she does become Dick's property. Heavenly's mother, a character similar to Amanda Wingfield, lives her life in the pursuit of social mobility and financial repose and dedicates herself to securing a proper mate for her daughter.

Although Heavenly is very beautiful and socially well placed, in her decision to be sexually intimate with Dick, she has significantly reduced her chance of becoming a respectable man's wife. Virginity is vital in the culture of Port Tyler, Mississippi. In admitting that she lost her virginity, Heavenly devastates her morally rigid mother. Still, Heavenly chooses to love Dick wholly without religious or moral constraints. She enjoys being the moral rebel, yet she wants a traditional family and home life once she is married. Unable to lower her standards to life on a river barge, she lets Dick go. She is now forced to make her life work with Arthur. When she discovers that Arthur killed Hertha, she decides to claim him and conceal his crime because in her mind it is better to be a murderer's wife than a spinster.

As do Blanche DuBois and Alma Winemiller, Heavenly rationalizes her sexuality through misguided desire and love. When Dick and Arthur leave her, Heavenly has two options for her life: She can, as do Blanche and Alma, become a prostitute, or she can repress her sexuality altogether, as Aunt Lila has. The end of the play leaves this decision open, but for the time being, Heavenly decides to wait on the porch until one of her beaus returns to claim her.

*Spring Storm* is one of Williams's posthumous gifts to contemporary theater. Although this play was written in 1937 and 1938, several years before Williams's first major success, THE GLASS MENAGERIE, it was never published or acknowledged in his lifetime. Williams wrote *Spring Storm* at the University of Iowa when he was a theater student in the late 1930s. The play was a homework assignment for a playwriting class he took with E. C. Mabie, and there are several different unpublished endings. Williams abandoned work on this script and began NOT ABOUT NIGHTINGALES, another college homework assignment. The "lost" script of *Spring Storm* was discovered in 1996 in Williams's papers at the University of Texas.

## PRODUCTION HISTORY

*Spring Storm* was first staged as a reading at the Ensemble Studio Theatre in 1996. It was directed by Dona D. Vaughn.

## PUBLICATION HISTORY

*Spring Storm* was published by New Directions in 1997.

## CHARACTERS

**Critchfield, Esmerelda** Esmerelda is the tiresome mother of Heavenly Critchfield. Esmerelda is obsessed with appearances and constantly advises her daughter on how to behave and dress. It is important to her that Heavenly marry the town's most eligible bachelor, Arthur Shannon. However, Heavenly has a lover, Dick Miles. Mrs. Critchfield knows that Heavenly will be ruined if she stays with Dick. This is a source of discord between the two women, who argue constantly.

**Critchfield, Heavenly** Heavenly is a beautiful young woman who desperately tries to tame her lover, Dick Miles. Heavenly is deeply in love with Dick, and she focuses all of her attention on keeping him and marrying him. Dick is a free spirit who wants to spend his life working on the Mississippi River. Heavenly is a respectable Southern gentlewoman with no patience for Dick's desire to be a vagabond on the river. Her relationship with Dick and her sexual relations with him have made her a subject of town gossip. Arthur Shannon, the wealthiest bachelor in Port Tyler, is also courting Heavenly. Heavenly is faced with the difficult decision of either living as a gypsy with Dick, the man she truly loves, or marrying Arthur and learning to appreciate him and live in luxury. Her greatest fear is that she, like her aunt, Lila Critchfield, will never marry. Bad times befall Heavenly and she is ultimately left to become an aging unmarried woman. As a lover, Heavenly resembles Serafina Delle Rose because she is proud of her passionate love for her boyfriend. She does not believe she is being promiscuous as she intends to marry Dick. She can also be viewed as a younger version of Amanda Wingfield, as she is a beautiful young woman who is courted by many suitors. She has many options, but in the end loses and resigns herself to being alone.

**Critchfield, Lila** Lila is the maiden aunt of Heavenly Critchfield. She is intelligent and has a close relationship with her niece. As Heavenly has, Lila had many suitors when she was young. Her one true love, Mr. Shannon, married another woman and broke her heart. She lives out the fate that Amanda Wingfield hopes to prevent for her daughter, Laura, that of being dependent upon the charity of her brother's wife and family. Lila finds solace in poetry and advises Heavenly to marry for love instead of status or money.

**Critchfield, Oliver** Oliver is the husband of Esmerelda Critchfield and father of Heavenly Critchfield. A cotton merchant, he is a traditional Southern man who has a sense of humor about gossip and protocol. He adores his daughter, and they share a deep connection, unlike his wife and daughter.

**Miles, Dick** Dick is a handsome young man and Heavenly Critchfield's boyfriend. Dick is a free spirit and is constantly seeking adventure. Although he loves Heavenly, Dick is in love with his freedom and the outdoors, and the Mississippi River in particular. Dick refuses to settle down and lead an ordinary life with a mundane office job. When he gets a job working for the government levee project, he wants to marry Heavenly and take her with him. Heavenly is horrified by this suggestion, as she desires a traditional Southern life: a husband with a stable job, a nice home, and children. Dick leaves Port Tyler, Mississippi, and Heavenly behind in order to pursue his dreams. Dick, as is Val Xavier, is wild at heart and seeks out adventure and new experiences.

**Neilson, Hertha** She is an intellectual young woman living in the socially oppressive environment of Port Tyler, Mississippi. Dreaming of adventure and of leaving her small hometown, Hertha identifies with a fellow dreamer, Dick Miles. However, unlike Dick, who does escape, Hertha is obligated to care for her alcoholic father. Hertha works at the public library and fantasizes about the town's most eligible bachelor, Arthur Shannon. One rainy night, Hertha encounters a drunken Arthur, who rapes and kills her in the freight yard.

**Shannon, Arthur** He is a wealthy young bachelor who has fallen in love with Heavenly Critchfield. Arthur was ridiculed in elementary school, particularly by Heavenly. Forced into boarding school to avoid further harassment, Arthur has returned home with romantic intentions toward his childhood foe. He becomes the second suitor for Heavenly and pressures her to choose him. Heavenly does not feel the same passion for Arthur as she does for Dick Miles, a free spirit who cannot stay in one place for long. Heavenly thinks she could love Arthur and his money. When Arthur commits rape and murder during a drunken rage, Heavenly advises him to deny his guilt and crime. He chooses to leave town. Heavenly loses both suitors and does not marry.

## *Stairs to the Roof*

Full-length play written between the years 1940 and 1942. The subtitle is *A Prayer for the Wild of Heart That Are Kept in Cages.*

## SYNOPSIS

The setting is expansive, ranging from the inside of a shirt factory, where a gigantic clock rules the employees, to street corners, office cubicles, a maze of buildings, and Gothic towers that represent a college campus. However, this expressionistic play remains minimal despite its varying settings.

*Scene 1: "Shirts and the Universe"*

In a department of Continental Shirtmakers, a large clock looms ominously over the workers.

In the office building of Consolidated Shirtmakers, Mr. Gum looks for Ben Murphy. Finding him returning from the elevator, Gum inquires about his disappearance. Ben tells his boss that he needed to get away from the stifling atmosphere of the office and found some "stairs to the roof." He philosophizes about the regimentation of the workplace and about the need for freedom from a grueling job. Gum tells Ben that he is reviewing his work file, as he questions whether Ben should continue to work at the factory. As the lights fade, Mr. E. laughs offstage.

*Scene 2: "No Fire Escape"*

The scene is the law office of Mr. Warren B. Thatcher, several floors down from the shirt factory.

In Thatcher's office a fire has started. Warren is on the phone with a female friend, telling her that there are no extinguishers, fire escapes, or volunteer firemen to be found. He arranges to meet her that night and begins to complain about his secretary, who is "on the verge of declaring her passion" for him. Hanging up, Warren calls for the Girl, who becomes flustered as he gives her instructions. Exasperated, he leaves for the rest of the day. The Girl (who remains nameless throughout the play) drafts a love letter to Warren. As the lights black out on the empty office, Mr. E. laughs offstage.

*Scene 3: "The Scene of Celebration"*

Two tables and a jukebox serve as the setting of a downtown bar in Saint Louis.

In the bar, Ben meets his longtime buddy and colleague, Jim. They converse about how different they dreamed their lives would be after college. As Ben pessimistically explains his job situation, he theorizes about the "inordinate lust for disintegration" of conscious life and predicts a rough night. After bidding Jim farewell, Ben goes home. Jim asks Bertha to dance and the lights go out.

*Scene 4: "Blue Heaven"*

A double bed is center stage.

As Ben enters his home, he steps on the cat and wakes Alma, his pregnant wife. She chastises Ben for his drinking habits, reminding him of his promise to save his beer money to buy a baby carriage. Ben begins to pontificate about the implications of child rearing and the moral responsibility entailed. He argues that a man should first better the world if he is going to raise a child. Alma suspects that Ben has had trouble at work, and as Ben rants, she grows hysterical, convinced that he has been fired. She threatens to leave him and Ben leaves, disgusted and frustrated. At the blackout, Mr. E. laughs offstage.

*Scene 5: "An Accident of Atoms"*

The set features a university quadrangle projected onto a screen and a large statue of an athlete with the inscription *youth.*

On a bench of a university campus, Ben sits, whiskey in hand, reminiscing about his college days. (The scene that proceeds is a "memory scene"—much like the motif used in THE GLASS MENAGERIE.) Cheering voices are heard faintly offstage, and from the dark steps Helen, Ben's college girlfriend, appears. She reminds him of the passion they once shared and quickly disappears. Jim appears as a ghost of his younger self and warns Ben not to marry Helen. A commencement speech is heard and Ben tells Jim that he has been offered a job at Consolidated Shirtmakers by the president himself, Mr. J. T. Faraway Jones. Jim urges Ben to take the job, proclaiming that he himself has accepted a job at the Olympic Light and Gas Company. Enraged by the memory of this conversation and angered by the reality of their present life, Ben hurls his whiskey into empty air and collapses into sobs. A Youth in military attire marches by, and Ben asks him whether he is prepared to take on the brutalities of real life. The Youth, careless and free, shrugs his shoulders and responds, "How do I know?" As the Youth exits, the music and lights dim and Mr. E. is heard sighing offstage.

*Scene 6: "White Lace Curtains"*

A chair, radio, and record player, with a fishbowl on top, are center stage.

Later in the night, Ben visits Jim at his house and discusses his "caged" existence. Ben wants to start anew and "refurnish" his life, but Jim urges him to stick to his middle-class lifestyle. Ben furiously rips down the white lace curtains hanging in Jim's kitchen, a stark symbol of their domesticated, repressed life. Jim only sighs and explains that his wife, Edna, will rehang the curtains in the morning. As Ben charges out of the house, Edna calls from the bedroom and tells Jim that Alma is leaving Ben. The lights fade and Mr. E. laughs offstage.

*Scene 7: "The Letter"*

A bedroom in a rooming house.

The Girl sits at home dreaming of Warren as her roommate, Bertha, raves about Jim. The Girl confesses to Bertha that she wrote a love letter to Warren and left it on his desk so that he would find it in the morning. Bertha insists that the Girl go to the office at once to retrieve the letter, regardless of her feelings. She warns the Girl that she is in danger of losing her job. At the blackout, Mr. E. laughs offstage.

*Scene 8: "Did Somebody Call the Night Watchman?"*

The scene is a downtown corner near the shirt factory at midnight.

The Girl appears at the doors of the Consolidated Shirtmakers office building, desperately knocking for the Night Watchman. An Officer appears, informing her that the Watchman is deaf and blind. Ben appears and asks her to feed his pigeons on the roof if he loses his job. Both suddenly see golden lights in the distance and travel off to investigate; Ben affectionately dubs the Girl "Alice," and she in turn calls him "Rabbit." They exit as the Watchman appears at the doorway. Sad, slow music begins to play, and Mr. E. laughs softly offstage.

*Scene 9: "Keys to the Cages"*

In a wooded section of the city park, a golden wheel can be seen through the trees and brush.

In search of the golden lights, Ben and the Girl come upon the park zoo, where the Zookeeper is tending to a pregnant fox. Outraged that the fox should have to give birth in captivity, Ben punches the Zookeeper and sets the fox free. He and the Girl run into the forest as the Zookeeper shouts for the police. As the lights fade, Mr. E. laughs uncontrollably offstage.

*Scene 10: "Every Girl Is Alice"*

Across a wide black lake, a carnival is visible.

Reaching the edge of a lake, Ben and the Girl rest from the chase. As they talk, she tells him about her love for her boss and about her feeling of being caged by the desperation of her situation. She wishes for love to be easy and "very white and cool-looking." Embracing her, Ben agrees to be her "Warren" if she will be his "swan." They lie down together in the grass as the lights dim and Mr. E. is "respectfully silent" offstage.

*Scene 11: "The Carnival—Beauty and the Beast"*

A carnival, with a ferris wheel, is seen. Below the stage a placard reads, "PETIT THEATRE PRESENTS 'BEAUTY AND THE BEAST.' PERFORMANCE: MIDNIGHT."

Proceeding toward the lights, Ben and the Girl arrive at a carnival, where "Beauty and the Beast" is being performed. As the play commences, a direct parallel between the stage action and the relationship between Ben and the Girl is evident. However, when it is time for the actors to bow, the Beast begins to choke Beauty. Ben intervenes quickly, speaking Russian to the foreign actor and calming him. Suddenly, the Zookeeper appears, but the Beast attacks him so that Ben can escape. The Girl is left alone as the carnival disperses. As she begins to sob, Ben returns to rescue her. He embraces her as the curtain falls. Mr. E. chuckles offstage.

*Scene 12: "This Corner's Where We Met"*

The street corner is the setting.

In the early morning light, Ben and the Girl approach the Consolidated Shirtmakers building. They part, each realizing that it is time to face reality. Ben explains that he is married and on the brink of losing his job. The Girl thanks him for a wonderful evening, and Ben kisses her before departing. At the blackout, Mr. E. chuckles offstage.

### *Scene 13: "I'm Worried about My Roommate"*

Scenes 13 through 16 are sidelines to the main-stage action. They are performed in swift succession. Lighting separates each mise-en-scène from the next.

Bertha is alarmed by the Girl's disappearance and tells Mrs. Hotchkiss, who remarks that she has probably "gone to the dogs!"

### *Scene 14: "Come Home to Mother"*

Alma calls her Mother to tell her that she is leaving Ben. Her Mother is delighted and welcomes her home.

### *Scene 15: "Rise and Shine"*

Edna wakes Jim, repetitiously shrilling, "Rise and shine!" Jim groans and covers his face with a pillow.

### *Scene 16: "Hello Again"*

Bertha and Jim meet on the street and discover that both their friends have disappeared. Bertha proposes that she and Jim do the same.

### *Scene 17: "Which Came First?"*

The action occurs in Mr. Thatcher's office.

The Girl charges into work and tells Warren that she is no longer in love with him. She immediately drops the wall clock into his wastebasket and tells him about the night she spent with Ben. Confidently, she goes about filing some papers, and then she tells an incredulous Mr. Thatcher that she is going to the roof for lunch. As she laughingly exits, Mr. E. is heard laughing "loud and close-by."

### *Scene 18: "Up to the Roof"*

In the office of the Continental Branch of Consolidated Shirtmakers, the huge clock says it is nearly noon.

The Consolidated Shirtmakers executives P, D, T, and Q rush into Gum's office, searching for Ben. They explain that he is a threat to the company because of his knowledge of the stairs to the roof. Gum proposes that they offer Ben a position which requires travel in exchange for his silence about the roof stairs. The men agree and proceed to search for the roof stairs and Ben. Mr. E. laughs very close by offstage.

### *Scene 19: "The Roof? What Roof?"*

Up on the roof, Ben is feeding the pigeons when the Girl arrives. She thanks him again for their evening together, and Ben expresses his repressed need to care for her. Suddenly, they hear great laughter and Mr. E. appears with thunder and lightning at his heels. The day turns to dusk, and stars appear in the sky as Mr. E. (with long flowing robes and a magical sparkler) proposes that Ben inhabit a new star world, a second world that Mr. E. wants to create. Ben agrees to go only if the Girl can accompany him. Mr. E. sends them off with a wave of his sparkler. Mr. E.'s laughter turns to silent weeping as he addresses the audience. He explains that he was ready to demolish the world until he saw Ben. Instead he decided to let Ben populate a new world, on a faraway star, so that now Ben has metaphorically gone "beyond the roof." P, D, Q, T, and Gum rush out onto the roof as Mr. E. disappears with a quick swish of his sparkler. Alarmed by the employees who have followed them onto the roof, the executives pretend to be welcoming, but the workers shout and cheer for Ben. From far away, Ben calls good-bye and the workers murmur on the roof about the dawning of "the Millennium." A band plays and the employees cheer as the curtain falls.

## COMMENTARY

The setting of Williams's *Stairs to the Roof* is minimalist at the start of the play; it grows more intricate as the protagonist himself travels further and further from reality. The lighting is complementary, the sets effective. Most props are pantomimed until the carnival scene—which requires gaudy toys and trinkets.

Williams draws largely from his own experiences working at the INTERNATIONAL SHOE COMPANY in SAINT LOUIS, MISSOURI, in the summer of 1936. Williams wrote this play after a mental breakdown caused by his monotonous existence at the factory. Thematically similar to *The Glass Menagerie, Stairs to the Roof* predates the Broadway hit that would make Williams famous.

*Stairs* possesses elements of sensationalism that make it a less weighty script. Its subtitle, *The Wild of Heart That Are Kept in Cages,* reminds us that the work is a social and political play, whereas *The Glass Menagerie* is more personal and has a less universal plot. In *Stairs to the Roof,* he creates a "moral earnestness" (afterword, 101), in his characters—characters trapped in a lifestyle they did not dream of, wishing for freedom from a caged existence.

As Ben Murphy is a slave to the factory and to the omnipresent clock that looms over the set, Tom Wingfield in *The Glass Menagerie* also feels he is a caged animal with an impotent rage toward his mother and economic responsibilities to his family. Both characters are provoked to grab control of their individual destiny. Ben Murphy becomes a savior to a people who are oppressed; Tom Wingfield breaks out of Saint Louis to pursue his own dreams. Both characters become defenders of the human spirit, collectively or otherwise. Ben Murphy, as is Tom Wingfield, is a reflection of Williams as a young man. As is Dick Miles in SPRING STORM, Ben Murphy is a dreamer who envisions a better way of life devoid of bureaucracies and mundane, stagnating work.

*Stairs to the Roof* is a precursor to CAMINO REAL, another Williams play endowed with sharp social and political commentary. Written in 1953 and based on a one-act play called TEN BLOCKS ON THE CAMINO REAL, *Camino Real* is sensational and absurd. It too is an expressionistic play in which Williams visits similar themes of entrapment, conformity, and cosmic magical realism that supersedes rational or literal happenings. *Stairs* is very similar to *Camino Real,* structurally, as Williams has written the play as several short acts or scenes that proceed within a framework (i.e., Mr. E's offstage laughter at the end of most scenes). *Stairs to the Roof* is one of Williams's apprentice plays, which, along with CANDLES TO THE SUN and NOT ABOUT NIGHTINGALES, illustrate his early talents and commitment to innovative and socially relevant drama.

## PRODUCTION HISTORY

*Stairs to the Roof* premiered at the Pasadena Playhouse on March 25, 1945, directed by MARGO JONES. It was produced after the success of *The Glass Menagerie* and received warm reviews, but it was clearly overshadowed by *Glass.* Similar in plot and theme, *The Glass Menagerie* triumphed as a play that could be more easily staged (*Stairs* would be technically and economically difficult to produce). *Stairs* was revived at the Pasadena Playhouse in 1947 but was then overshadowed by the huge success of the Broadway production of A STREETCAR NAMED DESIRE. Williams considered *Stairs* a play written and staged before its time. Allean Hale writes, "Its science-fiction ending, predating the inter-galactic explorations of *2001: A Space Odyssey* and *Star Trek I,* is on target today" (Hale, xviii).

## PUBLICATION HISTORY

*Stairs to the Roof* was published by New Directions in 2000.

## CHARACTERS

**Alma** The wife of Ben Murphy, an unhappy and disillusioned man. Alma decides to leave Ben when she becomes pregnant with his child.

**Bertha** She is the friend of the Girl. Bertha urges the Girl to retract the love letter her friend left for her employer, Mr. B. Warren Thatcher. Bertha accompanies her to the office in the middle of the night to retrieve the letter, and they encounter Ben Murphy, who befriends them.

**E, Mr.** Mr. E appears near the end of the play, wearing a long flowing robe and carrying a sparkling wand. He states that he was going to destroy the world until he met Ben Murphy. Because of Ben's feelings of discontent regarding his life as a factory worker, Mr. E. rescues Ben and his girlfriend, The Girl. He bellows a powerful laugh at the end of each scene of the play.

**Girl** She is the secretary of Mr. B. Warren Thatcher and madly in love with him. After she writes a love letter and leaves it on his desk, she is persuaded by her friend, Bertha, to retrieve the letter. The Girl and Bertha go to the office in the middle of the night and find Ben Murphy there. The Girl is chased by police for burglarizing the office building, but she evades them by running to the woods with Ben. There, she confesses that she is searching for a love that is "cool." Ben promises to be her Mr. Thatcher if she will in turn be his swan.

They consummate their relationship. The next day The Girl rushes to the roof of the factory building, where she finds Ben feeding pigeons. The magical Mr. E appears and rescues them from their desperate lives.

**Gum, Mr.** Gum is Ben Murphy's boss at the Consolidated Shirtmakers factory. He complains of Ben's negative attitude toward the factory and he chastises Ben for escaping to the roof for long breaks.

**Helen** She is the former girlfriend of Ben Murphy. Helen appears to Ben while he drunkenly sits on a park bench, reminiscing about the glory of his college days, when he nearly married Helen. She reminds him of the passion they once shared.

**Jim** He is the friend of Ben Murphy. Jim reminisces about their college days when life was free and they dreamed of being more than factory workers at Consolidated Shirtmakers.

**Murphy, Ben** Trapped in a factory job at Consolidated Shirtmakers, Ben dreams of a time when he can lead a more meaningful life. He escapes to the roof of the factory to breathe, write, and reminisce about the good old days of college, when he was carefree and the world was his. Ben leaves his pregnant wife, Alma, and becomes romantically involved with the Girl. She happens to be in love with the boss, Mr. B. Warren Thatcher. Ben and the Girl are kindred spirits whose dreams are finally fulfilled with the appearance of the godlike Mr. E. As does Tom Wingfield in *THE GLASS MENAGERIE,* Ben Murphy aspires to a happier life, and he is literally rescued from his mundane routine.

**Thatcher, Mr. B. Warren** The employer of the Girl, Mr. Thatcher is overwhelmed by his life and his job. The Girl, who is his secretary, is also in love with him, although he treats her badly. The Girl's attraction to him adds a bit of humor to his mundane existence.

## FURTHER READING

Hale, Allean. "Introduction: A Play for Tomorrow," in *Stairs to the Roof.* New York: New Directions, 2000.

# *Steps Must Be Gentle*

A dramatic reading for two performers written around 1980.

## SYNOPSIS

Two performers "representing" the American poet Hart Crane and his mother, Grace Hart Crane, engage in a nonrealistic, after-death duologue. Each performer stands behind a lectern facing the audience. Positioned behind the two performers is a large cyclorama, which displays an abstract design evoking the sea and sky.

Hart and Grace revisit their past and their often turbulent relationship. Grace confronts Hart about his suicide and tells him about the misery of her life after his death. She also seeks recognition from her son as the great "defender" of his poetry and reputation after his death. The two discuss the tension that developed between them because of Crane's sexuality, and Crane's absent father, who abandoned them both. Crane confesses his overwhelming, if unacknowledged, concern for his mother, and she painfully confesses that she ended her days in poverty as a scrubwoman.

## COMMENTARY

In *Steps Must Be Gentle* Williams pays tribute to Hart Crane, his favorite poet and most pervasive influence. (The play's title was taken from Crane's poem "My Grandmother's Love Letters.") For Williams, Crane served as a model, an inspiration, and in many ways a mirror of his own life, vocation, and ambition. Williams shared Crane's deeply ingrained loneliness, isolation, and detachment from a largely intolerant world. Williams and Crane also shared remarkable parallels in their background and family life, particularly their callous, emotionally absent, and unsupportive fathers and their neurotic and domineering mothers.

Crane's overwrought relationship with his mother, Grace Hart Crane, is the central motif of *Steps Must Be Gentle.* Reminiscent of various themes and situations that occur and are alluded to in *THE GLASS MENAGERIE* and *SUDDENLY LAST SUMMER,* the play depicts the rocky relationship between a sensitive young poet and his overbearing, but fiercely loyal mother. (The significantly absent father, who cares little for his sensitive poet-son, is also a recurring theme in each of these plays.) In *Steps Must be Gentle,* Crane and his mother establish a connection in the afterlife. (Hart Crane died April 26, 1932, and Grace Hart Crane died July 30, 1947.) The two characters are given the opportunity finally and frankly to speak their mind to one another and attempt to reconcile.

In many ways, Hart and Grace's relationship mirrors that of Williams and his own mother, EDWINA DAKIN WILLIAMS. Their relationship is depicted extensively in *The Glass Menagerie,* and in many of her tirades with her son, Grace Crane is often suggestive of Amanda Wingfield, particularly in her claim "Over-indulgence was my one fault as your mother." Grace's assertion that she "made it my dedication, my vocation, to protect your name, your legend. . . . Despite my age and illness, I have carried the stones to build your tower again" is a testament to her fierce loyalty and passionate belief in her son's greatness and creative genius. Her words resonate with those of Edwina Williams, who once stated, "I'm just like any mother who thinks her son is of course a genius always" (Brown, 118).

The figure of Williams's mother, possessed of a devotion to her children "to the point of obliteration" (Brown, 107), at once fiercely loyal, yet simultaneously hypercritical, is featured prominently throughout the Williams canon. She is a figure who, as a result of "too much love," reinforces her poet-son's sense of otherness and isolation and ultimately drives him away. This theme is vividly illustrated in *Steps Must Be Gentle,* in which, although Grace reiterates that she is in Hart's blood, and he in hers, and he confesses that Grace was the "central concern to my being as the heart of my body," their words cannot compensate for the vast emotional and physical distance that has long existed and continues to exist between them. Mother and son remain strangers even in death.

Although *Steps Must Be Gentle* was published in 1980, Gilbert Debusscher suggests that the play actually predates *The Glass Menagerie.* He makes a strong case that *Steps* served as an early template for *Menagerie.* However, the play's expressionistic style and undeniable maturity of voice place it squarely alongside the later works of Williams's dramatic canon. There are a finality and a feeling of coming full circle in the work, as if to reveal Tom and Amanda, Sebastian and Violet—and perhaps by extension Tennessee and Edwina—reunited years later.

The other important feature that makes *Steps Must Be Gentle* such an intriguing and significant work is its uncompromising treatment of homosexuality. Hart and Grace openly discuss their conflict over his sexual orientation, a point of discord in their life together. Crane's declaration and plea to his mother to acknowledge his sexual identity possess "a ring of authentic feeling, coupled with a characteristically Williamsian will to endure" (Debusscher, 475). As Debusscher notes, at no other point in Williams's published work is homosexuality presented "more honestly and simply."

## PRODUCTION HISTORY

There have been no professional production of *Steps Must Be Gentle.*

## PUBLICATION HISTORY

*Steps Must Be Gentle* was published in a limited edition by William Targ in 1980. Three hundred fifty copies were printed and signed by Williams.

## CHARACTERS

**Crane, Hart** (1899–1932) Historical figure and one of two characters in *Steps Must Be Gentle.* Hart Crane was one of Williams's most important literary influences. (Some scholars contend that Crane was Williams's most central influence and principal artistic inspiration.) Williams admired Crane above all American poets and believed Crane possessed one of the "purer voices in poetry" (Debusscher, 456). Williams ranked Crane's poetry with that of Shakespeare, Keats, and Whitman (*Where I Live,* 2–3).

Crane's poetry combined the influences of European literature with a particularly American sensibility. His major book-length epic poem, *The Bridge* (1930), expresses a vision of the historical and spiritual meaning of America. As did T. S. Eliot, Crane used the landscape of the modern industrialized city to create a powerful new and symbolic literature. Crane viewed himself as a marginalized figure as a result of his vocation as a poet within a capitalist economy and because of his sexual identity. As a result, a major theme in Crane's work is that of the artist as outcast in an urbanized world. In addition, he made a lifelong effort to find a means of expressing his sexuality and making it meaningful for his audience. These ideals and ideas greatly inspired Williams and surfaced throughout his dramatic works, such as *BATTLE OF ANGELS*, *THE GLASS MENAGERIE*, *CLOTHES FOR A SUMMER HOTEL*, *ORPHEUS DESCENDING*, *STAIRS TO THE ROOF*, *SUDDENLY LAST SUMMER*, and *SOMETHING CLOUDY, SOMETHING CLEAR*.

In Crane, Williams found a mirror of his own life, vocation, and ambition. He recognized their shared pain—a deeply ingrained sense of loneliness and isolation. Their mutual sense of detachment sprang from being gay men living in a largely intolerant world. Gilbert Debusscher is one of several scholars to note the "truly stunning similarity of [Williams's] and Crane's formative years, family situations, and aspirations" (Debusscher, 460). These parallels include similar small-town origins, families who consisted of a domineering mother and loving and saintly grandmother, and a callous, emotionally absent, and unsupportive father. Williams and Crane were plagued by the same professional and personal demons: fear of failure, periods of self-doubt and despair, and the continual fight for artistic legitimacy. Williams first had contact with Hart Crane's poetry while he was a student at Washington University in SAINT LOUIS, MISSOURI. He reportedly helped himself to a volume of Crane's collected poems that belonged to the university library. He took the book and kept it because it had not, in his opinion, received the readership it deserved (Debusscher, 456). Williams would later declare that this one volume was his "only library and all of it" (ibid.).

Debusscher has also extensively outlined the "clear traces of [Crane's] presence" in Williams's works, which include passing references in *YOU TOUCHED ME!* (Mathilda Rockley claims that the romantic poetry she has written is dedicated to Hart Crane) and *NIGHT OF THE IGUANA* (while painting a portrait of T. Lawrence Shannon, Hannah Jelkes recalls a famous portrait of Hart Crane). The motto of *A STREETCAR NAMED DESIRE* is from the fifth stanza of Crane's "The Broken Tower" (the poem Crane finished a month before his death). The motto for *SWEET BIRD OF YOUTH* was gleaned from Crane's poem "Legend." The title of Williams's play *SUMMER AND SMOKE* is from Crane's poem "Emblems of Conduct": "By that time summer and smoke were past / Dolphins still played, arching the horizons, / But only to build memories of spiritual gates" (Crane, 68). For Debusscher, Crane also "pervades the texture" of *The Glass Menagerie* without being explicitly mentioned or alluded to (Debusscher, 461). He also suggests that Williams shaped the play's title from Crane's poem "The Wine Menagerie." Both Debusscher and Nancy Tischler see Crane vividly represented in the dead poet son, Sebastian Venable, of *Suddenly Last Summer.*

Williams's most overt dramatic treatment of, or tribute to, Hart Crane is the play *Steps Must Be Gentle,* in which Crane appears as a character alongside his mother, Grace Hart Crane. The play's title is taken from Crane's poem "My Grandmother's Love Letters," which includes the line "Over the greatness of such space / Steps must be gentle" (Crane, 63). The play, which Williams called a dramatic reading for two performers, is an imaginary afterlife duologue between the poet and his mother. Hart Crane died on April 26, 1932, when he leapt from the stern of the ship *Vera Cruz* and plunged into the Caribbean Sea near the Florida coastline while sailing back to the United States from Mexico. In his will, Williams requested to be buried at sea near the location of Crane's suicidal leap. In *A Streetcar Named Desire* the character Blanche Dubois echoes this request.

In 1965, Williams recorded selections of Hart Crane's poetry for Caedmon Records (*Tennessee Williams Reads Hart Crane*). Williams also drafted the liner notes for the album's dust jacket. Many of his observations on the life and work of Hart Crane are strikingly appropriate for the playwright himself: "Crane had lived and worked with such fearful intensity—and without fearful intensity Crane was unable to work at all. . . . He lived in a constant inner turmoil and storm that liquor, which he drank recklessly, was no longer able to quieten, to hold in check." Williams's endearing closing lines of tribute to Crane are also equally appropriate for both the playwright and his poet-hero: "Still there remains about him so much that escapes understanding. But his poetry lives and burns and cries out with indestructible beauty."

**Crane, Grace Hart** The mother of the American poet Hart Crane, Grace conducts a fretful duologue with her son in the afterlife, and the two reminiscence about their troubled past together. Unable to confront her son previously about his suicide or his sexuality, Grace now addresses these points with Hart. She also declares herself his great defender and informs her son that after his death, she devoted her life to promoting his poetic genius and keeping his legend alive. In many ways, this character bears striking similarities to Amanda Wingfield in *THE GLASS MENAGERIE,* and by extension Williams's own mother, EDWINA DAKIN WILLIAMS. Her maternal ferocity in protecting her son's poetic legacy is also mirrored in Violet Venable in *SUDDENLY LAST SUMMER.* Williams became acquainted with Grace Hart Crane before her death in 1947, and she gave Williams a scarf and a fan that once belonged to her poet son.

### FURTHER READING

Brown, Dennis. *Shoptalk: Conversations about Theatre and Film with Twelve Writers, One Producer—and Tennessee Williams's Mother.* New York: Newmarket Press, 1992.

Crane, Hart. *The Complete Poems of Hart Crane,* edited by Waldo Frank. Garden City, N.Y.: Doubleday, 1958.

Debusscher, Gilbert. "Minting Their Separate Wills: Tennessee Williams and Hart Crane," *Modern Drama* 26, no. 4 (December 1983): 455–476.

Williams, Tennessee. "Hart Crane," *Tennessee Williams Reads Hart Crane,* Caedmon Records, TC 1206, 1965.

Williams, Tennessee. *Where I Live: Selected Essays,* edited by Christine R. Day and Bob Woods. New York: New Directions, 1978.

## *Stopped Rocking*

A screenplay written in 1977.

### SYNOPSIS

The action of this screenplay takes places in 1975 in Saint Carmine's Sanatorium, a mental institution near Saint Louis, and in various other locales in and around the city.

On Easter Sunday, Olaf Svenson arrives at Saint Carmine's Sanatorium to visit his wife, Janet Svenson. Olaf changes his mind and gives to Sister Grace the flowers he has for Janet. Sister Grim chastises Sister Grace for being very emotionally involved with patients' lives. Sister Grace delivers the flowers to Janet, who is heartily disappointed.

In a classroom at the community college, Alicia Trout has just finished a class. She stands near a window, wearing a sheer blouse. Stuart, one of her students, becomes so captivated by her beauty that he attempts to place his hands on her breasts. Alicia reprimands Stuart as Olaf enters the room. Alicia chastises Olaf for visiting Janet and for refusing to divorce her.

In the dayroom at Saint Carmine's, Janet plays bridge with Madge and Gloria. Janet and Madge notice that Sophie has slowed the pace of her rocking in her rocking chair. Madge fears that Sophie has "retired from life." Gloria discovers a note on her door indicating that Gloria will be given a series of shock therapy treatments the following day.

The next day Janet is summoned to see the head physician, Dr. J. Planter Cash. Dr. Cash makes Janet nervous and agitated. He observes her coldly and takes copious notes during their conversation. Dr. Cash informs Janet that he is going to allow her husband to take her for a weekend outing in the Ozark Mountains. On the day of the scheduled outing, Olaf does not arrive, and Janet is severely disappointed. Later, Dr. Cash informs Janet that Olaf has requested that Janet be transferred to another institution.

Alicia and Olaf sit watching television in their apartment. As Olaf tries to watch baseball, Alicia starts another argument about Janet. She wants Olaf to divorce Janet so that they can marry. Olaf decides that he will take Janet to the Ozarks the next weekend to break the news to her.

Olaf collects Janet from Saint Carmine's in his camper. As they travel to the Ozarks, Janet can hardly contain her excitement. Olaf stops to call

Alicia, who is in their apartment having an intimate dinner with her student, Stuart. As the journey continues, Olaf is distracted by Janet's behavior and they are involved in several nearly serious traffic incidents. After being hit by another car from behind, Olaf and Janet are so shaken that they both leave the camper and vomit in the bushes. Olaf calls Alicia; she and Stuart are slowly becoming more intimately involved.

Once they arrive at the Ozark campsite, Olaf and Janet try to connect and manage one poignant embrace, but ultimately their dialogue is unsuccessful. Olaf tells Janet his plans for the future with Alicia. Janet takes one of her tablets, and she and Olaf try to sleep. Janet wakes during the night. Olaf is severely irritated by Janet and her repeated requests that they drive higher into the mountains. When he reaches his wit's end, he forces Janet to take an excessive amount of her prescribed medication. The medication alters her severely. She rushes out of the camper and has a vision of the Apparition of Father O'Donnell. Father O'Donnell speaks kindly to her and assures her that she has been "absolved." Janet thanks Father O'Donnell but informs him that she "has to keep moving. Can't stop rocking." She runs toward the river and wades into the water. Olaf watches her from the trailer as she founders, splashes, and sinks in the water. Eventually he helps her and carries her back to the trailer.

The next day Olaf returns Janet to Saint Carmine's. Janet is now completely withdrawn. She has "stopped rocking" and has resigned herself to silence. She is whisked away in a wheelchair, as Dr. Cash orders that she be placed on the ninth floor, "the vegetable garden."

## COMMENTARY

In *Stopped Rocking,* Williams vividly and poignantly depicts the humiliation and indignities often suffered by patients in mental institutions. Janet's painful story is one of great loss, the loss of love, liberty, pride, and human dignity. Sister Grace is the only source of humanity and affection in Janet's world. However, Sister Grace is significantly outnumbered by those with more authority at the asylum, such as Sister Grim and Dr. Cash. Through this "dark work" Williams hoped to make audiences aware of the indignities mental patients suffer, in an effort to shift the balance toward "the light of humanity" (Williams, author's note, 295). As Richard Gilman suggests, it is not at all far-fetched to assume that Williams's loving sympathy for Janet and her fellow patients was largely informed by his enduring love of his sister, ROSE WILLIAMS, who suffered from mental illness.

## PRODUCTION HISTORY

*Stopped Rocking* has not been filmed or produced professionally.

## PUBLICATION HISTORY

*Stopped Rocking* was first published in *Stopped Rocking and Other Screenplays* (1984).

## CHARACTERS

**Apparition of Father O'Donnell** Father O'Donnell is the much-loved former head physician at St. Carmine's Sanatorium. All of his former patients, particularly Janet Svenson, remember him fondly. When her husband, Olaf Svenson, forces her to take an overdose of her medication, Janet has a vision of Father O'Donnell.

**Cash, Dr. J. Planter** The insensitive resident physician at St. Carmine's Sanatorium. Unlike his predecessor, Father O'Donnell, Dr. Cash is insensitive in his dealings with his mentally ill patients. His callousness frustrates and confuses his good-natured patient, Janet Svenson, and as a result, he refuses to believe that she is getting well.

**Gloria** She is a 72-year-old mental patient at Saint Carmine's. She disrupts Madge's bridge game when she discovers a sign on a door indicating that she will be given a series of electrical shock therapy treatments the following day.

**Madge** An aggressive mental patient at Saint Carmine's Sanatorium. Playing bridge is the only joy in Madge's life at Saint Carmine's. She becomes severely agitated when other inmates are too dazed or confused to play the game correctly or when they disrupt or halt her games.

**Sister Grace** She is a caring attendant at Saint Carmine's Sanatorium in Saint Louis. As her name suggests, she approaches the women in her care with delicacy and affection. She takes special care of one of her favorite patients, Janet Svenson. In this she sharply contrasts with her counterpart, Sister Grim.

**Sister Grim** As her name suggests, Sister Grim is a sour and unpleasant nun who reluctantly cares for patients at Saint Carmine's Sanatorium near Saint Louis. Unlike her counterpart, Sister Grace, Sister Grim badgers and antagonizes the mentally ill women in the asylum.

**Sophie** Sophie is an elderly mental patient in Saint Carmine's Sanatorium. The title of the screenplay is a reference to her. When first admitted to the asylum Sophie sat in her rocking chair each day and rocked ferociously. This action expressed her will and determination to live. As she lost that will, her rocking slowed, until she eventually stopped rocking altogether. Madge declares that Sophie has "retired from life."

**Stuart** Stuart is a community college student who is having an affair with his physics teacher, Alicia Trout. He visits Alicia while her long-term lover, Olaf Svenson, is away visiting his wife, Janet Svenson, at Saint Carmine's Sanatorium.

**Svenson, Janet** Janet is a mentally disturbed woman who has been an inmate at Saint Carmine's Sanatorium for five years. Her husband, Olaf Svenson, has moved on with his life and for the last five years has had a relationship with Alicia Trout. Olaf, however, does not have the heart to divorce or abandon Janet. Ultimately, he resorts to cowardly tactics to rid himself of her by arranging that she be transferred to an asylum away from Saint Louis. Before her transfer, Olaf takes Janet for a weekend outing in the Ozarks, and during the trip he forces her to take more medication than has been prescribed. Janet, who was formerly a speech therapist, met Olaf while helping him to overcome a speech impediment.

**Svenson, Olaf** Olaf is the tormented handsome husband of Janet Svenson. Janet is a long-term mental patient at Saint Carmine's Sanatorium. She has been in treatment for nearly five years. Olaf has established a long-term relationship with Alicia Trout, an attractive community college physics teacher, and is searching for a guilt-free way to terminate his relationship with Janet. Ultimately, he resorts to cowardly tactics to rid himself of her by requesting that she be transferred to an asylum away from Saint Louis. Before her transfer, Olaf takes Janet for a weekend outing in the Ozarks, and during the trip he forces her to take more medication than has been prescribed for her.

**Trout, Alicia** Alicia is an attractive community college physics teacher who has a complicated relationship with Olaf Svenson. Olaf's wife, Janet Svenson, is mentally ill and has been confined to a mental institution for five years. Olaf has moved on with his life and has been in a relationship with Alicia for the last five years. Much to Alicia's dismay, he does not have the heart to divorce or abandon Janet. Described as a "mathematical bombshell," Alicia has an unsentimental view of love. She delights in her own physical attractiveness and dallies with Stuart, one of her students, while Olaf is away visiting Janet.

## FURTHER READING

Gilman, Richard. "Introduction," in *Stopped Rocking and Other Screenplays.* New York: New Directions, 1984, p. xi.

Williams, Tennessee. "Author's Note," in *Stopped Rocking and Other Screenplays.* New York: New Directions, 1984, p. 295.

# *The Strangest Kind of Romance*

A one-act play written before 1946.

## SYNOPSIS

The setting is a boardinghouse in a factory town.

*Scene 1*

The Landlady (Mrs. Gallaway) shows Musso the room she has for rent. She warns him that the previous tenant had a terrible strain of luck caused by

Nitchevo, the stray cat that occupies the room. Musso takes a liking to the cat and, ignoring superstition, rents the room. Mrs. Gallaway explains that she has an invalid husband who also lives on the premises. She likes Musso so she decides to help him get a job at the local plant. When an Old Man enters the room, Mrs. Gallaway introduces him as her father-in-law. She promises to visit Musso.

### *Scene 2*

In late winter, Musso grows unhappy with his life. He hates the exhausting work at the plant, and his only friend is Nitchevo. While dressing for bed, he hears a knock at his door. Mrs. Gallaway appears wearing a soiled negligee. She admits that her husband is of no use to her sexually and hopes that Musso will have an affair with her, as had the man who previously rented the room. Musso warns her against becoming involved with him, as he is merely a "ghost of a man." Mrs. Gallaway tells Musso that "nature says—don't be lonely" as she caresses his shoulder.

### *Scene 3*

Late one winter night, Musso enters his room covered with snow. He sets out cream for Nitchevo, and the Old Man enters his room. The Old Man warns Musso not to become too devoted to Nitchevo and complains that the plant will not hire him because of his age. The Old Man becomes hysterical and breaks a windowpane. Mrs. Gallaway bursts through the door with a police officer. Musso seduces the woman in order to keep Nitchevo.

### *Scene 4*

Several months later, Musso has moved out of the boardinghouse. He returns in search of Nitchevo. There is a new lodger (the Boxer) in his old room. Musso explains to him that he was laid off at the plant and committed to a mental institution. Mrs. Gallaway informs Musso that his belongings have been stored for him. She proudly admits that she has gotten rid of Nitchevo. Musso insults her, and she slaps him. The Boxer intervenes by throwing Musso out the door. Unexpectedly, Musso finds Nitchevo in a nearby alleyway. Watching from the upstairs window, Mrs. Gallaway remarks that the "ghost of a man" and the cat are departing together—"the funniest pair of lovers!"

## COMMENTARY

In *The Strangest Kind of Romance* Williams illustrates the importance of love and trust in a ruthless, cold world. Musso is extremely lonely, to the point that his life has become transparent. He identifies himself as a ghost in the living world. Escaping the harshness of life is impossible for him. The bitter winter air swirls around him during his cruel days of factory work. His only source of emotional security is the cat, and the only times he feels alive are in the sexual encounters with his aggressive landlady. Musso is consumed by the mendacity of his life, and his source of companionship is Nitchevo, a stray animal.

The Old Man warns Musso of the fleeting nature of his relationship with Nitchevo, but Musso is so lonely that he disregards the advice. Teetering on the brink of insanity, Musso falls headlong into a state of mental frailty and is forced to leave without Nitchevo. When he recovers and goes in search of the cat, he finds that he has been replaced at the boardinghouse; the discovery supports his belief that he is insignificant, merely a ghost.

The factory town of *The Strangest Kind of Romance* resembles Saint Louis during Williams's life there. In this autobiographical mirroring, Williams creates a Musso who is lonely and emotionally fraught as well as physically trapped in an industrial and depressing setting. Williams often wrote of his miserable life in Saint Louis, where he was ridiculed and misunderstood. Musso is a drifter who lands himself in a city like Saint Louis of the 1930s and is negatively affected by the dinginess and desperation of a life in the dank factory. Williams's unhappy home life contributed to his misery in the metropolis, and his isolation is made manifest in Musso.

## PRODUCTION HISTORY

*The Strangest Kind of Romance* was first produced at Theatre de Champs Elysees, Paris, 1960.

## PUBLICATION HISTORY

This play was first published in *27 Wagons Full of Cotton and Other One-Act Plays* (1966). This one-act play is based on the short story, "The Malediction."

### CHARACTERS

**Landlady** The Landlady, who is also referred to as Miss Gallaway, is a middle-aged woman who runs a boardinghouse. Because her husband is an invalid, she seeks out sexual relationships with her male boarders. She plays the balalaika and hates Musso's cat, Nitchevo.

**Musso** A frail and weak man who is given the nickname "Musso" by his Landlady. When Musso moves into Miss Gallaway's boardinghouse he befriends the cat Nitchevo, who also occupies his room.

**Old Man** He is the father-in-law of the Landlady. An alcoholic, the Old Man is thrown out of the boardinghouse for fraternizing with the tenants late one night.

# *A Streetcar Named Desire*

A full-length play written in 1947.

### SYNOPSIS

The setting is an old house that has been turned into two apartments. It is located in Elysian Fields, a section of the French Quarter of New Orleans. The action takes place in the downstairs two-room apartment rented by the Kowalskis.

#### *Scene 1*

Stella Kowalski relaxes in a shabby armchair in the bedroom of the small apartment. She eats chocolates and reads a movie magazine. Stella's husband, Stanley Kowalski, enters, carrying a package of meat dripping with blood and yelling for his wife. Stanley tosses the meat to Stella, who catches it in a surprised reaction. Stanley leaves to go bowling with his friends, and Stella decides to tag along. She hurriedly primps in the living room mirror, quickly closes the apartment door behind her, and says hello to Eunice Hubbell and a Negro Woman who are sitting on the landing. As she exits, the two women laugh about Stanley's lack of manners.

Blanche DuBois enters. She is carrying a small suitcase and a piece of paper. She is a fading Southern belle, whose appearance suggests she is going to a garden party, but her search for her sister, Stella, has landed her in the slums of the French Quarter. Eunice notices the confused Blanche, and she asks whether she is lost. Blanche explains that she was instructed to take a streetcar named Desire to Elysian Fields via a streetcar called Cemetery. Eunice informs her that she is indeed in the right place. Eunice lets her into the Kowalskis' apartment to wait for Stella while the Negro Woman fetches Stella from the bowling alley. Blanche has arrived unannounced, and she is shocked to discover Stella living in such a dismal place.

Blanche searches for a drink, and Stella enters. The two sisters are ecstatic to be reunited. Blanche speaks excitedly, overwhelming Stella with criticism of the apartment. Stella is speechless and hurt by these remarks, and she notices that Blanche is shaking and anxious. Stella is concerned by her sister's behavior, and she attempts to calm her nerves by offering her a drink. Blanche urges Stella to explain why she is living in such depressing conditions. Blanche says she has taken a leave of absence from her high school teaching job. She says that she is having a difficult time and needed a break. Blanche mentions the weight Stella has gained, and she compliments her on her appearance; however, Stella knows that her sister is being critical. Blanche demands that Stella stand so she can fully analyze the size of her hips, her less than perfect haircut. She asks Stella about having a maid, but the Kowalskis' apartment only consists of two rooms. Blanche is horrified by this news. She pours another drink to curb her intolerance of the place. Blanche has been lonely; she feels her sister abandoned her when she left Mississippi and their father died. Blanche admits that she is not well. Stella insists that her sister stay at the apartment, and she directs her to a folding bed. She insists that Stanley will not mind the lack of privacy, as he is Polish. Stella advises her sister that Stanley is unlike the Southern gentlemen they knew back in Laurel, Mississippi. She confesses he is ill mannered, but she is madly in love with him.

Blanche confesses that she has lost Belle Reve, the family plantation. Blanche expresses her resentment of her sister because she was "in bed with [her] Polack" while Blanche scraped and clawed to hold on to Belle Reve. Stella is very upset to know that they have lost their homestead. Blanche bitterly blames the foreclosure on the many deaths in the family. Blanche is plagued with guilt, as well as being hopelessly adrift, and she projects her feelings of loss onto Stella, who runs into the bathroom to escape her sister's wrath.

Stanley returns home. He shouts to his friends, Steve Hubbell and Mitch (Harold Mitchell), from the stairwell. Blanche speaks to him before he notices her presence. Stanley is cordial to her and asks for Stella, who has locked herself away in the bathroom. He offers Blanche another shot of whiskey, noticing that the bottle has already been sampled. Blanche declines the offer, stating that she rarely drinks. Her obvious dishonesty spurs Stanley to ask some very personal questions regarding her past, namely, about her husband. He sheds his sweaty shirt to find relief in the summer heat and welcomes her to stay with them. Upset by his meddlesome inquiries, Blanche replies that her young husband is dead. She grows nauseous discussing this subject and has to sit down to regain her composure.

*Scene 2*

Around six o'clock the following evening, Blanche and Stella plan to have dinner out and see a movie while Stanley and his friends have a poker night in the apartment. While Blanche readies herself in the bathroom, Stella tells Stanley that Belle Reve has been lost. She also warns him not to mention that she is pregnant because Blanche is already so unstable. Stanley is most concerned with the loss of the estate. He suspects Blanche sold the plantation and kept all of the profits for herself. Referring to the Napoleonic Code, Stanley wants to know whether he has been swindled. To find proof of the foreclosure he rummages through Blanche's trunk. Appraising the furs and jewelry she has, he urges Stella to acknowledge that Blanche has deceived her. Stella fears the looming confrontation, so she escapes to the porch.

When Blanche emerges from her hot bath and realizes that Stella is not around, she flirts with Stanley as a means of winning him over; however, he is interested only in the profits from Belle Reve. When Stanley accuses Blanche of selling the plantation and keeping all of the money, she insists that she has never cheated anyone in her life. She says, "I know I fib a good deal. After all, a woman's charm is fifty percent illusion, but when a thing is important, I tell the truth." Stanley rifles through the trunk again, searching for documents that will prove Blanche is lying. Stanley discovers yellowing letters held together by aging ribbons, and he withholds these visibly precious items until she pulls two manila envelopes from her belongings. Blanche says that his touch has contaminated her cherished love letters. She tells Stanley that this paperwork is all that is left of the plantation, and he continues berating her by demanding to know how she could allow the foreclosure to happen. Blanche recoils with anger and retorts that the plantation has been lost by generations of negligent men who "exchanged the land for their epic fornications." Stanley intends to have the documents read by a lawyer friend, and Blanche invites him to do so. Now that Stanley has been proved wrong, he justifies his concern with the fact that Stella is pregnant. This is a happy digression for Blanche, who is genuinely excited by this information. When Stella returns, Blanche expresses her joy about the baby. She brags that she handled Stanley and even flirted with him. The two sisters leave as Stanley's friends arrive for their poker night.

*Scene 3*

Later that night in the Kowalski apartment, Stanley and his friends are still drinking and playing cards. Stella and Blanche return at 2:30 A.M., and Stanley asks them to visit Eunice until the game is over. When Stella does not comply, Stanley slaps her backside as a means of countering her disobedience in front of his friends. Blanche is intrigued by Mitch, who is uninterested in the poker game because he is worried about his ailing mother. Blanche is immediately attracted to his sensitivity. The two introduce themselves. Mitch offers her a cigarette, showing her the inscription on his cigarette case. She immediately recognizes it as the poetry of Elizabeth Barrett Browning. Mitch explains the case is from a former girlfriend who died. Mitch's story of his former lover resonates with Blanche's own sense of loss of her young husband, Allan Grey. She tells Mitch, "Sorrow makes for sincerity," and continues, "Show me a person that hasn't known sorrow and I'll show you a superficial person." She asks Mitch to cover the naked lightbulb with a Chinese lantern she recently purchased.

Stanley grows more inebriated and increasingly irritated by the music Blanche is playing. He crosses the room, rips the radio from the wall, and throws it out of the window. He hits Stella when she tries to stop him. Humiliated and stunned, Stella runs into the kitchen area and orders Stanley's friends to leave. Stanley chases and attacks Stella. Blanche begs Mitch to stop him, and the men restrain Stanley on the sofa. Blanche whisks Stella to Eunice's apartment upstairs while the men attempt to sober Stanley. After a cold shower, he stumbles out of the bathroom, goes out onto the porch, and yells up to Stella. He continues to shout for Stella, who descends the stairs and returns to him. Stanley falls to his knees, pressing his head against her legs. Kissing passionately, the couple retreat to their bedroom. Blanche runs down after Stella. When she discovers them making love, she is angered by her sister's weakness. Mitch calls out to Blanche. They share another cigarette. Blanche is thankful for Mitch's kindness.

### *Scene 4*

Early the next morning, Blanche returns to the Kowalski apartment after spending the night at Eunice and Steve's apartment. When she realizes Stella is alone, she hugs her with nervous concern. Stella, on the other hand, is cheerful and content. Stella blames liquor and poker for Stanley's behavior. She explains to her sister that she gets a thrill from her husband's extreme actions. Blanche is infuriated. She says Stella has married a "madman." While Blanche devises an escape plan for them, Stella tidies the apartment. Stella says she is happy with Stanley. Blanche is still bewildered by Stella's cool resignation.

Blanche remembers an old beau, Shep Huntleigh, whom she plans to call on for their escape, but Stella does not want to be rescued. Blanche compares Stanley to an ape. During this conversation, Stanley has returned unnoticed. He has heard everything that has been said. All of Blanche's persuading has been in vain: When Stella sees Stanley, she runs over and jumps into his arms.

### *Scene 5*

Blanche has been living at the Kowalskis' apartment for three months. While she finishes writing a letter to Shep about imaginary cocktail parties she has been attending, Stanley enters. He slams drawers and creates noise to express his irritation by Blanche's presence. To provoke Stanley, she asks him his astrological sign. He remarks that he is a Capricorn (the goat) and Blanche replies she is Virgo, the sign of the virgin. Stanley laughs and asks her about a man by the last name of Shaw who claims to have spent an evening with Blanche at the Flamingo Hotel. Blanche adamantly denies this accusation, but her face registers panic and alarm. Stanley is victorious and exits to go bowling.

Blanche becomes hysterical. She asks Stella whether she has heard rumors about her, but Stella gracefully denounces gossip. Blanche confesses that she did not maintain a good reputation when she was losing Belle Reve. She admits her fears of being a "soft" person, of needing people too much, and of her fading beauty. Blanche fears she will not be able to "turn the trick" much longer because she is visibly aging. She also confesses that she lied about her age to Mitch because she wants him to fall in love with her. Blanche has presented an illusion of herself as a prim and proper woman to Mitch. Stella is accustomed to Blanche's nervous tirades, and she pays little attention to what her sister is actually saying. Stella comforts her by pouring her a drink. A young boy stops by the apartment selling newspapers. On his way out, Blanche calls him back inside and kisses him. Blanche chastises herself for putting "her hands" on the boy. He leaves and Mitch arrives with a bouquet of roses for her.

### *Scene 6*

Later that night, Blanche and Mitch return from a disappointing date. Blanche blames herself for the dull evening. Mitch asks whether he may kiss her good night, and she consents but says their actions can go no further because she is a single woman. Stanley and Stella are not home, so Blanche invites

Mitch in for a nightcap. Blanche plays the coquette while Mitch perspires with desire for her. While she searches for a bottle of whiskey, Blanche asks Mitch in French whether he would like to sleep with her. She comments that it is a good thing Mitch does not understand French. She encourages him to take off his coat, but he is embarrassed by his sweatiness. Blanche asserts that he is just a healthy man.

When Mitch suggests that the four of them go out together sometime, Blanche makes it clear that Stanley hates her. She asks whether Stanley has said anything derogatory about her. Mitch replies that he does not understand how Stanley could behave so rudely to her. Blanche says she plans to leave as soon as Stella has the baby.

Mitch asks Blanche her age, and Blanche refuses to answer. He explains that he asks because he has been with his mother talking about her. Blanche presumes Mitch will be very lonely when his mother dies. She explains that she knows this sort of loneliness firsthand because her one true love has passed away. She tells Mitch about Allan's tenderness and sensitivity and says that she never understood him until she discovered he was having an affair with an older man. Blanche explains that Allan needed her to help him, but she could not see what was happening until it was too late. She confronted him while they were drunk at a dance at Moon Lake Casino. Her words provoked him to run to the edge of the lake and commit suicide. She can still hear the polka music that was playing during the time. Blanche cannot forgive herself for condemning Allan's desires and pushing him to such drastic measures. She compares her love for Allan to a

Production photograph for the Broadway production of *A Streetcar Named Desire,* starring Jessica Tandy as Blanche Du Bois, Marlon Brando as Stanley Kowalski, and Kim Hunter as Stella Kowalski. *(Photographer: Eileen Darby. Photograph courtesy of The Billy Rose Theatre Collection, New York Public Library)*

"blinding light." Mitch answers that they are both lonely, and they both need someone. The polka tune that continually plays in Blanche's mind ceases. Mitch and Blanche embrace with thoughts of marriage.

### Scene 7

Several weeks later, Stanley arrives home after a day of work to find the apartment decorated for Blanche's birthday party. He is disgruntled to know that Blanche is taking a hot bath, making the apartment even hotter and increasingly unbearable. Stanley proudly announces to Stella that he has found out the real story behind her sister's extended visit. She was fired from her teaching job because she had an indecent relationship with a 17-year-old boy and set up residency at the Flamingo Hotel, which she was then forced to leave because of her sexual excesses. She has become the laughingstock of Laurel, Mississippi. Stella is profoundly stunned by this information, and she tries to defend Blanche by explaining the tragic situation with Allan. Stanley informs Stella that he felt it was his duty to warn his friend about Blanche. Blanche calls for a towel and notices a strained expression on Stella's face, but Stella assures her nothing is wrong. Stella is fraught with worry about what will happen to Blanche now that Mitch is likely to abandon her. Stanley implies that Mitch may not be through with Blanche, but he certainly will not marry her. He remarks that he bought Blanche a bus ticket back to Laurel. Stanley yells for Blanche to get out of the bathroom so that he can use it. Sensing something is wrong, Blanche cautiously enters the room.

### Scene 8

Nearly one hour passes. Stella, Stanley, and Blanche are eating dinner. Blanche is trying to ignore the empty chair where Mitch would be sitting. Blanche tries to lighten the mood of the party by telling a joke, but no one finds it funny. Stella says Stanley is "too busy making a pig of himself." She instructs him to wash up and help her clean the table. Stanley flies into a rage, sweeping the table's contents to the floor, and declares that he is the king in his home. When Stanley leaves the table and goes out onto the porch, Blanche begs Stella to tell her what is going on. Blanche calls Mitch's home while Stella chastises her husband for passing rumors to Mitch. Stanley presents the bus ticket to Blanche. She runs into the bedroom crying. Stella yells at Stanley for being so terrible to Blanche. Stanley reminds his wife that she loves his commonness, especially at night in their bedroom. As he shouts for Blanche, Stella doubles over with pain. She is rushed to the hospital.

### Scene 9

Later that evening, Blanche sits alone in the darkness of the apartment drinking liquor. Mitch enters wearing his work uniform. Although he is dirty and unshaven, she admits that she is happy to see him, as his presence stops the polka music that otherwise persistently plays in her mind. She searches for more liquor to serve him, but he declines drinking Stanley's liquor. Mitch inquires why Blanche keeps the apartment so dark and insists on seeing him only at night. He wants to turn on the light, but Blanche begs him to allow the magic (illusions) to continue. When he wrenches the lantern off the lightbulb, Blanche's aged face is revealed. He proceeds to tell her what he has heard about her promiscuous life in Laurel. Blanche immediately pleads that after Allan and the loss of Belle Reve, she could only find relief from the pain in the arms of strangers. A vendor is heard outside selling flowers for the dead. This sparks Blanche to talk about all of the deaths in her life. She says she was "played out" when she finally landed in New Orleans. She found solace and love with Mitch, believing that she could possibly find happiness and rest. Mitch embraces her, and she pleads for marriage. Mitch says she is unsuitable. He pulls her hair and demands the physical intimacy she has denied him all summer. Blanche orders him to leave, and when he does not, she runs to the window and shouts, "Fire!" This action prompts Mitch to leave.

### Scene 10

A few hours later, Blanche is still alone and drinking heavily. She is wearing an old gown and a rhinestone tiara. Stanley enters carrying liquor. He informs Blanche that Stella will not have the baby before the morning, so he has come home. Blanche is nervous about being in the apartment alone with Stanley all night. Stanley laughs at her and questions her attire. Blanche announces that she has received a telegram from Shep Huntleigh, inviting her on a cruise to the Caribbean. Stanley retreats to the bedroom and collects the red silk pajamas he wore on his wedding night. When he returns, Blanche says that Mitch came by begging for forgiveness, but she simply could not forgive his cruelty. Stanley angrily denounces her lies. Blanche rushes to the telephone and pleads with the operator to connect her with Shep Huntleigh. When she puts down the phone, Stanley corners her. Blanche retreats to the bedroom, where she smashes a bottle to use as a weapon against him. Stanley lunges at her, grabs the bottle, and gathers Blanche in his arms. She fights him, but he overpowers her, stating that they have had this date with each other from the moment she arrived.

### *Scene 11*

Several weeks later, Stella cries as she packs Blanche's belongings. Eunice holds the baby while Stanley and his friends play poker. Stella wonders whether she is doing the right thing in sending her sister to the state institution. Eunice responds that if Stella wants to save her marriage, she must believe that Stanley did not rape her sister. Blanche enters from the bathroom with a "hysterical vivacity." She asks whether Shep has called while she dresses. The doorbell sounds and a doctor and attendant enter to collect Blanche. Blanche wants to leave the apartment, but she does not want to be seen by Mitch, Stanley, and the other men. When she sees that the man at the door is not Shep, she tries to run back into the apartment. Stanley blocks her way. He cruelly tells her that all she has left in this apartment is the paper lantern hanging over the lightbulb. He tears it down and hands it to her. Blanche screams, and Stella rushes to the porch, where Eunice comforts her. The doctor and attendant wrestle Blanche to the ground to restrain her.

Mitch attacks Stanley, blaming him for Blanche's condition. The men fight and their friends pull them apart. Blanche is helped to her feet. The doctor helps her to the door and she says that she has "always depended on the kindness of strangers." Stella is heartbroken by the scene. She sobs while the doctor escorts Blanche out of the apartment. Stanley consoles Stella by fondling her breasts. Steve announces the next round of poker.

## COMMENTARY

When asked about the meaning of *A Streetcar Named Desire,* Williams responded, "the ravishment of the tender, the sensitive, the delicate, by the savage and brutal forces of modern society" (Haskell, 230). All the characters in *Streetcar* have been ravished by life to some degree. Although Stanley clearly functions as the most damaging force against Blanche, he, too, has also been forced to grow up too quickly as he spent his youth as a soldier serving in World War II. Reintegration into a mundane, peaceful world does not keep him fulfilled. He is moody and restless, and his animalistic tendencies are challenged by the overly refined Blanche.

Stella is a submissive character, placed in the middle of a war between gentrified society, represented by Blanche, and the rugged, practical world of the working class personified by Stanley. In war there are the victors and the vanquished. Blanche ultimately suffers the most damaging defeat, being institutionalized, while Stanley continues to brutalize his way through life.

In the opening scene of the play, Stanley appears carrying a package of bloody meat, which immediately establishes his primitive nature. In stark contrast, Blanche enters the scene wearing white. Williams compares her to a moth, symbolically stressing her fragility, purity, and virtue. Her pristine attire serves as an effective camouflage for her sordid past. As Chance Wayne (in SWEET BIRD OF YOUTH), Sebastian Venable (in SUDDENLY LAST SUMMER), and Lot (in KINGDOM OF EARTH, OR THE SEVEN DESCENTS OF MYRTLE) do, by wearing white, Blanche uses her clothing to disguise her "degenerate" self-perception. Her name, which is French, literally means "white of the woods." Out of her unlucky and desperate wilderness, Blanche enters the Kowalski apartment a transformed, mothlike creature of nature, recast as a virginal character. Although she has been a prostitute, Blanche prefers to believe in her renewed chasteness. She lives in a world of illusion and believes that her sexual encounters with strangers never constituted love; therefore, she never forfeited any aspect of her true self.

As has Karen Stone in *THE ROMAN SPRING OF MRS. STONE,* Blanche has an aversion to being viewed in bright light that will reveal her true age. As early as the first scene, she asks Stella to turn off the overhead light. Blanche is most comfortable in the warm glow of a lamp that allows her to play the part of the innocent coquette completely. She lies about her age when she courts Mitch and avoids spending time with him in daylight. When Mitch returns in the final meeting with her, he insists on tearing the lantern off the overhead light so that he may finally have a good look at her. When Blanche asks why he wants the glare of bright light, he says he is just being realistic. Blanche replies:

> I don't want realism. I want—magic! . . . Yes, yes, magic! I try to give that to people. I do misrepresent things to them. I don't tell the truth, I tell what *ought* to be the truth. And if that's a sin, then let me be damned for it! *Don't turn the light on!*

Of course, Stanley has informed him that she has been lying about everything. However, her mothlike, youthful facade is not just used to fool Mitch; it is an integral part of who she is. Blanche wishes she could actually be what she pretends to be. She resigns from reality because it has been too harsh. The "magic" in which she chooses to dwell is her only means of survival, as her suffering has been so great. She fears that looking her age will further discredit her in a world that has already discarded her.

Blanche also drinks heavily, while pretending to adhere to a Southern gender code that restricts well-bred women from drinking in company or in public. This is another aspect of playing the innocent coquette. Late in the play, Mitch informs Blanche that Stanley has talked about how much of his liquor she has consumed, and she realizes that her subterfuge has failed.

Although it is a means of comfort and relief, alcohol has long been a source of shame and regret for Blanche. She particularly regrets her drunken criticism of Allan because she did not mean the words that drove him to take his own life. Leonard Berkman suggests:

> It is not the existence of Allan's homosexuality that signals the failure of Blanche's marriage; it is, rather, that Blanche must uncover this information by accident, that Blanche is incapable of responding compassionately to this information, that in short there never existed a marriage between them in which Allan could come to her in full trust and explicit needs. ("The Tragic Downfall of Blanche DuBois," 2)

Blanche responded to Allan's sexuality with a sense of wounded pride, and as Brick in *CAT ON A HOT TIN ROOF* does to his friend Skipper, she spends the rest of her life regretting that she did not love and accept him. Blanche responded too harshly. She loved Allan and truly believed in their marriage; however, she lived in a romantic world of delusion until she witnessed a real moment when Allan was having sex with another man, which completely shattered the illusion. As Blanche explains to Mitch:

> [Allan] was in the quicksand clutching at me—but I wasn't holding him out, I was slipping in with him! I didn't know that. I didn't know anything except I loved him unendurably but without being able to help him or help myself.

In this instance, it was Blanche who was cruelly responsible for the ravishment (or abuse) of one that was "tender, sensitive, and delicate."

Allan Grey's suicide scene is reminiscent of the final scene in *The Seagull* by ANTON CHEKHOV (see *THE NOTEBOOK OF TRIGORIN*). When Konstantin can no longer endure his life and the knowledge that he must live without the love he desires, he is drawn to the lake (like a seagull) and shoots himself. Konstantin and Allan are tragically similar characters, who are gravely misunderstood by those around them. Williams was enamored of Chekhov's characters, finding them dynamically flawed and powerfully present. Chekhov's dramaturgical influence is inherent in *Streetcar,* as the psychological reality of the characters creates the dramatic tension and fuels the action to an unavoidable conclusion.

Blanche tells the story of her homosexual husband to Mitch, who could very easily assume that Blanche and Allan's marriage was never consummated. Even through her tragically truthful tales

Blanche continues to create the illusion that she is prim and virginal. This makes the news of her promiscuous past more shocking and insulting to Mitch, who has respected her wish to abstain from sexual intimacy. Blanche presents the person she would like to be: naive, proper, and respectable. Blanche has found an Allan substitute in Mitch. She longs to have an opportunity to re-create that marriage and have a second chance to make up for her cruel past actions. Mitch is the answer as his sensitivity stops the haunting polka music in her mind (i.e., the painful memories of Allan's death).

Throughout the play, Blanche frequently takes long hot baths in the sweltering heat of a New Orleans summer. This symbolic act of baptism absolves her of her past sins and cleanses her body in preparation for her husband-to-be. She repeatedly purifies her body in water, and in her mind, by each ritual bathing, she creates more distance from the sullied strangers she encountered at the Flamingo Hotel in Laurel. In moments of desperation and self-doubt, Blanche bathes. This repeated action greatly annoys Stanley.

Stanley and Blanche are archenemies because they possess antithetical personalities, and each lays claim to Stella. Whereas Stanley respects complete honesty, Blanche delights in experiencing the world through rose-colored glasses. She spends much of her time rejecting the harshness of life, and Stanley is always there to make her acknowledge the truth. Blanche enjoys the protocol of the Old South; she is nostalgic about the tradition of Southern life, whereas Stanley hates sentimentality. In his production notebook, Elia Kazan writes of Blanche:

> Her problem has to do with her tradition. Her notion of what a woman should be. She is stuck with this "ideal." It is her. It is her ego. Unless she lives by it, she cannot live; in fact her whole life has been for nothing. (Kazan, 22)

Blanche defines her existence according to the traditions of the Old South. She is completely immersed in that world, whereas Stanley symbolizes the new or modern world that is obliterating that former way of living.

Early in the play these two characters clash over the subject of Belle Reve. It is Blanche's lost, beautiful dream, rich with family heritage and pride; Stanley is interested only in the property's material or monetary real estate value. He is happy in the loud, harsh, and dirty world of the Vieux Carré of New Orleans, whereas Blanche prefers finer accommodations, the bucolic setting of hundreds of acres of land and large white pillars on a grand veranda that provide lounging quarters out of the midday sun. Some critics see Blanche as Williams's most representative character, as she has lost the stability of her ancestral home and is now in exile.

According to Kazan, Blanche's emotional decline begins when she is stripped of her plantation:

> The things about the "tradition" in the nineteenth century was that it worked then. It made a woman feel important with her own secure positions and functions, her own special worth. It also made a woman at that time *one with her society*. But *today* the tradition is an anachronism which simply does not function. It does not work. So while Blanche must believe it because it makes her special, because it makes her sticking by Belle Reve an act of heroism, rather than an absurd romanticism, still *it does not work*. . . . She's a misfit, a liar, her "airs" alienate people, she must act superior to them which alienates them further. (Kazan, 22)

Blanche is one of Williams's "lost souls," those characters who are caught between an old and a new world. As are Amanda Wingfield (in THE GLASS MENAGERIE) and Alma Winemiller (in SUMMER AND SMOKE), who also delight in tradition, Blanche is lost in a modern, industrial society because in it she does not have a special position simply by virtue of being a Southern woman. Belle Reve is her identification or authentication as a person, and without it, she does not possess a self and therefore must rely on others to supply stability, security, and substance. Blanche only realizes that she is responsible for her own financial and social status when it is too late. Her "airs" are her tragic flaw in this new world, Stanley's world, a world that has been changed through hardship and struggles associated with industry, war, and economic depression. Blanche becomes "a last dying relic . . . now adrift in our unfriendly day" (Miller, 23). Although this situation may make her more pitiable, it does not make her less offensive to her peers.

Blanche's very vocal disapproval of Stanley serves to isolate her from Stella, the one sympathetic person in her life. Her critical opinion of the dismal apartment and of Stanley's brutish demeanor creates a chasm in the sisters' relationship, and her chances of familial bonding are sacrificed. Blanche demonstrates her racial prejudices when she calls Stanley a "Polack," and her gradual, yet persistent provocations lead to her ultimate violation. This act of rape wounds Blanche to a point of no return. The culmination of Stanley's victory over Blanche occurs when Stella refuses to believe that her sister has been assaulted. Stella sides with her husband as Blanche's past and world of illusions (or dishonesty) serve to silence her in her most desperate moment.

Williams's ability to "capture something of the complexity of the novel within the dramatic form, especially in the area of character probity and psychology" (Adler, 9), has set *Streetcar* apart and is the reason it merits its status not only as a modern classic, but s a watershed moment in U.S. theater history. Essentially, Williams created a new genre in the modern theater: a heightened naturalism that allows dreams (or nightmares) to coexist with reality.

Marlon Brando (Stanley Kowalski) and Kim Hunter (Stella Kowalski) embrace, as Jessica Tandy (Blanche DuBois) looks on, in the Broadway production of *A Streetcar Named Desire,* 1947 *(Eileen Darby)*

## PRODUCTION HISTORY

*A Streetcar Named Desire* opened at the Barrymore Theater, New York, on December 3, 1947, and electrified its audience. The cast, which included MARLON BRANDO (Stanley), KIM HUNTER (Stella), and JESSICA TANDY (Blanche), received a standing ovation that lasted a full half hour after their opening performance.

At this point in his career, Williams had only one other major success, *The Glass Menagerie* (on Broadway in 1945), which was revered as a delicate, elegiac, lyrical, and gentle play. By comparison, *Streetcar* was outrageously raw, sexual, and violent.

Critics immediately praised the first Broadway production, complimenting every facet of the production: acting, directing, and design. In his review of the first production Irwin Shaw wrote:

> As far as I am concerned, even the ushers and ticket-takers at the Ethel Barrymore Theater are beautiful these nights. . . . Such is the effect of a magnificent play, magnificently done. The play is "A Streetcar Named Desire," by Tennessee Williams, and the production is the result of Elia Kazan's direction, Jo Mielziner's scenery and lighting and, I suppose, Irene Selznick's money, all of which have my unqualifying blessing. (Miller, 45)

Shaw preferred *Streetcar* to *The Glass Menagerie* because he believed that in *Streetcar* Williams incorporated elements of "true tragedy" (Miller, 45). Some critics and audience members were shocked by the coarse nature of the play. They were not prepared for its overt sexuality or its protagonist, Blanche DuBois, a teacher turned prostitute. However the naysayers held the minority point of view.

*Streetcar* ran on Broadway longer than any other Williams play: 855 performances between December 1947 and December 1949. In addition,

Williams received both the Pulitzer Prize and the Drama Critics Circle Award for this play. Since its premiere, *Streetcar* has been produced more than 20,000 times, and worldwide it remains the most popular American play.

The film version of *A Streetcar Named Desire* (1951) popularized the play further. The film, as was the Broadway production, was directed by Elia Kazan. With the exception of VIVIEN LEIGH playing Blanche, the cast remained the same. The film took on a life of its own and sparked great controversy among censors, who deemed it "immoral, decadent, vulgar and sinful" (Sova, 285). Much to the chagrin of Kazan and Williams, the movie was censored after it had been shot and was altered without their consent. Several close-up shots were deleted to tone down the insatiable sexual dynamic between Stella and Stanley, and the scene in which Stanley rapes Blanche was cut, as were references to Blanche's promiscuous nature and several of Stanley's licentious comments to Blanche, such as his statement that she "might not be bad to interfere with." The most significant alteration in the move from stage to screen was Stella's final response.

Under pressure from the censors, who required that Stanley be punished for his violation of Blanche, the ending was altered significantly. Instead of remaining with Stanley, Stella takes her newborn baby in her arms, looks into the child's eyes, and exclaims, "We're never going back. Never, never back, never back again." She is last seen running up the stairs to seek refuge with Eunice and Steve Hubbell.

Vivien Leigh (Blanche), Karl Malden (Mitch), and Kim Hunter (Stella) all garnered Academy Awards (Oscars) for their performances in the film of *A Streetcar Named Desire.*

## PUBLICATION HISTORY

*A Streetcar Named Desire* was first published by New Directions in 1947.

## CHARACTERS

**DuBois, Blanche** Described in the opening scene as "mothlike," Blanche is an aging Southern belle. She is refined, delicate, and steeped in the traditions of Southern gentry. She first appears wearing white, symbolizing her feigned purity and virtuous nature. Blanche is one of Williams's dreamers, forfeiting reality for a magical or romantic approach to life. She is not concerned with truth, but rather "what ought to be the truth."

When she was a young woman, Blanche married her true love, Allan Grey. He was tender and sensitive, different from the other men in her life. Although he was not "the least bit effeminate looking," she learned of his homosexuality when she entered a room uninvited and found Allan having sex with an older male friend. Later that night, the three of them attended a dance at Moon Lake Casino. During this evening of heavy drinking, Blanche confronted Allan about his sexuality while a polka played and lovers danced around them. Devastated by Blanche's disgust toward him, Allan ran off the dance floor. He found refuge at the edge of the nearby lake, where he shot himself. Blanche is forever haunted by the guilt she feels over Allan's suicide. She cannot move beyond the loss of her husband, and in moments of desperation she still hears the polka waltz in her mind. She drinks whiskey to cope with her self-reproach, but the cruelty she displayed toward Allan forever torments her.

Blanche's life continues on a downward spiral with the deaths of several other family members. She is obligated to nurse them, witnessing the slow, torturous deterioration of life. Blanche is forced to earn her living as a high school English teacher because her ancestral home, Belle Reve (which means "beautiful dream" in French), in Laurel, Mississippi, is in danger of foreclosure. Severely lonely and desperate, she finds consolation in the embrace of strange men. When she is fired from her teaching position because of a "morally unfit" liaison with a 17-year-old boy, her reputation is completely ruined. Belle Reve is foreclosed and she is forced to live in a seedy hotel called the Flamingo. Because of her practice of entertaining men at the Flamingo, she is eventually forced to leave that establishment as well.

Destitute and homeless, Blanche travels to New Orleans, taking a "streetcar named Desire" to the slums of Elysian Fields, where her sister, Stella Kowalski, lives with her brutish husband, Stanley Kowalski. She arrives unannounced at the cramped two-room apartment. She immediately rejects Stanley because of his unrefined behavior and crude, straightforward response to life. Her worst opinions of Stanley are justified when she witnesses the beatings Stella suffers at the hands of her husband. Blanche believes that "a woman's charm is fifty percent illusion," and she clashes with Stanley, who is determined to catch Blanche in all of her lies. Her facade quickly positions her as Stanley's prime enemy. He is sickened by her exaggerations and false prudishness. Despite her past, Blanche remains married to the ideals of purity, creating the illusion of what she "ought to be."

Stanley triumphs over her when he finds out about her promiscuous past in Laurel. He destroys her only chance of comfort by relating her sordid past to Mitch (Harold Mitchell), her only and final marriage prospect. Stanley then rapes Blanche, presuming that she has had so many sexual encounters that one more will make no difference. After this act, a deed that Stella refuses to acknowledge, Blanche is wounded once and for all. She loses her grip on reality and finds consolation in a type of magical world that will not allow her to hurt anymore. This world places her at the mercy of "the kindness of strangers." The strange men in her life are replaced by the medical staff of a mental institution.

**Hubbell, Eunice** Eunice is the wife of Steve Hubbell. She and Steve are the upstairs neighbors of Stanley and Stella Kowalski. As do Stanley and Stella, Eunice and Steve have a volatile marital relationship. In many ways, the older couple (Eunice and Steve) mirror Stanley and Stella and offer a vision of what the young couple will be in the future. Eunice is a confidante to Stella, and Eunice eases the younger woman's transition into a life of denial and compromise. When Stella's sister, Blanche DuBois, accuses Stanley of rape, Eunice instructs Stella to disavow Blanche's claims for the sake of her marriage, her child, and her own sanity.

**Hubbell, Steve** Steve is the husband of Eunice Hubbell. He and Eunice are the upstairs neighbors of Stanley and Stella Kowalski. As do Stanley and Stella, Eunice and Steve have a volatile marital relationship. In many ways, the older couple (Eunice and Steve) mirror Stanley and Stella and offer a vision of what the young couple will be in the future.

**Kowalski, Stanley** He is a strong, brutish man of Polish descent. Stanley is a former soldier, who fought during World War II and who now lives in the mundane world of factory work. He is cruelly honest. His pastimes include bowling, drinking, playing poker with his friends and having sex with his wife, Stella Kowalski. Stanley enjoys the comforts of Stella's love. Although he is unrefined, loud, and quick-tempered, he possesses a simplicity which makes him desirable to Stella. There is also an animal attraction between Stanley and Stella, and their relationship is based not on communication but on physical attraction. In the stage directions of *Streetcar,* Williams describes him as a "gaudy seed bearer [who] sizes women up at a glance."

Stanley revels in the fact that Stella is from an old aristocratic Southern family and that she has rejected upper-crust society to live with him in a tenement house in the slums of New Orleans. Stanley functions with very basic objectives. He is strong-willed and responds to adversity with violence.

When his sister-in-law, Blanche DuBois, moves in, Stanley feels threatened by her presence and her rejection of his way of life. He does not like to share what is his: his wife, his liquor, and his apartment. When he finds out that the DuBois plantation, Belle Reve, has been foreclosed, he immediately demands proof that Blanche did not sell it and keep the money. Stanley expects to share any profits, as he is Stella's husband. Stella and Blanche are personally devastated by the loss of their ancestral home; Stanley is only concerned with the practical, monetary side of the situation. He has no way of comprehending the emotional loss of such a thing. In addition, Blanche's large personality leaves little room for him to be the center of attention. The two engage in a power struggle that draws out the worst in Stanley's personality. The tension created by Blanche's presence provokes Stanley to beat Stella and to seek a way to ruin his sister-in-law.

He triumphs over Blanche after searching for the truth of her disreputable past. When he has gathered this ammunition, he informs Blanche's only marriage prospect, Mitch (Harold Mitchell) of her sordid past. By this he is able to pierce the virginal facade that Blanche has used to manipulate and control. Stella defends her sister by explaining that she has had a tragic past and she is weak, but Stanley is interested only in survival of the fittest. He rapes Blanche and denies that he did to Stella. This is Stanley's ultimate triumph. In the end, Blanche is taken to a mental institution while Stanley comforts his wife by fondling her breasts.

**Kowalski, Stella** She is the wife of Stanley Kowalski and the sister of Blanche DuBois. Stella is a member of a very refined and dignified Southern family, who has chosen to cast off her social status in exchange for marriage to Stanley, a vulgar and often brutal simpleton. She is caught in the war between Stanley and Blanche, whose constant bickering and fighting leads to Stanley's sexually assaulting Blanche. Stella refuses to believe that her husband would rape her sister. After her accusations of rape, Stella commits Blanche to a mental institution. As does her sister, Stella glosses over harsh reality to live in the world of illusions to cope with Stanley's abhorrent behavior.

**Mitchell, Harold (Mitch)** A middle-aged man whose dedication to his ailing mother leaves him lonely and troubled. Mitch falls in love with Blanche Dubois, a refined, yet fading Southern belle. They engage in a respectable courtship, and Blanche insists on delaying sexual relations until they are married. When Stanley Kowalski informs Mitch of Blanche's sordid past as a prostitute, he is shocked and offended that she has made him wait for sexual intimacy.

### FURTHER READING


Adler, Thomas P. *A Streetcar Named Desire: The Moth and The Lantern.* Boston: Twayne, 1990.

Berkman, Leonard. "The Tragic Downfall of Blanche DuBois," *Modern Drama* 10, no. 2 (December 1967): 249–257.

Kazan, Elia. "Notebook for *A Streetcar Named Desire,*" in *Twentieth Century Interpretations of A Streetcar Named Desire: A Collection of Critical Essays,* edited by Jordan Y. Miller. Englewood Cliffs, N.J.: Prentice-Hall, 1971, pp. 21–26.

Shaw, Irwin. "Masterpiece," in *Twentieth Century Interpretations of A Streetcar Named Desire: A Collection of Critical Essays,* edited by Jordan Y. Miller. Englewood Cliffs, N.J.: Prentice-Hall, 1971, pp. 45–47.

Sova, Dawn B. *Forbidden Films: Censorship Histories of 125 Motion Pictures.* New York: Facts On File, 2001.


## *Suddenly Last Summer*

A one-act play written in 1958.

### SYNOPSIS

The setting is a Gothic-style Victorian mansion in the Garden District of New Orleans, one late afternoon between late summer and early fall

#### *Scene 1*

Mrs. Violet Venable, an aging aristocrat, entertains her guest, Doctor Cukrowicz (or Doctor Sugar), in the exotic gardens of her deceased son, Sebastian. She tries to persuade the neurosurgeon to perform a lobotomy on her niece, Catharine, who is ruining the family reputation with a sordid story about the particulars of Sebastian's death. In order to combat Catharine's story, Mrs. Venable had her niece committed to Saint Mary's Asylum.

Mrs. Venable tells Dr. Sugar that Sebastian was a locally famous poet who, with her unfaltering guidance, perfected one poem every summer. Mrs. Venable offers a detailed account of her travels with Sebastian. She then proposes to donate money for a neurosurgery wing at the Lion's View Hospital if Dr. Sugar will agree to silence Catharine. The doctor is ambivalent about agreeing to this deal when he has not yet met the patient. Catharine and her nurse, Sister Felicity, can be seen entering the house.

#### *Scene 2*

Miss Foxhill, Mrs. Venable's secretary, leads Catharine and her nurse outside while Mrs. Venable drinks her routine afternoon cocktail inside her home. While Catharine and her nurse argue about Catharine smoking a cigarette, Doctor Sugar spies on them from a nearby window. Catharine discovers him and shouts, "Lion's View Hospital,"

Publicity portrait of Williams *(Photograph courtesy of the Billy Rose Theatre Collection, New York Public Library)*

to let him know that she is aware of the torturous kind of medicine he practices. His blond hair reminds Catharine of the times Sebastian longed for blond men as if they were "items on a menu." Sister Felicity tries to quiet her. She speaks of his death, convinced that if he had held on to her hand, she could have saved him. Catharine's mother, Mrs. Holly, and her brother, George, arrive.

*Scene 3*

Mrs. Holly urges George to compliment Catharine, but he is uncooperative and more interested in talking to his sister in the nun's absence. Sister Felicity is hesitant to allow her patient out of her sight; however, Mrs. Holly persuades her to go inside until she is called. George berates Catharine about the drama that she has created around Sebastian's death. He begs her to refrain from telling her story to appease Mrs. Venable so that she will release the money Sebastian willed to them. Mrs. Holly intervenes when Catharine becomes upset, then attempts to convince Catharine lovingly to stop telling her "fantastical" story. George becomes very angry when Catharine insists that she is telling the truth, as he knows their aunt will make sure they never receive their inheritance.

*Scene 4*

Mrs. Venable enters and Miss Foxhill delivers a folder containing the police report of Sebastian's death. George and his mother ask Mrs. Venable to speed up the inheritance process, but she ignores their request and calls for the doctor to evaluate Catharine. When Doctor Sugar joins them after receiving an urgent telephone call, Catharine asks him whether he wishes to drill a hole in her head and cut out a piece of her brain. She mocks him by exclaiming that he must have her mother's permission for the surgery. Mrs. Venable announces that she is in charge because she is paying for the lobotomy, and she accuses Catharine of trying to take Sebastian away from her.

Doctor Sugar asks to speak with Catharine alone in order to assess her mental state fully. George goes to his aunt in another attempt to create peace within the family and secure his inheritance. Doctor Sugar and Catharine talk alone. Catharine admits that because Sebastian liked her, she loved him in a motherly way, the only way he would accept love from a woman. She tells a story about a man she met at a Mardi Gras ball who offered her a ride home. They stopped at the edge of the woods and had sex, and afterward the young man confessed to having a pregnant wife. He asked Catharine to keep their rendezvous a secret. Catharine was so upset that, after he took her home, she went back to the ball, found the young man, and created a public scene on the dance floor. Sebastian witnessed her outburst and escorted her home. Doctor Sugar gives Catharine an injection when she becomes agitated by her memories and asks her to tell him honestly what happened to Sebastian. Catharine stands up to deliver the graphic details of her cousin's death, but the drugs dizzy her. The doctors stands to help her regain her balance, and they embrace. Catharine forcefully kisses him as George returns to the garden. He angrily shouts at his sister about her lewd behavior.

Mrs. Venable, Sister Felicity, and Mrs. Holly enter. Doctor Sugar instructs Catharine to tell the true story once and for all. Catharine talks about the cruise to Europe, the wonderful stay in Paris, and Sebastian's lavish gifts to her. At the Cabeza de Lobo, he was uninterested in his poetry and spent his days scouring the beach for handsome young men. Mrs. Venable interrupts Catharine to say that she always protected him when she traveled with him. Catharine realized that she was procuring men for Sebastian by wearing a transparent bathing suit he bought for her and demanded she wear. As the summer progressed and the beach grew more crowded, he no longer needed her. Catharine was then allowed to wear a dark bathing suit and sit far away from him. She would meet him every day at five o'clock in the afternoon near the bathhouse. The homeless young men would follow him out of the bathhouse and onto the beach, where he paid them for their services. Each day the band of men became more aggressive in their pursuit of Sebastian until he became afraid to go to the beach.

The mob of young men recognize Sebastian in his white suit at a nearby café. Catharine notices Sebastian's fear through his need to take his heart medication. When they leave the café and Sebastian walks up the street, the mob attacks him, tears his body apart, and eats his flesh. Catharine runs to fight them off, but it is too late, as she witnesses his mangled body in horror. Mrs. Venable orders the doctor "to cut this hideous story out of her brain." When prompted to give his analysis, Doctor Sugar asserts that maybe Catharine is telling the truth.

## COMMENTARY

*Suddenly Last Summer* is considered Williams's most shocking drama, and as a result, the play is often a favorite target of "Williams attackers" (Hurley, 392). In its own time the play was simultaneously revered for its seemingly simple structure and detested for its "disturbing" content of homosexuality and cannibalism. Critical prudery blinded many critics to the fact that this play is one of Williams's "most richly and tightly written Gothic romances" (Canby, 17) and contains some of Williams's most evocative language.

Scholarship regarding *Suddenly Last Summer* has nearly exclusively focused on "one of the most successful creations of an offstage character in dramatic literature" (Harris, 11), the absent Sebastian Venable. In addition to venerating Sebastian, many critics view this character as a "stand-in" for Williams himself. At first glance, this appears to be Williams's most direct and autobiographical connection to the play, as both author and character are gay male literary artists.

There is no doubt that *Suddenly Last Summer* was a deeply personal work for Williams; another poignantly emotional and deeply autobiographical connection is provided by Catharine Holly, a character directly reminiscent of his sister, ROSE WILLIAMS, who had a prefrontal lobotomy performed in 1937. Williams was always haunted by the fact that his mother consented to this life-altering experiment; his lifelong regret was that he was not present to intervene and defend Rose. Some biographers have speculated that, as is Catharine's, Rose's lobotomy was prompted by the family's need to silence her allegations of sexual abuse levied against their father, CORNELIUS COFFIN WILLIAMS. *Suddenly Last Summer* is infused with the "blistering pain" (Brantley, 13) Williams felt at what his sister suffered in his absence.

As are *BATTLE OF ANGELS* and *ORPHEUS DESCENDING*, *Suddenly Last Summer* is a "tangle of Christian and mythical echoes" (Debusscher, 449). Scholars have extensively identified the connection between Sebastian Venable with the life and death of his namesake, the Roman martyr Saint Sebastian. According to legend, Saint Sebastian was an attractive young Roman who became the emperor Diocletian's lover. Upon his conversion to Christianity, Sebastian used his intimate and influential status to try to dissuade Diocletian from persecuting his fellow Christians. Feeling betrayed, when Sebastian's protests become more public and outspoken, Diocletian sentenced him to death. Sebastian was placed before a firing squad of Mauritanian archers. Although severely wounded by the shower of arrows, he miraculously survives and is nursed back to health by a pious widow. Sebastian returns to Diocletian's court to continue his advocacy on behalf of Christians. Diocletian swiftly orders that his lover be bludgeoned to death. After this torment Sebastian is mortally wounded and another pious woman collects his body and buries him.

Williams's familiarity with the legend of this martyred Roman Catholic saint is established by his poem "San Sebastian de Sodoma" written in 1948. Scholars have been thorough in tracing references to Saint Sebastian and his life and death in *Suddenly Last Summer.* Prompted by his name, Catharine's declaration that they spent much of their vacation on "a beach that's named for Sebastian's name saint," and the fact that Sebastian Venable's death is "carefully worded" (Debusscher, 450) to reflect the first death sentence (death by arrows) of the Roman martyr, "There were naked children along the beach, a band of frightfully thin and dark naked children that look like a flock of plucked birds, and they would come darting up. . . . Sebastian started to run and they all screamed at once and seemed to fly in the air." Gilbert Debusscher also notes a further similarity in the narratives of the two Sebastians: the presence of two female caretakers. He sees Mrs. Venable and Catharine Holly as modern versions of the two pious Roman widows who tended Saint Sebastian. A more invigorating approach to this concept is the idea that on the death of both Sebastians, two women are present to lay claim to the remains, literally in the case of Saint Sebastian and metaphorically (through reputation and legacy) in the case of Sebastian Venable.

Thomas Van Laan is one of many contemporary scholars to argue that *Suddenly Last Summer* deserves recognition as one of Williams's best plays. The basis of this critical reevaluation is the acknowledgment that the play "is not a study of Sebastian Venable, sensationalistic or otherwise," but rather "a conflict between opposing versions (or visions) of Sebastian, and especially a conflict for supremacy between the two who hold them" (Van Laan, 257). At the heart of this reassessment is a shift in emphasis to the character of Catharine, which sends the reader once again into the world of martyrs, myths, and legends.

Catharine Holly's name suggests "Holy Catharine." The name Catharine (or Catherine) itself literally means "pure" or "innocent." These inherent traits are underscored in the text by Williams's extensive lighting directions which concentrate direct light on Catharine while the other characters "sink into shadow." The effect is like an early Renaissance painting of a golden-haloed saint surrounded by heavenly light. Williams also insists, "During [her] monologue the light has changed, the surrounding area has dimmed out and hot white spot is focused on Catharine." It is clear from these instances that Catharine, as is her cousin, is inextricably linked to her name saint, Catherine of Alexandria.

As Sebastain had done in the court of Diocletian, Catherine of Alexandria, at the age of 18, presented herself to the emperor Maximinus and reprimanded him for his violent persecution of Christians. The emperor was so impressed by Catherine's intelligence and tenacity that instead of putting her to death, he assembled 50 of his court scholars and ordered them to outwit Catherine and prompt her to relinquish her faith. She was steadfast and emerged from the debate unaltered, with the added victory of having converted several of Maximinus's learnéd men to Christianity. As a result, Catherine was scourged and imprisoned. She continued her mission from her jail cell. From there she managed to convert Maximinus's wife and the captain of his army (both of whom were subsequently put to death). To silence her, Maximinus condemned Catherine to death by a torture device known as "the wheel." However, when Catherine laid her hand upon this instrument it miraculously disappeared. Refusing to be outdone, Maximinus had her beheaded. Angels were said to have carried Catherine's headless body to Mount Sinai. According to Catholic tradition, Saint Catherine is revered as one of the most helpful, and persuasive intercessory saints in heaven.

Catharine Holly shares her name saint's desire to impart her truth to others. Both she and her patron saint face a tyrannical adversary who has the power to sentence them to a literal or metaphoric death, respectively. As the emperor Maximinus does, Mrs. Venable, "a caged tiger" (Harris, 9), attempts to silence Catharine by having her scrutinized by the "learnéd men" of Saint Mary's Asylum (and by Dr. Sugar), imprisoned and tortured (drug therapy, insulin, and electric shock treatments). As Catharine Holly refuses to relinquish or recant her truth, Mrs. Venable attempts to orchestrate a symbolic "beheading" administered at the hands of Dr. Sugar: a lobotomy. Catharine's gift for persuasion is evident in Dr. Sugar's final hopeful line: "I think we ought at least consider the possibility that the girl's story could be true."

Ironically the two Catherines also share a similar logistical fate. In a strange quirk of canonical tradition, clerics have called into question the "authenticity" of the legend of Saint Catherine. As a result, many of the discourses that have been attributed to Saint Catherine may ultimately be "rejected as inventions, pure and simple" (Clugnet, 323). In *Suddenly Last Summer* Catharine Holly is also enmeshed in a controversy of truths, lies, and narratives. In addition, the validity and authenticity of both Catherines hinge on the significant details and circumstances concerning a death: For Saint Catherine the death in question is her own; for Catharine Holly it is that of her cousin, Sebastian. Ultimately, both women are exonerated.

Although some have contended that *Suddenly Last Summer* is one of the darkest and most bleak plays in Williams's dramatic canon, their assessment overlooks the fact that the play's ending is triumphantly hopeful. Unlike other "silenced" characters (most notably Blanche DuBois, in *A STREETCAR NAMED DESIRE*, who is similarly tormented and driven mad by a truth that others refuse to believe), Catharine is vindicated. Dr. Sugar, dressed in angelic white, becomes a sweet savior to her. It is also implied by their fierce embrace and Dr. Sugar's growing attachment to Catharine, that he, like the celestial beings in St. Catherine's legend, may very well spirit her away and carry her from his place of death.

Focusing on the character of Catharine Holly provides the play with an active and physically "present" center. By focusing on the character who is present (Catharine) instead of the absent non-character, Sebastian, *Suddenly Last Summer* shifts to become Williams's most hopeful revision of his sister Rose's tragic fate.

## PRODUCTION HISTORY

*Suddenly Last Summer* premiered in New York at the York Theatre in January 1958. It was produced in tandem with *SOMETHING UNSPOKEN* under the title *Garden District*. Herbert Machiz directed the production, which featured Anne Meacham as Catharine Holly and Hortense Alden as Mrs. Venable. *Suddenly Last Summer* was adapted for film in 1959; it featured ELIZABETH TAYLOR as Catharine Holly and Katharine Hepburn as Mrs. Venable.

## PUBLICATION HISTORY

*Suddenly Last Summer* was first published by New Directions in 1958.

## CHARACTERS

**Cukrowicz, Doctor** Also known as Doctor Sugar, Dr. Cukrowicz is a young neurosurgeon whom Violet Venable engages to evaluate her niece, Catharine Holly. In an effort to protect her dead son's reputation, Mrs. Venable would like Dr. Cukrowicz to perform a prefrontal lobotomy on Catharine to prevent her from revealing the circumstances surrounding her son's death. Mrs. Venable has offered Dr. Cukrowicz a sizable amount of research funding in exchange for treating Catharine. When Catharine is taken to the Venable home for the evaluation, Dr. Cukrowicz gives her a truth serum and ultimately decides that Catharine may be telling the truth.

**Doctor Sugar** See Cukrowicz, Doctor.

**Foxhill, Miss** She is Mrs. Violet Venable's secretary. She tries to maintain order when Mrs. Venable's relatives, George Holly and Mrs. Holly, pay her employer a visit.

**Holly, Catharine** Catharine is the niece of Violet Venable. Since her return from a European vacation with her cousin, Sebastian Venable, Catharine has been incarcerated in Saint Mary's Asylum. Her aunt has placed her in a state mental institution in an effort to silence her, to prevent her from revealing the true circumstances surrounding Sebastian's gruesome death.

**Holly, George** George is the brother of Catharine Holly. Along with his mother, Mrs. Holly, he visits his aunt, Mrs. Violet Venable, at her mansion in the Garden District of New Orleans, Louisiana. George and his mother hope to appease Violet and prevent Catharine from upsetting Violet further. As Mrs. Venable's poor relations, George and his mother are beholden to

Violet's charity and financial support. George arrives at the Venable mansion wearing a tailored suit previously owned by Mrs. Venable's deceased son, Sebastian. George's lavish attire serves as a cruel reminder to Violet of her dead son and the indebtedness of Catharine's family to her own. George urges Catharine to refrain from revealing the details of their cousin Sebastian's death. If Catharine will not refrain, their aunt has vowed to have her silenced by a prefrontal lobotomy, administered by Doctor Cukrowicz. George's motives for pleading with Catharine are not entirely altruistic: Their aunt has also vowed to cut them off financially if Catharine continues her tirades.

**Holly, Mrs.** Mrs. Holly is the mother of Catharine Holly and George Holly. Along with George, Mrs. Holly visits her sister-in-law, Violet Venable, at her mansion in the Garden District of New Orleans, Louisiana. Mrs. Holly and her son hope to appease Violet and prevent Catharine from upsetting her further. As Mrs. Venable's poor relations, Mrs. Holly and her children are beholden to Violet's charity and financial support.

**Sister Felicity** Sister Felicity is a caretaker at Saint Mary's Asylum near New Orleans, Louisiana. She is responsible for a young woman, Catharine Holly, who has been committed to the asylum by her aunt, Mrs. Violet Venable. Sister Felicity serves as a brisk guardian angel for Catharine. She tries to keep her young patient calm and still, and she disapproves of Catharine's smoking cigarettes.

**Venable, Violet** Mrs. Venable is a wealthy Southern widow who lives in a large mansion in the Garden District of New Orleans, Louisiana. She is the mother of the deceased, young poet Sebastian Venable. Violet strives to protect her dead son's legacy and reputation by placing her niece, Catharine Venable, in a mental institution. Catharine witnessed Sebastian's lascivious life and gruesome death while vacationing with him in Europe. Mrs. Venable does not want Catharine to reveal what she has seen. Using her wealth and affluence, she tries to persuade the young Dr. Cukrowicz (Dr. Sugar) to perform a lobotomy on her niece, literally to remove her story from her head.

### FURTHER READING


Brantley, Ben. "Tennessee Williams, Chilled Out," *New York Times*, December 10, 1994, p. 13.

Canby, Vincent. "Decadence, Ferns and Facades," *New York Times*, October 11, 1995, pp. C17–C18.

Clugnet, Leon. "St. Catherine of Alexandria," in *The Catholic Encyclopedia*, 3, edited by Kevin Knight. New York: Robert Appleton, 2003, 323–326.

Debusscher, Gilbert. "Tennessee Williams's Lives of the Saints: A Playwright's Obliquity," *Revue des Langues Vivantes* 40 (1974): 449–456.

Hurley, Paul J. "*Suddenly Last Summer* as 'Morality Play,'" *Modern Drama* 8, no. 4 (February 1966): 392–402.

Van Laan, Thomas. "'Shut Up!' 'Be Quiet!' 'Hush!' Talk and Its Suppression in Three Plays by Tennessee Williams," *Comparative Drama* 22, no. 3 (fall 1988): 257–263.


## *Summer and Smoke*

A play in two parts written in 1948.

### SYNOPSIS

The play is set in Glorious Hill, Mississippi, in summer, during the early years of the 20th century. A large, dominating fountain in the form of a stone angel called "Eternity" sits in the center of the stage.

#### *Prologue*

Alma Winemiller and John Buchanan Jr. begin the play as children. John teases Alma for her prudishness, and she introduces him to the stone angel of the fountain.

#### *Part 1*

#### *Scene 1*

Several years later on the fourth of July 1916, the Reverend and Mrs. Winemiller sit near the fountain enjoying fireworks. Alma can be heard singing an aria offstage. John Buchanan also stops at the fountain to listen. His father, Dr. Buchanan, appears, and John and his father have a heated exchange concerning John's unruly behavior. When Alma joins her parents by the fountain, she becomes agitated by John's presence. The Reverend Winemiller tries to maintain order, but Alma succumbs to a panic attack, as her mother cries out for ice cream.

When Alma's parents leave, John throws a lighted firecracker underneath her bench. Alma is startled by his prank. John offers her a drink of brandy from his flask, but she refuses. John is a medical doctor, and he diagnoses Alma's nervous palpitations as "an irritated Doppelgänger." Rosa Gonzales sashays toward the fountain, and John is taken aback by her seductiveness. Nellie Ewell walks over to congratulate Alma on her performance. Nellie also makes an appointment with John to discuss the facts of "nature" because she has recently fallen in love. John tells Alma that she is a source of ridicule in the Glorious Hill community. Alma is hurt by the news and retaliates by criticizing John's reckless behavior. Rosa Gonzales returns, luring John from Alma's side. Roger Doremus arrives to escort Alma home.

### *Scene 2*

The next day Mrs. Winemiller sits in her living room at the rectory. She primps in the mirror wearing a plumed hat that she has just stolen from a local shop. She quickly hides the hat when Alma enters to answer the telephone. Alma apologizes to the hat shop owner, finds the hat, and scolds her mother. She then calls John to invite him to a literary club meeting. Alma's mother harasses her about having a crush on John. Nellie arrives for her singing lessons and confesses her own interest in John. Alma chastises Nellie, but Mrs. Winemiller loudly declares Alma's infatuation. Alma promptly sends Nellie away and berates her mother. As they argue, the hat is destroyed.

### *Scene 3*

Later that evening, as Alma reads the minutes of the last meeting, John arrives and is welcomed into the literary group. Rosemary attempts to read her paper on the poet William Blake but is stopped short by Mrs. Bassett, who argues that Blake is an immoral poet. In Blake's defense, Alma recites his poem "Love's Secret," which expresses her feelings for John. Rosemary is encouraged to begin her paper again, but the episode has prompted John to escape the gathering of bickering members. Alma becomes angry with Mrs. Bassett for driving John out of the meeting.

### *Scene 4*

A few evenings later, John is cut in a fight. He goes into his father's office with Rosa, who bandages his wounded arm when Rosa leaves. Alma enters to see John's father, but John Jr. intercepts her. He gives her a sleeping tonic, unbuttons her blouse, and checks her heartbeat with a stethoscope. He says that inside her chest there is a little voice that says, "Miss Alma is lonesome." He makes a date with Alma for the following Saturday night and sends her home with a box of sleeping pills. Rosa returns as Alma exits. John kisses Rosa roughly.

### *Scene 5*

The following Saturday evening, Alma and her parents sit in their parlor and discuss John's impending visit. John whistles for Alma outside the house. She excitedly runs out to meet him.

### *Scene 6*

Outside the Moon Lake Casino, at an arbor with picnic tables, John and Alma drink wine. They converse and explore their differences: Alma is seeking a spiritual form of love and John is merely interested in physical satisfaction. Alma says she has been unsuccessful with men. John kisses Alma several times and asks her to forget she's "a preacher's daughter." Alma is offended and demands to go home. John abruptly shouts for a taxi to return her to the rectory.

## *Part 2*

### *Scene 7*

This scene alternates between the rectory and the doctor's office. On this Saturday evening in late summer, Roger Doremus shows to Alma a scrapbook of his mother's visit to Asia. Sounds of a raucous gathering at the Buchanan household can be heard. Mrs. Bassett enters to complain about the party at the Buchanan residence and to ask the Reverend Winemiller to call John's father, who is away at a fever clinic.

Mrs. Bassett gossips that John and Rosa have obtained a marriage license and are to be married the next day. Alma rushes to the telephone and calls John's father. In the doctor's office Rosa dances for John. He is disgusted with himself and remarks that he should have been castrated. Rosa's drunken father, Papa Gonzales, enters the doctor's office and collapses on the couch. Rosa urges John to rejoin the party with her. Instead, John goes to the rectory, seeking Alma's cold hands to cool the "fire" in his head. Alma holds John close. In the meantime, Dr. Buchanan returns to his office to find Rosa Gonzales and her father. He beats Rosa's father with his cane. Papa Gonzales responds by shooting Dr. Buchanan.

*Scene 8*
A few hours later, Alma takes John coffee as the Reverend Winemiller prays with John's father in the next room. Alma confesses that she phoned John's father, prompting his return. John drags Alma to the anatomy chart and forces her to look at it. Alma declares that the soul is the most important part of human beings and the part of her with which she has loved John is missing from his chart. Alma sings for Dr. Buchanan.

*Scene 9*
This scene alternates between the rectory and the doctor's office. On this late autumn afternoon, Alma sits on the love seat. Her hair is undone and she is still wearing her dressing gown. The Reverend and Mrs. Winemiller return from watching the parade given in John's honor. The Reverend Winemiller criticizes his wife's behavior and scolds Alma for her disheveled appearance. The parade marches past the Winemillers' window. Alma rushes to watch and collapses. John enters the doctor's office and places his trophy on his desk. Nellie slips into the office unnoticed. She flirts with John and kisses him. He orders her to leave before they get into "trouble."

*Scene 10*
On this afternoon in December, Alma sits in the park with the stone angel fountain to catch her breath. Mrs. Bassett discusses with her news about the literary circle. Nellie enters with a basket of Christmas presents. She gives Alma a beautifully wrapped box containing an exquisite lace handkerchief. Alma reads Nellie's Christmas card and from it learns of Nellie's engagement to John.

*Scene 11*
One hour later, at the doctor's office, Alma tells John about her recurring sore throat. She recalls his early diagnosis of Doppelgänger. John checks her pulse and her heart. Alma takes John's head in her hands and kisses him. Alma pleads with John to love her. Nellie enters the office, parading her engagement ring. She asks Alma to sing at their wedding.

*Scene 12*
At dusk of the same day, Alma encounters Archie Kramer, a young traveling salesman, who is drinking water from the fountain. Alma takes one of her sleeping pills and offers one to Archie. She flirts with him and offers to take him to Moon Lake Casino. He calls for a taxi while Alma bids farewell to the stone angel.

## COMMENTARY

Based on the short story "THE YELLOW BIRD," this delicate tragedy of missed romantic possibility illustrates an allegorical conflict of opposites. Alma Winemiller's ill-fated attempts to connect with John Buchanan personify a struggle of the spiritual versus the sensual, the body versus the soul, and purity versus carnality. John Buchanan, with his anatomy chart and hedonistic self-indulgence, is firmly grounded in the physical, sensual world; Alma—whose name is Spanish for "soul"—represents a rigid and repressive puritanism. At the heart of *Summer and Smoke* is a quest for self-awareness and discovery. In their awakening John and Alma face the extremity of their beliefs and behavior and ultimately reverse roles. He finds his higher calling and true vocation while she (as is Blanche DuBois) is left to find love and fulfillment through sex with strangers. The journey to self-knowledge provides solace for John, but only emptiness and regret for Alma.

Although she is largely identified with Amanda Wingfield in *THE GLASS MENAGERIE*, Williams's mother, EDWINA DAKIN WILLIAMS, also served as the prototype for Alma Winemiller. As is Alma, the young Edwina Dakin was a minister's daughter who loved to sing and play the piano, and her usual laugh was one of her well-noted mannerisms. Mrs. Williams recalled that her many gentleman callers would visit her at the Dakin home in Mississippi to hear her sing and play the piano. *Summer and Smoke* was, in fact, her favorite of her son's plays (Brown, 113).

## PRODUCTION HISTORY

*Summer and Smoke* was first produced by MARGO JONES in July 1947 at Theatre '47 in Dallas, Texas. Jones's production was generally very well received, and there were plans to have the production transferred immediately to Broadway. The Broadway run of *Summer and Smoke* was delayed, however, by the Broadway opening of *A STREETCAR NAMED DESIRE* on December 3, 1947. When the production finally made it to Broadway and premiered at the Music Box Theatre on October 6, 1948, it was unfavorably compared to *Streetcar.*

The Broadway production closed on January 1, 1949, after 100 performances. The most significant production of *Summer and Smoke* was the version directed by Jose Quintero in New York in 1952 at the Circle in the Square Theatre, which featured GERALDINE PAGE as Alma Winemiller. Page revived her portrayal of Alma Winemiller when the play was adapted for screen by James Poe and Meade Roberts and produced as a feature film in 1961. Page was nominated for an Academy Award (Oscar) for her performance as the fragile, lovelorn Alma. Page believed that with *Summer and Smoke* Williams had created "one of the most perfect things, both in form and content and everything else" (Steen, 239).

## PUBLICATION HISTORY

*Summer and Smoke* was first published in 1948. It was subsequently revised and rewritten as *THE ECCENTRICITIES OF A NIGHTINGALE* in 1951.

## CHARACTERS

**Alma** She is Alma Winemiller as a young girl. At the tender age of 10, Alma is already completely devoted to John. Noticing that he has had a bad cold, she gives him a box of handkerchiefs and leaves them on his school desk. John finds her at the fountain in the center of town and teases her for leaving the handkerchiefs on his desk. Alma introduces John to the stone angel of the fountain. She shows him how to read the angel's fading name in the stone by using his hands. The stone angel, Eternity, watches over Alma as John pulls her hair and kisses her. As her name (which is Spanish for "soul") implies, Alma has an innocent, angelic presence.

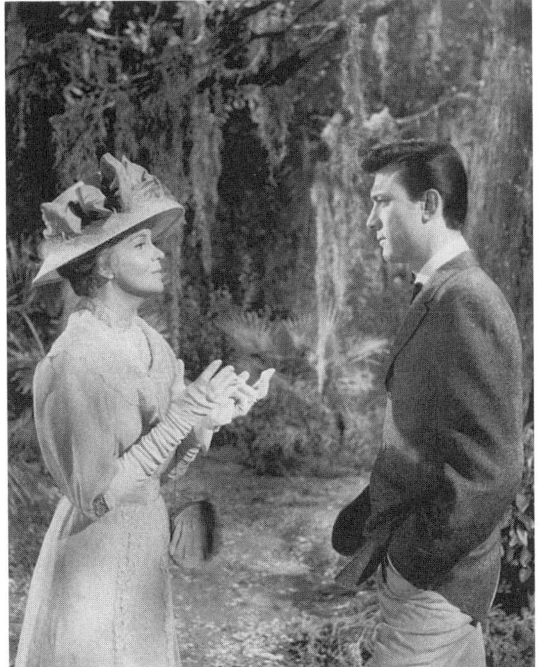

Geraldine Page (Alma Winemiller) and Laurence Harvey (John Buchanan, Jr.) in the film version of *Summer and Smoke* *(Paramount, 1961)*

**Bassett, Mrs.** An overbearing old widow who is a member of the literary circle in Glorious Hill, Mississippi, led by Alma Winemiller. At one of their meetings, she becomes irate when Rosemary tries to read her essay about William Blake. Mrs. Bassett's unreasonable and childish behavior embarrasses Alma in front of John Buchanan.

**Buchanan, Dr. John** Dr. Buchanan is a well-respected physician in the town of Glorious Hill, Mississippi. He is also John Buchanan Jr.'s father. He is greatly dismayed by his son's unruly and common behavior. As a result of John's folly, Papa Gonzales shoots Dr. Buchanan and kills him.

**Buchanan, John, Jr.** John is the crude, self-indulgent, and philandering son of Dr. John

Buchanan. He dallies with the affections of his lovelorn next-door neighbor, Alma Winemiller; He becomes engaged to Rosa Gonzales but ultimately decides to marry Nellie Ewell.

**Doremus, Roger** Roger is Alma Winemiller's only true friend in Glorious Hill, Mississippi. As is Alma, he is a musician: She is a singer and he plays the French horn. He is also a member of Alma's literary circle. Their relationship is solely platonic.

**Ewell, Nellie** Nellie is one of Alma Winemiller's vocal students. During the course of the play she matures from an awkward teenager into an attractive young woman. Initially, she frequents the Winemillers' home for private voice lessons with Alma. Nellie confesses that her crush on Miss Alma led her to take singing lessons. During one of her lessons she catches Alma spying on John Buchanan and admits her own attraction to the young doctor. Nellie goes away to college, and when she returns from Sophie Newcomb, she becomes John's fiancée.

**Gonzales, Papa** Papa Gonzales is the owner of the Moon Lake Casino, near Glorious Hill, Mississippi, and the father of Rosa Gonzales. Papa Gonzales strikes a deal with John Buchanan Jr. to help the young doctor settle his substantial debts at the casino. If John will marry Rosa, he will not have to repay Papa Gonzales. John accepts the deal and the couple promptly become engaged. The night before their wedding, John hosts a raucous party at the Buchanan home. In an effort to help John and to stop his impending marriage to Rosa, Alma Winemiller calls his father, Dr. John Buchanan Sr., who is out of town at a fever clinic. Dr. Buchanan returns home immediately and confronts Papa Gonzales. In a drunken rage, Papa Gonzales shoots Dr. Buchanan.

**Gonzales, Rosa** Rosa is Alma Winemiller's first rival for John Buchanan Jr.'s affection. A sensual Mexican beauty, she is likened to the tropical breezes that blow from the Gulf of Mexico: warm, languid, and fluid. She provides a stark contrast to the cold, rigid, and awkward Alma. Rosa's father, Papa Gonzales, forces John to propose to Rosa as compensation for John's gambling debts at the Moon Lake Casino, which Papa Gonzales owns. Rosa and John are engaged briefly but do not marry. On the evening before their wedding, her father shoots and fatally wounds John's father, Dr. John Buchanan Sr.

**John** He is John Buchanan Jr. as a young boy. During the prologue, John confronts Alma at the fountains. She has publicly humiliated him by leaving a wrapped box of handkerchiefs on his school desk. Alma left the gift as a token of her affection and concern for John, who has had a cold and is without a mother. Alma introduces John to the stone angel of the park fountain. She shows him how to read the angel's name with his fingers. John teases Alma for her awkward prudishness and kisses her roughly.

**Kramer, Archie** Archie is a traveling salesman who visits Glorious Hill, Mississippi. He encounters Alma Winemiller after she has decided to lead an uninhibited life. Alma eagerly escorts Archie to a part of town where they can rent a room for an hour. Archie is the parallel character to the Traveling Salesman in *THE ECCENTRICITIES OF A NIGHTINGALE*.

**Rosemary** A member of the literary circle in Glorious Hill, Mississippi, led by Alma Winemiller. She has written an essay on the poet William Blake, which she attempts unsuccessfully to read at the literary club meeting.

**Winemiller, Alma** She is the delicate daughter of the Reverend Winemiller and Mrs. Winemiller, who gives singing lessons in the rectory parlor. Although "prematurely spinsterish" and prudish, she is hopelessly in love with John Buchanan Jr. When she loses John to Nellie Ewell she seeks solace in the arms of Archie Kramer, a traveling salesman.

Although she is largely identified with Amanda Wingfield in *THE GLASS MENAGERIE*, Williams's mother, EDWINA ESTELLE DAKIN WILLIAMS, also served as the prototype for Alma Winemiller. As is Alma, the young Edwina Dakin was a minister's daughter who loved to sing and play the piano, and her laugh was one of her much-noted mannerisms. Mrs. Williams recalled that her many gentleman callers would visit her at the Dakin home in Mississippi to hear her sing and play the piano. *Summer and Smoke* was her favorite of her son's plays (Brown, 113).

**Winemiller, Mrs.** She is the mentally unbalanced mother of Alma Winemiller. Mrs. Winemiller's behavior toward her daughter and her husband, the Reverend Winemiller, is childishly cruel and malicious.

**Winemiller, Reverend** The Reverend Winemiller is the Episcopal minister of Glorious Hill, Mississippi, and the father of Alma Winemiller.

### FURTHER READING

Brown, Dennis. *Shoptalk: Conversations about Theatre and Film with Twelve Writers, One Producer—and Tennessee Williams's Mother.* New York: Newmarket Press, 1992.

Steen, Mike. *A Look at Tennessee Williams.* New York: Hawthorn Books, 1969.

## *Sweet Bird of Youth*

Full-length play written in 1952.

### SYNOPSIS

#### *Act 1, Scene 1*

The setting is a bedroom of an old, fashionable hotel in the Gulf Coast town of Saint Cloud, in the early morning.

Chance Wayne, a handsome man in his late 20s, watches a famous aging actress, Alexandra Del Lago, also known as Princess Kosmonopolis, sleep as he smokes his first cigarette of the day. He is interrupted by a delivery of coffee from room service. Church bells toll and Chance realizes that it is Sunday. The waiter, Fly, tells him it is Easter. Fly remembers Chance from the town dances that Chance attended with his girlfriend, Heavenly Finley. Chance is happy to recollect that time. The young town surgeon, George Scudder, appears outside the door, to tell Chance that he must leave Saint Cloud and never return. He asks Chance why he is back in town. Chance has returned to see his mother and his "girl," Heavenly. Scudder tells him that his mother died several weeks ago. Devastated, Chance asks why no one contacted him. Scudder says the whole town tried to track him down, and when they received no answer from several wires and letters, they pooled their funds together to pay for the funeral. Scudder accuses Chance of being unconcerned that his mother was seriously ill. He claims she was also "sick at heart" that Chance left. Scudder also says the whole town is angry at Chance and asks whether he has received a very important letter. Chance says he did not get the letter. Scudder informs him that Heavenly had a terrible experience. Despite Chance's pleas for more information, Scudder says he has to leave. He warns Chance to leave town before Heavenly's father, Boss Finley, hears that he is back. (Boss Finley has threatened to castrate Chance if he ever encounters him again.) Scudder says he is going to tell Mr. Hatcher at the front desk that Chance and the princess are checking out of the hotel this morning. Scudder calls Chance a "criminal degenerate" and informs him that Heavenly is no longer Chance's "girl," as she is now engaged to Scudder.

Chance immediately phones Aunt Nonnie, Heavenly's aunt. He tells her that he is at the Royal Palms and wants to speak to Heavenly. Aunt Nonnie is fearful of talking to him and hangs up the phone. Suddenly the Princess begins to cry in her sleep. Chance runs to her side to awaken her. She does not know who Chance is. She begs for her oxygen mask and begins to have a panic attack. Chance rummages through her luggage and finds the mask just in time. She takes a pink pill and washes it down with vodka. Chance calls down to the front desk to plead with Mr. Hatcher to allow them to stay. The Princess begins to drink heavily because she wishes to forget her name and her life. Chance admits that she has a good idea. He grabs a small tape recorder and goes to her bedside. He inquires about her illness. She panics at the mention of calling a doctor, as she has become a hashish addict now that her acting career is over. She informs Chance that she acquired her current stash by mail from Morocco. The Princess says this is not the kind of conversation that should be happening anywhere as public as a hotel room. She scoffs at the prospect of being arrested and sent to a prison for "distinguished addicts." She also laments her faded youth and the contemptible position of being an old actress. She confesses that her decision to retire from the screen was prompted by a box office failure. Chance responds that no one is young these days. He too understands aging and the loss of sex appeal.

Chance changes the subject to discuss the "second-rate" Hollywood studio that she owns. He proposes that she give him an acting contract. If she does not agree to launch his career, he will use the conversation about the Moroccan hashish to blackmail her. Chance expects her to offer Heavenly an acting contract as well. The Princess acknowledges that this is the first time Chance has ever tried anything such as blackmail. Chance encourages her to sign over some traveler's checks and lend him her Cadillac to find Heavenly. Princess Kosmonopolis demands that Chance draw the curtains, put on some sweet music, and pretend that they are youthful lovers.

### *Act 1, Scene 2*

In the darkened hotel room at the Royal Palms Hotel, Princess Kosmonopolis signs checks as Chance dresses. He begins to tell his life story: about being born in Saint Cloud, leaving with dreams of stardom, and becoming a kept young man of rich widows and bored wives of the aristocracy. Chance believes his past stole his youth. He confesses that he hated himself and couldn't handle the routine of pleasing others for a living. He left Heavenly to join the navy and was discharged when he had a nervous breakdown. He shows a nude photo of Heavenly to the Princess and delights in the recollection of the magical night he took the photo. He says that every time he left Saint Cloud and returned a failure, Heavenly was his cure. She nursed him back to emotional health. The Princess asks why he did not marry Heavenly if he loved her so much. Chance explains that Boss Finley would not allow it as he believed she could marry someone of better social standing, a man that could help his political career. The last time he returned to Saint Cloud, Heavenly called him a liar and said that she wanted nothing else to do with him. Chance hopes that the acting contract will win Heavenly back. The Princess is hesitant to help Chance as she wants to remain incognito. As Chance bids her farewell, the Princess says she loves him and that she will wait for him.

### *Act 2, Scene 1*

On the terrace of Boss Finley's Victorian house, Boss Finley is addressing Scudder. He tells him that Chance Wayne had sex with Heavenly when she was just 15 years old. He knows this because he found some photographs Chance took of Heavenly naked on the beach. Furious that Chance has returned despite his orders never to return, Boss Finley asks his son, Tom Finley Junior, to call the hotel and ask whether he has checked out yet. Tom Junior makes the call and tells his father that Chance is still in town. Boss Finley chastises Scudder for leaking the details about the surgery he had performed on Heavenly, which he calls a "whore's operation." Boss Finley orders Scudder to remove Princess Kosmonopolis to a hospital with a false diagnosis of a contagious disease. At this moment, Chance drives by honking his horn. He calls for Aunt Nonnie, who is afraid to go to him. Boss Finley corners Aunt Nonnie. She admits that she sent a message to the hotel warning him to leave Saint Cloud before Boss Finley found out. Boss threatens that Chance will leave, but not in a fancy Cadillac. Nonnie begs him to refrain from violence, and Boss Finley insults her. Boss blames Nonnie for Heavenly's involvement with Chance.

Boss and Tom Junior argue, as Tom feels unappreciated by his relentless and despotic father. He has dedicated himself to his father's campaign and organized the Youth for Tom Finley Club. Boss points out Tom Junior's recent arrest for drunk driving and flunking out of college. Tom Junior retorts with accusations that his father always had a mistress, Miss Lucy, even before the death of his mother. Boss denies the allegation, and Tom Junior follows by saying that Miss Lucy tells everyone that Boss is too old to be a good lover. She went so far as to write it on a mirror in the ladies' room. Boss Finley is embarrassed by Miss Lucy's betrayal. He addresses the audience with lofty banter about his political mission. He calls Heavenly, who has become despondent about her life. Boss forces her to listen while his servant reminds him of an appointment and hands him a gift.

Boss Finley is revived by Heavenly's beauty. Admiringly, he says that she is still beautiful despite what has happened to her. Heavenly refutes the compliment, calling herself a carcass after the surgery. Her father scolds her for talking in such a way, and he orders her to not to repeat such derogatory remarks because people listen. If more people knew that, at 15, Heavenly contracted a venereal disease from Chance Wayne and had to have a radical hysterectomy, his political career could be tainted. Angered by his self-centeredness, Heavenly blames her unhappiness on her father's refusal to allow her to marry Chance at the time. She faults her father for the empty life she is forced to live because Boss drove Chance out of town. She is embittered that her father attempted to marry her to a 50-year-old "money bag" to fuel his political campaigns. Heavenly says, "Papa, you married for love; why wouldn't you let me do it, while I was alive, inside, and the boy still clean, still decent?" Heavenly mentions Miss Lucy and says that the fact her father had a mistress broke her dying mother's heart.

Boss Finley tries to appease Heavenly by offering her a shopping spree. He tells her about the time when he bought her dying mother a diamond pin to prove to her that he did not believe she was so ill. He sent it back to the jeweler after she died. When Heavenly patronizes him about being such a kind, giving man, he reminds her that he has been heckled with shouts about her surgery from the campaign crowd. Heavenly apologizes for the embarrassment she has caused her family and suggests entering a convent. Boss Finley rejects the idea of her entering a Catholic convent: He will never be elected to office in this Protestant town if she does. He insists that she escort him and stand on the speaker's platform at the next campaign rally. She refuses and he threatens to hurt Chance if she does not. Boss Finley expresses his disdain for Chance and explains that he is trying to keep the pure white blood of the South unadulterated. He believes he was called by "the voice of God" to go down from the mountain and protect the aristocracy.

### *Act 2, Scene 2*

The setting is the cocktail lounge at the Royal Palms Hotel, where Chance Wayne used to work. Boss Finley has planned to hold his campaign rally there tonight.

Miss Lucy enters wearing an elaborate ball gown. She sits down at the bar and glares at the bartender, Stuff. She accuses Stuff of telling Tom Junior what she said about his father. Stuff defends himself by saying that she wrote it on the mirror in the ladies' room. A Heckler enters the lounge, to shout insults at Boss about Heavenly's sordid past. For revenge, Miss Lucy agrees to help him get into the rally.

Stuff gossips that Chance is staying at the hotel with the old movie star Alexandra Del Lago. Miss Lucy is intrigued. Chance walks into the lounge, shouting orders at Stuff. At this moment, Aunt Nonnie enters the lounge. Chance is very happy to see her, and she demands that he walk outside with her. She warns him to leave Saint Cloud. Chance takes a pill, which he washes down with liquor. Chance reminisces about a drama league production that he and Heavenly starred in.

Chance shows Aunt Nonnie the acting contracts signed by his traveling companion. She thinks they are fake and that this is another one of Chance's scams. He pleads with her to take him seriously, but she can only warn him against Boss Finley and exits. Two old friends, Bud and Scotty, enter the bar. Chance begins to feel high from the pills and alcohol. He sings with the piano, and everyone in the bar silently watches this sad spectacle. Miss Lucy announces herself to Chance as Bud and Scotty make fun of his nonexistent acting career. Miss Lucy points out changes in Chance's once youthful appearance. She cruelly teases him about being a beach boy in hotels in Florida.

Bud and Scotty tell Chance that an African-American man was recently castrated because he was out on the street after curfew. At the rally, Boss Finley is going to state his opinion on the matter. Chance calls this violent act "sex envy," and he predicts that Boss Finley will not be opposed to the crime. He becomes louder when he condemns Boss Finley as a hypocrite and a liar. Miss Lucy tries to calm him, but he refuses to desist. He continues to take pills and talk loudly about his devotion to Heavenly. A messenger is sent to collect Chance for Princess Kosmonopolis. When Chance does not respond, she enters. Miss Lucy introduces herself to the famous actress. The Princess calls for Chance as he rushes out of the lounge. The Princess can see that he has been defeated and is relieved that he has returned to her. Dan Hatcher, Tom Junior's friend, calls Chance's name from a distance. Chance tries to make an escape, but it is too late. Hatcher tells him that Tom Junior is waiting to speak with him. Chance refuses to move, forcing Tom Junior to appear. Chance demands to know what has happened to Heavenly while he was gone. Enraged by Chance's loyalty to Heavenly, Tom Junior tells him that Heavenly contracted a venereal disease, which Chance must have contracted in his occupation as a gigolo. Heavenly did not understand her illness until it was too late and she had to undergo extensive surgery. Chance is dumbfounded, as he swears he did not know that he had given the disease to Heavenly.

Geraldine Page (Alexandra Del Lago/Princess Kosmonopolis) embracing Paul Newman (Chance Wayne) in the 1959 Broadway production of *Sweet Bird of Youth* *(Eileen Darby)*

Tom Junior is bewildered by his stupidity. The Princess grows nervous waiting for the escalating fight to end. She begs Chance to leave the lounge with her. The Princess has another attack and is escorted out of the lounge in a wheelchair.

Boss Finley and his entourage enter. He loosens his tie and collar to catch his breath. A drum majorette ushers in the Youth for Tom Finley committee, accompanied by Finley, Tom Junior, and a reluctant Heavenly. Miss Lucy is seated beside the Heckler, who prepares his interruptions. Boss Finley proclaims himself the "colored man's best friend"; however, he follows this by explaining that he will also fight to prohibit "blood pollution." Boss Finley claims to have had no part in the recent castration. Chance shouts insults and heckles him from the audience. The Heckler joins in and inquires about Heavenly's surgery, and Boss Finley's gang of men beat him. Heavenly descends the platform and collapses.

### *Act 3, Scene 1*

Later that night in the hotel bedroom, the Princess paces the floor waiting for Chance. When he enters, she hysterically demands to get out of Saint Cloud. There is a knock on the door. Hatcher, Tom Junior, Bud, and Scotty enter the room in search of Chance, who hides down the corridor. They interrogate the Princess and leave. Chance comes out of hiding and demands that Princess Kosmonopolis phone some Hollywood executives on his behalf. She calls Sally Powers, from whom she learns that her last movie was not unsuccessful, as she had been led to believe. Princess Kosmonopolis discovers that she is still a celebrity and her career is very much alive.

The Princess's attitude toward Chance Wayne changes. She indicates that she is not concerned with the career of a pool boy. She can no longer be threatened by his blackmail because she is a superstar. Princess Kosmonopolis gives Chance advice on aging and youth before a driver arrives to take her to the airport. Tom Junior and his posse reenter to take Chance away. He says good-bye to the Princess, as he submits to the men.

## COMMENTARY

*Sweet Bird of Youth* is Williams's darkest exploration of fading youth and diminishing livelihood with the onset of age. Chance Wayne forfeits love for aspirations of becoming a movie star. This pursuit consumes his consciousness and his chance at happiness. As he searches for a way to fulfill his destiny, he loses his most valuable asset—his youth. Although he remains handsome and is still in his 20s, he is constantly reminded that he is not as striking as he used to be.

Decay is a primary theme in this play. Chance's opportunities fade with time, and he falls short of his dreams when he is forced to become a pool boy in order to survive. His refuge is his beauty, which grants him the luxury of older women, who are also searching for ways to retain their youth, beauty, and sex appeal. He does not give up on his desires to become a star, but his chances wane as a result of the passing of time and his youth.

Chance returns to Saint Cloud in order to reconcile with Heavenly for two reasons: He realizes that he loves Heavenly, and he wants to try to retrieve his youth by rekindling an innocent relationship and time in his life. This attempt to reconnect with the past and make it the present serves as Chance's tragic flaw, as his past actions were too destructive for him to ever regain access to Heavenly. Facing castration by Boss Finley, Chance accepts that his lifestyle has brought about the degradation of his life. Chance's days of being a virile, beautiful man are over, just as the dreams of a Hollywood career are. In his self-pity and self-loathing state of mind, Chance accepts punishment for his life's mistakes: castration by Boss Finley's henchmen.

Chance and the Princess are very similar characters. They are both battling life and time for a chance to remain among the beautiful people, without much regard for others. Princess Kosmonopolis's aging beauty propels her into a self-destructive cycle of drug addiction and meaningless sexual encounters. She feels the loss of her own youth and is comforted only through forgetful hashish episodes. As does Karen Stone in THE ROMAN SPRING OF MRS. STONE, the Princess decides to end her own glamorous career by taking flight. Using an alias, she steps out of life, but only to encounter fading youth and unfulfilled dreams in aging pool boys such as Chance. However, the Princess's hope is revived when she becomes aware that her last film was actually a huge success. Her retirement has been premature; her fate and her future is still promising. Unlike Karen Stone, she has strength of character and a fighting will to survive. Although Chance and Princess Kosmonopolis have a similar nature, the actress "towers over the other characters in her rage and in her lust, sharing none of their pettiness or vengefulness" (Tischler, 498). Without the vices of pettiness or vengefulness, Princess Kosmonopolis is free to return to the world and enjoy her life of celebrity and fame. She does not stoop to take a part in this troubled plot. Rage and lust, which are typically viewed as contemptible human qualities, prompt the downfall of the other characters in the play. They are, however, the Princess's saving graces.

Boss Finley is one of the most malevolent and racist characters in Williams's works. With his mission and fanatical belief that the white race should not be polluted, Boss Finely tries to separate himself from the violent crime against the African-American man. As it is established that he will castrate Chance Wayne, his involvement in the crime becomes glaringly obvious. Also, in his thirst for power he creates pawns of his children. As is his counterpart, Miss Lucy, Boss Finley is disloyal and quick to turn on the people closest to him. He is an all-consuming force that barks and bellows unpleasantness as does Big Daddy in CAT ON A HOT TIN ROOF. His hypocritical self-righteousness can be compared to that of Jabe of ORPHEUS DESCENDING. As does Jabe, Boss Finley dispenses what he perceives to be justice for the atonement of the sins of the small town. His power spans the community like that of "the Old Testament God of vengeance" (Adler, 658).

Because Williams continually revised and reworked his plays, remnants of *Sweet Bird of Youth* can be traced throughout his canon, including several one-act and full-length plays. There are distinct similarities and resonances between this work and the much earlier one-act THE PURIFICATION (1940). The two heroines, Heavenly and Elena, share a similar fate of being brutally victimized for loving the wrong man. Interestingly, both Heavenly and Elena (whose name is Greek, meaning "bright light" or "torch light") are ethereal characters whose lamentations permeate their respective communities.

## PRODUCTION HISTORY

*Sweet Bird of Youth* was first produced at the Studio M Playhouse in Coral Gables, Florida, April 16, 1956, directed and designed by George Keathley. The play was produced at the Martin Beck Theatre in New York on March 10, 1959, directed by Elia Kazan, designed by JO MIELZINER and Anna Hill Johnstone. This production starred Paul Newman as Chance Wayne and Geraldine Page as the Princess. Despite mixed reviews, *Sweet Bird* was very successful, with 383 performances. Geraldine Page was said to have given "a compelling, bravura performance as Alexandra" while "Paul Newman was superb in a role that requires him to be almost constantly repugnant" (Aston, 348). Critics complained of an uneven script, excessive symbolism, and Chance's concluding and heavily romantic plea. Williams himself admitted that this play "was in the works too long" and said, "Sometimes I wish I had not tried to deal with so much" (Devlin, 60).

The film version of *Sweet Bird* was produced in 1962, directed by Richard Brooks, again starring, Paul Newman and Geraldine Page. It won an Academy Award for Best Actor in a Supporting Role (Ed Begley) and a nomination for Best Actress in a Leading Role (Geraldine Page) and Best Actress in a Supporting Role (Shirley Knight). *Sweet Bird* required drastic textual revisions for the film version. As a result, according to Maurice Yacowar, "a tragedy of poison [became] a romance of rebirth" (97). Richard Brooks and his producers felt compelled to turn the dark tragedy into a positive story, whereby Chance merely suffers a broken nose from Boss Finley, rather than castration and implied death. Chance Wayne wins back Heavenly, and they leave Saint Cloud for Hollywood. Boss Finley is hated by everyone at the end of the film, and Miss Lucy becomes Alexandra Del Lago's driver. This hopeful adaptation omits the African American's castration and all references to the crime.

In 1989, a television version of this play was filmed, starring Elizabeth Taylor, Mark Harmon, and Valerie Perrine. This production returned to the Williams script and restored many of the original uncensored elements of the plot.

## PUBLICATION HISTORY

*Sweet Bird of Youth* was performed long before it was officially published. It first appeared in *Esquire*, April 1957, and was published as a book by New Directions in 1959 and by Penguin in 1962.

## CHARACTERS

**Aunt Nonnie** She is the sister-in-law of Boss Finley and the surrogate mother of her niece, Heavenly Finley. Aunt Nonnie sympathizes with Heavenly's longtime boyfriend, Chance Wayne, and when he returns to Saint Cloud to take Heavenly to Hollywood with him, Aunt Nonnie warns him that Boss Finley will kill him if he does not leave.

**Boss Finley** As his name suggests, Boss Finley is a domineering politician in the old Southern town of St. Cloud. Boss Finley is a womanizer who believes himself virtuous in his mission to maintain segregation and inequality in the African-American community. Like those of Big Daddy of *CAT ON A HOT TIN ROOF*, Boss Finley's expectations for his children cripple their ability to persevere in life. Heavenly Finley, as does Brick Pollitt, deteriorates under such despotism.

**Finley, Heavenly** She is a young beauty who loves a handsome young man, Chance Wayne. Contracting a venereal disease that is cured only through a hysterectomy, she prematurely ages because her life has been wrecked and her reputation tarnished. Devoid of ambition, she is harassed by her politician father, Boss Finley, who insists on dressing her in elaborate white dresses and presenting her on the campaign platform as his virtuous, pure example of white pride.

**Finley, Tom, Junior** The brother of Heavenly Finley. Tom Junior loathes Heavenly's recently returned lover, Chance Wayne, and he agrees with his father, Boss Finley, that Chance should leave town immediately. Tom Junior serves Boss Finley as one of his thuggish hired men.

**Heckler** He is a protester who attends Boss Finley's campaign rallies. The Heckler is the voice of reason, who serves to release the tension surrounding Finley's campaign of bigotry. He is beaten by the politician's henchmen when he points out Finley's hypocritical statements, heckling Boss Finley, and revealing the tyrannical nature of the politician.

**Miss Lucy** She is an aging beauty who has been clandestinely committed to the thuggish local politician Boss Finley. Miss Lucy tires of his infidelities and sabotages his campaign rally. She sympathizes with Boss Finley's archenemy, Chance Wayne.

**Princess Kosmonopolis** Also known as Alexandra Del Lago, she is an aging movie star who develops a hashish addiction after what she perceives as the failure of her latest movie and end of her acting career. She finds consolation in pool boys and gigolos, in particular Chance Wayne. Princess Kosmonopolis does not remember where she found him, but he quickly becomes her nurse and kept man. Princess Kosmonopolis wakes up in Chance's Gulf Coast hometown of Saint Cloud. She is pulled into a dramatic fight for Chance's love with Heavenly Finley. When she is blackmailed by Chance to gain an acting contract, she discovers that her last movie was a huge hit. With renewed confidence, Princess Kosmonopolis hires a driver and leaves Saint Cloud. Her need for Chance Wayne subsides, and she is restored by the knowledge that she is not too old to be attractive to moviegoers. Princess Kosmonopolis is very much like Karen Stone of *THE ROMAN SPRING OF MRS. STONE*, another aging actress who finds life in the arms of a beautiful young hustler. The Princess, however, is able to reestablish herself in the social circles that matter to her. With a reinstated career, she has a second chance in life.

**Wayne, Chance** He is a handsome young man who has lived life beyond his years. With dreams of a career in film, he has been a gigolo in the aristocratic circles at resorts near Saint Cloud, a Gulf Coast town. Chance's true love, Heavenly Finley, has suffered the brunt of his playboy days. At 15 years of age, she contracted a venereal disease from him and had a radical hysterectomy. Chance left Saint Cloud to pursue his dreams, but when he returns after several years, he discovers that he is no longer welcome in his hometown. As is Val

Geraldine Page as Alexandra Del Lago (Princess Kosmonopolis) in *Sweet Bird of Youth,* 1959 *(Eileen Darby)*

Xavier in *ORPHEUS DESCENDING,* he is the center of attention, but his virility has severely wounded his reputation as a good man. Heavenly's father, a politician named Boss Finley, threatens to castrate Chance. With the plan of taking Heavenly to Hollywood with him, he learns of her surgery and recoils in defeat. His traveling companion, Princess Kosmonopolis, also known as Alexandra Del Lago, leaves him to resume her film career. Chance is a fallen man who finally submits to Boss Finley's posse. He recognizes that after destroying Heavenly's life, his dreams are unattainable.

## FURTHER READING

Adler, Thomas P. "Culture, Power, and the (En)gendering of Community: Tennessee Williams and Politics," *Mississippi Quarterly* 48 (fall 1995): 649–665.

Aston, Frank. "Review of *Sweet Bird of Youth,*" *New York World-Telegram,* March 11, 1959, p. 30. Reprint in *New York Theatre Critics' Reviews* 20 (1959): 348.

Devlin, Albert J., ed. *Conversations with Tennessee Williams.* Jackson: University Press of Mississippi, 1986.

Tischler, Nancy. "A Gallery of Witches," in *Tennessee Williams: A Tribute,* edited by Jac Tharpe. Jackson: University Press of Mississippi, 1977, pp. 494–450.

Yacowar, Maurice. *Tennessee Williams and Film.* New York: Frederick Ungar, 1977.

# *Talk to Me Like the Rain and Let Me Listen*

A one-act play written around 1950.

## SYNOPSIS

A Woman sits in a chair drinking water and watching rain clouds through her window. She waits for the Man, who lies in bed, to wake up. When he finally does, he asks her the time. The Woman answers, "Sunday." A Child's Voice is heard, chanting the familiar rhyme "Rain, rain, go away! Come again some other day!"

The Man cannot find his unemployment check. The Woman tells him that she did not cash it and found his illegible note when she returned from scouring the city for him. He explains that he was out and woke up naked "in a bathtub full of melting ice-cubes and beer," and he pontificates on the abuse one endures when he is drunk in the city. The Man has been beaten, stripped naked, and was left in a trashed hotel room.

After relating his adventure, the Man begs the Woman to "talk to [him] like the rain and let [him] listen." He tells her that it has been too long since they were completely honest with each other. The Woman says she wants to go away without him. She wants to wear white, read poetry in a seaside hotel, and walk along the sea 50 years from now, letting the wind blow her "thinner and thinner." The Man asks her to return to bed as he caresses her throat and face. She cries, and the Man waits for her to calm down. She then asks him to return to bed. Slowly, he turns to her.

## COMMENTARY

The relationship Williams constructs between the Man and the Woman is one of hopelessness. The Woman is weary of life. She longs to remove herself from the worries and anxieties of the world and the relationship she shares with the Man. The Man attempts to escape through alcohol and parties, but he repeatedly suffers physical abuse as a result. This "hopeless[ly] inalterable" situation binds them. When the Woman finally reaches the brink of acting on her impulse to leave, she is drawn back to the Man. Similarly when the Man is ready to release her, resigning his hold emotionally, she pulls him back to bed. As do the characters One and Two in the play I CAN'T IMAGINE TOMORROW, the couple in *Talk to Me Like the Rain and Let Me Listen* are tormented by the need for change, but are inextricably locked in a routine cycle of coexistence.

## PRODUCTION HISTORY

*Talk to Me Like the Rain and Let Me Listen* was first produced at White Barn Theatre, Westport, Connecticut, in 1958. The play was revived in *Three by Tennessee,* Lolly's Theatre Club, New York City, in 1973.

## PUBLICATION HISTORY

This play was published in *27 WAGONS FULL OF COTTON AND OTHER ONE-ACT PLAYS* (1966).

## CHARACTERS

**Man** An unemployed drunkard, he is in a hopeless relationship with the Woman. There is an invisible wall between them, and an acceptance of things that cannot be changed.

**Woman** She is a frail, quiet woman who is in a hopeless relationship with the Man. She shares her fantasy of living alone in a seaside motel with the Man after he has passed a night of drunken parties. The Woman nearly musters the courage to leave the Man because of his irresponsible behavior, but she accepts him again by luring him back to bed with her.

# Ten Blocks on the Camino Real

A one-act play written in 1946.

## SYNOPSIS

The setting is a small town in Mexico.

### Block 1

The Guitar Player strikes a somber chord. A parched and ragged Peasant stumbles onto the stage and throws himself down near the plaza fountain when he realizes it is dry. He makes his way to a nearby cantina, but the owner, Mr. Gutman, blows a whistle for an Officer, who shoots the Peasant. Mr. Gutman and the Officer return to the cantina, and the bleeding body of the Peasant lies near the fountain.

### Block 2

Kilroy enters whistling. He sees a sign that says, "KILROY IS COMING," and he smudges out "COMING" and writes "HERE." Kilroy asks an Officer whether there is a Wells Fargo bank. When he is informed there is no bank, Kilroy explains that he won the boxing gloves that hang around his neck in the lightweight championship title. He has since retired after being diagnosed with a heart the size of a baby's head that is likely to explode under exertion.

The Officer refuses to tell Kilroy what town he is in. When Kilroy grabs his arm and asks again, the Officer punches him in the stomach as he curses and retires to the cantina. Kilroy recovers and is stopped by Rosita, a prostitute. He declines her services. Over a loudspeaker, the Gypsy asks Kilroy whether he is lost. In his confusion, Kilroy does not realize a Pickpocket has stolen his wallet.

Kilroy cries out for an Officer, who refuses to believe he has been robbed. He believes the American embassy will help him solve the crime. Exhausted, Kilroy leans against the wall, watching the Officer go inside the cantina with Rosita. In frustration, he declares, "This deal is rugged!" Kilroy walks toward the pawnshop, taking off his ruby-and-emerald-studded belt.

### Block 3

A woman sings in the plaza. Mr. Gutman enters and promotes his hotel and the local tourist attractions. Each time he finishes a sentence, the Guitar Player adds, "On the Camino Real," and strums his guitar. Mr. Gutman confesses that he cheats people of money and predicts that someday soon, the Streetcleaners will come for his body. Saddened by this thought, he rhetorically asks, "Is this what the glittering wheels of heaven turn for?" He directs his question to the Gypsy.

### Block 4

Jacques and Marguerite enter and sit at a little table. They are irritated by the strange music; however, Mr. Gutman replies that an "Indian died of thirst," and the Streetcleaners are collecting him. Marguerite tries to bribe them to leave quickly. Mr. Gutman cheers her by talking about the fiesta that will occur tonight. Held every full Moon, it publicly restores the virginity of the Gypsy's daughter, Esmerelda. She will dance on the roof and then choose a "hero to lift her veil." Mr. Gutman orders that a bottle of wine be delivered to the table and departs.

Marguerite confesses to Jacques that although she is comfortable with him, she still desires to be with someone who is in love with her. At that moment, Jacques receives a letter informing him that his cash flow has been depleted. He breaks the news to Marguerite, who excuses herself to fetch her shawl. Mr. Gutman reenters to tell Jacques that their reservations have been mixed up and they will have to find a different place to stay for the night. As Jacques follows him inside, the Guitar Player strums.

### Block 5

Kilroy enters and sees the Baron de Charlus. Mistaking the Baron for a "normal American in a clean, white suit," Kilroy approaches and proclaims, "It's wonderful to see you!" The Baron points out that his suit is pale yellow. He is French and an unusual man. Kilroy asks the Baron for a five-dollar loan because the pawnshop wanted only his lucky gloves. The Baron refuses to lend him money and returns to the inside of the hotel. Mr. Gutman tells Kilroy to hold on to anything that's "lucky" because there is no compassion for an unlucky man on the Camino Real. Confused, Kilroy asks what the Camino Real is, and Mr. Gutman tells him that he must discover that for himself.

Searching for an exit, Kilroy is directed to a crumbling archway called "The Way Out." Noticing that the Streetcleaners are eyeing Kilroy, Mr. Gutman tells him he should keep five dollars in his pocket lest the Streetcleaners remove him to the "laboratory" when he dies. Jacques enters the plaza, carrying his luggage. Kilroy asks him to spare five dollars, but Jacques tells him that he has no money, he has no place to stay, and his last friend has left him. Kilroy strolls across the plaza to the pawnshop. He removes his lucky gloves from around his neck. A strum from the Guitar Player signals the Streetcleaners' exit.

### *Block 6*

Later that night, the fiesta begins. Dancers in the square move as light falls on the roof of the Gypsy's house. Esmeralda appears and dances the flamenco. Kilroy suddenly enters from the pawnshop. He is mesmerized and dances beneath the roof. Esmeralda throws her flower to him, and the plaza erupts with cheers proclaiming Kilroy the hero. There is a shower of fireworks as the Gypsy appears at the door. She commands Kilroy to enter her house. The plaza empties and only Jacques and La Madrecita remain. Jacques cries for Marguerite and La Madrecita cries out, "Flores, flores para los muertos." ("Flowers, flowers for the dead.")

### *Block 7*

Kilroy is seated behind a scrim in the Gypsy's house where she performs a psychic reading. The Gypsy says he will die soon, but he will also find love. She strikes a gong and Esmeralda enters. She announces that her fee is $10. The Gypsy leaves to collect change. Esmeralda describes her dream of going to Acapulco. Kilroy promises to take her there in the morning if he can lift her veil. She begs him to "be gentle." Esmeralda gasps and moans while Kilroy lifts her veil, finally revealing her face. Once the veil has been lifted, both cry out, "I am sincere!" and lean back in exhaustion. Regaining his breath, Kilroy complains that he is tired and regrets spending his money. The Gypsy returns and says the price has gone up. Outraged, Kilroy asks, "What kind of deal is this?" He is answered with a gun pointed in his face and an assurance that the deal is "a rugged one!" Kilroy makes a quick exit as Esmeralda wipes away a tear that has trickled down her face.

### *Block 8*

Kilroy finds Jacques, La Madrecita, and the Guitar Player in the plaza. Kilroy and Jacques converse about love and drink a wine called "Tears of Christ." Jacques laments that he used to be a lover of many women, but since he's been in the Camino Real, his luck has changed: He has no women and no bed. Kilroy tells Jacques about his lovers and shows a picture of his former wife. The Streetcleaners approach Kilroy's table, making him nervous. He slumps back, having trouble breathing. He asks Jacques to hold his hand. Jacques laughs that "two old Casanovas" are holding hands, and they laugh until Kilroy falls over dead. Jacques moves away and leans against a wall as the Streetcleaners collect Kilroy's body. They search his pockets and, finding no money, take his corpse to the laboratory. Jacques returns to the table and finds the wine bottle empty. The Guitar Player strikes a somber chord.

### *Block 9*

La Madrecita is seated with Kilroy's body draped across her lap in the style of Michelangelo's *Pieta.* Downstage a doctor and his assistants stand over a sheeted corpse. As the doctor details the scientific particulars of the case, La Madrecita describes Kilroy's personal life. As the doctor moves to open the corpse's chest cavity, voices offstage start a lamentation at La Madrecita's request. Suddenly, La Madrecita touches Kilroy with one of her gaudy tin flowers and he awakens to the voices shouting, "Olé! Olé! The Chosen Hero!" Standing up, Kilroy asks where he is and only sees La Madrecita leaving via the alleyway. He approaches the doctors just as a glittering sphere is removed from the corpse's chest. The assistants wash the heart for further examination. They discover it is solid gold. Kilroy snatches his heart and rushes offstage. The doctor shouts, "Stop, thief! Stop, corpse!"

### *Block 10*

Esmeralda appears on the Gypsy's roof. Kilroy whistles to her, but she does not hear him. The fiesta scene of block 6 is replayed, this time in a hauntingly slow fashion. Kilroy throws his gold heart into the air to catch Esmeralda's attention, but she merely says, "Go away, cat." Kilroy rushes into the pawnshop to pawn his heart of gold. He emerges with gifts for Esmeralda: a fur coat, a gown of sequins, pearls, a rhinestone tiara, balloons, and two tickets to Acapulco. He begs her forgiveness and releases balloons that float up to her. Esmeralda disappears from the roof, and Kilroy rushes to the door to meet her. The Gypsy throws water in his face and orders him to leave. Kilroy leaves the gifts strewn on the street and sputters in disgust, "How do you like them apples!"

Don Quixote appears outside the cantina. Kilroy says, "The deal is rugged, you know?" Don Quixote invites Kilroy to join his journey. He calls for Sancho while Kilroy runs to change the sign to read, "Kilroy was here." Jacques sits at a table in the plaza. Marguerite enters to confess that she was only out looking for a bit of silver. She invites him to her room and he weeps. Sancho emerges from the cantina burdened with Don Quixote's knightly armor. He exits through the alleyway as the Guitar Player starts to play a tune. Sancho takes a final look around the Camino Real and stretches his arms in a gesture of wonder and finality.

## COMMENTARY

In his *Memoirs,* Williams recalled sending *Ten Blocks on the Camino Real* to his agent, Audrey Wood, who initially found the play to be "too coarse." She instructed Williams to put the play away and never show it to anyone. Williams was hurt by Wood's reaction but conceded that the play was very much ahead of its time. He felt theater audiences were not ready for his metaphors, abstractions, and poetic expressionism.

*Ten Blocks on the Camino Real* is a prime representative of the true genius of Williams's dramaturgy. The play invites the reader/audience to contemplate the scenes or "blocks" of the Camino Real, an existential wasteland. The play's beauty lies in its ambiguity. As metaphor is by nature subjective, this play, as does an abstract painting, becomes or "means" whatever the viewer/reader perceives it to be or mean. Beneath its surreal structure lies Williams's recurring social commentary. Kilroy's quest to find love results in the literal loss of his heart, but he regains his sense of adventure and purpose through his friendship with Don Quixote, who becomes his guide, out of this surreal land.

*Ten Blocks on the Camino Real* is significantly different from its more realist counterparts in the one-act play anthology, *AMERICAN BLUES;* however, it seems to have been Williams's favorite of this group. He continued to revise the play and developed it into the full-length play *CAMINO REAL* in 1948.

## PRODUCTION HISTORY

*Ten Blocks on the Camino Real* was produced as a film in 1966. Directed by Jack Landau, it starred Martin Sheen, Lotte Lenya, and Tom Aldredge.

## PUBLICATION HISTORY

*Ten Blocks on the Camino Real* was published in *American Blues* in 1948.

## CHARACTERS

**Casanova, Jacques** He is a notorious lover, but now he has only Marguerite Gautier for companionship in the Camino Real. Jacques experiences a strain of bad luck: Marguerite leaves him, he runs out of money, and then he is evicted from his hotel room. He befriends Kilroy, witnessing his strange journey and relationship with Esmeralda.

**Charlus, Baron de** A literary figure in Marcel Proust's *Remembrance of Things Past,* as a character in *Ten Blocks on the Camino Real.* He is a guest at the Siete Mares Hotel. Baron de Charlus has a brief encounter with Kilroy in which he asks him for the time and a light for his cigarette. Kilroy is unable to provide either. De Charlus is a stately Frenchman, dressed in a pale yellow suit.

**Esmeralda** She is the Gypsy's daughter. Esmeralda is a beautiful and highly desirable young woman. Though she is a lover of many men, her virginity is restored every month during a public ritual celebrating the full Moon. She woos Kilroy but rejects his affections. Esmeralda represents the regret all men feel for a desire that cannot be fulfilled. She is a part of the "rugged deal," or the unfortunate moments in Kilroy's life.

**Gautier, Marguerite** Marguerite is based on the character Marguerite Gautier in Alexandre Dumas's novel *La Dame aux camélias.* This elegant woman, once the most best dressed, most expensive, and most successful courtesan in Paris, is now Jacques Casanova's aging lover. Hints of her former glory remain in her grand demeanor and her attire, which includes a hat heaped with violets. She abandons Jacques early in the play but ultimately returns to him. In this highly symbolic play, Marguerite represents faithfulness and companionship.

**Guitar Player** He provides choruslike narration during particular scenes in the play, along with mood music (which he plays with his blue guitar) at appropriate times. In this expressionistic play, he serves as a master of ceremonies.

**Gutman, Mr.** Mr. Gutman is the proprietor of the Siete Mares Hotel. As does the Gypsy, he cheats his residents of their money. Mr. Gutman is sly, well dressed, and indifferent to the plight of the needy.

**Gypsy** She is a psychic and the mother of Esmeralda. The Gypsy consistently mistreats Kilroy. She cheats him of money, and when he complains, she holds him at gunpoint. She also throws water on him when he returns to Esmeralda.

**Kilroy** Kilroy is a 25-year-old boxer. He is a naive American who has wandered into the Camino Real. He has an abnormally large heart, which is said to be the size of a baby's head. This medical oddity prevents him from boxing and prevents him from being physically intimate with his wife. He is hailed as the "Chosen Hero," falls in love with Esmeralda, and loses all of his money trying to win her affection. Kilroy meets Don Quixote and decides to travel with him. In this symbolic drama, Kilroy represents the innocent young man who gives away his heart for love and is rejected.

**La Madrecita de Las Soledades** She hides her face with a blanket and disguises herself as a street figure for much of the play. La Madrecita reveals herself near the end. She wears a snow-white *rebozo* (a long, Mexican head scarf) and sells gaudy tin flowers that are used in Latin American funerals. Her voice is soft and musical and she is very old. Her name means "little mother of the lonely."

**Officer** He is a corrupt law enforcer who has a hostile encounter with Kilroy. In this play, the Officer is a criminal with authority: He shoots an "Indian" in the first scene, continuously consumes alcohol, and employs the services of the Prostitute.

**Panza, Sancho** Sancho accompanies Don Quixote. He appears in the final scene of the play. Sancho follows Quixote out of the Camino Real, carrying armor, and says the town is confusing and will remain a mystery.

**Peasant** He is a Native American man who stumbles into the town square in search of water. The Peasant is dying of thirst. When he investigates the dry fountain in the town square, he is unjustly shot and killed by the Officer.

**Quixote, Don** He is Sancho Panza's master. He makes a brief appearance at the end of the play. He gives Kilroy advice about life and love and invites him to venture out of the Camino Real with him.

**Singer** She is a performer who sings to set the tone of the scenes. The Singer's presence is described as a "softening" in the harsh city setting.

**Streetcleaners** They are the two public service workers who collect the dead bodies lying in the streets of the Camino Real. It is their decision whether a deceased body can be claimed by relatives or becomes property of the state, and they base their decision on the bribes they receive. They are fixtures in the corrupt power structure of the Camino Real. The Streetcleaners are also manifestations of the ever-present existential and foreboding tone that permeates the Camino Real.

# "Ten Minute Stop"

Short story written around 1936.

## SYNOPSIS

Luke travels from his home in Memphis to Chicago for a job interview, but when he finally arrives at the office, the secretary informs him that the boss is out of town on a cruise. He is due back at the end of the month. Luke is shocked by the news, as he has spent nearly all of his money on a bus ticket and is desperate for work. After making a scene in the office, Luke buys a pint of whiskey and boards the next bus back to Memphis.

He encounters a Young Negro boxer on the bus. Luke shares his whiskey with him, but he quickly tires of his new friend's talkative nature. Luke finally goes to sleep, but the Young Negro snores so loudly that he wakes. The bus makes a stop at Champaign, and the boxer exits. Luke gets off the bus and buys a glass of milk. As he boards the bus, he notices a billboard. It is an advertisement for a movie starring Jean Harlow and Stark Navle. He admires Harlow's breasts, while listening to the sound of crickets and drinking his milk. His mind wanders to thoughts of Restoration poets, the universe, and social injustice. Luke decides he should make a daring decision in his life, so he sells his bus ticket to a passerby and blissfully falls asleep on the grass under the poster of Jean Harlow.

## COMMENTARY

Luke is in search of something more in life than scraping together some sort of existence in his hometown of Memphis. He is an intellectual young man who has a promising future, and he recognizes his potential. His frustration lies in the knowledge that he could have a good job and better future if he could only somehow break through. Luke is seizing big opportunities, and he keeps waiting for something promising to happen. Going anywhere is better than going home, and when Luke makes the decision to stay in the town of the 10-minute stop, he is pleased that he has found another option.

Luke is reminiscent of several "drifter" characters in the Williams canon, such as Val Xavier in the *BATTLE OF ANGELS* and *ORPHEUS DESCENDING* and the protagonist of "THE GIFT OF AN APPLE."

## PUBLICATION HISTORY

"Ten Minute Stop" was published in *Collected Stories* (1985).

## CHARACTERS

**Luke** Luke is a young man desperate to find a job and have a stable, comfortable life. When his job plans in Chicago fall through, Luke is forced to board a train back to Memphis. He cannot accept that he is returning home so soon and without a job. What was originally a 10-minute bus stop in Champaign, Illinois, becomes Luke's permanent home.

**Young Negro** He befriends Luke on a bus traveling south from Chicago. The Young Negro is a boxer, who has won his first major fight. Luke admires him for the exciting future he is creating for himself.

# "Tent Worms"

Short story written in 1945.

## SYNOPSIS

It is a beautiful summer day in Cape Cod, Massachusetts. Billy Foxworth is obsessed by the tent worms that have infested the orchard of his summer home. His wife, Clara, ignores him in the hope that he will stop talking and let her relax in the sun. She secretly dreams about leaving him as he scolds her for not listening. Clara knows Billy is dying and will not return with her next summer. She is irritated that he is wasting his time thinking about the infestation.

Clara smells smoke and discovers that Billy is burning the worms by lighting the webs they form between the trees. Clara dreams of the coming winter, which will be a time of "expensive mourning." Clara receives a phone call from the doctor. She tells him that she cannot wait: She cannot take much more from her husband. He tells her to be patient and bide her time. He reminds her it will soon be over. She hangs up and resumes her position on the deck. Billy sits in the adjoining chair. He contemplates the tent worms and the summer house on the Cape, and he acknowledges that he will not return. Clara holds his hand. They both remember the wonderful love they once shared, a love as fleeting as the summer and now as fleeting as Billy's life.

## COMMENTARY

"Tent Worms" is a highly elusive and remarkable tale. It is an intricate study in oppositions: endings and beginnings, life and death, darkness and light. Billy and Clara personify these oppositional tensions. Billy, at the end of his life, spends his remaining days covered in the shade of the orchard, smoking out the worms that have infested his trees. This is his futile attempt to control the uncontrollable and a way of clinging to life. He literally tries to conquer the very trappings of death: worms and cobwebs. Clara, by contrast, dreams of new beginnings as she basks in the sunlight of her youth.

As are many other of Williams's works, "Tent Worms" is an exploration of the conflict between the soul and the flesh, or world of the spirit versus the material world. Billy, who is in essence already dead to Clara, has an almost ghostly existence in the story. His presence troubles Clara, as if he were a sort of meddlesome goblin. He is already firmly immersed in the realm of nature, connecting with the elements (fire and air) even before his body has been committed to the ground. Clara's place is very much in the material world, as she self-indulgently dreams of limousines, furs, and other trappings of "expensive mourning."

## PUBLICATION HISTORY

"Tent Worms" was published in *Esquire* (1980) and in *Collected Stories* (1985).

## CHARACTERS

**Foxworth, Billy** Billy is a writer from New York who is spending the summer in Cape Cod, Massachusetts, with his wife, Clara. During their summer holiday he has become obsessed with the tent worms that have infested his orchard. Billy tries to burn them out, an action which disturbs Clara, who is trying to relax on the deck. Billy and Clara have ceased to love one another; their relationship has become one of merely coexisting. Billy is aware that he is dying and that this will be his last visit to Cape Cod.

**Foxworth, Clara** Clara is the disgruntled wife of Billy, a New York writer. She and Billy are spending the summer in Cape Cod, Massachusetts. Clara is frustrated by Billy's obsession with the tent worms that have infested their orchard. She is irritated that he is spending his last summer days trying to find ways of killing the worms. She is bored and ignores his temper tantrums. Clara is also aware that Billy is dying; however, she is no longer in love with him. She begins to imagine the glamorous life she will have without him: love affairs, furs, and limousines.

# *This Is the Peaceable Kingdom or Good Luck God*

One-act play written around 1980.

## SYNOPSIS

The setting is a nursing home in Queens, New York, during a nursing home strike in 1978.

### *Scene 1*

A male (Ralston) and a female (Lucretia) patient in their 80s, confined to wheelchairs, peer out onto the audience in silence. On the wall above them is the inscription "Good Luck God." In a pantomimic performance, an old woman named Mrs. Shapiro is spoon-fed by her elderly daughter, Bernice, and son, Saul.

Bernice shouts at Saul about his uselessness. Saul admits that he cannot bear to see his mother in this condition. Bernice states that their mother is now incontinent. Lucretia repeats the word *incontinent.* Bernice says this in English so that her mother, who primarily speaks Yiddish, will not understand. Bernice begins to shout at her mother, asking her where she left her false teeth. Saul suggests that they ask Miss Goldfein, the nurse whom they pay extra for special attention.

Lucretia repeats "incontinent" to herself. Ralston inquires about her thoughts. Ralston says he gets out of bed to go to the toilet, but Lucretia reminds him that he soiled himself last week. Ralston snaps that he received someone else's laxative tablet in his pills. Bernice begs her mother to eat. Bernice tells Saul that the nurse phoned last week to say their mother lost her teeth down the toilet when she was vomiting. Saul does not understand why she asked when she already knew the answer to the question. Bernice suspects the nurse is robbing them and is asking to make certain the stories match. Bernice shouts at her mother to eat, and Lucretia scolds her for shouting. Saul and Bernice contemplate moving their mother to another nursing home. A Strange Voice over an intercom announces, "This is the Peaceable Kingdom; this is the Peaceable Kingdom."

Bernice drops the spoon she is using. Lucretia groans, and Ralston strokes her hand as "a delicate ray of light strikes his face with a glimmer of benignity." The Strange Voice repeats his message as a whisper. Lucretia tells Ralston that she has been in the nursing home for more than eight years. She thought her family forgot about her because they stopped visiting, but she learned over time that they were all dead.

Saul yells at Bernice for forcing food into their mother's mouth. The First Black Man and Second Black Man converse in the corner. They tell dirty jokes that offend Lucretia, who says that she is a moral Christian woman. Lucretia announces that she is neither black nor Jewish. Saul overhears this comment and is incensed. Bernice warns him to be careful about what he says. Ralston tries to quiet Lucretia, who announces the nursing home is Christian. The Strange Voice reverberates its "Peaceable Kingdom, the kingdom of love without fear" message.

Saul and Bernice decide to move their mother to another nursing home. Ralston warns Lucretia that she is being anti-Semitic. Saul presents Lucretia with a peace offering of knishes. Saul suffers a seizure. Bernice gives him a pill, which restores him. Saul speaks hatefully to his mother, who holds her withered hand out to him.

The Supervisor enters the room to announce that negotiations are being made. The First Black Man demands food, and the crowd erupts in a riot. Bernice panics and tries to figure out a way to get her mother out of the commotion. A Matron enters with a cart of plates of nuts and fruit. As she gives her speech about the donors of the snacks, Ralston grabs two of the plates. The Matron demands he return them, and he obeys. A mob of patients attack the Matron, throwing the plates and ripping her clothes.

In the midst of the chaos, Bernice wheels her mother into an adjoining room. She shouts and cries that her mother is dead, killed by the Nazis of the nursing home. The Strange Voice reiterates "This is the Peaceable Kingdom." A policeman escorts the Matron out of the home. Lucretia envies Mrs. Shapiro, who has died, and she bangs her head against the wall. Calling for last rites, the Strange Voice interrupts her pleas to remind her of the Peaceable Kingdom "of love without fear."

*Scene 2*

Time has elapsed and the nursing home is quiet. Ralston comforts Lucretia with thoughts of love and encouragement that they live for each other. Lucretia replies that love is not something in which to believe. Ralston serenades her with a song about love, but she is not moved by the sentiment. Lucretia is angry, hungry, thirsty, and has just "wet" herself. Ralston tells her that he is God, who has come to the nursing home to take care of her. Lucretia questions the horrible conditions around them and asks why if he is God would he allow this to go on. Ralston calls her "Daughter" and says that he is patiently biding his time.

Saul and Bernice wait for the funeral home to arrive to collect their mother's body. Ralston wheels Lucretia back to the ward. The Strange Voice announces the Peaceable Kingdom.

## COMMENTARY

In *This Is the Peaceable Kingdom* Williams bitterly satirizes the state of assisted care homes and social and racial divides that exist within them. As he does in *LIFE BOAT DRILL,* Williams writes of the tragedy of old age. Stephen Grecco writes that the elderly characters in these plays who are "usually near death's door, are parodies of human beings, grotesque puppets with only a dim awareness of a life that might have been at one time dignified and purposeful" (*World Literature Today*, 586). As in THE FROSTED GLASS COFFIN, whose characters are divested of essential humanity and are parodied by being identified as mere numbers (i.e., One, Two, or Three) rather than names, the senior citizens depicted in *This Is the Peaceable Kingdom* suffer repeated indignities and social isolation. With this work, Williams reasserted himself as an advocate of the outcast and the put aside.

## PRODUCTION HISTORY

This play has not been professionally produced.

## PUBLICATION HISTORY

*This Is the Peaceable Kingdom* was published in *The Theatre of Tennessee Williams*, volume 7, in 1994.

## CHARACTERS

**Lucretia** She is an elderly woman confined to a wheelchair. Lucretia has been living in a nursing home for eight years. In moments of extreme frustration about her quality of life and the tragedy of aging, Lucretia beats her head against the wall. She is often rescued by her friend, Ralston. During a workers' strike at the nursing home, Lucretia learns that Ralston is actually God, who is there to take care of her. She is skeptical but wants to believe that she will have a better life because God is with her.

**Ralston** He is an elderly man confined to a wheelchair. Ralston lives in a chaotic nursing home where a workers' strike is under way. Ralston is continually hopeful, whereas his friend, Lucretia, suffers depression caused by the deterioration of her body and the quality of her life at the nursing home. Ralston tells Lucretia that he is God and is there to take care of her.

**Shapiro, Bernice** She is the elderly daughter of Mrs. Shapiro, a woman who has been living in a nursing home. Bernice impatiently cares for her mother, who can no longer speak. During a workers' strike at the nursing home, Bernice experiences anti-Semitism and a patients' revolt. The pandemonium of the scene proves too much for Mrs. Shapiro. Bernice and her brother, Saul, witness the death of their mother during the strike.

**Shapiro, Saul** He is a university professor who visits his mother, Mrs. Shapiro, during a nursing home strike. Saul suffers seizures and fights with his sister, Bernice. He refuses to look at his mother in her current condition. A revolt breaks out at the nursing home, and Saul's mother dies.

## FURTHER READING

Grecco, Stephen. Book Review of *The Theatre of Tennessee Williams*. *World Literature Today* 7, no. 3 (1994): 586.

# *This Property Is Condemned*

A one-act play written before 1942.

## SYNOPSIS

The action of this play takes place on a railroad embankment in Mississippi. Near the tracks is an abandoned house, with a large sign indicating "THIS PROPERTY IS CONDEMNED."

Willie is a young girl dressed in a frilly woman's dress and children's shoes. She wears rouge and lipstick and carries a doll and a banana, which she has salvaged from the Dumpster of a café. Tom approaches Willie, carrying a kite. Willie balances on one rail as she approaches Tom. She asks what he plans to do with a kite on a windless day. Willie notices the sky, "white as a piece of paper," as she sings "My Blue Heaven."

Willie dropped out of grade school two years ago when her older sister, a prostitute, died. She tells Tom about her beautiful sister, who would house the railroad men. She says her sister died of "lung affection" and her mother and father are missing. Tom asks her about a rumor that she danced naked for Frank Waters. Willie tries to change the subject, but Tom asks whether she will dance for him. She refuses, explaining that she was lonely when she danced before, but she is "not lonesome now." Willie admits that she still lives in the condemned house, and that the railroad men visit her. Willie says good-bye, and Tom watches her walk away. As she sings to herself, he holds up a finger to test the wind.

## COMMENTARY

*This Property Is Condemned* reads as a sequel to the one-act play *HELLO FROM BERTHA*, or a retelling of Bertha's tale from a different perspective, if she had had a younger sister. Willie is another engaging, if brief, female character study in the Williams canon. As do Bertha and Blanche Dubois, Willie clings to the relics of her past and her family home as long she can.

Willie's isolation and incredible innocence are compelling, and Williams effectively captures Willie's odd position in the world. In many ways she is an older woman, trapped in a child's body. She entertains railway workers, and yet she still plays with dolls. Williams effectively evokes sympathy—without sentimentality—for this young, abandoned fugitive child.

## PRODUCTION HISTORY

*This Property Is Condemned* was first produced at the New School for Social Research in 1942. A film version starring Natalie Wood and Robert Redford was produced in 1966. The film focused on the life of Willie's sister Alva and her relationship with a railroad boss named Owen Legate.

## PUBLICATION HISTORY

*This Property Is Condemned* was first published in *American Scenes* in 1941. It was subsequently published in *27 WAGONS FULL OF COTTON AND OTHER ONE-ACT PLAYS* (1966).

## CHARACTERS

**Tom** Tom is a young boy who encounters a young girl named Willie. He questions her about her family because he is interested in her provocative behavior. Tom is slightly older than Willie and carries a red crepe-paper kite.

**Willie** Willie is a young orphaned girl who spends her days wandering the train tracks. She dresses in her late sister's clothes and waits for the railroad men. She is naive about their association with her; she likes the parties they take her to and does not realize they are prostituting her to other men. Although she lives in an adult world and has adult relationships, Willie still carries her doll.

# "Three Players of a Summer Game"

Short story written between the years 1951 and 1952.

## SYNOPSIS

Brick Pollitt, a thin, handsome former athlete, is married to Margaret, a former New Orleans debutante. After a couple of years of marriage, Brick has become an alcoholic. Margaret is forced to manage her husband's plantation. The timid, delicate debutante has transformed herself into an astute businesswoman.

Margaret goes to Memphis to attend a funeral. While she is gone, Brick's doctor becomes terminally ill of brain cancer. Brick visits Dr. Grey and his wife, Isabel Grey. Brick and Isabel sit at the doctor's bedside, and Brick helps her administer the hypodermic needle that ends her husband's anguish. When it is over Isabel and Brick lie side by side in a bed and hold hands. They lie still and silent, trying to comprehend that the doctor is dead.

Isabel and her 12-year-old daughter, Mary Louise, have very little money. Brick takes it upon himself to care for the widow and her child. At first the people of the town think he is noble, but after several weeks, gossip of an affair surfaces. He renovates her Victorian home, and he tries to quit drinking for her. When he does succumb to alcohol, he pontificates about the game of croquet. He believes it to be a sober man's sport, which he aspires to play.

Mary Louise spends the summer setting up the croquet game in the hope that Brick will play with her. He makes a spectacle of himself and the game when he is drunk. He leaps and runs wildly in the yard, disregarding what the neighbors are saying about his behavior. Mary Louise and her mother cower in embarrassment, begging him to stop. Eventually he passes out in the middle of the front lawn, partly dressed. The local police collect him, and an hour later, Isabel fetches him from jail.

As time passes, Brick's visits become less frequent. When he does happen to stop by, he is always with a group of people, drinking and partying. Isabel is forced to invite the entire party into her home, and the neighbors gossip about her. Isabel's car is repossessed, and she and Mary Louise move away. Late in the fall, the narrator sees Brick Pollitt in the backseat of his car, being chauffeured by his wife, Margaret.

## COMMENTARY

"Three Players of a Summer Game" is the source text for the drama *CAT ON A HOT TIN ROOF.* As in the later dramatic work, the short story is centered on the self-indulgent Brick Pollitt and his problematic relationship with his wife, Margaret.

In the short story, their marriage is strained by Brick's dying best friend, Dr. Grey, and his widow, Isabel. Isabel and Brick develop a psychological bond in the act of releasing Dr. Grey from his pain. They are prompted to commit euthanasia by their love for the dying doctor, and it is their love of him that brings them together as lovers. Brick's affection fills the void in Isabel's life left by her husband. For Brick, their romantic tryst is a delightful summer fling that takes him away from the responsibilities of being a land owner and running a plantation. Unlike his counterpart in *Cat,* in "Three Players of a Summer Game," Brick is able to carouse, play childhood games (croquet) and relive the frivolity of his youth. His indulgence comes at a high price for Isabel. Brick's wild antics tarnish her reputation in the small-town society, and she and her daughter are forced to move away.

Brick's wife, Margaret, is ever steadfast and determined in both the short story and the play. Margaret, as does her counterpart, "Maggie the Cat," shoulders the responsibility of their survival and success. She is shrewd in her business dealings and possesses the strength of will to literally and figuratively drive her wayward husband into maturity. The tension and distance that exists between them in the short story is expanded and heightened in the dramatic retelling.

## PUBLICATION HISTORY

"Three Players of a Summer Game" was published in the *New Yorker* (1952) and reprinted in *Best American Short Stories of 1953* (1953), *Hard Candy* (1954), *Stories of Modern America* (1961), *Fifty Best American Short Stories* (1965), and *Young Man Axelbord & Other Stories* (1975).

## CHARACTERS

**Grey, Dr.** Dr. Grey is a handsome young doctor, who is married to Isabel Grey and is the father of Mary Louise Grey. He is dying of brain cancer, and his best friend, Brick Pollitt, is present at his bedside during his final hours. Moments after his death, Dr. Grey's wife becomes Brick's mistress.

**Grey, Isabel** Isabel is married to Dr. Grey and is the mother of Mary Louise Grey. When her husband is diagnosed with brain cancer, his best friend, Brick Pollitt, arrives to comfort and assist the couple. Isabel falls in love with the handsome plantation owner and begins an affair with him moments after her husband dies. Brick helps Isabel manage her finances and she tries to help him overcome his alcoholism. When it becomes obvious that she has failed to help him, the pain is too much for her to bear. She and her daughter move away and are never heard from again.

**Grey, Mary Louise** She is the 12-year-old daughter of Isabel and Dr. Grey. Mary Louise loves to play croquet and takes the game very seriously. She often plays the game with her mother's lover, Brick Pollitt. However, when his heavy drinking interferes with their matches, she does not care for his participation.

**Pollitt, Brick** He is a handsome plantation owner who struggles in an unhappy marriage and through alcoholism attempts to escape reality. Brick's life is spent fighting the disease, and although two women love and support him, he cannot be good to either of them.

**Pollitt, Margaret** She is the wife of Brick Pollitt. Margaret has been forced to take control of their plantation because her husband's alcoholism has made him incapable of meeting the responsibility. Margaret was once a frail debutante, but she becomes a strong, astute businesswoman. Margaret is humiliated by Brick's affair with Isabel Grey, but she remains married to him and dedicated to taking care of him.

# *Tiger Tail*

A play in two acts written in 1977.

## SYNOPSIS

The play is set in the rural town of Tiger Tail, Mississippi. The action of the play takes place in and around the home of Archie Lee Meighan and his wife, Baby Doll Meighan.

### *Act 1, Scene 1*

The Meighan's furniture is being repossessed. Baby Doll places a call to the Kotton King Hotel. She makes a room reservation and explains her current situation with Archie Lee to the person on the other end. Baby Doll gives the details of her marital "agreement" with Archie Lee, a pact made by Archie Lee and Baby Doll's father in which Archie Lee promised Baby Doll's father that he would not attempt to consummate their marriage until she reached the age of 20.

An explosion is heard as a fire breaks out at the Syndicate Plantation across the road. Aunt Rose Comfort McCorkle rushes out of the house to find Baby Doll. Ruby Lightfoot and her son, Two Bits, deliver a gallon of liquor for Archie Lee. In need of refreshment, Baby Doll decides to go to Ruby Lightfoot's place to purchase some Coca-Colas. Aunt Rose tries to stop or at least accompany her, but Baby grabs a pistol for protection and sets off down the road alone. A shot is fired as Baby Doll serves a warning to a man hiding in the bushes. Baby Doll chastises Archie Lee for leaving her behind and causing her to miss the fire that he started at the plantation. He becomes irate and physically abusive. He corrects Baby Doll and reinforces his alibi with her by squeezing her arm. He tries to make peace and seduce Baby Doll by kissing her wounded arm. Archie Lee seizes her wrists sharply and sends her to bed.

### *Act 1, Scene 2*

The location is the same as in the previous scene, and the time is the next morning. Silva Vaccaro and his assistant, Rock, arrive at the Meighan home with 27 wagons of cotton. Rock discovers an empty kerosene can. Archie Lee eagerly accepts the opportunity to gin Vacarro's cotton. Archie Lee introduces Baby Doll to Silva and Rock and instructs her to entertain Silva while his cotton is being ginned. Baby Doll yawns and apologizes for her bad manners, stating that she and Archie were up very late the previous night. Silva, Rock, and Archie Lee notice the discrepancy between Baby Doll's statements and Archie Lee's. Archie Lee rushes back into the house and barks for Aunt Rose to make coffee for Silva. He returns and shakes Silva's hand confirming the "tit for tat," "good neighbor policy." Silva has strong suspicions that Archie lee destroyed his gin. After he and Rock have disappeared to start ginning cotton, Silva toys with Baby Doll to find out the truth. Baby Doll inadvertently lets it slip that Archie Lee left the house and did not return until after the fire at the Syndicate Plantation had started. When he questions her directly about Archie Lee's whereabouts, Baby Doll tries to retract her comments.

Silva teases and taunts Baby Doll. His advances awaken Baby Doll sexually. She runs to Archie for protection; he is infuriated by her disruption of his work and slaps her in front of all the gin workers. Archie Lee is frustrated by a piece of broken machinery and vents his rage on Baby Doll. Silva sends Archie Lee all over the state to fetch a new part for the machinery. Silva and Rock make arrangements to have the part taken from their cotton gin across the road. Silva takes this opportunity to pursue Baby Doll further.

### *Act 2, Scene 1*

Silva hopes to obtain a confession from Baby Doll. He intimidates her and tells her that the house she lives in is haunted. Silva engages Baby Doll in a game of hide-and-seek. He then terrorizes her to sign a statement verifying that Archie Lee burned down the Syndicate Gin. Baby Doll is disappointed when Silva is satisfied with nothing more than her signature. Silva decides that they have played enough "children's games." He kisses Baby Doll passionately and paddles her backside with his riding crop. She runs to the nursery; he follows and aggressively seduces her.

### *Act 2, Scene 2*

Silva and Baby Doll talk intimately after their encounter. Baby Doll inquires whether she and Silva will have "more afternoons" like the one they have spent. Baby Doll is delighted to learn that they will.

Archie Lee returns, and Baby Doll descends the stairs dressed in a silk slip. Archie Lee shouts about her appearance and refers to "useless women." Baby Doll counters by referring to "destructive men," who "blow things up and burn things down." Archie Lee is stunned and stung by her words. Baby Doll walks out onto the porch; Archie Lee follows her and switches on the porch light. The workers from the Syndicate Gin catch a glimpse of Baby Doll in her negligee and several men call out and whistle. Archie Lee defends what is "his," and Baby Doll warns him about taking his possession of her for granted. Ruby Lightfoot and her son make another delivery of liquor to Archie Lee. When Baby Doll questions whether he is celebrating his "criminal actions," he whacks her across the face in front of Ruby and Two Bits. Baby Doll cancels their agreement.

Archie Lee is shocked to discover Silva pumping water from the Lees' well. Baby Doll informs Archie Lee that Silva wants to establish a "good neighbor policy" whereby Archie Lee will gin cotton for him indefinitely. The one condition is that Baby Doll must entertain Silva every day. Aunt Rose Comfort calls everyone to supper. The meal is undercooked and unsatisfactory to Archie Lee. He accosts Aunt Rose Comfort and threatens her with eviction. Silva promptly offers her a job cooking for him.

Archie Lee collects his shotgun and chases Silva out of the house. Silva climbs a nearby pecan tree. Baby Doll phones the police and runs out of the house to join Silva in the tree. Archie Lee runs around the yard crying out for his "Baby Doll!" Sheriff Coglan and Deputy Tufts arrive and escort Archie Lee away. As Aunt Rose sings a hymn, the lovers remain in the tree.

## COMMENTARY

*Tiger Tail* holds a significant and unique place in the Williams canon. It evolved, as did a large percentage of Williams's full-length stage dramas, from what can be termed Williams's "three-tiered" writing method, whereby he initially shaped an idea into a short story, then used the short story as the basis for a one-act play, and then used the one-act as the foundation text for an expanded full-length play. The material was often then adapted or revised into a screenplay or produced as a film. However, *Tiger Tail* is Williams's only dramatic work which is a stage version of a screenplay. It is an adaptation of the controversial film *BABY DOLL*. Thus, this play is the final installment of a dynamic cycle of works detailing the complex and tumultuous relationships of a beautiful, voluptuous woman and two rival cotton gin operators.

## PRODUCTION HISTORY

*Tiger Tail* was first produced at the Alliance Theatre, Atlanta, Georgia, in 1978, under the direction of Harry Rasky.

## PUBLICATION HISTORY

*Tiger Tail* was first published, with the screenplay *Baby Doll*, in 1991.

## CHARACTERS

**Coglan, Sheriff** The chief law enforcement officer in Tiger Tail, Mississippi. Sheriff Coglan is summoned to the home of Archie Lee Meighan by his young wife, Baby Doll Meighan. He and Deputy Tufts take Archie Lee into custody for causing a public disturbance. Baby Doll calls the Sheriff's office when her husband grabs his shotgun and threatens to kill her lover and his business rival, Silva Vaccaro.

**Lightfoot, Ruby** She is a beautiful bootlegger and tavern hostess who sells illegal homemade distilled liquor in Tiger Tail, Mississippi. Her son, Two Bits, helps her to distribute her brew. Archie Lee

Meighan is one of her faithful customers. To the consternation of Aunt Rose Comfort McCorkle, Ruby's son, Two Bits, leaves a gallon of liquor on the porch for Archie Lee. As does Archie Lee's young wife, Baby Doll Meighan, Ruby repeatedly suffers verbal and physical abuse from the hotheaded Archie Lee.

**McCorkle, Aunt Rose Comfort** She is an adaptation of Aunt Rose Comfort McCorkle from the screenplay *BABY DOLL*. Aunt Rose is the elderly unmarried relative of Baby Doll Meighan. Aunt Rose Comfort lives with Baby Doll and her husband, Archie Lee Meighan, and makes herself "useful" by cooking for them. Archie Lee has grown tired of Aunt Rose Comfort, her "simple-minded foolishness," and her poor cooking skills. When Archie Lee threatens to throw her out, the rival cotton gin operator, Silva Vacarro, offers her a job cooking for him.

**Meighan, Archie Lee** He is a revision of the character Archie Lee Meighan in the screenplay *BABY DOLL*. Archie Lee is a severely frustrated man: He is going bankrupt because the Syndicate Cotton Gin is dominating the ginning business, and his wife, Baby Doll Meighan, refuses to consummate their marriage until she turns 20. After years of waiting and with only two days until Baby Doll's birthday, Archie Lee is forced to focus on his business. In desperation, he burns down the rival gin, but he pays dearly when he agrees to gin his rival's cotton and assigns Baby Doll the task of entertaining the man.

**Meighan, Baby Doll** She is a revision of the character Baby Doll Meighan in the screenplay *BABY DOLL*. She is the voluptuous 19-year-old virgin wife of Archie Lee Meighan. Her husband is down on his luck since the Syndicate Cotton Gin started to dominate the cotton business in the area.

After the fire at the Syndicate Plantation, her husband is given the opportunity to gin 27 wagons of cotton for Silva Vacarro, the Syndicate Plantation manager. Archie Lee orders Baby Doll to entertain Silva. During their visit Baby Doll accidentally contradicts Archie Lee's alibi. She essentially confirms for Silva that Archie Lee started the fire at his gin. Silva takes his revenge on Archie Lee by persuading Baby Doll to sign a statement confirming that Archie Lee started the fire. In the midst of their heated flirtations, Baby Doll is aroused sexually for the first time and surrenders to Silva's overpowering sexuality.

**Tufts, Deputy** He is a law enforcement officer in Tiger Tail, Mississippi. Deputy Tufts accompanies his boss, Sheriff Coglan, when he is summoned to the home of Archie Lee Meighan. Archie Lee's teenage wife, Baby Doll Meighan, calls the sheriff's office when her husband grabs his shotgun and threatens to kill her lover and his business rival, Silva Vacarro.

**Two Bits** He is the diminutive son of Ruby Lightfoot, a bootlegger in Tiger Tail, Mississippi. Two Bits assists his mother in distributing her illegal brew throughout the rural cotton town.

**Vaccaro, Silva** He is the handsome, virile, and volatile Italian manager of the Syndicate Plantation Cotton Gin in a small town in rural Mississippi. Silva's success has threatened other cotton gin operators in the area, and many have gone out of business as a result. His chief competitor is Archie Lee Meighan. After a fire destroys his cotton gin, Silva considers Archie Lee the primary suspect. When Silva takes his 27 wagons of cotton to Archie Lee to be ginned, his suspicions are confirmed. Delighted by his triumph over Silva, Archie Lee orders his full-figured, teenage, virgin wife Baby Doll Meighan to entertain Silva while the cotton is being ginned. During their conversation, Baby Doll innocently contradicts Archie Lee's alibi. Silva takes revenge on Archie Lee by aggressively seducing Baby Doll.

# The Travelling Companion

A one-act play written in 1981.

## SYNOPSIS

The play is set in the bedroom of a lavish New York hotel. The time is late evening, around midnight.

### *Scene 1*

Vieux, an aging writer, and Beau, his young traveling companion, have arrived at their suite in a posh hotel. Beau stares blankly at the double bed. Vieux suggests that Beau order two bottles of wine from room service, while he searches frantically for his medicine kit. Vieux takes note of the tasks Beau should undertake on future travels as his traveling companion. Beau is indifferent to Vieux's references to the future and "hereafter." Vieux continues to ramble nervously, while Beau remains frozen, staring at the large double bed. Beau demands that he be given his own room and threatens to make a scene downstairs in the hotel if Vieux does not accommodate his request. Vieux reminds Beau that he met him in a gay bar in San Francisco. Beau pretends that he did not know that the bar was for gays. Beau takes a quaalude tablet and calls the front desk, demanding a room of his own. Room service delivers their food and wine, and Beau explains that he would never have taken the job of being Vieux's traveling companion if he had known that it required physical intimacy. Vieux reminds Beau that the terms of their arrangement were "young companionship, [and] privilege of light caresses."

Beau takes another table and places a long-distance call to his boyfriend, Paul, who has recently returned to San Francisco from Alaska. During the call, he discovers that his friend Hank is trying to seduce Paul. He shows a picture of Paul to Vieux and collapses on the double bed until his single room is ready. Vieux watches him sleep.

### *Scene 2*

In the same location as scene 1, some time later, as Beau sleeps, Vieux contemplates him and ponders that "boys are fox-teeth in the heart." He reminisces about the care and attention good traveling companions should give, such as caring for laundry. New traveling companions neglect such details and are more attentive to their own needs; Vieux declares that they suffer from the "give-me's." He predicts that Beau will follow suit and be like the others. Beau awakens and mentions that he left his guitar in San Francisco. Vieux admonishes him for not telling him about the guitar before they left. Vieux lies down beside Beau on the double bed and turns out the light. Beau demands that Vieux call the front desk about his room. Vieux reminds Beau that he is his employer and as such should not be spoken to in such a callous manner. The hotel staff delivers a cot to Vieux's room for Beau. Beau concedes that he will stay with Vieux, if he buys him a new guitar.

## COMMENTARY

*The Travelling Companion* is similar in plot, theme, tone, and structure to the play AND TELL SAD STORIES OF THE DEATH OF QUEENS. However, *Companion* is an updated version of the story of a cold-hearted hustler abusing the romantic sensibilities of a delicate, lonely person longing for love. The theme of love as a mercantile exchange is vividly and poignantly explored throughout Williams's work. No longer able to use their fame or their beauty as commodities, Karen Stone (of THE ROMAN SPRING OF MRS. STONE), Sabbatha Veyne Duff-Collick (of "SABBATHA AND SOLITUDE"), and Trinket Dugan (of THE MUTILATED) are forced to secure their lovers's affection with financial incentives and rewards.

Metaphorically, *The Travelling Companion* is a tale of age versus youth. Vieux, whose name means "old" in French, is forced to contend with Beau, whose names is French for "handsome." Ironically, the word *beaux,* also pronounced *Beau,* means "male admirers." When they are viewed as two sides of a single character, Vieux and Beau in their conflict express the human struggle with aging and impending death. Vieux tries repeatedly to connect and make peace with youth, as fervently as Beau tries to escape aging. In the final scene, Vieux encapsulates their dilemma: "Being unable to go on alone and having no way to go back—where would I go back to? To me as difficult as reversing the way the earth turns." Whether Vieux and Beau are viewed as two separate characters or as the feuding sides of a single one, the apex of their conflict is that age cannot exist with youth or without youth, and vice versa. By having the front desk deliver to their room a cot for Beau, Williams comically illustrates that there is no reprieve from this eternal dilemma. The young man is not offered an escape. Beau and Vieux remain together and are forced to reach an uneasy compromise and ultimately find a way to lie together.

## PRODUCTION HISTORY

*The Travelling Companion* was first professionally produced in New York by the Irish Repertory Theatre in 1996.

## PUBLICATION HISTORY

*The Travelling Companion* was first published in *Christopher Street* magazine, in 1981.

## CHARACTERS

**Beau** Beau, whose name means "handsome" in French, is an attractive 25-year-old hustler. This blond youth is the traveling companion of Vieux, an aging writer. Beau has accompanied Vieux across the country from San Francisco to New York, but once they arrive at their suite in New York, he adamantly refuses to share a room with Vieux. Beau threatens Vieux and tries to call his boyfriend, Paul, back in San Francisco. Ultimately, he offers Vieux a compromise and establishes the mercantile terms of their intimacy.

**Vieux** Vieux, whose name means "old" in French, is an aging writer. He has engaged the company of Beau, a destitute young man, as a traveling companion. Once a beautiful youth himself, Vieux is now middle-aged and suffering from defective vision and a damaged liver. Beau is not physically attracted to Vieux, and when they arrive at their hotel in New York, he initially refuses to share a room with him. Accustomed to this routine, Vieux waits patiently while Beau rationalizes the mercantile terms of their intimacy.

# "Twenty-seven Wagons Full of Cotton"

A short story written in 1935.

## SYNOPSIS

The story takes place in rural Mississippi, on the front porch and inside the home of Mrs. Jake Meighan. The time is late afternoon during summer.

Mrs. Meighan has been given the task of "entertaining" the Syndicate Plantation Manager while his 27 wagons of cotton are being ginned by her husband, Jake. (He is unable to gin his own cotton, as his gin was destroyed by fire the evening before.)

Mrs. Meighan and the Plantation Manager sit together in the porch swing. It is an exceedingly hot day, and Mrs. Meighan is drenched in sweat. She is tired and would like to have an afternoon nap, but she is responsible for hosting the Manager. The Manager makes advances toward Mrs. Meighan, declaring that he likes "big women." Mrs. Meighan rejects the advances but is somewhat flattered by his desire. Their flirtation intensifies until Mrs. Meighan's defenses are weakened. He teases her by flicking her shapely legs with his riding crop. Confused and disoriented, Mrs. Meighan leans against the screen door and tries to go into the house. The Manager half forces and escorts her into the house. Mrs. Meighan, a "tremendous, sobbing Persephone," backs into the darkened hallway and halts breathlessly outside the Meighans' bedroom door. She fears that the Manager is going to beat her with his whip. She pleads with him not to hurt her as she throws her arms around him.

## COMMENTARY

"Twenty-seven Wagons Full of Cotton" is a concise and evocative tale of seduction. As in similar tales of overpowering desire (such as "DESIRE AND THE BLACK MASSEUR" and "GIFT OF AN APPLE") Williams employs the device of contrasts to underscore the magnetic attraction of the characters. In "Twenty-seven Wagons" he pairs an almost absurdly large woman ("You're bigger'n the whole southern hemisphere,") with a minuscule man; and the two share a sexual dynamic that borders on sadomasochism. Their relationship is a reversal of the "little and large" interplay which occurs in "Desire and the Black Masseur," a later short story.

Metaphorically, the exceedingly full-figured Mrs. Meighan, whose proportions are too large for the

Manager to encircle with his small hands, personifies the Manager's—and her husband's—ambition. She is also an embodiment of the American South and its great potential wealth. She, as is the land, is something to be idolized, possessed, seduced, or coerced into surrender.

"Twenty-seven Wagons Full of Cotton" is the basis of the one-act play *27 WAGONS FULL OF COTTON* and a source text for the screenplay *BABY DOLL* and the play *TIGER TAIL.*

## PUBLICATION HISTORY

"Twenty-seven Wagons Full of Cotton" was first published in *Manuscript* magazine in 1936. It was subsequently published in *Collected Stories* in 1985.

## CHARACTERS

**Meighan, Mrs. Jake** She is the extremely full-figured wife of Jake Meighan, a cotton gin owner and operator. Mrs. Meighan is ordered by her husband to spend the day hosting and entertaining the Syndicate Plantation manager, while her husband gins his 27 wagons of cotton. After rejecting his repeated sexual overtures, she ultimately allows herself to be seduced by the Manager.

**Syndicate Plantation Manager** He is the manager of the Syndicated Plantation Cotton Gin. As a result of a fire that destroyed his gin, the plantation manager has taken his 27 wagons of cotton to Jake Meighan to be ginned. While his cotton is being ginned, the manager has been left in the care of Mrs. Jake Meighan, an exceedingly full-figured woman. The manager has a fondness for "big women" and proceeds to seduce Mrs. Meighan.

# *27 Wagons Full of Cotton*

A one-act play written before 1946.

## SYNOPSIS

The action of the play occurs on the front porch of the home owned by Jake and Flora Meighan, near Blue Mountain, Mississippi. The time is early evening, in September 1936.

### *Scene 1*

Jake Meighan rushes out of the house and runs off the porch carrying a can of coal oil. He speeds away in his Chevy as Flora calls him from the house. An explosion is heard in the distance, and voices and sounds of confusion nearby. A voice calls out to Flora offering her a ride to see the fire at the Syndicate Plantation. Flora is startled by the news that the Syndicate gin is on fire. She sits on the front porch, waiting and watching the fire in the distance. Jake returns slowly from the side of the house. Flora chastises him for leaving her alone without a ride or Coca-Cola in the house. When she continues to accuse him of "disappearing," he becomes irate and physically abusive. He corrects Flora and reinforces his alibi with her by twisting her wrists. Flora accepts Jake's alibi. They decide to go into town to buy Coca-Cola.

### *Scene 2*

The location is the same; the time is just after noon, the next day.

Jake returns to the house with Silva Vacarro, the superintendent of the Syndicate Plantation. Jake calls for Flora. He introduces Silva to Flora as the man he wants her to "cheer up" for him. Silva is disgruntled about losing his gin. As the conversation turns to the fire, Jake diverts Silva and Flora's attention to Flora's well-proportioned body. He leaves them alone on the porch and gleefully departs to gin Silva's cotton.

Flora and Silva make an awkward attempt at conversation. She remarks on his bravery in sitting out in the sun. By lifting his shirt he shows her that his skin is "natcherally [*sic*] dark" and not merely sunburned. This level of intimacy with a stranger flusters Flora. She laughs and apologizes that she cannot offer Silva a soft drink. In explaining why they do not have any Coca-Colas, Flora inadvertently lets it slip that after dinner Jake "went off an' left her settin' on this ole po'ch" and did not return until after the fire at the Syndicate Plantation had started. Her admission of the truth is not lost on Silva. When he questions her directly about Jake's earlier whereabouts, she tries to retract her comments.

Silva joins Flora in the porch swing. Their conversation takes a "personal turn." Flora tries to cover her lapse in Jake's alibi. Silva becomes very flirtatious and starts teasing her with his riding crop. Silva notices the bruising on Flora's wrist and speculates that Jake twisted it and that Flora enjoyed it. Flora tries to retreat into the house, but Silva blocks her path and threatens to accompany her. Flora becomes confused and begins to cry. She is afraid that Silva is going to beat her with his whip. She pleads with him to leave his whip on the porch if he is going to follow her into the house. Silva orders her into the house; as she cries, she tries to reassure Silva that Jake did not destroy his gin. They enter the house. The sounds of a "despairing cry," a slamming door, and another scream are drowned out by the slow, steady thumping sound of the cotton gin across the road.

### *Scene 3*

The location is the same; the time is nine o'clock in the evening.

Flora stumbles onto the porch from the house. She has been severely beaten and raped. She hides in the shadows of the porch as Jake returns triumphantly from his cotton gin. He is too proud and vain to notice her. He thinks about the details of his most successful workday, when he pushed his workers harder than he ever had. Flora sits in the swing trying to restrain her growing hysteria. Flora gives Jake the news that Silva is going to allow him to gin all of his cotton for the rest of the season while Flora entertains him. Jake cannot believe his good luck. To celebrate, he offers to take Flora to see a movie. Flora waddles down the porch steps painfully. As she walks to the car she sings, "Rock-a-Bye-Baby."

## COMMENTARY

*27 Wagons Full of Cotton* is a dramatization of the short story "TWENTY-SEVEN WAGONS FULL OF COTTON." As does its predecessor, the play depicts the complex relationship of a woman caught between two rival cotton gin operators. Flora Meighan becomes a commodity that changes hands in the underhanded dealings of the two men. In exchange for the brutalization of his wife, Jake Meighan acquires Silva Vacarro's 27 wagons of cotton. Jake is too blinded by his own success and ambition to notice his wife's suffering. Her dignity and welfare are negligible to him. All that matters to Jake is the victory over his competitor.

Metaphorically, the full-figured Mrs. Meighan personifies Jake and Silva's ambition and its source, cotton. Both men associate and equate her with cotton, referring to her in cotton-related terminology (e.g., *big, soft,* and *white*). While doting on her and idolizing her for her cottonlike qualities, both men also verbally and physically abuse Flora. They each manipulate her to gain advantage over the other. In this regard, Flora also embodies the American South and its great potential wealth. She, as is the land, is to be possessed, dominated, and exploited.

*27 Wagons Full of Cotton,* along with THE LONG STAY CUT SHORT, OR THE UNSATISFACTORY SUPPER, serves as a source text for the screenplay BABY DOLL and the full-length play TIGER TAIL.

## PRODUCTION HISTORY

*27 Wagons Full of Cotton* was first produced in New Orleans at Tulane University in January 1955. Edward Ludlam directed the production, which featured MAUREEN STAPLETON as Flora Meighan. Stapleton also played Flora in the first New York production at the Playhouse Theatre in April 1955.

## PUBLICATION HISTORY

*27 Wagons Full of Cotton* was first published in *Best One-Act Plays of 1944* (1945) and subsequently in the anthology *27* WAGONS FULL OF COTTON AND OTHER ONE-ACT PLAYS (1966).

## CHARACTERS

**Meighan, Flora** She is the full-figured wife of Jake Meighan, a cotton gin owner in rural Mississippi. After a fire at the Syndicate Plantation, her husband is given the opportunity to gin 27 wagons of cotton for Silva Vacarro, the Syndicate Plantation manager. Flora is ordered to entertain Silva, to keep him out of Jake's way while the cotton is being ginned. During her conversation with Silva, Flora accidentally contradicts Jake's alibi. She essentially confirms that Jake did in fact start the fire at his gin. Silva takes his revenge on Jake by beating and raping Flora. Jake is so blinded by his "victory" over Silva that he does not notice that Flora has been harmed.

**Meighan, Jake** He is a cotton gin owner in rural Mississippi, the husband of Flora Meighan. Jake is described as a "fat man of sixty." After the fire at the Syndicate Plantation, he is given the opportunity to gin 27 wagons of cotton for his principal competitor, Silva Vacarro, the Syndicate Plantation manager. Jake orders his full-figured wife to entertain Silva, to keep him out of his way while the cotton is being ginned. During her conversation with Silva, Flora accidentally contradicts Jake's alibi. Flora confirms that Jake started the fire that destroyed Silva's gin. Silva takes his revenge on Jake by beating and raping Flora. Jake is so blinded by his "victory" over Silva that he does not notice that Flora has been harmed.

**Vacarro, Silva** He is the superintendent of the Syndicate Plantation near Blue Mountain, Mississippi. An Italian, Silva is described as "a rather small and wiry man of dark Latin looks." After a fire destroys the Syndicate Plantation cotton gin, Silva considers the primary suspect, his next-door neighbor and principal competitor, Jake Meighan. When Silva takes his 27 wagons of cotton to Jake to be ginned, his suspicions are confirmed. Jake orders his full-figured wife, Flora Meighan, to entertain Silva while the cotton is being ginned. During their conversation, Flora accidentally contradicts Jake's alibi. She confirms that Jake started the fire that destroyed Silva's gin. Silva takes his revenge by beating and raping Flora.

# *27 Wagons Full of Cotton and Other One-Act Plays*

A collection of 13 one-act plays published in 1966. The collection includes *27 WAGONS FULL OF COTTON, THE PURIFICATION, THE LADY OF LARKSPUR LOTION, THE LAST OF MY SOLID GOLD WATCHES, PORTRAIT OF A MADONNA, AUTO-DA-FÉ, LORD BYRON'S LOVE LETTER, THE STRANGEST KIND OF ROMANCE, THE LONG GOODBYE, HELLO FROM BERTHA, THIS PROPERTY IS CONDEMNED, TALK TO ME LIKE THE RAIN AND LET ME LISTEN*, and *SOMETHING UNSPOKEN*. This collection contains some of Williams's finest and most powerful shorter dramas. Each of these works illustrates Williams's insight into human nature and his gift for an evocative and poetic revelation of character.

## PUBLICATION HISTORY

*27 Wagons Full of Cotton and Other One-Act Plays* was published by New Directions in 1966.

# *The Two Character Play*

A play written between 1966 and 1975.

## SYNOPSIS

### *Act 1*

In an unspecified theater at an unspecified location, the stage is partially set for a performance. The design re-creates the interior of an old Victorian Southern house in summer. Through a window a field of tall sunflowers can be seen. Set pieces and properties from other productions also clutter the stage area. The stage is dominated by a statue of sinister-looking giant on a pedestal.

Felice, a young actor and playwright, enters the stage area and sits on a piano stool. He is the male star of a touring acting company. As he sits, he revises a monologue he has written about the power of fire and fear. His sister and costar, Clare, calls to him from offstage. Felice does not answer, but continues to draft his monologue. She calls again, and he finally responds. Clare enters the stage; she seems heavily medicated. She places a tiara, which is missing several stones, on her disheveled hair as she approaches her brother. Felice switches on a tape recorder, which plays previously recorded guitar music, and he and Clare rehearse a section of their lines to the music. Clare declares that she is ready to meet the press. Felice clarifies that they will not be meeting with the press before their performance. Clare is furious that a press reception has not been scheduled, as she believes she handles the press skillfully. Her brother criticizes her for getting drunk and raging against fascism in front of the press. Clare counters that he bores them with his discussions of "total theater."

She spots a cockroach on the stage and kills it by crushing it underfoot as she shouts "Cockroach!" Felice suggests she "drop an upper," but Clare believes she only needs strong coffee. Clare demands that Felice stay out of her affairs with other company members and stick to the business of the performance. Clare procrastinates, and Felice warns her that it is nearly time for the performance to begin. Clare discovers a prop throne on the stage and she pretends to be royalty. Felice is seized by a migraine. Clares inquires whether their tour is nearly over. Felice assures her that it will be over if they do not do well that evening. Clare expresses her frustrations about touring. Felice criticizes his sister's chemical dependencies and reminds her that her doctor has warned her that she runs the risk having a heart attack onstage. The two argue and insult each other bitterly.

Clare confesses that she wants to return home. Felice reminds her that the theater is their home and that they have no where else to go. Felice checks the production props, as Clare continues to complain. Clare recalls the bad reviews they received for a production of *Antony and Cleopatra* that they performed together. Clare and Felice turn their attention to the evening's performance of "The Two Character Play." The set is not complete, and Felice warns Clare that there will be a great deal of improvisation needed to perform the play successfully. Clare realizes that she and her brother have no lines of communication established between themselves and the front-of-house staff; they are isolated onstage.

Clare's persistent nagging that Felice end the tour prompts him to tell her the truth about their dire financial situation. He finally shares with her a telegram that he received from the other members of the company informing him that they have all quit. Clare decides they should quit too, but Felice believes the show must go on. Clare wants to return to her hotel room to relax, and Felice reminds her that they have no hotel rooms. The show has to go on because they have nowhere else to be. Felice orders Clare to remove her coat; as she is cold, she refuses. Felice abruptly snatches it off her. They bicker as their "audience" gathers in the theater. Felice attacks Clare, calling her a variety of crude names, and leaves her onstage. Before Clare can regain her composure, the "curtains" are opened and she is caught onstage by the "audience." The two actors struggle to perform their play, which recounts the death of their parents. Clare founders throughout the performance and Felice chastises her for "destroying the play." Clare falls apart completely when Felice utters the word "confined," which as far as she is concerned is a prohibited word and should not be included in the script. The curtain is drawn for a 10-minute intermission.

### *Act 2*

During the intermission Felice and Clare's fighting has continued. They return to the stage with cuts and bruises. They resume their "performance." Clare tends to Felice's wounded cheek. As she dabs his scratched cheek, Felice confesses that he has forgotten his lines. When Clare admits that she has forgotten hers too, he instructs her to improvise. Clare improvises on the tension that existed between her parents before the accident that caused their death. Her improvisation leads her parents to reveal that they are penniless because their father's life insurance payment was forfeited on a "legal technicality." The play begins to fall apart again, as the actors argue about life together following their parents' demise. They emphatically call "Line!" even though there is no one available to prompt them. They bicker over the whereabouts of their father's revolver. Clare recounts the time Felice spent in a state asylum. They endeavor to venture from the confines of their home. They each offer excuses and hesitate, until Felice forcibly maneuvers Clare out the door. They attempt a visit to Grossman's Market, a block away from their home. Clare succumbs to fear and scrambles to return to the house. Felice threatens that he will leave her, and Clare threatens that she will wait for him. Felice leaves the house. He speaks directly to the audience and tells them of his own cowardice and how he will return to the house. He re-enters the house, and he and Clare are too ashamed to look at one another. Clare concludes the performance and orders Felice to "come out of the play." Clare informs Felice that the audience has already left the theater. He blames the audience's retreat on Clare for her lack of concentration and for destroying the play's texture. They sit on the prop sofa, have a cigarette, and discuss their next move. Clare urges Felice to contact their manager, Fox, and obtain enough money for them to leave. They call out for Fox, and do not receive a reply. Clare speculates that "The Two Character Play" may not have an ending.

The pair makes plans to find a nearby hotel. Felice leaves Clare on the stage, only to return abruptly with the news that the stage doors and the front doors of the theater have been locked from the outside. There are no windows in the building, and the backstage phone is "as lifeless" as the prop telephone they use onstage. They both begin to recognize that the stage lights are dimming, and Felice is not controlling them. Sensing that they are completely trapped, Clare realizes "it's a prison, this last theater of ours." Their greatest fear, being confined, has finally come to pass. Clare resigns herself to the fact that "there is nothing to be done." Felice corrects his sister: They can return into the world of the play. They begin their performance again, speaking their lines rapidly in an attempt to "lose themselves" in the play. Clare swiftly grabs their father's revolver and aims it at Felice. He urges her to shoot him, but she hesitates. She allows the gun to slip from her hand. Felice retrieves it, aims it at Clare, and tries to pull the trigger. He cannot. Clare and Felice reach out for each other as the lights fade to total darkness.

## COMMENTARY

In this remarkable play Williams parodies his own dramaturgy, his life, the theater, and life itself. Structurally, the play is a composite of all the principal themes, motifs, situations, and relationships found in Williams's writings.

Felice and Clare's dilemmas (the unhappy marriage of their parents, abandonment, death, loss, emotional isolation, social rejection, madness, chemical dependency, poverty, hunger, lack of human connections, fear of confinement, fear of insanity, fear of the outside world, and fear of artistic failure) are concepts to which Williams repeatedly returned throughout his literary career. These are also issues that concerned Williams throughout his own life. The play inextricably meshes Williams's life and his art, to an even greater degree than in *The Glass Menagerie* and *Something Cloudy, Something Clear*.

The play features a pair of tormented siblings who are the product of a tempestuous home life. At the heart of Clare and Felice's drama is their role as unwilling participants in and traumatized witnesses to their parents' volatile marriage and the brutality it spawns. The Williamses' home in Saint Louis regularly brimmed with tension and hostility, which culminated in Rose Williams's accusation of sexual abuse against her father. She was institutionalized and received a prefrontal lobotomy shortly after making this claim.

In addition to representing or re-presenting elements of his life and works in *The Two Character Play,* Williams also spoofs his own characters in this drama about theater and acting (taking on roles). Felice, the poet-playwright, is obviously a stand-in for Williams. However, with his good looks, unkempt, shoulder-length hair, oversized greatcoat, and "period" shirt he is the quintessential actor, who seems on the brink of assaying Hamlet, that great and most existential dramatic role in Western drama. Felice's opening line ("To play with fire is to play with fire") is clearly a take on Hamlet's "To be or not to be" speech, and he states repeatedly that "theatre is a prison." Felice shares this connection to Hamlet with Constantine, another of Williams's struggling playwrights, in *The Notebook of Trigorin.* As does Constantine, Felice is dedicated to new innovations in the theater, and he postulates repeatedly on his theory of "total theatre."

Similarly, Felice's sister, Clare, is a serious caricature of many of Williams's dynamic and edgy women. She makes her first appearance wearing a tiara, a highly suggestive hint of Blanche DuBois (*A Streetcar Named Desire*), and her Victorian costume pieces, a parasol and gloves, seem fit for Alma Winemiller (*Eccentricities of a Nightingale*). It is easy to imagine that underneath her greatcoat she also wears a provocative slip, as does Maggie Pollitt (*Cat on a Hot Tin Roof*). Along with these external indicators, Clare's disposition belies her alignment with these and various other Williams characters. Clare's bedraggled restlessness is reminiscent of Gloria Bessie Greene (AT LIBERTY), Cassandra Whiteside (BATTLE OF ANGELS) and Carol Cutrere (ORPHEUS DESCENDING). Her frantic phone call to the Reverend Wiley is reminiscent of Blanche's final appeal to Shep Huntleigh. Clare's name, which is an anagram of the word "clear," her demeanor, and "apparitional look" resurface later in the character Clare in *Something Cloudy, Something Clear.*

In *The Two Character Play* not only does Williams satirize his own dramaturgy, he merges it with that of Luigi Pirandello and SAMUEL BECKETT. As a work about the theater, the theatrical (or performative) nature of human existence, and the drama of life itself, *The Two Character Play* is closely aligned with Pirandello's existential drama *Six Characters in Search of an Author.* As does the family of performers in Pirandello's work, Felice and Clare struggle to create a meaningful existence for themselves without any real guidance or a complete script, and they are trapped in the roles that have been assigned to them. As do Vladimir and Estragon in Beckett's classic *Waiting for Godot,* Clare and Felice find themselves alone in a desolate wasteland. Williams cleverly replaces Beckett's withered tree with a giant sunflower, which grows has high as a house, right outside their window. Felice and Clare's cheery sunflower-filled garden belies the pair's dark and desperate existence inside the house. As do Dorothy Simple's rigid double row of petunias in THE CASE OF THE CRUSHED PETUNIAS, Clare and Felice's border of sunflowers protects them from the outside world but also becomes a barrier that imprisons them. Similar to Beckett's transients, Clare and Felice cannot leave the place where they find themselves, nor are they satisfied to remain. They wait expectantly for help to arrive; their Godot-figure is Fox, a crafty production manager who fleeces them of their money and absconds. Both Beckett and Williams's works present a "fragmented world" and convey "that all we can do is act roles which will screen for a time our existential loneliness" (Cohen, 338). Both dramatists express the absurdity of the human condition and share the sentiment that all human beings are locked in the theater/prison of life.

While Felice merely strives to create "total theater" in his play-within-a-play ("The Two Character Play"), Williams succeeds in doing so in his. Through an evocative manipulation of his life story and his own unique dramaturgy, combined with significant and recognizable elements of theater history, Williams creates an existential masterpiece. This extraordinary work is at once a panoramic display of Williams's entire literary world and a snapshot that reveals a vision of the human condition and life itself.

## PRODUCTION HISTORY

*The Two Character Play* was produced at the Lyceum Theatre, in New York in March 1973. Peter Glenville directed the production, which featured Michael York and Cara Duff-MacCormick as Felice and Clare.

## PUBLICATION HISTORY

Williams began writing *The Two Character Play* in 1966. It was first published by New Directions in 1969. The play was revised under the title OUT CRY. This version of the play was published by New Directions in 1973. Williams extensively revised the work again, returning to the original title, *The Two Character Play.* This version, considered definitive, was published by New Directions in 1975.

## CHARACTERS

**Clare** Clare is an actor in a touring theater company. Her brother Felice is her costar, director, and the company playwright. She and Felice have been abandoned by their fellow company members and remain in an unspecified theater, in an unspecified location in the South. The two actors attempt to persevere by performing the play that Felice has written called "The Two Character Play." Much to Felice's chagrin, Clare continually forgets her lines and drops character repeatedly. She stops the performance when she realizes that the audience has left.

**Felice** Felice is a handsome young playwright who dreams of creating what he calls "total theatre." He is the leading member, director, and playwright for a touring theater company, and his sister Clare is his principal costar. When the rest of the ensemble deserts them, and their production manager, Fox, absconds with their money, Felice urges

Clare to persevere. The two of them attempt to perform a play Felice has written called "The Two Character Play." Once they have stopped their performance, Felice realizes that he and his sister have been locked in the theatre. As there is no means of escape, nor any way to communicate with the outside world, Felice suggests that he and Clare return to the world of the play.

### FURTHER READING

Cohn, Ruby. "Late Tennessee Williams," *Modern Drama* 27, no. 3 (September 1984): 336–344.

## "Two on a Party"

Short story written between the years 1951 and 1952.

### SYNOPSIS

Billy and Cora befriend each other in a Manhattan bar one night. As they are both cruising for men, they become best friends. Billy and Cora move in together and have sex once, but it is not fulfilling for either of them. They spend their time attending fantastic parties, and Cora falls in love with Billy (although she never discloses this information). They indulge in drugs and alcohol, and although they enjoy the frenetic pace of their life, they always arrive at an empty and lonely emotional state. One night they pick up a hitchhiker for Billy, but when Billy flirts with him, the hitchhiker attacks him. Cora distracts the hitchhiker with sexual advances. Billy and Cora are very shaken by the incident, but they are ultimately "two birds flying together against the wind, nothing real but the party, and even that's sort of dreamy."

### COMMENTARY

When Cora is asked why she parties so incessantly, she explains that she and Billy are just lonely people. The answer to loneliness for them is perpetual debauchery. Even when the circumstances become dangerous, Billy and Cora accept their roles and find ways to surf through them regardless of the wounds they suffer. Billy is beaten, slumped in the corner, and Cora seduces the hitchhiker as a means to an end. Their interest in young men is a solid bond between them. Billy and Cora live for the challenge of seduction, proving to themselves that they remain attractive and desirable. Donald Spoto claims that "Two on a Party" was Williams's tribute to and celebration of his "wild weeks on the road sharing liquor and men" with his friend Marion Black Vaccaro (62). Williams had hoped to create a film version of this story featuring Sylvia Miles and Joe Dallesandro.

### PUBLICATION HISTORY

"Two on a Party" was published in the collections *Hard Candy* in 1954, *Collected Stories* (1985), *The Other Persuasion: An Anthology of Short Fiction about Gay Men and Women* (1977), and *The Faber Book of Gay Short Fiction* (1991).

### CHARACTERS

**Billy** Billy is a young gay man who meets his best friend, Cora, in a bar. The two join forces in their quest for potential boyfriends. Billy and Cora love to party and dedicate themselves to the pursuit of pleasure.

**Cora** She is a wild young woman who loves to party. She and her best friend, Billy, actively scout for potential male lovers together.

### FURTHER READING

Spoto, Donald. *The Kindness of Strangers.* New York: Ballantine Books, 1985.

## "The Vengeance of Nitocris"

A short story written in 1928.

### SYNOPSIS

*Part 1*

The Egyptian god Osiris causes a great flood of the Nile River that washes out a bridge that would have allowed Egypt's Pharaoh to traverse the great river triumphantly. Angered by the flood, Pharaoh publicly denounces Osiris by beating the priests and defiling the sacred altars.

Fearing the wrath of the god, the Thebans rush the palace gates. Drawing his sword, the Pharaoh slashes the air ferociously and addresses the crowd, who demand he light the temple fires. The Pharaoh stands defiant and resolute. The mob retreats slightly, as they are taken aback by his fierce presence. The Pharaoh controls the mob with minimal effort, but he is careless of the crumbling steps beneath him. He tries to catch his balance, but he tumbles down the remaining steps, landing at the feet of the priests. Declaring this a sign from Osiris, the priests incite the mob once more. They kill the Pharaoh by dismembering his body with their hands and weapons. The Pharaoh's beautiful sister, Nitocris, witnesses this scene and vows to avenge her brother's death.

### *Part 2*

Soon after Nitocris's coronation, there are rumors that she has ordered the construction of a new temple, but the details remain secret. The people acknowledge the gift of the new temple on the banks of the Nile, as an apology for the Pharaoh's defilement.

A great banquet is announced. An extravagant celebration is held in honor of Nitocris. When she arrives at the gala, Thebans shout with excitement and appreciation. Nitocris remains steadfast in her welcoming expressions of gratitude and love. She smiles and exudes piety and beauty in the face of her enemies. Nitocris orders the lifting of a great wall, revealing a vault with splendid tables of delicacies. The Thebans rush down the steps and around the tables, devouring the feast and enjoying the music and the beautiful servants. Singing, laughing, and drinking intensify and the banquet becomes an orgy.

Nitocris sits on her throne and watches the festivities with cat eyes. At midnight, Nitocris rises from her seat. She surveys the room one final time and ascends the stairs. When she reaches the top, she looks back to be sure that her exit has been undetected. Nitocris leaves the banquet, motioning to the guards, who are waiting at their posts. They place a gigantic slab of rock over the vault, tightly enclosing the citizens. Nitocris feels an exhilarating tingle throughout her body as she draws the hood of her cloak around her feline face and exits. Using a secret passage, the empress and her guards walk to a stone pier at another point of the river. At the pier stand a number of levers. With an ecstatic glance into the night sky, she pulls back one lever and leaps to the edge to hear the water rush. Nitocris releases a victorious cry.

Inside the vault, the dancers freeze and gaze into the black abyss. The banquet grows silent as the thunderous rushing water advances. The banqueters are met with a tidal wave and terror abounds. The Pharaoh is avenged.

The next day, citizens block Nitocris's chariot, demanding an explanation for the people who did not return from the banquet. Nitocris ignores their insistence and lashes her horses forward. When she arrives at the palace, she orders her slaves to fill her chamber with fiery ashes. She locks herself in the room, and after a short period, she suffocates.

## COMMENTARY

In 1928, Williams entered a short story contest sponsored by *Weird Tales,* a science fiction and fantasy magazine. The story was published, and he won a $25 prize. In the *New York Times,* March 1958, Williams recalled that this story, his first published work, "set the keynote for most of the work that followed." Although some critics have found numerous shortcomings in the piece, it is an important example of Williams's thematic and poetic style.

The story contains themes such as revenge, sibling bonds, familial honor, societal violence, and self-sacrifice, all of which became staples in the Williams canon. This early fiction illustrates the promise of the mature Williams, who would write similar works such as the short story "DESIRE AND THE BLACK MASSEUR" and the plays *ORPHEUS DESCENDING* and *SUDDENLY LAST SUMMER.* Williams revisited themes and works many times, and his short stories often served as the framework and blueprint for his full-length plays. "The Vengeance of Nitocris" was the profound beginning of a prolific writer. This short story is based on a story in *The Persian Wars* by Herodotus.

## PUBLICATION HISTORY

Following its first publican in *Weird Tales* magazine in 1928, "The Vengeance of Nitocris" appeared in *La Venganza de Nitocris* (1968), *The Pulps: Fifty Years of American Pop Culture* (1970), *Collected Stories* (1985), *Masterpieces of Terror and The Supernatural* (1985), *First Fiction: An Anthology of the First Published Stories by Famous Writers* (1994), and *Into the Mummy's Tomb* (2001).

## CHARACTERS

**Nitocris** She is a regal, pious, and determined woman who becomes empress of Egypt when her brother is slaughtered. Her brother's body was dismembered by Thebans for defiling the temple of Osiris. Nitocris vows to avenge the death of her brother. She builds a new temple as a peace offering and invites the Thebans to a great banquet. The unsuspecting priests and citizens think Nitocris is atoning for her brother's actions; however, she traps them inside the vaultlike hall and floods it with the waters of the Nile. Nitocris then commits suicide to avoid being killed by the remaining Thebans.

**Pharaoh** The Pharaoh is the ruler of Egypt. He is a statuesque man who considers his nobility and divinity equal to those of the gods. Pharaoh's pride provokes him to defile the temple altars of Osiris. His citizens fear retribution for this act, so they storm the palace, attack Pharaoh, and dismember his body.

# *Vieux Carré*

Full-length play written in 1976.

## SYNOPSIS

The setting is a rooming house, No. 722 Toulouse Street, in the French Quarter of New Orleans. The rooming house has been transformed into a dank art gallery. The time is winter 1938 and spring 1939.

### *Part 1, Scene 1*

The Writer, who also serves as the narrator, informs the audience that the house was livelier at one time, but now it is inhabited by desperate characters who struggle to survive. He calls them "shadowy occupants like ghosts." The Writer also frames the story by explaining that the characters are also characters in his memory, and the recollection begins.

Mrs. Wire shouts at Nursie, the housemaid, who panics because bats are in the kitchen. As they grumble, Mrs. Wire notices a knapsack in the hallway. Nursie explains that a crazy man had arrived in search of accommodations, but when she told him there were no vacancies, he left the sack of belongings to be picked up the next day. Mrs. Wire notices the name *Sky* written in shiny letters on the sack, and she orders Nursie to carry it upstairs. Frustrated by her orders, Nursie announces that she is retiring to become a bag lady. Mrs. Wire refuses to placate her and Nursie refuses to follow the order. Mrs. Wire rests on a cot she has set up near the front door to monitor the comings and goings of her tenants.

The Writer appears in the entranceway. He has a confrontation with Mrs. Wire, who orders him to his room. Another tenant, Jane Sparks, enters the house. Mrs. Wire chastises her for being out in the Quarter so late at night. Mrs. Wire reminds her that when she rented the room, she agreed that a single woman should have a curfew of midnight. Jane angrily insists that she went out to purchase a can of insect repellent because the house is infested with cockroaches. As she storms out of the room, Mrs. Wire asks about the man who is living with her upstairs. Jane says the man is Tye McCool, as she leaves to join Nursie for coffee. Nightingale, a tenant and sketch artist, enters with a man he has picked up for the night. When Mrs. Wire accosts him, Nightingale claims the young man is his cousin, who is visiting New Orleans. She does not believe him and does not allow the man to go upstairs.

Mary Maude and Miss Carrie enter the kitchen, where they find the Writer, Nursie, and Jane. The two "crones" ask Nursie to store their leftover food in the icebox for them. Jane volunteers to let them use her icebox, but Nursie tells her that the women are starving and they have collected the greasy bag of food from the outside garbage can. She insists on discarding the bag. Jane decides to buy them groceries the next day. Jane pontificates about pride and confesses that she is living with a drug addict who works at a strip club. Tye enters with boxes of stolen merchandise to store in Jane's room.

*Part 1, Scene 2*

The Writer has undressed and lies in bed. He hears Nightingale's tubercular coughs in the nearby cubicle. The sound of Jane's sobbing permeates the rooms. Nightingale lights a cigarette and strikes up a conversation by criticizing their miserly landlady. Nightingale then talks about the sketches he does for the tourists who pay him to "prostitute" his artistic ability. The Writer says that he cries because his grandmother, Grand, died the previous month. The two men agree that loneliness is an affliction as Nightingale offers the Writer a cigarette and complains that bedbugs are "bleeding him like leeches." Nightingale makes sexual advances to the Writer, who initially declines. The Writer admits that he has not "come out completely" and says that he has had only one sexual experience, with a paratrooper. They pause for a moment to listen to the rain. The lights dim as Nightingale joins the Writer under his sheets.

The Writer then returns to his role as the narrator, and addresses the audience. He explains that an apparition of an old female saint visited him in the alcove of his room after this encounter. She was his deceased grandmother. She stared at him, and he wondered whether she witnessed their act. She gave no indication but stood indifferently. The apparition then forgave the Writer by lifting her cool, gray hand before he drifted to sleep.

*Part 1, Scene 3*

In the boardinghouse, the Writer encounters Jane and helps her take her groceries into her room. Jane insists he stay and have a cup of coffee with her. The Writer hesitates because Tye is sprawled out on the bed in a drug-induced slumber. Jane reassures him that Tye is asleep, though his eyes are not completely closed. Tye angrily awakens and accuses Jane of taking another man home. The Writer focuses on an elegant chess board to defuse the embarrassing situation. He asks whether Jane and Tye play chess together. Tye lewdly responds by rubbing his genitals and explaining that they "play" often. As they sit and drink coffee, Tye calls the Writer a "faggot" and continues to tell a story about his encounter with a gay man. Unable to tolerate more insults and discomfort, the Writer leaves. Jane reprimands Tye for his impolite behavior. Jane admits that she is attracted to Tye because she has never encountered anyone like him.

*Part 1, Scene 4*

Mrs. Wire prepares a pot of gumbo in her kitchen. It is midnight.

As the Writer enters the kitchen area, Mrs. Wire tells him that he has been evicted from her boardinghouse because he has not paid rent. He sits at the table in a state of desperate disbelief. He says that he applied for work on the Works Progress Administration (WPA) for writers but could not prove he was destitute, so he was considered ineligible. The aroma of the gumbo lures Miss Carrie and Mary Maude from their room. Tye enters the house in an inebriated state. The Writer helps him carry boxes up the stairs, and Tye collapses in the Writer's bed.

The Writer returns to the kitchen. Mrs. Wire asks him where he goes at night. She confesses that she has maternal feelings for him and worries about his well-being. She observes that he has changed since he arrived at the rooming house. She serves him a bowl of gumbo and asks him to pass out flyers for the restaurant she has decided to open in the rooming house. Tye's angry voice is heard from upstairs. It is followed by Nightingale's apologies for getting into bed with him.

*Part 1, Scene 5*

In the Writer's cubicle, Nightingale enters the room and complains about bedbugs. The writer is immediately irritated by his visit and the earlier situation with Tye. Nightingale starts an argument with the Writer. He is restless and does not want to be alone; however, the Writer is upset and prefers to be alone. The Writer suspects that Nightingale has a fever. Nightingale disrobes and asks to be held. When the Writer rejects him, Nightingale accuses him of being coldhearted. Infuriated, the Writer insists that Nightingale come to terms with his disease (tuberculosis).

*Part 1, Scene 6*

The next morning in Jane and Tye's room, the Writer delivers a letter to Jane, who has spent the morning working on her fashion designs. Tye is sprawled across the bed wearing only a pair of shorts. Jane invites the Writer to stay for coffee, but he declines. She begs him to stay, and the Writer realizes that she is disturbed by the letter. Jane begins to drink bourbon while the Writer gazes at Tye's body. Jane notices and covers him with a blanket. Tye calls for the cat in his semiconscious state. The Writer leaves.

### *Part 1, Scene 7*

The lights come up on the Writer as narrator. The Writer begins the scene with information about a distinguished photographer who leased the basement of Mrs. Wire's rooming house. When the Writer enters the house for the night, he is stopped by Mrs. Wire, who has been spying on the photographer's party below. She orders the Writer to help her boil water to pour through the hole in the floor that has exposed the orgiastic party. With talk of stamping out corruption in the Quarter, she is determined to end these parties permanently. The Writer refuses to participate in the scalding. Mrs. Wire pours the boiling water onto the floor and screams are heard as people can be seen running from the basement. Nightingale enters, and Mrs. Wire decides to blame the incident on him if the police arrive. Miss Carrie and Mary Maude enter as the police arrive.

The lights dim on the scene as the Writer appears in the witness box at night court. The Old Judge asks him whether he saw Mrs. Wire scald the partygoers. The Writer does not directly answer the question. The Old Judge finds her guilty anyway. The scene then dims and lights come back up on the kitchen. Mrs. Wire accuses the Writer of testifying against her. He is quick to say that he has returned to the house only to collect his belongings. Mrs. Wire says she is withholding his possessions until he pays his bill. She begins to pity him and offers him a drink.

Mrs. Wire states that the incident revealed to her that she is utterly alone in the world. She acknowledges that in her own home she is surrounded by strangers who loathe her. Nightingale enters the kitchen mimicking the Writer's court testimony.

### *Part 2, Scene 8*

In his cubicle, the Writer is working at his old typewriter. A man enters and introduces himself as Schuyler, or Sky. The Writer remembers the knapsack that appeared in the hallway nearly a year ago. Sky is a musician who is passing through town. He asks the Writer to leave with him and go west. Sky urinates out of the window overlooking the courtyard. Mrs. Wire sees him and shouts at him from downstairs. Nightingale is heard coughing from his cubicle, and Mrs. Wire begins to quarrel about him and his contagion. Nightingale calls her accusations lies, still denying that he has tuberculosis. Mrs. Wire informs him that she has heard that the cashiers at the Two Parrots have to scrub the pavement with lye where Nightingale works, as he coughs up blood and spits on the ground. Nightingale fiercely defends himself by locking himself in his room. The Writer asks Mrs. Wire to stop this arguing because Nightingale is near death. Mrs. Wire angrily demands that Nursie unlock his door and throw out everything in the room to get rid of the disease. When Mrs. Wire enters the room, Nightingale suffers a coughing spasm that leaves him prostrate on the floor. Mrs. Wire orders the furniture burned, and she tells Nightingale that he will be going to the charity ward at Saint Vincent's Hospital.

Mrs. Wire refuses to allow the Writer to leave. She says that she has adopted him since her son was taken away from her years ago. Sky and the Writer agree to meet at midnight to leave New Orleans.

### *Part 2, Scene 9*

Jane has been packing. She frantically tries to awaken Tye from an unnaturally deep sleep. She discovers a needle mark on his arm as he grunts with irritation. Jane slaps his face with a wet towel to stir him, and he threatens to beat her. She reminds him that he promised to quit his job at the strip club to find a more wholesome means of income, but he is indignant about his lifestyle. Jane hints that she is not healthy. Tye immediately assumes she is pregnant, and she quickly dispels the thought. He tries to entice her to bed, but she rejects him because he has lipstick smeared on his face and other places on his body. She also admonishes him for the needle mark on his arm. Jane urges Tye to get dressed and leave the studio, because she is expecting a call from a businessman from Brazil who propositioned her for a sexual encounter. He gave her $100, but she was so disturbed by the circumstances that she originally declined the offer. She thoughtfully questions how an educated woman ever ended up in such a dire situation as hers. Nursie is heard directing tourists in the courtyard, and this exasperates Jane. Tye tries to persuade her to get back into bed with him. When she tells him they are finished and that he is moving out, he rapes her. The Writer overhears Jane's cries of protest. He is so baffled that he does nothing. Mrs. Wire happens upon him and sarcastically disregards his concern, claiming the sounds do not mean that Jane is in pain. Mrs. Wire shouts at them to quit "that loud fornication." Tye shrieks at the old woman and jumps up to confront her. Jane intervenes, explaining that Tye is moving out of the rooming house.

*Part 2, Scene 10*

The Writer explains that this was his last Sunday in the Quarter. He served meals for Mrs. Wire and retired to his cubicle. He thought Nightingale was dead because there was silence, but he heard a soft cry. For the first time, the Writer returns his visits.

Nightingale tries to get dressed and leave Mrs. Wire's to avoid being committed to a charity ward. Nightingale shows the Writer his most prized possessions: a tortoiseshell comb with a mother-of-pearl handle and a silver-framed mirror that belonged to his mother. The Writer gives Nightingale a sleeping pill and instructs him to concentrate on the apparition in the alcove that has appeared to comfort him. The Writer returns to his room to pack for the West Coast.

*Part 2, Scene 11*

In Jane's studio, Jane cries on the bed while Tye rolls a joint and tries to assuage her after the rape. The conversation quickly becomes nasty when Tye insinuates that Jane is "less than a whore" because she has sex with him for free. Jane grows nauseous when Tye tells her a story about a stripper who was mauled to death by the owner's dogs because she threatened to leave him. Tye finally notices that Jane is losing weight and is always physically weak.

Portrait of Williams, 1977 *(Bill Viggiano)*

She is ambivalent about telling him that she has a blood disease that has been in remission for some time, but it is now rapidly progressing. Tye reads the test results and begins to dress. Nightingale is taken to the charity ward.

*Part 2, Scene 12*

The Writer observes that Jane's gaze was full of resentment. Mrs. Wire appears in the hallway. She appears disheveled and delusional. She calls the Writer "Timmy," the name of her son. Mrs. Wire leads him back to his room, tucking him in his bed and reasoning with him as if talking to a child. Nursie enters to help Mrs. Wire back to bed. As they exit, the apparition of Grand appears to the Writer. Jane watches Tye primp in the mirror, and she suspects he will not return to her now that he knows she is dying. Tye leaves for work, promising to be home early. She follows him into the hallway, where she collapses. The Writer helps her to her room. He begins to set up the chess board when Sky arrives to collect him for the trip. The Writer is hesitant to leave Jane in her state, but she insists he jump at this opportunity and get out of the Quarter. The Writer turns to leave Mrs. Wire's house.

## COMMENTARY

Williams often recalled his struggling youthful days in New Orleans in letters, calling it his "favorite city of America . . . of all the world, actually," and he boasted, "My happiest years were there" (Williams, 103). *Vieux Carré* is one of several Williams play set in New Orleans. As in *A STREETCAR NAMED DESIRE,* the eclectic nature of the French Quarter is captured through Williams's poetic language. Dank and dilapidated houses, decay and decadence, languorous and destitute drifters, and the desperation that thrived along with the burgeoning artists of the Vieux Carré in the 1930s, all create the atmosphere of suffocating despondency. This atmosphere was simultaneously tragic and beautiful, as the uniqueness of the memory as well as the eccentric nature of New Orleans enhance a coming of age story of exciting adventure and extreme hardship.

The dramaturgical evolution of *Vieux Carré* began with the short story "THE ANGEL IN THE ALCOVE," written in 1943. In this work, the writer is seduced by the tubercular artist and leaves the rooming house when the artist is evicted. The apparition of Grand appears only to the writer as a guide, much like Dante's Virgil. The Writer is far more bewildered by the angel in the alcove, and his actions are prompted by Grand's appearance. The short story also functions as a coming-out story from Williams to his deceased grandmother, as she (in her ghostly form) witnesses the sexual encounter of the artist and writer. The plot of the short story resurfaces as the one-act play *THE LADY OF LARKSPUR LOTION.* In this retelling Williams shifts the focus to include the ruthless Mrs. Wire, Mrs. Hardwick-Moore, and a writer who fancies himself as ANTON CHEKHOV. In The *Lady of Larskpur Lotion,* there is less mood surrounding the plot. Williams was hesitant to adapt this short story for the stage, because it was what he called a "story of . . . mostly mood and nostalgia" (*Conversations,* 301).

*Vieux Carré* is similar in tone and structure to *THE GLASS MENAGERIE.* Both plays center on narrative form and a strong sense of nostalgia that coincides with recollections of the past. Both plays are framed by a narrator (who is also a writer) and are derived from Williams's personal experiences. Whether *Vieux Carré* (as well as *The Glass Menagerie*) is strictly autobiographical is debatable, according to Williams's comments on the play:

> You can't do creative work and adhere to facts . . . there is a boy who is living in a house that I lived in, and undergoing some of the experiences that I underwent as a young writer. But his personality is totally different from mine. He talks quite differently from the way that I talk, so I say the play is not autobiographical. And yet the events in the house actually did take place. (*Conversations,* 300)

Robert Bray suggests that *Vieux Carré* "may be more profitably seen as a well-unified artistic and autobiographical sequel to *The Glass Menagerie*" (152). In this context, Tom's escape from his puritanical Saint Louis environment leads him to the bohemian French Quarter, where he becomes an openly gay artist. Tom the writer is rescued from the stifling oppression of Mrs. Wire by a fellow artist and adventure seeker. The apparition of Grand appears in two possible ways: as Tom's guilty conscience filtering past events or as a ghost. In either case, Grand absolves him of much more than being a gay man: She lets him know that he is forgiven for abandoning his responsibility in the Wingfield household.

Central themes found in *Vieux Carré* include loneliness, depression, and destitution in the crumbling South. Nightingale is a character who has been reduced spiritually as well as physically. He is an insomniac whose loneliness enraptures his sense of reality. Nightingale searches for comfort from the solitude caused by his disease. As a person who is marginalized by his sexuality, he is further isolated by his contagion. Jane Sparks wrestles with the mistakes she has made in the past, and they propel her toward similar ones in the future. As a result she is consumed by such a despicable man as Tye McCool. Jane's loneliness has driven her to Tye who does not fulfill her thirst for intellectual companionship.

The brutish Tye McCool is like Bill McCorkle of *SMALL CRAFT WARNINGS* in his homophobic response to the writer. He enjoys tormenting the writer for being gay and yet he reveals in drug-induced moments when he himself has had sex with men. Sex for Tye is merely a primal act in response to natural desires. He does not associate love with sex, or love with sex, but uses his virility as a means of dominating and subjugating Jane.

*Vieux Carré*'s Mrs. Wire is a dynamic character. She resents that her home has become a den of corruption and misfits, although she enjoys the financial benefits they bring her. As is Eloi Duvenet in AUTO-DA-FÉ, Mrs. Wire is obsessed with abolishing the amoral aspects of life in the French Quarter to the point of using force and causing physical harm. Her crusades are, however, contained within the walls of the rooming house, and her continual rampages are concentrated on the few dismal tenants.

## PRODUCTION HISTORY

*Vieux Carré* premiered at the Saint James Theatre, May 11, 1977, directed by Arthur Alan Seidelman and starring Richard Alfieri as the Writer, Tom Aldredge as Nightingale (or the Painter), and Sylvia Miles as Mrs. Wire. It was revived for a London production at the Playhouse Theatre, Nottingham, May 16, 1978. Directed by Keith Hack, the play starred Karl Johnson as the Writer, Richard Kane as Nightingale, and Sylvia Miles as Mrs. Wire.

## PUBLICATION HISTORY

*Vieux Carré* was published by New Directions in 1979.

## CHARACTERS

**Mary Maude** She is a starving unmarried woman who resides at the New Orleans rooming house of Mrs. Wire. Mary Maude occupies her time, along with Miss Carrie, by writing a Creole cookbook. Mary Maude refuses to admit that she is destitute and dying of malnutrition.

**McCool, Tye** A rough and handsome man who lives in the French Quarter of New Orleans with his girlfriend, Jane Sparks. Tye is a self-destructive drug addict whose lifestyle includes working nights at a strip club. He also deals in stolen merchandise as a side job. Tye is often in a drug-induced sleep, but his temper rages at Mrs. Wire and the Writer, and eventually he rapes Jane. When he learns that Jane is dying of a blood disease, he leaves her.

**Miss Carrie** She is a starving unmarried woman who resides at the New Orleans rooming house of Mrs. Wire. Miss Carrie is a member of a once respected family, who has fallen on hard times. All Miss Carrie has left is her pride, which prevents her from admitting that she is dying of malnutrition. She shares a room with her friend, Mary Maude.

**Nightingale** He is a lonely young artist struggling to survive by sketching tourists in New Orleans. Nightingale resides in the rooming house of Mrs. Wire, a wretched aging woman. His daily fights with her escalate when it becomes obvious he is dying of tuberculosis. Refusing to believe that he has the disease, he tells other tenants that he is suffering from asthma or a flu. Nightingale's loneliness increases with the progression of the disease. He finds some comfort in the arms of a young man called the Writer. Against his wishes and during his last days, Mrs. Wire commits Nightingale to the charity ward at the local hospital.

**Nursie** She is the maid and disregarded assistant of Mrs. Wire. Nursie is an aging woman who has grown tired of her employer's strange and harsh orders. She is responsible for the upkeep of a dilapidated rooming house in the French Quarter of New Orleans.

**Sky** He is a young musician who leaves his knapsack at the rooming house of Mrs. Wire and returns to claim it a year later. Sky befriends the Writer and invites him to leave the sordid French Quarter (and the dank rooming house) for the West Coast.

**Sparks, Jane** She is a woman who flees her New England home in search of a fresh start in New Orleans. With dreams of becoming a prominent fashion designer, Jane falls prey to a brutish drug addict named Tye McCool. His reckless and aggressive disposition excites her at first, but when she wants to end the relationship, he rapes her. Jane is dying of a blood disease that is rapidly progressing. She looks to the fellow tenants in Mrs. Wire's rooming house for companionship. Lonely and desperate, she urges her only friend, the Writer, to leave New Orleans when the chance arises. When Jane reveals the severity of her disease to Tye, he coldly disengages and leaves.

**Wire, Mrs.** She is the miserable landlady of a dilapidated rooming house in the French Quarter of New Orleans. Mrs. Wire terrorizes her tenants, considering it her duty to stamp out corruption and vice. These tenants also serve as her only source of family and income. Mrs. Wire is based on Williams's experience of various landladies in New Orleans when he was a young and struggling writer.

**Writer** A young man who has made his way to New Orleans in search of freedom from his controlling mother. The writer lives in the dank and desperate rooming house owned by Mrs. Wire. His encounters with the other tenants serve as material for his art after he escapes the hopeless scene for the West Coast with another drifter, Sky. The play is a coming of age story for the Writer, and desolate tenants such as Nightingale, Jane Sparks, and Tye McCool provide a jolting thrust into adulthood. Williams based this character on himself during the time in New Orleans when he was a young and struggling artist. The Writer also serves as the narrator of the play, which is his recollection of bygone days.

## FURTHER READING

Bray, Robert. "*Vieux Carré:* Transferring a Story of Mood," in *The Undiscovered Country: The Later Plays of Tennessee Williams,* edited by Philip Kolin. New York: Peter Lang, 2002, pp. 142–154.

Grauerholz, James. "Orpheus Holds His Own: William Burroughs Talks with Tennessee Williams," in *Conversations with Tennessee Williams,* edited by Albert J. Devlin. Jackson: University Press of Mississippi, 1986.

Leverich, Lyle. *Tom: The Unknown Tennessee Williams.* New York: Crown, 1995.

# "The Vine"

Short story written between the years 1939 and 1944.

## SYNOPSIS

Donald, a middle-aged actor, discovers his wife, Rachel has left him. He tries to move on, but his sanity depends on her. He searches all over the city for Rachel, intruding on friends and acquaintances, interrogating them about her whereabouts. Donald attacks one acquaintance when she says she has not heard from Rachel. Donald returns to his empty apartment to calm down and contemplate his life with Rachel. Donald goes to bed and cries himself to sleep on her pillow.

## COMMENTARY

As a brief tale of loneliness and loss, "The Vine" seems a precursor to a later short story, "THE INTERVAL." In that work, Jimmie the actor husband is the one who leaves, not the one who is abandoned. "The Vine" was inspired by ANTON CHEKHOV's short novel *My Life.* "The Vine" illustrates Williams's affinity with Chekhov, particularly in its psychological texture and tone. Williams often proclaimed the Russian writer as his primary artistic influence.

## PUBLICATION HISTORY

"The Vine" was published in *Mademoiselle* (1954) and included in *Hard Candy* (1954). It won the *Benjamin Franklin* magazine award in 1955. It was published in *Collected Stories* (1985).

## CHARACTERS

**Donald** Donald is a middle-aged actor, who is faced with being alone after many years with his lovely wife, Rachel. He is shattered by her departure, and he suspects she has left him because he is sterile and cannot give her the child she desires.

**Rachel** She is an actor and dancer who leaves her husband, Donald, who suspects she has left him because he is sterile.

# Where I Live

Williams's collection of essays written throughout his career. Spanning the years 1944–78, these essays vary in nature and tone and have largely served as prefaces to his published works. In this prose form, Williams grapples with such issues as success, the vocation of the poet, theatrical failures, the personal nature of his dramaturgy, and his beloved KEY WEST, FLORIDA. Included in the essays are Williams's additional thoughts on such works as *A STREETCAR NAMED DESIRE*, *THE ROSE TATTOO*, *CAMINO REAL*, and *SWEET BIRD OF YOUTH*. Throughout these essays, Williams presents his philosophies regarding the theater as well autobiographical meanderings.

## PUBLICATION HISTORY

*Where I Live* was published in 1978 by New Directions.

# Will Mr. Merriwether Return from Memphis?

Full-length play, estimated to be written during the 1950s.

## SYNOPSIS

The setting is Saint Louis, also known as "Tiger Town."

### *Act 1, Scene 1*

Louise and her daughter, Gloria, sit motionless and silent for several minutes. A banjo plays a ragtime piece. Louise then moves center stage and addresses the audience. She says that while she was preparing Mr. Merriwether's room for his return, a Gypsy appeared at her door and prompted her to ask her most pressing question. Louise asked whether in fact Mr. Merriwether would return from Memphis but received a puzzling answer: "He will never forget you." Louise refuses to believe that her boarder will not return, and she tells Gloria that Mr. Merriwether phoned her in the middle of the night, excited about returning. Gloria suggests that she dreamed the call, as he was elated to receive the promotion that called him away from the boardinghouse.

Louise scolds Gloria, who is scantily dressed. She warns her against her going to the library so late at night and about the young men who wait on the library steps for her. Nora (a plump, small woman of 50) enters carrying a bowl of strawberries and cream for Louise, who, she worries, is losing weight. Louise tells Nora about Gloria's outings to the library, where the boys wait for her, "like male dogs tagging after a female dog in heat." Nora suggests they summon an apparition to distract Louise from her problems. Nora says Mme. du Barry, a mistress of King Louis XV, visited her the previous night. Louise says Marie Antoinette visited her. The women both agree that the wind is right for receiving apparitions.

Louise and Nora chant for an apparition to appear. The Ghost of Vincent Van Gogh appears to them. He searches for light, brushes, and paint. He tells them that light is a tremendous gift, regardless of whether one paints, and disappears. Louise leaves to get a sweater, and Nora addresses the audience with the information that Louise is a widow who fell in love with a drummer (Mr. Merriwether). Louise returns, puts on her sweater, and says that she still feels chilled from the apparition's visit. Nora tells her a story about lepers who live in large cisterns on Bella Street, between the white and black sections of town. Every night the lepers get out of the cisterns and receive food their families have left them. They have sex together in the shadows of the old trees. Some of the lepers even give birth in the cisterns, making no sound, to prevent detection. Louise decides to say good night to Nora. She is disappointed that Mr. Merriwether did not return, and she hears a banjo playing in the distance.

### *Act 1, Scene 2*

Gloria speaks to the audience. She confesses that she wears light dresses and enjoys the masculine smell of her admirers, which permeates the classrooms. She becomes drowsy from the smell and watches them loll in their chairs. The boys are so unresponsive that the teachers become angry. She says that a piece of chalk becomes too heavy for them.

### *Act 1, Scene 3*

At the public library, the Librarian (a tense little woman wearing a pink dress) calls out to Gloria. She reprimands Gloria for her misuse of the library and scolds her for the nearly transparent dress she is wearing. Gloria retaliates by claiming to use the library to write her English papers. She says it is not her fault that boys follow her into the reference room and sit too close to her. The Librarian says that she sees what happens in the room and demands that Gloria stop using the library. Gloria is infuriated and threatens to call the superintendent. The Librarian says that she will do the same.

### *Act 1, Scene 4*

Louise secretly calls Mr. Merriwether. When he answers, she slams down the phone and lectures herself about being so impatient.

### *Act 1, Scene 5*

In the classroom at the library, Miss Yorke congratulates Gloria for a well-written paper. She asks Gloria to read it for the class. Gloria reads the paper, which details a class trip to search for fossils. She explains that she found five fossils in the rocks, and a boy chipped them out for her. The class left and she was alone with the boy. She began to cry and tremble. The boy had to escort her to town, and even when she arrived at home, she was still so shaken by the idea that she was holding ancient artifacts. Her mother did not care about the fossils, however. Gloria received a phone call from the boy who helped her with the fossils. She told him that she would be at the library later that evening to write the paper. She hoped she would understand why she was so affected by the fossils. Miss Yorke suggests that she realized the transitory nature of life. Gloria begins to cry again. The Handsome Youth who helped her with the fossils escorts her to the streetcar to go home.

### *Act 1, Scene 6*

Gloria and the Handsome Youth sit silently on a bench. Gloria eventually breaks the silence. The Youth admits that he becomes speechless at times. He says that speaking is torture. Gloria calls him Richard, and asks whether he feels that way even with her. Gloria recalls a time in Spanish class when he was asked to read. The Handsome Youth said he could not because he stutters. The teacher reassured him that the class is aware of that fact. Gloria thought the teacher was sympathetic; however, the Youth insists that it was condescension, and he was humiliated. Gloria reminds him that he is the most handsome boy in the school.

Gloria asks whether he would mind if she removed her dress, because she wishes to lie in the clover and does not want to stain the dress. The Youth awkwardly assures her that he does not mind. He says he has no experience, and she says she believes he should have some. She tells him that she loves him. Gloria asks him to close his eyes, and she removes her dress and hides. When the Youth opens his eyes, she tells him to find her; she is invisible to everyone in the world except him. A banjo is heard in the distance. The Youth begins to search for Gloria.

### *Act 1, Scene 7*

Three Crones enter, carrying wooden stools, sewing equipment, and a large hourglass. They speak with an Irish brogue.

One negatively surmises that they will have to introduce themselves as "The Fatal Sisters." Three reminds her that this is the assignment. Two adds that "a philosophical attitude" is a sign of old age. The Crones fight over a sausage Two eats. Three announces that they are the Fatal Sisters, who have been summoned to sew the fabrics of the initiation that is taking place in the field. A woman's voice howls like a wildcat's. One comments that the howl was the sound of a man hitting a woman. Three says that the woman tries to prevent the man from drinking, and One concludes that there is no use in making the effort. The man and woman fight openly, lowering their social status in their neighborhood.

Three reminds them to keep sewing, but One concludes that they are no more than a vaudeville turn in the play. Two reminds them that a poet spoke of them, as "The Eumenides." One says that his death was stitched with regret. Three announces that they are both now undressed in the field. One says that a boy with a stammer may not have an erection or may ejaculate prematurely. The Crones fight over which will turn the hourglass this time. They watch Gloria and the Youth in varying stages of undress. One comments on the state of her mother, who spends her life wondering whether Mr. Merriwether will return to her. They stitch the time away.

One exits and returns with tea. Three announces that Gloria has given the Youth "tender knowledge," ending his stammer for all time.

### *Act 1, Scene 8*

Nora and Louise enter and sit down to chat. Nora asks whether an apparition visited Louise the night before, and Louise disappointedly says no. Nora says she received a naked apparition. The French Club Instructor enters for their evening lesson. Mrs. Biddle enters for the club meeting. They converse about the dark doorway behind them, which represents their lives. The club is invested in learning French, but the women also gather to express what is on their minds. The Instructor leads them in the exercise. Louise begins to cry, and the Instructor advises her not to suppress her emotions. In French Nora tells her peers that although her husband has been dead for 20 years, she prepared a dinner for two the previous night. The Instructor states that even in dreams there is suffering. Louise tries to confess her emotions to the club. The Instructor says that he frequents the bus stop in search of the company of "youth in the military services." The police caught him and are forcing him to leave town before midnight. The Instructor is going to Memphis. Louise comments that Memphis is "a memory of a dream."

### *Act 2, Scene 1*

Louise and Nora summon an apparition. The poet Arthur Rimbaud, seated in a wheelchair, appears to the women. His sister, Isabelle, pushes him. Isabelle says that her brother became a poet at 16 and gave up at 20. Arthur rejects the occupation and tells the story of having his leg amputated. The apparitions talk of the mist between death and heaven. Arthur begins to recite poetry. He then demands a letter be dictated to a man in Aden to inquire about a job. Isabelle and Arthur exit.

### *Act 2, Scene 2*

Louise sits, drinking a cup of tea, when Nora enters her home. She tells Nora that she invited apparitions tonight, but the winds are not moving to permit their visit. Nora delivers upside-down cake and sets it on the table. Louise is perplexed, as she enjoys the deliberate composition of the table. Louise tells Nora that the empty spaces are just as important to the overall aesthetic as the objects that occupy space. Louise calls the vacant spaces plastic space. Louise tells her friend that Eleanor of Aquitaine visited her and commented on the composition of her table, particularly the starfish.

Nora realizes that she left the front door open when she entered, and she has heard someone else enter. Louise jumps up, hoping to greet Mr. Merriwether. However, Mrs. Eldridge enters. She is remarkably clothed, in an Oriental dress. Mrs. Eldridge suspects that her chauffeur has just died, and she called on Louise to help her get to the Bar Apache, where she is expected. When she leaves, Nora asks whether she was an apparition, and Louise explains that she is the richest living lady in Tiger Town. The banjo is heard in the distance.

### *Act 2, Scene 3*

Louise sits at her table while she listens to the banjo in the distance. Nora enters with a bowl of blancmange. Nora is upset when Louise takes it to the ice box and discovers that everything she gives Louise to eat remains untouched. When Louise says she has no appetite, Nora suggests that she is depressed. She also suggests that Louise take in a new boarder. Louise is offended and retorts that she is not promiscuous. Louise grows irate, and she shouts about Mr. Merriwether's leaving. She is interrupted when she hears a car stop. Mr. Merriwether enters through a window with a flower between his teeth. Louise falls with emotion. Mr. Merriwether says that he has returned to stay and asks for his old room. Louise tells him that her entire life is waiting for him. They embrace while Nora searches the house for something to calm Louise's nerves. Gloria and her Handsome Youth enter, and the two couples dance.

Nora realizes that she is now alone. She considers inviting an apparition just as the Apparition of her deceased husband appears. He confesses that he was always unfaithful to her, and she asks why. The Apparition begins to hum the banjo tune that has been heard throughout the play.

## COMMENTARY

Although *Will Mr. Merriwether Return from Memphis?* is meant to be a comedy, a rare commodity in the Williams canon, the dark and mournful atmosphere of Tiger Town, with its evocation of apparitions, seems to contradict its stated dramatic purpose. However, as are much of Williams's later works, and most of the drama of the THEATER OF THE ABSURD, the play is unpredictable; anything can happen in the realm of the supernatural.

In this fluid, ethereal, and dreamlike world where characters thrive on their intuition and emotional instability, Williams's dramaturgy comes full circle. His ideas about PLASTIC THEATRE (encapsulated in the scene concerning Louise's ponderously composed table) are coupled with his later innovations in absurdist and expressionistic techniques. In the preface to *THE GLASS MENAGERIE,* Williams makes the claim that all artistic measures available should be used to put forth the world of a play. To achieve this, Williams felt it necessary to build upon realist staging by creating expressionistic moments with new media and technology.

In *Will Mr. Merriwether Return from Memphis?* his expressionistic technique is guided more by the paranormal than the technological. Following August Strindberg's example in such works as *Ghost Sonata* and *A Dream Play,* Williams challenges the characters', and by extension the readers' (or spectators'), perception of reality. This technique is explored extensively in similar works, such as *CLOTHES FOR A SUMMER HOTEL* and *SOMETHING CLOUDY, SOMETHING CLEAR,* where Williams goes a step further and dispenses with a realistic concept of time. These three "ghost plays" go beyond the Williamsian "memory play," in which the past is recalled or actively reexamined; in these works, the past is lived simultaneously with the present. The mature Williams continued to experiment with theatrical forms, even inventing his own, and *Will Mr. Merriwether Return from Memphis?* is an example of his continued dramatic evolution.

## PRODUCTION HISTORY

*Will Mr. Merriwether Return from Memphis?* premiered at the Tennessee Williams Performing Arts Center, Florida Keys Community College, on January 25, 1980.

## PUBLICATION HISTORY

*Will Mr. Merriwether Return from Memphis?* was published in *Missouri Review,* in 1997.

## CHARACTERS

**Apparition** One of several apparitions that appear in the play, he is the spirit of Nora's deceased husband. Alone and dejected, Nora summons him to comfort her. When he arrives, he proceeds to confess that he was always unfaithful to her.

**Eldridge, Mrs.** Mrs. Eldridge is the wealthiest woman in Tiger Town. She enters Louise's house unannounced and demands that Louise assist her. Mrs. Eldridge's chauffeur has just died, and she needs to get to Bar Apache for an event. Nora is so stunned by this remarkable occurrence that she questions whether Mrs. Eldridge is an apparition.

**French Club Instructor** A foreign-language teacher who offers emotional support to his students, Nora and Louise. During their evening language session, the class becomes aware of the pain and suffering each person is enduring. They discuss their respective grievances in French.

**Ghost of Vincent Van Gogh** He is an apparition summoned by Nora and Louise. When he appears, he searches for light, brushes, and paint. Van Gogh's ghost advises Nora and Louise that "light" is a tremendous gift.

**Gloria** She is a young woman who delights in the attention she receives from young men. Gloria, known for her beauty, is constantly berated by her mother, Louise, for her escapades with the young men at the public library. Gloria lives freely, and during a sexual encounter with a Handsome Youth in a field of flowers, Gloria cures the young man of self-consciousness and a speech stammer.

**Handsome Youth** He cares for the beautiful Gloria. The Handsome Youth has his first sexual experience with her and is freed from a nervous stammer in his speech.

**Librarian** A prim, petite woman who works in the public library. She is appalled by Gloria's behavior in the library. The Librarian admonishes Gloria for coming to the library scantily clad and accuses her of luring boys into the reference section for indecent activities.

**Louise** She is a middle-aged woman who suffers depression after her boarder, Mr. Merriwether, leaves to take a job in Memphis. Louise is wilting away without him, and the attention her daughter, Gloria, draws from young men does not help her condition. Louise's only companion, a neighbor called Nora, tries to care for her, but Louise is irritated by her constant presence. The women share the hobby of summoning apparitions at night.

**Merriwether, Mr.** He is a young musician who boarded at the home of Louise. Mr. Merriwether accepted a position in Memphis, but he returns because he has become romantically attached to Louise. The couple are reunited at the end of the play, and they dance with joy.

**Nora** She is a middle-aged widow who likes to dabble in the world of the supernatural. She spends her time summoning apparitions of famous people with her neighbor, Louise. Nora tries in vain to help Louise, who is heartbroken because Mr. Merriwether has moved to Memphis.

**One** One of three Irish Crones known as "the Fatal Sisters." One introduces herself and her sisters to the audience. She provides a running commentary on the Handsome Youth's sexual encounter with Gloria.

**Rimbaud, Arthur** Historical figure and character in *Will Mr. Merriwether Return from Memphis?* This man of letters appears as an apparition along with his sister, Isabel, summoned by Nora and Louise. Rimbaud recites some of his poetry and discusses with his sister the "mist between death and heaven."

**Rimbaud, Isabel** She appears as an apparition with her brother, Arthur Rimbaud. The two are summoned by Nora and Louise. She escorts her brother, who is confined to a wheelchair, and recounts his life story to the two women.

**Three** She is one of three Irish Crones, known as "the Fatal Sisters." Three announces their function in the play to the audience. She declares that they have been summoned to sew the "fabrics of initiation" for Gloria's sexual encounter with the Handsome Youth. She has to remind her sisters to keep sewing, when they become repeatedly distracted.

**Two** One of three Irish Crones known as "the Fatal Sisters." Two greedily eats a sausage, which she does not share with her sisters. While her sister One introduces the siblings to the audience, Three informs the audience that that they are responsible for sewing the "fabrics of initiation" for Gloria's sexual encounter with the Handsome Youth. Two has loftier aspirations and reminds her sisters that a previous poet referred to them as "the Eumenides."

# "The Yellow Bird"

Short story written before 1947.

## SYNOPSIS

Alma Tutwiler is the descendant of Goody Tutwiler, a woman who was accused of practicing witchcraft. She was hanged during the Salem witch trials. Legend has it that Goody's yellow bird, Bobo, flew to her enemies and damned them to hell.

Alma, who is 30 years old, rebels against her father, the Reverend Tutwiler, a long-winded minister, and her rigid mother. She smokes cigarettes in her parents' home despite her mother's threats and publicly defies her father, who disowns her. In his rage, the Reverend Tutwiler slaps Alma, who then slaps him in return. She bleaches her hair, routinely stays at parties all night and dates Stuff, a wild, local soda jerk.

Alma moves to New Orleans, where she becomes a prostitute in the French Quarter. In New Orleans, she begins to feel the presence of some unseen person who is with her at all times. Her parents send a young woman from the church to call on her. Alma is pleased, because her parents will know how she is living.

Alma realizes that she is pregnant. She gives birth to a son, whom she names Johnnie. This child is magical, and he crawls out of the apartment every morning and returns late in the evening with his fists full of gold and jewels. Alma and John become rich and move north.

Johnnie grows up and becomes a sailor. Old and lying on her deathbed, Alma wishes for her son to appear. Instead, Alma's deceased lover, John, appears to her. He resembles Neptune, and he dumps riches over her bed. She leaves with him, and when her son returns, he donates the riches to the Home for Reckless Spenders. A monument is built in the town square in commemoration of Alma Tutwiler. On the monument is inscribed "Bobo."

## COMMENTARY

"The Yellow Bird" is the basis and source text for the plays SUMMER AND SMOKE and THE ECCENTRICITIES OF A NIGHTINGALE. As are the two later works, "The Yellow Bird" is a study of the conflict between the soul and the flesh, or spirituality versus carnality. In this version of events in Alma Tutwiler's life, the flesh has clearly triumphed over the soul. As a result, the short story's protagonist is strikingly—and thrillingly—different from her incarnations in the later two dramas. Here, in her vigorous and hedonistic pursuit of a life of pleasure, she becomes a kindred spirit of John Buchanan Jr., Alma Winemiller's "combatant" and love interest in *Summer and Smoke*.

Alma Tutwiler senses she is trapped in her small-town society and takes out her spiritual and sexual frustrations on her repressive and scandalized parents. She eventually breaks free of her puritanical confines and lives the life she chooses, without remorse or regret. Ironically, she is handsomely rewarded for her rebelliousness by the god Neptune, and her life of pleasure continues in the afterlife.

Williams reinvented Alma in the two later works, where she exhibits far more restraint and gentility. Alma's passions are significantly repressed, which subjects her to comments about her eccentricities and slightly odd and old-fashioned behavior. Had Alma remained as she is portrayed in "The Yellow Bird," the two dramas that evolved from this text would have become two very different tales. Although she is repressed in the later retellings of the Alma stories, the passionate essence of Alma Tutwiler resurfaces in such characters as Cassandra Whiteside (*BATTLE OF ANGELS*), Carol Cutrere (*ORPHEUS DESCENDING*), and Valerie Coynte (MISS COYNTE OF GREENE).

## PUBLICATION HISTORY

"The Yellow Bird" was published in *Town and Country* (1947), *One Arm* (1948), *Great Tales of the Modern South* (1955), *Collected Stories* (1985), and *Stories of the Modern South* (1986).

## CHARACTERS

**Stuff** Stuff is a soda jerk and lover of Alma Tutwiler. He is roughly 10 years younger than Alma. Although he has many girlfriends, Alma is his favorite.

**Tutwiler, Alma** At the beginning of the story, Alma is a quiet, reserved minister's daughter; later she breaks out of oppressive conservatism to become a free spirit. Alma moves to New Orleans, becomes a prostitute, moves north with her son, and dies as a rich old woman.

**Tutwiler, Mrs.** She is the Reverend Tutwiler's wife and the mother of Alma. Mrs. Tutwiler witnesses her daughter's rebellion and entry into a life of prostitution, which cause her spells.

**Tutwiler, Reverend Increase** He is a well-respected member of a small community. When his daughter, Alma, rebels against their conservative lifestyle, he is devastated that he can no longer control her.

# *You Touched Me!*

A play in three acts written with DONALD WINDHAM in 1942.

## SYNOPSIS

The action of the play takes place in a country mansion in rural England during the spring of 1942.

*Act 1, Scene 1*

The time is morning. Matilda Rockley and her aunt, Emmie Rockley, sit in the living room. Matilda mindlessly polishes silver while Emmie laments the presence of a fox that is terrorizing the local vicinity. Emmie describes the details of her impending visit from the rector, the Reverend Melton. The maid, Phoebe, delivers a wire from Matilda's adopted brother, Hadrian. He is a fighter pilot who is on leave and wishes to visit the Rockley estate. Emmie and Matilda despise and fear Hadrian because he has an unknown bloodline. Matilda's drunken father, Captain Cornelius Rockley, celebrates this news by drinking and singing old sailor tunes.

Hadrian sneaks into the house and startles Matilda. He hides behind furniture as Matilda rushes into the garden to assist Emmie with the captain. Emmie and the captain return to the living room bickering about Hadrian. He overhears them and plays his penny flute to reveal himself.

*Act 1, Scene 2*

A few hours later tea is served in the garden. Matilda rushes into the living room to escape interaction with Hadrian. Emmie follows her to say that she fears that the captain will leave his room and embarrass her in front of the Reverend Melton. Hadrian enters to find Matilda. Cornelius escapes from his room, and Phoebe hurries him into his cabin near the garden. Hadrian and the Reverend Melton join Emmie and Matilda in the living room. Emmie and Matilda try desperately to hide the fact that the captain is home. When Hadrian begins to talk about change and liberation, Matilda sends him to guard Captain Rockley.

The captain tells Hadrian tales of his seafaring days. Emmie and the Reverend Melton become better acquainted, discovering that they are similar. Cornelius escapes from the cabin and swears crudely as he chases Phoebe through the living room and into the kitchen. Emmie is mortified and runs up the stairs in tears.

*Act 2, Scene 1*

Later that evening Matilda and Emmie return from a women's meeting at the church. Hadrian and Cornelius hide in the cabin and eavesdrop on their conversation. When Emmie calls them out, Cornelius apologizes for his bad behavior. Emmie orders Cornelius to go to sleep in the cabin. She and Hadrian discuss the resentment and hostility that exist between them. Hadrian sends Cornelius up to his bedroom and takes his place in the cabin.

During the night there is a raucous in the henhouse. Matilda and Emmie hurry downstairs from their bedrooms. Emmie rushes into the garden with a shotgun. Matilda enters the cabin to check on her father. While caressing his forehead, Matilda discovers it is Hadrian's.

*Act 2, Scene 2*

The next morning, Palm Sunday, Matilda and Hadrian converse uncomfortably at the breakfast table. Hadrian joins Cornelius for coffee in the cabin. Matilda and Emmie eavesdrop on their conversation about Emmie's frigidity and Matilda's potential spinsterhood. Hadrian professes to the captain his romantic intentions toward Matilda, and Emmie barges in to confront him. Cornelius declares that unless Matilda weds Hadrian, she and and Emmie will be cut out of his will. Emmie rushes out to seek the Reverend Melton's assistance. Hadrian confesses his love to Matilda. Matilda tells him that Emmie has taught her to fear him. They talk about their past together, and Matilda agrees to marry him. When Emmie returns, she orders Matilda to her room. She fumes at Hadrian as he leaves to obtain a marriage license.

*Act 3, Scene 1*

Later that evening, Emmie sleeps in a chair in the living room. Phoebe awakens her with a telegram for Hadrian. Matilda creeps down the stairs from her bedroom. Emmie tells Matilda that she is going to commit Cornelius to an asylum for alcoholics. Emmie is trying desperately to hold on to her inheritance, so she tells her niece that Hadrian wants to marry her only for her money. She then hurries Matilda back upstairs as Hadrian and Cornelius return from a drunken spree. Cornelius discusses his views about frigid virginity with Hadrian. The

Reverend Melton arrives to persuade Cornelius to attend a Christian retreat. Cornelius becomes violent and bloodies Melton's nose.

Hadrian tricks Matilda to open her bedroom door and step out into the hallway. As he rushes into Matilda's bedroom, Emmie races out of her room and locks Matilda's door, locking Hadrian inside. Emmie calls the police, and she and Cornelius fight ferociously on the stairs. Hadrian climbs out the bedroom window and reenters the house through the front door. As they wait for the police to arrive, the fox makes another appearance in the henhouse. Cornelius provokes Emmie to grab the shotgun and kill the fox. Hadrian takes Matilda in his arms as two gunshots ring out. A Policeman arrives to collect Hadrian, but Matilda dismisses him. To ponder her options, Matilda leaves for the night.

### *Act 3, Scene 2*

At dawn the next morning, Matilda returns. She and Hadrian embrace as Emmie is heard calling for Phoebe. Matilda runs to her room to gather some of her belongings. Hadrian waits outside as Cornelius and Emmie discuss his abrupt departure. Cornelius tells Emmie that the Reverend Melton has asked for permission to marry her. Matilda and Hadrian make a gleeful escape and Emmie departs for church services stunned and elated.

## COMMENTARY

Inspired by a D. H. Lawrence short story of the same title, *You Touched Me!* is a romantic comedy in which Williams (in collaboration with Donald Windham) explores the conflict between soul and flesh. That allegorical struggle resurfaces throughout Williams's work. This theme is most prominently featured in the argument about spiritual love versus physical love that occurs in both *SUMMER AND SMOKE* and *THE ECCENTRICITIES OF A NIGHTINGALE*.

Adoption is not a common theme for Williams; however, here he uses it as a vehicle to explore the fading importance of class structure and family heritage. Hadrian is a young man who understands familial ties through a veil of strain, resistance, and turmoil. Williams exposes the injustices created by living with a system of ideals based on pedigrees. Hadrian is an orphan, who rejects his role as a "charity boy" and becomes a decorated war hero. He shatters the rubric of class and social standing as he is virtuous, dutiful, and gentlemanly.

Emmie is persistent in belittling Hadrian, making him feel low-bred. She closely resembles other Williams characters, such as Mrs. Critchfield and Amanda Wingfield, who live by an arbitrary system of class and protocol, regardless of how miserable it makes them or those around them.

Hadrian's character is rooted in the life of the Roman emperor Hadrian (A.D. 76–138), a famous leader and the protégé and adopted son of Trajan. When he became emperor, Hadrian immediately met resistance and resentment among older military and political leaders. His peers immediately plotted against him, as Emmie and Matilda plot against Williams's Hadrian. Captain Rockley mirrors Trajan: He delights in the idea of having a protégé despite the apparent and unhealthy obstacles that Hadrian faces. Much to the chagrin of his sister, Emmie, and his daughter, Matilda, Hadrian becomes a Rockley, the male heir to the family estate.

## PRODUCTION HISTORY

MARGO JONES directed the first production of *You Touched Me!* at the Playhouse in Cleveland, Ohio, in October 1943. The first New York production of the play was in September 1945 at the Booth Theatre. Guthrie McClintic and Lee Shubert directed the production with Montgomery Clift in the role of Hadrian.

## PUBLICATION HISTORY

*You Touched Me!* was first published in 1947 by New Directions.

## CHARACTERS

**Melton, Reverend Guildford** The Reverend Melton is a pompous Anglican vicar. He pursues a platonic compassionate relationship with Emmie Rockley. He is only amused by his own wit, intellect, and humor.

**Phoebe** She is a servant in the home of Cornelius and Emmie Rockley. Phoebe is a simple woman who tolerates her drunken boss, Cornelius

Rockley, and the constant war between Cornelius and his sister.

**Rockley, Captain Cornelius** Cornelius is a retired British sea captain. He is the biological father of Matilda Rockley and the adoptive father of Hadrian. Cornelius adopted Hadrian as a way of giving meaning to his life. He also took this orphan home as an ally against the tyranny of his spinster sister, Emmie Rockley. When Hadrian leaves the estate, Cornelius becomes a drunk. Hadrian returns as a war hero and helps Cornelius fight Emmie.

**Rockley, Emmie** Emmie is a prim, middle-aged British spinster, who lives with her brother, Captain Cornelius Rockley, and her niece, Matilda Rockley. Emmie is lonely and unhappy, and as a result, she is harsh and judgmental to Cornelius and Matilda. Emmie despises her adopted nephew, Hadrian Rockley, and she mistreats him to the point that he leaves as soon as he is old enough to join the military. Proud of her virginity, Emmie is smitten by the Reverend Melton and hopes to marry him.

**Rockley, Flight Lieutenant Hadrian** Hadrian is the adopted son of Cornelius Rockley. He is a dashing young pilot in the Royal Canadian Air Force during World War I. Hadrian returns to the Rockley estate as a decorated war hero. He introduces a progressive worldview to challenge their classist and archaic perspectives on society, suffering, and war. Abhorred by his oppressive aunt, Emmie Rockley, and feared by his adopted sister, Matilda Rockley, Hadrian extends warmth and respect to the only family he has known. He is met with resistance from Emmie but wins the heart of Matilda.

**Rockley, Matilda** Matilda is the timid and naive daughter of a former sea captain, Cornelius Rockley. She lives a sheltered life under the watchful eye of her aunt, Emmie Rockley. Matilda is afraid of adventure and of her adopted brother, Hadrian Rockley, who ultimately wins her heart.

# PART III

# *Related Entries*

**Albee, Edward** (1928– ) *American playwright, producer, and director; literary peer and friend of Williams's.* Edward Albee entered the American theater scene in the late 1950s. Albee's plays, which exposed the agonies and disillusionment of contemporary American life, startled critics and audiences alike and changed the landscape of American drama. Many critics and scholars have hailed Albee as the most immediate successor to Williams's theatrical legacy. As do Williams's, Albee's dramas form a body of work that is recognized as unique, uncompromising, controversial, elliptical, and provocative.

During the early 1960s Williams, Albee, and their fellow playwright WILLIAM INGE were all targeted by conservative critics for the "queer material" these critics perceived in their works. Drama critics such as Howard Taubman warned audiences that these three gay playwrights were "purveying an unwholesome version of masculinity and femininity" by depicting "weak male and strong female characters" (Woods, 11) onstage.

Albee's masterpiece, *Who's Afraid of Virginia Woolf?* (1962), which is centered on the theme of illusion, appearance, and reality, is said by some to be a continuation of the conflictual marriage of Margaret (Maggie the Cat) and Brick Pollitt in *CAT ON A HOT TIN ROOF.* Albee's other works include *The Zoo Story* (1959) and *A Delicate Balance* (1966).

### Further Reading

Woods, Gregory. "The 'Conspiracy' of the 'Homintern.'" *The Gay & Lesbian Review Worldwide* 10, no. 13 (May–June 2003): 11–13.

**The American** The principal legitimate theater in SAINT LOUIS, MISSOURI. Touring productions from Broadway were performed at the American and provided Saint Louis audiences with an opportunity to see prominent actors, such as TALLULAH BANKHEAD and LAURETTE TAYLOR, in exceptional productions. Williams regularly attended performances at the American while growing up in Saint Louis. His most profound experience was seeing ALLA NAZIMOVA playing Mrs. Alving in HENRIK IBSEN's *Ghosts* in 1934.

**American Academy of Arts and Letters** An honorary academy of notable U.S. artists, writers, and composers. Founded in 1904, the American Academy of Arts and Letters was created to recognize American achievement in the arts. In 1944, Williams was awarded a grant of $1,000 in recognition of his dramatic achievements. Williams was recommended for the honor by the New Directions chief executive, JAMES LAUGHLIN, who praised him as the most talented and promising young writer being published by New Directions. Admission into the academy is considered one of the highest honors an American artist can achieve.

**antagonist** The major character opposing a hero or a protagonist. Williams possessed an amazing ability to weave antagonistic traits into many of his characters so that the lines of good and evil are often blurred. Dramatic friction is caused by the characters' unpredictability. Williams believed that his poet-characters were always "tragic antagonist[s]," because they searched for the pure in an impure world, fighting against the tide of social order.

**antihero** A protagonist lacking heroic qualities such as courage, idealism, and honesty. Williams presents many antiheroes in his pursuit to portray people as realistically as possible. He claims the antihero is an appropriate image of modern humankind, seeking a moral truth, but devoid of a natural path. The antihero or "negative saint" is faced with a different and more dangerous world in the modern age. Driven more from within than without, Williams's antihero acts according to his or her own social constraints, pressures, and personal anxieties. The results are not necessarily heroic but are always characteristic. He once stated, "I don't believe in villains or heroes—only right or wrong ways that individuals have taken, not by choice but by necessity or by certain still-uncomprehended influences in themselves, their circumstances, and their antecedents." Tom Wingfield of *THE GLASS MENAGERIE* is a prime example of a Williams antihero who chooses to serve himself by escaping his obligations to his mother and sister. Tom does not soldier on and assume the responsibility of the breadwinner; instead, he escapes the pressure and oppressive atmosphere, to be forever haunted by this choice. Tom succeeds in preserving his life and mental well-being but certainly does not respond to his moral dilemma with traditional heroics.

**Ashley, Elizabeth** (1939– ) *American actor.* Elizabeth Ashley is one of the premier interpreters of Williams's female characters. A close friend of the playwright's, Ashley made a promise to him to assay as many of his female roles as possible. In the late 1970s, Williams elicited "a blood oath" (Evans, 8) from Ashley (with her mother serving as the witness) whereby she promised she would continue to work on his plays indefinitely.

Williams was particularly keen for her to perform the leading roles in *THE MILK TRAIN DOESN'T STOP HERE ANYMORE*, *THE RED DEVIL BATTERY SIGN*, *SWEET BIRD OF YOUTH*, and *THE GLASS MENAGERIE*. Her 2001 portrayal of Amanda Wingfield in *The Glass Menagerie* (Hartford Stage Company, Hartford, Connecticut) marked a quarter-century of Ashley's distinguished work on Williams's plays. She shares Williams's Southern background (she was born in Florida and raised in Louisiana), and she was notably the first Southerner to play Maggie Pollitt ("Maggie the Cat") in *CAT ON A HOT TIN ROOF*. It was during the successful Broadway revival of *Cat on a Hot Tin Roof* in 1974 that the two became acquainted.

### Further Reading

Evans, Everett. "Role of a Lifetime: Actress Elizabeth Ashley Honors Commitment to Tennessee Williams," *Houston Chronicle*, August 26, 2001, p. 8.

**awards** Williams was the recipient of numerous national and international awards, which included two fellowships from the Rockefeller Foundation (1939 and 1940); a grant from the American Academy of Arts and Letters (1944); the New York Drama Critics Circle Award for *THE GLASS MENAGERIE* (1945), *A STREETCAR NAMED DESIRE* (1948), *CAT ON A HOT TIN ROOF* (1955), and *THE NIGHT OF THE IGUANA* (1962); the Sidney Howard Memorial Award for *The Glass Menagerie* (1945); the Donaldson Award for *A Streetcar Named Desire* (1948); the Pulitzer Prize for *A Streetcar Named Desire* (1948) and *Cat on a Hot Tin Roof* (1955); the Brandeis University Creative Award (1965); the Gold Medal for Drama by the American Academy of Arts and Letters and the National Institute of Arts and Letters (1969); the National Theatre Conference Annual Award (1972); the Centennial Medal of the Cathedral Church of Saint John the Divine (1973); the Medal of Honor for Literature by the National Arts Club (1975); and the Entertainment Hall of Fame Award (1974). In addition, Williams received two honorary degrees, from the University of Missouri (doctor of humanities, 1969) and the University of Hartford, Connecticut (doctor of literature, *honoris causa,* 1972). The citation for the Centennial Medal of the Cathedral Church of Saint John the Divine recognized Williams as the "foremost dramatist of our day, whose compassion for the suffering of others has served to increase the sensitivity of an insensitive age, and replace stones with human hearts."

# B

**Bankhead, Tallulah** (1903–1968) *American actor, friend of Williams's.* Williams first met Tallulah Bankhead, a fellow Southerner, in Provincetown, Massachusetts, in 1940. Williams had hoped that Bankhead would perform the role of Myra Torrance in *BATTLE OF ANGELS,* his first professionally produced work. Bankhead refused, and the role was played by Miriam Hopkins. Years later, Bankhead did play another part Williams wrote for her, BLANCHE DUBOIS in *A STREETCAR NAMED DESIRE.* Bankhead performed in *Streetcar* at the Coconut Grove Playhouse in Miami, Florida, and the City Center Theater in New York in 1956. After her Miami performance, Williams languished over what he called Bankhead's assault upon the role of Blanche. Williams's remarks about Bankhead's performance were subsequently reprinted in *Time* magazine. Williams apologized to Bankhead publicly in the *New York Times.* On opening night of the run at the City Center Theater in New York, Williams knelt at Bankhead's feet and apologized again. Bankhead is said to have accepted his apologies and two dozen roses with queenly dignity. These two incidents are referenced in Williams's autobiographical work, SOMETHING CLOUDY, SOMETHING CLEAR, in which Bankhead is represented by the character Tallulah.

**Beckett, Samuel** (1906–1989) *Nobel Prize–winning Irish playwright, poet, and novelist.* Beckett achieved international fame with his landmark play *Waiting for Godot.* Written in 1949 and published in English in 1954, *Waiting for Godot* established Beckett as the leading voice of the THEATER OF THE ABSURD. Williams admired the work of Beckett and was instrumental in introducing him to U.S. audiences. Beckett's works are concerned with human suffering and survival and expose the existential anguish of the 20th-century human being.

Although Williams is not generally considered a member of the Absurdist school of thought, many of his works possess elements and techniques similar to those of Beckett. Both writers often depict characters beset by guilt and loss of purpose, individuals who struggle against meaninglessness in a world that is little more than a desolate void. This is most apparent in the later works of the Williams dramatic canon, notably *IN THE BAR OF A TOKYO HOTEL, OUT CRY, THE TWO CHARACTER PLAY,* and *I CAN'T IMAGINE TOMORROW.*

**Bowles, Jane** (1917–1973) *American novelist, playwright, literary colleague, and friend of Williams's.* Her works include *Two Serious Ladies* (1943), *A Quarrelling Pair* (1945), *In the Summer House* (1953), and *Plain Pleasures* (1966). Williams regarded Bowles as "the finest writer of fiction" in the United States. He admired her "unique sensibility," which he found even more appealing than that of CARSON MCCULLERS (*Memoirs,* 159–160). Williams was particularly fond of Bowles's play *In the Summer House* and named the gazebo of his Key West home "the Jane Bowles Summer House." Williams met Bowles and her husband, PAUL BOWLES, in Mexico in 1940.

### Further Reading

Williams, Tennessee. *Memoirs.* Garden City, N.Y.: Doubleday, 1975.

**Bowles, Paul** (1910–1999) *American composer, author, and translator.* Bowles was one of the preeminent composers of music for the U.S. theater. He created numerous musical compositions for Williams's plays, including *THE GLASS MENAGERIE, SUMMER AND SMOKE, SWEET BIRD OF YOUTH,* and *THE MILK TRAIN DOESN'T STOP HERE ANYMORE.* Bowles greatly admired Williams's dramatic works, but he also found Williams to be an excellent lyricist. Paul Bowles set four of Williams's poems ("Heavenly Grass," "Lonesome Man," "The Cabin," and "Sugar in the Cane") to music for the suite *Blue Mountain Ballads,* published by Schirmer in 1946. Bowles's composition for Williams's poem "Heavenly Grass" was used as incidental music in *ORPHEUS DESCENDING.* Paul Bowles and his wife, JANE BOWLES, met Williams in Acapulco in 1940. They all remained lifelong collaborators and close friends.

Marlon Brando as Stanley Kowalski and Jessica Tandy as Blanche DuBois in the Broadway production of *A Streetcar Named Desire (Eileen Darby)*

**Brando, Marlon** (1924–2004) *American actor.* Marlon Brando achieved international acclaim through his portrayal of Stanley Kowalski in the 1951 film of *A STREETCAR NAMED DESIRE,* directed by ELIA KAZAN. Brando originated the role on Broadway in 1947. His acting style, characterized by sexual dynamism, physical vibrancy, and a brooding intensity, became legendary. Brando's performance is considered the definitive portrayal of the character, and all other "Stanleys" are measured by his success.

For Williams, Brando was possibly the "greatest living actor . . . greater than Olivier" (Williams, 83). He believed Brando possessed an onstage presence and charisma that corresponded to that of LAURETTE TAYLOR in its "luminous power" (Williams, 131). Brando also brought this legendary charisma and vigor to his portrayal of Val Xavier in the film version of *ORPHEUS DESCENDING,* entitled *THE FUGITIVE KIND* (1960).

### Further Reading

Williams, Tennessee. *Memoirs.* Garden City, N.Y.: Doubleday, 1975.

**Breton, André** (1896–1966) *French poet, essayist, critic, editor, and chief promoter of surrealism.* Breton began his career as a dadaist but soon turned to SURREALISM as a medium of artistic expression. Breton's manifestos are the most important statements of this artistic movement. Breton and the surrealists drew from the works of French poets Charles Baudelaire and Arthur Rimbaud. Williams was strongly influenced by the surrealists' use of vivid imagery, ambiguous sexuality, and inclination toward severe despair. The results of these influences are evident in *THE NIGHT OF THE IGUANA, SUDDENLY LAST SUMMER,* and *SWEET BIRD OF YOUTH,* among others. Williams's trademark is his talent for combining the fantastical tones of the surrealists with a REALISM much like that of Anton Chekhov. Breton and his brand of surrealism emphasized the unconscious mind's wealth of thoughts, opinions, and intellect as the true response to life. In his *Manifeste du surréalisme* (published in 1924), he defines *surrealism* as an expression of the authentic thought process, without the confines of reason. Williams adopts a surrealist stance in his creation of unconventional characters who determine their own boundaries and exist outside the limitations of their respective societies.

**Byron, George Gordon, Lord** See Lord Byron, in CAMINO REAL.

**Capote, Truman** (1924–1984) *American novelist, celebrated man-about-town, and literary associate of Williams's.* Capote is best known for his novella *Breakfast at Tiffany's* (1958). Williams met Capote in 1948 aboard a luxury liner bound for New York. Williams was on his way to the Broadway premiere of SUMMER AND SMOKE. The two became friends and often traveled abroad together. Like Williams, Capote was a Southerner and the Deep South provided the setting and background for much of Capote's fiction. The friendship soured significantly when excerpts of Capote's then novel in progress, *Answered Prayers* (published posthumously in 1986), was published in *Esquire* magazine in 1975–76. It contained passages about a character called "Mr. Wallace," an acclaimed U.S. playwright from the South, who was described as "a chunky, paunchy, booze-puffed runt with a play moustache glued above laconic lips." It was very apparent that Capote's "Wallace" was a cruel send-up of Williams. In response to Capote's attack, Williams composed a very curt letter to the magazine's editor. However, he was advised to maintain a dignified silence and was dissuaded from sending the letter.

**Cassidy, Claudia** (1905?– ) *Influential U.S. arts critic and cultural writer for the* Chicago Tribune. Cassidy has written commentaries that have greatly influenced the course of music, dance, and theater in Chicago for more than seven decades. She attended the Chicago premiere of THE GLASS MENAGERIE at the Chicago Civic Theatre on December 26, 1944. For her *The Glass Menagerie* was a "tangible, taut and tentacled play . . . that gripped players and audiences alike, and created one of those rare evenings in theatre that make 'stage struck' an honorable word" (Cassidy, *Tribune*). Her enthusiastic reviews and regular support of the play were instrumental in preventing an early closure of the production because of poor box office receipts. She championed the play and predicted its overwhelming future success. Audiences eagerly responded to Cassidy's personal crusade for the play, and a complete turnaround at the box office resulted: Tickets became virtually impossible to obtain. The play was a huge success, proceeded to Broadway, and became one of the most famous modern American plays. Claudia Cassidy's perceptive eye changed the course of Williams's career and American theater history.

### Further Reading

Cassidy, Claudia. "Fragile Drama Holds Theater in Tight Spell" *Chicago Daily Tribune*, December 27, 1944, p. 11.

**Chekhov, Anton Pavlovich** (1860–1904) *Great Russian playwright and short fiction writer.* His work often depicts the provincial aristocracy during the period before the Russian Revolution. The stifling and oppressive atmosphere that Chekhov creates in such works as *Three Sisters* and *The Cherry Orchard* is echoed in Williams's depiction of the plight of the gentry in the modern American South. In his *Memoirs*, Williams writes, "It has often been said that [D. H.] Lawrence was my major literary influence. . . . Lawrence was, indeed, a highly simpatico figure in my literary upbringing, but Chekhov takes precedence as an influence." It was during the summer of 1934 that Williams became enamored of the "delicate poetry" he found in the works of Chekhov, particularly in his short stories.

Williams believed that Chekhov's play *The Seagull* was "the greatest of modern plays." In 1980, Williams paid homage to his predecessor in his adaptation of *The Seagull*, called *THE NOTEBOOK OF TRIGORIN*. Chekhov is also the name given to the character known as the Writer in *THE LADY OF THE LARKSPUR LOTION*.

**Clurman, Harold** (1901–1980) *Stage director, critic, author, and teacher who shaped modern American theater.* Clurman was the founder of the GROUP THEATRE, along with Irwin Shaw and Molly Day Thacher. The organization was already very well known for being EUGENE O'NEILL's resident theater as well as for introducing CLIFFORD ODETS's talent to the theater world when it awarded Williams the prize of $100 for three plays in the collection *AMERICAN BLUES*. Through this association, Williams was introduced to his longtime literary agent, AUDREY WOOD.

**Crane, Hart** See Crane, Hart, in *STEPS MUST BE GENTLE*.

# D

**Dakin, Reverend Walter Edwin** (1857–1955) Walter Dakin was born April 23, 1857, in Harveysburg, Ohio. He studied at Eastman Business College in Poughkeepsie, New York, and subsequently found work as an accountant in Marysburg, Ohio, where he met his future wife, ROSINA ISABEL OTTE DAKIN. They were married on October 10, 1883. Less than a year later, on August 19, 1884, their only daughter, Edwina Estelle, was born. Walter attended seminary for the Episcopalian ministry at the University of the South in Sewanee, Tennessee, and obtained his teaching license in the late 1880s; on March 23, 1895, he was ordained to the Episcopal deaconate.

During the early years of his ministry, he moved at least six times, from Ohio to Tennessee to Mississippi, until he was appointed to Saint Paul's Church, Columbus, Ohio, in 1905, and the family settled in the rectory in Second South Street in Columbus. In 1913, he was appointed to the Church of the Advent in Nashville, Tennessee; after two years, the family relocated to Canton, Mississippi. On December 31, 1915, the Dakin family, including his married daughter (EDWINA ESTELLE DAKIN WILLIAMS) and two grandchildren (ROSE ISABEL WILLIAMS and Thomas Lanier [Tennessee] Williams), moved to Clarksdale, Mississippi, where "life was a stencil of gracious living in the Old South" (Spoto, 10). The Reverend Dakin remained in Clarksdale, at Saint George's Church, for 14 years, until his retirement in 1931, after which he and Rosina moved to Memphis, Tennessee.

Variously described as a bon vivant and as selfish and self-important, he also was known to be kind, liberal, and erudite. Walter Dakin became a surrogate father to his grandchildren, Rose and Tom, in whom he sparked an interest in the written word early on. Despite his seemingly traditional religious background, his philosophy and outlook were broad-minded. The Bible stories he told to the children were interspersed with recitations from Milton, Homer, Shakespeare, and Poe, and he instilled a lifelong love of travel in his elder grandson. In the summer of 1928, Tom accompanied him on a parish tour of Europe, which was preceded by a visit to New York and, importantly, Tom's first experience of Broadway.

In the summer of 1935, Williams's "fantastically unworldly grandfather" (Leverich, 151) entrusted his and Rosina's life savings to a pair of unknown con men, and as a result the elderly couple became financially dependent on Edwina and her temperamental spouse, CORNELIUS COFFIN WILLIAMS. In 1941, he and Rosina moved to SAINT LOUIS, MISSOURI, to live with their daughter and resentful son-in-law. The situation became even more unbearable after the death of Rosina in 1944 and the reverend's virtual blindness. In 1948, Tom took his grandfather to KEY WEST, FLORIDA, and, the following year, bought a house for him on Duncan Street near his and FRANK MERLO's home. Walter Dakin loved his grandson unconditionally and was accepting of his sexual orientation. He was intrigued by "gay culture," which he found rather elite and stylish.

In the fall of 1949, the Reverend Dakin was treated for minor skin cancer. He died on February 14, 1955, at Saint Barnes Hospital, Saint

Louis. Williams donated $1,000 to the University of the South in Sewanee in memory of his grandfather, who, unlike his father, accepted, inspired, and encouraged him. This gentle man is also remembered in the character Nonno (Jonathan Coffin), the world's oldest poet in *THE NIGHT OF THE IGUANA*.

### Further Reading

Leverich, Lyle. *Tom: The Unknown Tennessee Williams.* New York: W. W. Norton, 1995.

Spoto, Donald. *The Kindness of Strangers.* Boston: Da Capo, 1997.

**Dakin, Rosina Isabel Otte** (1863–1944) Rosina was born in 1863 in Buffalo, New York, the daughter of German immigrants. Raised in Marysville, Ohio, she attended the Roman Catholic boarding school in Youngstown and subsequently the Conservatory of Music in Cincinnati. After her return to Marysville, she met WALTER EDWIN DAKIN, whom she married on October 10, 1883. Their daughter, Edwina Estelle, was born on August 19, 1884.

While her husband studied for the Episcopal ministry, she began to augment the family income by working as a music teacher and seamstress, activities she never abandoned, even after the family's financial situation improved. From 1909, when EDWINA ESTELLE DAKIN WILLIAMS returned to her parental home, to 1918, when Edwina's husband, CORNELIUS COFFIN WILLIAMS, moved his family to SAINT LOUIS, MISSOURI, Rosina cared for her grandchildren, ROSE ISABEL WILLIAMS and Thomas Lanier (Tennessee) Williams, allowing Edwina to resume her active social life. When Edwina became seriously ill after the birth of her last child, DAKIN WILLIAMS, in 1919, her mother moved to Saint Louis to care for the children again, much to the delight of Rose and Tom. For them the move and the separation from their grandparents had been traumatic. Reserved, serious, and frugal, "Grand"—as Tom and Rose would always call her—was the counterpoise to their grandfather's extrovert personality, and in many ways she became her grandson's conscience and angel.

The question "What would Grand think of this?" (Spoto, 12) turned into a moral guideline. Throughout her life she financially supported her grandchildren, enabling Edwina and the children to take a holiday in the summer of 1925 and paying for Rose's violin lessons and her tuition at Hosmer Hall as well as Tom's college fees. It was she and the Reverend Dakin to whom Tom turned after his nervous breakdown in 1935, when he stayed with them in Memphis to recover. Tom discovered in November 1941 that she had lung cancer, when she visited Saint Louis to consult specialists. Over the next two years she would slowly waste away from the disease, and her grandson would pay at least some of her medical expenses after he began a job as a contract writer for METRO-GOLDWYN-MAYER. She died at the Williams home in Saint Louis on January 6, 1944, after a horrific hemorrhage. Williams was present when his grandmother died, but poignantly he scheduled an eye operation for the day of her funeral, because he could not bear to see dead the "only member of my family that I cared for very deeply" (Leverich, 432). Williams paid tribute to his grandmother in several of his works, such as "GRAND," "ANGEL IN THE ALCOVE," "ORIFLAMME," and *THE LONG STAY CUT SHORT, OR THE UNSATISFACTORY SUPPER*.

### Further Reading

Leverich, Lyle. *Tom: The Unknown Tennessee Williams.* New York: W. W. Norton, 1995.

Spoto, Donald. *The Kindness of Strangers.* Boston: Da Capo, 1997.

**Dowling, Eddie (Joseph Nelson Goucher)** (1889–1976) *Pulitzer Prize–winning American producer, playwright, songwriter, director, and actor.* Eddie Dowling codirected the premiere production of *THE GLASS MENAGERIE* with MARGO JONES in 1945. Dowling also originated the role of Tom Wingfield in this production, which also featured LAURETTE TAYLOR as Tom's overbearing mother, Amanda Wingfield.

**Dramatists Guild** In 1940 the Dramatists Guild awarded Williams $1,000 to return to New York (he was in Saint Louis) to work on his plays. He was invited by John Gassner to attend a play writing seminar at the New School for Social Research.

# E–G

**expressionism** A 20th-century literary and artistic movement, which evolved in part as a reaction against realism and naturalism, and in part as a revision of impressionism. In expressionism, the artist's gaze is turned inward, and emphasis is placed upon the thoughts and images rooted within the artist's mind over those that precisely reflect the outside world. The results are often distorted, dreamlike, or nightmarish. The origins of expressionism lay in the works of such painters as Wassily Kandinsky (1866–1944) and Oscar Kokoschka (1886–1980) and the playwright AUGUST STRINDBERG (1849–1912). In American literature, expressionism appeared most prominently in the dramatic writings of EUGENE O'NEILL (1888–1953) and Elmer Rice (1892–1967). In fine art, JACKSON POLLOCK (1912–56) was the exemplar of abstract expressionism. Many of Williams's dramatic works, particularly his later plays, are prime examples of the expressionistic tradition, particularly *CAMINO REAL* and *SOMETHING CLOUDY, SOMETHING CLEAR.*

**Flanner, Janet (Genet)** (1892–1978) *American novelist, translator, and journalist.* Flanner is best known for her fortnightly "Letter from Paris," which she contributed to the *New Yorker* magazine from 1925 to 1978, under the pen name Genet. A prominent figure in the American lesbian expatriate community of Paris, Flanner met Williams and his partner, FRANK MERLO, in Rome during the summer of 1949. Flanner's life partner, the Italian writer Natalia Danesi Murray, developed a working relationship with Williams and served as the dialect coach and personal assistant to Italian screen star ANNA MAGNANI during the filming of *THE ROSE TATTOO* and *ORPHEUS DESCENDING.* Flanner greatly admired Williams's dramatic writings and declared him "the strangest theatre contributor of our time, anywhere. He makes the angry young men of London seem merely furious socialists and Red Brick College (i.e., poor boys) graduates" (Flanner, 308–309). The plucky American journalist Meg Bishop in *THE ROMAN SPRING OF MRS. STONE* is a portrait of the feisty Janet Flanner.

### Further Reading

Flanner, Janet. *Darlinghissma: Letters to a Friend.*, edited by Natalia Danesi Murray. New York: Random House, 1985.

**García Lorca, Federico** (1898–1936) *Spanish playwright and poet.* Williams admired García Lorca's acute imagery and employment of universal characters. As García Lorca incorporated elements such as water, the Moon, the Earth, and blood in his literature, Williams followed suit in such works as *THE PURIFICATION* and *THE ROSE TATTOO.* Williams was also influenced by García Lorca's extreme use of the tragic form to convey deep emotion regarding inherent injustice in the world. These elements coupled with ritualized actions produce drama with an ancient and epic quality.

**The Group Theatre** An American theater company founded in 1931 by HAROLD CLURMAN, Lee Strasberg, and Cheryl Crawford. The Group was a pioneering theater collective dedicated to presenting "new American plays of social significance" (Wilmeth, 212). The Group Theatre organized an annual playwriting competition to develop and promote the works of young playwrights. This competition launched Williams's career. In 1939, Williams submitted a collection of three one-act plays, *MOONY'S KID DON'T CRY*, *THE DARK ROOM*, and *THE CASE OF THE CRUSHED PETUNIAS* to the competition and won the $100 prize. His work garnered the attention of AUDREY WOOD, who became his longtime agent.

## Further Reading

Wilmeth, Don B., and Tice L. Miller, eds. *Cambridge Guide to American Theatre*. Cambridge: Cambridge University Press, 1993.

# H

**Hellman, Lillian** (1905–1984) *One of the leading U.S. playwrights of the 20th century.* During Williams's first professional visit to New York City in 1939, he saw the Broadway production of Hellman's *The Little Foxes,* a play that centers on a traditional Southern family at odds with modern changes or the "New South." Starring TALLULAH BANKHEAD, the play won the Drama Critics Circle Award and was lauded for its Chekhovian (see ANTON CHEKHOV) texture. Williams was strongly inspired by this performance, and in his own dramaturgy, he would push the boundaries and complexities of Southern culture beyond Hellman's treatment. In 1968, Hellman presented to Williams the National Institute of Arts and Letters Gold Medal for Drama.

**Hemingway, Ernest** See Hemingway, Ernest, in *CLOTHES FOR A SUMMER HOTEL.*

**homosexuality, gay literature, and Williams** Over the past several years critics and scholars of gay literature and queer theory have fallen into two camps regarding Williams's works. At the center of their debate is the question whether Williams's works should be characterized as exhibiting an "internalized homophobia" or lauded as progressive and revolutionary. As this debate continues, there is little doubt that the latter will ultimately be proven the more accurate assessment, as critics and scholars (re)examine the historical and sociopolitical context surrounding Williams's works and delve more deeply into his entire canon them, beyond the more well-known dramatic works.

GORE VIDAL outlined the historical context (and conflict) surrounding Williams's sexuality and his works in his introduction to Williams's *Collected Stories:*

> It has suited the designers of moral life in the American republic to pretend that there are indeed two teams, one evil and sick and dangerous, and one good and "normal" and straight. . . . Although Tennessee came to feel a degree of compassion for his persecutors, they never felt any for him. For thirty years he was regularly denounced as a sick, immoral, vicious fag and . . . in the fifties, the anti-fag brigade mounted a major offensive. (pp. xxi, xxiii)

The 1960s did not prove much more tolerant, as Gregory Woods recalled:

> In the early 1960s, like-minded critics whipped up a flurry of disquiet around the plays of Williams, WILLIAM INGE and EDWARD ALBEE. That the three major American dramatists were known to be gay was bad enough; that they were purveying an unwholesome version of masculinity and femininity—creating weak male and strong female characters—was seen as intolerable. (p. 11)

In 1963, Howard Taubman, drama critic of the *New York Times,* warned his readers of the need to police dramatic works for putatively "queer" material. Given such open and public hostility in the 1950s and 1960s, it is remarkable that Williams continued to write at all. However, even at the height of his career, in the late 1940s, his works were considered "dangerous." In 1947, *A STREETCAR NAMED DESIRE* "hit the public like a bomb [and] . . . brought the American stage into adulthood because of its sex and hint of homosexuality" (Gardner, A.01).

Homosexuality is more than hinted at in many of Williams's lesser-known and often later dramatic works (such as *NOW THE CATS WITH JEWELLED CLAWS; SOMETHING UNSPOKEN; AND TELL SAD STORIES OF THE DEATH OF QUEENS; THE TRAVELLING COMPANION; STEPS MUST BE GENTLE; SOMETHING CLOUDY, SOMETHING CLEAR;* and *THE REMARKABLE ROOMING-HOUSE OF MME. LE MONDE*) and in his fiction (such as "DESIRE AND THE BLACK MASSEUR," "MISS COYNTE OF GREENE," "SABBATHA AND SOLITUDE," "THE KILLER CHICKEN AND THE CLOSET QUEEN," "ONE ARM," "HARD CANDY," "THE INTERVAL," and "HAPPY AUGUST THE TENTH"). These works are remarkably bold and unapologetic in their treatment of homosexuality. Interestingly, "Happy August the Tenth," which concludes with its two principal female characters' nestling comfortably into a loving lesbian relationship, is one of the few instances of a mutually affirming romantic relationship in Williams's canon. Rightfully, Williams is considered the most important gay writer of the pre-1969 (Stonewall) era.

Williams's most overt and personal treatment of homosexuality is in his *Memoirs* (1973), which is largely a discourse about his "amatory activities." He explained that this emphasis was largely due to the fact that he was "late in coming out, and when I did it was with one hell of a bang" (*Memoirs*, 50). During these later years Williams found pride in his sexuality and in his community, as he stated: "There is no doubt in my mind that there is more sensibility—which is equivalent to more talent—among gays of both sexes than among the 'norms'" (*Memoirs*, 51). Williams saw the gay rights movement as a "serious crusade to assert for its genuinely misunderstood and persecuted minority, a free position in society which will allow them to respect themselves" (*Memoirs*, 50).

### Further Reading

Gardner, Elysa. "Tennessee Williams Is Hotter Than Ever," *USA Today*, October 25, 2003. p. A.1.

Vidal, Gore. "Introduction," in *Tennessee Williams: Collected Stories*. New York: New Directions, 1985, pp. xix–xxv.

Williams, Tennessee. *Memoirs*. Garden City, N.Y.: Doubleday, 1975.

Woods, Gregory. "The 'Conspiracy' of the 'Homintern.'" *The Gay & Lesbian Review Worldwide*. 10, no. 13 (May–June 2003): 11–13.

**Hunter, Kim (Janet Cole)** (1922–2000) *American stage, film, and television actor.* Hunter made her Broadway debut in 1947 as Stella Kowalski in the premiere production of *A STREETCAR NAMED DESIRE*, directed by ELIA KAZAN. She reprised this role in the 1951 film, also directed by Kazan. Hunter won an Oscar (Academy Award) as Best Supporting Actress for her portrayal of this engaging Williams character.

# I

**Ibsen, Henrik** (1828–1906) *Norwegian playwright.* Generally credited as the "father of modern drama," he demonstrated the power of psychological realism. His masterpieces include *Peer Gynt* (1867), *A Doll's House* (1879), *An Enemy of the People* (1883), *The Wild Duck* (1884), and *Hedda Gabler* (1891). His plays often depict individuals in bitter conflict with the norms of their society.

Ibsen's dramatic convention of the "unmasking of a guilty secret" (Spoto, 38) became a major facet of Williams's dramaturgy and is a prominent feature of such works as *A STREETCAR NAMED DESIRE, CAT ON A HOT TIN ROOF, KINGDOM OF EARTH, THE MUTILATED,* and *SUDDENLY LAST SUMMER,* among others.

Ibsen's dramas inspired Williams on the stage as well as on the page. Williams recalled that his most profound encounter in the theater as a young man was attending a production of Ibsen's *Ghosts,* starring Alla Nazimova, at the American Theatre in SAINT LOUIS, MISSOURI, in 1934. *Ghosts* has been described as Ibsen's greatest play, invested with the intensity and fatalism of a Greek drama and the first play to deal with both euthanasia and a clinical comprehension of heredity.

### Further Reading

Spoto, Donald. *The Kindness of Strangers: The Life of Tennessee Williams.* New York: Ballantine Books, 1985.

**Inge, William Motter** (1913–1973) *Pulitzer Prize–winning U.S. playwright and a literary associate and friend of Williams's.* Inge began his theatrical career as a drama critic. In 1943, he moved to SAINT LOUIS, MISSOURI, and joined the staff of the *St. Louis Star-Times.* In December 1944, he was asked to interview Williams, the "local boy" whose play *THE GLASS MENAGERIE* was being produced in Chicago. Inge immediately admired Williams, and when he ventured to Chicago to cover the premiere of *Menagerie,* the two became romantically involved.

Shortly after seeing Williams and *Menagerie* in Chicago, Inge wrote his play *Farther Off from Heaven* and sent it to Williams. Williams liked the play and gave it to his agent, AUDREY WOOD, whose response was less positive than Williams's. Williams introduced Inge to MARGO JONES, who produced *Farther Off from Heaven* in Dallas, Texas, in 1947. His success was confirmed with his next work, *Come Back, Little Sheba.* Williams, Jones, and Wood all loved the work, which premiered in New York in 1950. Williams was instrumental in launching Inge's career. Inge never forgot this and thanked Williams for his support and encouragement by dedicating *The Dark at the Top of the Stairs* (1957), his last work, to Williams. Inge's other works include *Picnic* (1953) and *Bus Stop* (1955).

### Further Reading

Cuoco, Lorin, and William Gass, eds. "William Inge," in *Literary St. Louis: A Guide.* St. Louis: Missouri Historical Society Press, 2000, pp. 203–207.

**International Shoe Company (I.S.C.)** Williams worked from 1931 to 1934 at a branch of the International Shoe Company, located at Fifteenth and Delmar Streets in SAINT LOUIS, MISSOURI. After spending three years at the UNIVERSITY OF MISSOURI and failing the Reserve Officers Training Corps (ROTC) course there, Williams was forced by his father, CORNELIUS COFFIN WILLIAMS, to withdraw from the university. Cornelius financed a short typing course for his son and then promptly obtained a position for him as a clerk/typist at the warehouse of the Continental Shoe Makers, earning $65 per month.

Williams detested the position and referred to it as his "season in hell." The work was monotonous and tiring: dusting hundreds of pairs of shoes each morning, carrying heavy cases of them across town in the afternoon, and typing endless lists of figures. What he did enjoy about the position was the camaraderie with his coworkers, the daily exchange of talk about movies, stage shows, and radio programs. He began to write at night, scheduling himself one short story a week. Occasionally he would write poetry in the lid of shoe boxes during the day at work.

His time at the shoe warehouse was invaluable to him as a writer. He learned firsthand the fate of the white-collar worker trapped in a hopelessly routine job. The experience endowed him with a compassion for the working class. Williams deducted the three years he spent at the International Shoe Company from his actual age, as he felt he did not truly live during those years. This has been a source of confusion for biographers and researchers. The International Shoe Company (as I.S.C. and/or Continental Shoe Makers) is referenced in several works such as *THE GLASS MENAGERIE*, *A LOVELY SUNDAY FOR CREVE COEUR*, and *STAIRS TO THE ROOF.*

**Isherwood, Christopher** (1904–1986) *British-born U.S. novelist, pioneer of the gay liberation movement, friend and literary associate of Williams's.* Isherwood is best known for *The Berlin Stories* (1933), a series of stories about life in pre–World War II Germany. Isherwood's vivid and vibrant tales are the basis for the play *I Am a Camera* and the popular musical *Cabaret.* Williams considered Isherwood one of his most valued friends and allies.

# J

**Jones, Margo** (1911–1955) *American director, producer, and friend of Williams's.* Jones was the originator of the regional theater movement in the United States. She founded Theatre '47 in Dallas, Texas, the name changing with the year; it became the Margo Jones Theatre, after her death. Jones maintained that theater should be happening in every community of the United States. She believed that every locale "with a population of over one-hundred-thousand could sustain a theatre," and it was the responsibility of "competent theatre people to go to such an area and create a fine theatre" (Lea, 481). For Jones, theater in America needed to be more than exclusively a Broadway experience.

Margo Jones, artistic director of Theatre '47, Dallas, Texas *(Photograph courtesy of the Billy Rose Theatre Collection, New York Public Library)*

Although she was devoted to producing classical plays, particularly those of HENRIK IBSEN, Jones was also a champion of new U.S. playwrights and new play development. Jones was a loyal promoter of Williams's work throughout her life. She nurtured him and directed the premieres of many of his works, including *YOU TOUCHED ME!* (1943), *THE PURIFICATION* (1944), *THE GLASS MENAGERIE* (codirected with EDDIE DOWLING, 1945), and *SUMMER AND SMOKE* (1947).

Williams and Jones had a lifelong professional relationship and friendship. The two had similar personalities and were very close friends. Because Jones accompanied Williams to numerous public engagements, rumors spread that they were romantically involved. However, their relationship was strictly platonic. It has been said that Williams's one-act play *SOMETHING UNSPOKEN* details Jones's relationship with a wealthy, older woman, whom she accompanied on a worldwide tour as her secretary and companion. Williams playfully described this "strong-willed, magnetic and fiery" (Spoto, 99) woman as a "Texas tornado" (ibid.).

## Further Reading

Lea, Florence M. "Margo Jones," in *Notable Women in the American Theatre,* edited by Alice M. Robinson, Vera Mowry Roberts, and Milly S. Barranger. New York: Greenwood Press, 1989.

Sheehy, Helen. *Margo: The Life and Theatre of Margo Jones.* Dallas: Southern Methodist University Press, 1989.

Spoto, Donald. *The Kindness of Strangers: The Life of Tennessee Williams.* Boston: Little, Brown, 1985.

# K

**Kazan, Elia** (1909–2003) *American stage and film director.* Elia Kazan was considered by many to have been the foremost American director of stage and screen. He won two Best Director Academy Awards for his direction of *Gentleman's Agreement* (1947) and *On the Waterfront* (1954). He collaborated with Williams frequently and successfully throughout his career. His work with Williams included stage and screen versions of *A STREETCAR NAMED DESIRE* (staged 1947, filmed 1951) and *BABY DOLL* (1956). Kazan's directorial style was noted for its psychological and emotional depth. In his work with actors, such as MARLON BRANDO, Kazan focused on the development of an on-screen life that possessed a high-charged intensity and profound sexual vibrancy. Kazan's style of direction matched the intense realism of Williams's dramas. Of Williams's writing Kazan once stated:

> One comes out of his plays feeling that particular mixture: sadness transmuted into joy, the two together or the one unexpectedly following the other. Also this: that despite ourselves we may have a chance after all. One feels—gratitude. His concern is humanity and what can be found there to sing about and respect. Still he is anything but bland: his words have sharp teeth. (Spoto, 378–379)

### Further Reading

Spoto, Donald. *The Kindness of Strangers: The Life of Tennessee Williams.* Ballantine Books: New York, 1985.

**Key West, Florida** An island located at the southwestern end of the Florida Keys, 55 miles from mainland Florida and 90 miles from Havana, Cuba. The town of Key West, the southernmost city in the

Tennessee Williams in Key West *(Don Pinder)*

United States, was incorporated in 1828. Key West was then, and is now, a mecca for painters, writers, and artists, a "haven for those who choose to drop out of conventional society" (Williams, "Homage," 162). For Williams, this tropical locale was a paradise, where "time past has a wonderful way of remaining time present. I once wrote a line, 'The day turns holy as though God moves through it.' That's the way I feel about Key West" (Lang, 66).

Williams's attachment to Key West began when he arrived in 1941, at a time when the island was "still affected by the presence of Ernest Hemingway" ("Homage," 160). Williams sought solace and refuge in Key West after the first important disaster in his career (see *BATTLE OF ANGELS*). In 1950, Williams and his life partner, FRANK MERLO, bought a small Bahamian house at 1431 Duncan Street.

Key West was Williams's favorite setting in which to write, and he became one of the island's favorite residents. In 1970, Williams was made an honorary "Conch" (Key West native) by Mayor Gerald Staundberg. In 1980, the Florida Keys Community College established the Tennessee Williams Fine Arts Center, which opened with the premiere production of *WILL MR. MERRIWETHER RETURN FROM MEMPHIS?* (1964), which Williams himself directed. Key West is referenced in Williams's late play *THE GNÄDIGES FRÄULEIN*, which is set in the fictional "Cocaloony Key." As did Williams, the principal character of the play retreats to this tropical isle to recover from an artistic disaster and reinvent herself.

### Further Reading

Lang, John. "In Key West, They Like to Live on the Edge." *U.S. News & World Report,* April 9, 1984, 64–66.

O'Reilly, Jane. "In Key West: Where Writers Get Top Billing," *Time,* February 6, 1984, 11–13.

Williams, Tennessee. "Homage to Key West," in *Where I Live: Selected Essays,* edited by Christine R. Day and Bob Woods. New York: New Directions, 1978, pp. 160–164.

# L

**Lanier, Sidney** (1842–1881) *American poet and musician.* An ancestor of Williams, Sidney Clopton Lanier was born February 3, 1842, in Macon, Georgia. Educated at Atlanta's Olgethorpe College, he was inspired by the works of Byron, Tennyson, Scott, and other romantic writers. Known as America's "Sweet Singer of Songs," Lanier created poetry that is marked by its melodic verse and extravagant conceits. His haunting and musical poetry reflected his love of nature and the Old South of his boyhood and is among the best Southern writing of the 19th century. Lanier's first novel, *Tiger-Lilies,* published in 1867, was based on his experiences during the Civil War. His study of the interrelation of music and poetry, *The Science of English Verse,* was published in 1880. His *Poems* was published posthumously in 1887. He died at the age of 39, a victim of tuberculosis contracted during the war.

Williams was quite proud of his literary ancestor. Through the Lanier family line, Williams was also a descendant of Valentine Xavier, the younger brother of Saint Francis Xavier, whose name Williams would take when he converted to Roman Catholicism. As a fledgling writer, Williams briefly called himself Valentine Xavier.

**Laughlin, James, IV** (1914–1997) *U.S. publisher, friend of Williams's.* Laughlin founded New Directions publishing house in 1936, while he was still an undergraduate at Harvard University. With New Directions he went on to publish, often the first to do so, such authors as Williams Carlos Williams, Vladmir Nabokov, Dylan Thomas, FEDERICO GARCÍA LORCA, Yukio Mishima, Djuna Barnes, Rainer Maria Rilke, Lawrence Ferlinghetti, Henry Miller, and Ezra Pound.

Laughlin quickly gained a reputation for publishing innovative works by unconventional and daring writers. In 1944, he published an anthology of poetry entitled *Five Young American Poets,* which included poems by such young writers as Williams and CLARK MILLS. Williams contributed 40 pages of poetry to the anthology. This collaboration was the start of a lifelong author-publisher relationship.

**Lawrence, D. H.** See Lawrence, D. H., in *I RISE IN FLAME, CRIED THE PHOENIX.*

**Leigh, Vivien (Vivian Mary Hartley)** (1913–1967) *Award-winning British actor.* Leigh is noted as one of the most successful interpreters of Williams's female characters. Williams described Leigh as "an actress of great talent which has steadily grown through meeting the challenge of many classical roles, Greek, Shakespearean, Restoration, and Shaw, while still appearing so masterfully in such American films as *Gone with the Wind* and A STREETCAR NAMED DESIRE" (Williams, *Where I Live,* 127–128). Leigh will always be remembered for her Academy Award (Oscar)–winning portrayal of two of the most compelling women in American literature, Scarlett O'Hara and Blanche DuBois.

Leigh first appeared as Blanche in the first British production of *A Streetcar Named Desire* in 1949. She was then selected to play the role in the 1951 film version of the play. Leigh was chosen for the film over JESSICA TANDY, who had originated the role on the U.S. stage in 1947. Leigh had the advantage of being a recognizable screen name over the then relatively unknown Tandy. Many also believe Leigh was chosen because of her highly successful portrayal of the quintessential Southern heroine, Scarlett O'Hara. John Russell Taylor acknowledged that the role of Blanche was in many ways a "natural successor" (Taylor, 86–87) to Scarlett, as the two shared an obsession with their ancestral home (Tara and Belle Reve) and suffered from the rapid decay of the South. These two roles proved to be the "twin peaks" (ibid.) of Leigh's career. Vivien Leigh's performance as Blanche was considered by many, including Williams, to be the definitive portrayal of that character.

In 1961, Leigh appeared in the screen version of *THE ROMAN SPRING OF MRS. STONE*. Leigh's portrayal of the complicated Karen Stone, another romantically tragic character, who is desperate for love and denied the "consolations of beauty, peace and spiritual grace," is said to have been "one of [Leigh's] finest" (Quirk, 181).

### Further Reading

Quirk, Lawrance J. *The Great Romantic Films.* Secaucus, N.J.: Citadel Press, 1974.

Taylor, John Russell. *Vivien Leigh.* London: Elm Tree Books, 1984.

Williams, Tennessee. "Five Fiery Ladies," in *Where I Live: Selected Essays,* edited by Christine R. Day and Bob Woods. New York: New Directions, 1978, pp. 127–128.

**Mabie, E. C.** Williams studied playwriting under Professor Mabie at the UNIVERSITY OF IOWA. Their relationship was rocky, as Mabie often cruelly referred to Williams as "the sissy." Despite Mabie's contempt for Williams and his distaste for Williams's dramaturgy, Williams respected him. Williams also admired Mabie's intellect as well as his contributions to the Federal Theatre Project (Mabie was the regional director as well as a founding designer of the Works Progress Administration program).

### Further Reading

Leverich, Lyle. *Tom: The Unknown Tennessee Williams.* New York: W. W. Norton, 1995.

**Magnani, Anna** (1908–1973) *Award-winning Italian actress.* Anna Magnani was renowned for her portrayals of earthy, passionate female characters. Williams first met Anna Magnani in Rome in 1950, while there on holiday with his life partner, FRANK MERLO. Merlo, who was Italian American, mediated between the two. Magnani and Williams became immediate and lifelong friends.

Williams introduced Magnani to U.S. audiences in the film version of *THE ROSE TATTOO* (1955). Her portrayal of the fiery Serafina Delle Rose was considered the highlight of her acting career. Critics and audiences were enthralled by her great beauty and her remarkable film presence. She won the Academy Award (Oscar) for Best Actress for her performance. Magnani captivated U.S. audiences again when she portrayed the strong-willed Lady Torrance in THE *FUGITIVE KIND,* the screen version of *ORPHEUS DESCENDING,* in 1959. The film, directed by Sidney Lumet, paired Magnani with MARLON BRANDO.

Anna Magnani died of cancer at the age of 65. Williams sent 20 dozen roses for her cortege. Williams's 25-year friendship with Magnani is the subject of Franco D'Alessandro's play *Roman Nights* (2002).

**McCullers, Carson** (1917–1967) *American novelist, poet, and playwright.* One of Williams's dearest friends, Carson McCullers was a leading figure in Southern fiction and American literature. She is renowned for her exploration of spiritual and social alienation in a Southern milieu. Her works include *The Heart Is a Lonely Hunter* (1940), *The Member of the Wedding* (1946), *The Ballad of the Sad Cafe* (1951), *The Square Root of Wonderful* (1958), *Clock without Hands* (1961), and *Sweet as a Pickle, Clean as a Pig* (1965). Kindred in spirit to Williams's, McCullers's works offer sensitive and compassionate depictions of individuals in isolation. Her characters, as Williams's, are usually outcasts and misfits whose need for love is never fulfilled.

In 1940, after reading *The Heart is a Lonely Hunter,* Williams wrote to McCullers, stating that he wanted to meet her. He invited her to spend the summer with him on Nantucket. The two writers spent the summer working together at the ends of a long table. Williams drafted *SUMMER AND SMOKE,* while McCullers—at Williams's suggestion—adapted her novel *The Member of the Wed-*

Anna Magnani and Williams in Key West, Florida, during the filming of *The Rose Tattoo* *(Photograph courtesy of the Billy Rose Theatre Collection, New York Public Library)*

*ding* for the stage. This was the start of a lifelong friendship. McCullers developed a strong connection with Williams and his sister, ROSE ISABEL WILLIAMS. The three spent several Christmases together at McCullers's home in Nyack, New York. Williams referred to McCullers as "Sister-Woman," and Rose simply called her "C."

McCullers's life was as complex as her fiction. She married, divorced, and remarried the same man, Reeves McCullers. Carson and Reeves were both openly and actively bisexual. Williams witnessed and recorded in his *Memoirs* episodes of their turbulent relationship, which ended with Reeves's suicide in 1953. Reeves's death was but one of the many tragedies in McCullers's life. Williams often wrote to MARIA ST. JUST about his concern for McCullers: "[She has had] so much tragedy in her life that it scares you almost into feeling indifferent to her, as if she were hopelessly damned and you couldn't afford to think about it: the way I feel for my sister." (St. Just, 113).

Williams clearly understood McCullers's "isolation and longings" (ibid., 116). In the introduction to her novel *Reflections in a Golden Eye,* he wrote:

> If artists are snobs it is . . . not because they wish to be different and hope and believe that they are, but because they are forever painfully struck in the face with the inescapable fact of their difference which makes them hurt and lonely enough to want to undertake the vocation of artists . . . [with] a sense, an intuition, of an underlying dreadfulness in modern experience.

In the preface to her novel *The Heart Is a Lonely Hunter* he declared that McCullers possessed a great "heart and the deep understanding of it, but in addition she had that 'tongue of angels' that gave her power to sing of it, to make of it an anthem." As did his sister, Rose, Carson McCullers's artistry and fragile, tragic beauty served as inspiration to Williams and surfaced continually in his work. For example, in the preface to THE ROSE TATTOO, Williams cites the concluding line of one of McCullers's lyric poems: "Time, the endless idiot, runs screaming 'round the world."

### Further Reading

St. Just, Maria, ed. *Five O'Clock Angel: Letters of Tennessee Williams and Maria St. Just, 1948–1982*. New York: W. W. Norton, 1990.

Williams, Tennessee. "Introduction," in *The Heart Is a Lonely Hunter.* Boston, Houghton Mifflin, 1967.

———. "Introduction," in *Reflections in a Golden Eye.* New York: Bantam, 1974.

**Merlo, Frank Philip** (1922–1963) *Williams's life partner of 16 years.* Williams and Merlo met in Provincetown, Massachusetts, in the summer of 1947. Their relationship began at nearly that very moment and lasted until Merlo's death in 1963. Merlo, a handsome, self-educated navy veteran of Sicilian descent, was born and raised in Brooklyn, New York. His union with Williams provided the playwright with emotional stability and a real and much-needed sense of "home." The couple bought a house in KEY WEST, FLORIDA, at 1431 Duncan Street, in 1950. Locals still recall Merlo as a kind and gentle soul and a man who possessed a real sense of civility and "humanity." Merlo was a positive and stabilizing force in William's hectic and often self-destructive life. Artistically, Merlo served as a muse for Williams. Merlo opened the world of Italian, and particularly Sicilian, culture to Williams, which he embraced wholeheartedly. This exposure to the culture of Italy, with the help of a native son as a guide, was the catalyst for Williams to create such works as THE ROSE TATTOO and THE ROMAN SPRING OF MRS. STONE and the source for the Italian/Sicilian elements found in such works as ORPHEUS DESCENDING and BABY DOLL. Williams dedicated the *The Rose Tattoo* to Merlo in honor of his sharing his culture with the author.

In the early 1960s their relationship began to deteriorate as a result of Williams's repeated infidelities with other men. Merlo was diagnosed with lung cancer and succumbed to the disease in 1963. Williams was at Merlo's bedside when he died, and the playwright memorialized that traumatic time—Merlo's final days—in a scene in the highly autobiographical play, SOMETHING CLOUDY, SOMETHING CLEAR! Williams was devastated by the loss of the greatest love of his life, and as a result he slipped into a severe depression. He turned to drugs and alcohol to ease his pain. Williams referred to the period following Merlo's death as his "stoned age." In his MEMOIRS Williams wrote: "As long as Frank was well, I was happy. He had a gift for creating life, and, when he ceased to be alive, I couldn't create a life for myself. So I went into a seven-year depression" (194). Donald Spoto believes that the two female lovers in the short story "HAPPY AUGUST THE TENTH" were modeled on Williams and Merlo and that the delicate love story of Horne and Elphinstone is in fact a "gentle tribute" (Spoto, 294) to their relationship. A similar connection can also be drawn to the dashing, young male couple in NOW THE CATS WITH JEWELLED CLAWS. David P. Foley offers a dramatic rendering of Williams and Merlo's long-term relationship in his play *Sad Hotel.*

### Further Reading

Foley, David P. *Sad Hotel.* New York: Theatre Communications Group, 1999.

Spoto, Donald. *The Kindness of Strangers: The Life of Tennessee Williams*. Boston: Little, Brown, 1985.

Williams, Tennessee. *Memoirs*. Garden City, N.Y.: Doubleday, 1975.

**Metro-Goldwyn-Mayer (MGM)** With the help of his agent, AUDREY WOOD, Williams became a scriptwriter for MGM in 1943. Williams was suspended from scriptwriting duties when he did not complete the work he was assigned. Williams despised this position, calling the Hollywood writers around him "hacks." Williams resisted writing the neatly packaged scripts with happy endings that MGM required. He hoped that his screenplay "The Gentleman Caller" (later developed into THE GLASS

MENAGERIE) would relieve him from his contractual obligations at MGM, such as having to write what he termed a "celluloid brassiere" for Lana Turner.

**Mielziner, Jo** (1901–1976) *American theatrical designer.* Mielziner made his Broadway debut in 1924. He worked on more than 200 Broadway productions designing sets and often lighting. Mielziner designed the production of nine plays for Williams: A STREETCAR NAMED DESIRE, CAMINO REAL, SWEET BIRD OF YOUTH, and CAT ON A HOT TIN ROOF. In appreciation, Williams dedicated his play SUDDENLY LAST SUMMER to his memory.

**Miller, Arthur** (1915–2005) *Pulitzer Prize–winning American playwright, novelist, and a literary associate of Williams's.* In comparing these two great American playwrights, Kenneth Tynan stated:

> Miller's plays are hard, "patrist," athletic, [and] concerned most with men. Williams's are soft, "matrist," sickly, [and] concerned mostly with women. What links them is their love for the bruised individual soul and its life of "quiet desperation." (Tynan, 141)

Miller, whose most noted works are *All My Sons* (1947), *Death of a Salesman* (1949), and *The Crucible* (1953), believed that Williams was a truly revolutionary artist whose lasting gift to the American theater was a profound sense of "eloquence and an amplitude of feeling" (Centola, 203). The American theater, according to Miller, never truly recognized or fully appreciated its indebtedness to Williams's first success, THE GLASS MENAGERIE. The works of Williams, Miller once stated, are "as permanent in the vision of this century as the stars in the sky" (203).

Williams held a similar admiration for Miller. He once stated that he "looked up to" Miller (Devlin and Tischler, 234) and felt a bona fide and "unmistakable beam of satisfaction" (ibid., 235) upon learning that Miller's play *Death of a Salesman* had been well received by the press. Williams himself found the work "a deep, human play, warmly felt and written with a great simple dignity which comes out of Miller's own character." (ibid.). ELIA KAZAN, who directed the premiere of *Salesman,* acknowledged that Miller had "learned from *Streetcar* how easily nonrealistic [theatrical] elements" in a drama "could be blended with the realistic ones" (Kazan, 361).

### Further Reading

Centola, Steven, ed. *Arthur Miller: Echoes down the Corriodor—Collected Essays 1944–2000* New York: Viking, 2000.

Devlin, Albert J, and Nancy M. Tischler. *The Selected Letters of Tennessee Williams,* vol. 11, *1945–1957.* New York: New Directions, 2004.

Kazan, Elia. *Elia Kazan: A Life.* New York: Alfred A. Knopf, 1988.

Tynan, Kenneth. *Tynan on Theatre.* Baltimore: Penguin Books, 1961, p. 141.

**The Mummers** A small theater group that flourished in SAINT LOUIS, MISSOURI, during the 1930s. Willard Holland, director of the Mummers, asked Williams to write a brief sketch for his company. Williams wrote a 12-minute antimilitary play called *Headlines.* It was presented as a curtain raiser with Irwin Shaw's *Bury the Dead* in 1936. Williams also wrote a full-length play, CANDLES TO THE SUN, for the Mummers. It was a powerful story about coal miners in Alabama.

# N–O

**New Orleans, Louisiana** Williams migrated to New Orleans in 1938 in the hope of being recognized by the Federal Writers Project, a branch of President Roosevelt's New Deal during the depression. In New Orleans, Williams finally found a city in which he could live freely and without the suffocatingly puritanical and depressing atmosphere of SAINT LOUIS, MISSOURI, his hometown. Williams remarked, "It was a period of accumulation, I found the kind of freedom I had always needed, and the shock of it, against the Puritanism of my nature, has given me a subject, a theme, which I have never ceased exploring" (Spoto, 68).

In New Orleans Williams was awakened to a different way of living and viewing the world. He found the eccentric and the downtrodden, the old aristocrats, as well as prostitutes and passerby sailors, living and enjoying the rich culture of the French Quarter. New Orleans provided fodder for his writing and became a distinct setting for many of his plays. His New Orleans literature includes *VIEUX CARRÉ*, "ANGEL IN THE ALCOVE," *AUTO-DA-FÉ*, *AND TELL SAD STORIES OF THE DEATH OF QUEENS*, *LORD BYRON'S LOVE LETTER*, and the most famous, *A STREETCAR NAMED DESIRE*.

### Further Reading

Spoto, Donald. *The Kindness of Strangers: The Life of Tennessee Williams*. Boston, Little, Brown, 1985.

**O'Neill, Eugene** (1888–1953) *Nobel and Pulitzer Prize–winning American playwright.* O'Neill is recognized as one of America's greatest, and possibly its most bleak and pessimistic, dramatists. His later, and most renowned, naturalistic dramas deal with the inevitability of fate: *The Iceman Cometh* (1939), *Long Day's Journey into Night* (1941), and *A Moon for the Misbegotten* (1943). His other significant works include *Anna Christie* (1920), *Desire under the Elms* (1924), and *Ah, Wilderness!* (1933). He won the Pulitzer Prize four times and, in 1936, the Nobel Prize in literature.

Williams and O'Neill share many characteristics in their style and subject matter. In addition they also shared a remarkable coincidental experience. In the spring of 1907, O'Neill attended a production of HENRIK IBSEN's *Hedda Gabler*, with Alla Nazimova playing the title role. According to O'Neill biographer Louis Sheaffer, the playwright was so taken by the production and Nazimova's performance that he saw the play 10 times. Ibsen's play and Nazimova's performance deeply moved and inspired O'Neill and guided his conception of modern theater. It was also Nazimova's commanding performance in Ibsen's *Ghosts* at the American Theatre in Saint Louis, in 1934, which so electrified and transfixed Williams as a youth that he knew immediately he had to write for the stage.

### Further Reading

Sheaffer, Louis, *O'Neill: Son and Artist*. Boston: Little, Brown, 1973.

Sheaffer, Louis. *O'Neill: Son and Playwright*. Boston: Little, Brown, 1968.

# P–R

**Page, Geraldine** (1924–1987) *Prominent American actor.* Page is noted as one of the most successful interpreters of Williams's female characters. Her first notable success was in the role of Alma Winemiller in the 1951 Broadway production of SUMMER AND SMOKE. Hers was considered by many, including Williams himself, the definitive portrayal of this character. Page is said to have brought the character to life precisely as Williams had envisioned her (Steen, 225). Page approached the role of Alma with the philosophy that beneath Alma's extreme femininity and delicacy lie a "will of steel" (Steen, 240). Page re-created the role for film and was nominated for an Academy Award (Oscar) as Best Actress.

Page is also noted for her performance as Princess Kosmonopolis (Alexandra Del Lago) in the play SWEET BIRD OF YOUTH. She won the New York Drama Critics Award and was nominated for the Antoinette Perry (Tony) Award and the Sarah Siddons Award for her performance in the 1959 Broadway production of *Sweet Bird of Youth.* The production, which also featured Paul Newman as Chance Wayne, ran for 375 performances. Page and Newman re-created their roles for the film version of the play in 1962, and Page was again nominated for an Academy Award as Best Actress.

Ironically, Page's first encounter with Williams's work occurred when, as a young woman, she worked as an usher at the Civic Theatre of Chicago during the first, highly successful, run of THE GLASS MENAGERIE in 1945. Page subsequently credited LAURETTE TAYLOR's performance as Amanda Wingfield in that production as the impetus that propelled her into a career on the stage. Williams described Geraldine Page as "the most disciplined and dedicated of actresses, possibly the one fate will select as an American Duse" (*Where I Live,* 128–129).

Anna Magnani with Geraldine Page (right) backstage after a performance of *Sweet Bird of Youth,* 1959 *(Wide World Photos, Inc.)*

### Further Reading

Roberts, Vera Mowry, and Mark Hall Amitin. "Geraldine Page," in *Notable Women in the American Theatre: A Biographical Dictionary,* edited by Alice M. Robinson, Vera Mowry Roberts, and Milly S. Barranger. New York: Greenwood Press, 1989, pp. 709–712.

Steen, Mike. *A Look at Tennessee Williams.* New York: Hawthorn Books, 1969.

Williams, Tennessee. *Where I Live: Selected Essays,* edited by Christine R. Day and Bob Woods. New York: New Directions, 1978.

Young, William C., ed. *Famous Actors and Actresses on the American Stage: Documents of American Theater History.* Vol 2. K–Z. New York: R. R. Bowker, 1975, pp. 901–909.

***Pictorial Review Magazine*** A women's magazine that Williams sold door-to-door in the summer of 1930, during the Great Depression. As were so many other salesmen during this difficult period, Williams was largely unsuccessful in his efforts. His experience selling magazine subscriptions was immortalized in Amanda Wingfield's efforts to sell *The Homemaker's Companion* to her friends in *THE GLASS MENAGERIE.*

**Pinter, Harold** (1930– ) *British dramatist, screenwriter, director, and actor.* Harold Pinter is one of the leading dramatists of the THEATER OF THE ABSURD. His most noted works are *The Birthday Party* (1958), *The Dumb Waiter* (1959), and *The Homecoming* (1965). Williams once stated that he both admired and envied Pinter. Their admiration was mutual and their literary concerns were quite similar. The works of both Williams and Pinter expose the human struggle against victimization.

In 1981, the playwrights shared the honor of being joint recipients of the Commonwealth Award for "excellence and outstanding achievement in various fields of human endeavour" (Billington, 301). In 1985, Pinter directed *SWEET BIRD OF YOUTH,* which featured Lauren Bacall as the aging Alexandra De Lago (Princess Kosmosnopolis), at the Theatre Royal, Haymarket. Pinter's work on Williams was driven not only by his admiration of Williams, but also by his awareness of the sociopolitical dimension of Williams's work—a dimension Pinter believed was "largely ignored by British critics" (ibid.).

### Further Reading

Billington, Michael. *The Life and Work of Harold Pinter.* London: Faber and Faber, 1996.

**plastic theatre** A term Williams used to describe his unconventional theater aesthetic. In his preface to *THE GLASS MENAGERIE,* Williams explains this concept as the incorporation of many theatrical styles such as EXPRESSIONISM and REALISM and the use of different media and poetry to present the fullest artistic expression on the stage. Williams delighted in these unorthodox marriages, calling the results "plastic" and their effect "closer to the truth." Although he considered realism a foundation for his work and often cited ANTON CHEKHOV (a leading figure of the genre) as his primary influence, this dramatic style was not always vivid enough for his dramaturgy.

Ever experimenting with forms to create new and organic art, Williams believed the conventional forms of the U.S. theater ill represented a modern culture. In *WILL MR. MERRIWETHER RETURN FROM MEMPHIS?,* Louise contemplates the theory of plastic space in fine art by strategically composing a table of objects as a painting whose free space or plastic space is just as important as the objects that exist within the space. Richard E. Kramer suggests that Williams was influenced by the artist Hans Hoffman, who coined the term *plastic space.* The principles of plastic theater are also at work in such works as *CAMINO REAL* and *THIS IS THE PEACEABLE KINGDOM.*

### Further Reading

Kramer, Richard E. "The Sculptural Drama: Tennessee Williams's Plastic Theatre," *The Tennessee Williams Annual Review* 5 (2002): 1–10.

**Pollock, Jackson** (1912–1956) *American painter.* Pollock was the leading figure of the abstract expressionist movement (see EXPRESSIONISM). Pollock developed an artistic technique in which he rhythmically "dripped" paint onto enormous horizontal canvases. His physically active style of painting led to the creation of the term *action painting.* Williams first met Pollock while he was writing *THE GLASS*

MENAGERIE in Provincetown, Massachusetts, during the summer of 1944. In many ways the two were kindred spirits: They shared a similar background of disjointed childhoods, dramatic sibling relationships, fluid sexuality, and chronic artistic frustration. Williams and Pollock became close friends and shared a playful association.

Williams greatly admired Pollock, an artist he believed was a heroic and self-destructive figure, who could "paint ecstasy as it could not be written" (*Memoirs*, 250). Williams commemorates Pollock in the character of Mark Conley, the tormented artist at the center of the play *IN THE BAR OF A TOKYO HOTEL*. Many scholars also contend that Pollock, who was often drunk and violent and had a turbulent relationship with his wife, Lee Krasner, may have served as the model for Stanley Kowalski in *A STREETCAR NAMED DESIRE*.

### Further Reading

Naifeh, Steven, and Gregory White Smith. *Jackson Pollock: An American Saga.* New York: C. N. Potter, 1988.

Ruas, Charles. *Conversations with American Writers.* New York: Alfred A. Knopf, 1985, pp. 75–90.

Williams, Tennessee. *Memoirs.* Garden City, N.Y.: Doubleday, 1975.

**Redgrave, Vanessa** (1937– ) *British actress and political activist.* MARIA BRITNEVA, LADY ST. JUST, gave Redgrave a copy of one of Williams's earliest works, *NOT ABOUT NIGHTINGALES*. Redgrave was so taken with the text that she prompted a major production of the work in London in 1998. Redgrave's efforts sparked a revival of interest in the earlier works of Williams. She is also noted for her portrayal of Lady Torrance in *ORPHEUS DESCENDING*.

# S

**St. Just, Maria Britneva, Lady** (?–1994) *Russian-born actress and close friend of Williams's.* Williams and St. Just first met in London in 1948, at a party celebrating the London production of THE GLASS MENAGERIE. The two remained close friends until Williams's death in 1983. They often traveled together, and even when they were not together, they corresponded extensively. In fact, their relationship is recorded in 35 years of letters. St. Just played Blanche DuBois in a 1955 revival of A STREETCAR NAMED DESIRE. Williams loved her interpretation of the character. He wrote to her, "I hope that you are still playing Blanche as well as you can with your whole heart and complete understanding and no intrusive annoyances from the management" (St. Just, 113).

Williams was a frequent guest at St. Just's home, Wilbury Park, where he would relax and write. When Williams died, St. Just was devastated; she claimed never to have fully recovered from the loss of Williams. A cotrustee of his estate, St. Just guarded Williams's unpublished writings and correspondence. She was known for her strident ferocity in protecting and maintaining Williams's reputation and for her strict control over access to Williams's published and unpublished works. She also championed unsuccessfully an attempt to preserve his home in KEY WEST, FLORIDA, as a historic site. St. Just was said to have been the model for Maggie Pollitt in CAT ON A HOT TIN ROOF.

### Further Reading

St. Just, Maria. *Five O'Clock Angel: Letters of Tennessee Williams to Maria St. Just 1948–1982.* New York: Knopf, 1990.

**Saint Louis, Missouri** Williams spent 16 years of his life in Saint Louis (1918–29 and 1932–37). The Williams family moved there from Mississippi in 1918, when Williams's father, CORNELIUS COFFIN WILLIAMS, accepted a position at the INTERNATIONAL SHOE COMPANY. The family lived in a boardinghouse on Lindell Street temporarily then settled in an apartment at 4633 Westminster Place. Williams recalled this location as a "perpetually dim little apartment in a wilderness of identical brick and concrete structures with no grass and no trees" (Cuoco and Gass 1951–69). It was a far cry from his idyllic Southern childhood in rural Mississippi.

In this new locale he also became aware of the fact that there were "two kinds of people, the rich and the poor, and that we belonged more to the latter" (Cuoco and Gass 196). The building has since been renamed the Glass Menagerie Apartments in Williams's honor. The family moved twice more, finally to a cramped apartment at 6254 Enright Avenue. This tenement building is the model for the Wingfield home in THE GLASS MENAGERIE.

Williams was educated at the Eugene Field Public School and Stix School. He attended high school at Blewett School, Soldam High School, and University City High School and then entered Washington University (1936–37). He also spent three years at the University of Missouri at Columbia (1929–32).

Saint Louis also served as Williams's training ground as a dramatist. There he encountered Williard Holland and his theatre company, THE MUMMERS. Williams described the troupe as a dynamic, if disorderly theater group that guided his "professional youth" (Cuoco and Gass 199). The Mummers produced Williams's first theatrical efforts and encouraged his development as an artist.

Ultimately, however, Saint Louis would always represent all the dreadful experiences of his life, such as his parents' marital strife, his sister's mental breakdown, his frequently ailing health, his time spent at the International Shoe Company, and his brief hospitalization in Barnes Psychiatric Hospital. He maintained that Saint Louis was a cold, materialist, "middle-American" sort of place that had no vestige of the romantic aura of the Deep South. His time spent in Saint Louis was "the bitter education" that taught him about the "inequities of society," the starting point of the social consciousness that developed as an inherent feature of Williams's writing (Cuoco and Gass 197).

David Merrick, the theatrical producer and a friend of Williams's, who shared his Saint Louis upbringing, recalled they "received no encouragement from the city" (Brown, 103). Against his wishes and express directives in his will, Williams was buried in Calvary Cemetery, in Saint Louis, beside his mother, EDWINA DAKIN WILLIAMS.

Many of Williams's plays and fiction take place in and around Saint Louis, such as *STOPPED ROCKING*, *ALL GAUL IS DIVIDED*, *A LOVELY SUNDAY FOR CREVE COEUR*, *THE GLASS MENAGERIE*, *THE IMPORTANT THING*, "THE FIELD OF BLUE CHILDREN," and *A PERFECT ANALYSIS GIVEN BY A PARROT*.

## Further Reading

Brown, Dennis. *Shoptalk: Conversations about Theatre and Film with Twelve Writers, One Producer—and Tennessee Williams's Mother*. New York: Newmarket Press, 1992.

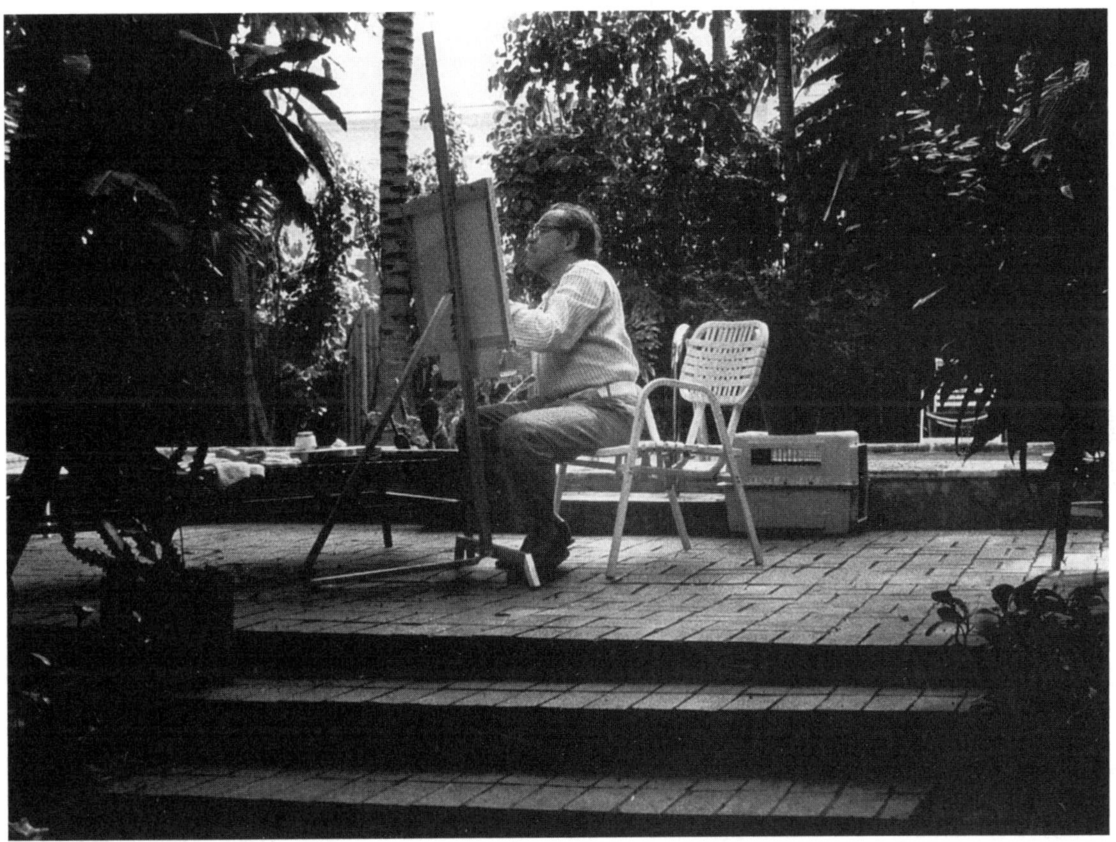

Williams painting in the back garden of his Key West home, 1979 *(Bill Viggiano)*

Cuoco, Lorin, and William Gass, eds. "Tennessee Williams," in *Literary St. Louis: A Guide.* St. Louis: Missouri Historical Society Press, 2000, pp. 194–202.

**the South and Williams** Williams proudly described his ancestors as "pioneer Tennesseeans," and he honored his forebears by claiming "Tennessee" as his nom de plume. Williams's pride in his Southern heritage is also reflected in his writing. He once explained:

> Excuse me for writing mostly about my folks. My own life seems relatively prosaic. I left the South when I entered high school, but frequently returned, home being where you hang your childhood . . . and Mississippi to me is the beauty spot of creation, a dark, wide, spacious land that you can breathe in. (Kozlenko, 174)

The "dark, wide, spacious land" of the American South is prominently featured throughout Williams's dramatic and fictive canon. His works illustrate his cultural identification with and connection to this region. Born in northern Mississippi, raised there and in SAINT LOUIS, MISSOURI, Williams also centered his life in the Southern cities NEW ORLEANS, LOUISIANA, and KEY WEST, FLORIDA.

The Southern landscapes that appear in Williams's works are invested with Williams's deep-set affection and disdain for the region. In his works this part of the world is simultaneously revered and reviled as "the beauty spot of creation" (ibid.) and as "dragon country, the country of pain, . . . an uninhabitable country which is inhabited" (Williams, *Tomorrow,* 138). In numerous plays and short stories, Williams chronicles and depicts a vividly dichotomous South.

The beauty of the South and its romantic, chivalric past are most often chronicled by Williams through memory. The "Old South" is a stinging longed-for dream and a genteel illusion that serves as an escape and a buffer for individuals unable to cope with their tragic realities, such as Amanda Wingfield (in *THE GLASS MENAGERIE*) and Blanche DuBois (in *A STREETCAR NAMED DESIRE*). By contrast, the "new South" is depicted as an active landscape, as opposed to a fantasy dreamscape. This terrain is often a harsh wasteland rife with cruelty, isolation, bigotry, hatred, exploitation, brutality, and racial injustice. This view of the South is revealed in such works as *BABY DOLL, ORPHEUS DESCENDING, THIS PROPERTY IS CONDEMNED, 27 WAGONS FULL OF COTTON, SWEET BIRD OF YOUTH, SOMETHING UNSPOKEN, AT LIBERTY,* and *SUDDENLY LAST SUMMER.*

It has been said that Williams's appreciation of this dichotomous tension in Southern culture was the key to his success. His ability to vividly (and often brutally) convey Southern cultural myths and simultaneously deconstruct these very same myths is considered his greatest achievement as a writer.

### Further Reading

Williams, Tennessee. "Landscape with Figures: Two Mississippi Plays," in *American Scenes,* edited by William Kozlenko. New York: John Day, 1941.

**Stapleton, Maureen** (1925– ) *American actor.* Maureen Stapleton is one of the premier interpreters of Williams's female characters. She has completed an impressive and successful range of Williams's female roles, such as Serafina Delle Rose in *THE ROSE TATTOO* (1951), Flora Meighan in *27 WAGONS FULL OF COTTON* (1955), and Lady Torrance in *ORPHEUS DESCENDING* (1957).

In 1951, she won the Antoinette Perry (Tony) Best Supporting Actress Award for her performance as the passionate and complex Serafina Delle Rose, and in 1969 she received a National Institute of Arts and Letters Award. Stapleton was one of Williams's favorite performers, and he often wrote his plays with her in mind, specifically *STOPPED ROCKING* (which is dedicated to her) and *KINGDOM OF EARTH, OR THE SEVEN DESCENTS OF MYRTLE.* For Williams, Stapleton was a magnanimous performer who possessed an extraordinary gift for characterization.

**State University of Iowa** Williams attended the University of Iowa in 1937. He was drawn to the University of Iowa, as he believed it had the best writing program in the country. At that time the theater program was under the direction of Profes-

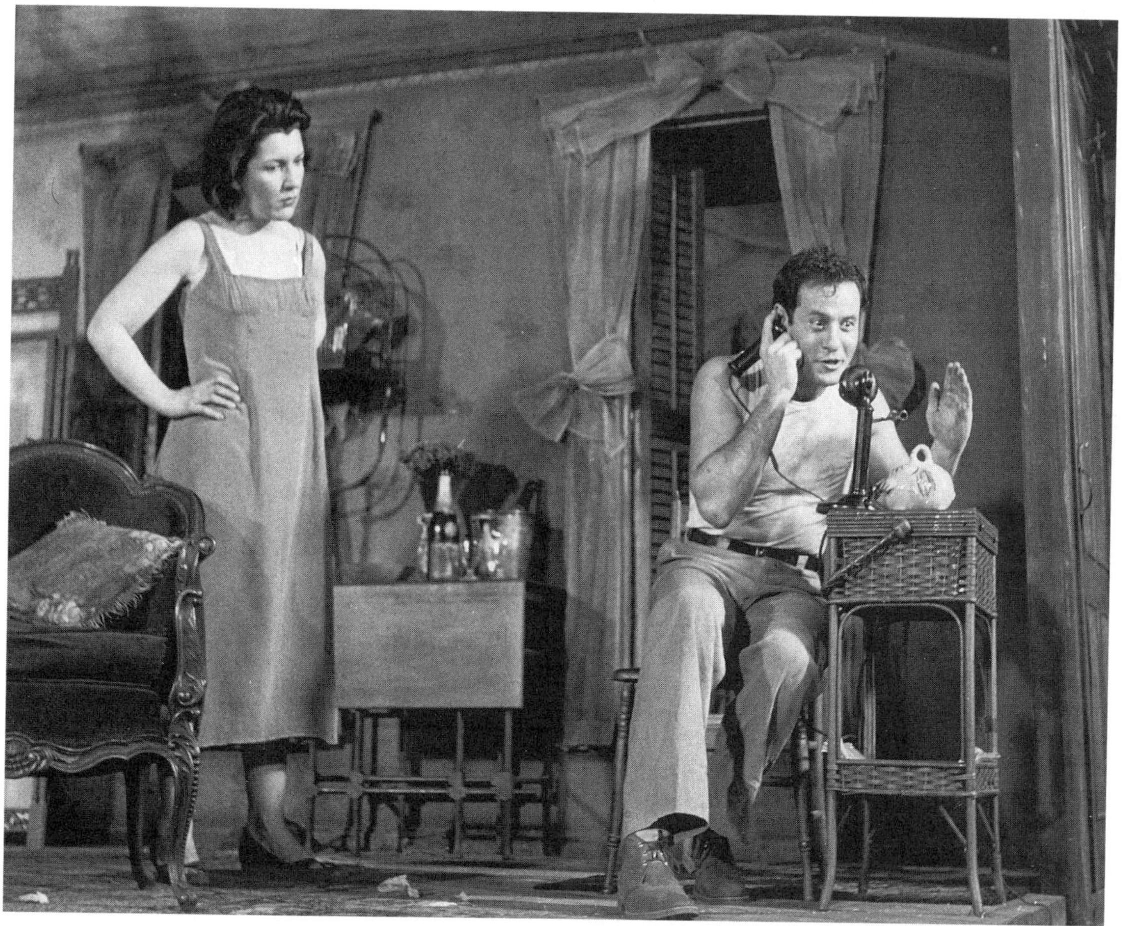

Maureen Stapleton as Serafina Delle Rose and Eli Wallach as Alvaro Mangiacavallo in the Broadway production of *The Rose Tattoo*, 1951 *(George Karger)*

sor E. C. Mabie and Elsworth P. Conkle. (The State University of Iowa is now the University of Iowa.) Here, Williams was relieved of the familial feuds that plagued his family in SAINT LOUIS, MISSOURI, and he was free to embark seriously on his playwriting. During his time at Iowa, Williams wrote *NOT ABOUT NIGHTINGALES* and *SPRING STORM* and revised the *FUGITIVE KIND*.

# T

**Tandy, Jessica** (1909–1994) *British-born American actor.* Tandy was one of the greatest actresses of the 20th-century American stage. After seeing her as Lucretia Collins in *PORTRAIT OF A MADONNA* in 1946, Williams demanded that Tandy be given the lead female role in the production of his latest play,

Jessica Tandy as Blanche DuBois in the Broadway production of *A Streetcar Named Desire,* 1947 *(Eileen Darby)*

*A STREETCAR NAMED DESIRE.* Her portrayal of Blanche DuBois in the original Broadway production of *Streetcar* (1947) was praised overwhelmingly by critics. This role successfully launched Tandy to Broadway stardom, and she won an Antoinette Perry (Tony) Best Actress Award for her portrayal of Williams's most famous female character. Despite her remarkable success in the part, she was not chosen to play Blanche DuBois in the film version of *Streetcar.* The role was given to VIVIEN LEIGH, who was at the time a better-known star.

**Taylor, Elizabeth** (1932– ) *Award-winning English-born American screen actor.* Taylor rose to stardom in the 1950s, after her success in *National Velvet* (1944), *Little Women* (1955), and *Father of the Bride* (1950). At the age of 15, Taylor was declared "the most beautiful woman in the world" (Sonneborn, 213). Taylor contributed her remarkable talent and striking good looks to her legendary performance of Margaret Pollitt ("Maggie the Cat") in the 1958 film version of *CAT ON A HOT TIN ROOF* and received her second Academy Award (Oscar) nomination for her portrayal of Williams's sultry powerhouse. Williams considered Taylor to be one of the greatest cultural phenomena in America, and possibly the "finest raw talent on the Hollywood screen" (*Where I Live,* 131).

### Further Reading

Sonneborn, Liz. "Elizabeth Taylor," in *A to Z of American Women in the Performing Arts.* New York: Facts On File, 2002, pp. 212–214.

Elizabeth Taylor as "Maggie the Cat" in the film version of *Cat on a Hot Tin Roof (MGM, 1958)*

Williams, Tennessee. "Five Fiery Ladies," in *Where I Live: Selected Essays,* edited by Christine R. Day and Bob Woods. New York: New Directions, 1978, pp. 127–132.

**Taylor, Laurette Cooney** (1884–1946) *American actor.* Taylor originated the character of Amanda Wingfield in THE GLASS MENAGERIE for the play's Chicago premiere in 1944 and on its subsequent run on Broadway in 1945. Taylor's performance became legendary and a benchmark for subsequent performers of the role, including Helen Hayes (1956), MAUREEN STAPLETON (1965), and JESSICA TANDY (1983).

Her portrayal of the faded Southern matriarch was considered her greatest acting success and was also her triumphant return to the stage after a considerable absence following the death of her husband, J. Hartley Manners, in 1927. She was so grief-stricken by his death that she withdrew from the stage. Taylor was in her 60s and a confirmed alcoholic when Williams's play reached her. She immediately refused the part, believing her illustrious career had ended, but was prevailed upon to accept it.

Rehearsals for *The Glass Menagerie* were plagued by Taylor's drinking and her reluctance to learn her lines. However, when the production opened in December 1944, Taylor was at the height of her powers and on her way to "creating a legend" (Spoto, 111). Taylor's portrayal of Amanda Wingfield was voted "best performance" of 1945 by the readers of *Variety* magazine. Perhaps the highest praise for Taylor's performance was that by Williams's mother, EDWINA DAKIN WILLIAMS, the prototype for Amanda Wingfield. Mrs. Williams greatly enjoyed Taylor's performance and declared her "a real genius" (Brown, 116). Mrs. Williams admired Laurette Taylor's skill for "adequately capturing the pathos" (Brown, 116) of the character and she proclaimed her the definitive Amanda Wingfield.

### Further Reading

Brown, Dennis. *Shoptalk: Conversations about Theatre and Film with Twelve Writers, One Producer—and Tennessee Williams's Mother.* New York: Newmarket Press, 1992.

Kullman, Colby H. "Laurette Cooney Taylor," in *Notable Women in the American Theatre: A Biographical Dictionary,* edited by Alice M. Robinson, Vera Mowry Roberts, and Milly S. Barranger New York: Greenwood Press, 1989, pp. 857–861.

Spoto, Donald. *The Kindness of Strangers: The Life of Tennessee Williams.* Boston: Little, Brown, 1985.

Young, William C., ed. *Famous Actors and Actresses on the American Stage: Documents of American Theater History,* Vol 2. K–Z. New York: R. R. Bowker, 1975, pp. 1,041–1,053.

**theater of the absurd** A term coined by Martin Esslin to describe a group of dramatic works that strive to expose the absurdity of the human condition. Dramas of this kind present a view of human perplexity and spiritual anguish through a series of connected incidents and patterns of images that present human beings as "bewildered beings in an incomprehensible universe" (Harmon, 2). These plays are generally devoid of a realistic plot or linear time frame, while also possessing a dreamlike or nightmarish quality; they often contain language that consists of "incoherent babblings" and strikingly unusual characters who can be perceived as "mechanical puppets" (Esslin, 21–22).

Eugene Ionesco's play *The Bald Soprano* (1950) is considered by many to be the first genuine example of absurdist drama. The best-known work of this school of thought is Samuel Beckett's *Waiting for Godot* (1955). Other absurdist playwrights who flourished in Europe and the United States in the 1950s and 1960s include HAROLD PINTER and Jean Genet. Although Williams is not widely acknowledged as a principal writer within this genre, many of his dramatic works—particularly those of his late period—exhibit absurdist qualities or undeniably possess an absurdist aesthetic. Thematically, all of Williams's dramatic works exude the fundamentally absurdist philosophy that human beings are very often creatures living in "meaningless isolation in an alien environment" (Harmon, 2).

## Further Reading

Esslin, Martin, *Theatre of the Absurd.* London: Penguin Books, 1961.

Harman, William, and C. Hugh Holman, eds. *A Handbook to Literature.* Upper Saddle River, N.J.: Prentice-Hall, 1996.

# U–V

**University of Missouri** Williams attended the University of Missouri at Columbia between the years 1929 and 1932. At the university, the Dramatic Arts Club produced his then-controversial one-act play *BEAUTY IS THE WORD.* The play centers on a missionary and his family who live among the natives of the South Pacific. The scandalous aspect of the play occurs when the missionary's daughter says that fear and God are dichotomous ideas; her God is one of beauty. Williams also became known for his short story, "THE LADY'S BEADED BAG," published in the college magazine. When Williams failed Reserve Officers Training Corps (ROTC) for the third time, his father, CORNELIUS WILLIAMS, forced him to quit school and take a clerical position at the INTERNATIONAL SHOE COMPANY.

**Vidal, Gore** (1925– ) *novelist, playwright, essayist, literary associate and friend of Williams's.* His major works include *The City and the Pillar* (1948), *The Judgment of Paris* (1953), and *United States* (1993). Williams met Vidal in Rome, Italy, in 1948, shortly after Vidal had achieved fame for his second novel *The City and the Pillar,* which was one of the first national best-sellers to feature an openly gay main character. Vidal wrote the introduction to *Collected Stories,* an anthology of Williams's short stories, published in 1985, two years after Williams's death. Vidal's essay is a remarkable piece of literary and social criticism of Williams's life and art. In it he states:

> [Williams] is not a great short story writer like Chekhov but he has something rather more rare than mere genius. He has a narrative tone of voice that is totally compelling. The only other American writer to have this gift was Mark Twain . . . you cannot stop listening to either of these tellers no matter how tall or wild their tales.

### Further Reading

Vidal, Gore. "Introduction," in *Tennessee Williams: Collected Stories.* New York: New Directions, 1985, pp. xix–xxv.

# W

**Washington University** During the years 1936–37, Williams made his mark as a budding poet and aspiring playwright at Washington University, in SAINT LOUIS, MISSOURI. As members of a literary circle called the Saint Louis Poets Workshop, Williams and his peers sent out poetry to publishers, and Williams was by far the most successful. Seven of his poems were published in *College Verse,* four in *Poetry,* and nine in *The Eliot.* During this time, Williams was also awarded first place in a one-act play competition for *THE MAGIC TOWER,* and he ferociously studied works by August Strindberg, ANTON CHEKHOV, and his favorite poet, Hart Crane (later to appear as a character in Williams's play *STEPS MUST BE GENTLE*). When Williams submitted *ME, VASHYA!* to a college competition and did not win, he furiously withdrew from Washington University and transferred to IOWA STATE UNIVERSITY.

**Webster, Margaret** (1905–1972) *British-born American director.* Renowned for her notable and provocative productions of Shakespeare's plays in America, Margaret Webster directed the premiere production of *BATTLE OF ANGELS,* Williams's first professional produced work, for the Theatre Guild in 1940. Although the production was a professional disaster, Webster was captivated by the play and the talent of its young playwright. To Webster, Williams's drama featured an extraordinary dramaturgy, which possessed "naturalistic dialogue penetrated with poetic diction, the clashing of impassioned central characters, a pervasive sense of humor, and remarkable technical innovations" (Barranger, 112).

### Further Reading

Barranger, Milly S. *Margaret Webster: A Life in the Theatre.* (Ann Arbor: University of Michigan Press, 2004).

**Williams, Cornelius Coffin** (1879–1957) Cornelius Coffin Williams was born in Knoxville, Tennessee, to an old Tennessee family. His father was Thomas Lanier Williams, who traced his lineage to French Huguenots; his mother, Isabel Coffin, was descended from colonists who settled Virginia. Cornelius had two older sisters, Ella and Isabel. His mother died of tuberculosis in 1884, when he was five years old.

He attended Rogersville Synodical College and later Bell Buckle Military Academy, from which he was dismissed. After two years of law studies at the University of Tennessee, he volunteered to serve in the Spanish-American War, during which he acquired a taste for drinking, gambling, and women. He was demobilized as an officer and initially worked in a paralegal position for the telephone company in Memphis after the war. On June 3, 1907, he married EDWINA ESTELLE DAKIN (WILLIAMS) at her father's church in Columbus, Mississippi. The first 18 months of their marriage was spent in Gulfport, Mississippi. His wife returned to her paternal home, and he visited her regularly there. By 1910 his lifestyle, specifically his drinking and gambling, became a topic of public interest in Columbus.

In early summer 1918 he obtained a managerial position with the Friedman-Shelby branch of the INTERNATIONAL SHOE COMPANY in SAINT LOUIS, MISSOURI, and moved his family there in July 1918. Although known and respected among his peers as a shrewd businessman, he began to behave irresponsibly and violently in the domestic sphere. He had little interest in his two elder children, ROSE ISABEL WILLIAMS and Thomas Lanier (Tennessee) Williams, and often called Tom "Miss Nancy," as the boy preferred reading or writing to sports. His youngest son, WALTER DAKIN WILLIAMS, clearly his favorite, was the only one of his children to whom he related. He spent hours listening to sports events on the radio with Dakin. His obvious disappointment in his "unmanly" son was confirmed when Tom failed Reserve Officers Training Corps (ROTC) in 1935. Cornelius reacted by taking his son out of college and getting him a job at International Shoe, which Tom resented to the point of having a nervous breakdown. In 1946 Cornelius retired from the shoe business, with nothing to do but drink and gamble and make life a misery for his wife and despised father-in-law, REVEREND WALTER EDWIN DAKIN, whom he referred to as "the Parson," who had by this time joined them at Arundel Place in Saint Louis.

When Cornelius returned home from the hospital, where he had been admitted after a drunken spree, his wife refused to see him; shortly thereafter she divorced him. In an act of surprising generosity, he gave Edwina the house at Arundel Place as well as half his stock in International Shoe, although the royalties she received from her son's highly successful play *THE GLASS MENAGERIE* (1945) had made her independently wealthy. Cornelius initially lived with his sister, Ella, in Knoxville and then moved into an apartment hotel. Eventually he met a widow from Toledo, Ohio, who became his drinking partner and constant companion until his death in 1957.

**Williams, Edwina Estelle Dakin** Edwina Estelle Dakin was born August 19, 1884, in Marysville, Ohio. She was the only child of REVEREND WALTER EDWIN DAKIN and ROSINA ISABEL OTTE DAKIN. From 1897 she attended Harcourt Place Seminary, Gambier, Ohio. Academic activities, however, took second place to the school chorus, dances, and local parties, not to mention her male admirers at Kenyon College, the local military academy, and the theological school. Between 1901 and 1905 Edwina records no fewer than 45 beaux in her diary. Although she nursed a secret ambition to become an actress, her most successful performance was that of a quintessential Southern belle.

In 1906, while appearing in an amateur production of *The Mikado* in Columbus, she met CORNELIUS COFFIN WILLIAMS, whom she married on June 3, 1907, at her father's church. The couple moved to Gulfport, Mississippi, and the 18 months they spent there were possibly the happiest of their marriage. Pregnant with her first child, ROSE ISABEL WILLIAMS, Edwina returned to her parental home in 1909 and stayed there for the next nine years, regularly visited by Cornelius. In 1910 she became pregnant with their second child, Thomas Lanier (Tennessee) Williams, who was born March 23, 1911.

Edwina Dakin Williams with her children, Rose and Tom *(George Freedley)*

Beautiful, strong-willed, and ambitious, Edwina showed very little talent or inclination for housekeeping duties, but she devoted part of each day to her children, reciting old ballads and acting out folk tales for them. When Tom had a near-fatal bout of diphtheria in 1916 she cared for him around the clock. The lasting psychological effect of this illness was a deep emotional attachment between mother and son. The idyll ended when Cornelius took his family to Saint Louis in 1918. Edwina became pregnant for the third time, and constant financial constraints forced a massive change in her life. Her quest for Southern gentility was sublimated in an unending hunt for better living accommodations that forced numerous moves within Saint Louis. The birth of WALTER DAKIN WILLIAMS on February 21, 1919, sparked a string of illnesses, culminating in the miscarriage of her fourth child in 1921 and incipient tuberculosis.

Edwina and Cornelius spent two weeks on the West Coast in the hope of warding off the disease. The trip was financed by Paul Jamison, Cornelius's employer, who was clearly attracted to Edwina, although their relationship remained platonic. Her marital relationship, however, deteriorated from icy politeness to open hostility, with incidents of physical abuse. Despite this, Edwina attempted to encourage Tom's writing and increasingly presented a cheerful front to protect her children from the effects of the family situation. This was not enough to prevent Rose's increasingly apparent mental illness. Rose was hospitalized repeatedly and for long periods, and in 1943 Edwina gave consent for her daughter to have a prefrontal lobotomy. Although he never forgave his mother for this decision, in 1946 Williams signed over to her half of his royalties for *THE GLASS MENAGERIE,* the play that she inspired. Financially independent at last, she separated from her abusive husband but continued to live at Arundel Place in Saint Louis.

With the assistance of Lucy Freeman, Edwina wrote her memoir, *Remember Me to Tom,* in 1963. Her mental state began to deteriorate, and from the early 1970s onward she was increasingly disoriented and entered a nursing home. When she died in 1980, Williams refused to accept his brother's telephone call notifying him of her death. However, he imported 2,000 English violets—Edwina's favorite flower—to cover her coffin, thus commemorating a relationship characterized by love and resentment.

In addition to Amanda Wingfield in *The Glass Menagerie,* Edwina Dakin Williams is mirrored in such characters as Grace Hart Crane in *STEPS MUST BE GENTLE,* Violet Venable in *SUDDENLY LAST SUMMER,* and Sally McCool in the short story "COMPLETED." Edwina is said to have greatly enjoyed her stage persona Amanda Wingfield, and she particularly favored LAURETTE TAYLOR's interpretation of the part. She considered Taylor "a real genius," who adequately captured the "pathos" of the character (Brown, 116). Alma Winemiller in *SUMMER AND SMOKE* was also fashioned after Edwina and is said to have been her favorite of all her son's characters, in her favorite of his plays. Edwina Dakin Williams was exceedingly proud of her internationally successful son. She once declared, "I'm just like any other mother who thinks her son is of course a genius always" (Brown, 118).

### Further Reading

Brown, Dennis. *Shoptalk: Conversations about Theatre and Film with Twelve Writers, One Producer—and Tennessee Williams's Mother.* New York: Newmarket Press, 1992.

Williams, Edwina Dakin, with Lucy Freeman. *Remember Me to Tom.* New York: Putnam, 1963.

**Williams, Rose Isabel** (1909–1996) Rose Isabel Williams was the first child of CORNELIUS COFFIN WILLIAMS and EDWINA ESTELLE DAKIN WILLIAMS. She was born November 17, 1909, in Columbus, Mississippi. Rose spent her early years under the care of her maternal grandmother, ROSINA OTTE DAKIN, who was known as "Grand." A highly imaginative child, she enjoyed with her brother, Thomas Lanier (Tennessee) Williams, or Tom, a sheltered upbringing as the minister's granddaughter. The family's move from this idyllic locale to the industrial inner city of SAINT LOUIS, MISSOURI, in July 1918 was devastating for Rose. She began absenting herself from school, sitting in the dark, and waiting for Tom to return home. Her father's drunken volatility became extremely unsettling for her, and she increasingly identified with her mother, Edwina, during her long period of illness at this time. In an attempt to take Rose's mind off the family situation, Edwina arranged for her to take violin lessons, which were financed by Grand, an experiment which ended when Rose froze with terror at the Costume Violin Recital in 1922. (This incident is chronicled in the short story "THE RESEMBLANCE BETWEEN A VIOLIN CASE AND A COFFIN.")

Her time as a student at Soldan High School also produced a failure, and she left the school permanently during the first quarter of 1924. Subsequently, she attended Hosmer Hall, a private junior high, and, when Edwina could no longer cope with her rebellious and erratic behavior, she was sent to the All Saints Episcopal junior college in Vicksburg, Mississippi. Upon her return to Saint Louis she was enrolled in Rubicam's Business College to learn stenography. Unable to cope with the workload and unsympathetic teachers, she again missed class and eventually quit. She then attempted two brief subsequent stints of employment, which also did not last. By this time, 1926, she was suffering increasingly from psychosomatic gastric trouble, a condition her mother sought to remedy by a combination of church visits and gentleman callers. Alternating between sexual ravings and a withdrawal that estranged her even from her brother Tom, she was finally confined to a private sanatorium in 1929.

During the early 1930s her mental state declined consistently, and the psychological counseling she received in 1936 did little to halt the process. After she alleged that Cornelius had sexually abused her, she was admitted to a state asylum in Farmington, diagnosed with schizophrenia, and given electric shock therapy treatments in the summer of 1937. She remained at Farmington, where six years later, with her mother's consent, she received a prefrontal lobotomy that left her practically autistic and in need of permanent institutionalization. Her brother Tom was not informed of the procedure until afterward and alternately blamed his mother and himself for not preventing the surgery. Racked with guilt and constantly afraid that the specter of mental illness would affect him, he did not visit Rose until November 1948.

In 1951, Williams had his sister transferred to Stony Lodge in Ossining, New York, and continued to visit her frequently, taking her out for trips and shopping excursions. His attempt to move her out of Ossining altogether in 1979 failed, but he did successfully move her into a private residence in KEY WEST, FLORIDA, for a short time. He engaged one of their cousins as her companion, but the arrangement lasted for less than a year, and Rose returned to Stony Lodge. Rose Williams died on September 4, 1996, having outlived Tom by 13 years. She was buried beside him in the Calvary Cemetery in Saint Louis, and her headstone reads: "Blow out your candles, Laura."

Many of Williams's female characters were created in homage to his fragile and much-beloved sister Rose, such as Rosemary McCool in "COMPLETED," Sister in "Resemblance between a Violin Case and a Coffin," and Laura Wingfield in "PORTRAIT OF A GIRL IN GLASS" and *THE GLASS MENAGERIE*. Roses, in many forms (rose bushes, rose petals, and rose oil), repeatedly serve as symbols of love, beauty, and grace throughout Williams's work, as in *THE ROSE TATTOO*, *SOMETHING UNSPOKEN*, and *THE LONG STAY CUT SHORT, OR THE UNSATISFACTORY SUPPER*.

**Williams, Walter Dakin** (1919– ) Walter Dakin Williams was born February 21, 1919, in SAINT LOUIS, MISSOURI. He was the third child of CORNELIUS COFFIN WILLIAMS and EDWINA ESTELLE DAKIN WILLIAMS, and the only one to whom his father was able to relate. Consistently good at schoolwork and interested in sports, he clearly was the son Cornelius always wanted. Dakin graduated from high school third in his class and went on to college, where, unlike his brother, Thomas Lanier (Tennessee) Williams, or Tom, he did not fail Reserve Officers Training Corps (ROTC). Dakin studied law at WASHINGTON UNIVERSITY and graduated in April 1942. He continued his studies at Harvard University, where he studied business administration as part of his officer training. Drafted into the army as a noncommissioned officer, Dakin was dispatched to duty in the Pacific in 1943 and to Asia in 1944.

During his time in the armed forces, Dakin converted to Catholicism. After his demobilization he became a legal adviser to his family. In this capacity, he drafted his parents' separation agreement and administered the trust fund Tom established for their sister, ROSE ISABEL WILLIAMS (based on half the royalties from his brother's play *SUMMER AND SMOKE*) in 1948. Together with AUDREY WOOD, Dakin managed the legal and financial aspects of his brother's career. In 1968, he persuaded his brother to convert to Catholicism, hoping to cure his chemical dependency. Dakin continued to care for his brother and, in 1969, after a near-fatal incident, had him hospitalized for his chemical addiction. During his withdrawal period, Williams suffered three grand mal seizures and nearly died. As a result, he never forgave Dakin for the enforced hospitalization and permanently removed him from his will.

**Windham, Donald** (1920– ) *U.S. novelist, memoirist, editor, and longtime friend of Williams's.* Windham is best known for such works as *Dog Star* (1950), *The Hero Continues* (1960), *The Warm Country* (1962), *Emblems of Conduct* (1963), *Tennessee Williams's Letters to Donald Windham 1940–1965* (1976), and *Lost Friendships: A Memoir of Truman Capote, Tennessee Williams, and Others* (1987). Windham and Williams met in January 1940. Windham had recently arrived in New York City from Atlanta, Georgia, with his companion, Fred Melton. Windham and Williams were both youthfully optimistic about the future. Whereas Windham and Melton were struggling to survive and Windham's literary aspirations were still dreams, Williams's career had already become promising and somewhat financially fruitful. He had been awarded a Rockefeller Foundation fellowship of $1,000, and THE GROUP THEATRE prize of $100 for his collection *AMERICAN BLUES*. While Windham and Melton secured temporary odd jobs to pay the rent, Williams traveled and explored and wrote many letters to his newly established family of choice, Windham, Melton, and others.

Williams and Windham collaborated in 1942 to create the play *YOU TOUCHED ME!*, an adaptation of D. H. LAWRENCE's short story of that title. When *You Touched Me!* was produced on Broadway in 1945, it was brutally and unfavorably compared to Williams's most recent success, *THE GLASS MENAG-*

Williams and Donald Windham, in Times Square, New York City, early 1940s *(Photograph courtesy of the Billy Rose Theatre Collection, New York Public Library)*

ERIE. Although this close friendship would become strained and distant over the years, Windham remained fascinated by, and in many ways enamored of, Williams's vulnerability, genius, and what he called his "mysteriousness." This is evident in Windham's book *Tennessee Williams's Letters to Donald Windham 1940–1965.* Windham wrote in the introduction, "A great deal of my life would have been different if Tennessee and I had not known each other. He remains the rarest, the most intoxicating, the most memorable flower that has blossomed in my garden of good and evil."

### Further Reading

Kellner, Bruce. *Donald Windham: A Bio-Bibliography.* Westport, Conn.: Greenwood Press, 1991.

Leverich, Lyle. *Tom: The Unknown Tennessee Williams.* New York: Crown, 1995.

Windham, Donald. *Lost Friendships: A Memoir of Truman Capote, Tennessee Williams, and Others.* New York: William Morrow, 1987.

———. *Tennessee Williams's Letters to Donald Windham 1940–1965.* New York: Penguin Books, 1976.

**Wood, Audrey** (1905–1985) *Leading literary and talent agent in American theater during the 20th century.* Wood was introduced to Williams through THE GROUP THEATRE founder, Molly Day Thacher, in 1939. After reading the one-act play collection AMERICAN BLUES, Wood became not only his agent, but his caretaker and protector. Williams relied on Woods for emotional and financial support during times of crisis. This close and famous relationship would last more than 30 years, spanning Williams's years of commercial success.

In 1971, after many failures at the box office and the death of his long-term partner, FRANK MERLO, Williams experienced severe depression coupled with excessive chemical dependency. In this destructive period in his life, Williams became extremely fearful and angry. He focused his aggression on Wood, and he "turned on her the way one can turn on a parent" (Spoto, 330), accusing her of neglecting his work and blaming her for the decline in his career. This was the episode that finally ended their professional and personal relationship. Later Williams would write in MEMOIRS:

> To me she was much like a family member on whom I was particularly dependent. . . . Perhaps if my feelings for her had been limited to professional ones, I would not have been so disturbed and finally so outraged when her concern for me—once so great and sincere . . . appeared to ebb, so that I found myself alone as a child lost or an old dog abandoned. (229)

Williams would continue to praise Wood as an outstanding theater professional. Neither Wood nor Williams ever recovered from the loss of this relationship, which has been described as "one of the most lengthy, loving and finally tragic creative relationships in American theatre history" (Spoto, 81).

### Further Reading

Spoto, Donald. *The Kindness of Strangers: The Life of Tennessee Williams.* New York: Ballantine Books, 1985.

Williams, Tennessee. *Memoirs.* New York: Doubleday, 1975.

**Works Progress Administration Federal Writers' Project** Federal government program under the Works Progress Administration (WPA) to provide gainful employment for out-of-work writers during the Great Depression. Early in his career Williams attempted to secure a place in the WPA Federal Writers' Project but was unsuccessful because the project administrators felt that his work lacked significant social and political content. Also, Williams could not prove that his family was destitute. He recalled that he had "a touch of refinement in my social behavior which made me seem frivolous and decadent to the conscientiously rough-hewn pillars of the Chicago Project" (81). Williams refers to his experience with the Writers' Project in his essay "The Past, the Present and the Perhaps," which serves as the preface to ORPHEUS DESCENDING. Also, in VIEUX CARRÉ, the Writer describes the experience to his landlady, Mrs. Wire, when she threatens him with eviction.

### Further Reading

Williams, Tennessee. "The Past, the Present and the Perhaps," in *Where I Live: Selected Essays*, edited by Christine R. Day and Bob Woods. New York: New Directions, 1978, pp. 81–88.

# CHRONOLOGY OF LIFE AND WORKS

**1911**
March 26, Thomas Lanier Williams (Tennessee Williams) is born to Cornelius Coffin and Edwina Dakin Williams in Columbus, Mississippi.

**1918**
The Williams family moves to Saint Louis, Missouri.

**1927**
Williams's first published work, "Can a Good Wife Be a Good Sport?" (essay), appears in *Smart Set* magazine.

**1928**
Short story "The Vengeance of Nitocris" is published in *Weird Tales.*

**1929**
Williams attends the University of Missouri at Columbia.

**1931**
Williams's father forces him to withdraw from college and take a job with him at the International Shoe Company.

**1935**
July 13, *Cairo! Shanghai! Bombay!* is produced in Memphis, Tennessee.

**1936**
Williams enrolls in Washington University, Saint Louis, Missouri. *The Magic Tower* and *Headlines* are produced.

**1937**
*Candles to the Sun* is produced in Saint Louis. Williams leaves Washington University to attend the University of Iowa, Iowa City. His sister, Rose Williams, has a prefrontal lobotomy. *The Fugitive Kind* is produced in Saint Louis.

**1938**
Williams graduates from the University of Iowa. He submits four short plays, *Moony's Kid Don't Cry, The Dark Room, Case of the Crushed Petunias,* and *The Long Stay Cut Short, or The Unsatisfactory Supper,* (which together with *Ten Blocks on the Camino Real* make up the collection *American Blues*), to a play contest sponsored by The Group Theatre, New York City.

**1939**
Williams is awarded $100 for *American Blues.* Audrey Wood becomes his agent. *Not About Nightingales* is produced in Saint Louis. "The Field of Blue Children" is published in *Story* magazine; this is the first time his work appears under the name Tennessee Williams. He receives a Rockefeller Foundation grant of $1,000 and moves to New York City. He lives a vagabond life, traveling and writing.

**1940**
*The Long Goodbye* is staged in New York City. *Battle of Angels* is produced in Boston.

**1941**
*Battle of Angels* closes after a disastrous run.

1942
*This Property Is Condemned* is produced in New York City.

1943
Williams signs a six-month contract as a screenwriter with Metro-Goldwyn-Mayer. He writes *The Gentleman Caller,* the prototype for *The Glass Menagerie. You Touched Me!* (collaboration with Donald Windham) opens in Cleveland, Ohio.

1944
*The Purification* is produced in Pasadena, California, in July. *The Glass Menagerie* opens in Chicago on December 26.

1945
*Stairs to the Roof* is produced in Pasadena, California, on March 25. *The Glass Menagerie* opens in New York City to critical acclaim and earns Williams a New York Critics Circle Award. *You Touched Me!* opens in New York City.

1947
Williams meets Frank Merlo, who becomes his partner for the next 16 years. *A Streetcar Named Desire* opens in New York City.

1948
*One Arm* is published on July 28, and *The Glass Menagerie* opens in London.

1949
*A Streetcar Named Desire* is produced in London.

1950
*The Roman Spring of Mrs. Stone* is published, and the film of *The Glass Menagerie* is released. *The Rose Tattoo* opens in Chicago on February 3.

1951
*The Rose Tattoo* opens in New York City and earns Williams a Tony Award. The film of *A Streetcar Named Desire* is released.

1952
The film *A Streetcar Named Desire* film wins a New York Film Critics Award. On April 24, *Summer and Smoke* opens in New York City.

1953
*In the Winter of Cities* is published. *Camino Real* opens in New York.

1954
*Hard Candy* is published.

1955
*Cat on a Hot Tin Roof* opens in New York City on March 24. It wins a Pulitzer Prize and Drama Critics Circle Award. The film of *The Rose Tattoo* is released.

1956
*Baby Doll,* the screenplay that fuses two one-act plays, *27 Wagons Full of Cotton* and *The Long Stay Cut Short,* is released and instantly blacklisted by the Catholic Church.

1957
*Orpheus Descending* opens in New York on April 8. *Camino Real* is produced in London.

1958
*Cat on a Hot Tin Roof* opens in London on January 30. *Garden District* opens in New York and London. The film *Cat on a Hot Tin Roof* is released.

1959
*The Rose Tattoo* is produced in London on January 15. *Sweet Bird of Youth* opens in New York on April 14. *I Rise in Flame, Cried the Phoenix* is produced in New York. *Orpheus Descending* is produced in London on May 14. The film *Suddenly Last Summer* is released.

1960
*Period of Adjustment* opens in New York on November 10. *The Fugitive Kind* (the film of *Orpheus Descending*) is released.

**1961**
*The Night of the Iguana* is produced in New York on December 29. The films of *Summer and Smoke* and *The Roman Spring of Mrs. Stone* are released.

**1962**
*The Night of the Iguana* wins the New York Critics Circle Drama Award. *Period of Adjustment* becomes Williams's first British hit on June 13. *The Milk Train Doesn't Stop Here Anymore* premieres at the Spoleto Festival, Italy. The film versions of *Sweet Bird of Youth* and *Period of Adjustment* are released.

**1963**
*Remember Me to Tom,* by Williams's mother, Edwina Williams, is published. *The Milk Train Doesn't Stop Here Anymore* is produced in New York on January 16. Frank Merlo dies.

**1964**
The film *The Night of the Iguana* is released.

**1965**
*The Night of the Iguana* is produced in London and wins the London Critics Award for Best Foreign Play.

**1966**
*The Knightly Quest* is published on February 22. *Slapstick Tragedy* opens in New York City. The film of *This Property Is Condemned* is released.

**1967**
*The Two Character Play* premieres in London.

**1968**
*Kingdom of Earth* (also entitled *The Seven Descents of Myrtle*) opens in New York. *Sweet Bird of Youth* and *The Milk Train Doesn't Stop Here Anymore* are produced in England. *BOOM!* (film version of *Milk Train*) is released.

**1969**
Williams is baptized in the Roman Catholic Church. *In the Bar of a Tokyo Hotel* opens in New York. Williams is committed for three months to a psychiatric hospital. *The Last of the Mobile Hot Shots* (film version of *Kingdom of Earth*) is released. Williams is awarded a doctorate in humanities by the University of Missouri and the Gold Medal for Drama by the American Academy of Arts and Letters.

**1971**
*Confessional* is produced in Maine. *Out Cry* (revised version of *The Two Character Play*) opens in Chicago. Williams fires Audrey Wood, his agent of more than 30 years.

**1972**
*Small Craft Warnings* opens in New York in April. Williams wins the National Theatre Conference Annual Award, and the University of Hartford awards him a doctorate in humanities.

**1973**
*Small Craft Warnings* opens in London. *Out Cry* opens in New York on March 1.

**1974**
*Eight Mortal Ladies Possessed* is published. Williams is awarded the Medal of Honor for Literature by the National Arts Club and the Entertainment Hall of Fame Award.

**1975**
*Moise and the World of Reason* and *Memoirs* are published.

**1976**
*The Red Devil Battery Sign* opens in Boston and closes after 10 days. *Eccentricities of a Nightingale* (rewritten version of *Summer and Smoke*) opens in New York. *Androgyne, Mon Amour* is published.

**1977**
*The Demolition Downtown* is produced in London. *Vieux Carré* is produced in New York. *The Red Devil Battery Sign* is produced in London. Tennessee Williams Performing Arts Center is dedicated at the Florida Keys Community College, Key West.

1978
*Kingdom of Earth* and *Vieux Carré* are produced in London. *Tiger Tail* (stage version of *Baby Doll*) is produced in Atlanta.

1979
*Creve Coeur* has a New York premiere.

1980
*Will Mr. Merriwether Return from Memphis?* is produced at the Tennessee Williams Performing Arts Center on January 25. *Clothes for a Summer Hotel* opens in Chicago.

1981
*Something Cloudy, Something Clear* is produced in New York.

1982
*A House Not Meant to Stand* is produced in Chicago. *Now the Cats with Jewelled Claws* is commissioned by New World Festival of the Arts. *It Happened the Day the Sun Rose* is published.

1983
On February 24, Williams is found dead in his room at the Hotel Elysée, New York City.

# Festivals, Internet Resources, and Important Libraries for Research on Williams

**Columbia University Library**
Butler Library, 6th Floor East
535 West 114th Street
New York, NY 10027
212/854-5153
www.columbia.edu/cu/lweb/

This collection includes the personal archive from Tennessee Williams's Key West home: letters, manuscripts, typescripts, annotated books, photographs and ephemera documenting the final years of Williams's life, as well as 66 miscellaneous pieces of artwork, among them paintings by the playwright and his sister, Rose. Correspondence in the Key West collection includes letters from Paul Bowles, Marlon Brando, and Carson McCullers, as well as postcards and notes from fans, agents, and editors.

Items from Williams's personal library include his copies of Kafka's diaries, Hart Crane's *Collected Poems,* the plays of Pirandello, and Rilke's *Duino Elegies,* all with extensive notes and dialogue on the endpapers and flyleaves. His copies of Irene Nemirovky's *Life of Chekhov* (1950) and an edition of Chekhov, *The Personal Papers* (1948), include pages of handwritten notes and poetry. Other marked and annotated works include Edith Hamilton's *The Greek Way* (1953), Beverly Nichols's *All I Could Never Be* (1952), novels by Faulkner and Ernest Hemingway, and Santayana's *Character and Opinion in the United States.*

**Billy Rose Theatre Collection at the New York Public Library for the Performing Arts**
40 Lincoln Center Plaza
New York, NY 10023
212/870-1639
www.nypl.org/research/lpa/

The Billy Rose Theatre Collection includes an extensive photograph collection, including portraits of Williams and various production photographs. The collection also includes newspaper clippings of production reviews, programs, and playbills.

**Harry Ransom Humanities Research Center at the University of Texas at Austin**
21st and Guadalupe
P.O. Box 7219
Austin, TX 78713
512/471-8944
www.hrc.utexas.edu

The extensive collection at the Ransom Center includes paintings, drawings, and prints by and related to Tennessee Williams. The collection is organized into works by Tennessee Williams, portraits of Williams by other artists, and works related to Williams.

The collection also includes numerous drafts and copies of Williams's literary works, including theatrical and radio plays, television and motion picture scripts, short stories, poetry, anthologies, reviews, journalistic essays, personal journals, notes, and academic assignments. Also present are newspaper clippings, photographs, and correspondence (including letters, telegrams, postcards, and Christmas cards).

**University of Delaware Library**
Newark, DE 19717
302/831-2229
www.lib.udel.edu

The Tennessee Williams Collection, spanning the years 1939 through 1994, includes correspondence, photographs, poems, essays, programs, playbills, theatrical and film ephemera, plays, notes, fiction, posters, clippings, page proofs, articles, and reviews.

The Ralph Delauney Papers related to Tennessee Williams's *The Rose Tattoo,* spanning the years 1947–53, comprise the playscript and revisions, correspondence, bills and receipts, budgets, clippings, notes, itineraries, theater programs, and sketches of the set. The material was gathered by Ralph Delauney in his role as stage manager for both the 1950 world premiere production of Williams's *The Rose Tattoo* at Erlanger Theatre in Chicago and the 1951 New York run at the Martin Beck Theatre. *The Rose Tattoo* playscript, with its numerous revisions, includes more than 10 variant endings to the play. Tennessee Williams, present during auditions and early rehearsals, as well as several actual productions, was continually rewriting the ending of the play.

**Mississippi Writers Page Online at the University of Mississippi**
www.olemiss.edu/mwp/index.html

The Mississippi Writers Page is a versatile Internet resource about writers associated with the state of Mississippi. The site includes a collection of articles about Williams's life, a comprehensive list of published titles, various awards and honors, and a selected bibliography of additional resources.

**Tennessee Williams/New Orleans Literary Festival**
www.tennesseewilliams.net

Every March, scholars, writers, performers, educators, and booksellers gather in New Orleans to celebrate and study Tennessee Williams and the art of writing. As Williams was greatly inspired by New Orleans throughout his career, the festival also celebrates the uniqueness of the city of New Orleans.

**Tennessee Williams Society in Key West**
www.tennesseeinkeywest.com

An annual festival celebrating the life and works of Tennessee Williams is held at the Tennessee Williams Theatre in Key West, Florida. The festival is dedicated to celebrating the works of Williams, educating the general public about his works, and supporting the works of his contemporaries and literary heirs. The festival includes theatrical productions, plays, readings, movies, lectures, and discussions.

# Bibliography of Williams's Works

## Plays and Screenplays

*All Gaul Is Divided* (c. 1950; published in *Stopped Rocking and Other Screenplays,* with an introduction by Richard Gilman [New York: New Directions, 1984]).

*American Blues* (a collection of five of Williams's one-act plays [New York: Dramatists Play Service, 1948]. The collection comprises *Moony's Kid Don't Cry; The Dark Room; The Case of the Crushed Petunias; The Long Stay Cut Short, or The Unsatisfactory Supper;* and *Ten Blocks on the Camino Real* [discussed later]; reprinted in 1968 and 1976 [New York: Dramatists Play Service].

*And Tell Sad Stories of the Death of Queens* (date of composition unknown; published with *Not About Nightingales* [discussed late] in *Political Stages: Plays That Shaped a Century,* edited by Emily Mann and David Roessel [New York: Applause Books, 2002]).

*At Liberty* (before 1940; published in *American Scenes: A Volume of New Short Plays,* edited by William Kozlenko [New York: John Day Company, 1941]).

*Auto-Da-Fé* (1938; published in *27 Wagons Full of Cotton, and Other One-Act Plays* [Norfolk, Conn.: New Directions, 1945]; reprinted in 1953, 1966, and 1981 [New York: New Directions]).

*Baby Doll* (1956; published with the two one-act plays that suggested it, *27 Wagons Full of Cotton* and *The Long Stay Cut Short, or The Unsatisfactory Supper* [New York: New Directions, 1956]; reprinted with *Something Unspoken* and *Suddenly Last Summer* [Harmondsworth, England: Penguin, 1968]; and in *Baby Doll and Tiger Tail: A Screenplay and Play* [New York: New Directions, 1991]).

*Battle of Angels* (1939; first published by Pharos [Murray, Utah: 1945]; reprinted in *Orpheus Descending with Battle of Angels: Two Plays* [New York: New Directions, 1958]; *The Theatre of Tennessee Williams* [New York: New Directions, 1971]; *Battle of Angels, The Glass Menagerie and A Streetcar Named Desire* [New York: New Directions, 1971]; and in *Plays 1937–1955,* edited by Mel Gussow and Kenneth Holdich [New York: Library of America, 2000]).

*Beauty Is the Word* (1930; unpublished).

*Cairo! Shanghai! Bombay!* (1935; unpublished).

*Camino Real* (1946; first published in 1953 [New York: Dramatists Play Service]; reprinted in 1976 and 1981 [New York: Dramatists Play Service]; reprinted in 1953 and 1970 [New York: New Directions]; reprinted in *Four Plays* [London: Secker & Warburg, 1957]; *The Rose Tattoo and Camino Real* [Harmondsworth, Penguin Books in association with Secker & Warburg, 1958]; *Three Plays of Tennessee Williams* [New York: New Directions, 1959]; *Six American Plays for Today,* edited by Bennett Cerf [New York: Modern Library, 1961]; *Three Plays: The Rose Tattoo, Camino Real, and Sweet Bird of Youth* [New York: New Directions, 1964]; *The Eccentricities of a Nightingale, Summer and Smoke, The Rose Tattoo and Camino Real* [New York: New Directions, 1971]; *The Rose Tattoo, Camino Real, Orpheus Descending* [Harmondsworth, England. New York: Penguin Books, in association with Secker & Warburg, 1976]; and *The Theatre of Tennessee Williams,* Volume 2 [New York: New Directions, 1976]).

*Candles to the Sun* (1935; first published in 2004 [New York: New Directions]).

*The Case of the Crushed Petunias* (1939; first published in 1948 in *American Blues* [see previous discussion] [New York: Dramatists Play Service); reprinted in 1968 in *Upstage and Down,* edited by Daniel P. McGarity [Toronto: Macmillan of Canada]).

*Cat on a Hot Tin Roof* (1955; [New York: New Directions, 1955]; [New York: New American Library, New York, 1955]; [New York: Penguin, 1955];

reprinted in [New York: New Directions, 1971 New York in *Cat on a Hot Tin Roof, Orpheus Descending and Suddenly Last Summer* in *Cat on a Hot Tin Roof: A Play in Three Acts* [New York: Dramatists Play Service, 1958, 1983, 1986]; included in *The Theatre of Tennessee Williams, Volume 3,* [New York: New Directions, 1991] and in *The Glass Menagerie, A Streetcar Named Desire, Cat on a Hot Tin Roof and Suddenly Last Summer* [New York: Quality Paperback Book Club, 1994]).

*Clothes for a Summer Hotel* (1980; [New York: Dramatists Play Service, 1981]; [New York: New Directions, 1983]; included in *The Theatre of Tennessee Williams,* Volume 8 [New York: New Directions, 1992]).

*Confessional* (1967; published in *Dragon Country,* [New York: New Directions, 1970]).

*Creve Coeur* See *A Lovely Sunday for Creve Coeur.*

*The Dark Room* (c. 1939; published in *American Blues,* [New York: Dramatists Play Service, 1948]).

*The Demolition Downtown* (before 1971; published in *Esquire,* 75, no. 6, [June 1971]): 124–127.

*Dragon Country* (collection of one-acts) [New York: New Directions, 1970]).

*The Eccentricities of a Nightingale* (1951 [New York: New Directions, 1964]); reprinted as *The Eccentricities of a Nightingale and Summer and Smoke: Two Plays* [New York: New Directions, 1964]; included in *The Theatre of Tennessee Williams Volume 2* [New York: New Directions, 1971, 1990]; [New York: Dramatists Play Service, 1977, 1992]).

*The Frosted Glass Coffin* (1941; published in *Dragon Country,* [New York: New Directions, 1970]); *In the Bar of a Tokyo Hotel and Other Plays,* [New York: New Directions, 1981]).

*The Fugitive Kind* (1936–38; [New York: New American Library, 1960]); [New York: New Directions, 2001]).

*Garden District* (published as *Garden District Two Plays: Something Unspoken and Suddenly Last Summer* [London: Secker & Warburg, 1959]; *Baby Doll and Other Plays* [London: Penguin, 1968, 2001]).

*The Glass Menagerie* (1944; published [New York: Random House, 1945]; [New York: New Directions, 1945]; [New York: Penguin Press, 1945]; [London: Methuen, 1945]; reprinted [New York: New Directions, 1949, 1970, 1966, 1971, 1999]; [New York: Dramatists Play Service, 1948, 1972, 1975, 1976]; [London: Heinemann Educational, 1968]; included in *Four Plays by Tennessee Williams* [London: Secker & Warburg, 1956]; included in *Four Plays* [London: Secker & Warburg, 1957, 1968]; [New York: New American Library, 1972, 1987]; [New York: Penguin, 1987]; included in *Sweet Bird of Youth, A Streetcar Named Desire, and The Glass Menagerie* [Harmondsworth, England: Penguin Press, 1962, 1982]; included in *The Glass Menagerie, A Streetcar Named Desire, and Suddenly Last Summer* [New York: Quality Paperback Book Club, 1994]; included in *The Theatre of Tennessee Williams Volume 1* [New York: New Directions, 1971, 1990]; [London: Methuen, 2002]).

*The Gnädiges Fräulein* (1965; included in *Slapstick Tragedy* [along with *The Mutilated*], *Esquire,* 64, no. 2, pp 95–102, 130–134 [August 1965]; [New York: Dramatists Play Service, 1967]). (Included in *In the Bar of a Tokyo Hotel and Other Plays.* New York: Dramatists Play Service, 1981.)

*Grand* (1964; [New York: House of Books, 1964]).

*Hello from Bertha* (1941; published in the collection *27 Wagons Full of Cotton and Other One-Act Plays* [Norfolk, Conn.: New Directions, 1945]; reprinted [New York: New Directions, 1953, 1954, 1966, 1981]).

*Hot Milk at 3 a.m.* (1930) See *Moony's Kid Don't Cry.*

*I Can't Imagine Tomorrow* (1966; published in *Esquire* 65 [March 1966]; included in *Dragon Country* [New York: New Directions, 1970]; *The Best Short Plays, 1971* [Radnor, Pa.: Chilton Book Co., 1971]; *In the Bar of a Tokyo Hotel and Other Plays* [New York: New Directions, 1981]).

*I Rise in Flame, Cried the Phoenix* (1939–41; published [New York: New Directions, 1951, 1981]; [New York: Dramatists Play Service, 1951, 1964, 1979]; in *Ramparts* 6 pp 14–19 [Jan. 1968]); included in *Dragon Country* [New York: New Directions, 1970]; in *Plays 1937–1955* [New York: Library of America, 2000]).

*In the Bar of a Tokyo Hotel* (1960s; published [New York: Dramatists Play Service, 1969]; included in *Dragon Country* [New York: New Directions, 1970]; *The Theatre of Tennessee Williams Vol. 7* [New York: New Directions, 1971–92]; [New York: New Directions, 1981].

*The Kingdom of Earth* (one-act) (1967; published in *Esquire,* 67 [February 1967]).

*The Kingdom of Earth, or The Seven Descents of Myrtle* (full-length) (1967; published [New York: New Directions, 1954]; reprinted [New York: New Directions, 1968]; published [New York: Dramatists Play Service, 1969]; reprinted [New York: Dramatists Play Service, 1975, 1997]; published *The Milk Train*

*Doesn't Stop Here Anymore, Kingdom of Earth (The Seven Descents of Myrtle); Small Craft Warnings, The Two-Character Play* [New York: New Directions, 1976]; included in *The Theatre of Tennessee Williams Vol. 5* [New York: New Directions, 1971–92]).

*The Lady of Larkspur Lotion* (before 1942; published in *The Best One-Act Plays of 1941* [New York: Dodd, Mead, 1942]; included in *27 Wagons Full of Cotton and Other One-Act Plays* [New York: New Directions, 1945]).

*The Last of My Solid Gold Watches* (before 1946; published in *27 Wagons Full of Cotton and Other One-Act Plays* [New York: New Directions, 1945]; *Best One-Act Plays of 1942* [New York: Dodd, Mead, 1943]; included in *Great American One-Act Plays* [Stuttgart: Ernst Klett Verlag, 1985]).

*Lifeboat Drill* (c. 1970; published in *In the Bar of a Tokyo Hotel and Other Plays* [New York: New Directions, 1981]; included in *The Theatre of Tennessee Williams Vol. 7* [New York: New Directions, 1971–92]).

*The Long Goodbye* (1940; published in *27 Wagons Full of Cotton and Other One-Act Plays* [New York: New Directions, 1945]).

*The Long Stay Cut Short* (before 1945; published as *The Unsatisfactory Supper* in *The Best One-Act Plays of 1945* [New York: Dodd, Mead, 1946]; in the collection *American Blues* [New York: Dramatists Play Service, 1948]; in *Baby Doll; the Script for the Film, Incorporating the Two One-Act Plays Which Suggested It: 27 Wagons Full of Cotton [and] The Long Stay Cut Short; or The Unsatisfactory Supper* [New York: New Directions, 1956]).

*Lord Byron's Love Letter* (before 1946; published in the collection *27 Wagons Full of Cotton and Other One-Act Plays* [New York: New Directions, 1945]; included in *The Best American One-Act Plays* [Tokyo: Kaibunsha, 1964]).

*The Loss of a Teardrop Diamond* (1950s; published in *Stopped Rocking and Other Screenplays* [New York: New Directions, 1984]).

*A Lovely Sunday for Creve Coeur* (1976; [New York: New Directions, 1980]; included in *The Theatre of Tennessee Williams Vol. 8* [New York: New Directions, 1971–92]; *Plays 1957–1980* [New York: Library of America, 2000]).

*Me, Vashya!* (1937; unpublished).

*The Milk Train Doesn't Stop Here Anymore* (1959–62; published in *The Best Plays of 1962–1963: The Burns Mantle Yearbook* [New York: Dodd, Mead, 1963]; [Norfolk, Conn.: New Directions, 1964]; [New York: Dramatists Play Service, 1964]; *The Milk Train Doesn't Stop Here Anymore and Cat on a Hot Tin Roof* [Harmondsworth, England: Penguin, 1969]; included in *The Theatre of Tennessee Williams Vol. 5* [New York: New Directions, 1971–92]; *Cat on a Hot Tin Roof, The Milk Train Doesn't Stop Here Anymore, and The Night of the Iguana* [Harmondsworth, England: Penguin, 1976]; *The Milk Train Doesn't Stop Here Anymore; Kingdom of Earth (The Seven Descents of Myrtle); Small Craft Warnings; The Two-Character Play* [New York: New Directions, 1976]; *Plays 1957–1980* [New York: Library of America, 2000]).

*Moony's Kid Don't Cry* (1930; published in *American Blues* [New York: Dramatists Play Service, 1948]; included in *The Best One-Act Plays of 1940* [New York: Dodd, Mead, 1941]).

*The Mutilated* (1965; included in *Slapstick Tragedy* [along with *The Gnädiges Fräulein*], *Esquire*, 64, no. 2 [August 1965] p. 95–102, 130–134; published [New York: Dramatists Play Service, 1967; included in *Dragon Country* [New York: New Directions, 1970]; *The Theatre of Tennessee Williams Vol. 7* [New York: New Directions, 1971–92]; *In the Bar of a Tokyo Hotel and Other Plays* [New York: New Directions, 1981]; *Plays 1957–1980* [New York: Library of America, 2000]).

*The Night of the Iguana* (1959; published [New York: New Directions, 1961]; [New York: New American Library, 1961]; [Harmondsworth, England: Penguin Books 1961]; *The Best Plays of 1961–1962* [New York: Dodd, Mead, 1962]; *The Best Plays of 1961–1962: The Burns Mantle Yearbook* [New York: Arno Press, 1962]; [New York: Dramatists Play Service, 1963]; [London: Secker & Warburg, 1963]; reprinted [New York: Dramatists Play Service, 1964]; reprinted [Harmondsworth, England: Penguin Books, 1964]; *The Night of the Iguana and Orpheus Descending* [Harmondsworth, England: Penguin, 1968]; *Sweet Bird of Youth, Period of Adjustment, The Night of the Iguana* [New York: New Directions, 1972]; reprinted in *The Best Plays of 1961–1962: The Burns Mantle Yearbook.* [New York: Arno Press, 1975]; *Three by Tennessee: Sweet Bird of Youth, The Rose Tattoo, The Night of the Iguana* [New York: New American Library, 1976]; *Cat on a Hot Tin Roof, The Milk Train Doesn't Stop Here Anymore, and The Night of the Iguana* [Harmondsworth, England: Penguin, 1976]; *Selected Plays* [Franklin Center, Pa.: Franklin Library, 1977]; *Eight Plays* [Garden City, N.Y.: Doubleday, 1979]; reprinted *Cat on a Hot Tin Roof, The Milk Train*

*Doesn't Stop Here Anymore, and The Night of the Iguana* [New York: Penguin Books, 1985]; reprinted [New York: Dramatists Play Service, 1991]; *The Theatre of Tennessee Williams Vol. 4* [New York: New Directions, 1993]; *Plays 1957–1980* [New York: Library of America, 2000]).

*Not About Nightingales* (1938; published [New York: New Directions, 1998]; [London: Methuen Drama, 1998]; [New York: Samuel French, 1999]; included in *Plays 1937–1955* [New York: Library of America, 2000]).

*The Notebook of Trigorin* (1981–83; published [New York: New Directions, 1997]; [New York: Dramatists Play Service, 1997]).

*Now the Cats with Jewelled Claws* (1981; included in *The Theatre of Tennessee Williams Vol. 7* [New York: New Directions, 1981]).

*One Arm* (1960s; published in Stopped *Rocking and Other Screenplays* [New York: New Directions, 1984]).

*Orpheus Descending* (1957; published [New York: New Directions, 1958]; [London: Secker & Warburg, 1958]; included in *The Best Plays of 1956–1957: The Burns Mantle Yearbook* [New York: Arno Press, 1957]; [New York: Dramatists Play Service, 1959]; *Orpheus Descending with Battle of Angels: Two Plays* [New York: New Directions, 1958]; *Five Plays* [London: Secker & Warburg, 1962]; *Five More Plays* [London: Secker & Warburg, 1962]; *Five More Plays* [London: Secker & Warburg, 1962]; *The Night of the Iguana and Orpheus Descending* [Harmondsworth, England: Penguin Books, 1968]; *Cat on a Hot Tin Roof, Orpheus Descending, Suddenly Last Summer* [New York: New Directions, 1971]; reprinted [New York: New Directions, 1971]; *The Theatre of Tennessee Williams Vol. 3* [New York: New Directions, 1971]; reprinted (in *The Best Plays of 1956–1957: The Burns Mantle Yearbook*) [New York: Arno Press, 1975]; *Four Plays* [New York: Signet Classic, 1976]; *Tennessee Williams, Four Plays: Summer and Smoke, Orpheus Descending, Suddenly Last Summer, and Period of Adjustment* [New York: New American Library, 1976]; *The Rose Tattoo, Camino Real, Orpheus Descending* [Harmondsworth, England: Penguin Books, 1976]; *Eight Plays* [Garden City, N.Y.: Doubleday, 1979]; reprinted [New York: Dramatists Play Service, 1983, 1987]; reprinted in *The Theatre of Tennessee Williams Vol. 3* [New York: New Directions, 1991]; *Plays 1957–1980* [New York: Library of America, 2000]).

*Out Cry* (1973; published [New York: New Directions, 1973]; included in *Plays 1957–1980* [New York: Library of America, 2000]).

*A Perfect Analysis Given by a Parrot* (1958; published [New York; Dramatists Play Service, 1958); *Esquire* 50, no. 4 [October 1958] pp. 131–135; included in *Dragon Country* [New York: New Directions, 1970]; *In the Bar of a Tokyo Hotel and Other Plays* [New York: New Directions, 1981]; *The Theatre of Tennessee Williams Vol. 7* [New York: New Directions, 1971–92]).

*Period of Adjustment* (1957; published in *Esquire*, 54, no. 6 [December 1960], pp. 210–276; reprinted [New York: New Directions, 1960]; [London: Secker & Warburg, 1960]; [New York: Dramatists Play Service, 1961, 1989]; [New York: New American Library, 1962]; [New York: Signet, 1962]; [New York: Four Square Books, 1963]; included in *The Theatre of Tennessee Williams, vol. 4* [New York: New Directions, 1971, 1993]; *Sweet Bird of Youth, Period of Adjustment, and The Night of the Iguana* [New York: New Directions, 1972]; *Four Plays* [New York: Signet Classic, 1976]; *Four Plays* [New York: New American Library, 1976]; *Period of Adjustment, Summer and Smoke, Small Craft Warnings* [Harmondsworth, England: Penguin, 1982]; *Plays 1957–1980* [New York: Library of America, 2000]).

*Portrait of a Madonna* (before 1946; published in *27 Wagons Full of Cotton and Other One-Act Plays* [Norfolk, Conn., New York: New Directions, 1945, 1953, 1966, 1981]).

*This Property Is Condemned* (before 1942; published in *27 Wagons Full of Cotton and Other One-Act Plays* [Norfolk, Conn., New York: New Directions, 1945, 1953, 1966, 1981]).

*The Purification* (1940; published in *27 Wagons Full of Cotton and Other One-Act Plays* [Norfolk, Conn., New York: New Directions, 1945, 1953, 1966, 1981]).

*The Red Devil Battery Sign* (1975–76; published [New York: New Directions, 1988]; reprinted *The Theatre of Tennessee Williams, vol. 8* [New York: New Directions, 1992]).

*The Remarkable Rooming-House of Mme. Le Monde* (date of composition uncertain; published in limited edition [New York: Albondocani Press, 1984]).

*The Rose Tattoo* (1950; published [New York: New American Library, 1950]; reprinted [1955, 1956]; reprinted [New York: New Directions, 1951]; [New York: Dramatists Play Service, 1951, 1965, 1966, 1979]; [London: Secker & Warburg, 1954];

included in *The Rose Tattoo and Camino Real* [Harmondsworth, England: Penguin Books in association with Secker & Warburg, 1958, 1968]; *Three Plays: The Rose Tattoo, Camino Real, and Sweet Bird of Youth* [New York: New Directions, 1959, 1964]; *Best American Plays, series 4* [New York: Crown Publishers, 1958, 1968]; *Five Plays* [London: Secker & Warburg, 1962, 1970]; *Five More Plays* [London: Secker & Warburg, 1962]; *The Eccentricities of a Nightingale, Summer and Smoke, The Rose Tattoo, and Camino Real* [[New York: New Directions, 1971]; *Three by Tennessee: Sweet Bird of Youth, The Rose Tattoo, and The Night of the Iguana* [New York: New American Library, 1976]; *The Theatre of Tennessee Williams, vol. 2* [New York: New Directions, 1976]; *Eight Plays* [Garden City, N.Y.: Doubleday, 1979]; *Three by Tennessee* [New York: Penguin, 1976]; *The Rose Tattoo, Camino Real, and Orpheus Descending* [Harmondsworth, England, New York: Penguin Books in association with Secker & Warburg, 1976]; *Selected Plays* [Franklin Center, Pa.: Franklin Library, 1977]; *Plays 1937–1955* [New York: Library of America, 2000]).

*Slapstick Tragedy* (1965; published in *Esquire* 64, no. 2 [August 1965]; 95–102, 130–134). (See *The Gnädiges Fräulein* and *The Mutilated.*)

*Small Craft Warnings* (1971; published [New York: New Directions, 1972]; reprinted [New York; McClelland & Stewart, 1972]; [London: Secker & Warburg, 1973]; included in *The Best Plays of 1971–1972* [New York: Dodd, Mead, 1972]; *The Theatre of Tennessee Williams, vol. 5* [New York: New Directions, 1976]; *Plays 1957–1980* [New York: Library of America, 2000]).

*Something Cloudy, Something Clear* (1979; published [New York: New Directions, 1995]; reprinted [1996]; reprinted [London: Methuen Drama, 1995]; [New York: Dramatists Play Service, 1995]).

*Something Unspoken* (before 1953; published in *27 Wagons Full of Cotton and Other One-Act Plays* [Norfolk, Conn., New York: New Directions, 1953, 1966, 1981]; *The Best Short Plays of 1955–1956,* edited by Margaret Mayorga [Boston: Beacon Press, 1956]; *Baby Doll: The Script for the Film, Something Unspoken, and Suddenly Last Summer* [Harmondsworth, England, Baltimore: Penguin, 1959, 1968, 1976, 1982, 1984, 2001]; *Garden District: Two Plays—Something Unspoken and Suddenly Last Summer* [London: Secker & Warburg, 1959]; *Orpheus Descending: Something Unspoken, Suddenly Last Summer* [Harmondsworth, England: Penguin, 1961]; *Five Plays* [London: Secker & Warburg, 1962, 1970]; *Five More Plays* [London: Secker & Warburg, 1962]; *Baby Doll and Other Plays* [London: Penguin, 1968, 2001]).

*Spring Storm* (1937–38; published [New York: New Directions, 1999]; reprinted *Plays 1937–1955* [New York: Library of America, 2000]).

*Stairs to the Roof* (1940–42; published [New York: New Directions, 2000]).

*Steps Must Be Gentle* (1980; published in a limited edition [New York: William Targ, 1980]; reprinted in *27 Wagons Full of Cotton and Other Short Plays* [New York: New Directions, 1981]).

*Stopped Rocking* (1977; published in *Stopped Rocking and Other Screenplays* [New York: New Directions, 1984]).

*The Strangest Kind of Romance* (1946; first published in *27 Wagons Full of Cotton and Other One-Act Plays* [Norfolk, Conn., New York: New Directions, 1945]; reprinted [1953, 1966, 1981]).

*A Streetcar Named Desire* (1945–47; published [New York: New Directions, 1947]; reprinted [New York: New Directions, 1980]; reprinted [New York: New American Library, 1947]; reprinted [New York: New American Library, 1972, 1973, 1980, 1984, 1988]; [New York: Dramatists Play Service, 1953]; reprinted [New York: Dramatist Play Service, 1974, 1981]; with an introduction by Jessica Tandy [New York: Limited Editions Club, 1982]; included in such collections as *The Burns Mantle Best Plays of 1947–48 and the Year Book of the Drama in America* [New York: Dodd, Mead, 1948]; *The Theatre of Tennessee Williams, Vol. 1* [New York: New Directions, 1971]; *Battle of Angels, The Glass Menagerie and A Streetcar Named Desire* [New York: New Directions, 1971]; *Eight Plays,* with an introduction by Harold Clurman [Garden City, N.Y.: Doubleday, 1979]; *The Glass Menagerie, A Streetcar Named Desire, Cat on a Hot Tin Roof and Suddenly Last Summer* [New York: Quality Paperback Book Club, 1994]; *Plays 1937–1955* edited by Mel Gussow and Kenneth Holdich [New York: Library of America, 2000]. The filmscript of the play was published by Charles K. Feldman Group Productions, Los Angeles, CA for Warner Brothers, 1951]; Script City, Calif.: Hollywood, 1951]; the screenplay was reprinted in *Film Scripts One,* compiled by George P. Garrett [New York: Appleton-Century-Crofts, 1971]. The libretto and text of an opera of the play were published [San Francisco: San Francisco Opera, 1998]).

*Suddenly Last Summer* (1958; published [New York: New Directions, 1958]; reprinted [New York: New Directions, 1980]; reprinted [New York: New American Library, 1958]; reprinted [New York: New American Library, 1964]; [New York: Dramatists Play Service, 1986]; included in *Garden District: Two Plays—Something Unspoken and Suddenly Last Summer.* [London: Secker & Warburg, 1959]; *Five Plays* [London: Secker & Warburg, 1962]; *Baby Doll: The Script for the Film; Something Unspoken and Suddenly Last Summer* [London: Penguin Books, 1968]; reprinted as *Baby Doll and Other Plays* [London: Penguin, 2001] *Cat on a Hot Tin Roof; Orpheus Descending; Suddenly Last Summer* [New York: New Directions, 1971]; *The Theatre of Tennessee Williams, Vol. 3.* [New York: New Directions, 1971]; *Four Plays: Summer and Smoke, Orpheus Descending, Suddenly Last Summer, Period of Adjustment* [New York: New American Library, 1976]; *Four Plays* [New York: Signet Classic, 1976]; *The Glass Menagerie, A Streetcar Named Desire, Cat on a Hot Tin Roof, and Suddenly Last Summer* [New York: Quality Paperback Book Club, 1994]; *Plays 1957–1980,* edited by Mel Gussow and Kenneth Holdich [New York: Library of America, 2000]. The screenplay, written by Gore Vidal, was published [London: Scripts Limited, 1959]).

*Summer and Smoke* (1948; published [New York: New Directions, 1948]; reprinted under the title *The Eccentricities of a Nightingale and Summer and Smoke: Two Plays,* [New York: New Directions, 1964]; reprinted [New York: Belgrave Press, 1948]; [New York; Dramatists Play Service, 1950]; reprinted [New York: Dramatists Play Service, 1975, 1977, 1978]; [London: J. Lehmann, 1952]; [New York: New American Library, 1961]; included in *Best American Plays,* edited by John Gassner [New York: Crown Publishers, 1952]; reprinted [1968]; *Four Plays by Tennessee Williams: The Glass Menagerie, A Streetcar Named Desire, Summer and Smoke, Camino Real* [London: Secker & Warburg, 1956]; *The Eccentricities of a Nightingale, Summer and Smoke, The Rose Tattoo and Camino Real* [New York: New Directions, 1971]; *The Theatre of Tennessee Williams, Vol. 2* [New York: New Directions, 1976]; *Four Plays: Summer and Smoke, Orpheus Descending, Suddenly Last Summer, Period of Adjustment* [New York: New American Library, 1976]; *Four Plays* [New York: Signet Classic, 1976]; *Eight Plays,* with an introduction by Harold Clurman [Garden City, N.Y.: Doubleday, 1979]; *Period of Adjustment, Summer and Smoke, Small Craft Warnings* [Harmondsworth, England: Penguin, 1982]; *The Eccentricities of a Nightingale, Summer and Smoke, The Rose Tattoo, Camino Real* [New York: New Directions, 1990]; *Plays 1937–1955,* edited by Gussow and Holdich [New York: Library of America, 2000]. The screenplay was published [Hollywood, Calif.: Paramount Pictures, 1961]. The libretto and text of an opera (music by Lee Hoiby and libretto by Lanford Wilson) were published [New York: Belwin-Mills, 1972, 1976]; [Long Eddy, N.Y.: Rock Valley Music Co.: [2000]).

*Sweet Bird of Youth* (1952; first published in *Esquire* 51, no. 4 [April 1959]: pp. 114–115; reprinted, [New York: New American Library, 1959; 1962]; [New York: New Directions, 1959, 1972, 1975]; [London: Secker & Warburg, 1961]; [New York: Dramatists Play Service, 1962, 1987, 1992]; included in *A Streetcar Named Desire and Other Plays* [London: Penguin in association with Secker & Warburg, 1962, 1992]: *Sweet Bird of Youth, A Streetcar Named Desire, The Glass Menagerie* [Harmondsworth, England: Penguin in association with Secker & Warburg, 1962, 1982]; *Three Plays: The Rose Tattoo, Camino Real, Sweet Bird of Youth* [New York: New Directions, 1964]; *The Theatre of Tennessee Williams, Vol. 4* [New York: New Directions, 1971]; *Sweet Bird of Youth, Period of Adjustment, and The Night of the Iguana* [New York: New Directions, 1972]; *Three by Tennessee: Sweet Bird of Youth, The Rose Tattoo, and The Night of the Iguana* [New York: New American Library, 1976]; *Three by Tennessee* [New York: Signet Classic, 1976]; *Selected Plays* [Franklin Center, Pa.: Franklin Library, 1977]; *Eight Plays,* with an introduction by Harold Clurman [Garden City, N.Y.: Doubleday, 1979]; *Plays 1957–80* edited by Gussow and Holdich [New York: Library of America, 2000]. The screenplay was published [Culver City, Calif.: Metro-Goldwyn-Mayer, 1961]).

*Talk to Me Like the Rain and Let Me Listen* (1950; published in *27 Wagons Full of Cotton and Other One-Act Plays,* 3d ed. [Norfolk, Conn.: New Directions, 1953]; reprinted 1958, 1966, 1981, 1992]).

*Ten Blocks on the Camino Real* (1946; published in *American Blues* [New York: Dramatists Play Service, 1948]; reprinted [1968, 1976]).

*This Is the Peaceable Kingdom* (1980; published in *In the Bar of a Tokyo Hotel and Other Plays* [New York: New Directions, 1981]).

*This Property Is Condemned* (before 1942; published in *27 Wagons Full of Cotton and Other One-Act Plays* [Norfolk, Conn., New York: New Directions, 1945, 1953, 1966]).

*Tiger Tail* (1977; published in *Baby Doll & Tiger Tail: A Screenplay and Play* [New York: New Directions, 1991]).

*The Travelling Companion* (1981; published in *Christopher Street* 5, no. 10 [November 1981]: 32–40).

*27 Wagons Full of Cotton* (before 1946; published [Norfolk, Conn.: New York: New Directions, 1945]; reprinted [1946, 1949, 1953, 1954, 1958, 1966, 1981, 1992]; [London: J. Lehmann, 1949]; included in *Baby Doll: The Script for the Film, Incorporating the Two One-Act Plays Which Suggested it—27 Wagons Full of Cotton, and The Long Stay Cut Short, or The Unsatisfactory Supper* [New York: New Directions, 1956]; *The Theatre of Tennessee Williams*, vol. 6 [New York: New Directions, 1971]; *Plays 1937–1955* [New York: Library of America, 2000]).

*The Two-Character Play* (1968; published [New York: New Directions, 1969, 1979]; included in *The Theatre of Tennessee Williams*, Vol. 5 [New York: New Directions, 1976]). (See also *Out Cry*.)

*The Unsatisfactory Supper*. See *The Long Stay Cut Short*.

*Vieux Carré* (1976; published [New York: New Directions, 1979]; reprinted [2000]; [New York: Golden Eagle Productions, 1979]; included in *The Theatre of Tennessee Williams, Vol. 8* [New York: New Directions, 1992]; *Plays 1957–1980* [New York: Library of America, 2000]).

*Will Mr. Merriwether Return from Memphis?* (1950; published *The Missouri Review*, 20, no. 2 [1997]; 79–131).

*You Touched Me!* (1942; published [New York: Samuel French, 1947]; reprinted [1993]).

## Fiction, Essays, and Poetry

*Androgyne, Mon Amour* (1977; poetry collection [New York: New Directions]).

*Blue Mountain Ballads* (c. 1943; poetry collection published as lyrics for musical score, with musical composition by Paul Bowles, under the title *Heavenly Grass* [New York: G. Schirmer, 1943]; reprinted [New York: G. Schirmer, 1946]; reprinted as *Blue Mountain Ballads* [New York: G. Schirmer, 1946]; *Sugar in the Cane* [New York: G. Schirmer, 1946]; Lonesome Man [New York: G. Schirmer, 1946]; Cabin [New York: G. Schirmer, 1946]; *Heavenly Grass and Cabin* [New York: G. Schirmer, 1979]; *Blue Mountain Ballads* [New York: G. Schirmer, 1979]).

*Eight Mortal Ladies Possessed* (poetry collection published [New York: New Directions, 1974]; [London, Secker & Warburg, 1975]).

*In the Winter of Cities* (poetry collection; published [Norfolk, Conn.: New Directions, 1956]; [Norfolk, Conn.: J. Laughlin, 1956]; reprinted [New York: New Directions, 1964]).

*The Knightly Quest* (before 1966; published as *The Knightly Quest: A Novella and Four Short Stories (Mama's Old Stucco House, Man Bring This Up Road, The Kingdom of Earth, Grand)* for J. Laughlin [New York: New Directions, 1966]; [London: Secker & Warburg, 1968]; as *The Knightly Quest, A Novel* [New York: New Directions, 1968]).

*Moise and the World of Reason* (before 1975; [New York: Simon & Schuster, 1975]; [London: W. H. Allen, 1975]; [New York: Bantam Books, 1975]; [Taipei: Imperial Book, Sound & Gift Co., 1975]; reprinted [W. H. Allen, 1976]; [Bantam Books, 1976]).

*The Roman Spring of Mrs. Stone* (around 1950; published [New York: New Directions, 1950]; [New York: Ballantine Books, 1950]; [London: Secker & Warburg, 1950]; [London: J. Lehmann, 1950]; [New York: Bantam Books, 1950]; [New York: New American Library, 1950]; [London: Vintage, 1950]; [St. Albans, Panther, 1950]; [Harmondsworth, England: Penguin, 1950]; [London: English Library Ltd., 1960]; [Hollywood, Calif.: Warner Bros. Pictures, 1961]; reprinted [New York: New American Library, 1952, 1959, 1961]; [London: Secker & Warburg, 1957, 1971, 1972]; [Penguin, 1969]; [New York: New Directions, 1969, 1993]; [Bantam Books, 1976]; [St. Albans: Panther, 1976]; [New York: Ballantine Books, 1985]; [London: Vintage, 1999]).

*27 Wagons Full of Cotton and Other One-Act Plays* (before 1945; published [New York: New Directions, 1945]; reprinted [New York: New Directions, 1949, 1953, 1954, 1966, 1992]).

*Where I Live* (collection of essays; published [New York: New Directions, 1978]).

*Memoirs* (before 1975; published by Doubleday [Garden City, N.Y., 1975]; Bantam Books [New York, 1975]; Star Books [London, 1975]; W. H. Allen [London, 1976]; reprinted Bantam Books [New York, 1976]; W. H. Allen [London, 1977]; Star Books [London, 1977]; Doubleday [Garden City, N.Y., 1983].

### Short Stories

"The Accent of a Coming Foot" (1935; first published in *Collected Stories,* [New York: New Directions, 1985]; in *Collected Stories* [New York: Bantam Books, 1986]; reprinted *Collected Stories* [New York: Bantam Books, 1994]).

"The Angel in the Alcove" (1943; first published in the short story collection *One Arm: and Other Stories* [New York: New Directions, 1948]; reprinted in *Three Players of a Summer Game and Other Stories* [London: Secker & Warburg, 1960]; *Collected Stories* [New York: New Directions, 1985]; *The Night of the Iguana and Other Stories* [London: J. M. Dent, 1995]).

"Big Black: A Mississippi Idyll" (1931–32; published in *Collected Stories* [New York: New Directions, 1985]; reprinted in *Collected Stories* [New York: Ballantine Books, 1986]).

"Chronicle of a Demise" (1947; first published in the collection *One Arm, and Other Stories* [New York: New Directions, 1948]; in *Collected Stories* [New York: New Directions, 1985]; in *Collected Stories* [New York: Bantam Books, 1986]; reprinted in *One Arm, and Other Stories* [New York: New Directions, 1967]; *Collected Stories* [New York: Bantam Books, 1994]).

"The Coming of Something to Widow Holly" (around 1943; published in *New Directions in Prose and Poetry,* (Vol. 14) [New York: New Directions, 1953]; in *Hard Candy, A Book of Stories* [New York: New Directions, 1954]; in *The Kingdom of Earth with Hard Candy: A Book of Stories* [New York: New Directions, 1954]; in *Hard Candy, A Book of Stories* [Norfolk, Conn.: J. Laughlin, 1954]; in *Three Players of a Summer Game: and Other Stories* [London: Secker & Warburg, 1960]; in *Three Players of a Summer Game, and Other Stories* [London: J. M. Dent, 1960]; in *Collected Stories* [New York: New Directions, 1985]; in *Collected Stories* [New York: Ballantine Books, 1986]; in *The Night of the Iguana and Other Stories* [London: J. M. Dent, 1995]; reprinted in *Hard Candy: A Book of Stories* [New York: New Directions, 1959, 1967]; reprinted in *Three Players of a Summer Game and Other Stories* [London: J. M. Dent, 1984]; reprinted in *Collected Stories* [New York: New Directions, 1994]).

"Completed" (1973; published in *Eight Mortal Ladies Possessed* [New York: New Directions, 1974]; in *Collected Stories* [New York: New Directions, 1985]; in *Collected Stories* [New York: Ballantine Books, 1986]; reprinted in *Collected Stories* [New York: New Directions, 1994]).

"The Dark Room" (around 1940; published in *Collected Stories* [New York: New Directions, 1985]; in *Collected Stories* [New York: Ballantine Books, 1986]; reprinted in *Collected Stories* [New York: New Directions, 1994]).

"Das Wasser ist kalt" (1973–79; published in *Collected Stories* [New York: New Directions, 1985]; in *Collected Stories* [New York: Ballantine Books, 1986]; reprinted in *Collected Stories* [New York: New Directions, 1994]).

"Desire and the Black Masseur" (1942–46; published in *New Directions in Prose and Poetry,* (Vol. 10) [New York: New Directions, 1948]; in the collection *One Arm, and Other Stories* [New York: New Directions, 1948]; in *Collected Stories* [New York: New Directions, 1985]; in *Collected Stories* [New York: Bantam Books, 1986]; reprinted in *One Arm, and Other Stories* [New York: New Directions, 1967]; *Collected Stories* [New York: Bantam Books, 1994]).

"The Field of Blue Children" (1937; published in *Story* magazine [Vol. 15, no. 79 (September–October 1939); pp. 66–72]; in the collection *One Arm, and Other Stories* [New York: New Directions, 1948]; in *Housewife* magazine [Vol. 14, no. 10 (October 1952) pp. 38, 83, 85–86]; in *Three Players of a Summer Game, and Other Stories* [London: Secker & Warburg, 1960]; in *Three Players of a Summer Game, and Other Stories* [London: J. M. Dent, 1960]; in *Collected Stories* [New York: New Directions, 1985]; in *Collected Stories* [New York: Bantam Books, 1986]; reprinted in *One Arm, and Other Stories* [New Directions, 1967]; *Collected Stories* [New York; Bantam Books, 1994]); in *The Night of the Iguana and Other Stories* [London: J. M. Dent, 1995]).

"Gift of an Apple" (1936; published in *Collected Stories* [New York: New Directions, 1985]; in *Collected Stories* [New York: Bantam Books, 1986]; reprinted *Collected Stories* [New York: Bantam Books, 1994]).

"Grand" (around 1964; published in *The Knightly Quest: A Novella and Four Short Stories (Mama's Old Stucco House, Man Bring This Up Road, The Kingdom of Earth, Grand)* [New York: New Directions for J. Laughlin, 1966]; in *Collected Stories* [New York: New Directions, 1985]; in *Collected Stories* [New York: Bantam Books, 1986]; reprinted *Collected Stories* [New York: Bantam Books, 1994]).

"Happy August the Tenth" (1970; published in *Antaeus* no. 42 (1971) pp. 22–23; in *Eight Mortal Ladies Possessed* [New York: New Directions, 1974]; in *Collected Stories* [New York: New Directions, 1985]; in *Collected Stories* [New York: Ballantine Books, 1986]; reprinted in *Collected Stories* [New York: New Directions, 1994]).

"Hard Candy" (1953; published in *Hard Candy, a Book of Stories* [New York: New Directions, 1954]; in *Hard Candy, a Book of Stories* [Norfolk, Conn.: J. Laughlin, 1954]; in *The Kingdom of Earth with Hard Candy: A Book of Stories* [New York: New Directions, 1954]; [Tokyo: Kinseido, 1961]; in *Collected Stories* [New York: New Directions, 1985]; in *Collected Stories* [New York: Ballantine Books, 1986]; reprinted in *Collected Stories* [New York: New Directions, 1994]).

"The Important Thing" (1945; published in *Story* magazine 27, no. 116 (1945) pp. 17–25; *One Arm, and Other Stories* [New York: New Directions, 1948]; in *Collected Stories* [New York: New Directions, 1985]; in *Collected Stories* [New York: Bantam Books, 1986]; reprinted in *One Arm, and Other Stories* [New York: New Directions, 1967]; *Collected Stories* [New York: Bantam Books, 1994]; in *The Night of the Iguana and Other Stories* [London: J. M. Dent, 1995]).

"In Memory of an Aristocrat" (1940; published in *Collected Stories* [New York: New Directions, 1985]; in *Collected Stories* [New York: Bantam Books, 1986]; reprinted in *Collected Stories* [New York: Bantam Books, 1994]).

"The Interval" (1945; published in *Collected Stories* [New York: New Directions, 1985]; in *Collected Stories* [New York: Bantam Books, 1986]; reprinted in *Collected Stories* [New York: Bantam Books, 1994]).

"The Inventory at Fontana Bella" (1972; published in *Playboy*, no. 172 (1973) pp. 76–78; in *Eight Mortal Ladies Possessed* [New York: New Directions, 1974]; *Collected Stories* [New York: New Directions, 1985]; in *Collected Stories* [New York: Bantam Books, 1986]; reprinted in *Collected Stories* [New York: Bantam Books, 1994]).

"It Happened the Day the Sun Rose" (before 1981; published [Los Angeles: Sylvester & Orphanos, 1981]).

"The Killer Chicken and the Closet Queen" (1977; published in *Christopher Street*, 3, no. 1 (1978) pp. 17–26; in *Collected Stories* [New York: New Directions, 1985]; in *Collected Stories* [New York: Bantam Books, 1994]).

"The Kingdom of Earth" (1942; published in *The Kingdom of Earth with Hard Candy: A Book of Stories* [New York: New Directions, 1954]; in *The Knightly Quest: A Novella and Four Short Stories (Mama's Old Stucco House, Man Bring This Up Road, The Kingdom of Earth, Grand)* [New York: New Directions for J. Laughlin, 1966]; in *Collected Stories* [New York: New Directions, 1985]; in *Collected Stories* [New York: Bantam Books, 1986]; reprinted *Collected Stories* [New York: Bantam Books, 1994]).

"A Lady's Beaded Bag" (1930; published in *Columns*, University of Missouri literary magazine, 1, no. 3 (May 1930) pp. 11–12; in *Collected Stories* [New York: New Directions, 1985]; in *Collected Stories* [New York: Bantam Books, 1986]; reprinted *Collected Stories* [New York: Bantam Books, 1994]).

"The Malediction" (before 1945; published in *One Arm, and Other Stories* [New York: New Directions, 1948]; in *Three Players of a Summer Game, and Other Stories* [London: Secker & Warburg, 1960]; in *Three Players of a Summer Game, and Other Stories* [London: J. M. Dent, 1960]; in *Collected Stories* [New York: New Directions, 1985]; in *Collected Stories* [New York: Bantam Books, 1986]; reprinted in *One Arm, and Other Stories* [New York: New Directions, 1967]; *Collected Stories* [New York: Bantam Books, 1994]; in *The Night of the Iguana and Other Stories* [London: J. M. Dent, 1995]).

"Mama's Old Stucco House" (before 1965; published in *Esquire* 62, no. 1 (January 1965) 87–90; in *Weekend Telegraph*, no. 33, (7 May 1965) pp. 49–54; in *The Knightly Quest: A Novella and Four Short Stories (Mama's Old Stucco House, Man Bring This Up Road, The Kingdom of Earth, Grand)* [New York: New Directions for J. Laughlin, 1966]; in *Collected Stories* [New York: New Directions, 1985]; in *Collected Stories* [New York: Bantam Books, 1986]; reprinted *Collected Stories* [New York: Bantam Books, 1994]).

"Man Bring This Up Road" (1953; published in *Mademoiselle*, 49, no. 3 (July 1959) pp. 56–61; in *International*, 1, no. 2 (spring 1965) pp. 61–65; in *The Knightly Quest: A Novella and Four Short Stories (Mama's Old Stucco House, Man Bring This Up Road, The Kingdom of Earth, Grand)* [New York: New Directions for J. Laughlin, 1966]; in *Collected Stories* [New York: New Directions, 1985]; in *Collected Stories* [New York: Bantam Books, 1986]; reprinted *Collected Stories* [New York: Bantam Books, 1994]).

"The Mattress by the Tomato Patch" (1953; published in *The London Magazine,* 1, no. 9 (October 1954) pp. 16–24; in *The Kingdom of Earth with Hard Candy: A Book of Stories* [New York: New Directions, 1954]; in *Hard Candy, A Book of Stories* [Norfolk, Conn.: J. Laughlin, 1954]; in *Collected Stories* [New York: New Directions, 1985]; in *Collected Stories* [New York: Bantam Books, 1986]; reprinted *Collected Stories* [New York: Bantam Books, 1994]).

"Miss Coynte of Greene" (1972; published in *Eight Mortal Ladies Possessed* [New York: New Directions, 1974]; in *Collected Stories* [New York: New Directions, 1985]; in *Collected Stories* [New York: Ballantine Books, 1986]; reprinted in *Collected Stories* [New York: New Directions, 1994]).

"Mother Yaws" (1977; published in *Collected Stories* [New York: New Directions, 1985]; in *Collected Stories* [New York: Ballantine Books, 1986]; reprinted in *Collected Stories* [New York: New Directions, 1994]).

"The Mysteries of Joy Rio" (1941; published in *The Kingdom of Earth with Hard Candy: A Book of Stories* [New York: New Directions, 1954]; in *Hard Candy, A Book of Stories* [Norfolk, Conn.: J. Laughlin, 1954]; in *Collected Stories* [New York: New Directions, 1985]; in *Collected Stories* [New York: Ballantine Books, 1986]; reprinted in *Collected Stories* [New York: New Directions, 1994]).

"Night of the Iguana" (1946–48; published in *One Arm, and Other Stories* [New York: New Directions, 1948]; in *Three Players of a Summer Game, and Other Stories* [London: Secker & Warburg 1960]; in *Three Players of a Summer Game, and Other Stories* [London: J. M. Dent, 1960]; in *Hard Candy, A Book of Stories* [Norfolk, Conn.: J. Laughlin, 1954]; in *Collected Stories* [New York: New Directions, 1985]; in *Collected Stories* [New York: Bantam Books, 1986]; reprinted *Collected Stories* [New York: Bantam Books, 1994]).

"One Arm" (1942–45; published in *One Arm, and Other Stories* [New York: New Directions, 1948]; in *Three Players of a Summer Game, and Other Stories* [London: Secker & Warburg, 1960]; in *Three Players of a Summer Game, and Other Stories* [London: J. M. Dent, 1960]; in *Hard Candy, A Book of Stories* [Norfolk, Conn.: J. Laughlin, 1954]; in *Collected Stories* [New York: New Directions, 1985]; in *Collected Stories* [New York: Bantam Books, 1986]; reprinted *Collected Stories* [New York: Bantam Books, 1994]; in *The Night of the Iguana and Other Stories* [London: J. M. Dent, 1995]).

"Oriflamme" (1944; published in *Eight Mortal Ladies Possessed* [New York: New Directions, 1974]; in *Collected Stories* [New York: New Directions, 1985]; in *Collected Stories* [New York: Ballantine Books, 1986]; reprinted in *Collected Stories* [New York: New Directions, 1994]).

"The Poet" (before 1948; published in *One Arm, and Other Stories* [New York: New Directions, 1948]; in *Collected Stories* [New York: New Directions, 1985]; in *Collected Stories* [New York: Ballantine Books, 1986]; reprinted in *Collected Stories* [New York: New Directions, 1994]).

"Portrait of a Girl in Glass" (1942; published in *One Arm, and Other Stories* [New York: New Directions, 1948]; in *Three Players of a Summer Game, and Other Stories* [London: Secker & Warburg, 1960]; in *Three Players of a Summer Game, and Other Stories* [London: J. M. Dent, 1960]; in *Collected Stories* [New York: New Directions, 1985]; in *Collected Stories* [New York: Ballantine Books, 1986]; reprinted in *Collected Stories* [New York: New Directions, 1994]; in *The Night of the Iguana and Other Stories* [London: J. M. Dent, 1995]).

"A Recluse and His Guest" (early 1970s; published in *Collected Stories* [New York: New Directions, 1985]; in *Collected Stories* [New York: Ballantine Books, 1986]; reprinted in *Collected Stories* [New York: New Directions, 1994]).

"The Resemblance between a Violin Case and a Coffin" (1949; published in *Flair New York City,* 1, no. 1 (February 1950) pp. 40–41, 126–128; in *The Best American Short Stories of 1951* [Boston: Houghton Mifflin, 1951]; in *Hard Candy, A Book of Stories* [Norfolk, Conn.: J. Laughlin, 1954]; in *The Kingdom of Earth with Hard Candy: A Book of Stories* [New York: New Directions, 1954]; in *Three Players of a Summer Game, and Other Stories* [London: Secker & Warburg, 1960]; in *Three Players of a Summer Game, and Other Stories* [London: J. M. Dent, 1960]; in *Collected Stories* [New York: New Directions, 1985]; in *Collected Stories* [New York: Bantam Books, 1986]; reprinted in *One Arm, and Other Stories* [New York: New Directions, 1967]; *Collected Stories* [New York: Bantam Books, 1994]); in *The Night of the Iguana and Other Stories* [London: J. M. Dent, 1995]).

"Rubio y Morena" (before 1948; published in *Partisan Review,* 15, no. 12 [1948] pp. 1293–1306; in *New Directions in Prose and Poetry,* 15, no. 12 (1949); in *Hard Candy, A Book of Stories* [Norfolk, Conn.: J. Laughlin, 1954]; in *The Kingdom of Earth with Hard Candy: A Book of Stories* [New York: New

Directions, 1954]; in *Collected Stories* [New York: New Directions, 1985]; in *Collected Stories* [New York: Bantam Books, 1986]; reprinted in *Collected Stories* [New York: Bantam Books, 1994]).

"Sabbatha and Solitude" (1973; published in *Playgirl*, 1, no. 4 (1973); in *Eight Mortal Ladies Possessed* [New York: New Directions, 1974]; in *Collected Stories* [New York: New Directions, 1985]; in *Collected Stories* [New York: Ballantine Books, 1986]; reprinted in *Collected Stories* [New York: New Directions, 1994]) 6 pages in various pagings.

"Sand" (before 1976; published in *Collected Stories* [New York: New Directions, 1985]; in *Collected Stories* [New York: Ballantine Books, 1986]; reprinted in *Collected Stories* [New York: New Directions, 1994]).

"Something About Him" (before 1946; published in *Mademoiselle*, 23, no. 2 (1946) pp. 168–169, 235–239; in *Collected Stories* [New York: New Directions, 1985]; in *Collected Stories* [New York: Ballantine Books, 1986]; reprinted in *Collected Stories* [New York: New Directions, 1994]).

"Something by Tolstoi" (1930–31); published in *Collected Stories* [New York: New Directions, 1985]; in *Sunday Times* (London, England), August 3, 1986, pp. 26–28 in *Collected Stories* [New York: Ballantine Books, 1986]; reprinted in *Collected Stories* [New York: New Directions, 1994]).

"Ten Minute Stop" (around 1936; published in *Collected Stories* [New York: New Directions, 1985]; in *Collected Stories* [New York: Ballantine Books, 1986]; reprinted in *Collected Stories* [New York: New Directions, 1994]).

"Tent Worms" (1945; published in *Collected Stories* [New York: New Directions, 1985]; in *Collected Stories* [New York: Ballantine Books, 1986]; reprinted in *Collected Stories* [New York: New Directions, 1994]).

"Three Players of a Summer Game" (1951–52); published in *Hard Candy, A Book of Stories* [Norfolk, Conn.: J. Laughlin, 1954]; in *The Kingdom of Earth with Hard Candy: A Book of Stories* [New York: New Directions, 1954]; in *Three Players of a Summer Game, and Other Stories* [London: Secker & Warburg, 1960]; in *Three Players of a Summer Game, and Other Stories* [London: J. M. Dent, 1960]; in *Collected Stories* [New York: New Directions, 1985]; in *Collected Stories* [New York: New Directions, 1985]; in *Collected Stories* [New York: Bantam Books, 1986]; reprinted in *Collected Stories* [New York: Bantam Books, 1994]; in *The Night of the Iguana and Other Stories* [London: J. M. Dent, 1995]).

"Twenty-seven Wagons Full of Cotton" (1935; published in *Collected Stories* [New York: New Directions, 1985]; in *Collected Stories* [New York: Bantam Books, 1986]; reprinted in *Collected Stories* [New York: Bantam Books, 1994]).

"Two on a Party" (1951–52); published in *Hard Candy, A Book of Stories* [Norfolk, Conn.: J. Laughlin, 1954]; in *The Kingdom of Earth with Hard Candy: A Book of Stories* [New York: New Directions, 1954]; in *Three Players of a Summer Game, and Other Stories* [London: Secker & Warburg, 1960]; in *Three Players of a Summer Game, and Other Stories* [London: J. M. Dent, 1960]; in *Collected Stories* [New York: New Directions, 1985]; in *Collected Stories* [New York: Bantam Books, 1986]; reprinted in *Collected Stories* [New York: Bantam Books, 1994]; in *The Night of the Iguana and Other Stories* [London: J. M. Dent, 1995]).

"The Vengeance of Nitocris" (1928, published in *Weird Tales*, 12, no. 2 (1928) pp. 253–260; in *The Pulps: Fifty Years of American Pop Culture* [New York: Chelsea House, 1970]; in *Collected Stories* [New York: New Directions, 1985]; in *Masterpieces of Terror and the Supernatural* [New York: Doubleday & Co., 1985]; in *Collected Stories* [New York: Bantam Books, 1986]; reprinted in *Collected Stories* [New York: Bantam Books, 1994]; *First Fiction: An Anthology of the First Published Stories by Famous Writers* [Boston: Little, Brown, 1994]; and *Into the Mummy's Tomb* [New York: Berkley Books, 2001]).

"The Vine" (1939–44; published in *Mademoiselle*, 39, no. 3 (July 1954) pp. 25–30; *Hard Candy, a Book of Stories* [Norfolk, Conn.: Laughlin, 1954]; in *The Kingdom of Earth with Hard Candy: A Book of Stories* [New York: New Directions, 1954]; in *Collected Stories* [New York: New Directions, 1985]; in *Collected Stories* [New York: Bantam Books, 1986]; reprinted in *Collected Stories* [New York: Bantam Books, 1994]).

"The Yellow Bird" (before 1947; published in *One Arm, and Other Stories* [New York: New Directions, 1948]; in *Three Players of a Summer Game, and Other Stories* [London: Secker & Warburg, 1960]; in *Three Players of a Summer Game, and Other Stories* [London: J. M. Dent, 1960]; in *Collected Stories* [New York: New Directions, 1985]; in *Collected Stories* [New York: Bantam Books, 1986]; reprinted in *Collected Stories* [New York: Bantam Books, 1994]); in *The Night of the Iguana and Other Stories* [London: J. M. Dent, 1995]).

# Bibliography of Secondary Sources


Adamson, Eve. "Introduction," in *Something Cloudy, Something Clear.* Tennessee Williams. New York: New Directions, 1995.

Adler, Jacob H. "*Night of the Iguana:* A New Tennessee Williams?" *Ramparts* 1, no. 3 (1962): 59–68.

Adler, Thomas P. "Culture, Power, and the (En)gendering of Community: Tennessee Williams and Politics," *Mississippi Quarterly* 48 (fall 1995): 649–665.

———. "The Dialogue of Incompletion in Tennessee Williams's Later Plays," *Quarterly Journal of Speech* 61 (February 1975): 48–58.

———. A Streetcar Named Desire: *The Moth and the Lantern.* Boston: Twayne, 1990.

———. "Tennessee Williams's Poetry: Intertext and Metatext," *The Tennessee Williams Annual Review* (1998): 63–72.

Adler, Thomas P., Judith Hersh Clark, and Lyle Taylor. "Tennessee Williams in the Seventies: A Checklist," *Tennessee Williams Newsletter* 2, no. 1 (spring 1980): 24–29.

Arnott, Catherine M. *Tennessee Williams on File.* London: Methuen, 1985.

Asibong, Emmanuel B. *Tennessee Williams: The Tragic Tension.* Elms Court; London: Arthur H. Stockwell, 1978.

Babcock, Granger. "*The Glass Menagerie* and the Transformation of the Subject." *Journal of Dramatic Theory and Criticism* 14, no. 1 (fall 1999): 17–36.

Bak, John S. "From '10' to 'Quarter Past Eight Foot'": Tennessee Williams and William Inge, 1957," *American Drama* 7, no. 1 (fall 1997): 19–29.

Barbera, Jack. "Strangers in the Night: Three Interior Dramatic Monologues by Tennessee Williams," *The Southern Quarterly* (fall 1999): 71–80.

Beaurline, Lester A. "*The Glass Menagerie:* From Story to Play," *Modern Drama* 8 (1965): 143–149.

Berkman, Leonard. "The Tragic Downfall of Blanche DuBois," in *Modern Drama* 10, no. 2 (December 1967): 249–257.

Bibler, Michael P. "'A Tenderness Which Was Uncommon': Homosexuality, Narrative, and the Southern Plantation in Tennessee Williams's *Cat on a Hot Tin Roof,*" *The Mississippi Quarterly* 55 no. 3 (summer 2002): 381.

Bloom, Harold, ed. *Tennessee Williams.* Bloom's Major Dramatists: Comprehensive Research and Study Guide Broomall, Pa.: Chelsea House, 2000.

Boxhill, Roger, *Tennessee Williams.* New York: Macmillan, 1988.

Bradham, JoAllen. "Reprising *The Glass Menagerie:* William Inge's *My Son Is a Splendid Driver,*" *American Drama* 11 no. 1 (winter 2002): 58.

Bray, Robert. "*Battle of Angels* and *Orpheus Descending,*" in *Tennessee Williams: A Guide to Research and Performance,* edited by Philip C. Kolin. Westport, Conn.: Greenwood, 1998, pp. 22–33.

———, ed. "Looking at the Late Plays of Tennessee Williams," *Tennessee Williams Annual Review* 5 (2002) Available online. URL: http://www.tennesseewilliamsstudies.org/archives/2002/1panel_lateplays.htm

———. "Moise and the Man in the Fur Coat," *The Southern Quarterly,* 38, no. 1 (fall 1999): 58–70.

———. "*Sweet Bird of Youth,*" in *Tennessee Williams: A Guide to Research and Performance,* edited by Philip C. Kolin. Westport, Conn.: Greenwood, 1998, pp. 137–148.

———. "Tennessee Homecoming," *The New Orleans Historical Collection Quarterly* 19, no. 3 (summer 2001): pp. 1–5.

———. "*Vieux Carré:* Transferring a Story of Mood," in *The Undiscovered Country: The Later Plays of*

*Tennessee Williams,* edited by Philip Kolin. New York: Peter Lang, 2002, pp. 142–154.

Brown, Cecil. "Interview with Tennessee Williams," in *Conversations with Tennessee Williams,* edited by Albert Devlin. Jackson: University of Mississippi Press, 1986, pp. 251–283.

Brown, Dennis. *Shoptalk: Conversations about Theatre and Film with Twelve Writers, One Producer—and Tennessee Williams's Mother.* New York: Newmarket Press, 1992.

Bruhm, Steven. "Blackmailed by Sex: Tennessee Williams and the Economics of Desire," *Modern Drama* 34 (1991): 532–533.

Brustein, Robert. "Robert Brustein on Theatre: Orpheus Condescending." *The New Republic,* October 30, 1988, 25–27.

Burnett, Hallie. *On Writing the Short Story.* New York: Harper & Row, 1983.

Cahir, Linda Costanzo. "The Artful Rerouting of *A Streetcar Named Desire,*" *Literature Film Quarterly* 22, no. 2 (1994): 72.

Canby, Vincent. "Decadence, Ferns and Facades," *New York Times,* October 11, 1995, pp. C17–C18.

Cardullo, Bert. "The Blue Rose of St. Louis: Laura, Romanticism, and *The Glass Menagerie,*" *Tennessee Williams Annual Review* 1 (1998): 81–92.

Carter, Cassie. "*Period of Adjustment: High Point over a Cavern: A Serious Comedy,*" in *Tennessee Williams: A Guide to Research and Performance,* edited by Philip C. Kolin. Westport, Conn.: Greenwood, 1998, pp. 204–210.

Cluck, Nancy Anne. "Showing or Telling: Narrators in the Drama of Tennessee Williams," *American Literature* 51, no. 1 (March 1979): 84–93.

Clum, John M. "*Something Cloudy, Something Clear:* Homophobic Discourse in Tennessee Williams," in *Displacing Homophobia: Gay Male Perspectives in Literature and Culture,* edited by Ronald R. Butters, John M. Clum, and Michael Moon. Durham, N.C.: Duke University Press, 1989, pp. 149–168.

Cobbe, Elizabeth C. "Williams's," *Explicator* 61, no. 1 (fall 2002): 49.

Cohn, Alan M. "More Tennessee Williams in the Seventies: Additions to the Checklist and the Gunn Bibliography," *Tennessee Williams Review* 3, no. 2 (spring–fall 1982): 46–50.

Cohn, Ruby. "The Garrulous Grotesques of Tennessee Williams," in *Tennessee Williams—a Collection of Critical Essays,* edited by Stephen Stanton. Englewood Cliffs, N.J.: Prentice-Hall, 1977, pp. 45–60.

———. "Late Tennessee Williams," *Modern Drama,* 27, no. 3 (September 1984): 336–344.

Colanzi, Rita. "Caged Birds: Bad Faith in Tennessee Williams's Drama," *Modern Drama* 35 (1992): 456–458.

Cole, Toby, and Helen Krich Cinoy. *Directors on Directing.* New York: Bobbs Merrill, 1963.

Conlon, Christopher. "'Fox-Teeth in Your Heart': Sexual Self-Portraiture in the Poetry of Tennessee Williams," *The Tennessee Williams Annual Review* 4 (2001). Available online. URL: http://www.tennesseewilliamsstudies.org/archives/2001/5conlon_htm.

Corrigan, M. A. "Memory, Dream, and Myth in the Plays of Tennessee Williams." *Renascence* (spring 1976): 155–167.

———. "Realism and Theatricalism in *A Streetcar Named Desire,*" *Modern Drama* 19, no. 4 (1976): 392.

Corrigan, Robert W. "Tennessee Williams," in *Contemporary Dramatists,* edited by K. A. Berney. London: St James, 1993, pp. 825–830.

Costello, Donald P. "Tennessee Williams's 'Conjure Man' in script and screen," *Literature–Film Quarterly* 27, no. 4 (October 1999): 263.

Crandell, George W. "*Cat on a Hot Tin Roof,*" in *Tennessee Williams: A Guide to Research and Performance,* edited by Philip C. Kolin. Westport, Conn.: Greenwood, 1998, pp. 109–125.

———. "The Cinematic Eye in Tennessee Williams's *The Glass Menagerie,*" *Tennessee Williams Annual Review* 1 (1998): 1–12.

———, ed. *The Critical Response to Tennessee Williams.* Westport, Conn.: Greenwood Press, 1996.

———. "'Echo Spring': Reflecting the Gaze of Narcissus in Tennessee Williams's *Cat on a Hot Tin Roof,*" *Modern Drama* 42 (fall 1999): 427.

———. "Misrepresentation and Miscegenation: Reading the Racialized Discourse of Tennessee Williams's '*A Streetcar Named Desire,*'" *Modern Drama* 40, no. 3 (fall 1997): 337.

———. "*The Night of the Iguana,*" in *Tennessee Williams: A Guide to Research and Performance,* edited by Philip C. Kolin. Westport, Conn.: Greenwood, 1998, pp. 148–157.

———. "Peeping Tom: Voyeurism, Taboo, and Truth in the World of Tennessee Williams's Short Fiction," *Southern Quarterly* 38, no. 1 (fall 1999): 28–35.

———. *Tennessee Williams: A Descriptive Bibliography.* Pittsburgh: University of Pittsburgh Press, 1995.

Cuoco, Lorin, and William Gass, eds. "Tennessee Williams," in *Literary St. Louis: A Guide.* St. Louis: Missouri Historical Society Press, 2000, pp. 194–202.

Cuoco, Lorin, and William Gass, eds. "William Inge," in *Literary St. Louis: A Guide.* St. Louis: Missouri Historical Society Press, 2000, pp. 203–207.

Daniel, Lanelle. "*The Two-Character Play* and *Out-Cry*," in *Tennesse Williams: A Guide to Research and Performance,* edited by Philip C. Kolin. Westport, Conn.: Greenwood, 1998, pp. 176–182.

Davis, David A. "'Make the Lie True': The Tragic Family in *Cat on a Hot Tin Roof* and *King Lear,*" *The Tennessee Williams Annual Review* 5 (2002). Available online. URL: http://www.tennesseewilliamsstudies.org/archives/2002/2davis.htm.

Debusscher, Gilbert. "'Minting their Separate Wills': Tennessee Williams and Hart Crane," *Modern Drama* 26, no. 4 (December 1983): 455–476.

———. "Tennessee Williams's Dramatic Charade: Secrets and Lies in *The Glass Menagerie,*" *Tennessee Williams Annual Review* 3 (2000): 57–68.

———. "Tennessee Williams's Lives of the Saints: A Playwright's Obliquity," *Revue des Langues Vivantes* 40 (1974): 449–456.

———. "'Where Memory Begins': New Texas Light on *The Glass Menagerie,*" *Tennessee Williams Annual Review* 1 (1998): 53–62.

Dervin, Daniel. "The Absent Father's Presence in Modern and American Gay Drama," *American Imago* 56, no. 1 (1999): 53–74.

Devlin, Albert J., ed. *Conversations with Tennessee Williams.* Jackson: University Press of Mississippi, 1986.

———. "'The Selected Letters of Tennessee Williams': Prospects for Research," *Tennessee Williams Annual Review* 1 (1998): 23–32.

Di Cintio, Matt. "Ordered Anarchy: Writing as Transitional Object in *Moise and the World of Reason,*" *Tennessee Williams Annual Review* 5 (2002). Available online. URL: http://www.tennesseewilliamsstudies.org/archives/2002/4dicinto.htm.

Donahue, Francis, *The Dramatic World of Tennessee Williams.* New York: Ungar, 1964.

Dorff, Linda. "'All very [not!] Pirandello': Radical Theatrics in the Evolution of *Vieux Carré,*" *Tennessee Williams Annual Review* 3 (2000): 1–23.

———. "Babylon Now: Tennessee Williams's Apocalypses," *Theater* 29, no. 3 (fall 1999): 115.

———. "Chamber Music: Four Artists Reflect on the Late Plays of Tennessee Williams," *American Theatre* 15, no. 8 (October 1998): 22–25.

———. Disfigured Stages: The Late Plays of Tennessee Williams, 1958–1983. Ph.D. Diss., New York University, 1997.

———. "'I Prefer the Mad Ones': Tennessee Williams Grotesque-Exegetical Poems," *Southern Quarterly* 38 (fall 1999): 81–93.

———. "Theatricalist Cartoons: Tennessee Williams's Late, 'Outrageous' Plays," *Tennessee Williams Annual Review* 2 (1999): 13–34.

Draya, Ren. The Fiction of Tennessee Williams's, in *Tennessee Williams: A Tribute,* edited by Jac Tharpe. Jackson: University Press of Mississippi, 1977, p. 647.

———. "The Frightened Heart: A Study of Character and Theme in The Fiction, Poetry, Short Plays, and Recent Drama of Tennessee Williams." Dissertation, University of Colorado, 1977.

Dubbe, P. D. "Feminism in *A Streetcar Named Desire,*" in *New Waves in American Literature,* edited by Desai Mutalik, V. K. Malhotra, T. S. Anand, and Prashant K. Sinha. New Delhi: Creative, 1999, pp. 53–56.

Duprey, Richard A. "Tennessee Williams's Search for Innocence," *Catholic World* 189 (1959): 191–194.

Durham, Leslie Atkins, and John Gronbeck-Tedesco. "*The Rose Tattoo,*" in *Tennessee Williams: A Guide to Research and Performance,* edited by Philip C. Kolin. Westport, Conn.: Greenwood, 1998, pp. 90–99.

Dusenbury, Winifred. "*Baby Doll* and 'The Ponder Heart,'" *Modern Drama* 3 (1961): 393–395.

Ensana, Joel. "Dancing with Waters," *Harvard Gay and Lesbian Review* 6, no. 2 (spring 1999): 12–14.

Evans, Everett. "Role of a Lifetime: Actress Elizabeth Ashley Honors Commitment to Tennessee Williams," *Houston Chronicle,* 26 August 2001, p. 8.

Falk, Signi. *Tennessee Williams.* New York: Twayne, 1978.

Fanatsu, Tatsumi. "Blanche's Loneliness in *A Streetcar Named Desire,*" *American Literature* 5 (June 1961): 36–41.

Fedder, Norman J. *The Influence of D. H. Lawrence on Tennessee Williams.* The Hague: Mouton, 1966.

Fleche, Anne. *Mimetic Disillusions: Eugene O'Neill, Tennessee Williams, and U.S. Dramatic Realism.* Tuscaloosa: University of Alabama Press, 1997.

———. "When a Door Is a Jar, or Out in the Theatre: Tennessee Williams and Queer Space," *Theatre Journal* 47, no. 2 (May 1995): 253–268.

Fisher, James. "An Almost Posthumous Existence: Performance, Gender and Sexuality in *The Roman Spring of Mrs. Stone,*" *Southern Quarterly* 38, no. 1 (fall 1999): 46–51.

———. "'The Angels of Fructification': Tennessee Williams, Tony Kushner, and Images of Homosexuality on the American stage." *The Mississippi Quarterly* 49, no. 1 (winter 1995): 13.

———. "*Camino Real*," in *Tennessee Williams: A Guide to Research and Performance,* edited by Philip C. Kolin. Westport, Conn.: Greenwood, 1998, pp. 100–108.

Ford, Marilyn Claire. "*Suddenly Last Summer*," in *Tennessee Williams: A Guide to Research and Performance,* edited by Philip C. Kolin. Westport, Conn.: Greenwood, 1998, pp. 126—136.

Fordyce, William. "Tennessee Williams's Tom Wingfield and Georg Kaiser's Cashier: A Contextual Comparison," *Papers on Language & Literature* 34, no. 3 (summer 1998): 250.

Foster, Verna. "Desire, Death, and Laughter: Tragicomic Dramaturgy in *A Streetcar Named Desire*," *American Drama* 9, no. 1 (fall 1999): 51–68.

Funke, Lewis, and John E. Booth. "Williams on Williams," *Theatre Arts* (January 1962): 72.

Gardner, Elysa. "Tennessee Williams Is Hotter Than Ever," *USA Today,* 25 October 2003. p. A1.

Gassner, John. "Tennessee Williams: Dramatist of Frustration," *College English* 10, no. 1 (October 1948): 1–7.

———. "Tennessee Williams: 1940–1960," in *Theatre at the Crossroads: Plays and Playwrights of the Mid-Century American Stage,* edited by John Gassner. New York: Holt, Rinehart & Winston, 1960, pp. 77–91.

Gianakaris, C. J. "Tennessee Williams and *Not About Nightingales:* The Path Not Taken." *American Drama* 9, no. 1 (fall 1999): 69–91.

Gilman, Richard. "Introduction," in Stopped Rocking *and Other Screenplays.* New York: New Directions, 1984, 11–18.

Goff, David H. "Tennessee Williams's Films," in *Tennessee Williams: A Guide to Research and Performance,* edited by Philip C. Kolin. Westport, Conn.: Greenwood, 1998, pp. 242–253.

Grauerholz, James. "Orpheus Holds His Own: William Burroughs Talks with Tennessee Williams," in *Conversations with Tennessee Williams,* edited by Albert J. Devlin. Jackson: University Press of Mississippi, 1986.

Grecco, Stephen. "World Literature in Review: English," *World Literature Today* 69, no. 3 (summer 1995): 586–591.

Grierson, Patricia. "An Interview with Dr. Margaret Walker Alexander on Tennessee Williams," *The Mississippi Quarterly* 48, no. 4 (fall 1995): 587.

———. "Tennessee Williams's Poetry," in *Tennessee Williams: A Guide to Research and Performance,* eidted by Philip C. Kolin. Westport, Conn.: Greenwood, 1998, pp. 232–241.

Griffin, Alice. *Understanding Tennessee Williams.* Columbia: University of South Carolina Press, 1995.

Gronbeck-Tedesco, J. "Ambiguity and Performance in the Plays of Tennessee Williams," *The Mississippi Quarterly* 48, no. 4 (fall 1995): 735.

Grosch, Robert J. "Memory as Theme and Production Value in Tennessee Williams's *The Red Devil Battery Sign.*" *Tennessee Williams Annual Review* 1 (1998): 119–124.

Gross, Robert F. "Consuming Hart: Sublimity and Gay Poetics in *Suddenly Last Summer*," *Theatre Journal* 47, no. 2 (May 1995): 229.

———. "The Gnostic Politics of *The Red Devil Battery Sign*," in *The Undiscovered Country: The Later Plays of Tennessee Williams,* edited by Philip C. Kolin. New York: Peter Lang, 2002.

———, ed. *Tennessee Williams: A Casebook.* New York: Routledge, 2002.

Gunn, Dewey Wayne. *Tennessee Williams: A Bibliography.* Metuchen, N.J.: Scarecrow Press, 1980.

Hale, Allean. "The Clock and the Cage: An Afterword about *A System of Wheels*," *Michigan Quarterly Review* 38, no. 4 (fall 1999): 512–513.

———. "Introduction: A Call for Justice," in *Not About Nightingales.* New York: New Directions, 1998, pp. 13–22.

———. "Introduction: A Play for Tomorrow," in *Stairs to the Roof.* New York: New Directions, 2000.

———. "The Secret Script of Tennessee Williams," *The Southern Review* 27, no. 2 (April 1991): 363–375.

———. "Tennessee Williams's St. Louis Blues," *The Mississippi Quarterly* 48, no. 4 (fall 1995): 609.

———. "Tennessee Williams: The Preacher's Boy," *Southern Quarterly* 38, no. 1 (fall 1999): 10–20.

———. "Tom Williams, Proletarian Playwright," *Tennessee Williams Annual Review* 1 (1998): 13–22.

Hall, Joan Wylie. "The Stork and the Reaper, the Madonna and the Stud: Procreation and Mothering in Tennessee Williams's Plays," *The Mississippi Quarterly* 48, no. 4 (fall 1995): 677.

Haller, Scot. "The Twilight of Tennessee Williams: A Portrait of the Playwright in the Last Stage of a Great Career." *People Weekly*, March 14, 1983, 60.

Haskell, Molly. *From Reverence to Rape: The Treatment of Women in the Movies*. Chicago: University of Chicago Press, 1987.

Hassan, Ihab. *Contemporary American Literature: 1945–1972*. New York: Frederick Ungar, 1973.

Hayman, Ronald. *Everyone Else Is an Audience*. New Haven, Conn.: Yale University Press, 1993.

Hays, Peter L. "Tennessee 'Outs' Scott and Ernest," in *The Author as Character: Representing Historical Writers in Literature*, edited by Frank Franssen and Ton Hoenselaars. Madison, N.J.: Fairleigh Dickinson University Press, 1999, pp. 253–263.

Helbig, Jack. "*Something Cloudy, Something Clear.*" *Booklist*, September 15, 1995, p. 131.

Heller, Scott, et al., eds. "Encore, Encore: Tennessee Williams Still Has Not Spoken His Last," *Chronicle of Higher Education* 48, no. 13 (2000): A14.

———. "Tennessee Williams's Last Play Finally Sees Print," *Chronicle of Higher Education* 47, no. 13 (2000): A14.

Henderson, Cathy. "*I Rise in Flame, Cried the Phoenix*," in *Tennessee Williams: A Guide to Research and Performance*, edited by Philip C. Kolin. Westport, Conn.: Greenwood, 1998, pp. 211–219.

Hicks, John. "Bard of Duncan Street: Scene Four," in *Conversations with Tennessee Williams*, edited by Albert Devlin. Jackson: University Press of Mississippi, 1986, pp. 318–324.

Hitchcock, Frances Oglesby. "*The Milk Train Doesn't Stop Here Anymore*," in *Tennessee Williams: A Guide to Research and Performance*, edited by Philip C. Kolin. Westport, Conn.: Greenwood, 1998, pp. 158–165.

Holditch, W. Kenneth. *Tennessee Williams and the South*. Jackson: University Press of Mississippi, 2002.

———. "Tennessee Williams in New Orleans," in *Magical Muse: Millennial Essays on Tennessee Williams*, edited by Ralph Voss. Tuscaloosa: University of Alabama Press, 2002, pp. 193–206.

Hoffman, Peter. "The Last Days of Tennessee Williams," New York, (25 July 1983): 41–49.

Hubbard, Kim. "The Original Maggie the Cat, Maria St. Just, Remembers her Loving Friend Tennessee Williams." *People Weekly*, (April 2, 1990) 93.

Hunter, Christina. "A Tennessee Williams Bibliography, 1998–2001," *Tennessee Williams Annual Review* 4 (2001).

Hurley, Paul J. "*Suddenly Last Summer* as 'Morality Play,'" *Modern Drama* 8, no. 4 (February 1966): 392–402.

Hurrell, John D., ed. *Two Modern American Tragedies: Reviews and Criticism of* Death of a Salesman *and* A Streetcar Named Desire. New York: Scribner's, 1961.

Isaac, Dan. "Big Daddy's Dramatic Word Strings," *American Speech* 40, no. 4 (December 1965): 272–278.

Jackson, Esther M. *The Broken World of Tennessee Williams*. Madison: University of Wisconsin Press, 1965.

Johnstone, Monica. "*The Roman Spring of Mrs. Stone*." *Studies in Short Fiction* 31, no. 4 (fall 1994): 714.

Jones, David Richard. *Great Directors at Work: Stanislavsky, Brecht, Kazan, and Brook*. Berkeley: University of California Press, 1986.

Kahn, Michael. "Introduction," in *Political Stages: Plays That Shaped a Century*, edited by Emily Mann and David Roessel. New York: Applause Books, 2002, pp. 391–392.

Baer, William, ed. *Elia Kazan: Interviews*. Jackson: University of Mississippi Press, 2000.

———. "Notebook for *A Streetcar Named Desire*," in *Twentieth Century Interpretations on* A Streetcar Named Desire: *A Collection of Critical Essays*, edited by Jordan Y. Miller. Englewood Cliffs, N.J.; Prentice-Hall, 1971, pp. 21–26.

King, Kimball. "Tennessee Williams: A Southern Writer," *The Mississippi Quarterly* 49 (fall 1995): 627–647.

Kolin, Philip C., ed. *American Plawyrights Since 1945: A Guide to Scholarship, Criticism, and Performance*. New York: Greenwood, 1989.

———. "Civil Rights and the Black Presence in *Baby Doll*," *Literature-Film Quarterly* 24 (January 1996): 2–11.

———. "Compañero Tenn: The Hispanic Presence in the Plays of Tennessee Williams," *Tennessee Williams Annual Review* 2 (1999): 35–52.

———. *Confronting Tennessee Williams's* A Streetcar Named Desire: *Essays in Critical Pluralism*. Westport, Conn.: Greenwood Press, 1993.

———. "Echoes of Reflexivity in Tennessee Williams's *A Perfect Analysis Given by a Parrot*," *Notes on Contemporary Literature* 30, no. 3 (2000): 7–9.

———. "'Isolated': Tennessee Williams's First Extant Published Short Story," *Tennessee Williams Annual Review* 1 (1998): 33–40.

———. "*Kingdom of Earth/The Seven Descents of Myrtle*," in *Tennessee Williams: A Guide to Research and Performance,* edited by Philip C. Kolin. Westport, Conn.: Greenwood, 1998, pp. 166–175.

———. "Lost in a Sea of Words: Tennessee Williams's *Lifeboat Drill*," *The Mississippi Quarterly* 53, no. 1 (winter 1999): 57.

———. "'Night, Mistuh Charlie': The Porter in Tennessee Williams's 'The Last of My Solid Gold Watches' and the Kairos of Negritude," *The Mississippi Quarterly* 47, no. 2 (spring 1994): 215.

———. "'No Masterpiece Has Been Overlooked': The Early Reception and Significance of Tennessee Williams's 'Big Black: A Mississippi Idyll,'" *ANQ* 8, no. 4 (fall 1995): 27.

———. "*Not About Nightingales.*" *World Literature Today* Vol. 72, no. 4 (autumn 1998): 833–834.

———. "*The Remarkable Rooming-House of Mme. LeMonde:* Tennessee Williams's Little Shop of Comic Horrors," *Tennessee Williams Annual Review* 4 (2001). Available online. URL: http://www.tennesseewilliamsstudies.org/archives/2001/3kolin.htm.

———. "Roland Barthes, Tennessee Williams and *A Streetcar Named Desire*/Pleasure," *Centennial Review* 43 (spring 1999): 289–304.

———. "'*Something Cloudy, Something Clear*': Tennessee Williams's Postmodern Memory Play," *Journal of Dramatic Theory and Criticism* 12, no. 2 (spring 1998): 35–55.

———. "*Spring Storm,*" *World Literature Today* 74, no. 2 (spring 2000): 369–370.

———. "*Stairs to the Roof,*" *World Literature Today* Vol. 74, no. 4 (autumn 2000): 816–817.

———, ed. *Tennessee Williams: A Guide to Research and Performance.* Westport, Conn.: Greenwood Press, 1998.

———. "Tennessee Williams: Fugitive Kind," *World Literature Today* 76, no. 1 (winter 2002): 151–152.

———. "Tennessee Williams's 'Interval': MGM and Beyond," *Southern Quarterly* 38, no. 1 (fall 1999): 21–27.

———, ed. *The Undiscovered Country: The Latter Plays of Tennessee Williams.* New York, Peter Lang, 2002.

———. *Williams:* A Streetcar Named Desire. Cambridge: Cambridge University Press, 2000.

———. "Williams in Ebony: Black and Multi-Racial Productions of *A Streetcar Named Desire,*" *Black American Literature Forum* 25, no. 1 (spring 1991): 147–181.

———. "Williams's *Cat on a Hot Tin Roof,*" *Explicator* 60, no. 4 (summer 2002): 215.

———. "Williams's *The Demolition Downtown,*" *Explicator* 62, no. 1 (fall 2003): 30.

———. "Williams's *The Frosted Glass Coffin.*" *Explicator* 59, no. 1 (fall 2000): 44–46.

———. "Williams's *Will Mr. Merriwether Return from Memphis?*" *Explicator* 60, no. 2 (winter 2002): 97.

Konkle, Lincoln. "Puritan Paranoia: Tennessee Williams's *Suddenly Last Summer* as Calvinist Nightmare," *American Drama* 7, no. 2 (spring 1998): 51–72.

Kontaxopoulos, Jean. "Orpheus Introspecting: Tennessee Williams and Jean Cocteau," *Tennessee Williams Annual Review* 4 (2001). Available online. URL: http://tennesseewilliamsstudies.org/archives/2001/1Kontaxopoulos.htm.

Korda, Michael. "That's It, Baby: What Happened When Tennessee Williams Decided That He Would Like to Publish His Fiction," *The New Yorker,* March 22, 1999, 60.

Kozlenko, William, ed. *American Scenes: A Volume of New Short Plays.* New York: John Day, 1941, pp. 174–182.

Kramer, Richard E. "'The Sculptural Drama': Tennessee Williams's Plastic Theatre," *Tennessee Williams Annual Review* 5 (2002). Available online. URL: http://tennesseewilliamsstudies.org/archives/2002/3kramer.htm.

———. Kramer, Richard E. "*Summer and Smoke* and *The Eccentricities of a Nightingale,*" in *Tennessee Williams: A Guide to Research and Performance,* edited by Philip C. Kolin. Westport, Conn.: Greenwood, 1998, pp. 80–89.

Kullman, Colby H. "*The Red Devil Battery Sign,*" in *Tennessee Williams: A Guide to Research and Performance,* edited by Philip C. Kolin. Westport, Conn.: Greenwood, 1998, pp. 194–203.

———. "Rule by Power: 'Big Daddyism' in the World of Tennessee Williams's plays," *The Mississippi Quarterly* 48, no. 4 (fall 1995): 667.

———. "Tennessee Williams's Mississippi Delta: A Photo Essay," *Southern Quarterly* 38, no. 1 (fall 1999): 124–140.

Kundert-Gibbs, John. "Barren Ground: Female Strength and Male Impotence in *Who's Afraid of Virginia Woolf?* and *Cat on a Hot Tin Roof,*" in *Staging the Rage: The Web of Misogyny in Modern Drama,* edited by Katherine H. Burkman and

Judith Roof. Madison, N.J.: Fairleigh Dickinson University Press, 1998, pp. 230–247.

Lahr, John. "The Belle of Bethel: Tennessee Williams's Sister Rose Williams," *The New Yorker,* September 23, 1996, 34.

Lang, John. "In Key West, *They Like to Live on The Edge.*" *U.S. News & World Report,* April 9, 1984, 64–66.

Lea, Florence M. "Margo Jones," in *Notable Women in the American Theatre,* edited by Alice M. Robinson, Vera Mowry Roberts, and Milly S. Barranger. New York: Greenwood Press, 1989.

Leavitt, Richard F., ed. *The World of Tennessee Williams.* London: W. H. Allen, 1978.

Lester, Neal A. "*American Blues,*" in *Tennessee Williams: A Guide to Research and Performance,* edited by Philip C. Kolin. Westport, Conn.: Greenwood, 1998, pp. 13–21.

———. "*27 Wagons Full of Cotton* and Other One-Act Plays," in *Tennessee Williams: A Guide to Research and Performance,* edited by Philip C. Kolin. Westport, Conn.: Greenwood, 1998, pp. 1–12.

Leverich, Lyle. *Tom: The Unknown Tennessee Williams.* New York: W. W. Norton, 1995.

Levin, Lindy. "Shadow into Light: A Jungian Analysis of *The Night of the Iguana,*" *Tennessee Williams Annual Review* 2 (1999): 87–98.

Levy, Eric P. "'Through Soundproof Glass': The Prison of Self-Consciousness in *The Glass Menagerie,*" *Modern Drama* 36, no. 4 (December 1993): 529–537.

Londré, Felicia Hardison. "Tennessee Williams and His Favorite Writer," *Tennessee Williams Literary Journal* 4, no. 2 (fall 1999): 21–32.

———. *Tennessee Williams: Life, Work, and Criticism.* New York: F. Ungar, 1979.

Lutz, Jean, and Harold Bloom. *Tennessee Williams: Bloom's Bio Critiques.* Broomall, Pa.: Chelsea, 2001.

Lux, Mary F. "Tenn among the Lotus Eaters; Drugs in the Life and Fiction of Tennessee Williams," *Southern Quarterly* 38, no. 1 (fall 1999): 117–23.

MacMullan, Hugh. "Translating *The Glass Menagerie* to Film," *Hollywood Quarterly* 5, no. 1 (fall 1950): 14–35.

Martin, Robert A. *Critical Essays on Tennessee Williams.* London: Prentice-Hall International, 1997.

Mattews, Kevin. "The Evolution of *Night of the Iguana:* Three Symbols in the Manuscript Record," *Library Chronicle of the University of Texas* 25, no. 2 (1994): 70–85.

Maxwell, Gilbert. *Tennessee Williams and Friends.* Cleveland: World Publishing, 1965.

Mayberry, Neal. "A Study of Illusion and the Grotesque in Tennessee Williams's *Cat on a Hot Tin Roof,*" *Southern Studies* 22 no. 4 (winter 1983): 359–365.

McCann, John S. *The Critical Reputation of Tennessee Williams: A Reference Guide.* Boston: G. K. Hall, 1983.

Miller, D. A. "Visual Pleasure in 1959," in *Out Takes: Essays on Queer Theory and Film,* edited by Ellis Hanson. Durham, N.C.: Duke University Press, 1999, pp. 97–125.

Montague, Mary. "He Died in Winter," *The Mississippi Quarterly* 48, no. 4 (fall 1995): 591.

Monteiro, George. "'Strict and Savage Heart on a Taffeta Sleeve': Emily Dickinson in the Plays of Tennessee Williams," *Tennessee Williams Literary Journal* 4, no. 2 (fall 1999): 37–44.

Murphy, Brenda. *Tennessee Williams and Elia Kazan: A Collaboration in the Theatre.* Cambridge: Cambridge University Press, 1992.

Myers, Eric. "Making *Streetcar* Sing," *Opera News* 63 no. 3 (September 1998). pp. 34–36.

Naifeh, Steven, and Gregory White Smith. *Jackson Pollock: An American Saga.* New York: C. N. Potter, 1988.

Nelson, Benjamin. *Tennessee Williams: The Man and His Work.* New York: Ivan Obolensky, 1961.

Neumann, Claus Peter. "Tennessee Williams's Plastic Theatre: *Camino Real,*" *Journal of American Drama and Theatre* 6, nos. 2–3 (spring–fall 1994): 93–111.

O'Connor, Jacqueline. *Dramatizing Dementia: Madness in the Plays of Tennessee Williams.* Bowling Green, Ohio: Bowling Green State University Press, 1997.

———. "'Living in This Little Hotel': Boarders on Borders in Tennessee Williams's Early Short Plays," *Tennessee Williams Annual Review* 3 (2000): 1–23.

———. "The 'Neurotic Giggle': Humor in the Plays of Tennessee Williams," *Studies in American Humor* 3, no. 6 (1999): 37.

Ohi, Kevin. "Devouring Creation: Cannibalism, Sodomy, and the Scene of Analysis in *Suddenly Last Summer,*" *Cinema Journal* 38, no. 3 (1999): 27–49.

O'Quinn, Jim. "Springtime for Tennessee," *American Theatre* 15, no. 6 (July–August 1998): 54.

O'Reilly, Jane. "In Key West: Where Writers Get Top Billing," *Time,* February 6, 1984, 11–13.

Pagan, Nicholas. *Rethinking Literary Biography: A Postmodern Approach to Tennessee Williams.* London, N.J.: Fairleigh Dickinson University Press, 1993.

———. "Tennessee Williams's Theatre as Body," *Philological Quarterly* 72, No. 1 (winter 1993): 97.

Paller, Michael. "The Couch and Tennessee," *Tennessee Williams Annual Review* 3 (2000): 37–55.

———. "The Day on Which a Woman Dies: *The Milk Train Doesn't Stop Here Anymore* and Noh Theatre," in *The Undiscovered Country: The Later Plays of Tennessee Williams*, edited by Philip Kolin. New York: Peter Lang, 2002, pp. 25–39.

Palmer, R. Barton. "*Baby Doll:* The Success of Scandal," *Tennessee Williams Annual Review*, 4 (2001). Available online. URL: http://www.tennesseewilliamsstudies.org/archives/2001/2palmer.htm.

———. "Chance's Main Chance: Richard Brooks's *Sweet Bird of Youth*," *Tennessee Williams Annual Review* 3 (2000): 25–36.

Palmer, Barton. "Elia Kazan and Richard Brooks Do Tennessee Williams: Melodramatizing *Cat on a Hot Tin Roof* on Stage and Screen," *Tennessee Williams Annual Review* 2 (1999): 1–11.

Paran, Janice. "Music in the Lower Depths," *American Theatre* 15, no. 5 (May–June 1998): 45.

Parker, Brian. "Bringing Back Big Daddy," *Tennessee Williams Annual Review* 3 (2000): 91–99.

———. "A Developmental Stemma for Drafts and Revisions of Tennessee Williams's *Camino Real*," *Modern Drama* 39, no. 2 (summer 1996): 331.

———. "Documentary Sources for *Camino Real*," *Tennessee Williams Annual Review* 1 (1998): 41–52.

———. "Multiple Endings for *The Rose Tattoo* (1951)," *Tennessee Williams Annual Review* 2 (1999): 53–68.

"A One-Act Version of *The Night of the Iguana* (An Introduction)," *Tennessee Williams Annual Review* 4 (2001). Available online. URL: http://tennesseewilliamsstudies.org/archives/2001/Oparker.htm

"A Provisional Stemma for Drafts, Alternatives, and Revisions of Tennessee Williams's *The Rose Tattoo*" (1951), *Modern Drama* 40, no. 2 (summer 1997): 279.

———. "Tennessee Williams and the Legends of St. Sebastian," *University of Toronto Quarterly* 69, no. 3 (summer 2000): 634.

———. "A Tentative Stemma for Drafts and Revisions of Tennessee Williams's *Suddenly Last Summer* (1958)," *Modern Drama* 41, no. 2 (summer 1998): 303–326.

Parker, Dorothy, ed. *Essays on Modern American Drama: Williams, Miller, Albee, and Shepherd.* Toronto: University of Toronto Press, 1987.

Parker, R. B. The Glass Menagerie: *A Collection of Critical Essays.* Englewood Cliffs, N.J.: Prentice-Hall, 1983.

Peden, Williams. *The American Short Story.* Boston: Houghton Mifflin, 1975.

Phillips, Gene D. *The Films of Tennessee Williams.* Philadelphia: Art Alliance Press, 1980.

Phillips, Rod. "'Collecting Evidence': The Natural World in Tennessee Williams's *The Night of the Iguana*," *The Southern Literary Journal* 32, no. 2 (spring 2000): 59.

Picano, Felice. "Tennessee Williams/New Orleans Literary Festival," *Lambda Book Report* 8, no. 10 (May 2000): 11.

Plimpton, George, ed. *Playwrights at Work: The Paris Review.* New York: New York Modern Library, 2000.

Plumley, William. "Tennessee Williams's Graphic Art: 'Two on a Party,'" *The Mississippi Quarterly* 48, no. 4 (fall 1995): 789–803.

Presley, Delma Eugene. *The Glass Menagerie.* Boston: Twayne, 1990.

———. "The Search for Hope in the Plays of Tennessee Williams," *The Mississippi Quarterly* 25 (1971): 31–43.

Price, Marian. "*Cat on a Hot Tin Roof:* The Uneasy Marriage of Success and Idealism," *Modern Drama* 38, no. 3 (fall 1995): 324–335.

Rader, Dotson. "The Art of Theatre. V. Tennessee Williams," *Paris Review* 81 (fall 1981): 145–185.

Ramaswamy, S. "Geriatrics: The Treatment of Old Age in Tennessee Williams's Play," *Indian Journal of American Studies* 28, nos. 1–2 (winter–summer 1998): 1–6.

Rasky, Harry. *Tennessee Williams: A Portrait in Laughter and Lamentation.* New York: Dodd, Mead, 1986.

Raymond, Gerard. "Tennessee Waltzes On," *The Advocate*, September 28, 1999, 89.

Razak, Ajmal M. "Note on a Line of Tennessee Williams's *Suddenly Last Summer*," *English Language Notes* 37, no. 2 (December 1999): 68.

Reynolds, James. "The Failure of Technology in *The Glass Menagerie*," *Modern Drama* 43, no. 4 (December 1991): 522–527.

Riddel, Joseph N. "*A Streetcar Named Desire:* Nietzsche Descending," *Modern Drama* 5 (spring 1963): 426.

Rizzo, Frank. "Raising Tennessee," *American Theatre* 15, no. 8 (October 1998): 20–25.

Rocha, Mark W. "*Small Craft Warnings, Vieux Carré,* and *A Lovely Sunday for Creve Coeur*," in *Tennessee Williams: A Guide to Research and Performance,* edited by Philip C. Kolin. Westport, Conn.: Greenwood, 1998, pp. 183–193.

Roessel, David, and Nicholas Moschovakis, eds. *The Collected Poems of Tennessee Williams.* New York: New Directions, 2002.

Rogers, Ingrid. *Tennessee Williams: A Moralist's Answer to the Perils of Life.* Frankfurt: Peter Lang, 1976.

Roudané, Matthew, ed. *The Cambridge Companion to Tennessee Williams.* Cambridge: Cambridge University Press, 1997.

Ruckel, Terri Smith. "A 'Giggling, Silly, Bitchy Voluptuary': Tennessee Williams's *Memoirs as Apologia pro Vita Sua,*" *Southern Quarterly* 38, no. 1 (fall 1999): 94–103.

Saddik, Annet. *The Politics of Reputation: The Critical Reception of Tennessee Williams's Later Plays.* Madison, N.J.: Farleigh Dickinson University Press, 1999.

———. "Tennessee Williams," *Mississippi Quarterly* 53, no. 1 (winter 1999–2000): 185–188.

———. "The (Un)Represented Fragmentation of the Body in Tennessee Williams's 'Desire and the Black Masseur' and *Suddenly Last Summer,*" *Modern Drama* 41, no. 3 (fall 1998): 347.

Sahayam, V. Sam. "How Broadway Proved Williams Wrong: A Comparative Study of *The Eccentricities of a Nightingale* and *Summer and Smoke,*" in *A Mosaic of Encounters,* edited by Desai Mutalik, V. K. Malhotra, T. S. Anand, and Prashant K. Sinha. New Delhi: Creative, 1999, pp. 15–20.

St. Just, Maria, ed. *Five o'Clock Angel: Letters of Tennessee Williams and Maria St. Just, 1948–1982.* New York: W. W. Norton, 1990.

Sarote, Georges-Michel. "Fluidity and Differentiation in Three Plays by Tennessee Williams: *The Glass Menagerie, A Streetcar Named Desire,* and *Cat on a Hot Tin Roof,*" in *Staging Difference: Cultural Pluralism in American Theater and Drama,* edited by Marc Maufort. New York: Peter Lang, 1995, pp. 141–156.

Saur, K. G., Erika J. Fischer, and Heinz Dietrich Fischer, eds. *Drama/Comedy Awards, 1917–1996: From Eugene O'Neill and Tennessee Williams to Richard Rogers and Edward Albee.* Vol. 12. New York: Saur, 1998.

Savran, David. *Communists, Cowboys, and Queers: The Politics of Masculinity in the Work of Arthur Miller and Tennessee Williams.* Minneapolis: University of Minnesota Press, 1992, p. 137.

Schiavi, Michael R. "Effeminacy in the *Kingdom:* Tennessee Williams and Stunted Spectatorship," *Tennessee Williams Annual Review* 2 (1999): 99–113.

Schlatter, James. "*Red Devil Battery Sign:* An Approach to Mytho-Political Theater," *Tennessee Williams Annual Review* 1 (1998): 93–102.

Schrecker, Ellen. *Many Are the Crimes: McCarthyism in America:* Boston: Little, Brown, 1998.

Sengupta, Ashis. "*The Glass Menagerie:* Bits of Shattered Rainbow," in *A Mosaic of Encounters,* edited by Desai Mutalik, V. K. Malhotra, T. S. Anand, and Prashant K. Sinha. New Delhi: Creative, 1999, pp. 21–28.

Shackelford, Dean. "'The Ghost of a Man': The Quest for Self-Acceptance in Early Williams," *Tennessee Williams Annual Review* 4 (2001):49–58.

———. "Is There a Gay Man in This Text?: Subverting the Closet in *A Streetcar Named Desire,*" in *Literature and Homosexuality,* edited by Michael J. Meyer. Amsterdam: Rodopi, 2000.

———. "The Transmutation of Experience," *Southern Quarterly* 38, no. 1 (fall 1999): 104–116.

———. "The Truth That Must Be Told: Gay Subjectivity, Homophobia, and Social History in *Cat on a Hot Tin Roof,*" *Tennessee Williams Annual Review* 1 (1998): 103–118.

Shalland, Irene. *Tennessee Williams on the Soviet Stage.* Lanham, Md.: University Press of America, 1987.

Shaw, Irwin. "Masterpiece," in *Twentieth Century Interpretations on* A Streetcar Named Desire: *A Collection of Critical Essays,* edited by Jordan Y. Miller. Englewood Cliffs, N.J.: Prentice-Hall, 1971, pp. 45–47.

Sheppard, Philippa. "An Annual Bibliography," *Modern Drama* 13, no. 2 (1999): 59–93.

Shewey, Don. "*Small Craft Warnings.*" *The Advocate,* June 20, 2000, 124.

Shukri, Muhammad. *Tennessee Williams in Tangier.* Santa Barbara, Calif.: Cadmus Editions, 1979.

Siebold, Thomas, ed. *Readings on the* Glass Menagerie. *The Greenhaven Companion to American Literature.* San Diego: Greenhaven, 1998.

Siegel, Robert. "The Metaphysics of Tennessee Williams," *American Drama* 10, no. 1 (winter 2001): 11–37.

Simon, John. "Damsels Inducing Distress," New York, April 7, 1980, 82, 84.

Single, Lois Leathers. "Flying the Jolly Roger: Image of Escape and Selfhood in Tennessee Williams's *The Glass Menagerie,*" *Tennessee Williams Annual Review* 2 (1999): 69–85.

Sklepowich, Edward A. "In Pursuit of the Lyric Quarry: The Image of the Homosexual in Tennessee

Williams's Prose Fiction," in *Tennessee Williams: A Tribute*, edited by Jac Tharpe. Jackson: University Press of Mississippi, 1977, pp. 525–544.

Smith, Bruce. *Costly Performances. Tennessee Williams: The Last Stage.* New York: Paragon House, 1990.

Sofer, Andrew. "Self Consuming Artifacts: Power, Performance, and the Body in Tennessee Williams's *Suddenly Last Summer*," *Modern Drama* 38 (1995): 342–345.

Sova, Dawn B. *Forbidden Films: Censorship Histories of 125 Motion Pictures.* New York: Facts On File, 2001, pp. 26–29.

Spoto, Donald. *The Kindness of Strangers: The Life of Tennessee Williams.* Boston: Little, Brown, 1985.

Stanton, Stephen S., ed. *Tennessee Williams: A Collection of Critical Essays.* Englewood Cliffs, N.J.: Prentice-Hall, 1977.

Steen, Mike. *A Look at Tennessee Williams.* New York: Hawthorn Books, 1969.

Stein, Roger B. "*The Glass Menagerie* Revisited: Catastrophe without Violence," *Western Humanities Review* 18, no. 2 (spring 1964): 141–153.

Styan, J. L. "Tennessee Williams: America's Chekhov," *Tennessee Williams Review* 4, no. 1 (spring 1983): 8–11.

Summers, Claude J. "'The Charm of the Defeated.': The Early Fiction of Truman Capote and Tennessee Williams," in *Gay Fictions: Wilde to Stonewall—Studies in a Male Homosexual Literary Tradition.* New York: Continuum, 1990.

———. *Gay Fictions: Wilde to Stonewall—Studies in a Male Homosexual Literary Tradition.* New York: Continuum, 1990.

Sutton, Brian. "Williams's *The Glass Menagerie* and Uhry's *The Last Night of Ballyhoo*," *Explicator* 61, no. 3 (spring 2003): 172.

Taylor, Helen. "'An Archaeological Dig': Tennessee Williams in the 1990's," *Critical Survey* 9, no. 2 (May 1997): 43.

Taylor, William E. "Tennessee Williams: The Playwright as Poet," in *Tennessee Williams: A Tribute*, edited by Jac Tharpe. Jackson: University Press of Mississippi, 1977, pp. 609–623.

Terkel, Studs. *The Spectator: Talk about Movies and Plays with the People Who Make Them.* New York: New Press, 1999.

Thompson, Judith J. *Tennessee Williams's Plays: Memory, Myth, and Symbol.* New York: Peter Lang, 1987.

Tharpe, Jack, ed. *Tennessee Williams: A Tribute.* Jackson: University Press of Mississippi, 1977.

———. *Tennessee Williams's Plays: Memory, Myth, and Symbol.* New York: Peter Lang, 1987.

Timpane, John. "Gaze and Resistance in the Plays of Tennessee Williams," *The Mississippi Quarterly* 48, no. 4 (fall 1995): 751.

Tischler, Nancy M. *The Student Companion to Tennessee Williams.* Westport, Conn.: Greenwood Press, 2000.

———. "Tennessee on Tennessee," *The Mississippi Quarterly* 51, no. 4 (fall 1998): 649.

———. *Tennessee Williams.* Austin: Steck-Vaughn, 1969.

———. *Tennessee Williams: Rebellious Puritan.* New York: Citadel Press, 1961.

———. "Tennessee Williams: Vagabond Poet," *Tennessee Williams Annual Review* Vol. 1 (1998): 73–79.

Tynan, Kenneth. "Papa and the Playwright." *Playboy,* May 1964, 138–141.

———. "Valentine to Tennessee Williams," in *Drama and the Modern World: Plays and Essays,* edited by Samuel Weiss. Lexington, Mass.: D.C. Heath, 1964, pp. 455–461.

Van Duyvenbode. "Darkness Made Visible: Miscegenation, Masquerade and the Signified Racial Other in Tennessee Williams's *Baby Doll* and *A Streetcar Named Desire*," *Journal of American Studies* 35, no. 2 (August 2001): 203.

Van Laan, Thomas. "'Shut Up!' 'Be Quiet!' 'Hush!' Talk and Its Suppression in Three Plays by Tennessee Williams," *Comparative Drama* 22, no. 3 (fall 1988): 257–263.

Vannatta, Dennis. *Tennessee Williams: A Study of the Short Fiction.* New York: G. K. Hall, 1988.

Vidal, Gore. "Introduction," in *Collected Stories by Tennessee Williams.* New York: New Directions, 1985, pp. xix–xxv.

Voss, Ralph F., ed. *Magical Muse: Millennial Essays on Tennessee Williams.* Tuscaloosa: University of Alabama Press, 2002.

———. "Tennessee Williams and William Inge: Friends, Rivals, Great American Playwrights," *The Tennessee Williams Literary Journal* 4, no. 2 (fall 1999): 9–20.

Wallace, Jack E. "The Image of Theatre in Tennessee Williams's *Orpheus Descending*," *Modern Drama,* 27, no. 3 (September 1984): 324–335.

Weales, Gerald Clifford. *Tennessee Williams.* Minneapolis: University of Minnesota Press, 1965.

Whelan, Gerard. *Spiked: Church–State Intrigue and* The Rose Tattoo. Dublin: New Island, 2002.

Wilhelmi, Nancy O. "The Language of Power and Powerlessness: Verbal Combat in the Plays of Tennessee Williams," in *The Text Beyond: Essays in Literary Linguistics,* edited by Cynthia Goldin Bernstein. Tuscaloosa: University of Alabama Press, 1994, pp. 217–226.

Williams, Dakin. *Tennessee Williams: An Intimate Biography.* New York: Arbor House, 1983.

Williams, Edwina Dakin, with Lucy Freeman. *Remember Me to Tom.* New York: G. P. Putnam's Sons, 1964, p. 134.

Williams, Tennessee. "Author's Note," in Stopped Rocking *and Other Screenplays.* New York: New Directions, 1984, p. 295.

———. "Landscape with Figures: Two Mississippi Plays," in *American Scenes,* edited by William Kozlenko. New York: John Day, 1941.

———. *Memoirs.* Garden City, N.Y.: Doubleday, 1975.

———. *Where I Live.* New York: New Directions, 1978.

Winchell, Mark Royden. "Come Back to the Locker Room Ag'in, Brick Honey!" *The Mississippi Quarterly* 48, no. 4 (fall 1995): 701–712.

Windham, Donald, *Tennessee Williams: Letters to Donald Windham, 1940–1965.* Athens: University of Georgia Press, 1977.

———. *Lost Friendships: A Memoir of Truman Capote, Tennesee Williams, and Others.* New York: W. Morrow, 1987.

Wolter, Jürgen C. "Strangers on Williams's Stage," *The Mississippi Quarterly* 49, no. 1 (winter 1995): 33.

———. "Tennessee Williams's Fiction," in *Tennessee Williams: A Guide to Research and Performance,* edited by Philip C. Kolin. Westport, Conn. Greenwood, 1998, pp. 220–31.

Woods, Gregory. "The 'Conspiracy' of the 'Homintern,'" *The Gay & Lesbian Review Worldwide* 10, no. 13 (May–June 2003): 11–13.

Yacowar, Maurice. *Tennessee Williams and Film.* New York: Frederick Ungar, 1977.

Young, Michael C. II. "The Play of Memory: Reflections from *The Glass Menagerie*—an Interview," *The Tennessee Williams Newsletter* 2, no. 2 (fall 1980): 32–35.

Zeineddine, Nada. *Because It's My Name: Problems of Identity Experienced by Women Artists, and Breadwinners in the Plays of Henrik Ibsen, Tennessee Williams, and Arthur Miller.* Braunton, England: Merlin Books, 1991.

# INDEX

Page numbers in **boldface** indicate main entries. Page numbers in *italic* indicate photographs.

## D

## M

## S

## U



## V